CC 81 .F66 1985

For concordance in
archaeological analysis

FOR CONCORDANCE
IN ARCHAEOLOGICAL ANALYSIS

CONTRIBUTORS

Robert Bettinger

David P. Braun

Christopher Carr

James A. Farley

Bruce G. Gladfelter

C. Marshall Hoffman

Marcia L. Jones

Arthur S. Keene

Kenneth L. Kvamme

W. Fredrick Limp

Sandra Parker

Dwight W. Read

David Hurst Thomas

Clifford E. Tiedemann

Leonard Williams

For Concordance in Archaeological Analysis

BRIDGING DATA STRUCTURE, QUANTITATIVE TECHNIQUE, AND THEORY

Christopher Carr
GENERAL EDITOR

WESTPORT PUBLISHERS, INC.
in cooperation with the Institute for Quantitative Archaeology,
University of Arkansas

© 1985 Westport Publishers, Inc., 330 W. 47th Street, Kansas City, Missouri, 64112. All rights reserved. No part of this publication may be produced, stored in a retrieval system, or transmitted in any form or by any means, electronic, mechanical, photocopying, recording, or otherwise, without the written prior permission of the Westport Publishers, Inc.

LIBRARY OF CONGRESS CATALOGING IN PUBLICATION DATA

Main entry under title:

For concordance in archaeological analysis.

    Includes bibliographies and index.
    1. Archaeology—Statistical methods—Addresses, essays, lectures.
I. Carr, Christopher, 1952-   .   II. University of Arkansas, Fayetteville. Institute of Quantitative Archaeology.
CC81.F66   1985   930.1'028'5   85-8861
ISBN 0-933701-00-4

Printed in the United States of America

To
JANIS
for her love and patience

And to
GEORGE, ANNA, and TONY
for giving history and meaning to my structures

Table of Contents

Preface   xv

Acknowledgements   xix

PART I. GENERAL INTRODUCTION

1. Perspective and Basic Definitions   *Christopher Carr*   1

    The Problem of Analytic Concordance in Philosophical Perspective   4
        The Nature of and Requirements for Meaningful Scientific
            Investigation   4
        Technique in Relation to Data Structure   5
        Technique in Relation to Theory   6
    Two Kinds of Discrepancies between Data Structure and Technical
        Assumption   7
    Definition of Terms Concerning Data Structure   10
    Postscript: A Comment on Metaphysical Viewpoint   12
    References   16

PART II. PHILOSOPHICAL FRAMEWORK

2. Getting into Data: Philosophy and Tactics for the Analysis of Complex
   Data Structures   *Christopher Carr*   18

    A Cause of Logical Inconsistencies between Data Structure, Technique,
        and Theory   20
    The Problem of Getting into Data   24
    Solutions for Maintaining Logical Consistency between Data Structure
        and Technique   25
        Deductive Specification of Potentially Relevant Variables and
            Observations, and an Appropriate Technique   26
        "Constrained" Exploratory Data Analysis   30
        Entry Models   34
        Stepwise, Cyclical Analytic Designs   39
    The Logic of Analysis vs. the Logic of Published Analysis   40
    Conclusion   41
    References   42

3. The Substance of Archaeological Analysis and the Mold of Statistical Method: Enlightenment Out of Discordance? *Dwight W. Read* 45

    Analogical Paradigm 48
        General Overview of the Inadequacy of the Analogically Based Paradigm 51
        Probabilistic Foundation for the Statistical Framework 53
            Example of the Application of the Statistical Conceptual Framework 54
        Inadequacy of the Analogically Based Paradigm from the Perspective of Probability Theory 58
        Preanalysis to Circumvent the Discordance in an Analogically Formatted Analytical Scheme 60
        Resolution of the Discordance by Preanalysis of the Data Base 61
            Examples of Preanalysis of Data with NWD Populations and NWD Variables 63
    Conclusion 80
    Notes 81
    References 82

PART III. DATA ORGANIZATION AND DATA BASE MANAGEMENT

4. Introductory Remarks on Data Base Management *Christopher Carr* 87

    Data Base Management as Analysis 87
    References 90

5. Archaeological Data Base Management as Conceptual Process
Sandra Parker, W. Fredrick Limp, and James A. Farley 91

    Background 92
    Problems, Goals, and Properties: A General Perspective on Data Base Management Systems in Archaeology 92
    Data Models and Data Structures in Archaeology 96
        Conceptual Models 98
        Physical Models and Physical Data Base Structure 107
    Conclusion 111
    References 111

PART IV. REGIONAL ANALYSIS

6. Introductory Remarks on Regional Analysis *Christopher Carr* 114

    Theoretical Foundation 114
    Methodological Advances 116
        The Multivariate Logistic Regression Approach in Total 117

Comparison to Other Inductive Approaches to Predictive Modeling of
  Settlement Location   118
Global vs. Local Analysis of Settlement Decision Process   120
The Future of Logistic Regression in Settlement Analysis   122
In Historical Perspective   124
References   126

7. The Analysis of Decision Making: Alternative Applications in
Archaeology   *W. Fredrick Limp and Christopher Carr*   128

A Philosophical Perspective: Fundamental Characteristics of any Theory
  Relevant to Archaeology   130
A General Theory of Rational Choice   132
  Preference, Ordering, and Selection   132
  Sets   133
  Physical Properties and Conditional Preference Aspects   134
  Dimensional and Primary Physical Properties   135
  Production Frontiers and Trade-Offs   136
  Altering Production Parameters and Constraints   137
  Measurability and Marginality   138
  Implications of Variable Measurability   139
  K-fold Partitioning   140
  Evaluation of the Relevance of the General Theory of Rational Choice
    to Archaeology   141
Historical Perspective: Decision Analysis in Archaeology, Anthropology,
  and Economics   142
  The Formalist-Substantivist Debate   142
  The Unsatisfactory Satisficer   145
  Additional Disagreements   148
Empirical Applications and the Concordance of Theory, Method, and
  Data Structure   150
  Emic Symmetry, Etic Coherence, and Data Accessibility   150
  Cost Function Analysis: Alternative Resource Choice   150
  Cost Function Analysis: Evaluation of the Concordance between
    Theory, Method, and Decision Process   156
  Hierarchical Choice Models: An Application to Settlement Location
    Analysis   157
  Hierarchical Choice Analysis: Evaluation of the Concordance between
    Theory, Method, and Decision Process   162
A Brief Introduction to and Assessment of Other Select Methods of
  Economic Analysis for Archaeology   164
  Linear Programming   164
  Statistical Decision Theory Using Decision Trees   165
  Game Theory   166

Appropriate Contexts of Use of the Diversity of Economic Theories
    and Methods   166
Conclusion   168
References   169

8. Predictive Modeling of Site Settlement Systems Using Multivariate
   Logistics   *Sandra Parker*   173

   Theoretical Foundation   174
   The Multivariate Logistic Approach to Predictive Modeling   176
       Data Requirements for Logistic Regression   178
   Settlement Model in the Sparta Research Area   179
       The Sparta Environment   179
       Operationalizing the Logistics Model in Sparta: Choice of Units and
           Variables   182
       Operationalizing the Logistics Model: The Surveyed Sample   186
       Predictive Model   187
       Model Validation   190
   Comparison of Multivariate Logistics to Other Predictive
       Methodologies   199
       Discriminant Function Analysis   199
       Trend Surface Analysis   201
       Kriging   202
   References   205

9. Determining Empirical Relationships between the Natural Environment
   and Prehistoric Site Locations: A Hunter-Gatherer Example   *Kenneth L.
   Kvamme*   208

   Methodological Perspective   209
   The Glenwood Project Data Base   210
       Sampling Design   210
       Site Types   213
       Environmental Data   215
   Environmental Features Important to Hunter-Gatherer Site Locations in
       the Glenwood Area   217
       Univariate Analysis   217
       Multivariate Analysis   224
       Differences between Site-Types in Locational Patterning   227
   A Model for Hunter-Gatherer Site Selection   228
       Site Selection Model   230
       Testing the Model   232
   Prospects and Problems   235
   Conclusion   236
   References   237

10. Constraints on Linear Programming Applications in Archaeology
    Arthur S. Keene 239

    On the Nature of Models 240
    Introduction to Linear Programming Models 243
      Building a Linear Programming Model 243
      Linear Programming in Prehistoric Subsistence Studies 252
    Benefits of Linear Programming 253
      Computational Burden 254
      Consistency 254
      Heuristic Advantages 255
    Limitations of Linear Programming 255
      Mechanical Limitations 255
      Conceptual Limitations 258
      Epistemological Considerations 268
    References 270

11. Notions to Numbers: Great Basin Settlements as Polythetic Sets
    Leonard Williams, David Hurst Thomas, and Robert Bettinger 274

    1985 Preface 274
    The Nature of Polythetic Entities 277
    The Reese River Ecological Project 281
    Another Loop in the Cycle 282
    Operational and Polythetic Definitions 283
    Survey Results 286
    Summary 292
    Acknowledgements 293
    References 294

PART V. INTRASITE SPATIAL ANALYSIS

12. Introductory Remarks on Intrasite Spatial Analysis
    Christopher Carr 297

    New Techniques 297
    Entry Models and Polythetic Organization of Depositional Sets 299
    Future Research 301
    References 301

13. Alternative Models, Alternative Techniques: Variable Approaches to
    Intrasite Spatial Analysis *Christopher Carr* 302

    Basic Assumptions and Philosophy of Analysis 305
      Evaluation and Expansion of the Goals of Intrasite Spatial
        Analysis 305

Evaluation of Logical and Operational Frameworks for Intrasite Spatial Analysis   316
Models of Organization of Depositional Sets and Activity Sets   328
  Basic Terminology   328
  Mathematical Concepts and Dimensions of Organization   330
  Building the Models   334
Linking the Models of Organization with Formation Processes   347
  Processes Leading to Forms of Organization in the Behavioral Domain   348
  Processes Leading to Forms of Organization in the Archaeological Domain: The Monothetic-Polythetic Dimension   351
  Processes Leading to Forms of Organization in the Archaeological Domain: The Nonoverlapping-Overlapping Dimension   355
Linking the Models of Organization with Spatial Analytic Techniques   356
  General Perspective   356
  AVDISTM   359
  Ratio and Rank-Scale Correlation Coefficients   361
  Jaccard's and Cole's Similarity Coefficients   363
  AVDISTLP1, AVDISTGP, AVDISTLP2   366
  Higher-Level Pattern Searching Algorithms   373
  A New Clustering Algorithm Allowing Cluster Overlap: OVERCLUS   380
Illustration of the Proposed Analytic Framework and New Techniques   384
  Overview of Pincevent   385
  Data Base   391
  Identification of Formation Processes and Their Effects on Artifact Organization   398
  Formal Linkage of the Pincevent Spatial Data Set to Techniques Appropriate for Its Analysis   407
  Depositional Sets at Habitation No. 1   408
Experimental Investigations of the Behaviors of the New Techniques Using the Pincevent Data   430
  Effects of Incongruencies between Relevant Data Structure and the AVDIST Coefficients   430
  Effects of Including Ubiquitous Types in Multidimensional Scalings Using Different AVDIST Coefficients   439
The Importance of Acknowledging Artifact Type Asymmetries and Polythetic Organization in Spatial Analysis: Illustration with the Pincevent Data   441
Conclusion   451
Notes   452

References 452
Appendix A. Computer Programs for Calculating the Similarity
   Coefficients, AVDISTGM, AVDISTLP1, and AVDISTGP 460

14. The Contiguity-Anomaly Technique for Analysis of Spatial
    Variation *Bruce G. Gladfelter and Clifford E. Tiedemann* 474

   Spatial Autocorrelation 476
      Non-Contiguity Measures 477
      Contiguity Measures 478
      Limitations of the Statistics 479
   The Contiguity-Anomaly Method 480
   Potential Application in Archaeology 488
      Pre-excavation Spatial Distributions 489
      Excavated Spatial Distributions 492
   Summarizing Remarks and Continuing Research 494
   Appendix A 496
      Comments on Moran's I and Geary's C Statistics 496
      Moran's I and Geary's C Statistics 498
   Appendix B 499
      Extracting Statistical Outliers 499
   References 500

PART VI. ARTIFACT ANALYSIS

15. Introductory Remarks on Artifact Analysis *Christopher Carr* 502

   Deductive Specification of Seriation Criteria 502
   Inductive Specification of Seriation Criteria 503
   New Methods for Seriation: Time Series Approaches 504
   Deductive Specification of Classification Criteria 505
   New Methods for Artifact Classification 506
   References 507

16. Absolute Seriation: A Time-Series Approach *David P. Braun* 509

   Some Problems in Absolute Dating and Seriation 510
   A Time-Series Approach for Solving the Problems 512
   A Midwestern Woodland Example 518
   Problems and Prospects 534
   References 537

17. The Use of Technological Indices: A Case Study for the Levantine
    Mousterian *Marcia L. Jones* 540

   The Sites 544
      Rosh Ein Mor 544

Nahal Aqev   545
Measurement Techniques and Methods of Analysis   546
Statistical Analyses   547
    Testing the Significance of Index Variation among Artifact Classes   547
        Intra-Assemblage Analyses   550
        Inter-Assemblage Analyses   559
Discussion   563
References   565

18. Projectile Point Maintenance and Typology: Assessment with Factor Analysis and Canonical Correlation   *C. Marshall Hoffman*   566

    Theoretical Orientation   567
    Projectile Points: Definitions and Terminology   569
    Normative-Empiricist Point Typologies of the Southeastern United States   570
    Point Use-Life and Maintenance   573
        Changes in the Stem   574
        Changes in the Blade   574
    Tool Maintenance and Point Typology: The Blade Shape/ Point Use-Life Hypothesis and its Traditional Alternative   577
        Operationalizing the Concept of Use-Life: The Point Blade Size/ Blade Edge Angle Hypothesis   581
    The Analysis   583
        The Sample   583
        Measurement Techniques   583
        Data Screening   588
        R-Mode Factor Analysis   590
        Canonical Correlation Analysis   599
        Comparison of Factor Analysis and Canonical Correlation   602
        Evaluating the Hypotheses   603
        Conclusions of the Analysis   605
    Perspective on Typology   605
    Conclusion   607
    References   608

Index   613

About the Contributors   619

Preface

The subject of this book is the relatively unexplored middle ground between philosophy of science, statistics, and archaeological and anthropological theory. Whereas the past two decades have witnessed the preoccupation of American archaeology with each of these concerns *individually*, and with theory building in the guiding light of philosophy of science, this book focuses on the integration of all three concerns. It calls for archaeologists to develop and make explicit the logical arguments and propositions that link theory, quantitative technique, and data to each other and the phenomenon of interest during the course of research design and analysis. What is the theoretically expectable nature of organization of the phenomenon of interest? What scales of measurement, variables, and observations within a data set most directly reflect the phenomenon and its organization? What techniques are algorithmically sensitive to aspects of the data that reflect the phenomenon of interest?

Arguments pertaining to questions such as these often are not formulated explicitly in archaeological analyses. They remain "implicit auxiliary hypotheses." Yet it is precisely these arguments, and the tailoring of theory, technique, and data to each other and the phenomenon of interest during the course of their explication, that ensure that analysis is logically concordant and meaningful. *Explicit justification* of the selection of data and methods for analysis, in relation to the expected and empirical nature of the phenomenon of interest, is one means by which logical inconsistencies and false premises in current theory are revealed, inadequacies in current techniques are uncovered, and new theories and methods are suggested. It is toward the location of such false premises and technical deficiencies, and the building of new theoretical frameworks and methods that bring greater concordance between theory, method, data, and phenomena, that this book is dedicated.

AUDIENCE AND CLASSROOM USE

Most of the chapters in this work assume, in one place or another, that the reader has some familiarity with multivariate analytic techniques—both the motivation behind their use and their procedures at a general level. However, in discussing the logic involved in applying technique to data or in linking technique to theory, the mathematical concepts necessary to understand such relationships have been explained more fully or exemplified. Thus, the focus of this volume on developing and maintaining consistency during analysis is accessible to a wide audience.

This book can serve as a reader in graduate level courses on archaeological research design or quantitative methods. Of fundamental concern in such courses is teaching the student the general nature of logic involved in analysis. Also of importance are the particular arguments that are useful for specifying the kinds of data (variables, observations, and scales of measurement) that should be collected and selected for analysis and the quantitative methods that should be used in various empirical contexts. These concerns are the primary focus of this volume. They are illustrated in relation to a wide diversity of problem areas that currently are being researched actively in archaeology. These include data base management; predictive modeling of subsistence and settlement decision making; intrasite spatial analysis of activities and formation processes; and ceramic and lithic artifact technology and chronometry.

The chapters in this work are organized into two major groups: those in Parts I and II, and those in the remaining four parts. The chapters in Parts I and II discuss the general nature of logic involved in the analysis of complex data structures. They present certain common, logical problems that characterize the analysis of complex data and some means by which they can be overcome. The chapters in the remaining parts of the book discuss specific instances of these problems and solutions in relation to the areas of current research mentioned previously. The chapters in these sections have been arranged by subject matter in order to stress the common structural features that are shared by data pertaining to similar phenomena, the common problems that those structures pose in analysis, and the similar bridging arguments about choice of technique and data that characterize the analysis of those structures.

THE INSTITUTE FOR QUANTITATIVE ARCHAEOLOGY

In a large way, this book is the product of many extended discussions, cooperative research projects, and a general research milieu in which a number of faculty and graduate students at the University of Arkansas have participated over the past six years. These include faculty in the Departments of Anthropology, Mathematical Sciences, and Geography, and the Arkansas Archeological Survey.

This network of cooperating faculty was crystallized in 1984 with the establishment of the Institute for Quantitative Archaeology within the Fulbright College of Arts and Sciences, University of Arkansas. Among the objectives of the Institute are 1) to train graduate students within the Department of Anthropology and non-degree visiting students within the university in creative, relevant approaches to quantified archaeological research, both basic and applied; 2) to offer conferences and workshops to train practicing professional archaeologists in the same; and 3) to facilitate funding and publication of multidisciplinary, quantitative research. Many of the educational goals are achieved through regularly offered coursework, tutorial study, and hands-on experience in a variety of research projects involving the Institute's faculty. Additionally, the Institute sponsors visits, lectures, and workshops by distinguished scholars through its Albert C. Spaulding Lectures Program. Other educational opportunities include a formal program of study on cartographic communication theory, computer mapping, and remote sensing, leading to certification by the Fulbright College of Arts and Sciences.

The subjects in which current faculty of the Institute have expertise include intrasite spatial analysis, quantitative modeling of intrasite formation processes, predictive modeling of settlement location choice, economic modeling and theory, quantified socio-stylistic analysis of artifacts, continuous-scale chronometry with artifacts, archaeometry, mathematics of geophysical prospecting, data base management, computer mapping, digital image interpretation, simulation, and linear programming. Many of these topics are discussed in this book.

Christopher Carr
University of Arkansas
September 10, 1984

Acknowledgements

First and foremost, I want to thank the contributors to this volume. They were both patient with and accepting of the suggestions I made for themes and argumentation within their chapters, and in a few cases, chapter topics, in order to illustrate the philosophical and topical themes of the volume. The extended discussions we had during manuscript preparation and the criticisms they offered of my ideas on analytic process were tremendously thought-provoking and of great help to me in refining them.

Equally important to the creation of this volume were Eugene, Gerri and Barbara Strauss. It is through their concern for and support of this work that its publication was possible.

I am deeply indebted to Robert Whallon and Michael Schiffer for the many ideas on quantitative analysis and logic that they have shared with me through the years. What they taught me forms the foundation for this work and provided its rationale. I also want to thank my father, James Matthews, and Roy Coleman, for teaching me at an early age the fundamentals of scientific procedure and attitude, and how to use mathematics in both exploratory and deductive manners as part of scientific process. These thought-patterns have served as a framework ever since.

I cannot thank Fred Limp and Sandy Parker enough for our six years together at Arkansas. Their intellectual company helped me—required me—to broaden my theoretical framework and allowed me to appreciate the richness that paradigmatic differences give to thought and life. Through work and friendship, their intellectual stimulation and spiritual support have been the breath of life for me.

To my present and former students in Research Methods and Archaeological Method and Theory, I send a warm thank you. Their criticisms of my ideas and eagerness for answers to issues that I had not fully thought out helped me to grow.

I owe a special thanks to Allen McCartney, former Chair of the Department of Anthropology, University of Arkansas, for his support and encouragement of my research over five years. The release time, physical facilities, and secretarial support that he made available to me through the department greatly facilitated my studies. I also want to thank Mary Herrington for her careful work and patience during the seemingly endless typing of papers, tables, and corrections, which were required for this volume.

Teaching, as one experience involving the integration of knowledge and love, requires much energy. This book, envisioned and written to share with others some kinds of thought-patterns for analyzing data and thinking about theory, could never have been realized without the knowledge, love, and energy that was so generously given by so many. Gary, Nancy, Fred, and Janis, thank you for your love and energy when I needed it most.

PART I: GENERAL INTRODUCTION

1

Perspective and Basic Definitions

CHRISTOPHER CARR

In the last twenty years, archaeology has made major strides in its ability to explain complex variability in the archaeological record. Theory from general anthropology, economics, ecology, genetics, and general systems approaches, as well as frameworks concerned specifically with the formation of the archaeological record, have all been utilized, further substantiated, and in some cases, extended.

In part, this growth in the use of theory and in theory building can be attributed to the great attention that archaeologists have paid to the nature of explanation and theory, as specified by various philosophers of science. Archaeologists have grown familiar with the nature of the logical constructs they wish to build and the forms of inductive and deductive argumentation by which they can be constructed and tested (e.g., Salmon, 1982; Renfrew et al., 1982). Early starts—commendable, yet troubled—now lie behind us. Some of these include Binford's (1968) call for a primarily deductive approach to archaeology; Watson, LeBlanc, and Redman's (1971) lack of clarity over the differences between explanation and description (Read & LeBlanc, 1979); and Flannery's (1973) and Meehan's (1968) contention that a systems explanation does not involve covering laws (Spaulding, 1973; Salmon & Salmon, 1979).

Parallel to these developments, particularly during the last fifteen years, progress has been made in the use of quantitative methods to describe and model complex archaeological variation. For instance, the application of linear programming methods to model subsistence systems (Reidhead, 1981; Keene, 1981), the development or application of numerous techniques for analyzing intrasite artifact distributions (Whallon, 1973, 1974, 1984; Peebles, 1971; Carr, 1984) and regional settlement distributions (Hodder & Orton, 1976), and advances in the procedures of artifact typology and seriation (Spaulding, 1953; Whallon, 1972; Christenson & Read, 1977; Marquardt, 1978) show promise for the profession.

I wish to thank David Braun, Michael Schiffer, and Dwight Read for their very useful comments that guided my writing of this introduction.

Nevertheless, the pace of progess along both the theoretical and methodological lines of advance has been constrained by the limited effort that has been devoted to integrating them. Until very recently (e.g., Whallon & Brown, 1982; Moore & Keene, 1983; Carr, 1984), little attention has been given to formally developing and maintaining, during analysis, *logically consistent* relationships between the theoretical developments, technical developments, and the data and phenomena of interest (but see Spaulding, 1953). *Yet it is precisely this concordance between theory, technique, data, and phenomenon that is required for analysis, theory building, and technical development to be relevant, accurate, meaningful, and efficient.*

It is toward understanding and circumventing this problem of developing and maintaining logical concordance in archaeological analysis that this volume is dedicated. Each of the chapters is concerned with one or more of the following:

1) elucidating the structural nature of various kinds of behavioral and archaeological phenomena and data, including both empirical and theoretically expectable structures;

2) evaluating standard quantitative methods for their constraining assumptions and their appropriateness for analyzing specific forms of archaeological data that reflect specific phenomena of interest;

3) introducing new analytic techniques that are more consistent with the relevant structure of archaeological data than ones previously used;

4) evaluating choices of the kinds and scales of variables and the kinds of observations that are used to monitor specific phenomena of interest;

5) introducing new methods for screening archaeological data and modifying their structure such that it reflects the phenomenon of interest more directly and meets the assumptions of higher-level techniques;

6) making explicit the bridging arguments that are useful in linking technical assumption to empirical data structure or theoretical framework;

7) elucidating, in philosophical and statistical theoretical terms, the logical processes that are involved in the analysis of complex data that typify archaeology.

These issues are addressed for several rapidly developing fields: data base management; predictive modeling of settlement and subsistence decision making; intrasite spatial analysis; and artifact technology, typology, and chronometry.

In addition to the primary theme of developing analytic concordance, various secondary themes are explored for two or more fields. Some of the more important ones include:

1) the embedding of *multiple, implicit structures* within a data base, only

some of which are relevant to and concordant with the phenomenon of interest and one's theoretical framework (chapters 1, 2, 5, 7, 13, 18);

2) the constraining of the range of methods that are appropriate for an analysis ultimately by the *empirical* nature of the phenomenon of interest, and by the data representing that phenomenon, rather than by theory or theoretical expectations about the phenomenon (chapters 2, 6);

3) the idea of *alternative techniques* that are useful in different empirical and theoretical contexts, rather than universally preferable techniques (chapters 1, 2, 7, 13, 18);

4) the nature of and means for overcoming what can be termed *the methodological double bind:* a situation in which the researcher needs some information about the structure of a data set to choose relevant variables and observations, to screen it in preparation for analysis, and to choose an appropriate analytic technique, yet is seemingly unable to obtain this information except by applying some pattern-searching technique to the unscreened data in a possibly discordant manner;

5) the complementary, stepwise, and cyclical uses of *inductive and deductive strategies* for acquainting oneself with a data set's structure and for analyzing it (chapters 2, 7, 11, 13, 15, 16, 17);

6) the logical problems with and limitations of the philosophy of *exploratory data analysis* when investigating complex data, resulting in the need to use a *constrained exploratory data analysis* approach instead (chapters 2, 13);

7) the use of *entry models* for choosing appropriate analytic techniques and in theory building (chapters 2, 13);

8) the role of *induction* (in the form of data exploration and choice of scales, variables, and observations) in "deductive" hypothesis-testing phases of scientific process when data are complex (chapters 2, 3, 6);

9) the *polythetic organization* of archaeological entities (chapters 6, 11, 13);

10) the distinction between *local structure* and *global structure* within a data set and the need for the development and application of techniques sensitive to the former in certain contexts (chapters 5, 6, 12, 13, 14);

11) the use of *multivariate statistical techniques* (factor analysis, canonical correlation) to identify and help assign meaning to the relevant structure of a data set, which allows one to overcome the methodological double bind (chapters 3, 18); and

12) the use of *time series analysis* and *spatial filtering* techniques to smooth data and reveal relevant patterning (chapters 13, 16).

THE PROBLEM OF ANALYTIC CONCORDANCE IN PHILOSOPHICAL PERSPECTIVE

This book considers only certain aspects of the logical, philosophical basis of meaningful scientific investigation. It is desirable, therefore, to place its content in a larger, philosophical perspective.

The Nature of and Requirements for Meaningful Scientific Investigation

First, it is necessary to comment on the nature of meaningful scientific investigation that is assumed here. A scientific study and its results are taken to be meaningful if the results 1) give *accurate* insight into a problem and lead to the development of theory, 2) allow the accurate testing of models or hypotheses that represent extant theory, or 3) allow a particular case to be accurately and logically subsumed under extant theory, constituting an accurate explanation. More informally, a meaningful scientific study produces results that allow or lead to the assignment of appropriate meaning to phenomena of interest, or to explanation of them. (The accuracy of insight, testing, or subsumption and the appropriateness of the assignment of meaning, of course, are not absolute qualities; they can be assessed only within the limits of the researcher's guiding paradigm. See postscript, pp. 12-16.)

By implication, the theories, models, or hypotheses that are developed or evoked in a meaningful scientific investigation and that allow or lead to the assignment of appropriate meaning must, themselves, be meaning*ful*. A meaningful proposition or construct is taken here to be not only *testable and confirmable* in the minimal, least-demanding usage of the term in philosophy of science (Carnap, 1936, pp. 420-427), but also *nontrivial*. It is taken to have "worthwhile" content from the perspective of the goals of the researcher's paradigm (Read & LeBlanc, 1978, pp. 307-308, 332; Salmon & Salmon, 1979, p. 72) and to organize information efficiently and parsimoniously (Hemple, 1966, pp. 40-45; van der Leeuw, 1978, p. 328).

For a scientific investigation to produce results that are meaningful within the limits of a researcher's paradigm, three conditions are minimally required. These are 1) that at least some aspects of the *data brought forward* for study be relevant to the researcher's problem domain and accurately represent the phenomenon of interest (i.e., a population or process) and its nature; 2) that those *aspects* of the data's structure that reflect the phenomenon of interest and its nature be identified, and that they be accurately represented when summarized as patterning; and 3) that these *patterns* be interpreted in a manner consistent with the nature of the phenomenon of interest. The first two conditions ensure the *accuracy* of results and lay the foundation needed to make results meaningful. However, they are not sufficient by themselves for the derivation of *meaningful* results, which depends on the third condition, too.

These minimal requirements, in turn, necessitate that the theories, models, hypotheses, test implications, mathematical techniques, data collection methods, and/or the data that are involved in an investigation be relevant to and logically consistent with each other and the phenomenon of interest. How to develop and maintain relevance and logical consistency between these constructs and entities at different levels of abstraction is a subject matter of philosophy of science that involves a great diversity of topics. Some examples include the correct forms of a logical deduction and induction; the role of auxiliary hypotheses and assumptions in operationalizing higher-level abstractions in terms of observables; the use of bridging arguments in making logical deductions and inductions; and the setting of boundary conditions to generalizations, hypotheses, models, and theories.

The chapters in this volume have been brought together in relation to a concern over only a small subset of the philosophical issues that are involved in developing and maintaining the logical consistency that is needed to reach meaningful results in scientific investigations. At the same time, they discuss some issues concerned with developing and maintaining consistency that philosophers of science typically have not explored in depth.

In particular, this volume focuses on the *logic of application of quantitative methods* of analysis and computerized methods of data storage to archaeological data, within the context of theory. It stresses the importance, during analysis, of developing and maintaining a) logical consistency between the assumptions that underlie a technique and those aspects of the structure of archaeological data that reflect the phenomenon of interest, and b) logical consistency between the assumptions that underlie a technique and the theoretical framework that guides analysis. Logical consistency between the entities in the first relationship is necessary for the accurate identification and summary representation of facets of the data that reflect the phenomenon of interest (condition 2, above). Consistency between entities in the second relationship is necessary for the meaningful interpretation of the patterns that are identified and represented (condition 3, above). Let us consider both of these relationships in greater detail in the next two sections.

Technique in Relation to Data Structure

The necessity of maintaining logical consistency between technique and some facets of data structure during analysis, in order to obtain accurate and potentially meaningful results, can be seen in the following way. By the nature of its procedures and design, a quantitative method can be sensitive to and accurately represent only certain aspects of the total structure of the data to which it is applied. In this regard, the application of a technique to data implies assumptions that only certain, specific aspects of the data are important for representation and evaluation whereas others are not—that certain aspects of the data accurately reflect the phenomenon that is of interest and its nature whereas others do not. For example, a technique might be sensitive to ratio scale patterns of covariation among variables, but not to nominal scale patterns of association among variables. Application of such a technique to a data set would imply an assumption that only ratio scale patterning in the data is of interest, in being concordant with the nature of the phenomenon of interest and accurately reflecting the phenomenon. Likewise, a method might be sensitive to monothetic relationships of similarity among items as opposed to polythetic ones. Application of such a method to a data set would imply an assumption that only the monothetic relationships in the data are of interest, in being concordant with the nature of the phenomenon of interest and accurately reflecting the phenomenon. In either case, if those data patterns that reflect the phenomenon of interest are not those to which the applied technique is sensitive, the results of analysis will not be accurate. They will neither reflect the relevant patterns in the data accurately nor allow accurate insight into the phenomenon of interest. Thus, the assumptions that a technique encompasses, concerning which aspects of the data's structure reflect the phenomenon of interest and its nature, must concord with those aspects of the data's structure that do, *indeed*, reflect the phenomenon of interest and its nature. Only in this way can analytic results accurately represent the phenomenon of interest and have the potential for meaningful interpretation. *Accurate quantitative analysis requires logical concordance between technical assumption and relevant aspects of data structure.*

Technique in Relation to Theory

At the same time, a data set's relevant structure, as revealed through the application of a technique that is sensitive to it, can be assigned an appropriate meaning only if the theoretical framework that guides or emerges from analysis is logically concordant with that technique and those relevant aspects of the data. If those patterns within a data set that are relevant to the phenomenon of interest are accurately revealed using an appropriate technique that implies one set of assumptions, but the patterns are interpreted within a theoretical framework that makes a different set of assumptions, then the meaning assigned to the patterns will probably be incorrect. For example, two tool types within the same tool kit might only associate rather than correlate in their spatial distributions over a site as a result of the operation of certain post-depositional disturbance processes over that same area. Appropriately, they might also be found to associate using spatial techniques that are sensitive to nominal scale relations among types and not to correlate using techniques that are sensitive to ratio scale relations. It is not likely, however, that these results would be assigned appropriate meanings—the existence of the tool kit and the operation of the post-depositional processes—if it were expected theoretically that tool types within tool kits always covary over space and that the effects of disturbance processes on this relationship are minimal (Carr, 1977; 1984). Thus, it is possible to identify, within data, patterns that accurately reflect the phenomenon of interest, but to then impart inappropriate meaning to the patterns, if one's guiding theoretical framework is not logically consistent with the data's relevant structure and the structure that is assumed relevant by the applied technique. *Meaningful quantitative analysis requires logical concordance between technique and theory as well as between technique and data.*

The logically consistent relationship between technical assumption and theoretical framework that is necessary to meaningful scientific investigation can be envisioned in a manner that is different from the above and more in line with discussions of philosophy of science. The assumptions that are implied by the application of a technique to data and that pertain to which aspects of the data's structure reflect the phenomenon of interest and its nature can be treated as *auxiliary assumptions* within the employed theoretical framework (Hempel, 1966, pp. 22-23; Salmon, 1982, p. 36). This is true whether one is building hypotheses and theory, testing them, or using them to explain a particular case. Thus, meaningful investigation can be said to require logical consistency between these auxiliary assumptions and other aspects of the theoretical framework, i.e., *internal* theoretical consistency.

Although this viewpoint is strictly correct, it focuses undue attention on the need for concordance between technical assumption and theoretical constructs; it does not imply the equally important need for concordance between technique and data. It also makes it difficult to discuss the need for and the nature of concordance between technique and data separate from consideration of other aspects of the theoretical framework. Consequently, in this volume, technique, and technical assumption about the nature of the phenomenon of interest that a technique is expected to monitor during its application, are considered to constitute an ideological construct in their own right—separate from theory, model, hypothesis, and test implication, and serving to interface test implication with data. In this way, both the relationship between technique and data and that between technique and theoretical framework—as well as the degree of concordance involved in each relationship—can be appropriately emphasized and more easily visualized and discussed.

A similar separation and positioning of technique in relation to theoretical framework and data is used by Limp and Carr (chapter 7) for these reasons. There, the term *etic coherence* is used to refer to the degree of concordance between theoretical framework and quantitative technique, whereas the term *emic symmetry* is used to refer to the degree of concordance between quantitative technique and the nature of the phenomenon of interest as expressed in data.

TWO KINDS OF DISCREPANCIES BETWEEN DATA STRUCTURE AND TECHNICAL ASSUMPTION

The data that are brought forward for analysis in early stages of a scientific project and the techniques that are used to explore them typically have a high potential for being logically discordant. This discordance results from the manner in which the data and technique are chosen. Most frequently, the variables and observations that are initially chosen for analysis are selected for their potential pertinence to a *broad problem domain* that involves *multiple, potential phenomena of interest*, rather than a single phenomenon of interest. They are also selected *deductively* on the basis of the *expected* nature of the potential phenomena of interest rather than their actual nature, which remains to be investigated. Likewise, the technique of analysis is selected deductively on the basis of the concordance between its assumptions and the expected nature of one or more of the potential phenomena of interest and the way in which they might be reflected in the data.

Two kinds of discordances between data structure and technical assumption can result from these selection processes.

Discordance 1. This discrepancy centers on the number of processes and populations to which the data and technique pertain. Being chosen in relation to a broad problem domain, the variables and observations that are brought forward for analysis typically reflect *multiple processes* that define *multiple populations*. As Cowgill (1982, p. 39) notes:

> In theory we may base our selection of variables and their possible values entirely on considerations of their relevance for specific purposes, but in practice . . . the tendancy seems to be to begin with a sizable number of *possibly relevant* variables and to decide that the truly relevant ones are those variables that in fact do, in terms of their patterning within the assemblage, show some sort of structure. (stress by Cowgill)

In contrast, many statistical techniques and the theory on which they are based assume a model that specifies some *single process* to be responsible for the variability within the data to be analyzed and a *homogeneous population* defined with respect to that process. For example, tests of model sufficiency in linear regression assume that the observations and variables that are under consideration refer to a single, multivariate normal population.

Equivalently, many statistical techniques and their theoretical foundations can be viewed as assuming a model that allows multiple processes to be responsible for the variability within the data, but these processes must be *parallel* and *coterminous* in the range of observations that they affect, so as to still define only one homogeneous population rather than multiple populations (Carr, in press). In other words, the outcomes of the multiple processes can be analytically combined as if they were the outcomes of a single process, effectively, which defines a single homogeneous population, despite the conceptual distinction of the processes. An example of parallel processes would be an activity that leads to the deposition of two tool types (a tool kit) in constant proportions over an archaeological site, and one or more post-depositional processes that operate over an area of similar expanse and that alter the constant proportions to simple co-occurrence relationships among the two types over the whole area.

Inasmuch as the model that underlies a statistical technique assumes a single process and population, or parallel processes and a single population, whereas the deduced set of possibly relevant variables and observations pertain to multiple processes that define multiple populations, technique and data will be logically discordant and the results of analysis of the data need not be meaningful. Analytic results will reflect an uncontrolled mix of several kinds of relationships among observations: relationships among observations within populations, which may differ from one population to another, and the relationship of populations to each other (Christenson & Read, 1977, p. 170). This problem and its solution are the subject of chapter 3 by Read and chapter 2 by Carr.

Discordance 2. This kind of discrepancy between data and technique, like the first, results from the manner by which they are selected. It concerns the *nature of organization* of the phenomenon of interest and how it is *actually expressed* structurally within the data compared to how it is *expected to be expressed,* as implied by the assumptions made by the technique being used and the kinds of variability to which it is sensitive. Of all the different kinds of relationships that occur within a data matrix between variables and observations (e.g., nominal, ordinal, or ratio scale relations; monothetic or polythetic relations; overlapping or nonoverlapping relations) only some will indicate the phenomenon of interest. The particular manifestation of the phenomenon of interest within the data will depend on the phenomenon's nature of organization. For example, in our tool kit illustration above, the two artifacts within the same tool kit might have covaried in their frequencies within the behavioral domain. This covariation would reflect the nature of their functions and organization for use and the nature of organization of the tool kit (the phenomenon of interest) in that domain. However, as a result of parallel, coterminous post-depositional formation processes, the two types might only co-occur in the archaeological domain, and the tool kit (the *same* phenomenon of interest) would have a different organization: a nominal scale organization rather than a ratio scale organization. Given a data matrix composed of the densities of each of the two artifact types within grid cells over the site, the membership of the two types in the same tool kit and the existence of the tool kit would not be expressed accurately by the ratio relationship among the densities of the types over the grid cells. Instead, they would be indicated by the nominal scale relationship among the presence-absence states of the types over grid cells that is *implicit* in the density data. The phenomenon of interest would be expressed in only certain aspects of the total information that is contained within the data matrix.

When a technique of analysis is selected deductively, any discordance between the *actual* nature of organization of the phenomenon of interest and its expression in the data, on the one hand, and its *postulated* nature of organization as implied by this choice, on the other, will result in a discordance between the chosen technique and those relevant aspects of the data that reflect the phenomenon of interest. This discordance will lead to quantitative results that are not necessarily meaningful or interpretable. Continuing the example above, suppose that a researcher expects that artifact types in the same tool kit will covary in their frequencies over a site as a result of their use and discard in constant proportions while achieving a task. Suppose that he also expects the randomizing effects of post-depositional disturbance processes on artifact organization to be minimal. He then might logically use the above-described matrix of artifact type densities within grid cells as given, along with correlation analysis, to search for covarying artifact types and tool kits over the site. The use of correlation analysis, however, would be discordant with the actual nominal scale nature of organization of the archaeological tool kits containing the types, and with those aspects of the total information implicit in the density matrix which reflect that organization. Not being consistently sensitive to nominal scale patterning among variables, correlation methods would not necessarily lead to the discovery of the tool kit. Thus, discordance between how a phenomenon of interest is actually expressed within data structurally, and how it is expected to be expressed—as a result of deductive selection of technique—can lead to a logical incongruence between technical assumption and relevant aspects of the data. Consequently, results may be questionable in meaning. This problem and its solution are discussed by Carr in chapter 2.

In sum, the manner in which data and technique are selected during initial stages of research can lead to two kinds of discordances between them. One pertains to the *number* of phenomena reflected in the data as compared to that assumed by the applied technique. This discordance arises from the way in which *data* are selected. The second pertains to the nature of the phenomenon of interest's *organization* which is assumed by the chosen technique as compared to the phenomenon's actual form of organization and expression in the data. This discordance arises from the way in which *technique* is selected. Both kinds of discordances typify early stages of analysis when a single phenomenon of interest has not been defined and little is known about the number or nature of the phenomena that are responsible for the data or their manner of expression in the data. The same two kinds of discordances can also occur, however, in later stages of analysis, depending on the success that the researcher has had in formulating specific questions that pertain to some single phenomenon and in coming to understand the kinds and causes of variability in the data (see Carr, chapter 2).

DEFINITION OF TERMS CONCERNING DATA STRUCTURE

In recognition of the multitude of phenomena and relationships that data can express, as well as the two kinds of discordances between data and technique that can occur, two pairs of contrasting terms are used throughout this volume.

These are 1) *total data structure* vs. *relevant data structure,* and 2) *relevant subset structure* vs. *relevant relational structure.*

Total data structure (or simply, data structure). This term is used to refer to all the variables, observations, and the relationships among them within a data set, regardless of whether or not they reflect the phenomenon of interest. A data structure may include "extra" variables or observations and relationships among them that are not pertinent to a single process (or parallel processes) and a single population of interest, as well as those that are. It may also include, simultaneously, multiple kinds of relationships among the *same* variables or observations (e.g., nominal scale and ratio scale relationships, monothetic and polythetic relationships)—only some relationships of which reflect the nature of organization of the phenomenon of interest. For example, ratio scale data simultaneously express interval, ordinal, and nominal scale relationships among variables, not all of which need be relevant.

Relevant data structure. In contrast to the term, total data structure, the term relevant data structure is reserved for those aspects of a data set that reflect the *single phenomenon of interest.* A data set's relevant structure includes variables and observations that pertain to a single process or parallel, coterminous processes that define a homogeneous population. It includes only those kinds of relationships among variables and observations that reflect the phenomenon of interest and its nature of organization.

A data set's relevant structure, particularly for archaeological data, usually will not have a physical correlate in a specific set of data items. This results partly from the fact that a single variable may reflect multiple processes (underlying dimensions of variability) and stochastic variation. It also relates to the fact that data at a measurement level higher than the nominal scale simultaneously reflect relationships at that higher-level scale and relationships at all lower-level scales. Finally, it can reflect a more fundamental circumstance that pertains to the organization of phenomena of interest in the physical world, as opposed to data about them. A phenomenon of interest (population or process) may not exist separate from other phenomena; it may be possible to isolate it only analytically, not physically. (See postscript, p. 14, for an example.)

Relevant subset structure vs. *relevant relational structure.* The relevant structure of a data set has two distinguishable, usually cross-cutting components. These are the relevant subset structure of the data set and its relevant relational structure. Consider a matrix of variables and observations that have been selected in regard to a broad problem domain rather than as a reflection of some single phenomenon of interest. The relevant subset structure of that matrix can be defined as the *subset of data items* that pertains to variables and observations reflecting the phenomenon of interest, although not necessarily only that phenomenon (see above). A data matrix that is defined in regard to a problem domain will usually have multiple relevant subset structures, each pertinent to different phenomena.

In contrast, the relevant relational structure of a data matrix is comprised of those *relationships among variables and observations* that are of a kind that reflect the organizational nature of the single phenomenon of interest. A data matrix may simultaneously contain several relational structures pertinent to several phenomena, even if the matrix has but one relevant subset structure. For example, recall the tool kit illustration. The matrix of cell densities of each of the two artifact types contains a nominal-scale relevant relational structure, which is pertinent to their organization as a tool kit, and a ratio scale relevant relational structure, which is pertinent to the disorganization of the types due to postdepositional disturbance processes.

Bringing this discussion full circle, then, one can relate the manner in which *data are selected* in early stages of research, the *number of phenomena* that a data set reflects, and the number of relevant *subset structures* that comprise the data set. During early stages of research, variables and observations are usually chosen in regard to some general problem domain, reflect multiple phenomena (processes and populations), and are comprised of multiple potentially relevant subset structures. One can also relate the manner in which *technique is selected*, the *nature of organization* of the phenomenon of interest that is assumed by the chosen technique, and the particular relevant *relational structure* of the data to which the technique is sensitive. During early stages of research, technique is often chosen deductively, with its assumptions reflecting the expected nature of organization of the phenomenon of interest and how that organization is expected to be expressed as relevant relational structure within the data.

It is the transformation of data structure into relevant subset and relational data structure, and the selection or design of technique in regard to relevant relational data structure, that are the focus of this volume.

POSTSCRIPT: A COMMENT ON METAPHYSICAL VIEWPOINT

The contributors to this volume represent a moderate range of world views that fall between the extremes of logical positivism and a phenomenological perspective. In this introduction and the chapters to follow, I take a particular perspective that I have found useful in developing the volume themes, but one that is not necessarily shared completely by all the contributors. This perspective I wish to make explicit.

In discussing the relationships of theory and technical assumption to data and phenomena of interest, I imply the distinction between several categories of information:

1) a portion of the real world

2) a phenomenon of interest—either a population or a process

3) data brought forward for study of a problem domain that includes the phenomenon of interest, i.e., total data structure

4) aspects of the data that are truly relevant to only the phenomenon of interest, i.e., relevant data structure

5) aspects of the data that are expected to be relevant to the phenomenon of interest.

The first four categories—as they are defined here—hold, in part, a nested, hierarchical relationship to each other. Among these categories, lower-level (higher-numbered) ones embody decreasing amounts of information on the real world as a result of the partially controllable processes of selective observation and analysis. The distinction between the last category and the first four reflects the difference between theoretical concepts about the real world, and the real world itself or selected information on it.

The first category, a portion of the real world, is the broadest category of information. It is the subset of *entities* or objects in the real world that the researcher selects for study in relation to his paradigmatic orientation and his more particular problem domain. Similar concepts are the research universe or study area.

Although a portion of the real world may be selected for study with a purpose in mind and in regard to certain of its characteristics, it is taken to have, simultaneously, a very large number of characteristics (properties, structures, organizations, natures) that are determined by a very large number of processes. This gives any portion of the world many *facets* or *phenomena*, such that it can be explored from many different perspectives and paradigms.

An example of a portion of the real world is an earthen archaeological site. This land parcel would have a large number of characteristics—e.g., artifactual, topographic, pedological, hydrological, archaeomagnetic, and others—only some of which might have served as a basis for selecting it for study. The site could be studied from many different perspectives and paradigms.

The second category, a phenomenon of interest, is that one facet within a portion of the real world—among its many facets—that is the object of study. Like the portion of the real world that is selected for study, the phenomenon of interest is chosen in relation to the researcher's paradigmatic orientation and problem domain.

A phenomenon of interest can be either a homogeneous population or a single process (or equivalently, parallel, coterminous processes that are analytically definable as one process). If the phenomenon of interest is a population, its organizational *nature* is determined by the process(es) that structure it—one or several of the many processes that structure the portion of the world of which the phenomenon is a part. If the phenomenon of interest is a process, its *form* is determined by the constraints that define it—a subset of the many constraints within the portion of the world of which the phenomenon is a part.

An example of a phenomenon of interest is a population of several archaeological tool kits (deposits) of some one kind (e.g., a hideworking set of knives, scrapers, and borers). This population of tool kits is the set of outcomes of a single process—an activity, hideworking. The organizational nature of the population of tool kits—for example, whether their constituent tool types are symmetrically or asymmetrically distributed or whether the tool types covary or only co-occur over the multiple tool kits—is determined partially by the nature of the hideworking depositional process.

Note that the same population of interest can have different forms of organization if parallel, coterminous processes structure it and if some of these processes are optional. This was exemplified earlier in this chapter (see p. 9), when it was suggested that a population of archaeological tool kits (deposits) might be characterized by either constant proportions among the artifact classes comprising them, or by simply co-occurrence relationships among the artifact classes. The first form of organization might reflect simply the nature of the activity in which the artifact classes were used and which led to their deposition; the second might reflect this depositional process plus the effects of one or more parallel, post-depositional disturbance processes that operated over the same area and altered proportional relationships to co-occurrence relationships.

A phenomenon of interest may or may not exist separate from other phenomena in the real world, and it may or may not be possible to isolate it physically. Sometimes the isolation of a phenomenon is possible only analytically. For example, in our tool kit example, the kinds of knives, scrapers, and/or borers that were involved in the population of hideworking tool kits might also have been used in other activities (e.g., working wood or bone), so as to define additional populations of tool kits (woodworking tool kits, boneworking tool kits). The spatial distributions of the multipurpose tool classes would then reflect these other activities (processes) and kinds of tool kits (populations) in addition to the hideworking tool kits as the phenomenon (population) of interest and hideworking as the process defining it. Isolation of the hideworking tool kits from the boneworking and woodworking tool kits might be possible only analytically (see below). This potential inability to physically segregate a phenomenon of interest from other phenomena contrasts with the physically discrete nature of portions of the real world that are chosen for study.

The third category, data brought forward for study, usually involves more and less information than that pertinent to the single phenomenon of interest. Data brought forward for study often include variables and cases that pertain to multiple phenomena (populations or processes), rather than a single phenomenon. In part, this can result from the data having been selected in relation to a broad problem domain and phenomena generally of interest, rather than a single, declared phenomenon of interest. It can also result from the inability to physically isolate the phenomenon of interest from other phenomena in the real world (see above). Data brought forward for study also usually express less than all the information that is pertinent to a single phenomenon of interest. This can result from the shortsightedness of research and data collection designs, the inadequacies of the theoretical frameworks used to plan them, and practical economic limitations. Finally, data brought forward for study may include information on undesirable processes, such as observation and data-recording biases and errors. In this chapter, the term, total data structure, has been used to refer to the complex structure of data items that has been brought forward for study—which includes relevant and irrelevant observations and relationships between data items, and probably also excludes some pertinent information.

An example of data brought forward for study, to continue our tool kit illustration, would be the spatial distributions of the multipurpose knives, scrapers, and borers. These data would reflect multiple phenomena of potential interest—multiple populations of tool kits that reflect multiple kinds of activities (processes). The data also would simultaneously include ratio, ordinal, and nominal scale spatial relationships among classes, whereas only one of these scales would be pertinent for revealing any one of the populations of tool kits. Finally, the data might lack information on the spatial locations of some items as a result of their incomplete recovery during excavation.

In contrast to a data set brought forward for study are those aspects of it that are relevant to some one phenomenon of interest and that comprise its relevant subset structure and relevant relational structure. Note that those aspects of the data that are relevant to the phenomenon of interest often express only a portion of the information that is potentially available and pertinent to the phenomenon of interest. This is a product of the constrained manner in which data that are brought forward for study are collected and selected.

Relevant data structures within a data set brought forward for analysis can be exemplified in the case of the artifact distribution palimpsests of multipurpose knives, scrapers, and borers that were previously described. Here, one relevant subset data structure would be the spatial locations of only those artifacts that were used and deposited together as hideworking tool kits (the population of interest) during hideworking (the defining process). A second relevant subset data structure would be the spatial locations of only those artifacts that were used and deposited together during woodworking, and a third would pertain to the locations of only boneworking artifacts that were deposited together. Use-wear or Fourier procedures (Carr, in press; this volume, chapter 13) might be used to analytically segregate these several relevant subset data structures from the data brought forward for study.

Finally, it is necessary to distinguish those aspects of a data set's structure that are expected to be relevant to a phenomenon of interest and its nature from those that are actually relevant to the phenomenon. Aspects of a data set's structure that are expected to be relevant are derived from some theoretical-interpretive framework and are expressed in the form of a model of relevant structure (see Read, chapter 3, schema D; Carr, chapter 13). They may bear little similarity to aspects of the data that actually reflect the phenomenon of interest, depending on the adequacy of both the primary premises and auxiliary assumptions within the theoretical framework. In the above illustration, for example, the population of hideworking tool kits (phenomenon of interest) might be manifested as nominal scale spatial relationships between knives, scrapers, and borers (as a result of the particular nature of the depositional process), whereas it might be expected that the population of tool kits would be defined in ratio scale spatial relationships.

In sum, the metaphysical framework that has been used in developing this book's themes postulates the multifaceted, multistructured nature of the real world, but also the concreteness of its facets (phenomena of interest), which can be explored within the constraints of different paradigms. This viewpoint leads to some important qualifications as to how, in this book, analytic concordance is taken to be assessable. In particular, from the viewpoint of the assumed metaphysical framework, it is impossible to speak in absolute terms about the accuracy, appropriateness, or relevance of a theoretical construct, analytic technique, or data structure in relation to the *real world* or a *portion of the real world*. It *is* possible, however, to speak in relative terms about the accuracy, appropriateness, or relevance of a theoretical construct, analytic technique, or data structure in relation to a *phenomenon of interest* as a selected but actual facet of a portion of the real world. It is also possible to speak in relative terms about the *expected* appropriateness or relevance of an analytic technique or data structure to the image of a phenomenon of interest, as expressed in theory.

REFERENCES

Binford, L.R. (1968). Archaeological perspectives. In S.R. Binford & L.R. Binford (Eds.), *New perspectives in archaeology* (pp. 5-32). Chicago: Aldine Publishing Co.

Carnap, R. (1936). Testability and meaning. *Philosophy of Science 3*(4), 420-471.

Carr, C. (1977). *The internal structure of a Middle Woodland site and the nature of organization of the archaeological record.* Unpublished preliminary examination paper, University of Michigan, Ann Arbor.

Carr, C. (1984). The nature of organization of intrasite archaeological records and spatial analytic approaches to their investigation. In M.B. Schiffer (Ed.), *Advances in archaeological method and theory* (Vol. 7) (pp. 103-222). New York: Academic Press, Inc.

Carr, C. (in press). Dissecting intrasite artifact palimpsests using Fourier methods. In S. Kent (Ed.), *Method and theory for activity area research: An ethnoarchaeological approach.* New York: Columbia University Press.

Christenson, A.L., & Read, D.W. (1977). Numerical taxonomy, R-mode factor analysis, and archaeological classification. *American Antiquity 42,* 163-179.

Cowgill, G.L. (1982). Clusters of objects and association between variables: Two approaches to archaeological classification. In R. Whallon & J.A. Brown (Eds.), *Essays on archaeological typology* (pp. 30-55). Evanston, IL: Center for American Archaeology Press.

Flannery, K.V. (1973). Archaeology with a capital s. In C.L. Redman (Ed.), *Research and theory in current archaeology.* New York: John Wiley & Sons, Inc.

Hempel, C.G. (1966). *Philosophy of natural science.* Englewood Cliffs, NJ: Prentice-Hall, Inc.

Hodder, I., & Orton, C. (1976). *Spatial analysis in archaeology.* Cambridge: Cambridge University Press.

Keene, A.S. (1981). *Prehistoric foraging in a temperate forest.* New York: Academic Press, Inc.
Marquardt, W.H. (1978). Advances in archaeological seriation. In M.B. Schiffer (Ed.), *Advances in archaeological method and theory* (Vol. 8) (pp. 257-314). New York: Academic Press, Inc.
Meehan, E. (1968). *Explanation in social science—a system paradigm.* Homewood, IL: The Dorsey Press.
Moore, J.A., & Keene, A.S. (1983). *Archaeological hammers and theories.* New York: Academic Press.
Peebles, C.S. (1971). Moundville and the surrounding sites: Some structural considerations of mortuary practices. In J.A. Brown (Ed.), Approaches to the social dimensions of mortuary practices. *Memoirs of the Society for American Archaeology 25.*
Read, D.W., & LeBlanc. S.A. (1978). Descriptive statements, covering laws, and theories in archaeology. *Current Anthropology 19*(2), 307-335.
Reidhead, V.A. (1981). *A linear programming model of prehistoric subsistence optimization: A southeastern Indiana example.* Indianapolis: Indiana Historical Society.
Renfrew, C., Rowlands, M.J., & Segraves, B.A. (1982). *Theory and explanation in archaeology: The Southampton conference.* New York: Academic Press.
Salmon, M.H. (1982). *Philosophy and archaeology.* New York: Academic Press.
Salmon, M.H., & Salmon, W.C. (1979). Alternative models of scientific explanation. *American Anthropologist 81*(1), 61-74.
Spaulding, A.C. (1953). Statistical techniques for the discovery of artifact types. *American Antiquity 18,* 305-313.
Spaulding, A.C. (1973). Archaeology in the active voice: The new anthropology. In C.L. Redman (Ed.), *Research and theory in current archaeology* (pp. 337-354). New York: Wiley.
van der Leeuw, S.E. (1978). Comment on: Read, D.W., & LeBlanc, S.A., descriptive statements, covering laws, and theories in archaeology. *Current Anthropology 19*(2), 328-329.
Watson, P.J., LeBlanc, S.A., & Redman, C.L. (1971). *Explanation in archaeology.* New York: Columbia University Press.
Whallon, R. (1973). Spatial analysis of occupation floors I: Application of dimensional analysis of variance. *American Antiquity 38,* 320-328.
Whallon, R. (1974). Spatial analysis of occupation floors II: The application of nearest neighbor analysis. *American Antiquity 39,* 16-34.
Whallon, R. (1984). Unconstrained clustering for the analysis of spatial distributions in archaeology. In H.J. Hietala, (Ed.), *Intrasite spatial analysis* (pp. 242-277). Cambridge: Cambridge University Press.
Whallon, R., & Brown, J.A. (Eds.). (1982). *Essays on archaeological typology.* Evanston, IL: Center for American Archaeology.

PART II: PHILOSOPHICAL FRAMEWORK

2

Getting into Data: Philosophy and Tactics for the Analysis of Complex Data Structures

CHRISTOPHER CARR

In Chapter 1, I argued that a quantitative analysis can produce meaningful results only when two conditions are met. First, there must be logical concordance between the assumptions that a chosen technique makes about which aspects of a data set's structure reflect the phenomenon of interest, and those aspects that actually are relevant in this way. This concordance ensures the accurate *representation* of the data. Second, there must be logical concordance between the theoretical framework that guides or emerges from analysis, and the assumptions that underlie the chosen analytic technique. This is necessary for appropriate *meaning to be assigned* to the analytically derived representation of the data.

Discordance between technical assumption and a data set's structure can be of two kinds. First, the model that underlies the statistical technique to be employed may require data that pertains to a single process or parallel, coterminous processes that define a single population, whereas the data to be analyzed may actually reflect the effects of multiple processes that define multiple populations. This discordance usually arises when the variables and observations that are brought forward for analysis are defined too broadly and reflect a general problem area rather than a specific phenomenon of interest. The relevant and irrelevant variables, dimensions, and observations that are suggested by this discordance define the data's relevant and irrelevant *subset structures*. Second, the aspects of the data's structure that reflect the phenomenon (e.g., the scale of measurement of relevant relationships between

---

The ideas in this chapter stem from conversations I have had with W. Fredrick Limp, Michael Schiffer, Robert Whallon, David Braun, Dwight Read, and many graduate students at the University of Arkansas over the past five years. For their stimulation, for the way they have enriched my life, I am most grateful. I also wish to thank David Braun, Dwight Read, and Michael Schiffer for a number of excellent comments that helped me in the revision of this chapter.

variables, the monothetic or polythetic nature of relevant relationships among observations) may not be those which are assumed relevant by the analytic technique and to which the technique is sensitive. This discordance often arises when there is inconsistency between the expected nature of organization of the phenomenon of interest (used as a basis for choosing the technique) and the actual nature of its organization. It suggests the distinction between the data's relevant and irrelevant *relational structures*.

In this chapter, the cause of such discordances between data structure, technical assumption, and theoretical framework is examined in philosophical terms. The cause is made clear by comparing the logical processes that are involved in analyzing *complex* data sets, which requires mathematical pattern recognition procedures, to those that are involved in analyzing *simple* data sets, which requires only mental pattern recognition abilities.

The complexity of a data set is defined here to be a function of its size (number of variables and observations), the number and complexity of patterns within it, and the strength of patterning. A complex data set can be either of two kinds. The first is a *multivariate* data set in which the number of variables, observations, and patterns among them are too large for the patterns and meaning of variation among data items to be assessed mentally. A data set having a structure resolvable only by principal components analysis would be an example. The second kind of complex data set is a *univariate* response to multiple factors, which forms a time or space series that is too complicated for mental dissection. To investigate a data set having this structure, Fourier analysis, spatial filtering techniques, or time series analysis would be required (Carr, 1982b, in press). In contrast to these complex data sets, a *simple* data set is taken to be one having a very limited, mentally manageable number of variables and observations that exhibit uncomplicated patterning.

It is important to emphasize that the dichotomy drawn here between complex and simple data sets pertains to only those of their characteristics that determine whether mathematical procedures are necessary to *recognize patterns* within them, as just described. The distinction is not used to refer to other data characteristics, which determine the *ease with which appropriate meaning is assignable* to the patterns found within them. These additional characteristics include, for example, the number and complexity of assumptions involved in collecting, subsampling, and/or screening the data. In regard to these kinds of characteristics, all data sets are more or less complex (Schiffer, personal communication, 1983).

Once the cause of the discordances that can occur between data structure, technique, and theoretical framework during the analysis of complex data structures has been clarified, the occasions when such discordances arise will be discussed. Although such problems can potentially occur at all stages of analysis, they are particularly notable in the initial stages when little is known about the relevant aspects of a data set's structure. At this time, the researcher may find himself in a *methodological double bind*: he cannot choose an appropriate technique of analysis and an appropriate subset of the data for analysis without some knowledge about the data set's relevant relational and subset structures; yet he cannot obtain this knowledge without applying some pattern searching technique to summarize the data's structure in a simpler form that is more comprehendable by the human mind. In short, the researcher has a problem of "getting into the data."

Finally, several solutions to the problem of getting into data and maintaining logical consistency in analysis thereafter are offered. The solutions—some standard, others not—are complementary. None is completely adequate. Each, however, focuses on precise *specification* of the phenomenon of interest and its nature, and explicit *justification* of the variables, observations, and techniques to be used in analysis relative to the phenomenon and its nature. As a consequence, they facilitate the formalization of bridging arguments, which characterize a mature discipline, and the development of theory; they represent a fundamental source of scientific advance.

A CAUSE OF LOGICAL INCONSISTENCIES BETWEEN DATA STRUCTURE, TECHNIQUE, AND THEORY

The fact that archaeology seeks to reconstruct and understand nonobservables (past behavior and ideas) through the discovery and investigation of patterning among observables (archaeological phenomena) places archaeological method within the realm of scientific method, involving the generating and testing of hypotheses or models (complexes of hypotheses). Hypotheses or models that are concerned with nonobservable activities and ideas are formulated through the discovery of patterns (generalizations) and are tested through the seeking of specific patterns (test implications) in archaeological observables.

The logic that is involved in formulating or testing hypotheses can vary in its consistency and potential for leading the researcher to accurate and meaningful conclusions. The degree of logical consistency that is realized and the accuracy of the conclusions that are reached depend minimally on two factors. The first is a *technical determinant*, which involves the complexity of the phenomenon, observables, and data set under investigation, and thus whether pattern-seeking mathematical techniques (e.g., factor analysis) are required during pattern-searching stages of research.

The second is a *theoretical determinant*, which involves the accuracy of the auxiliary assumptions that are used in assigning meaning to recognized patterns. For the sake of argument, the second, theoretical determinant will be held constant. It will be assumed that the auxiliary assumptions that are used in assigning meaning to recognized patterns are correct. Instead, attention will be focused on variation in the technical determinant and its effects on the consistency and accuracy of hypothesis formulation or testing.

Two kinds of situations, varying in the logic that they involve, can arise. In the first, a researcher studies relatively simple phenomena of interest. Observables and data observations pattern themselves clearly such that the researcher can observe the patterns by him/herself, without the aid of mathematical pattern-searching algorithms. In this case, the logic involved in the formulation or testing of hypotheses can be carried out with consistency between data structure, generalization/test implication, and hypothesis and can lead to accurate and meaningful conclusions. This can be done in the manner envisioned by philosophers of science (Hempel, 1966; Hanson, 1972). In the second situation, the phenomena studied are relatively complex. Observables and data observations pattern themselves in ways that require the researcher to use pattern-finding mathematical techniques rather than his own senses and mental capabilities, alone, to search for pattern. In this case, logical inconsistencies between data structure, technique, test implication, and hypothesis can creep into the analysis. Inaccurate quantitative results and distorted understanding may be derived.

Let us see how the study of complex phenomena and patterning among observables with mathematical techniques presents a problem in logic, whereas the study of simpler phenomena and patterning among observables with one's own mental capabilities does not. We can do this by comparing the two approaches, varying only the technical determinant of consistency and accuracy.

In the analysis of either simply or complexly structured data, the researcher's task is twofold: to *find* patterns inherent in the data and *interpret* them with regard to the phenomena that produced them. Interpretation of an empirical pattern can be achieved in two ways. The first involves comparing the empirical pattern to those patterns implied by extant predictive laws or models and then matching it to one of the expected patterns (Toussaint, 1978, pp. 191-192). This allows the logical subsumption of the specific case under the accepted general law or model (i.e., explanation). Alternatively, interpretation of a pattern can be achieved through the formulation of a new hypothesis/model that implies an expectable pattern which matches the one found (theory/hypothesis building), followed by logical subsumption of the specific case under the new general principle. This amounts to explanation only if the new principle can be confirmed with other, independent data. The problem with the logic of analysis of complex data sets is most apparent in those analyses that require the second means of interpretation—hypothesis generation—but also is an aspect of analyses that involve the application of extant laws/models for interpretation. Let us first consider analysis involving hypothesis generation.

For simply structured data sets with simple patterning among observations, the tasks of finding patterns and interpreting them through the generation of adequate explanatory hypotheses can be done with a *single* mental operation called *abduction* (Hanson, 1972). Abduction is the simultaneous discovery of a *pattern* and its *significance* in suggesting a hypothetical cause of the pattern, as one searches data. Abductive reasoning is the simultaneous dawning that a pattern exists in one's data, and that "the pattern could be explained if hypothesis X were true."

Abduction is more than induction—the process by which generalizations (patterns) are formulated (Hempel, 1966). Abduction involves the realization of the higher-level *meaning* of a generalization (i.e., the development of an hypothesis) as well as the formulation of the generalization, itself. Abduction is also more than retroduction—the process of understanding that a pattern could be explained if a given, new hypothesis were true. (Here, I depart from Hanson's [1972] use of the term retroduction.) Abduction involves the *perception* of a new pattern—previously unperceived—as well as the retroduction of a new explanatory hypothesis. Abduction, then is the seeming "conceptual gestalt" by which, simultaneously, new hypotheses are born and patterning in data suddenly becomes clear and explicable.

For more complexly organized observables, the processes of discovering patterns among data items and inferring the phenomenon that produced those patterns is a more intricate, *multistep, serialized* task. In the most common approach to analysis, first, sophisticated, pattern-finding mathematical techniques are used to search the data for multidimensional patterns and to summarize those patterns in two or three dimensional representations that humans can visualize, or with a few statistics (but see the "entry model" approach to data analysis, described below). This step, which involves the generalization of patterns among observables, is equivalent to logical *induction*. Second, the patterns that are found and summarized are then interpreted in terms of the phenomena that produced them. This step, which involves the logic that a pattern would be explicable if a given, new hypothesis were true, is equivalent to logical *retroduction*.

The difference between the multistep, serialized logic of analysis of complex data structures and the single-step logic of analysis of simple data structures is critical. It involves a *separation* of the process of *finding patterns* from the process of *interpreting patterns*, by the mathematical technique used to search the data. *This separation has the fundamental consequence of leaving room for the development of logical inconsistencies between data structure, pattern-finding technique, and interpretive framework during the course of analysis. These inconsistencies, in turn, may result in the distorted definition of relevant patterning and the drawing of false conclusions.*

To elaborate on this point, in the simple abductive process, data are searched for patterns by a human mind that both *knows* what kinds of patterns are possibly meaningful and expectable from an interpretive standpoint, and *searches* the data for precisely those patterns in some appropriate way. At the same time as the data are searched, the interpretive framework, the set of possibly meaningful patterns (the aspects of the data's structure considered relevant), and the mode of search are questioned and reformulated continuously, in light of the patterns found in the data. Feedback is instantaneous and continuous between data structure, mode of pattern searching, and interpretive framework, which brings and keeps all three in logically consistent relationships with each other. This feedback and logical consistency is possible only because the mental activities of searching for patterns and interpreting pattern occur simultaneously, in parallel, as part of the process of abduction.

In the case where mathematical techniques are used to search for patterns in complexly structured data items that pertain to complex phenomena, such feedback does not occur on a continuous basis. Data are not searched for patterns by a human mind with a *variable* search strategy, a variable theoretical framework, and a variable list of potentially relevant aspects of the data's structure—all of which may change as knowledge is gained about the data's structure during the search. Rather, data are searched by a mathematical technique with a *fixed* search strategy that is consistent with and implies a fixed interpretive framework and a fixed list of aspects of the data's structure that are considered relevant—none of which change when applied to the data. Critically, whether or not the technique produces mathematical results that accurately represent the relevant structure of the data depends on the degree of logical consistency between aspects of the data that are assumed relevant by the technique and those that actually are relevant. Interpretation then *follows* the search for patterning, *after* logical inconsistencies between relevant data structure, technique, and implied theoretical framework, as well as misrepresentation of the data, have had a chance to be incorporated in the analysis. Interpretations and conclusions of questionable accuracy and meaning may be derived. Thus, logical inconsistencies in analysis and erroneous conclusions can result from the *separation and serialization* of the processes of searching for pattern and interpreting pattern, and the inopportunity in a single search-pass over data for *feedback* between the currently known aspects of their structure and the nature of the search technique and interpretive framework.

The separation of the processes of searching for pattern and interpreting pattern by technique, and the undesirable effects of this separation on the logic of analysis, characterizes not only analyses that involve the formulation of new hypotheses for interpretation. It also characterizes analyses that involve the application of extant laws/models for interpretation. First, test implications are deduced from alternative models/laws that might have interpretive value for the specific case under investigation. Then the data are searched by mathematical techniques having assumptions that are concordant with the theoretical framework, rather than the relevant aspects of the data, in order to find patterns that match one or more of the test implication(s) and that allow the logical subsumption of the specific case under one or more of the explanatory models/laws. The patterns that are found within the data by the search technique may represent the relevant aspects of the data's structure with varying degrees of accuracy, depending on whether the technique's design and the assumptions it makes are logically consistent with the relevant aspects of the data. The matches obtained between found pattern and deduced test implications, and the interpretations made, will correspondingly vary in accuracy and meaning. Once again, in a single search-pass over the data, there is no opportunity for feedback between currently known aspects of the structure of the data, on the one hand, and the search technique and interpretive model implied by it, on the other. Logical inconsistencies are allowed to develop between data and technique, and erroneous conclusions are allowed to be drawn.

If one considers that in a real analysis, an interpretive framework involves uncertain auxiliary assumptions in addition to the primary hypotheses/laws or models, the problem of how to analyze a complex data set with logical consistency and how to define relevant patterns within it that have potential for being assigned appropriate meaning becomes all the more apparent and troublesome. In a real analysis, choice of analytic technique and the patterning in the data that is revealed may be influenced by the auxiliary premises as well as the primary premise assumed true. A delay in the feedback between known aspects of data structure and the interpretive framework (including the auxiliary assumptions) may result in a poorer choice of techniques for searching the data, a greater potential for inconsistency in analysis, and the definition of less relevant patterning. This circumstance will increase the possibility of inaccurately assigning meaning to analytic results, additional to the effects of any inaccuracies in the auxiliary assumptions, themselves.

In sum, maintaining logical consistency during the analysis of complex data sets often cannot be achieved for any single pass over the data. This problem does not result from the use of a pattern finding technique, per se. Both mental scanning of simple data sets and mechanical scanning of complex ones require the use of some search technique, yet the effectiveness of the latter may not match that of the former. Rather, the problem with the analysis of complex data, as typically approached, results from separating and serializing the processes of finding pattern and interpreting pattern, which does not allow continuous feedback between data structure, search technique, and theoretical framework. For circumstances involving hypothesis formulation as opposed to hypothesis testing, the problem posed by complex data sets, compared to simple ones, can be summarized in logical terms. *Analysis of complex data requires inductive and retroductive logic, whereas analysis of simple data can be achieved through abduction.*

THE PROBLEM OF GETTING INTO DATA

The serial process of finding pattern and interpreting pattern that is commonly involved in the analysis of complex data sets can result in the two potential kinds of discordance between data, technique, and theory that are described in this chapter's introduction. In brief, an analytic technique and the interpretive framework with respect to which it is chosen may assume that the data of interest pertain to a single process and population (relevant subset structure) and have a certain organization (relevant relational structure) when in actuality the data may reflect multiple processes and populations and have a different relevant relational structure.

These kinds of discordance can occur at any stage in the analysis of complex data sets. They are particularly problematic, however, at the beginning of the analytic process. At this point, little may be known about the relevant aspects of the data's structure. As a consequence, the researcher is put in a bind. He cannot choose an appropriate analytic technique and an appropriate subset of the data for analysis without some knowledge about the data set's structure; yet he cannot obtain this knowledge without applying some pattern-searching technique to summarize the data's structure in a simpler form that is comprehendable by the human mind. If the researcher uses an inappropriate technique and subset of the data, the patterns that are found may not be an accurate representation of the data's relevant structure, nor meaningful. Furthermore, these distorted patterns—if used as the basis for making basic transformations of the data (screening it) in order to bring concordance in later analytic steps—can instead focus the analysis in a direction of greater discordance.

A very simple example of this bind during the initial stages of analysis of complex data is given by Christenson and Read (1977, p. 171). Concerned with the typology of a set of projectile points, they note that they could not do an R-mode factor analysis of the data to determine relevant dimensions of morphological variability without first eliminating extreme cases and defining a homogeneous population. (To not eliminate such cases would introduce distortions in the magnitudes of the correlation coefficients serving as a basis for the factor analysis.) At the same time, proper multivariate (as opposed to univariate) identification of the outliers required that the dimensions of variability present in the data be known.

Thus, complex data pose to the researcher a problem of how to enter or "get into" them without violating the relevant aspects of their structure. To circumvent this problem, at least four different strategies of analysis can be used. These are discussed in the remaining sections of this chapter and the following chapter by Read.

SOLUTIONS FOR MAINTAINING LOGICAL CONSISTENCY BETWEEN DATA STRUCTURE AND TECHNIQUE

To enter unknown, complex data yet maximize consistency between relevant aspects of its structure and technical assumption, four complementary strategies of analysis can be used:

1) deductive specification of potentially relevant variables and observations, and an appropriate technique;
2) "constrained" exploratory data analysis;

3) the "entry model" approach; and
4) stepwise, cyclical analytic designs.

Each of the strategies improves the researcher's chance of 1) selecting a subset of variables and observations that reflect the phenomenon of interest, and 2) choosing an analytic technique that is concordant with and sensitive to the relevant structure of the data. In this way, the strategies help to resolve the two potential kinds of discordances that can occur between data and technique, which were summarized in the beginning of this chapter, and to overcome the methodological double bind.

Deductive Specification of Potentially Relevant Variables and Observations, and an Appropriate Technique

One direct strategy for improving the degree of logical consistency within an analysis is to deductively specify that subset of the available data and that analytic technique which are *likely* to be relevant to the phenomenon of interest. This is done on the basis of extant theory about the nature of that kind of phenomenon in general. To the extent that the expected nature of the phenomenon of interest does not concord with its actual nature, irrelevant variables and items may be included in analysis and some meaningful ones may be deleted. In addition, the technique that is chosen for analysis may assume that certain kinds of relationships among variables or observations are relevant, when in fact other kinds reflect the phenomenon of interest more accurately (see Carr, chapter 1).

This strategy is usually employed at the beginning of a multistep analysis, when little is known about the structure of the specific data that are available for analysis. It can be followed by more inductive exploration of the chosen data using techniques that are justified on the basis of the initial insight that is obtained into the data's structure.

In archaeological studies, middle range theory (e.g., Binford, 1977a; Schiffer 1976; Raab & Goodyear, 1984) is frequently used to deduce the subset of data and/or the technique that is likely to be appropriate for analysis. Middle range theory is useful in this regard because it specifies the archaeological observables that are expected to manifest particular phenomena of interest, and/or their expected nature of organization. Let us consider some examples of this application of middle range theory.

Middle Range Theory Used to Specify Relevant Subsets of Variables and Observations

Artifact Style Analysis. One area of currently active research, in which middle range theory has been used to deduce potentially relevant variables and observations for analysis, is artifact style analysis for the purpose of testing or formulating propositions about prehistoric social organization. Wobst's (1977) information exchange theory of style specifies the characteristics of items that are likely to indicate group affiliation through their morphology, thereby suggesting the *observations* that are probably relevant to the study of prehistoric social organization. Items having this potential are those that 1) probably were used in contexts ensuring their visibility to all members of the group and members of other nearby groups, as opposed to items used in the domestic sphere; 2) are long-lived, making their expression of group affiliation efficient over time; and 3) probably were not exchanged between groups.

Voss (1980a, p. 4), following Wobst, goes on to specify, for such items, the different kinds of stylistic *variables* that are often useful for determining group affiliation versus group interaction. Discrete characteristics that are highly visible and that thus can function effectively as symbols, such as discrete design elements and configurations (Fredrick, 1970; Stanislawski & Stanislawski, 1978), are more likely to be accurate measures of group affiliation. In contrast, continuous stylistic variables that encompass the "nuances" of style, such as the dimensions of design zones and counts of design element repetitions, are more likely to be accurate measures of group interaction. Finally, Braun and Plog have suggested that the stylistic characteristics of an artifact define a hierarchy. Attributes at different levels of the hierarchy represent different stages of the decision process that are involved in the manufacture of the artifact (Plog 1978, p. 161), but are also sensitive to different social factors and groups (Braun & Plog, 1982, p. 511), perhaps at different geographic scales (Braun, 1980, pp. 12-13).

In total, these middle range principles define a very powerful framework. From it, the kinds of observations and variables in an artifact style data set that are likely to be relevant to the study of prehistoric social organization can be deduced with a great degree of specificity. When applied within the bounds of their limitations (see Wiessner, 1983 for a discussion of limitations), these principles suggest the subset of variables and observations that probably pertain to a single social process, or a limited range of social processes, and that tend to be accommodated to statistical techniques based on models assuming some single process. Thus, in this case, deductive specification of variables and observations can improve the likelihood of concordance between data structure and technique.

Some studies of prehistoric social organization that have used these principles in this manner include those of Braun (1977, 1980), Plog (1976, 1978, 1980), Voss (1980a, 1980b), and Hinkle (1984). We may also note that Spaulding's emphasis on using nominal scale measures (or higher-scale measures reduced to a nominal scale) as the basis for artifact typologies, derives from conclusions of his that are concordant with the information exchange theory. Spaulding (1982, pp. 5-6, 10) argues that it is nominal scale (discrete) variables that indicate culturally imposed patterns of artifact manufacture and that may be used to define types having cultural significance (i.e., indicating the group affiliation of the artifact's makers).

In other fields of study, middle range theoretical arguments similarly allow one to deduce variables and observations that are probably relevant to some phenomenon of interest.

Principles of lithic technology. In this volume, Hoffman (chapter 18) uses principles of lithic technology to select several variables for investigating morphological variation in a set of projectile points that is relevant to maintenance and reduction processes. These include measures of blade edge angle and blade size.

Mortuary analysis. Braun (1979, p. 69) argues that the archaeological variables that are relevant to the identification of ascriptive, hierarchical social distinctions include grave good classes that do not occur in village middens, that occur rarely overall within burials, that involve a relatively substantial labor input to produce, and that do not associate with age or sex. He also argues (p. 67) that it is qualitative rather than quantitative burial ritual attributes that symbolize formal authority and hereditary ranking. These arguments were then used by Braun to select a potentially relevant subset of variables from a burial set for factor analysis. O'Shea (1981, p. 42) has made similar arguments specifying the kinds of mortuary variables that are likely to distinguish horizontally or vertically differentiated social segments. These, in turn, were used to select potentially relevant variables for a factor analysis.

Middle Range Theory Used to Specify the Nature of the Phenomenon of Interest, Relevant Relational Data Structure, and Appropriate Technique

Over the past ten years, there has been a growing, general concern about the proper use and misuse of higher-level quantitative techniques (Thomas, 1971, 1978; Cowgill, 1977; Hole, 1980; Vierra & Carlson, 1981; Scheps, 1982; Moore & Keene, 1983). These concerns have been met by active research into the nature of organization of the archaeological record and the relevant structure of archaeological data in various contexts, the development of middle range theory about that organizational variation, and specification of the contexts in which applications of various quantitative techniques are appropriate.

Intrasite spatial analysis. Carr (1984) has reviewed most spatial quantitative methods that are currently used in intrasite studies in regard to their concordance with a model of intrasite artifact organization that commonly typifies archaeological sites. The model specifies that depositional sets may be polythetic and overlapping in organization. It also specifies that depositional areas may vary in their size, shape, orientation, spacing, artifact density and composition, border crispness, and in whether they overlap and are hierarchically arranged in space. Similarly, Whallon (1984) has modeled the kinds of variability encompassed by depositional areas, and has evaluated the use of factor analysis and other global methods in relation to it.

Seeing the discordance between most currently used techniques of intrasite spatial analysis and the structure of intrasite archaeological records, both

Whallon (1979, 1984) and Carr (1977, 1981, 1982b, 1984) have formulated new analytic methods that exhibit greater concordance with and sensitivity to the behaviorally relevant aspects of intrasite artifact distributional variability. In chapter 13 of this volume, Carr continues to enumerate additional mathematical models of intrasite artifact organization, some behavioral and natural contexts in which intrasite artifact organization can be expected to concord with those models, and some quantitative techniques (new and old) that are appropriate for use in those contexts. In this way, with a limited understanding of the behavioral and natural context of a site, it is possible to deduce the probable relevant organization of artifacts within it and the techniques most likely concordant with that organization.

The progress that has been made in these studies is based on nearly a decade of previous research that has focused on evaluating the response of various techniques to different spatial organizations of artifacts. These earlier studies, however, did not involve the construction of models of artifact organization that allow particular sites to be subsumed under them and that specify the techniques appropriate in those instances. For example, Schiffer (1975), through simulation, assessed the ability of factor analysis to reconstruct depositional sets of artifact types when the percentage of multipurpose (as opposed to single purpose) types becomes large and when correlation coefficients based on type counts within grid cells are used as the factored coefficients of similarity. Speth and Johnson (1976, pp. 50-53), using grid cell counts of artifact types, evaluated the response of intertype correlation coefficients to different artifact arrangements that result from different depositional processes.

Economic analysis. Another area of active modeling of the nature of organization of the archaeological record and behavior, and the techniques appropriate to their analysis, is economic analysis of settlement location choice and subsistence resource choice. Limp and Carr, Parker, Kvamme, and Keene (chapters 7, 8, 9, 10, respectively) each propose models of the nature of such decision processes and evaluate the concordance between various quantitative methods and those models. Among the technical assumptions considered in the evaluations are the level of information that is assumed accessible to the decision unit, the information processing capabilities that are implied of the decision unit, the assumed degree of continuity of settlement locations over space, and the implied degree of importance of social and ideological factors in subsistence and settlement decisions. These studies parallel previous evaluations of the concordance between technique and decision process in economic anthropology (e.g., Gladwin, 1975) and archaeology (Reidhead, 1979). It should be noted that in all these studies, general anthropological and economic theory, rather than middle range theory, is used to specify the appropriate analytic technique.

Mortuary analysis. Braun (1977), for example, has argued that ascribed and achieved status positions differ in the *predictability* (institutionalization) that is demanded of the behaviors associated with them and, hence, the constancy of mortuary ritual treatments of individuals that occupy those positions. He also suggests (1979, p. 67) that ascribed status is symbolized at death by *multiple, redundant* forms of variation in burial ritual. On the basis of these postulates, Braun deduces that factor analysis can be a useful technique for identifying indications of ascribed status within a mortuary data set.

Artifact typology. Hodson (with Doran 1975; 1982, pp. 25-26) and Spaulding (1977, 1982, p. 18) have debated the appropriateness of object clustering techniques relative to attribute clustering techniques for creating artifact typologies. Cowgill (1982, pp. 45, 47-48, 50-53) argues that the two approaches can product equivalent or complementary results, and that the preferability of one approach over the other can vary. This depends on whether the data are measured on a nominal scale or continuous scale, and the data's particular structure (e.g., the distribution of marginal frequencies in the case of nominal data in contingency table format).

In sum, during the initial stages of analysis, the relevant structure of the data in hand is not often well-known. In this circumstance, deductive specification, from theory, of the subset of data and the technique that are likely to be relevant to the phenomenon of interest can be a powerful means for getting into the data and reducing the degree of discordance between data and technique. As theory develops—particularly middle range theory—and evaluation of the response of various techniques to different kinds of relevant archaeological data structures continues, we can expect this means for getting into data to become more helpful.

"Constrained" Exploratory Data Analysis

Deductive arguments can help one to narrow the range of variables and observations within a data set to those having greatest potential for reflecting the phenomenon of interest. They can also suggest a technique that is most apt to be concordant with the relevant aspects of the data's structure. However, deductive argumentation is seldom sufficient. Individual data sets need not—usually will not—conform to expectation in every way. If the theory employed to make deductions does not have strong predictive capabilities, the phenomenon of interest may manifest itself in unsuspected sets of variables and observations and forms of relationships among them (e.g., association rather than covariation). The same problem can arise if the predictive theory is incorrectly applied beyond the limits of its boundary conditions or if the auxiliary assumptions that are made when relating the theory to the data at hand are wrong. For example, consider the auxiliary assumptions that are made about sources of variation that are supposedly controlled during data collection. When unsuspected extraneous factors as well as those of interest affect the measurements brought forward for study, the data set's relevant structure may take an unexpected form. An expected linear relationship between two natural environmental variables, for example, might instead take the form of a cyclical function with a linear trend, as a result of the compounding of diurnal variation with the variation of interest. Thus, totally deductive specification of the variables and observations to be analyzed and the techniques to be used need not ensure the complete relevance of the selected data to the phenomenon of interest, nor the concordance of the selected technique with the data's relevant structure.

To compensate for these problems—to get into the data more successfully—it is necessary to supplement the deductive strategy with an inductive one that examines the data on its own terms. *"Constrained" exploratory data analysis* (CEDA), having at least two variants that differ in the kinds of techniques they employ, is useful for this purpose.

CEDA vs. Exploratory Data Analysis

As defined here, CEDA includes all the analytic approaches for getting into data that comprise exploratory data analysis (Tukey, 1977; Hartwig & Dearing, 1979; Clark, 1982) but only a *portion* of the philosophy of exploratory data analysis that motivates their use. Like exploratory data analysis, CEDA is an inductive approach to recognizing patterns in a data set. Both have the goal of finding "any unanticipated structures or relationships that occur within a data set, regardless of expectation" (Tukey & Wilk, 1970, p. 371). Both involve searching for any patterning in the data in order to reach a better understanding of the nature and causes of its total structure. Unlike in exploratory data analysis, however, in CEDA, this understanding of the data's total structure is sought in order to *isolate* the *relevant* aspects of it—*those that reflect some one explicitly specified phenomenon of interest as defined deductively* by the larger theoretical framework or paradigm of the researcher. In contrast, in exploratory data analysis, understanding of the total data structure is sought explicitly in order to generate new ideas, problem areas, and hypotheses (Tukey, 1979, p. 122; 1980, pp. 23-24) within a primarily inductive framework. Discovery of *many* relevant data structures pertinent to many phenomena, rather than the *single* structure pertinent to the single phenomenon of interest, is the goal of exploratory data analysis. Because CEDA is undertaken within a larger deductive framework and is more focused in its aim, whereas exploratory data analysis occurs within an inductive, less focused context, the designation *constrained* exploratory data analysis is used.

Whereas exploratory data analysis was developed by Tukey in reaction to the strongly deductive, "confirmatory" mode that dominates theoretical statistics (Tukey, 1979), CEDA is meant to articulate with it. Analysis is begun in a deductive manner with the specification of variables and observations that are probably relevant or irrelevant to the phenomenon of interest. Data items that are thought to be irrelevant are dropped from analysis. The search for relevant and irrelevant data items is continued in an inductive manner with CEDA procedures. The subset of the data that results from *both* the deductive and CEDA steps can then be used in either hypothesis testing or hypothesis formulation. In either case, both data screening steps are motivated by the researcher's larger theoretical framework, which specifies the phenomenon of interest. *CEDA, then, is an inductive middle-step within a stepwise analytic design that has an overall deductive orientation and that is begun with deduction.* In contrast, exploratory data analysis is an inductive approach for initiating analytic process. (See Carr, chapter 13 for a discussion of the strengths and weaknesses of exploratory data analysis in this capacity.)

To examine the total structure of a data set and determine those aspects of it that are probably relevant to the phenomenon of interest, CEDA uses the same methods as exploratory data analysis, plus some additional ones. First, to view the multiple structures within a data set, CEDA involves the re-expression of the data on various scales of measurement (e.g., nominal, ratio, logarithmic, square root) and the examination of the re-expressed data with different techniques that are concordant with those scales of measurement (Tukey, 1980, p. 24; Hartwig & Dearing, 1979, p. 10). Also, techniques assuming multiple mathematical models are used to investigate the data from multiple perspectives. An effort is made to find any patterns in the data, regardless of whether they reflect the phenomenon of interest, and to consider how potentially relevant structure in the data then might be isolated from irrelevant patterning (e.g., removal of outliers, selection of variables, expression of the data on a particular scale, use of a technique that is sensitive to the scale most likely appropriate to the relevant structure). Second, CEDA, like exploratory data analysis, stresses the importance of graphic representations of the data (e.g., histograms, crossplots, the box and whisker, maps) in aiding the search for patterns (Tukey, 1970, p. 372; Hartwig & Dearing, 1979, p. 9).

CEDA vs. Data Screening

CEDA and exploratory data analysis involve many of the same techniques and operations traditionally used to *screen* data in preparation for the application of higher-level statistical techniques. These include histograms; crossplots; simple univariate descriptive statistics; bivariate techniques of association, rank correlation, and correlation analysis; elimination of outlying observations; segregation of modalities for separate analysis, should the data be composed of observations within several suspected populations; and transformation of the form of the frequency distributions of individual variables or the functional relationships between variable pairs. All of these techniques and operations can be used in CEDA to obtain a basic understanding of the data to be analyzed. However, CEDA departs from traditional data screening in that these methods are not applied in order to transform the structure of the data into a form that is concordant with some particular analytic technique to be used. Data are not screened to *fit to technique*. Rather, the data set is examined to find and isolate the potentially relevant aspects of its structure, *in regard to which an appropriate technique of analysis is chosen or developed.*

Two Forms of Constrained Exploratory Data Analysis

CEDA encompasses two variants, which differ to some extent in the nature of the techniques they encompass. The first variant emphasizes the use of techniques that make *minimal assumptions* about the data's structure when displaying it for pattern-searching. The second variant emphasizes the use of techniques that are capable of handling *a heavy load of irrelevant variables or observations, or variation in general*—a common characteristic of data sets that have been screened only by deductive selection.

A good example of a technique that makes minimal assumptions and that might be used with a CEDA framework, but which to date has been used in only an exploratory data analysis framework, is Whallon's (1984) *unconstrained clustering* method of intrasite spatial analysis. As Whallon (1984, p. 275) notes, unconstrained clustering "is hardly more than an elaborate approach to a descriptive summary or display of the data or a series of such summaries and displays." (For a more detailed discussion of the method in relation to exploratory data analysis see Carr, chapter 13.) Other examples of techniques that make minimal assumptions include other graphic displays—such as the stem-and-leaf display, the box-and-whisker, and scatterplots—and certain "resistant" descriptive statistics— such as the trimmed mean, the Winzorized mean, and the median absolute deviation (Tukey, 1977; Hartwig & Dearing, 1979, pp. 16-26). These various techniques can be used to determine the variables, observations or the relationships among them that are probably relevant to the phenomenon of interest.

One example of a technique that is capable of handling a heavy load of irrelevant variables, but that does not make minimal assumptions, is *R-mode factor analysis.* Although it can be used for multiple purposes, R-mode factor analysis is ideally suited for defining clusters of variables, making it "easier to decide upon their relevance to a problem" (Christenson & Read, 1977, p. 174) with a CEDA framework.

Christenson and Read (1977, pp. 167, 170-174) have used factor analysis along with a multivariate identification-of-outliers program explicitly this way in preparation for developing a projectile point typology with cluster analysis. A factor analysis of projectile point data was used to identify two dimensions of morphological variability (groups of variables) that seemed relevant to the researchers' typological goals, and other dimensions that seemed irrelevant. The two relevant dimensions were then selected as the "variables" to be used in creating the point typology. The following chapter by Read continues discussion of this approach. It illustrates how factor analysis and scatterplots of factor scores can be used in an alternating, iterative manner to refine the selection of variables (factors) and set of observations that are chosen to represent the one or more phenomena of interest that are potentially reflected in a data set's structure.

A second example of a technique that is capable of handling a heavy load of irrelevant variation but that does not make minimal assumptions is *spectral analysis*. This technique allows the researcher to identify multiple forms of variability of different scales that are compounded within the track of a *single* response variable over time or space. The results of a spectral analysis can be used by a researcher to design "filters" that allow the extraction and isolation of these individual forms of variation from the compounded response variable, which in turn are defined as new variables. Those of the new variables that are considered to reflect the phenomenon of interest can then be subjected to further analysis, free of the confusing effects of the other, irrelevant sources of variation.

Carr (1982b) has used spectral analysis in this manner to identify and analyze several sources of variability within an intrasite resistivity survey data set. He has also suggested its use for identifying the different kinds of depositional processes that are responsible for artifact density variation within a composite artifact distribution (a palimpsest) that has been formed by the partial spatial overlap of multiple depositional processes (e.g., different kinds of activities of different scales). Artifact density variation that is thought pertinent to each of the depositional processes of interest (relevant data structure) can then be extracted from the palimpsest for individual study using filtering techniques (Carr, 1982a; 1984; 1986 this volume, chapter 13).

In conclusion, analysis of complex data sets often requires inductive as well as deductive specification of the variables, observations, and relationships among them that are likely relevant to the phenomenon of interest, and a concordant analytic technique. In this regard, in the case of complex data, phases of scientific investigation that are concerned with hypothesis testing and that are supposedly "deductive" are seldom *completely* deductive. Theory may be used to deduce a model or hypothesis, but the formulation of a test implication—which states an expectable relationship among observables in *terms of the variables, cases, and technique that is selected for analysis*—is a process that often requires both deductive and inductive logic. The expectable relationship follows from the theoretical framework, but its expression depends on the data and technique to be used, which often must be selected in part by induction.

Entry Models

A third strategy for getting into an unknown data set while maximizing consistency between its relevant structure and technical assumption involves the construction and use of what may be termed *entry models* and *parallel data sets*. This strategy involves both inductive and deductive logic, and requires the use and development of middle range theory. It gives the researcher insight into the organizational nature of the phenomenon of interest and the relevant relational structure of the data set (e.g., nominal vs. ratio scale organization), thereby allowing the researcher to choose an analytic technique which is more concordant with that form of organization. It does not necessarily involve the selection of relevant observations and variables, though it may. The strategy is summarized in Figure 1.

An entry model has three essential components: 1) The most critical is a *general mathematical model* or description of the *form of organization* of the archaeological observables that represent the phenomenon of interest. An example would be a model that specifies the form of spatial organization of coarranged artifact types within a site as monothetic or polythetic. To this organizational model are linked the other two components of the entry model.

2) The second component is an *enumeration of the kinds of processes* that could lead to the archaeological observables being organized in the way that the mathematical model specifies. These classes of processes will always include cultural and natural formation processes of the kind documented by middle range archaeological theory (e.g., curation, lithic reduction and maintenance processes, means by which rank is symbolized in mortuary remains). However, they may also include processes to which general anthropological theory pertains (e.g., the pattern and tempo of fission-fusion of hunter-gatherer bands). Continuing our intrasite spatial example, above, a list of processes that can cause coarranged artifact types to be organized monothetically or polythetically might include differential artifact preservation, artifact curation, artifact recycling, misclassification of artifacts, or the occurrence of alternative tool types within a tool kit (see Carr, chapter 13). Although specification of such linkages between form of archaeological organization and process may be difficult, it is currently the subject of active research on middle range archaeological theory.

3) The last component is an inventory of the quantitative techniques that are concordant with the mathematical model of organization of the archaeological observables. For example, some kinds of "polythetic association" methods of spatial analysis (Carr, chapter 13) would be concordant with a polythetic coarrangement of artifact types.

An entry model usually is one of a series of such models. Each entry model specifies a different mathematical model of the organizational form of the archaeological observables that represent the phenomenon of interest. The differences between the mathematical models of organization in the various entry models reflect the different effects of different classes of formation processes or higher-level processes, which are enumerated by the entry models. The entry models will also specify different quantitative techniques that are concordant with their different mathematical models of organization. For example, Carr (chapter 13) defines six alternative entry models. They involve different mathematical models of possible organizations of "tool kits" that have been deposited in the archaeological domain (archaeological observables) and that represent activities (the phenomenon of interest). The different mathematical organizations of the "tool kits" reflect the different effects that various kinds of formation processes, which are enumerated by the entry models, would have. The entry models also specify different sets of quantitative techniques that are concordant with the different organizations of "tool kits" and that can be used to search for them in archaeological data.

Entry models are useful when two circumstances occur. 1) The data set that documents the phenomenon of interest and that is slated for analysis is very complex. As a result, the researcher is unable initially to specify—by simple inspection of the data—the aspects of its structure that are likely to be relevant, the probable organization of the archaeological observables that represent the phenomenon of interest and that are expressed in the data, and an analytic technique that probably is appropriate. 2) There exists a simpler, *parallel data set* that gives the researcher insight into the processes that are responsible for the archaeological observables, their consequent organization, and the relevant and irrelevant structural aspects of the complex data set. In these two circumstances, it is possible for the researcher to learn something about the complex data set's relevant relational structure (e.g., the relative frequency of monothetic or polythetic relationships of association among coarranged artifact types) and to specify an analytic technique that is likely to be appropriate by examining the *parallel* data set and using the entry model. This is done in lieu of *directly* but possibly discordantly examining the *complex* data with a higher-level pattern-searching technique. In this way, the researcher is removed from the bind of not being able to choose an appropriate analytic technique without knowledge of the complex data set's structure, yet not being able to obtain this knowledge without applying some pattern-searching technique to the complex data.

The logical process involved in the use of a parallel data set and an entry model is shown in Figure 1 and can be described as follows:

1) Archaeological observables that reflect the phenomenon of interest are described in two separate data sets: a complex one that is the ultimate target of analysis and a simple, parallel one that is sensitive to the processes of formation of the archaeological observables in the complex one. An example of a complex data set would be a matrix of point locations of artifacts of many classes within a hunter-gatherer site. Examples of a simple data set that parallel this complex one and gives insight into the complex data's organizational nature would be (a) one that contains information on intrasite spatial variation in soil acidity (reflecting the potential for differential preservation of bone artifacts over space), (b) one that documents the orientation and dip of artifacts (indicating the possibility of disturbance in the spatial distribution of artifacts by fluvial activity), or (c) one that describes the grain of the surrounding environment (suggesting the likelihood of tethered mobility patterns, repeated reuse of the site, and the palimpsest nature of the artifact distribution).

2) The processes that are responsible for the archaeological observables to be

studied in the complex data set are reconstructed on the basis of information in the parallel data set. This reconstruction can be accomplished by logical deduction, in which case the specific patterns within the parallel data set are subsumed under general, accepted models of the observable consequences of formation processes. It can also be achieved by abduction from patterns within the parallel data set, followed by testing of one's conclusions with other, independent data that also comprise the parallel data set. For example, in deductive mode, the disturbance of an intrasite artifact distribution by fluvial processes might be determined by noting patterns in the orientation, dip, and size sorting of artifacts and then subsuming such patterns under established models of fluvial displacement of artifacts (Behrensmeyer & Hill, 1980; Shackley, 1978). This step conforms to Schiffer's (1983) call for "up front" identification of the processes that are responsible for archaeological observables, prior to behavioral interpretation.

3) The specific processes that are found to be responsible for the archaeological observables within the parallel data set and that are also pertinent to the organization of the complex data set are then matched with processes that are enumerated in a more general way in one or more of the entry models.

4) On the basis of (a) the association of the archaeological observables in both the parallel and complex data sets with a particular entry model via common processes and (b) the model's specification of both the effects of formation processes on the organization of archaeological observables in the complex data set and the analytic techniques that are concordant with that organization, two

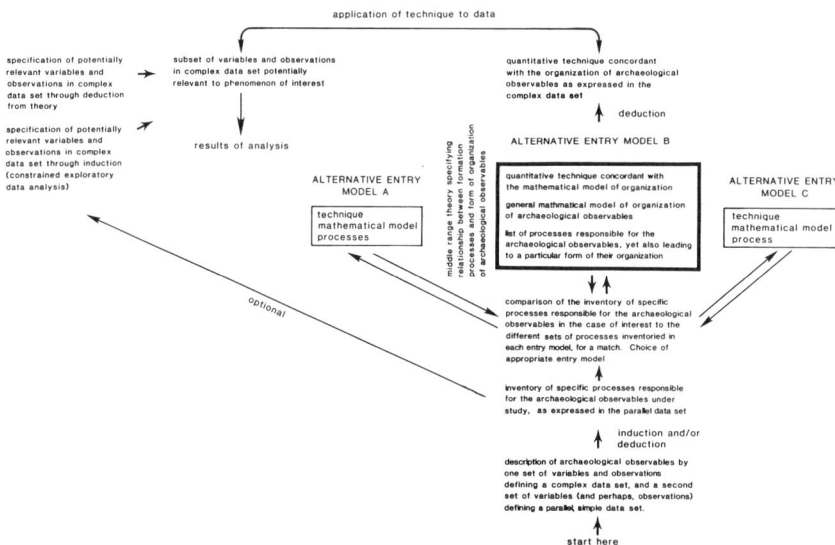

Fig. 2.1. The use of entry models and parallel data sets to get into a complex data set.

things are concluded. These are 1) the probable general nature of organization of the archaeological observables in the complex data, which is specified in mathematical terms, and by implication, some aspects of the complex data's relevant relational structure, and 2) the techniques of analysis that are most likely appropriate for investigating the archaeological observables in the complex data set. Note that information in the *parallel* data set is used to determine the appropriate entry model, whereas information on the relevant structure of the *complex* data set is derived from the entry model. Also note that the process of associating the archaeological observables in the parallel and complex data sets with a given entry model is equivalent to logically subsuming them under the entry model.

An example of the steps that have just been outlined is given in chapter 13 by Carr. Here, the target, complex data set is composed of the spatial distributions of many artifact types within a site. Formation processes that would have affected the nature of organization of spatially coarranged artifact classes within the site are identified with various kinds of aspatial data, which constitute a parallel data set. These processes are matched to those that are enumerated in two of several alternative entry models, which also include mathematical models of the organizational form of coarranged artifact types. From this match are concluded the two most probable forms of spatial organization of coarranged artifact types within the site, which is specified in mathematical terms (relevant relational structure), and the two techniques that are most apt to be appropriate for analyzing the artifact type distributions.

5) The quantitative technique that is determined to be most probably concordant with the relevant relational structure of the complex data is applied to that data, or some subset of its variables and observations that is thought potentially relevant to the phenomenon of interest. The potentially relevant subset might have been specified by deduction from theory or by inductive examination of the parallel data set. For example, again consider the application of the entry model strategy used by Carr in chapter 13. The artifact type, flint pebbles, might have been removed from the complex data set of artifact type distributions, and from the search for tool kits in that set, on the basis of an aspatial piece of information in the parallel data set: the fact that many of the smaller pebbles were probably of natural, fluvial origin, and thus, irrelevant to behavioral reconstruction.

In sum, the entry model strategy can be a powerful approach for getting into a complex data set while minimizing the violation of relevant aspects of its structure by an applied technique. The strategy allows the researcher to determine the probable general nature of the data set's relevant structure, and thus, the technique(s) that are most likely appropriate for its analysis, *without directly analyzing it with some possibly discordant method.* This is accomplished through the examination of a parallel data set for the processes of formation of the archaeological observables in both the parallel and the complex data sets, rather than through a direct, inductive examination of the many facets of the complex data set's structure using multiple techniques. In essence, the entry model strategy allows one to investigate a complex data set by "slipping in a side door," which is provided by parallel data on formation processes, rather than by affronting it.

Although the entry model strategy can be more powerful and bring greater concordance between data and technique than the deductive or CEDA strategies, the entry model approach has a disadvantage. It requires a good foundation of middle range theory on the processes that are responsible for the archaeological and behavioral variability of interest, and also processes that are not of interest. As this foundation broadens, it will become more practicable (see Schiffer, 1983).

Stepwise, Cyclical Analytic Designs

A final means for improving consistency between data structure, technique, and theoretical framework, during analysis, is the well known stepwise, cyclical process of scientific investigation, itself (Fig. 2). This process requires repeated analysis of a data set—including modification of the data, the analytic technique(s), and/or the interpretive framework that guides analysis, with each pass over the data—such that all three approach greater concordance with each other. Modifications of these three entities with each cycle are made in light of 1) discrepancies between expectable results and those obtained (external inconsistencies), 2) discrepancies between the interpretive implications of different

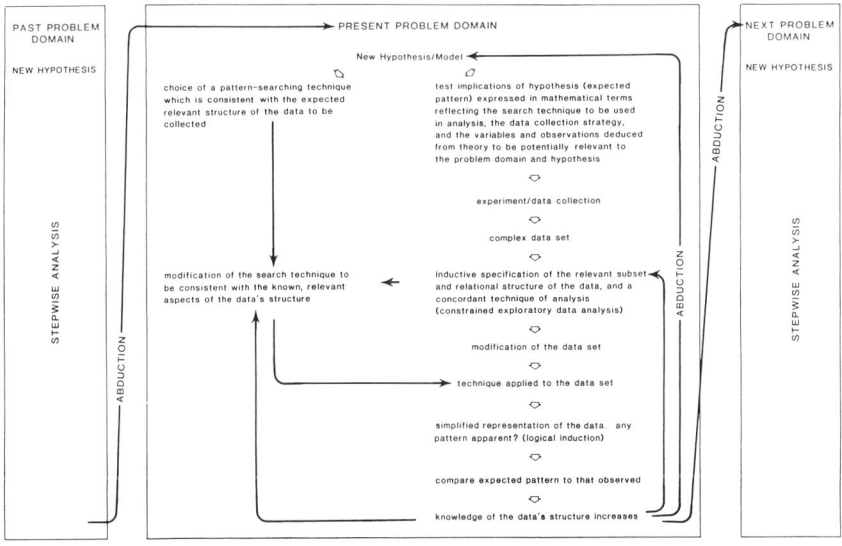

Fig. 2.2. The sequential, stepwise, cyclical process of scientific investigation.

subsets of the results that are obtained (internal inconsistencies), 3) whether the discrepancies increase or decrease from trial run to trial run, and 4) knowledge that is gained about the data's relevant structure. In short, the stepwise approach to data analysis is a logical process that *simulates*, in serial format, the continuous, simultaneous feedback between data, technique, and theoretical framework that characterizes the mental process of abduction.

THE LOGIC OF ANALYSIS VS. THE LOGIC OF PUBLISHED ANALYSIS

Successful analysis of complex data sets usually requires and involves deductive, inductive, *and* stepwise strategies for getting into the data and developing concordance between data, technique, and theory. It can also involve the use of parallel data sets. Nevertheless, if we were to look at a typical journal article that reports research on a phenomenon that is described by complex data, we would probably find, instead, a more deductive tenor. Justifications of the variables, observations, and technique(s) that are used would more likely refer to theoretical considerations than to patterns noted in the data or to insightful discrepancies between expectation and result in trial runs. We might also find simply a report of the problem of interest and associated hypotheses, data collection design, data, results of analysis, and conclusions, without explicit justification of the data items that were analyzed as opposed to those that were collected, or of the technique that was employed. In either case, the reader is left with the impression of a primarily deductive analytic process that has one or a few steps, as opposed to the more complex, multistep, multistrategy process that typifies the analysis of complex data as just described (see Binford & Sabloff, 1982 for a discussion of this effect in the New Archaeology of the 1960s-1970s).

This difference, which often occurs between the logic implied by the format of published scientific investigations and the logical processes by which such investigations are achieved, results from at least two factors. First, as a result of publication expense and limitations on space, it is often impossible to include in a report of investigation the multiple, sometimes complex reasons for deleting certain observations or variables, or for selecting one technique over another. Second, broad, general, deductive justifications of variables, observations, and technique can often be stated more succinctly than inductive justifications, which may have multiple idiosyncratic or contextual facets to them that can be conveyed only at length. (For examples of the latter, see Whallon, 1984; Read, chapter 3; Carr, chapter 13; Braun, chapter 16.) Thus, if any justifications of analytic strategy are included in a research report, it is the deductive ones, which can be expressed most briefly, that tend to be reported.

It is important to realize the difference between the deductive-tending logic of published analyses of complex data and the logic by which those analyses are accomplished. To confound published logic with the logic of analysis and to proceed with the analysis of complex data in a largely deductive, single-step manner can have at least two negative consequences. First, by limiting one's strategies for getting into data to a deductive approach—by not also using an inductive constrained exploratory approach and iterative processing—the researcher greatly decreases his capabilities for identifying the relevant aspects of his data and for selecting data and technique so as to maximize concordance between them.

Second, by not examining data in an inductive constrained exploratory manner, one decreases the opportunity for discovering unexpected data patterns that suggest new problem areas or alternative interpretive frameworks. The importance of constrained exploratory data analysis in the discovery of new problem domains and in escaping the blinding "tyranny" of an accepted theoretical framework and paradigm has been stressed by many authors (e.g., Hanson, 1972; Tukey, 1980; Clarke, 1972:8; Binford & Sabloff, 1982).

It also is important—in a groping, growing discipline like archaeology—that the analytic logic by which data and technique have been selected and justified be reported as much as possible, instead of reporting only succinctly statable deductive arguments or none at all. Many of the arguments that are used by a researcher to select certain observations, variables, or techniques imply (if they are not stated as such) formal *bridging arguments* (Hempel, 1966, pp. 72-75) that link the nonobservables of a theoretical framework to observables. Importantly, they involve the assumed nature of the phenomenon of interest. In an established discipline, where these bridges are well known and part of accepted theory and methodology, it is superfluous and too expensive to repeatedly report their use. However, in a quickly growing discipline where such bridges are not yet formalized and accepted, it is critical that they be stated explicitly and reported openly for criticism. *It is partly through explicit justification of the observations, variables, and techniques that are used in analysis and criticism of such justifications that the strong bridges between theory, method, and data, which typify a well established discipline, are built and communicated to the discipline at large.* Also, because such justifications pertain to the relevant structure of a data set, and thereby to the nature of the phenomenon of interest, *their refinement and formalization as bridging principles leads to or goes hand in hand with the refinement of theory and scientific advance* (e.g., Read, 1974).

Finally, in circumstances where bridging arguments are not well formalized or generally accepted, explicit statements of justification of the variables, observations, and techniques that are used in an analysis must be reported, if the analysis is to be assessable for its validity.

CONCLUSION

As a result of human limits to pattern recognition, the analysis of complex data sets cannot proceed with the same logic as the analysis of simple data sets. A sequential approach is required. This allows data structure and pattern-searching technique to become discordant with each other and causes a problem, for the researcher, of how to get into data without violating its relevant structure. Several solutions to this problem are discussed in this chapter. All can be summarized in a word: JUSTIFICATION. The analysis of complex data requires the researcher to make a conscientious attempt to justify explicitly— through deductive or inductive argument—the relevance of the variables and observations that are brought forward for analysis to the phenomenon of interest. It also requires the researcher to justify the chosen analytic technique in relation to what is known about the data set's relevant relational structure, which is a reflection of the nature of the phenomenon of interest. Only when data and technique are concordant with each other and the phenomenon of interest can the results of an analysis accurately represent the phenomenon of interest, in turn laying the foundation for the assignment of appropriate meaning to the results.

"Fine tuning" of an analytic design, which involves the explicit justification of data and technique, however, has value beyond the scope of any single analysis. It is a critical aspect of the process of scientific advance. It is one means by which logical inconsistencies and false premises in current theory are uncovered and inadequacies in traditionally used analytic techniques are unveiled, and, hence, is a driving force behind the formulation of new theories and techniques.

REFERENCES

Behrensmeyer, A.K., & Hill, A.P. (Eds.). (1980). *Fossils in the making: Vertebrate taphonomy and paleoecology.* Chicago: University of Chicago Press.

Binford, L.R. (1977). *For theory building in archaeology.* New York: Academic Press, Inc.

Binford, L.R., & Sabloff, J.A. (1982). Paradigms, systematics, and archaeology. *Journal of Anthropological Research* 38(2), 137-153.

Braun, D.P. (1977). *Middle Woodland-early Late Woodland social change in the prehistoric midwestern U.S.* Unpublished doctoral dissertation, University of Michigan, Ann Arbor.

Braun, D.P. (1979). Illinois Hopewell burial practices and social organization: A reexamination of the Klunk-Gibson mound group. In D. Brose & N. Greber (Eds.), *Hopewell archaeology: The Chillicothe conference* (pp. 66-79). Kent, OH: Kent State University Press.

Braun, D.P. (1980, April). *Neolithic regional cooperation: A midwestern example.* Paper presented at the annual meetings of the Society for American Archaeology, Philadelphia, PA.

Braun, D.P., & Plog, S. (1982). Evolution of "tribal" social networks: Theory and prehistoric North American Evidence. *American Antiquity,* 47(3), 504-525.

Carr, C. (1977). *The internal structure of a Middle Woodland site and the nature of the archaeological record.* Unpublished preliminary examination paper, University of Michigan, East Lansing.

Carr, C. (1981, April). *The polythetic organization of archaeological tool kits and an algorithm for defining them.* Paper presented at the annual meetings of the Society for American Archaeology, San Diego, CA.

Carr, C. (1982a, April). *Dissecting intrasite artifact distributions as palimpsests.* Paper presented at the annual meetings of the Society for American Archaeology, Minneapolis, MN.

Carr, C. (1982b). *Handbook on soil resistivity surveying: Interpretation of data from earthen archaeological sites.* Evanston, IL: Center for American Archaeology.

Carr, C. (1983, June). *A design for intrasite research.* Paper presented at the National Park Service Research Seminar in Archaeology, Fort Collins, CO.

Carr, C. (1984). The nature of organization of intra-site archaeological records and spatial analytic approaches to their investigation. In M.B. Schiffer (Ed.), *Advances in archaeological method and theory* (Vol. 7) (pp. 103-222). New York: Academic Press.

Carr, C. (in press). Dissecting intrasite artifact palimpsests using Fourier methods. In S. Kent (Ed.), *Method and theory for activity area research: An ethnoarchaeological approach* (chap. 5). New York: Columbia University Press.

Christenson, A.L., & Read, D.W. (1977). Numerical taxonomy, R-mode factor analysis, and archaeological classification. *American Antiquity 42*(2), 163-179.

Clark, G.A. (1982). Quantifying archaeological research. In M.B. Schiffer (Ed.), *Advances in Archaeological Method and Theory* (Vol. 5) (pp. 217-273). New York: Academic Press, Inc.

Clarke, D.L. (1972). Models and paradigms in contemporary archaeology. In D.L. Clarke (Ed.), *Models in archaeology* (pp. 1-60). London: Methuen Publications.

Cowgill, G.C. (1977). The trouble with significance tests and what we can do about it. *American Antiquity 33*, 367-375.

Cowgill, G.C. (1982). Clusters of objects and associations between variables: Two approaches to archaeological classification. In R. Whallon & J.A. Brown (Eds.), *Essays on archaeological typology* (pp. 30-55). Evanston, IL: Center for American Archaeology Press.

Doran, J.E., & Hodson, F.R. (1975). *Mathematics and computers in archaeology.* Cambridge, MA: Harvard University Press.

Doran, J.E., & Hodson, F.R. (1982). Some aspects of archaeological classification. In R. Whallon & J.A. Brown (Eds.), *Essays on archaeological typology* (pp. 21-29). Evanston, IL: Center for American Archaeology Press.

Friedrich, M.H. (1970). Design structure and social interaction: Archaeological implications of an ethnographic analysis. *American Antiquity 35*, 332-343.

Gladwin, H. (1975). Looking for an aggregate additive model in data from a hierarchical decision process. In S. Plattner (Ed.), *Formal methods in economic anthropology* (Special publication) (pp. 159-196). Washington, DC: American Anthropological Association.

Hanson, N.R. (1972). *Patterns of discovery.* Cambridge: Cambridge University Press.

Hartwig, F., & Dearing, B.E. (1979). *Exploratory data analysis.* Beverly Hills: Sage Publications.

Hemple, C.G. (1966). *The philosophy of natural science.* Englewood Cliffs, NJ: Prentice Hall.

Hinkle, K.A. (1983). *Ohio Hopewell textiles: A medium for stylistic and social information exchange.* Unpublished master's thesis, University of Arkansas, Fayetteville.

Hole, B.L. (1980). Sampling in archaeology: A critique. *Annual Review of Anthropology 9*, 217-234.

Moore, J.A., & Keene, A.S. (1983). Archaeology and the law of the hammer. In S.A. Moore & A.S. Keene (Eds.), *Archaeological hammers and theories* (pp. 3-13). New York: Academic Press, Inc.

O'Shea, J. (1981). Social configurations and the archaeological study of mortuary practices: A case study. In R. Chapman, I. Kinnes, & K. Randsborg (Eds.), *The archaeology of death* (pp. 39-52). Cambridge: Cambridge University Press.

Plog, S. (1976). Measurement of prehistoric interaction between communities. In K.V. Flannery (Ed.), *The early Mesoamerican village* (pp. 255-272). New York: Academic Press, Inc.

Plog, S. (1978). Social interaction and stylistic similarity: A reanalysis. In M.B. Schiffer (Ed.), *Advances in archaeological method and theory* (Vol. 1) (pp. 144-182). New York: Academic Press, Inc.

Plog. S. (1980). *Stylistic variation in prehistoric ceramics.* Cambridge: Cambridge University Press.

Raab, M.L., & Goodyear, A.C. (1984). Middle-range theory in archaeology: A critical review of origins and applications. *American Antiquity 49*(2), 255-268.

Read, D.W. (1974). Some comments on the use of mathematical models in anthropology. *American Antiquity 39*(1), 3-15.

Reidhead, V. (1979). Linear programming models in archaeology. *Annual Review of Anthropology 8*, 543-578.

Scheps, S. (1982). Statistical blight. *American Antiquity 47*(4), 836-850.
Schiffer, M.B. (1975). Factors and "tool kits": Evaluating multivariate analysis in archaeology. *Plains Anthropologist 20*, 61-70.
Schiffer, M.B. (1976). *Behavioral archaeology*. New York: Academic Press, Inc.
Schiffer, M.G. (1983). Toward the identification of formation processes. *American Antiquity 48*(4), 675-706.
Shackley, M.L. (1978). The behavior of artifacts as sedimentary particles in a fluvial environment. *Archaeometry 20*, 55-61.
Spaulding, A.C. (1977). On growth and form in archaeology: Multivariate analysis. *Journal of Anthropological Research 33*, 1-15.
Spaulding, A.C. (1982). Structure in archaeological data: Nominal variables. In R. Whallon & J.A. Brown (Eds.), *Essays on archaeological typology* (pp. 1-20). Evanston, IL: Center for American Archaeology Press.
Speth, J.D., & Johnson, G.A. (1976). Problems in the use of correlation for the investigation of tool kits and activity areas. In C. Cleland (Ed.), *Cultural change and continuity* (pp. 35-75). New York: Academic Press, Inc.
Stanislawski, M.B., & Stanislawski, B.B. (1978). Hopi and Hopi-Tewa ceramic tradition networks. In I. Hodder (Ed.), *The spatial organization of culture* (pp. 61-76). Pittsburgh: University of Pittsburgh Press.
Thomas, D.H. (1971). On use of cumulative curves and numerical taxonomy. *American Antiquity 36*, 206-209.
Thomas, D.H. (1978). The awful truth about statistics in archaeology. *American Antiquity 43*, 231-244.
Toussaint, G.T. (1978). The use of context in pattern recognition. *Pattern Recognition, 10*, 189-204.
Tukey, J.W. (1977). *Exploratory data analysis*. Reading, MA: Addison-Wesley.
Tukey, J.W. (1979). Comment to "Nonparametric statistical data modeling." *Journal of the American Statistical Association 74*, 121-122.
Tukey, J.W. (1980). We need both exploratory and confirmatory. *American Statistician 34*(1), 23-25.
Tukey, J.W., & Wilk, M.B. (1970). Data analysis and statistics: Techniques and approaches. In E.R. Tufte (Ed.), *The quantitative analysis of social problems* (pp. 370-390). Reading, MA: Addison-Wesley.
Vierra, R.K., & Carlson, D.L. (1981). Factor analysis, random data, and patterned results. *American Antiquity 46*(2), 272-283.
Voss, J.A. (1980a). *Tribal emergence during the Neolithic of northwestern Europe*. Unpublished doctoral dissertation, University of Michigan, Ann Arbor.
Voss, J.A. (1980b, April). *The measurement and evaluation of change in the regional social networks of egalitarian societies: An example from the Neolithic of northwestern Europe*. Paper presented at the annual meetings of the Society for American Archaeology, Philadelphia.
Whallon, R. (1979, April). *Unconstrained clustering in the analysis of spatial distributions on occupation floors*. Paper presented at the annual meetings of the Society for American Archaeology, Vancouver.
Whallon, R. (1984). Unconstrained clustering for the analysis of spatial distributions in archaeology. In H.J. Hietala (Ed.), *Intrasite spatial analysis* (pp. 242-277). Cambridge: Cambridge University Press.
Wiessner, P. (1983). Style and social information in Kalahari San projectile points. *American Antiquity 48*(2), 253-275.
Wobst, M.H. (1977). Stylistic behavior and information exchange. In C. Cleland (Ed.), *For the director: Research essays in honor of James B. Griffin* (Anthropological papers 61) (pp. 317-342). Ann Arbor: University of Michigan, Museum of Anthropology.

3

The Substance of Archaeological Analysis and the Mold of Statistical Method: Enlightenment Out of Discordance?

DWIGHT W. READ

Creativity is a state of mind, and it is most widely expressed by very young children, because their confrontation with their environment is constantly made up of original discoveries and inventions. In time, through social pressures to conform and the repetition of experience, most of them lose this sense of wonder and become less and less creative, trapped in a concrete mold not of their own making.

Fabun

The past three decades have seen Spaulding's (1953, 1960) seminal articles, establishing statistical methods as a legitimate part of archaeological theorizing, become a virtual torrent of applications (Thomas, 1976, p. 4; Clark & Stafford, 1982). The chapters in this volume are alone ample testimony to the richness of Spaulding's visionary projection. Yet the results of the enterprise have not been without critics (e.g., Hole, 1980), and even some of the proponents of that methodological revolution (Dunnell, 1982) have had moments of uncertainty about the quality, substance, and correctness of application of statistical methods at the technical level (e.g., Thomas, 1978).

While one can often properly criticize specific applications of statistical methods at the technical level of violation of underlying assumptions (e.g., Hole, 1980; Benfer & Benfer, 1981; Schleps, 1983), these are but surface manifestations of a far deeper issue (cf. Voorrips, 1982, p. 94). This issue centers around application of the conceptual framework of one domain to another domain (Schiffer, 1981), in this case concepts from the domain of *statistical theory* to the domain of *archaeological reasoning*.

Statistical theory has been defined by Fisher (1954, p. 1) as "mathematics applied to observational data." It will be taken here as a mathematical framework defining formal connection between measurement observations and models of underlying processes (cf., Mood et al., 1974, p. 8).

Archaeological theory, with the goal of formulating satisfactory explanatory theory at the level of process (Read & LeBlanc, 1978), and statistical theory, providing a conceptual framework for mathematically expressing the implications of processes for data observations (Cox & Hinkley, 1974, p. 5), evidently have commonality at the level of process. This commonality can be profitably developed, it will be argued, by viewing statistical theory as a conceptual framework within which one can define, represent, and characterize properties of processes (e.g., Ingold, 1980) said to be explanatory for data within the purview of archaeological theory: "important to archaeology . . . is the qualitative capacity of statistical and numerical *concepts* [italics added] in abstract model building" (Clarke, 1968, p. 144). Thus analysis of data using statistical methods can more effectively elucidate an underlying process when there is concordance between the conceptual frameworks associated with the two domains.

Concordance, however, is likely to be the exception rather than the rule when statistical methods are uncritically based on a transformation commonly made of the statistical conceptual framework in order to allow application of the methods to data that do *not necessarily represent any single process* (let alone a homogeneous population with respect to a single process).[1] The transformation redefines the conceptual framework away from a form where data are assumed to represent a common underlying process to a form that can include data brought forward for study but not in relation to a common structuring process: "we shall study procedures that permit confrontation of the mathematical [probability] model with empirical data" (Lukacs, 1972, p. 136). In essence, the transformation takes the analyst's more arbitrary formulation of a *data set* and defines a process for which the data set can be treated as a *homogeneous population* representing the newly defined process. Brunk (1960, pp. 97-100) gives the transformation explicitly (see also Hoel, 1966, p. 81).

The transformation is not a necessary part of application of the statistical conceptual framework. Its use reflects whether the framework is to be employed to *describe* observations or to represent the *processes responsible* for them: "parameters are to be regarded sometimes as representing underlying properties . . . and sometimes as giving concise descriptions of observations . . ." (Cox & Hinkley, 1974, p. 5; see also Earle, 1976, p. 201).

When a transformation of the statistical conceptual framework is employed in the application of statistical methods, the degree of discordance it brings between the two domains of statistical theory and archaeological reasoning may vary. At best, the transformation may only introduce a slight distortion. At worst, the transformation becomes reified and taken to be equivalent to the conceptual framework for statistical theory.

Some archaeologists have unwittingly accepted this reification by stipulating an unnecessary, if not distorting, rigid separation and unidirectional relation between the archaeological and statistical domains, asserting that analytic argumentation leads only from archaeological concepts to statistical methods. "Statistical methodology comes into play *only after* [italics added] the relevant populations have been defined to suit the research objectives" (Thomas, 1978, p. 35). This separation is unnecessary, as it is based on reification of the transformation of the statistical framework. It also eliminates rewarding interplay between the statistical conceptual framework and the archaeological domain (Clarke, 1968, p. 547) precisely at the level most fruitful for theory: the concept and definition of a population (cf. Spencer, 1980, pp. 144-146).

The separation between the two domains as expressed in the quote is, however, consistent with an analogical paradigm used to connect the two domains. Thus, the separation is not a simple problem of *error of application*, but a deeper and more general issue centered around the distinction between *borrowing by analogy and argumentation by principles*. By the latter is meant isomorphic (see Mitchell, 1980, p. 21) translation of fundamental principles from one domain into the language of another domain (cf. Read, 1984). In this case, the principles to be translated are those used to construct the probablistic foundation for statistical theory, and they are to be imbedded into the archaeological domain. This probabilistic foundation is "concerned . . . with the study of the *method of thinking* [italics added] that can be used in the study of random phenomena (i.e., individually non-deterministic phenomena that exhibit regularity in the aggregate)" (Parzen, 1960, p. 8).

The more common procedure of borrowing through the use of persuasive analogies rests on a tenuous assumption: the analogy captures the totality of relevant relations (Hesse, 1974, p. 217), even though only a partial set of the full set of relations is expressed in the analogy.

This chapter has several objectives. First to be shown is the precise manner in which the analogical argument used to connect the archaeological and statistical domains is insufficient and can lead to erroneous perceptions about the proper application of statistical concepts. The distinction between a *data base* brought forward for analysis in order to evaluate an *archaeological model*, and a *population* defined in relation to a *statistical model*, will be stressed as the basis for inadequacy of the analogical argument. An archaeological data base and an archaeological model often pertain to multiple processes, whereas a population defined in relation to a statistical model pertains to a single process. The tenuousness of uncritical analogical argument in archaeological reasoning in general has been stressed by a number of authors (e.g., Binford, 1967; Godfrey & Cole, 1979; Gould, 1980; Schiffer, 1981, Price, 1982) and will not be elaborated here.

Second, a brief review will be made of the probabilistic foundation for statistical theory in order to clarify the role of a model and a population in the statistical framework. This framework implies that a more arbitrarily selected data base, defined by analogy as a population, will probably be in discordance with the notion of a population as the set of outcomes of a single process.

Next, a resolution of the discordance introduced by this analogical argument, involving several different modes of analysis, will be presented. The implications of the statistical conceptual framework for these modes of analysis will be shown by example. The results will be used to argue that concordance between the statistical and archæological frameworks at the common level of process leads to a more enlightened analysis of data for theory construction.

ANALOGICAL PARADIGM

The following simplified diagram of a general research paradigm (e.g., Clarke, 1968, pp. 34-35; Pelto, 1970, pp. 335-337; Doran & Hodson, 1975, p. 6) schematically shows the primary features of a form of argument common to most research:

$$\cdots \begin{bmatrix} \text{Previous} \\ \text{Results} \end{bmatrix} \rightarrow \begin{bmatrix} \text{Research} \\ \text{Problem} \\ \text{plus} \\ \text{Data Base} \end{bmatrix} \rightarrow \begin{bmatrix} \text{Data} \\ \text{Set} \end{bmatrix} \rightarrow \begin{bmatrix} \text{Analysis} \end{bmatrix} \rightarrow \begin{bmatrix} \text{Interpretation} \\ \text{of Results} \end{bmatrix} \cdots \quad (A)$$

The three dots at the beginning and end of the schema indicate that research is a continuous, cyclical process. Results obtained at the end of a cycle of data analysis become part of the environment of previous results which guide the formulation of research problems and, perhaps, the revision of an earlier hypothesis (e.g., Barrett, 1976) in the next cycle of analysis (cf. Clarke, 1968, p. 444).

Prior to Spaulding's introduction of statistical methods as an integral part of archaeological argumentation, the content and definition for each aspect of the schema was defined primarily through an archaeologically based conceptual framework that guided notions about proper methods for research and argumentation. Spaulding's seminal papers, in conjunction with Binford's (1964, 1968) and Clarke's (1968) persuasive arguments for an explicitly scientific form of archaeology, radically altered perceptions about proper archaeological argumentation by introducing, in part, statistical methods. This changed Schema A into the following:

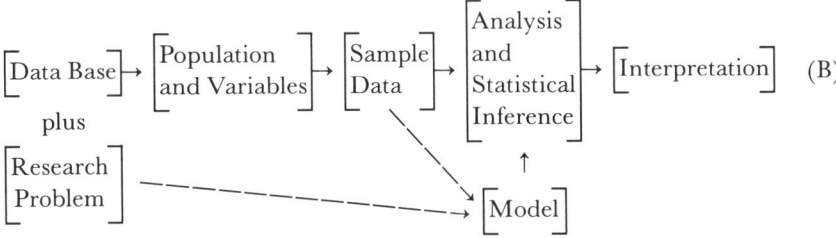

The shift to a mixed archaeological/statistical framework has been justified by an analogical argument. The argument presumes—incorrectly it will be shown—a particular form for imbedding statistical methods into archaeological arguments. The analogical argument relates the archaeological domain and the statistical domain via the following analogy equation:

Sample : Population :: Data Set : Data Base   (1)

This leads to perceiving the data base as a population (e.g., by defining a site or assemblage as a population of artifacts, or a regional system of sites as a population of sites), with archaeologically distinguished and defined units recast as nominal, ordinal, interval, or ratio variables. It also leads to defining the data set as a (probabilistic) sample of data from the population that has been formulated.

The specific form of the sample is established by a relation that characterizes the left side of the equation:

Random Sample : Population   (2)
            Objective Inference

Given "objective inference" as a goal within archaeological argumentation, it follows from the analogy that the next equation describes the proper method for achieving "objective inference":

Random Sample : Population   (3)
         Objective Inference
:: Random Sample (Artifacts, Sites) : Population (Artifacts, Sites)
                  Objective Inference

The analogy creates "objective inference" at the level of archaeological data and fills out the previous schema to make for a purportedly adequate form of argumentation:

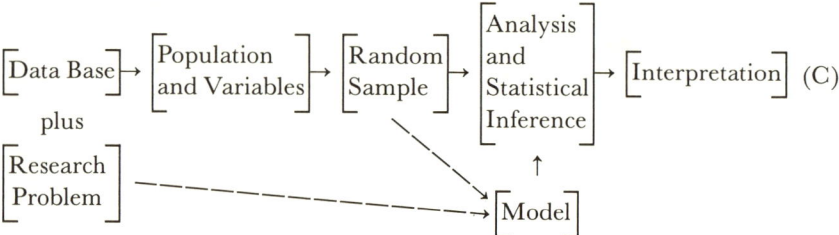

"Objective inference" is imbedded in the argument by Equation 3.

The statistical terms in the schema are the *translation* of the archaeologically defined notions of research problem, data base, and data set into the language of statistical methods. The schema leads naturally to the division of the originally unitary, archaeologically defined Schema A into two parts: archaeological and statistical. The new Schema C includes the definition and statement of the research problem and identification of a data base as part of the archaeological domain (cf. Parker et al., chapter 5), while the analysis of sample data in the context of a population, set of variables, and random sample belong to the statistical domain. The interpretation of results obtained from the statistical analysis includes a translation of the statistical conclusions into their meaning in the archaeological domain. The motivation for seeing *unidirectionality* in the analytical argument, as did Thomas (1978, p. 35), is immediately apparent from the schema.

A model has been explicitly introduced in Schemas B and C, but not in Schema A. An explicitly stated model is not necessary in nonstatistical analyses of the form given in Schema A, whereas it is necessary in analysis using statistical inference, as in Schema C, to go from the properties of sample data to population characteristics. The dashed lines in Schemas B and C, connecting the terms "research problem" and "sample data" to the model, indicate that the model can be formulated on the basis of either an inductive argument (e.g., Hietala & Stevens, 1977; Kintigh & Ammerman, 1982), such as postulating a relation between two variables from an apparent relation in a scattergram plot of sample data, or a deductive argument formulated in accord with current archaeological theory (e.g., Thomas, 1973; Wilmsen, 1973; Zubrow, 1975; Bettinger, 1975; Binford, 1977; Read, 1977; Wood, 1978; Hamblin & Pitcher, 1980; Renfrew & Cooke, 1981; Christenson, 1982; Steponaitis, 1982; Hastorf, 1983; see also references given in Carr, chapter 2).

In both the cases of inductive generalization and deductive specification, the same format for statistical analysis is used once the model is specified; divergence only occurs when interpretation is made of the results. The format consists of 1) a test for goodness of fit for the model, 2) estimation of parameters in the model and construction of confidence limits for those estimates; and 3) tests of hypotheses about parameter values. A model postulated on the basis of theoretical arguments is said to provide confirmation for that theory if it is statistically accepted, whereas statistical acceptance of an inductively generated model only defines it to be adequate as description of the data and need not confirm any theory.

General Overview of the Inadequacy of the Analogically Based Paradigm

The paradigm illustrated in Schema C is straightforward, but the initial transformation of the statistical conceptual basis is carried into the archaeological domain by analogical argument. This form of argumentation may introduce incongruity between models aimed at representing underlying processes as defined by archaeological theory and the population which the processes are said to represent. Obscured in the analogy is the critical fact that the left side of the analogy in Equation 3 is not the conceptual basis for statistical theory. Instead, it is a convenient relationship which allows restatement of properties of measurements made over sample data in the form of mathematical arguments that refer to the probabilistic foundation of statistical theory. This relationship on the left side of Equation 3, and its analog on the right, can be altered *so long as the relations basic to the mathematical argument are maintained*,[2] as is done in sampling theory (e.g., Cochran, 1977).

Schema C thus obscures the fact that statistical theory is based on its own conceptual framework for relating a model to a population and variables, apart from that of archaeological theory. ". . . [I]t is necessary to have a mathematical model for the experiment. The model must be able to account for the variation found when an experiment is repeated under essentially the same conditions, and for this the model is based on the ideas of probability" (Fraser, 1962, p. 4). Consider the middle part of Schema C, which belongs to the statistical domain. Within statistical theory, a model can be introduced via identification of a single underlying "experiment" or process that the model is intended to mathematically represent:

$$\begin{bmatrix} \text{"Experiment"} \\ \text{or Process} \end{bmatrix} \rightarrow \begin{bmatrix} \text{Model} \end{bmatrix} \\ \downarrow \\ \begin{bmatrix} \text{Population} \\ \text{and Variables} \end{bmatrix} \rightarrow \begin{bmatrix} \text{Random} \\ \text{Sample} \end{bmatrix} \rightarrow \begin{bmatrix} \text{Statistical} \\ \text{Inference} \end{bmatrix} \quad \text{(D)}$$

In Schema D, the *population is defined through the model* and underlying process, not separately from it, as in Schema C. In Schema D, the population is the set of entities that are the consequence of the process or experiment and has structure as defined by the model and process; whereas, in Schema C, this need not—and often is not—true.

If Schemas C and D are put together, the following schema is obtained:

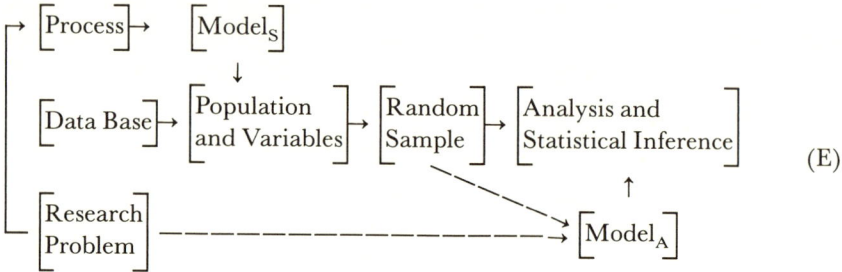

(E)

Observe that there are *two* models in Schema E, call them M_S and M_A. The two models need not be identical. The statistical model M_S is a representation of a *single* process (see Note 1) that has been identified (e.g., Hill, 1978), whereas the archaeological model M_A is based on a research problem that, in its full generality, is typically a series of processes (the multicausal "model"). A model M_A based inductively on properties of a random sample, of course, need not have any direct relationship to a process (Draper & Smith, 1967, p. 2). The model M_S for a single process roughly corresponds to a principle within so-called middle range theory (e.g., Binford, 1977), aimed at explication of a portion of a larger context.

There is no reason to expect consistency between the analogical definition of a population, dependent on an archaeological model, and the statistical framework definition of a population, dependent on a statistical model. The former has no constraints other than the archaeologist's intuition of what data base is relevant to the research problem. Some of the entities in this data base may result from the same process, but other entities are likely to be the consequence of different processes. Yet the analysis implicitly assumes, in the form of an analogy, that all entities in the population are the result of the same process.

A classic example of the dilemma occurs with the 10-square-meter relationship between the number of persons and the amount of living area in agricultural groups, which was defined by Naroll (1962) on the basis of a sample of such societies. The relationship, although correct as a *description* of the population from which the sample was taken, does not represent (except perhaps by chance) the relationship *within* any of the societies making up the population. Each society is likely to have very different processes that affect how living areas are constructed. Hence, taking the data base as a population contradicts the notion of a population as a set of entities resulting from the *same* process.

The potential discordance between the two ways a population can be specified is removed in standard statistical arguments by making a transformation of the statistical conceptual basis. The transformation eliminates the model M_S and substitutes a trivial model M_T that is necessarily consistent with the model

M_A, so as to artifically create internal consistency. (M_T is trivial in the sense of possibly not having theoretical content.) *The logical consequence of this transformation, however, is to reduce deductively determined models to descriptive statements about an arbitrary population in the statistical analysis. Thus, the statistical test need no longer be confirmation of theory.* Even when there is consistency between the models M_S and M_A, the transformation still allows a definition of a population that may be incorrect for the model. To understand the nature of this transformation and to complete the argument on the inadequacy of the analogic paradigm, it is necessary to diverge, for a moment, and introduce the reader to the probabilistic foundation of the statistical conceptual framework.

PROBABILISTIC FOUNDATION FOR THE STATISTICAL FRAMEWORK

Statistical theory has a probabilistic foundation with primitive notions (i.e., terms undefined within the theory) as follows: The domain for the theory is a finite[3] set Ω whose elements $e_1, e_2, \ldots$ are called *outcomes* or *elementary events*. Any set E of outcomes (i.e., a subset of Ω) is called an *event*. It is assumed that to each outcome e_i is assigned a nonnegative number p_i satisfying two conditions: 1) $0 \leq p_i \leq 1$ for each i and 2) $\Sigma p_i = 1$. The number p_i assigned to the outcome e_i is called the *probability* of the outcome e_i and one writes $\Pr[e_i] = p_i$. For any event E, one defines $\Pr[E] = \Sigma_{e \in E} \Pr[e]$. The set Ω along with a set $\{p_i\}$ of probabilities form a *probability* (or *sample*) *space*.

This framework is given interpretation for the context of a theory relating to a process P by letting the outcomes e_i represent precisely the set of all possible outcomes when the process P occurs (Parzen, 1960, p. 8; Feller, 1968, p. 14; Lukacs, 1972, p. 3; Mood et al., 1974, p. 9) and by assigning the probabilities p_i in accordance with the theory. A simple genetic example illustrates the procedure. In the mating of two heterozygote individuals, say $Aa \times Aa$, the outcomes can be defined genotypically as AA, Aa, or aa, making $\Omega_G = \{AA, Aa, aa\}$ the set of outcomes. Or the outcomes might be defined in terms of the phenotypic outcomes, symbolized by $A-$ ($=AA$ or Aa) and aa, in the case of a dominant allele A. In this case the set of outcomes is $\Omega_P = \{A-, aa\}$. The probabilities are assigned to the outcomes in these two examples according to genetic theory in a manner that makes the probability space a representation of the genetic mating process of heterozygote individuals.

The probabilities are determined first by the probabilistic interpretation that when the event E certainly occurs (i.e., the process must "produce" an outcome in the set E), $\Pr[E] = 1$. Thus, for example, $\Pr[\Omega] = 1$. When the event E cannot occur, $\Pr[E] = 0$. Second, the probabilities are determined by the interpretation that if two events E and F are said to be equally likely by the theory, probabilities p_i are assigned in such a fashion that $\Pr[E] = \Pr[F]$. In the example of the set Ω_G, the events AA and aa are equally likely and the outcome Aa is twice as likely as either AA or aa according to genetic theory. Hence,

Pr $[AA]$ = Pr $[aa]$ = Pr $[Aa]$ /2, so that Pr $[AA]$ = Pr $[aa]$ = $\frac{1}{4}$ and Pr $[Aa]$ = $\frac{1}{2}$. For the set Ω_P, since the outcome $A-$ is the event $\{AA, aa\}$, it follows that Pr $[A-]$ = Pr $[AA]$ + Pr $[Aa]$ = $\frac{3}{4}$ and Pr $[aa]$ = $\frac{1}{4}$.

Observe that the theoretical assignment of probabilities to outcomes is a fundamental means by which the resulting probability space becomes a representation of that theory.

The probability space also provides a basis for models representing a process in the form of relations among measures made over the outcomes. These measures are mathematically represented, using the concept of a random variable. A *random variable* X defined over a probability space Ω is a mapping (or rule) from Ω to the real numbers R, satisfying the condition that the mapping assigns exactly one real number (which need not be distinct) to each $e \in \Omega$. The value x assigned by the random variable X to the outcome e is the *value* of X at e, and one writes $X(e) = x$. A *probability distribution* for X is determined first by defining the event $E_x = \{e \in \Omega : X(e) = x\}$ (i.e., E_x is the set composed of all outcomes e for which the value x is assigned by the random variable X) and then defining Pr $[X = x]$ = Pr $[E_x]$. Note that if there is no $e \in \Omega$ such that $X(e) = x$, then E_x is the empty set and, by default, no outcome in this set can occur. Hence, Pr $[X = x]$ = 0 in this case.

To continue the genetic example, one random variable of interest for the space Ω_G is the variable X which assigns to a genotype the number of A alleles in the genotype. Thus $X(aa) = 0$, $X(Aa) = 1$, and $X(AA) = 2$, and the respective probabilities are $\frac{1}{4}$, $\frac{1}{2}$, and $\frac{1}{4}$ for these three values in the case of a heterozygote mating. In this example, the random variable X directly measures an aspect of the genetic process by identifying how many alleles of a given type are likely to be found in an offspring of the mating of heterozygotes.

Example of the Application of the Statistical Conceptual Framework

Now consider a situation within the purview of the archaeologist. The example is based on viewing a real world process as a natural experiment, in the sense that each instance of an entity produced by the process can be thought of as one result of "doing" that experiment. The outcomes of the "experiment" are just the distinct *possible* outcomes of the real world process: "The sample space ($=\Omega$) provides a model of an ideal experiment in the sense that, by definition, *every thinkable outcome of the experiment is completely described by one, and only one, sample point* (= one outcome)" (Feller, 1968, p. 14). (Note that a distinction is made between the entity produced by the experiment and the outcome that the entity represents. Different entities may represent the same outcome.)

The example is the construction of a camp by a group of !Kung San. The natural experiment can be identified as the process of camp construction. It includes decisions (some conscious, others not) concerning, for example: how the huts will be constructed (traditionally of branches and dried grass); how they will be spatially arranged (traditionally in a circular arrangement); how many will be constructed (generally equal to the number of nuclear families in the camp); and who will be next to whom, which reflects both kinship and other social relations. The outcomes can be characterized in several ways in reference to the process of camp construction. Here the set Ω will be the different possible spatial arrangements of the huts in camp, under the restriction that the arrangements conform to the single process of concern here: traditional camp construction. This process has as an idealized outcome a circular arrangement of huts with adjacent huts equidistant from one another, possibly reflecting egalitarianism in the spatial arrangement of huts. Thus, the set of outcomes Ω is a list of the distinct circular arrangements of huts, starting with camps having but one hut.

For this example, it is not immediately evident how to assign the probabilities, as a relevant theory does not yet exist. The domain for that theory can be established by deducing some of the consequences of the probabilities. Assume, for the moment, that probabilities have been assigned. The probabilities $\{p_i\}$ for the set Ω represent the likelihood that when a camp is constructed, it has a particular spatial arrangement of huts. Since the number of huts is assumed to be equal to the number of nuclear families, the probabilities $\{p_i\}$ are also a statement about the process by which !Kung society becomes divided into living groups, both on a short-term basis including temporary visitors (Marshall, 1976; Yellen, 1976, 1977; Lee, 1979) and on a long-term basis primarily involving rules of camp membership (Marshall, 1976, p. 182; Weissner, 1977; Lee, 1979). This suggests that the appropriate theory for defining the probabilities in this example involves a process that determines group fission and fusion. The number of families that comprises a camp presumably results from both the distribution of persons among camps according to the camps' roles as social units in the organization of the whole society, and the relationship between the number of persons in camp and its implications for the procurement of resources. Thus, the probabilities are related to a broader context that involves the complex issue of the way in which a hunting and gathering society is subdivided into a set of living groups, as well as the dynamics of temporary relocation of persons among these living groups (see discussion and references in Conkey, 1980). Observe that while the probabilities cannot yet be established from theory, consideration of the statistical conceptual framework nonetheless leads to identification of both the domain for that theory and the issues to be addressed (cf. Read, 1974a; Vierra, 1982, p. 166).

A natural random variable in this context is the mapping N which assigns to each outcome the number of huts in the spatial arrangement. Another random variable is the following (Read, 1978). Measure the distance L between adjacent huts as the nonstochastic part (see Discussion of Projectile Point Classification Example, p. 78) of the arc distance along the circumference of the camp from one adjacent hut to the next. Since it is assumed that, in the ideal, adjacent huts are equidistant, there will be a single value l that is computed for a given outcome. Assign this value to that outcome. This defines the random variable L. Another random variable of interest is the mapping A which assigns the nonstochastic part of the area a of the camp to an outcome.

For each of these random variables, N, L, and A, the respective probability distribution is determined from the set of probabilities associated with the outcomes making up Ω.

In the absence of adequately developed theory for determining the probabilities, one can assign the probabilities via repetition of the experiment. In this context, one repetition is one instance of a group of !Kung constructing a camp. If one observes n instances of !Kung camps (e.g., Yellen, 1977) and finds that the configuration with i huts occurs n_i times, then the ratio $n_i/n = \hat{p}_i$ is taken as an *estimate* of the probability p_i for the outcome defined by the spatial arrangement of a camp with i huts. The true value of p_i would be the value towards which the ratio n_i/n converges as the number of repetitions of the experiment increases indefinitely ($p_i = \lim_{n \to \infty} n_i/n$). In other words, p_i is an abstract concept (Nagel, 1936) that represents what would happen if it were possible to keep constant the factors structuring how the !Kung decides to construct a camp, and then repeat the experiment indefinitely[4] (or at least a large number of times, as might be done with computer simulation when the factors structuring the process are sufficiently well-identified, along with values of relevant parameters [e.g., Thomas, 1973; Howell & Lehotay, 1978].) As Fisher (1954, pp. 6-7) has commented, "Even in the simplest of cases the values . . . before us are interpreted as a random sample of a *hypothetical infinite population of such values as might have arisen in the same circumstances* [italics added] (see also Cox & Hinkley, 1974, p. 5; Cowgill, 1969, p. 162).

Observe that keeping the factors structuring camp construction constant is critical to the estimation of the probabilities $\{p_i\}$ through repetition of the experiment (cf. Fraser, 1962, p. 7; Mood et al., 1974, p. 9) if an instance of an actual !Kung camp is to constitute one instance of repetition of the experiment. This implies two things: First, it defines which camps can be taken as data to be used in the construction of the ratio n_i/n. A camp can be included as a datum only if its construction involved a set of factors and parameter values consistent with those of other camps used as data. Second, it conversely defines what data cannot be included, such as camps where construction involved other factors or different parameter values. For example, traditional !Kung camps are roughly circular, leading to the above ideal of a circular camp. However, !Kung with ties to the Herero pastoralists in the area often constructed camps that were not circular (Read, personal observation), and huts that imitated the wattle and daub techniques used by the Herero. These camps, even though they are !Kung camps, are not an instance of a repetition of the experiment of camp construction involving factors that determine how traditional camps were constructed, since a different set of "rules" or process is involved.

Thus, at the level of a *description* of !Kung camps, all !Kung camps and only !Kung camps would be considered. Distinctions might be made between "traditional" and "nontraditional" camps in the description, but all camps are part of the data base and are to be included in the description. At the level of the *statistical framework of an experiment and outcomes*, the data base would consist of instances of camp construction involving only a given set of factors or rules that define a single process. Thus, the data might include only some !Kung camps.

In other words, the framework of experiment and outcomes defines the *relevant population* of data for estimating the probabilities $\{p_i\}$ and measuring a random variable X as all entities that are the result of repetitions of the same experiment. The data base for the population is the actual set of instances that resulted from the experiment, and no other data (see Carr, chapter 2). Contrariwise, the translation of a collection of artifacts within a set of sites into a population defined as the set of all artifacts at the sites need not be (and most likely is not [Schiffer, 1976]) a set of entities resulting from a single process.

Just as the researcher must be careful to include in a data set only those observations relevant to the process of interest, so must the researcher make a careful selection of random variables in relation to that process (see Carr, chapter 2). The choice of a random variable is ultimately guided by its effectiveness in elucidating the properties of the process leading to the outcomes. Some choices of a random variable are of little value for the process in question (e.g., measuring an aspect that is only coincidental [Sackett, 1966; Brown, 1982, p. 186] such as an attribute relationship due only to mechanical contingency), while other choices may be highly illuminating. As Klejn (1977, p. 12) comments: "For the meaningful construction of systems we need a preliminary selection and hierarchy of traits . . ." (see also Read, 1974b).

A nontrivial example of a random variable elucidating a process is the random variable defined above as the nonstochastic part of the arc length distance between !Kung huts. At first glance, the measure would not seem to be of primary interest, yet empirically, it assigns a statistically constant value to each distinct outcome in the case for !Kung camps (Read, 1978). This indicates that the spatial arrangement of huts, as viewed upon entering the camp circle, is kept constant, regardless of the number of huts. It suggests that the !Kung perceives that the space between huts at the periphery of the camp, defining entries to the camp, should have a fixed spatial arrangement, despite the number of huts. In other words, the random variable L is apparently sensitive to an aspect of !Kung conceptualization about the proper construction of a camp. Other measures, such as distance between fires in front of the huts, are at first glance seemingly more relevant but do not yield a constant value over all outcomes; they vary with the number of huts (Read, 1978).

INADEQUACY OF THE ANALOGICALLY BASED PARADIGM FROM THE PERSPECTIVE OF PROBABILITY THEORY

Having reviewed the probabilistic foundation of statistical theory, it is now possible to complete the argument on the inadequacy of the analogic paradigm and discuss the transformation of the statistical conceptual framework often made in the application of a statistical technique to a data base.

A model, in the context of statistical theory (M_S, above), stands as a posited set of relations for a series of random variables defined over the set Ω of outcomes and associated probabilities $\{p_i\}$ for an experiment or process. The aim of the model is to represent, in a concrete form, the process that underlies the set of outcomes, so that its logic and underlying principles can be uncovered and expressed. From this viewpoint, a "correct" model defines how the set of outcomes is structured in terms of the random variables that have been defined (cf. Schact, 1980, p. 789). Equivalently, it may be said that the data relevant to the process are the data that have been generated in accordance with the model (see also Clark, 1979, p. 171; Carr, chapter 1).

In Schema C, a model is either a consequence of archaeological theory or inductively derived from data observations from the population. In this schema, the population represents the data base deemed relevant to the problem being investigated. On the contrary, it has just been argued that the model, from the statistical viewpoint, defines the set of data as instances of the model, in the sense of repetitions of the experiment for which the model is a representation. There is no a priori reason to assume that these two definitions are automatically consistent with one another, and in general, they are not. As noted before, the definition of a population simply as the data base carries no assurance that all data in it are the consequence of a process defined by the model (e.g., Evans, 1980; Munday & Lincoln, 1979) and by that process alone. As will be shown below by example, the discordance that is introduced in an analysis by taking the population to be equivalent to the data base without further consideration, need not be minor; it can lead to a misleading analysis.

The potential discordance between the concept of a set of outcomes of a single process and the definition of a population as the data base is removed artificially in order to apply statistical methods to the analysis of arbitrary data sets. The cost of this, however, is to reduce the analysis to the level of description.

The potential discordance is removed by defining a new process that has precisely the data base as outcomes, with a random variable defined by the rule that assigns to the outcomes the values determined by the variable that has been measured (see Brunk, 1960, pp. 97-100, for details). For example, suppose a population is defined as the set of lithic artifacts at a site, and the measures of archaeological concern are the length (l), width (w), and thickness (t) of each lithic artifact. (Variables have been chosen for simplicity of illustration only.) Define a process P in the following manner. Let the process P consist of listing each lithic in the site (e.g., a site catalogue). Then, the outcomes of this process are precisely the lithics in the site, and each instance of listing a lithic can be interpreted as one instance of repeating the process. Assign probabilities to the outcomes as follows: Because each artifact in the list is equally probable (that is, all artifacts are assumed to be listed and none are to be excluded), assign $1/N$ as the probability associated with each outcome, where $N =$ Population Size or total number of lithics in the site. Define random variables L, W, and T in correspondance to the measures l, w, and t by assigning to each outcome in the catalogue (= one lithic) the number obtained by the measurement l, w, or t, respectively. (Note that in contrast to the random variables defined for the !Kung camps, these random variables include the stochastic part of the measure.)

As a variant on this procedure, one might list lithics according to a classification. In this case, the outcomes would be the type class to which the lithic belongs, and the probabilities of the outcomes or types p_t are given by counting the total number of instances, n_t of type t in the population of N lithics, and setting $p_t = n_t/N$. Note that here the ratio n_t/N is the actual value of p_t.

For this definition of a process, the statistical framework precisely characterizes the process of listing artifacts in terms of archaeologically relevant information on types of lithics in the site and frequency of each type. The set of type outcomes Ω is just the list of all possible types, corresponding to the idea that a repetition of the "experiment" consists of identifying a lithic according to its type; the probabilities $\{p_i\}$ give precisely the probabilities that a lithic will be of a given type when the lithics are classified. Consequently, the statistical framework of a set of outcomes and of a random variable, as a mapping from the outcomes to the real numbers, has been preserved by this process. At the same time, the characterization exactly matches the *description* of the site at the level of either individual artifacts or artifact types.

Lost in the procedure, however, is any theory about site formation. The role of a model in the statistical analysis, as representing the *internal process* by which the data are generated, has been removed. For example, if one were to inductively find a linear relationship between the length and width of the lithics, the interpretation at the level of the process, defined as listing the lithics in a site, would be only a trivial one. The process can be described as one in which the result of listing the artifacts leads to a linear relationship between two variables. This result has no serious content for it completely begs the question of why a linear relationship should exist or whether the relationship is spurious and merely a result of the definition of the data base. Or, conversely, *failure* to fnd a relationship between variables may also be spurious in this situation. Because the collection of all lithics at a site is not the result of a single process, a model defined for the population of lithics at a site cannot be a characterization of each process underlying lithic manufacture and site formation; it therefore is spurious at the level of explanation. Hence the analysis has been shifted to the level of description.

This conclusion suggests that the common procedure of *arbitrarily* defining a population (in the sense of using criteria other than outcomes of a single process) and *arbitrarily* defining variables (in the sense of not establishing that the variables directly measure and effectively illuminate properties of the process at the level of outcomes) does not, by itself, lead to characterization of an underlying process. This is true even though the analytic scheme can be placed into the format of a set of outcomes and random variables defined over these outcomes.

PREANALYSIS TO CIRCUMVENT THE DISCORDANCE IN AN ANALOGICALLY FORMATTED ANALYTICAL SCHEME

The discordance between the concept of a set of outcomes as a single process and the definition of a population as the data base, as part of the analogically formatted analytical scheme, stems from two aspects: 1) The *population*, initially defined as equivalent to the data base, may contain data that are the result of several distinct processes; and 2) The *variables*, initially defined as the measures of interest, may not directly measure outcomes of an underlying process. These two aspects of the discordance suggest four modes of analysis, one not involving the discordance and three which do require the use of preanalytic screening of the data. The particular mode of analysis depends on whether or not the population is well-defined, in the sense of only containing entities that are the result of the same process, and whether or not the variables are well-defined, in the sense of effectively expressing properties of an underlying process (Read, 1983). The four modes are: 1) well-defined (WD) population and well-defined variables, 2) WD population and not well-defined (NWD) variables, 3) NWD population and WD variables, and 4) NWD population and NWD variables.

Examples of these four modes of analysis, drawing from the !Kung camp illustration above, would be as follows:

Mode 1 (WD population, WD variables). The population is formed of traditional !Kung camps. The variables are measures such as N, the number of huts in the camp, and L, the distance between huts along the perimeter of the camp. The underlying process is the set of decisions affecting construction of a camp in terms of its spatial arrangement. This circumstance does not involve discordance and does not require preanalytic screening of data of the kind discussed here. The remaining modes of analysis do involve discordance and require preanalytic screening.

Mode 2 (WD population, NWD variables). The population is composed of traditional !Kung camps, but variables such as distance between fires or area of the camp are used. As argued above, both of these variables are approximations of the variables in the previous example; hence, they are NWD variables with respect to the process of camp construction.

Mode 3 (NWD population, WD variables). The data set consists of !Kung traditional and nontraditional camps, with variables as given in the Mode 1 example. As argued above, the traditionally and nontraditionally constructed camps reflect different decision processes.

Mode 4 (NWD populations, NWD variables). This very common situation often occurs when the population is defined as the data base and variables are selected separately from identification of processes which generated these data (e.g., many schemes for measurement of artifacts, such as Thomas, 1970; Gunn & Prewitt, 1975; Benfer & Benfer, 1981). Two examples will be discussed below in detail. The first is the data set and variables used for application of factor analysis to determine "toolkits" within artifact assemblages (Binford & Binford, 1966). The second is the data set and variables used to critique numerical taxonomy procedures for artifact-type identification (Christenson & Read, 1977).

Because only Mode 1 corresponds to the conceptual framework of statistical theory for representation of a process, it follows that preanalysis of data, in order to eliminate NWD variables and/or redefine the original population into subpopulations that are WD populations, should precede analysis of data aimed at constructing models at the explanatory level. As Whallon (1982, p. 160) notes, the "identification of underlying dimensions and measurement along them . . . is *the* critical stage, because it is in the degree to which we can or cannot directly measure along these underlying dimensions of variation that the choice of all further analytical methods and techniques ultimately must be based." The methods of preanalysis, required to modify data as a part of analytic Modes 2, 3, and 4, will now be outlined.

RESOLUTION OF THE DISCORDANCE BY PREANALYSIS OF THE DATA BASE

A direct method for resolving the discordance identified by Modes 2, 3, and 4 consists of redefining variables and/or populations according to theoretical properties (e.g., Ericson et al., 1971; Weissner, 1973; Odell, 1981; Vierra, 1982, pp. 168-173). This requires 1) identifying what are believed to be the structuring factors for the context, 2) establishing that certain variables directly measure those factors, and 3) showing that the data are the consequence of precisely those factors (cf. Salmon & Salmon, 1979, pp. 68-69).

This direct approach for resolving discordance has two limitations. First, it requires adequate theory, which may not exist. In these instances, the analysis may have as partial goal elucidation of precisely those properties which must be known in order to define WD variables and populations. Second, even in situations where an appropriate, theoretical argument exists, the matter of population definition is often slighted by failing to establish that all cases in the population are a result of exactly one and the same process (see Carr, chapter 1). Hence, the methodological problem is to establish procedures that allow restructuring of data sets and redefinition of variables (cf. Voorrips, 1982) in a manner that, in the absence of adequate theory, more closely matches the conditions of Mode 1 analysis. This depends on identifying general properties, which relate NWD variables to WD variables, and general characteristics, which WD populations should exhibit with respect to WD variables. Each of Modes 2, 3, and 4 will now be reviewed in turn.

First, consider Mode 2 analysis involving NWD variables and a WD population. NWD variables arise when the underlying process is not well understood and variables are chosen in approximation of the (unknown) dimensions characterizing the process that gives rise to the WD population. Often many variables are measured, using the rationale that some of the measures approximate the unknown dimensions and that the full set of variables is measuring at least the desired dimensions. This leads naturally to techniques aimed at dimensional construction such as factor analysis (in the generic sense) and multidimensional scaling. But given that factor analytic procedures presume a *linear* relationship of the higher-level derived factors to the lower-level original variables, one cannot merely assume that the desired underlying dimensions can be recovered as factors. The underlying dimensions of relevance may be related in a nonlinear way to the measured variables, and not be recoverable. For example, it is well known that the first factor or first principal component over metric measurements of objects tends to be a size dimension, regardless of other properties, when the objects have considerable size differences among themselves. Or, with frequency counts, if some units have large numbers of artifacts and others have small quantities, the first factor tends to measure quantity of material as a dimension. In either case, the factors or principal components need not have interpretative significance at the level of a process, even if they are statistically significant. Conversely, shape is often seen as a single dimension, but none of the factors can be assumed to be a precise measure of that dimension.

As an alternative to these dimension-construction techniques, one may formulate new variables using other techniques that satisfy certain considerations deemed to be important for that class data. For example, if the goal is to measure the morphological shape of artifacts, one can define variables that directly measure the components of shape without redundancy (see Read, 1982). Or if, instead of the overall shape, certain relationships within shapes, such as constancy of ratios for certain measurements (see Whallon, 1982), are deemed important, then new variables can be defined as ratios of the original variables. Note that in neither of these two cases are the new variables recoverable from factor analysis of sets of measures such as length, width, thickness, height, diameter, etc. (cf. Whallon, 1982, p. 151), since in both cases the new variable cannot be expressed as a linear combination of these measures.

Obviously these two approaches do not exhaust all possibilities. Spaulding (1977, 1982) has argued, for example, that the critical measures should be defined at a nominal, rather than an interval, level. Odell (1981), Read (1982), and Whallon (1982), for instance, have used this procedure to form a paradigmatic classification starting with ratio scale variables. It has been argued by Spaulding (1953, 1977, 1982) and Read (1974, 1982) that paradigmatic classes ought to be analysed at the level of relations, which leads to combining together certain of the classes in the paradigmatic classification, using Spaulding's well-known "nonrandom association of attributes" as a means to define types (see Read, 1974, 1982 for a methodology; Cowgill, 1982 for further discussion). Read (1982) has shown that the result of that type of analysis can be a set of types that presumably are acting as units measuring distinctions made in the conceptual domain, and hence, are identifying a new, relevant, dimension or "well-defined variable."

Now consider the third mode of analysis, with WD variables and a NWD population. Here, the problem is to subdivide a population into subpopulations that are each the consequence of a single process. The basic method stems from identifying criteria that indicate whether or not a given subdivision is in the direction of WD populations. One procedure, discussed elsewhere (e.g., Clarke, 1968, p. 159; Read, 1974b; Cowgill, 1982, pp. 54-55) and used below, is a division of a data set by the antimodes in a histogram of a variable across the data set (e.g., Odell, 1981; Read, 1982; Whallon, 1982), with straightforward extension of the procedure to the multivariate case.

Finally, for analyses involving NWD variables and a NWD population, there is no single method, since the techniques for Mode 2 and Mode 3 analyses (discussed above) are dependent on either the variable being WD or the population being WD. It is suggested that an iterative procedure, alternating between the two sets of techniques until there is convergence such that neither set of techniques permits further reduction of either the subpopulations or the set of variables (see discussion by Read, 1974), be used. An example of the iterative procedure will be given in detail in the next section.

Examples of Preanalysis of Data With NWD Populations and NWD Variables

Two applications of these concepts to Mode 4 data will be given. The first is the data set used by Binford and Binford (1966) in their seminal use of factor analysis in the study of assemblage structure. The second will be the data set used by Christenson and Read (1977) to show the inadequacy of the numerical taxonomy method for typological construction.

Factor Analysis of Mousterian Sites

Binford and Binford (1966) introduced factor analysis as a possible statistical method for finding what they termed "tool kits," implicitly using the following analogical equation:

$$\text{Variables : Factors :: Artifacts : Tool Kits} \qquad (4)$$

Because factor analysis is a method for going from variables to factors, Binford and Binford argued that when artifact counts are taken as variables, the factor analysis should lead to factors which can be interpreted as tool kits. Thus, they argued for the following analogical relationship:

$$\underbrace{\text{Variables : Factors}}_{\text{Factor Analysis}} :: \underbrace{\text{Artifact Counts : Tool Kits}}_{\text{Factor Analysis}} \qquad (5)$$

The correctness of the left-hand side of the equation was used as the implicit justification for the right-hand side of the equation.

While the specific results and subsequent application of factor analysis to other contexts (e.g., Hill, 1970) has received much discussion (see review by Vierra, 1982, pp. 272-273), most of the criticism has been on a technical level (e.g., Lischka, 1975; Christenson, 1981) that will not be discussed here. Instead, I will show that the data set used by Binford and Binford is a NWD population with NWD variables. I will begin with the variables.

Although, in principle, variables defined as artifact frequency counts should be well-defined measures of the process defined by Binford and Binford for formation of assemblages, actual artifact frequencies are the consequence of a variety of effects (Schiffer, 1975; Speth & Johnson, 1976; Odell, 1981; Carr, 1984, chapter 13), including different patterns of curation of artifacts (Binford, 1973, p. 242). Furthermore, Bordes' typology, which is used in the factor analysis, has been criticized on the basis of internal functional heterogeneity (Odell, 1981). These criticisms strongly argue that the variables used by Binford and Binford are NWD variables for the process of assemblage formation.

Next, it will be shown that the set of sites used in the analysis is not a WD population. In this example, well-defined data would be instances of the *single* process of assemblages being formed via artifacts used together as tool kits in activities. Both the set of tools making up a tool kit and the relative proportion of tools in each tool kit would be constant. The model for tool type frequencies, as a consequence of tool kits and activity frequencies, can be expressed as follows: Let $t_1, t_2, \ldots, t_n$ be the tool types. Let $K_1, K_2, \ldots, K_m$ be the tool kits, with the ith tool kit composed of the tool types $t_{i1}, t_{i2}, \ldots, t_{in_i}$. Let $A_1, A_2, \ldots, A_p$ be the activities and let α_{ij} denote the conversion between the number of times activity A_i is performed and the number of tools of type t_j that will become part of the assemblage because of the performance of activity A_i. This gives the probabilistic relationship:

$$t_j = \alpha_{1j}A_1 + \alpha_{2j}A_2 + \ldots + \alpha_{pj}A_p + \epsilon_j \qquad (6)$$

for each tool type t_j, $1 \leq j \leq n$, where ϵ_j is an error term.[5] From this model it follows that the tool types in tool kits, the set of tool kits, and the conversion factor relating the number of occurances of activities to the number of tools which become part of the assemblage must be constant over all assemblages that are to be data points for the process. Otherwise, the results of the analysis will be ambiguous (cf. Cohen et al., 1980, p. 662).

The data used by Binford and Binford come from three sites: Jabrud and Mugharet Es-Shubbabiq in the Near East and Houppeville in France. The eight data points from Jabrud included in the analysis were levels 2-10 in that site and the seven cases from Shubbabiq were seven excavation units; Houppeville constituted a single case, giving a total of 16 cases with 40 artifact types as variables.

Clearly, excavation units from a single assemblage do not constitute separate outcomes of a single process. Further, there is no particular reason to assume that all of these assemblages would have precisely the same tool kits represented. Indeed, Binford and Binford comment that Houppeville is not comparable to the Near East sites: "The material from Houppeville is not directly relevant to a study of the Mousterian of the Near East." Nevertheless, the site was included in the data set in order to "increase [their] sample size" (1966, p. 289).[6]

If Bordes and de Sonneville-Bordes' (1971) well-known interpretation of the Mousterian—that the different assemblages represent different cultures doing similar tasks—is correct, then the assumption of constant tool kits over all assemblages is obviously false. By definition, the different groups of peoples would have been doing similar tasks with different types of artifacts.

If Binford and Binford's hypothesis—that the different assemblages distinguished may represent functional differences reflected in different activities at the site locations—is correct, then it may be possible to maintain the constancy of tool kits at a global level, but not at the local level of each assemblage; the absence of tool kits in a site does not give information regarding their composition. It follows that, under either interpretation of the assemblages, not all of the data are from the same process. The implicit population of all Mousterian assemblages, even if narrowed to the Near East, is thus a NWD population. Hence, the results of the factor analysis are unreliable, and interpretation of the factors may be biased to an unmeasured degree. To avoid this problem, the factor analysis should have been restricted at least to the level of Mousterian assemblages of a single type, as defined by Bordes' cumulative frequency diagrams. These subpopulations represent a constant set of activities under either interpretation, although Binford (1973, p. 246) suggests that these may lack homogeneity.

Projectile Point Classification

In the following section, a second example of analysis of data constituted by a NWD population and NWD variables will be given. The iterative approach for preanalyzing data of this sort, as described above, will be outlined and illustrated.

The data to be examined are the projectile point data reported by Christenson and Read (1977). The data set consists of 64 projectile points from a California site, Ven 39, with nine measurements made on the points: length, width, thickness, length of base, angle of point, fineness of flaking, and distance from maximal width to proximal limits (see Christenson & Read, 1977 for a more detailed description of the data set and measures).

The iterative procedure that will be outlined here consists basically of alteration between redefinition of variables using factor analytic techniques (or possibly other means of dimensionality reduction) and subdivision of the data set into subpopulations using the new variables defined from the factor analytic techniques. This cycle is continued until there is convergence in the sense that the constructed variables have good archaeological interpretation and/or no further nonarbitrary subdivision of the data is possible.

The dimensionality reduction phase of each cycle of the iterative procedure, involving redefinition of variables, is a means for weighting variables appropriately in analysis in the absence of theoretical arguments for weighting them. This strategy differs from that used in numerical taxonomic approaches, which encourage equal weighting of variables and thus need not lead to interpretable results. For example, in Christenson and Read, it was shown that cluster analysis of the original data set—a numerical taxonomic approach involving equal weighting of variables—gave ambiguous results, at best, and incorrect subdivision of the data set, at worst. The failure of the numerical taxonomy approach[7] is not surprising, as the results obtained here will show that the variables are not well-defined in the sense discussed above, and therefore, require differential weighting. This is so, even though the variables were chosen according to suggested measurement schemes (e.g., Thomas, 1970).

Now consider the iterative procedure:

Step 1: Initial screening of the data set for outliers. Outliers are points in a data set that fall outside of the distribution defined by the bulk of the data. They are problematic, in that they have an undue effect on correlation coefficients, and consequently, need to be removed from analyses that are based on correlation coefficients. At the same time, they cannot be dismissed casually, since they are part of the data set. The approach used here is to remove outliers when their presence significantly alters the results obtained from a particular statistical method, and then compare the outliers, as separate individual cases, to the results obtained from the bulk of the data. In their original analysis, Christenson and Read found nine outliers in the data set and removed them prior to dimensional reduction by principal component analysis. Here, they will not be removed at the initial stage in order to demonstrate their biasing effects.

Step 2: Dimensionality reduction on the screened data. Principal component analysis[8] is used because it is a model free method that makes no assumptions about

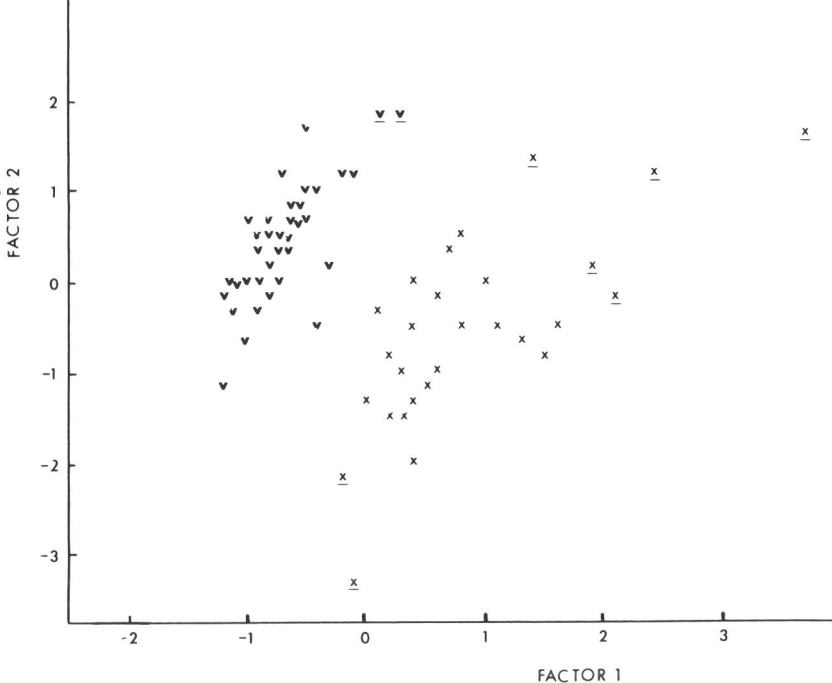

Fig. 3.1. Scattergram plot of Factors 1 and 2 for 64 projectile points from VEN 39. Factor scores are normalized values. In this, and Fig. 2-4, the factors are determined by a varimax rotation of a principal component solution using an eigenvalue of 1.0 as a cutpoint for the number of principal components. Underlined points were determined to be outliers in a previous analysis of these data. Symbols: x—convex base points; v—concave base points.

any structuring of the data (see also Benfer, 1979). For the data examined by Christenson and Read, with outliers excluded, the initially ambiguous data configuration has a three-dimensional factor solution, with the data distributed in a nonoverlapping bimodal manner along the first dimension or principal component (see also Fig. 4 in Aldenderfer, 1982, p. 69). The principal component analysis is repeated here, but without removal of the outliers. Figure 1 gives a scattergram plot of the first two principal components after varimax rotation. The outliers sufficiently bias the analysis so that the projection of the data onto the first principal component leads to an overlapping bimodal distribution. Nonetheless, a clear separation of the data into two groups is still evident in Figure 1.

The factor loadings for the rotated solution are given in Table 1. Three principal components were chosen as a solution using Kaiser's criterion of 1.0 as a cutpoint for eigenvalues. All loadings with value less than 0.25 have been

Table 3.1

Factor Loadings (Principal Component Analysis, Varimax Rotation) for 64 Projectile Points from VEN 39[1,2]

Variables	Factor 1	Factor 2	Factor 3	Communality
Thickness	0.889	0.0	0.0	0.81
Proximal Distance	0.864	−0.410	0.0	0.92
Number of Flakes	−0.819	0.0	0.0	0.73
Length	0.803	0.0	−0.406	0.85
Base Length	0.787	−0.364	0.0	0.75
Width	0.748	0.346	0.497	0.93
Base Width	0.0	0.870	0.273	0.86
Convergence	0.0	−0.822	0.429	0.88
Angle	0.0	0.0	0.957	0.93
Eigenvalue[3]	4.09	1.96	1.61	
Percent Variance	0.45	0.21	0.18	

[1] In this, and Tables 3.2-5, factor loadings less than 0.25 have been replaced by 0.0 and variables have been ordered according to the magnitude of their variance.
[2] Outliers have not been removed.
[3] $x^2 = 461.1$, df $= 36$, $p < .001$.

replaced by zeros in this and all subsequent tables. Variables are ordered by decreasing loading on the first factor. The main point to be made about the factors is that none of them have a simple interpretation.

When one examines Figure 1, it is apparent why the factors are difficult to interpret. The factors do not measure any single dimension that could correspond to an underlying process; rather, they respond to two separate dimensions: one which separates the groups and the other, at approximately right angles to the first, which displays variation within each of the two groups. The factor solution is an analytical compromise between these two independent dimensions. Thus, the factors each represent at least two, if not several, dimensions that structure the data set.

Accordingly, the variables, as originally measured, have frequency distributions that reflect both 1) the structure of projectile points in each group separately (with each group possibly having a different structure) and 2) the dimension along which there is group separation. Neither of these is completely

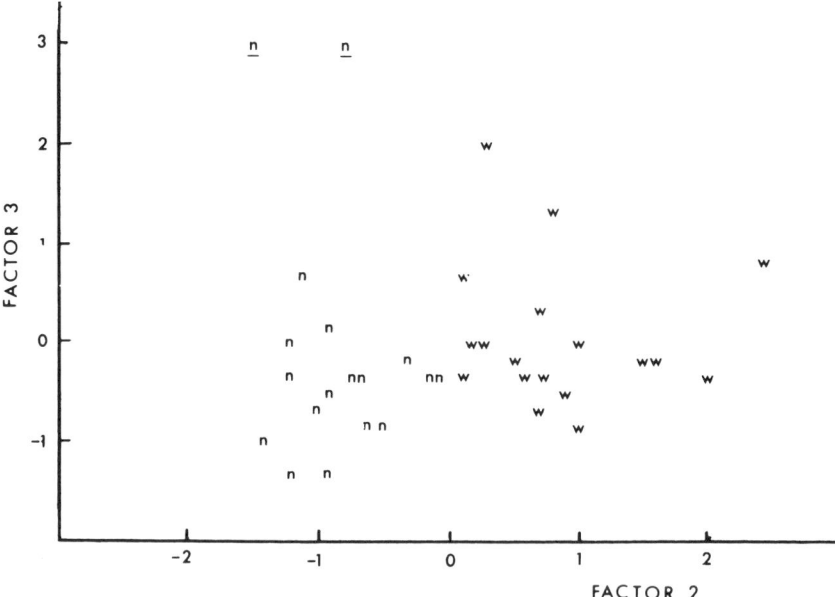

Fig. 3.2. Scattergram plot of Factors 2 and 3 for 36 concave base projectile points from VEN 39. Outliers removed in subsequent analyses are underlined. Symbols: *n*—narrow concave base points; *w*—wide concave base points.

measured by any single variable (excluding the dichotomized, nominal coding of base length). Thus the variables, as originally measured, are NWD variables.

Step 3: Subdivision of the population into subpopulations. To achieve this task, one can apply cluster techniques to the factors in the above step taken as variables. In this case, however, the results are obvious from inspection of Figure 1. The two groups correspond precisely to the two groups initially distinguished visually as convex base points (the left group in Fig. 1) and concave base points (the right group in Fig. 1) and are shown in Figures 4 and 5. Hence, the initial population of points is now divided into two subpopulations: concave base points and convex base points. The next step is to repeat Step 2, but for each of the subpopulations separately.

Step 4: Dimensional reduction over each subpopulation. Each of the two subpopulations is analyzed separately, using the principal component procedure. The results are given in Figure 2 (concave base points) and Figure 3 (convex base points). The factor loadings are given in Tables 2 and 3.

When these tables are compared to each other and to Table 1, it can be seen that the factors are radically different in each table. This occurs because the original principal component analysis, over all the data, fitted factors to oppos-

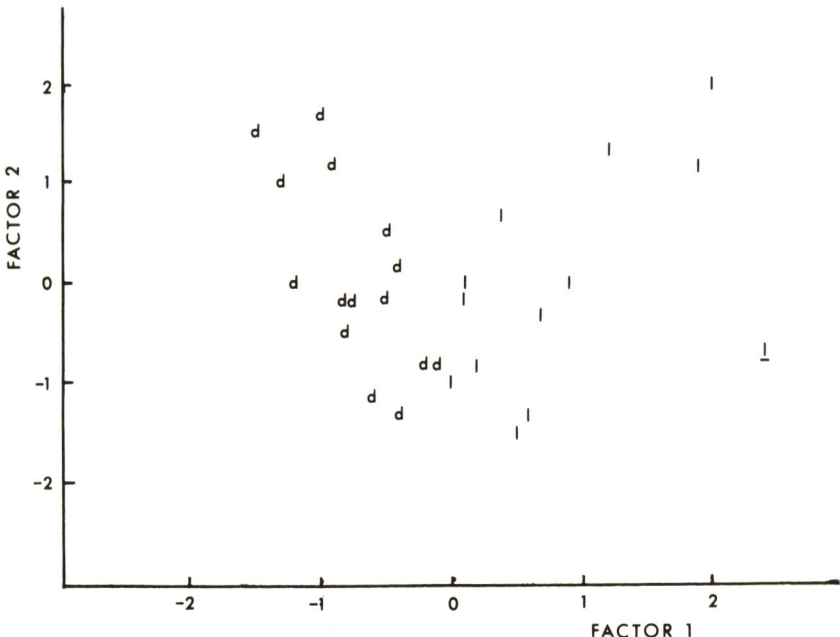

Fig. 3.3. Scattergram plot of Factors 1 and 2 for 28 convex base projectile points from VEN 39. Outliers removed in subsequent analyses are underlined. Symbols: *l*—leaf shaped convex base projectile points; *d*—needle/leaf shaped convex base points.

ing dimensions, whereas the principal component analyses done separately for each group do not include the effect of the dimension separating the groups.

Observe that in Tables 2 and 3 the factors begin to have interpretability, especially in Table 2. In Table 2, the first factor seems to be measuring the angle of the point (as an approximate shape dimension); the second factor is a width dimension; and the third factor is a measure of base size. In Table 3, Factor 1 seems to be a shape measure; Factor 2 is a size measure; and Factor 3 is a base shape measure.

Step 5: Further subdivision of the population. Figures 2 and 3 show that both of the two subpopulations (concave base points and convex base points) can be subdivided further. In Figure 2, it is evident that there are two subgroups without internal structure separated primarily along the second factor. This suggests that this group of points can be interpreted as representing a single, nominal-scale dimension with the groups representing polar extremes (cf. Leone, 1982) along the narrow/wide dimension. This matches Spaulding's (1977) argument for the primacy of nominal variables in defining artifact classes. In Figure 3, a very different pattern is displayed. The pattern matches that found by Whallon (1982, Fig. 6.12) in his analysis of pottery from a Swiss

Table 3.2

Factor Loadings (Principal Component Analysis, Varimax Rotation) for 36 Concave Base Projectile Points from VEN 39[1]

Variables	Factor 1	Factor 2	Factor 3	Communality
Angle	0.917	0.0	0.0	0.89
Length	−0.848	0.0	0.0	0.75
Convergence	0.796	−0.298	0.0	0.73
Thickness	−0.655	0.0	0.0	0.49
Width	0.0	0.936	0.0	0.89
Base Width	0.0	0.933	0.0	0.90
Flake	0.365	−0.523	0.0	0.44
Proximal Distance	0.0	0.0	0.885	0.85
Base Length	0.337	0.0	0.795	0.75
Eigenvalue[2]	2.901	2.29	1.51	
Percent Variance	0.32	0.25	0.17	

[1] Outliers have not been removed.
[2] $x^2 = 177.4$, df $= 36$, $p < .001$.

Late Neolithic site: a single connected group composed of distinct "arms." Here, there are two arms, approximately at right angles to each other, with a linear relationship that passes near the point (0, 0) so that there is an approximately constant ratio between the two factors defining the scattergram plot. This suggests that there are two distinctive shapes represented by the two arms, with size (Factor 3) the main dimension of variation for each arm.

The next step, therefore, is to subdivide each of the two subpopulations into further subpopulations, and then to make a dimensional study of the resultant subpopulations. At this juncture, outliers, as measured by a X^2 test for Mahalanobis's D^2 distance measure for a case from the group centroid, are removed from the data set. The biasing effects of outliers becomes more pronounced with each subdivision of the data. For one of the subgroups, a single outlier completely changed the principal component solution (not shown) in the next step. Three outliers are removed: cases 26, 29 and 53.

Step 6a: Dimensional reduction for the concave base points. Each of the two subgroups for these points, wide and narrow based points, show little internal patterning. (Note that "base width" and "width" are structurally the same

Table 3.3

Factor Loadings (Principal Component Analysis, Varimax Rotation) for 28 Convex Base Projectile Points from VEN 39[1]

Variables	Factor 1	Factor 2	Factor 3	Communality
Width	0.822	0.403	0.0	0.87
Angle	0.818	−0.332	0.0	0.78
Proximal Distance	0.797	0.406	0.0	0.82
Flake	−0.786	0.0	0.0	0.65
Length	0.0	0.909	0.0	0.88
Convergence	0.285	−0.738	−0.338	0.74
Thickness	0.503	0.585	0.344	0.71
Base Length	0.0	0.0	0.855	0.76
Base Width	0.0	0.0	0.834	0.77
Eigenvalue[2]	2.98	2.24	1.77	
Percent Variance	0.33	0.25	0.20	

[1] Outliers have not been removed.
[2] $x^2 = 144.11$, df = 36, $p < .001$.

measures, loading highly on Factor 2, for these points.) The variable correlations for the wide points are low in each subgroup, with only 7 out of 36 correlations for the wide points and 4 out of 36 correlations for the narrow points being greater than 0.60 (approximately the smallest correlation coefficient significant at $\alpha = 0.05$ for sample sizes corresponding to these data sets). Bartlett's procedures were used to test the null hypothesis that the correlation matrix is identical to the identity matrix—one having off-diagonal entries of zero and diagonal entries of one (see Bartlett, 1950; Vierra, 1982; Healan, 1984 for details of the test). The test exhibited a significant value for the wide base points ($X^2 = 92.9$, df = 36, $p < .001$). It has moderately significant value for the narrow base points ($X^2 = 76.2$, df = 36, $p < .01$). Although the matrices are significant, the communalities of the variables in the principal component solution are low (wide points, median communality = 0.81; narrow points, median communality = 0.72).

A step-wise discriminant analysis of the two groups shows that only the width measure discriminates the two subgroups (wide points, $\bar{x}$ (mean width) = 13.1 mm, S.E. = 0.28, $n = 18$; narrow points, $\bar{x}$ (mean width) = 10.6 mm,

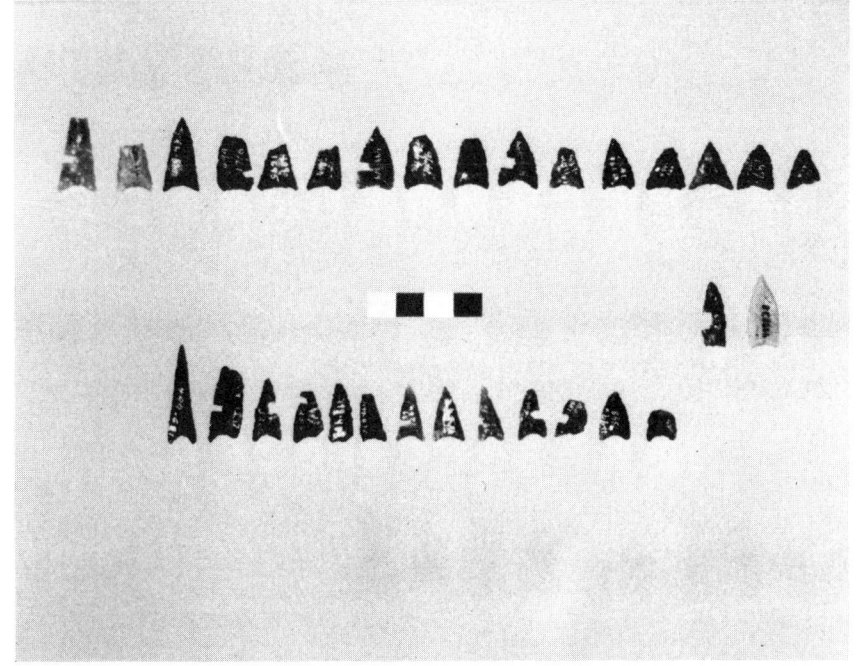

Fig. 3.4. Photograph of the concave base points from VEN 39. The top group of points is the wide base points, ordered by length (length of broken points was estimated). The wide points are case nos.: (left to right) 32, 31, 13, 27, 6, 30, 22, 21, 23, 20, 8, 35, 18 (missing), 9, 12 (missing), 36, 3 (missing). The bottom group of points is the narrow base points, ordered by length. The narrow points are case nos.: (left to right) 34, 33, 24 (missing), 25, 11, 16, 19, 14, 15, 28, 17, 10, 5, 2, 1, 7, 4. The two points on the right of the photograph are outliers (case nos. 26 and 29) removed from the analysis.

S.E. $= 0.20$, $n = 16$; $F = 52.2$; df $= 1, 32$; $p < .001$). The coefficient of variation for the width measure is 0.08 for the wide points and 0.07 for the narrow points, indicating that the value for this dimension was under tight constraint (see Read, 1982). In sum, these two subgroups can best be interpreted as distinguishable by a nominal dimension with two attribute values, Narrow and Wide, while other measures generally vary independently of each other within general constraints on the possible shape range, as can be seen in Figure 4.

Step 6b: Dimensional reduction for the convex base points. One of the two subgroups distinguished on the basis of the two-armed cluster (the right arm in Fig. 3) shows considerable internal patterning. This subgroup is well defined by a principal component analysis with the first factor (see Table 4), comprising most of the metric measurements, relating to size. Shape, measured primarily by the angle of the point, is measured independently by Factor 2. The marked drop in

Table 3.4

Factor Loadings (Principal Component Analysis, Varimax Rotation) for 12 Leaf Shape Convex Base Projectile Points from VEN 39[1]

Variables	Factor 1	Factor 2	Factor 3	Communality
Length	0.954	0.0	0.0	0.97
Proximal Distance	0.950	0.260	0.0	0.92
Thickness	0.895	0.0	0.370	0.94
Width	0.789	0.508	0.0	0.90
Convergence	−0.690	0.490	0.0	0.74
Flake	−0.556	−0.573	0.0	0.40
Angle	0.0	0.972	0.0	0.96
Base Length	0.0	0.0	0.935	0.92
Base Width	0.303	0.637	0.677	0.96
Eigenvalue[2]	4.16	1.90	1.66	
Percent Variance	0.46	0.21	0.18	

[1] Outliers have been removed.
[2] $x^2 = 99.7$, df = 36, $p < .001$.

eigenvalues between the first and the second factors suggests that shape is relatively constant and the main dimension of variation is size. That the points have an approximately constant leaf shape across the points in this group can be seen in Figure 5 (lower group of points).

The second subgroup of the two-armed cluster (the left arm) is more difficult to characterize, but it appears to be the antithesis of the first group, in that size and shape covary. The angle of the tip for these points varies inversely with length (see Table 5), making the shape more needle-like for the large points and leaf-like for the small points in the group. (Recall from Step 4 that the two subgroups overlap for small points, as shown in Fig. 3.)

For the group of leaf-shaped points, 12 out of 36 correlations are greater than 0.60, and the median communality is 0.92. Bartlett's test gives $X^2 = 99.0$, df = 36, $p < .001$. These findings suggest strong internal patterning for the leaf-shaped points. For the second group of points with the needle/leaf shape, only 3 out of 36 correlations are greater than 0.60, the median communality is 0.82, and Bartlett's test gives $X^2 = 50.2$, df = 36, $p > .05$, making the factor solution little more than what would be expected for random data (see Christenson,

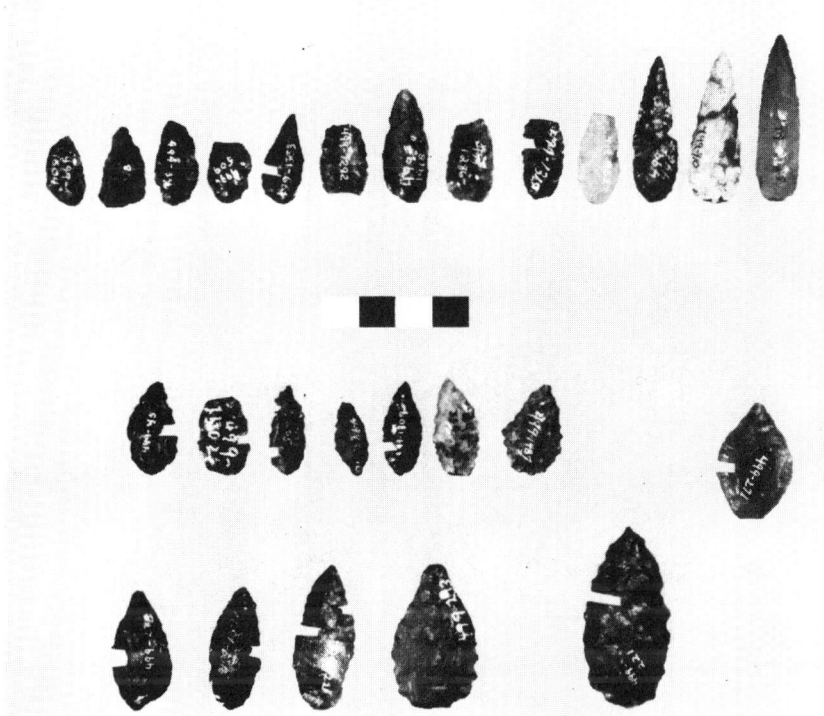

Fig. 3.5. Photograph of the convex base points from VEN 39. The top group of points is the needle/leaf shaped points, ordered by their relative position along the linear fit to the left "arm" in Fig. 3. These points are cases nos.: (left to right) 39, 41, 38, 43, 48, 44, 46 (missing), 57 (missing), 62, 40, 50, 42, 59, 60, 58. The bottom group of points is the leaf shaped points, represented by the right arm in Fig. 3 and separated into 3 subgroups by the size dimension (see Fig. 6). In the first two of the three subgroups the points are ordered by their relative position on the linear fit to the clusters in Fig. 6. The linear fit is essentially a measure of the length of the base of the point. The group with a single case is an outlier along the size dimension and may be a preform. The small leaf shaped points in the first subgroup are cases nos.: (left to right) 51, 55, 49, 37, 47, 45, 54. The large leaf shaped points in the second subgroup are cases nos.: (left to right) 52, 61, 64, 56. The single large point forming the third subgroup is case no. 63. The point on the far right of the photograph is an outlier (case no. 53) removed from the analysis.

1979; Vierra, 1982). This suggests a structure for the needle/leaf-shaped points that is not well expressed in the factor analytic format.

A step-wise discriminant analysis finds that the angle of the tip of the point ($F = 27.4$; df = 1, 25; $p < .01$), distance from maximal width to proximal limits ($F = 8.98$; df = 1, 24; $p < .01$), and number of flakes ($F = 4.32$; df = 1, 23;

Table 3.5

Factor Loadings (Principal Component Analysis, Varimax Rotation) for 15 Needle Shape Convex Base Projectile Points from VEN 39[1]

Variables	Factor 1	Factor 2	Factor 3	Factor 4	Communality
Length	−0.899	0.0	0.0	0.0	0.86
Angle	0.871	0.0	0.0	0.0	0.79
Convergence	0.764	−0.395	0.0	0.0	0.62
Base Width	0.0	0.896	0.0	0.0	0.91
Width	0.0	0.866	0.0	0.0	0.87
Flake	0.0	0.0	−0.785	0.0	0.75
Base Length	0.0	0.363	0.740	0.0	0.70
Thickness	−0.389	0.327	0.598	0.0	0.62
Proximal distance	0.0	0.0	0.0	0.975	0.96
Eigenvalue[2]	2.42	2.05	1.59	1.21	
Percent variance	0.27	0.23	0.18	0.13	

[1] Outliers have been removed.
[2] $x^2 = 50.2$, df $= 36$, $p < .05$.

$p < .05$) are the variables significantly distinguishing the two groups ($\alpha = 0.05$).

Scattergram plots of the factors for the needle/leaf-shaped points do not suggest any further subdivision of these points. However, one of the scattergram plots for the leaf-shaped group of points shows that this group should be further subdivided (see Fig. 6).

Step 7: Subdivision of the leaf-shaped points. The scattergram plot of Factors 1 and 3 for the leaf-shaped points (see Fig. 6) shows two distinct groups and a single outlier falling on the same dimension that separates the groups. The dimension separating the subgroups is size, with the perpendicular dimension being essentially base length. Note that Factor 1, though a size factor, does not precisely measure the dimension separating the subgroups. The points forming these subgroups are shown in Figure 4 (bottom part of the photograph), and their separation into distinct size categories is immediately evident. The large outlier is possibly a preform (Christenson, personal communication, 1983). Because of the small sample sizes in the subgroups, dimensionality reduction was not repeated for these subgroups.

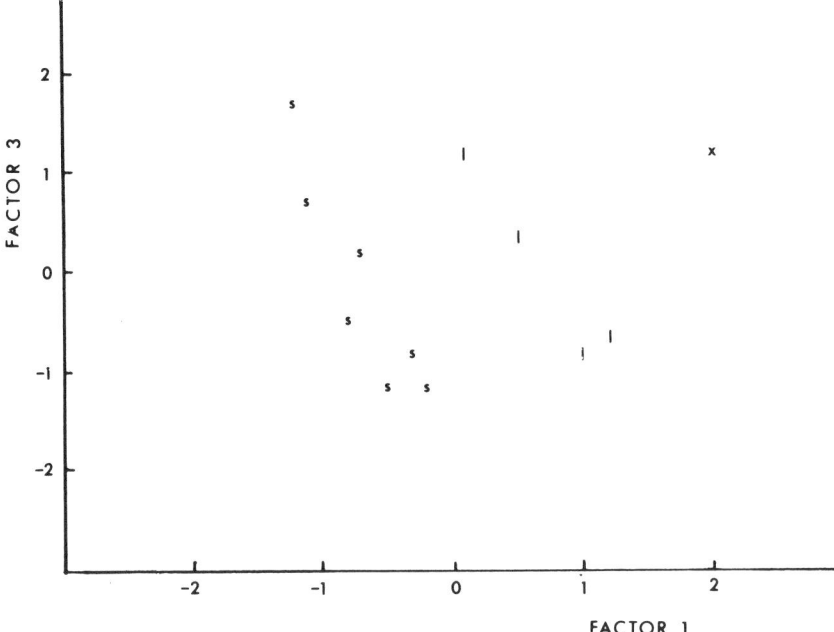

Fig. 3.6. Scattergram plot of Factors 1 and 3 for 12 leaf shaped convex base points from VEN 39. The underlined point is an outlier for this scattergram plot. Symbols: *s*—small leaf shaped convex base points; *l*—large leaf shaped convex base points; *x*—exceptionally large leaf shaped convex base point.

In sum, the convex base points represent two, overlapping subgroups. For one, size is the main dimension of variation (leaf-shaped points with length and tip angle independent). For the other, an inverse size-shape relation holds, with length and tip angle negatively correlated (the larger are more needle-like and the smaller are more leaf-like points). The two groups overlap with both having small, leaf-like points. Also, the leaf-shaped points are divided by a nominal dimension with two attribute values: Small and Large.

Overall, five subpopulations have been distinguished: 1) Narrow Concave Base Points, 2) Wide Concave Base Points, 3) Small Leaf-Shaped Convex Base Points, 4) Large Leaf-Shaped Convex Base Points, and 5) Needle/Leaf-Shaped Convex Base Points, with overlap between subpopulations 3 and 5. Dimensions that have been distinguished are the nominal dimension of width for the concave points only, and the nominal dimension of size for leaf-shaped convex points only. In addition, the ratio of size to shape distinguishes the needle/leaf- and leaf-shaped groups of points. Other measures vary independently within the shape contraints which characterize these points, or what Read (1982, p. 74) calls "empirical qualitative" distinctions.

The outliers (case nos. 26, 29, and 53) may now be compared to the five groups, and it is evident by inspection (see Figs. 4 & 5) that the outliers are idiosyncratic cases with respect to these groups. This both justifies and necessitates their exclusion from the statistical analysis.

Discussion of Projectile Point Classification Example

It has been demonstrated that the initial data set, defined as projectile points from Ven 39, consists of five distinct subpopulations. This raises the question of the relationship of these subpopulations to one another. At one extreme is the interpretation that they represent five distinct processes and are unrelated. At the other extreme is the interpretation that they are five outcomes of one process (with the process assumed to have more content than merely "the manufacture of projectile points"). The analysis suggests an interpretation between these two extremes.

1) The concave base points seem to be the result of a single process with two outcomes, Narrow and Wide, since the width measure is a significant structural dimension for these points and width is highly constrained within each group (as indicated by the small CV values). Given the interpretation of a process with two outcomes, Narrow and Wide, the corresponding set of outcomes is the set $\Omega = \{\text{Narrow, Wide}\}$. The probabilities p_N and p_W for the two outcomes are estimated from the data: $\hat{p}_N = n_N/n = {}^{16}/_{34}$ and $\hat{p}_W = n_W/n = {}^{18}/_{34}$. These estimates suggest that Narrow and Wide concave points are equally likely, or $p_N = p_W = \frac{1}{2}$.

The discriminate analysis indicates that measures other than width have a distribution independent of the two values, Narrow and Wide, for the concave base points. Two interpretations can be given. The first and simplest is that variation in these measures is pure error (in the regression model sense), with the deterministic (or nonerror) part of each measure a constant value for each of the outcomes. This agrees with the conclusion from the F-test where there is no significant difference in means for each of these measures for the Narrow and Wide groups of concave base points. The second interpretation is that some measure, perhaps length, also defines a series of outcomes, but with essentially the same probability distribution for each of the two groups. For example, it might be postulated that the outcomes are Narrow + Length and Wide + Length, where Length takes on a continuum of outcomes, as might be the case if there is a regular change in length of points through time. In the absence of supporting archaeological evidence, the second interpretation is at the moment only a logical possibility.

If the first interpretation is the more reasonable one, then variation in the measures of length, thickness, etc. for the concave points does not represent different values for a random variable defined over the space $\Omega = \{\text{Narrow},$

Wide}, but the measure of the amount of error that is "allowed" in the manufacture of these points. Variation in these measures would thus be explained as manufacture error within global constraints that define the basic shape for these points.

2) For the convex base points, the distinction between the two subpopulations is more complex. It seems to be defined for the leaf-shaped points by a size dimension (length, width, thickness, and proximal distance) independent of tip angle (see Table 4); i.e., size varies while shape remains constant (see Fig. 5, bottom part of the photograph). On the other hand, for the needle/leaf group of points, the inverse relation between angle (θ) and length l) (see Table 5) indicates that

$$l \times \theta = c, \tag{7}$$

where c is a constant. This hypothesis is confirmed by a scattergram plot of log (l) versus log (θ) (not shown) with the scatter of points well fitted by the linear relationship $\log \theta = -\log l + \log c$, the log-log transformation of Equation 7.

While the points in these two groups have a convex basal shape in common and there is overlap in the groups, it is not clear whether the two groups represent two values on a single shape dimension, or two processes that only overlap because of the logic of the two relations defining the two groups. Note that in a coordinate system defined by l and θ, the curve representing $l \times \theta = c$ for the needle/leaf-shaped points and the curve $\theta = d$ (a constant) for the first leaf-shaped group of points will necessarily intersect for some value l_0 at the lower end of the range of values for the variable l. Hence, the overlap in the groups may be mathematically necessary but culturally coincidental.

Given the interpretation that the two groups represent two separate processes, the data for the leaf-shaped points suggest a nominally defined size dimension, creating the set of outcomes $\Omega = \{\text{Large, Small}\}$. For this set, $\hat{p}_L = 4/11$ and $\hat{p}_S = 7/11$. These values suggest that the Small points are twice as likely as the Large points, or $p_S = 2/3$ and $p_L = 1/3$.

3) Finally, this example suggests how a random variable, based on a measurement (e.g., width, length) and defined over a respective set of outcomes (e.g., $\Omega = \{\text{Narrow, Wide}\}$ or $\Omega = \{\text{Large, Small}\}$), should be interpreted. The example stresses the distinction between the *descriptive* parameters of a data set taken as a population, and the parameters of a population defined by a *process*.

Taking the set $\Omega = \{\text{Narrow, Wide}\}$ with its associated population of concave base points as an example, a random variable of interest can be defined as the rule that assigns to an outcome a quantity representing the *norm* for points of that kind. The assumption is made here that a nominal distinction on a continuum, with highly constrained range of values in each class of the set of distinctions, reflects an emic normative categorization (Spaulding, 1977, 1982). The measure width, for example, does not directly conform to the definition of a random variable for the concave base points with the set of outcomes given above. It does *not* assign a value representing a norm to the outcomes Wide and Narrow; the actual width of a point represents both the normative value (the deterministic part of the measure) and manufacture error (the stochastic part of the measure). The values w, taken on by the width measure over the several points, can be modelled by the stochastic relation

$$w = w_N + \epsilon \qquad (8)$$

for the Narrow concave base points, where w_N is the posited normative value and ϵ is the measure of manufacture error, and by the stochastic equation

$$w = w_W + \epsilon \qquad (9)$$

for the Wide concave base points, where w_W is the posited normative value for the wide points. Under the usual assumption that the error terms will have mean (or expected) value 0, it follows that $\mu_N = E(w) = E(w_N + \epsilon) = E(w_N) + E(\epsilon) = w_N$, since w_N is a constant where μ_N is the expected or mean width of the concave base points under investigation and "$E(\ )$" represents the expected value of the random variable in the parentheses. Similarly, $\mu_W = w_W$. These results indicate that the parameters μ_N and μ_W for the width measure w have the desired normative characteristic, and that the desired random variable is the rule that assigns the outcomes, Narrow or Wide, respectively, to the real numbers μ_N and μ_W.

The actual values of μ_N and μ_W are not known and would not be known, even if all concave base projectile points manufactured by the individuals who inhabited Ven 39 were recovered and measured, since this is still a sample of the infinite population, to which Fisher (1954, p. 5) refers (see also the discussion by Read, 1982, pp. 69-70). Instead, the values are estimated from the sample data using standard statistical procedures, as has been done above: $\bar{x}_N$ (mean width of narrow, concave base points) = 10.6 mm; $\bar{x}_W$ (mean width of wide, concave base points) = 13.1 mm.

In conclusion, the numbers $\bar{x}_N = 10.6$ mm and $\bar{x}_W = 13.1$ mm should *not* be interpreted as estimates of population parameters defined for a data set taken as a population, which is a *descriptive* interpretation. Rather, they should be interpreted as estimates of the normative values w_N and w_W that define, in part, the *process* that underlies manufacture of these points.

CONCLUSION

The term *preanalysis* has been chosen for the type of analysis just exemplified, since the results prepare the way for archaeological analysis aimed at interpretation of the *meaning* of these phenomena (Binford & Sabloff, 1982, p. 147). The preanalysis is not an end, but a beginning. The data set used in the example is small, but it has an unsuspected richness at the level of expressing a set of processes that would be difficult to uncover without the conceptual framework provided by statistical theory at the level of representation of processes.

Statistical theory is not just method applied to data, but a framework that demands the uncovering of precisely the phenomena deemed to be at the basis of archaeological theory: *underlying processes that structure the formation of the entities comprising the archaeological record*. The conceptual framework of statistical theory does not solve the quest for construction of satisfactory theory, but puts the empirical basis for that theory into order so that archaeological theory will be well founded. As analysis of archaeological data includes more complex techniques, the need for a solid foundation becomes all the more crucial.

Any technique presupposes a model, which in turn presupposes a process. The challenge is to identify such processes, and then, order data in concordance with them.

NOTES

1. "Single" is meant in the sense of a process definable by a fixed set of relations and parameter values for all entities asserted to be part of the population subject to the process. A discriminant function would be an example of a model defining a single process, even though the process might distinguish two subpopulations.

2. For example, random sampling is a sufficient but not a necessary condition for assuring that the sample mean follows an approximately normal distribution, a property used extensively in statistical inference. But in the language of probability theory, the Central Limit Theorem, upon which this conclusion is based, does not mention random samples. Instead, the Central Limit Theorem states that the sum of independent random variables having a common mean, μ, and a common, finite variance, σ^2, will tend to have a normal distribution (cf. Feller, 1968, p. 229). Random sampling is introduced as a means to satisfy these conditions by first defining a process under which a sample mean for a measurement x can be treated as the sum of random variables. This is done by defining the process P to be: "Take a sample of size n from a population," so that the sample in hand is one outcome of the process. Then define random variables $X_1, X_2, \ldots, X_n$ by the following operation: the ith random variable X_i assigns to the outcome (= the sample) the value of the measurement x for the ith entity in the sample, $1 \le i \le n$. The sample mean $\bar{x}$ is now just the value assigned to the outcome by the random variable $\bar{X} = X_1/n + X_2/n + \ldots + X_n/n$. For a random sample, the random variables just defined satisfy the conditions for the CLT.

Another way the conditions can be satisfied is through independent repetition of an experiment. Thus, in the example to be discussed below, each instance of a !Kung San camp can be interpreted as a repetition of the experiment, "Construct a traditional !Kung camp." So long as each instance is an independent repetition of the same experiment, the conditions for the CLT are satisfied. Thus a data set composed of n independent repetitions of an experiment will equally assure the analogical relations given in Equation 3.

3. For simplicity, it is assumed that the set Ω is finite. For nonfinite sets of outcomes, a slightly modified procedure is used to define probability distributions for the set Ω. (See Lukacs, 1972, for an introduction to axiomatic probability theory.)

4. Note the difference between interpreting a probability as part of the definition of a process, and interpreting a probability as part of the description of a population. In the latter case, $p = n_e/N$, where n_e is the number of instances of the elementary event e in the population and N is the population size, whereas in the former case, $p = \lim_{n \to \infty} n_e/n$, where n is the number of repetitions of the experiment.

5. Although Equation 6 is formally similar to the factor analysis model, assumptions underlying

techniques such as varimax rotation may not be in accord with archaeological arguments about processes such as curation that affect the formation of assemblages.

6. The small sample size is indeed a problem (see Cowgill, 1969) since the correlation matrix is singular when the number of cases is less than the number of variables. Automatically, there will be at most $n - 1$ factors, where n is the sample size, regardless of any structure in the data. This condition makes interpretation of the factors useless when the sample size is smaller than the number of variables. Use of principal component analysis for dimensionality reduction (without interpretation of principal components), however, would still be possible (cf. Benfer, 1979).

7. Hodson (1982) has objected to this conclusion, arguing that some other unspecified and untried cluster algorithm would have worked. However, the k-means algorithm favored by Hodson gives a 2-cluster solution with about a 25% error rate, and a 3-cluster solution has 2 clusters that are approximately correct, but the third cluster crosscuts the concave and convex base points. While Hodson rejects Christenson and Read's use of their intuition that concave base and convex base points ought to be separated (see Figs. 4 & 5) as a basis for testing the cluster solutions, he contradictorily notes the need for "classifying artifacts by eye, *as we usually must* [italics added]" (p. 28). Cowgill (1982) suggests that perhaps the average linkage solution mentioned by Christenson and Read may have some validity, but Aldenderfer (1981) aptly makes the point that any cluster solution must have independent verification. The so-called factor analysis results of Christenson and Read are validated by the fact that the factors define a reduced set of dimensions in which the two types of projectile point types are clearly exhibited as separate clusters.

8. All analyses were done with the BMDP (Dixon, 1981) series of computer programs. The following programs were used: P4M (Factor Analysis), P7M (Stepwise Discriminant Analysis) and PKM (K-Means Clustering).

REFERENCES

Aldenderfer, M. (1982). Methods of cluster validation for archaeology. *World Archaeology 14*, 61-72.

Barrett, S. (1976). The use of models in anthropological fieldwork. *Journal of Anthropological Research 32*, 161-181.

Bartlett, M. (1950). Tests of significance in factor analysis. *British Journal of Psychology, Statistical Section 3*, 77-85.

Benfer, R. (1979). Sample size in multivariate analyses: Some corrections of Davis' review of *Sampling in archaeology. Plains Anthropologist 83*, 91-94.

Benfer, R., & Benfer, A. (1981). Automatic classification of inspectional categories: Multivariate theories of archaeological data. *American Antiquity 46*, 381-396.

Bettinger, R. (1975). *The surface archaeology of Owens Valley, Eastern California: Prehistoric man-land relationships in the Great Basin*. Unpublished doctoral dissertation, University of California, Riverside.

Binford, L. (1964). A consideration of archaeological research design. *American Antiquity 29*, 425-441.

Binford, L. (1967). Smudge pits and hide smoking: The use of analogy in archaeological reasoning. *American Antiquity 32*, 1-12.

Binford, L. (1968). Archeological perspectives. In S. Binford & L. Binford (Eds.), *New Perspectives in Archeology* (pp. 5-32). Chicago: Aldine Publishing Co.

Binford, L. (1973). Interassemblage variability: The Mousterian and the "functional" argument. In C. Renfrew (Ed.), *The explanation of culture change: Models in prehistory* (pp. 227-254). London: Duckworth.

Binford, L. (1977). General Introduction. In L. Binford (Ed.), *For theory building in archaeology* (pp. 1-10). New York: Academic Press, Inc.

Binford, L., & Binford, S. (1966). A preliminary analysis of functional variability in the Mousterian of Levallois Facies. *American Anthropologist 68*, 238-295.

Binford, L., & Sabloff, J. (1982). Paradigms, systematics and archaeology. *Journal of Anthropological Research 38*, 137-153.
Bordes, F., & de Sonneville-Bordes, D. (1971). The significance of variability in paleolithic assemblages. *World Archaeology 2*, 61-73.
Brown, J. (1982). On the structure of artifact typologies. In R. Whallon & J. Brown (Eds.), *Essays on archaeological typology* (pp. 176-190). Evanston, IL: Center for American Archaeology Press.
Brunk, H. (1960). *An introduction to mathematical statistics.* New York: Ginn and Co.
Cahen, D., Keelev, L., & Van Noten, F. (1980). Stone tools, toolkits and human behavior in prehistory. *Current Anthropologist 20*, 661-683.
Carr, C. (1984). The nature of organization of intrasite archaeological records and spatial analytic approaches to their investigation. In M.B. Schiffer (Ed.), *Advances in archaeological method and theory* (Vol. 7). New York: Academic Press, Inc.
Christenson, A. (1979). On the virtues of simplicity: Some comments on statistical analysis in anthropology. *Plains Anthropologist 83*, 35-38.
Christenson, A. (1982). *The evolution of subsistence in the prehistoric midwestern United States.* Unpublished doctoral dissertation, University of California, Los Angeles.
Christenson, A., & Read, D. (1977). Numerical taxonomy, R-mode factor analysis and archaeological classification. *American Antiquity 42*, 162-179.
Clark, A., & Stafford, C. (1982). Quantification in American archaeology. *World Archaeology 14*, 61-72.
Clark, J. (1979). Modelling trade in non-literate archaeological contexts. *Journal of Anthropological Research 35*, 170-190.
Clarke, D. (1968). *Analytical archaeology.* London: Metheuen and Co.
Cochran, W. (1977). *Sampling techniques.* New York: J. Wiley & Sons, Inc.
Conkey, M. (1980). The identification of prehistoric hunter-gatherer aggregation sites: The case of Altimira. *Current Anthropology 21*, 609-630.
Cowgill, G. (1969). Some sampling and reliability problems in archaeology. In *Archeologie et Calculateurs: Problemes Semiologiques et Mathematiques* (pp. 161-172). Paris: Centre National de la Recherche Scientifique.
Cowgill, G. (1982). Clusters of objects and associations between variables: Two approaches to archaeological classification. In R. Whallon & J. Brown (Eds.), *Essays on archaeological typology* (pp. 30-55). Evanston, IL: Center for American Archaeology Press.
Cox, D., & Hinkley, D. (1974). *Theoretical statistics.* London: Chapman and Hall.
Dixon, E. (Ed.). (1981). *BMDP statistical software.* Berkeley: University of California Press.
Doran, J., & Hodson, F. (1975). *Mathematics and computers in archaeology.* Cambridge: Harvard University Press.
Draper, N., & Smith, H. (1967). *Applied regression analysis.* New York: John Wiley & Sons, Inc.
Dunnell, P. (1982). Dilemma of modern archaeology. *Journal of Anthropological Research 38*, 1-25.
Earle, T. (1976). A nearest-neighbor analysis of two formative settlement systems. In K. Flannery (Ed.), *The early Mesoamerican village* (pp. 196-223). New York: Academic Press, Inc.
Ericson, J., Read, D., & Burke, C. (1971). Research design: The relationship between the primary functions and the physical properties of ceramic vessels and their implications for ceramic distributions on an archaeological site. *Anthropology UCLA 3*, 84-95.
Evans, S. (1980). Spatial analysis of basin of Mexico settlements: Problems with the use of the central place model. *American Antiquity 45*, 866-875.
Feller, W. (1968). *Introduction to probability theory and its applications. Volume I.* New York: John Wiley & Sons, Inc.
Fisher, R. (1954). *Statistical methods for research workers.* London: Oliver & Boyd.
Fraser, D. (1962). *Statistics, an introduction.* New York: John Wiley & Sons, Inc.
Godfrey, L., & Cole, J. (1979). Biological analogy, diffusionism, and archaeology. *American Antiquity 81*, 37-45.

Gould, P. (1980). *Living archaeology.* Cambridge: Cambridge University Press.

Gunn, J., & Prewitt, E. (1975). Automatic classification: Projectile points from west Texas. *Plains Anthropologist 20*, 139-149.

Hamblin, R., & Pitcher, B. (1980). The classic Maya collapse: Testing and class conflict hypothesis. *American Antiquity 45*, 246-267.

Hastorf, C. (1983). *Prehistoric agricultural intensification and political development in the Jauja region of central Peru.* Unpublished doctoral dissertation, University of California, Los Angeles.

Healan, D. (1984). Errors in Vierra and Carlson's presentation of Bartlett's Test of Significance. *American Antiquity 49*, 626-627.

Hesse, M. (1974). *The structure of scientific inference.* Berkeley: University of California Press.

Hietala, H., & Stevens, D. (1977). Spatial analysis: Multiple procedures in pattern recognition studies. *American Antiquity 42*, 539-559.

Hill, J. (1970). Broken K pueblo: Prehistoric social organization in the American southwest *(University of Arizona Archaeological Papers, No. 18).* Tucson: University of Arizona Press.

Hill, J. (1978). Individuals and their artifacts: An experimental study in archaeology. *American Antiquity 43*, 245-257.

Hodson, F. (1982). Some aspects of archaeological classification. In R. Whallon & J. Brown (Eds.), *Essays on archaeological typology* (pp. 21-29). Evanston, IL: Center for American Archaeology Press.

Hoel, P. (1966). *Elementary statistics.* New York: John Wiley & Sons, Inc.

Hole, B. (1980). Sampling in archaeology: A critique. *Annual Review of Anthropology 9*, 217-234.

Howell, N., & Lehotey, V. (1978). AMBUSH: A computer program for stochastic microsimulation of small human populations. *American Anthropologist 80*, 905-922.

Ingold, T. (1980). Statistical husbandry: Chance, probability and choice in a reindeer management economy. In J. Mitchell (Ed.), *Numerical techniques in social anthropology* (pp. 37-116). Philadelphia: ISHI.

Kintigh, K., & Ammerman, A. (1982). Heuristic approaches to spatial analysis in archaeology. *American Antiquity 47*, 31-63.

Klejn, L. (1977). A panorama of theoretical archaeology. *Current Anthropology 18*, 1-42.

Lee, R. (1976). !Kung spatial organization. In R. Lee & L. De Vere (Eds.), *Kalahari hunter-gatherers* (pp. 73-97). Cambridge: Harvard University Press.

Lee, R. (1979). *The !Kung San.* Cambridge: Cambridge University Press.

Leone, M. (1982). Some opinions about recovering mind. *American Antiquity 47*, 742-760.

Lischka, J. (1975). Broken K revisited: A short discussion of factor analysis. *American Antiquity 40*, 220-227.

Lowe, J. (1982). On mathematical models of the classic Maya collapse: The class conflict hypothesis re-examined. *American Antiquity 47*, 643-652.

Lukacs, E. (1972). *Probability and mathematical statistics.* New York: Academic Press, Inc.

Marshall, L. (1976). *The !Kung San of Nyae Nyae.* Cambridge: Harvard University Press.

Mitchell, J. (1980). Introduction. In J. Mitchell (Ed.), *Numerical techniques in social anthropology* (pp. 1-29). Philadelphia: ISHI.

Mood, A., Graybill, F., & Boes, D. (1974). *Introduction to the theory of statistics.* New York: McGraw-Hill, Inc.

Munday, F., & Lincoln, T. (1979). A comment on Bettinger: Problem in archaeological interpretation. *American Antiquity 44*, 345-351.

Nagel, E. (1936). The meaning of probability. *Journal of the American Statistical Society 31*, 10-30.

Naroll, P. (1962). Floor area and settlement pattern. *American Antiquity 27*, 587-589.

Odell, G. (1981). Meaning in lithic tool types. *Journal of Anthropological Research 37*, 319-342.

Parzen, E. (1960). *Modern probability theory and its application.* New York: John Wiley & Sons, Inc.

Pelto, P. (1970). *Anthropological research.* New York: Harper and Row Publishers, Inc.

Price, B. (1982). Cultural materialism: A theoretical review. *American Antiquity 47*, 709-741.

Read, D. (1947a). Some comments on the use of mathematical models in anthropology. *American Antiquity 39*, 3-15.
Read, D. (1947b). Some comments on typologies in archaeology and an outline of a methodology. *American Antiquity 39*, 216-242.
Read, D. (1978). Towards a formal theory of population size and area of habitation. *Current Anthropology 19*, 312-317.
Read, D. (1982). Toward a theory of archaeological classification. In R. Whallon & J. Brown (Eds.), *Essays on archaeological typology* (pp. 56-92). Evanston, IL: Center for American Archaeology Press.
Read, D. (1983). From multivariate statistics to natural selection: A reanalysis of plio/pleistocene hominid dental material. In G. Van Vart & W. Howells (Eds.), *Multivariate statistical methods in physical anthropology* (pp. 377-413). Amsterdam, The Netherlands: D. Reidel.
Read, D. (1984). An algebraic account of the American kinship terminology. *Current Anthropology 25*, 417-449.
Read, D., & LeBlanc, S. (1978). Descriptive statements, covering laws and theories in archaeology. *Current Anthropology 19*, 307-312.
Renfrew, C., & Cooke, K. (Eds.). (1979). *Transformations: Mathematical approaches to culture change*. New York: Academic Press, Inc.
Sackett, J. (1966). Quantitative analysis of upper palaeolithic stone tools. *American Anthropologist 68*, 356-392.
Salmon, M., & Salmon, W. (1979). Alternative models of scientific explanation. *American Antiquity 81*, 61-74.
Schact, R. (1980). Two models of population growth. *American Antiquity 82*, 782-798.
Schiffer, M. (1975). Factors and "toolkits": Evaluating multivariate analyses in archaeology. *Plains Anthropologist 67*, 61-70.
Schiffer, M. (1976). *Behavioral archaeology*. New York: Academic Press, Inc.
Schiffer, M. (1981). Some issues in the philosophy of archaeology. *American Antiquity 46*, 899-908.
Schleps, S. (1982). Statistical blight. *American Antiquity 47*, 836-851.
Spaulding, A. (1953). Statistical techniques for the discovery of artifact types. *American Antiquity 18*, 305-314.
Spaulding, A. (1960). Statistical description and comparison of artifact assemblages. In R. Heizer & S. Cook (Eds.), *The application of quantitative methods in archaeology* (Viking Fund Publications in Anthropology No. 28) (pp. 60-92). New York: Wenner-Gren Foundation for Anthropological Research.
Spaulding, A. (1977). On growth and form in archaeology: Multivariate analysis. *Journal of Anthropological Research 33*, 1-15.
Spaulding, A. (1982). Structure in archaeological data: Nominal variables. In R. Whallon & J. Brown (Eds.), *Essays on archaeological typology* (pp. 1-20). Evanston, IL: Center for American Archaeology Press.
Spencer, P. (1980). Polygyny as a measure of social differentiation in Africa. In J.C. Mitchell (Ed.), *Numerical techniques in social anthropology* (pp. 117-162). Philadelphia: ISHI.
Spethe, J., & Johnson, G. (1976). Problems in the use of correlations for the investigation of toolkits and activity areas. In C. Cleland (Ed.), *Cultural change and continuity: Essays in honor of James Bennett Griffin* (pp. 35-57). New York: Academic Press, Inc.
Steponaitis, V. (1981). Settlement hierarchies and political complexity in nonmarket societies: The formative period of the valley of Mexico. *American Anthropologist 83*, 320-338.
Suppe, F. (1972). What's wrong with the received view on the structure of scientific theories? *Philosophy of Science 39*, 1-19.
Thomas, D. (1970). *Archaeology's operational imperative: Great Basin projectile points as a test case* (University of California Archaeology Survey Annual Reports No. 12). Los Angeles: University of California.

Thomas, D. (1973). An empirical test for Steward's model of Great Basin settlement patterns. *American Antiquity 38*, 155-176.
Thomas, D. (1976). *Figuring anthropology*. New York: Holt, Rinehart & Winston.
Thomas, D. (1978). The awful truth about statistical archaeology. *American Antiquity 43*, 231-244.
Vierra, R. (1982). Typology, classification and theory building. In R. Whallon & J. Brown (Eds.), *Essays on archaeological typology* (pp. 162-175). Evanston, IL: Center for American Archaeology Press.
Vierra, R., & Carlson, D. (1981). Factor analysis, random data and patterned results. *American Antiquity 46*, 272-283.
Voorrips, A. (1982). Mambrino's helmet: A framework for structuring archaeological data. In R. Whallon & J. Brown (Eds.), *Essays on archaeological typology* (pp. 93-126). Evanston, IL: Center for American Archaeology Press.
Whallon, R. (1982). Variables and dimensions: The critical step in quantitative typology. In R. Whallon & J. Brown (Eds.), *Essays on archaeological typology* (pp. 127-161). Evanston, IL: Center for American Archaeology Press.
Wiessner, P. (1977). *Hxaro: A regional system of reciprocity for reducing risk among the !Kung San*. Unpublished doctoral dissertation, University of Michigan, Ann Arbor.
Wiessner, P. (1983). Style and social information in Kalahari San projectile points. *American Antiquity 48*, 253-276.
Wilmsen, E. (1973). Interaction, spacing behavior and the organization of hunting bands. *Journal of Anthropological Research 29*, 1-31.
Wood, J. (1978). Optimal location in settlement space: A model for describing location strategies. *American Antiquity 43*, 258-270.
Yellen, J. (1976). Settlement patterns of the !Kung. In R. Lee & I. De Vere (Eds.), *Kalahari hunter-gatherers* (pp. 47-72). Cambridge: Harvard University Press.
Yellen, J. (1977). *Archaeological approaches to the present*. New York: Academic Press, Inc.
Zubrow, E. (1975). *Prehistoric carrying capacity: A model*. Menlo Park, NY: Cummings.

PART III: DATA ORGANIZATION AND DATA BASE MANAGEMENT

4

Introductory Remarks on Data Base Management

CHRISTOPHER CARR

DATA BASE MANAGEMENT AS ANALYSIS

The term *data base management* often brings to mind the image of complex programming of a computer to *store* data. However, it involves much more than that. For projects that encompass large amounts of data of diverse classes, data base management (DBM) involves the careful consideration of the particular variables, kinds of observations, and kinds of relationships among them—of the infinite ones that are possible—that have potential analytic value within the paradigm of the researcher and that should be preserved for later analysis. This is true whether the information to be preserved is stored with computer technology or with written records, photographs, maps, or other storage techniques (Chenhall, 1982, p. 6). In the perspective of the previous two chapters, then, DBM is *the* initial step of analysis. It is concerned with defining the total data structure which has potential relevance to a broad problem domain, and from which certain aspects will later be selected deductively or inductively for analysis in order to investigate particular questions. To the extent that this initial step can considerably limit the kinds of variability and relationships that can be investigated later, as well as the quantitative means for doing so, it is of fundamental importance.

Once the data base manager has decided what variables, kinds of observations, and kinds of relationships should be preserved, the task more often associated with DBM remains: determining a means for storing such information within the physical constraints of computer technology so that it is preserved completely and accurately, and can be retrieved and added to with accuracy. The logic that is required for success in this aspect of DBM is analogous to that required in selecting and applying a statistical technique to data. Just as a statistical technique must be logically concordant with and sensitive to the relevant aspects of a data set that reflect the phenomenon of interest and its nature, so, too, the means by which data are stored on a computer must be logically concordant with and allow for the preservation of all information that is of potential interest and that reflects the phenomena of potential interest and their natures. In both cases, method must not *constrain* the form of the data as they are processed.

DBM, then, has two aspects. One is concerned with problem definition, specifying the phenomena of potential interest and their nature, and *modeling* the data entities and relationships that reflect those phenomena. The second is concerned with *preserving* that model. The segregation and stepwise nature of these two phases of DBM, as well as the top-down, theory-to-system approach to the design of DBM systems that this implies, is emphasized in the following chapter by Parker, Limp, and Farley. The authors suggest that the successful design of a DBM system requires the stepwise development of two models of the data: 1) a *conceptual model* which stipulates the entities, attributes, and relationships of potential interest, and 2) a *physical model* which specifies how that information is to be preserved. The conceptual model is the product of the data modeling phase of DBM, whereas the physical model is the logically equivalent transformation of the conceptual model, which is achieved through the use of principles of DBM (e.g., the process of normalizing a hierarchy of relationships).

The conceptual process that is advocated by Parker et al. for designing a DBM system differs to some degree from that described by Chenhall (1982). Both sets of researchers emphasize the necessity of carefully considering, prior to the design of a system, its purpose and the questions it is to answer. However, Chenhall organizes his operations of system development around the *research activities* in which the system is to participate; different files are established upfront for different activities. The data categories and relationships to be stored within each file are determined only after the initial inventory of files is specified (Chenhall, 1982, p. 5). In contrast, Parker et al. organize their operations of system development around the *nature of the data* that the system is to preserve; data modeling is fully completed before the consideration of files. The latter approach seems preferable in that the nature of the data base can play a somewhat more important role in the programmer's consideration of how to structure the system so that it can store and retrieve the desired information with the least storage and search costs.

The viewpoint that the structure of a DBM system should be logically concordant with the nature of the data to be preserved has naturally led Parker et al. to consider the general nature of archaeological data, and thus, the general structure required of an archaeological DBM system. Defining archaeological data in the broadest sense as the kind that is generated by multiyear, regional research and CRM programs, as opposed to site-specific data, alone (Brown et al., 1982; Gaines, 1974), Parker et al. suggest that archaeological data bases have a number of characteristics that pose management problems. In particular, they

1) are very large;
2) are complex, having multiple, overlapping relationships of both the object-clustering and attribute-clustering kinds;
3) involve diverse kinds of entities of different social scales (e.g., regions, sites, proveniences, artifacts) which are described by diverse kinds of attributes (e.g., soil type, edge angle) on different measurement scales (nominal, ordinal, interval);
4) define a matrix that has a high percentage of empty or zero cells;
5) are continually added to; and
6) are accessed in multiple, diverse subsets to investigate diverse hypotheses.

These characteristics, in combination, cause problems in storing, retrieving, and updating data in a manner that is accurate and complete, yet also parsimonious and economical. To overcome these management problems, Parker et al. advise the use of a *relational* DBM system, as opposed to one structured with pointers. Basic concepts of the relational approach are illustrated with the Arkansas Archeological Survey's AMASDA-DELOS system. Thus, the chapter by Parker et al. evaluates quantitative methodology for its logical concordance with data structure, as do many other chapters in this book.

In addition to the several themes mentioned previously, a number of other important points are made by Parker et al.

1) A physical data base structure that has logical concordance with the data to be preserved need not be a *natural* structure—a mirror representation of the data that involves empty cells and path dependencies. It can be an unnatural structure (e.g., a set of relational files) that has been transformed from the natural one to make storage and search economical.

2) Development of a conceptual model of the data that is to be preserved has *heuristic* advantages. It requires the researcher to consider relationships between variables and kinds of entities that might not otherwise be considered. (See also Chenhall, 1982, p. 2; Keene, chapter 10).

3) The common motivation behind the development of DBM systems and archaeological typologies is discussed. The limitations of the latter, in terms of data preservation and retrieval, are enumerated.

4) A DBM system can serve both inventory and research purposes. This is illustrated by the AMASDA-DELOS system. It is capable, for example, of inventorying the locations and dates of excavation of sites, yet also can retrieve ecological data that is useful in settlement modeling studies. (For a contrasting opinion on function segregation, see Chenhall, 1982, p. 2).

Finally, it is necessary to mention the importance of a DBM system of the encompassing kind that is discussed by Parker et al. The value of such a system extends beyond its capability of simply *preserving* information of potential relevance. It also extends beyond its capability of allowing the researcher to simply *extract*, in a purely deductive fashion, portions of a data base that are to be used in quantitative analysis when solving specific problems (Chenhall, 1982, p. 8; Brown et al., 1982, pp. 76-78). When used to its full potential, a DBM system can also serve as a *data screening device* within the context of an exploratory data analysis or constrained exploratory data analysis framework (see Carr, chapter 2). It allows the researcher to inventory the kinds of network relationships that do exist between variable states within the data set—of all those relationships that could be present in the data, as specified by the conceptual and physical models. In addition, it allows the researcher to determine the commonness of the network relationships that do occur between variable states. In this way, the researcher is provided with a summary of the nominal scale structure of the data base, which would be impractical to establish from a listing of the raw data, itself. Such a summary can be used to increase the efficiency with which more elaborate data screening procedures (e.g., crossplots, correlation analysis) are applied to the data at later stages of analysis. It can also be used to ensure that no significant relationships are overlooked (Farley, 1983).

REFERENCES

Brown, J.A., Clayton, S., Wendt, T., & Werner, B. (1982). The Koster project information retrieval application. In S.W. Gaines (Ed.), *Data bank applications in archaeology* (pp. 67-79). Tucson: University of Arizona Press.

Chenhall, R.G. (1982). Computerized data bank management. In S.W. Gaines (Ed.), *Data bank applications in archaeology* (pp. 1-8). Tucson: University of Arizona.

Farley, J.A. (1983). *Data base management, systematics, and their relationship to the analytical process in archaeology.* Unpublished master's thesis, University of Arkansas, Fayetteville.

Gaines, S.W. (1974). Computer-aided decision-making procedures for archaeological field problems. *American Antiquity 39*(3), 454-462.

5

Archaeological Data Base Management As Conceptual Process

SANDRA PARKER
W. FREDRICK LIMP
JAMES A. FARLEY

Basic concepts and their implications are often controversial simply because they are basic. They are buried in common sense, and it is in the nature of common sense to be almost beyond analysis; in effect, we relegate our primitive ideas to a level of unanalyzed givens so that we can get on with the job instead of succumbing to paralysis induced by uncertainty on where and how to begin.

A.C. Spaulding

Archaeological data sets are often of massive size, with multiple levels of integration, complex permutations, and wide covariations. These properties make effective computerized information processing an integral element of successful archaeological investigations. An effective computerized system, however, can be derived only from an intensive examination of the general structure of archaeological data itself. Careful, "top down" consideration of the nature of the archaeological data must logically precede the design of the data base to be preserved. The data base design, in turn, leads to the actual development of data processing software. This "top down" approach can be contrasted with the common "bottom up" approach, in which the limitations of existing programs or coding formats guide the development of a system.

The theme of this chapter, therefore, is not about the structure of archaeological data alone, nor is it only about archaeological data base management; rather, it is about the *connectedness* of both of these. The concepts presented will be illustrated with operational examples taken from the AMASDA and DELOS systems, data base management systems that have been developed by the Arkansas Archeological Survey.

BACKGROUND

During the 1960s, a large number of computer applications for processing archaeological information appeared (cf. Chenhall, 1965, 1967, and 1971; Brown, 1973; Cowgill, 1973; Irwin-Williams & Clark, 1973; Scholtz & Chenhall, 1976). In the early days of computer system development, archaeologists spoke of data banks or, perhaps, management information systems. The first applications were of two general types: 1) specialized files of archaeological data, computerized as aids for specific research applications and 2) vast pools of archaeological data in which researchers could "go fishing" for answers to questions of interest (see Whallon, 1972; Scholtz & Chenhall, 1976 for surveys of applications). Both of these types of applications served some useful purpose, but at the same time, suffered from limitations. The specialized file was of significant research utility in the project for which it was designed, but, lacking generality, it did not often prove useful in other projects. The general purpose data bank, on the other hand, rather than being too specialized was usually too general to be of much utility. Frequently, researchers found that the data relevant to answering their questions were either not encoded or encoded inappropriately for their purposes.

Undaunted by the limitations of the early applications, archaeologists continue to develop information systems for their research. As observed by Gaines (1981, p. vii): ". . . archaeology is in its adolescence in terms of computerized data management and information systems." This lack of maturity suggests that it is desirable and necessary to examine and make explicit the principles that should guide the design of data base management systems in archaeology.

PROBLEMS, GOALS, AND PROPERTIES: A GENERAL PERSPECTIVE ON DATA BASE MANAGEMENT SYSTEMS IN ARCHAEOLOGY

Although archaeologists may hold to different paradigms, connecting them with different kinds of phenomena and relationships among phenomena, it is clear that archaeologists, nonetheless, deal with a recurring set of generalized data structures. These data structures tend to share certain characteristics that in turn present a common set of data management problems which, to some extent, can be overcome through the application of principles of data base management (Martin, 1977).

Some common, general characteristics of archaeological data structures are the following:

1. They are *large*, often involving many observations, each of which is described by a large number of variables.
2. They are *complex*, involving associations and covariations among variables and similarities among observations that may be multidimensional and overlapping. The relationships among observations may be hierarchical or define a plex or network structure (see below). Importantly,

the structure of an archaeological data set may vary locally among different sets of observations and variables, rather than be globally uniform. This complexity, in part, relates to the diverse kinds of units that an archaeological data structure may encompass (e.g., geographic regions, sites, proveniences, artifacts) and the diverse scales along which their attributes are measured (nominal, ordinal, interval, or ratio). However, it also relates to the often fluid manner in which even a restricted set of archaeological phenomena may be organized (e.g., spatial relations among artifacts within a site; see Carr, chapter 13).

3. They often involve a high percentage of empty or *zero cells* when fully enumerated as a matrix of observations against variables.

4. They are often used for *multiple purposes* to investigate diverse hypotheses.

5. They are often *open-ended*, i.e., they must be added to continually as work and analysis proceed. Updating a data structure may be two-dimensional, involving addition of both new observations and new variables.

These general characteristics of archaeological data, either individually or in combination, pose a set of problems involving data storage, including preservation of all potentially important relationships within the data in an efficient manner; retrieval of and access to the data in multiple formats and subsets; and updating of the data set. These problems must be surmounted if efficient and encompassing analysis of the data is to be allowed.

As will be seen below, the historic response of archaeologists to these data management problems was the development of archaeological systematics. Variations and covariations within archaeological data were summarized within various kinds of "types," including artifact types, settlement types, cultures, and assemblages, based on their physical or spatial properties (Binford, 1982, p. 27; Struever, 1968, p. 287; Bordes 1968, pp. 28-29). This approach to "data management" helps alleviate, to some extent, the problems of data storage associated with the voluminous, complex, empty-celled nature of archaeological data by reducing the amount of information that has to be recorded. At the same time, it is not an optimal solution to the problem, for only some kinds of observations and relationships—those coterminous with the type—are preserved. This is particularly true if the types are defined intuitively. In this case, the limitations of the human mind in simultaneously considering large numbers of dimensions of variability selects against the many forms of variability that occur in a data set being greatly included in the constructed types (see Hoffman, chapter 18).

Classification as an approach to data management also suffers in that it neither facilitates the retrieval of those relationships used (or unused) to create the classes nor easily allows the created data base structure to be updated. Substantial analytical effort may be expended in careful observations in order to define a type, but once such a mental construct is achieved, it tends to stand in place of the observation, hampering access to the very kinds of variability used to define it. Neither is the definition of such a construct easily altered to encompass a broader or differing subset of variability as new archaeological finds are made and new kinds of variation require "storage." This point was recognized by even so confirmed a typologist as Philip Phillips:

> Once you begin to play with numbers, itself a dangerously fascinating pastime, typological afterthoughts are not welcome; anything learned about types through their use only makes for awkward complications. Thus classification and site analysis tend to become separate operations to the detriment of both. (1970, p. 247)

Although classification has its important roles in archaeology (see Hoffman, chapter 18), computerized data base management systems can provide a more efficient, flexible, and accurate solution to the problems of data storage, retrieval, and updating. When properly structured, a data base management system can increase the efficiency with which large quantities of complexly structured data can be recorded, accessed, and manipulated in a manner compatible with specific user-defined applications. It can allow the same information to be examined from a number of perspectives without required alteration of the system programs themselves. Likewise, new information can be augmented to the system without altering the management programs. By providing a standard framework for preserving and displaying archaeological data, a data base management system allows the development of comparable bodies of data between projects. Comparable data bases are crucial in regional-oriented studies which are emphasized currently in archaeology.

The success or failure of any particular data base management system in overcoming the problems of storing, retrieving, and updating archaeological data depends on the degree of concordance between the nature of the programs comprising the system and the structure of the data being managed. Given the certain general structural properties of archaeological data (above), and the desired basic functions of a data base management system, it is thus possible to state some preferable general properties of an archaeological data base management system. These properties are as follows:

1. *Top-down theoretical orientation.* A data-base system designed with a top-down theoretical orientation is one in which the variables relevant to the research question of concern (or likely concern) and relationships between those variables have been defined prior to program development. A system designed top-down requires that the entities, attributes, and relationships among them, all of which are apt to be found in the archaeological data to be managed and be important, be identified and *modeled* first. (The term *entity* in this chapter refers to a class of observations or a unit of analysis, such as a site or artifact class; the term *attribute* refers to a property of an entity or observation, synonymous with the term *variable*. See below.) Then management programs may be designed to

accommodate such entities, attributes, and relationships. By designing a management system from the top down, the likelihood of preserving *more* of the relationships within archaeological data increases; the complexity of archaeological data is accommodated. Moreover, by preserving the relationships that are *relevant* to a broad theoretical orientation, a data base is created that allows multiple access for addressing the questions of that orientation, making it a productive data base. This top-down approach to the development of a data base management system differs from a bottom-up approach in which data are recorded on the computer and are expected to be useful in some unidentified research applications—a strategy not likely to produce fruitful results (Scholtz & Chenhall, 1976).

It should be noted that a top-down approach to developing a data base management system is not synonymous with an *a priori, deductive* approach to data preservation and subsequent analysis. Success in modeling the data to be preserved prior to program design depends on one's degree of familiarity with the data and the clarity with which one envisions his or her theoretical orientation and potential questions of relevance.

Key notions (discussed below) in relation to the top-down approach to the development of a data base management system include data modeling, the conceptual model of data structure, the physical model of data base structure, data independence, and normalization.

2. *Open-ended.* Any data base management system with a generalized design has the potential for not including some necessary entities, attributes, or relationships that might be relevant to a particular theoretical orientation. For this reason, a data base management system should be open-ended, allowing the encoding of additional entities and attributes, and the definition of new relationships in the data, without necessitating redesign and reprogramming of the software system. Sets of data, or files should be structured such that attributes and entities can be added to them without changing the data relationships that already exist in the files. New files should be integrated easily with established ones. Only minimal programming changes, such as the addition of new attribute names or new file names, should be required by such changes, leaving unaltered the basic integrity of the software system supplying file storage and retrieval functions.

This feature of a data base management system is necessary to accommodate not only the open-ended nature of archaeological data structures, but also their complexity. Some relevant entities, attributes, and relationships may be deleted in the process of modeling the data prior to program design. Their importance may become apparent only when the encoded data are examined more thoroughly with the aid of the management system and statistical operations. At this point, it is preferable for the new entities, attributes, and relationships to be incorporated in the data base with ease.

3. *Parsimony.* A data base management system for archaeology should be

judged on the basis of its parsimony, in terms of the amount of storage space and computer time it requires compared to its utility and flexibility. An efficient management system will eliminate the necessity of storing the information-devoid zero cells that usually occur frequently in a fully enumerated matrix of attributes and observations pertaining to multiple scales of archaeological organization (region, site, provenience, artifact). At the same time, this will be achieved with minimal introduction of data redundancy in the form of "linking identifiers" that must be stored, and will involve minimal search and processing costs. As shown below, a partially hierarchical, partially plex conceptual model of archaeological data structures, represented by a relational file-storage structure, is one efficient approach for reaching the desired balance.

4. *Flexibility.* A successful data base management system will preserve all currently known covariations among entities and allow these multiple permutations to be accessed and documented easily. This is necessary if diverse hypotheses consistent with the orientation of the data base are to be tested, and multiple kinds of tables for reports are to be generated.

5. *Accuracy.* An effective data base management system should allow scanning and retrieval of chosen portions of the data so that correct representations of the data are obtained. The selection and extraction of some or all property values of some or all of the entities within a data base, on the basis of some search criterion, should maintain "semantic integrity" (Martin, 1977, p. 222); that is, displays that do not contain false relationships or invalid combinations of data items, sometimes called "false drops," should be produced (Heller, 1974, p. 3).

DATA MODELS AND DATA STRUCTURES IN ARCHAEOLOGY

Having discussed very generally the preferred characteristics of an archaeological data base management system, in light of the storage, retrieval, and updating problems posed by archaeological data, let us consider in greater detail the process of developing a management system and its structural characteristics.

Using a top-down approach, the construction of a data base management system requires several, stepwise operations: These are 1) extensive consideration of the potential questions which might be asked of the data (developing the problem domain); 2) the identification of entities, attributes, and relationships required to address these problems (modeling data relationships); 3) formation of conventions for data documentation (data standardization); and 4) consideration of the manner in which entities and attributes will be associated with one another and stored on the computer (physical data organization). These operations represent two essentially discrete processes: the development of a data base, and the creation of a series of computer programs which are logically concordant with the data base in that they operate upon it in a manner responsive to an original set of problems. The segregation of these two processes permits the data base developer to focus initial attention on creating an optimal level of integration within the data, while deferring any consideration of program design to a subsequent stage of development. This condition is known as *data independence* (Martin, 1977). It is a desirable strategy for developing a management system because it allows a system with the greatest range of application and open-ended structure to be formed.

The processes of developing a data base and designing managing programs are correspondingly associated with the development of two kinds of models of the structure of archaeological data to be examined: the *conceptual model* and the *physical model*. The conceptual model is a product of the prior experience of the archaeologist and the particular theoretical paradigm under which the archaeologist operates. It specifies the *kinds of units* or entities to be described (e.g., sites, artifacts) and their *relationship* (e.g., hierarchical, nested). It also specifies the data's attributes or properties which are pertinent for study and which should be preserved in the management system, given the theoretical orientation of the archaeologist and the kinds of questions he anticipates asking. Finally, it specifies the *pairs or sets of attributes* having relationships of probable interest, that should be preserved and retrievable for investigation.

In dealing with kinds of units rather than the total array of observations within the data set, the conceptual model does not map the properties of and relationships among each observation. It is a *model* of the relevant structure of the data rather than a *complete enumeration* of that structure. The complete enumeration of the data's structure implied by the model may be called the *conceived data structure*.

Note that the conceived data structure will usually contain only those attributes, observations, and relationships of the data relevant to the paradigm and questions of the archaeologist, as opposed to all potentially relevant attributes, observations, and relationships from the perspective of all possible paradigms. The totality of information in a data set is termed its *data structure*, in accord with its usage in this book.

It is important to realize that although the conceptual model of the data is often generated in relation to a specific set of data, it may describe the structure of a number of similar data sets. This results from the general nature of the conceptual model and its close relationship to the theoretical orientation of the archaeologist as opposed to the data-specific nature of the conceived data structure.

The physical model of the structure of an archaeologist data set stipulates the framework in which the various kinds of entities, attributes, and relationships among them in the conceptual model will be preserved on the computer so as to be compatible with it. It is a general construct and may be contrasted with how each observation in the data set and their relationships are stored, which may be called the *physical data base structure*. The physical model can be envisioned as a structural transformation of the conceptual model through the use of the principles and constructs of data base management. Likewise, the physical data base structure can be envisioned as a structural transformation of the conceived data structure, although this transformation is only implied by the former.

Inasmuch as the conceptual model of the data to be examined is constructed in a generalized way and models many archaeological data sets, and the physical model of the data successfully preserves all aspects of the conceptual model, the resulting data base management system will have wide applicability. This is a desirable circumstance, affording comparability among many data sets and minimizing the work effort involved in system development. Thus, both models should be constructed with forethought as well as concern for present usage to the degree possible.

Although the two processes of developing a conceptual model and transforming it into a physical model have been characterized as independent processes, it must be stressed that these processes are carried out in a stepwise manner, in accord with a top-down approach. The results of one stage depend on those of the previous stages. Decisions made during the process of identifying important entities, attributes, and relationships and developing the conceptual model constrain the decisions that can be made in the development of the physical model as well as the forms and amount of variability it may encompass. In this way, increased regularity (Ashby, 1956; Clarke, 1968) is brought into the creative process by stages. The validity of the results obtained at any given stage is contingent on the cumulative accuracy or error introduced by the constraining decisions which precede them. The degree to which these constraints are justifiable and produce accurate representations of the portion of archaeological variability that is focused on within the data depends on the familiarity of the archaeologist with that data, related data sets, and the methods of data base management.

With this overview of the process of developing a computerized data base management system in mind, we may now examine the nature and manner of generation of conceptual models and physical models in greater detail.

Conceptual Models

A key part of the process of establishing a conceptual model is the recognition of the *entities* and their properties, both of which define the data being modeled. Entities are those items about which data are to be collected, e.g., an object, place, event, or abstract construct. Properties of entities are referred to as attributes, variables, or data categories. Some variables have a special significance because they *identify* entities, whereas others merely *describe* them.

In an archaeological application, the data entities are those constructs that serve as units of analysis. The exact nature and definition of the units will depend on several factors (discussed below) but some common analytical units in archaeology are sites, geographic units (which may include sites), provenience units, objects, and other entities with properties that may be observed and analyzed to answer questions of archaeological interest.

Scholtz and Chenhall (1976) point out that effective design of a computerized information retrieval system must follow a thorough consideration of the nature of the data to be encoded, the types of questions to be addressed, and the requirements of the potential user. Ideally, all attributes would be measured over all entities pertinent to any given set of research questions. If this were a realistic endeavor, successful data base management would simply require extensive consideration of entities and their properties, and the subsequent measurement of all properties identified. However, identification and documentation of a potentially infinite number of variables is in no way a realistic expectation. Thus, the task becomes one of implementing a series of cost-benefit decisions with regard to the information which will be included in the data base.

This limitation makes it imperative that the selection of entities and their properties be made on the basis of their ability to contribute to the entire set of problems that one hopes to address. It requires 1) identification of essential, nonnegotiable data entities and attributes; 2) postulation of the likely relationships among them; and 3) elimination of attributes that measure the same phenomena or closely related phenomena. The latter process, identified by Martin (1977) as the reduction of data redundancy, is necessary to produce an efficient data management system. It defines a mini-max strategy for retaining attributes where attributes are evaluated on the basis of their ability to make the *maximum* contribution to the problems being considered while incorporating the *minimal* amount of redundancy in the data being recorded.

All three operations mentioned above are part of a process called *data modeling*, in that they ultimately lead to the formulation of a conceptual model of the archaeological data in hand and similar data. Data modeling is accomplished through extensive consideration of questions of potential interest within the problem domain, and the entities and qualities of entities necessary to address those questions. It also requires the researcher's intimate familiarization with the data in hand and related data sets. It is an interactive process, requiring simultaneous consideration of the problem domain and the data.

Once an acceptable model of the data has been refined, a form of data standardization is required to complete the conceptual model. This necessitates the development of a procedural guideline for data documentation and the design of a format for recording data to serve as the basis for data input. Both the documentation conventions and the recording format are derivatives of the data modeling process and as such, should reflect any superordinate-subordinate relationships extant within that model. The logical relationships between entities and properties and their relative importance (if any), as defined by the modeling process, should be preserved. Examples of such documentary procedures, as they are applied to archaeological research, are provided by Newell and Vroomans (1972), Limp (1978), Moore-Jansen, Parker, and Million (1981), Limp and Parker (1983), and in the SELGEM recording manual published by the University of Arizona in 1974.

Toward Optimal Conceptual Models of Archaeological Data in General

As mentioned above, a conceptual model results from the simultaneous consideration of the researcher's theoretical orientation and the kind of data to be managed. In archaeological research, any conceptual model can be considered the product of three such theoretical or substantive dimensions: 1) the theoretical orientation of the archaeologist; 2) the spatial relationships among artifacts, features, and environment; and 3) the physical properties of archaeological materials and sites. In this section, the potential complexity of each of these three dimensions is discussed, and the necessity of accommodating such complexity within the conceptual models upon which archaeological data base management systems are built is emphasized. The result is the formulation of criteria for evaluating the optimality of conceptual models and the specification of two general structural properties of conceptual models that can be used in helping them meet these criteria.

Different theoretical orientations result in different analytical constructs involving complex permutations of patterning among the physical and spatial properties of archaeological materials (Binford, 1982, p. 27). Binford has classified most archaeological analytical constructs as *assemblage-based* versus *association groups*. Briefly, Binford defines an assemblage-based construct as one based on "content summaries" or "inventories" of entity types within units of observation, each having some minimal degree of associational integrity. An example would be a Paleolithic culture based on similarities in the artifact type inventories of several assemblages (the unit of analysis). In contrast, an association group is a construct based on attributes that have continuity in their presence or covariation over space. A New World archaeological culture defined by culture traits having continuity over space would be an example (Binford, 1982, p. 27; Binford & Sabloff, 1982).

Binford has argued that both assemblage and association-group approaches to archaeological data inherently lead to problems in recognizing the full range of variability in the artifact data, particularly as it pertains to spatial analysis. He argues that the problems associated with these two approaches are a result of the theoretical orientation—the problem domains—of earlier workers who did not focus on the complex issues of evolutionary change and diversity.

Despite Binford's discussion of the problems with assemblage and association-group analytical constructs, we argue that such constructs have utility in archaeology and in the conceptual models of data base management applications when not used as "summary constructs." The problems that Binford cites with assemblage and association-group analytic constructs stem not only from the theoretical orientation of early workers, but also from the use of assemblages or associational groups as "summarizing" devices. Most humans are unable to simultaneously consider a large number of multiple dimensions of observation. As a result, a complex covariation of artifact attributes is summarized in a "type," whereas a complex set of objects and spatial corelationships are distilled into an "assemblage." As mentioned before, the practical effect of this operation is that it becomes easier to use the constructed classes than the original data upon which they are based; the original data, thus, are seldom accessed. In many instances, the difficulty is further exacerbated by a reification of the construct—it becomes real and *replaces* the observations from which it was derived. While no data base management approach can eliminate the potential for reification, we believe that the increased accessibility of the original data through the various retrieval procedures offered by management systems does reduce the emphasis placed on the summary constructs; thus, they can play a useful role in the development and structuring of such systems.

On initial consideration, it might appear that the second and the third dimensions of the conceptual model, spatial and physical properties, are less complex than the theoretical dimension. Such is not the case, however, since 1) the interrelationships between the spatial and physical properties may be observed at a number of levels of resolution and 2) the entities or properties selected for observation are themselves, in part, defined by the analytical approach of the archaeologist.

Clarke has proposed that there are three levels of resolution of spatial properties pertaining to archaeological materials: micro (within structures, such as houses or graves); semimicro (within sites); and macro (between sites) (1977, p. 11ff). The spatial properties define associations between and among archaeological materials which are critical to the interpretation of cultural process and culture history.

The physical properties of archaeological materials may be observed at the object level or the attribute level (Whallon, 1982; Spaulding, 1982; Hodson, 1982). Classification at the object level involves the evaluation of an item with respect to a set of previously defined item-cluster descriptions. An item sharing the item-cluster characteristics, either fully or partially, is a member of that cluster (Hodson, 1982, p. 24). In attribute clustering, co-occurrences of attributes are used to define the class (Spaulding, 1982, p. 6ff). Cowgill (1982), Read (1982), and Voorrpis (1982) have emphasized that both approaches may be used and can be expected to produce productive insight into the nature of an archaeological data set (cf. Brown, 1982).

For a conceptual model of archaeological data structure to be optimal, it must accommodate the complexities of the three theoretical or substantive dimensions of variation just described. The most useful conceptual model of archaeological data structure, thus, is a *generalized* one, permitting observations that allow both assemblage and type-based analysis (as defined by Binford, 1982) as well as object and attribute classification (as defined by various authors in Brown & Whallon, 1982). Furthermore, the model should permit the investigation of association of these observations at the micro, semimicro, and macro levels of spatial resolution.

An optimal conceptual model, then, must minimally meet the criterion of *flexibility*—one of the characteristics preferred of a data base management system discussed at the opening of this chapter. It must accommodate the complexities of archaeological data structures and theoretical orientations just discussed, allowing the recording of all possible currently known covariations of interest. At the same time, to be effective in the construction of an optimal data base management system, a conceptual model must have other preferred characteristics of management systems: It will be *parsimonious*, in not demanding the inclusion of "impossible states" or zero cells; *open-ended*, so that previously unrecognized combinations of variables may be added when observed; and structurally will reflect the recognized *discontinuities* in the data.

Two structural properties that can be incorporated in a conceptual model of archaeological data to help it meet these criteria (particularly 1 and 2) are a *hierarchical structure*, as opposed to a complete enumeration of a full matrix of alternative attributes and objects; and a *plex structure*. A completely enumerated matrix retains all potentially relevant relationships, but it is the least parsimonious approach to data recording and retrieval. It is possible, however, to reduce such a matrix to a more parsimonious structure, while simultaneously retaining the necessary data relationships, by formulating it in a hierarchical fashion (Fig. 1a). While the full matrix is inclusive, the hierarchical structure is exclusive. Each level of the hierarchy corresponds to an assumption concerning the relevant properties which have defined membership, and each descendant has but one parent. Hierarchical structures are characterized by *path dependency*, i.e., the interpretation of any lower node in the hierarchy is at least partially dependent on the information contained in its parent (higher) nodes (Martin, 1977).

The second structure, which may be useful in modeling archaeological data, is the plex (Fig. 1b). Although the plex is similar to a hierarchy with path dependencies, in the plex, any descendant may have multiple parents. As a

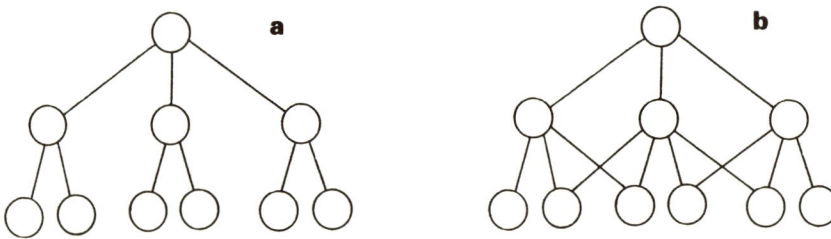

Fig. 5.1. (a) Hierarchical structure. (b) Plex structure.

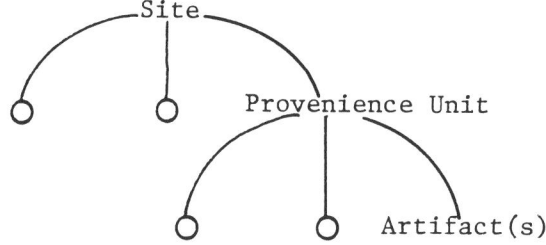

Fig. 5.2. Hierarchically structured archaeological data.

result, the plex structure may permit the retention of more information on the variability of and covariation among attributes of entities. The plex structure allows for flexibility in classification. However, it also increases the complexity of the classification of entities because they may be classified in multiple ways simultaneously and classes may be overlapping.

An optimal conceptual model of archaeological data will probably contain both hierarchical and plex structures, although these will not be sufficient for guaranteeing its optimality. To illustrate these properties in practice, aspects of the conceptual model of the AMASDA and DELOS data base management system will be presented.

An Example of an Archaeological Conceptual Model

In the conceptual model of archaeological data used in the AMASDA and DELOS systems, data entities are identified at three levels of observation: 1) the site level, 2) the provenience unit level, and 3) the artifact level. This structure presents that of a hierarchy (Fig. 2), in which a node in each higher level may point to many nodes in the next lower level. The AMASDA system is the portion of the total data management system which is designed to handle data at the highest, or site, level. The subsystem designed for information processing at the provenience and artifact levels is DELOS.

The structure of the AMASDA/DELOS conceptual model, however, is considerably more complex and flexible than a simple hierarchy. It recognizes that analysis may require the organization of provenience units into multiple, overlapping analytical units intermediate between the provenience units—into horizontal strata, excavation units, site areal units, and interpretive structures (e.g., houses, graves, activity areas, or other spatially/behaviorally recognized units). This presents a plex structure where each provenience unit node may point up to a number of intermediate level nodes (Fig. 3). The organization of these units into multiple overlapping units permits analysis to be either *assemblage* or *type*-based, or of intermediate character, because the various associational relationships allow diverse combinations of objects in complex spatial associations.

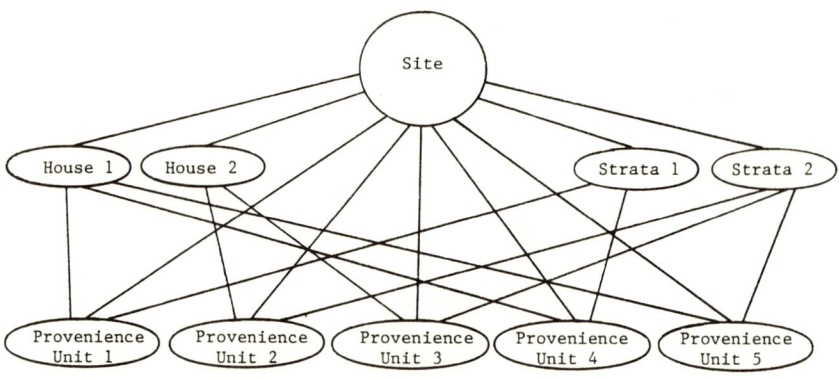

Fig. 5.3. Plex structured archæological data.

Given this overview of the conceptual model of archæological data structure at the foundation of AMASDA/DELOS, we will now discuss structural aspects of the model and the form of data standardization employed at each of the entity levels. Selection of these specific entity levels was based on their overwhelming primacy in archæological data, and requires little, if any, further justification. Such is not the case, however, for the properties observed for the entities.

The site entity level is the most inclusive. Numerous properties of sites are recognized. Beyond the obvious "managerial" data (e.g., site ownership, various dates, and other such categories of data) selection of the properties of the site entity was guided primarily by an ecological paradigm. These properties include physical descriptive data, associated biophysical data, interpretive cultural data, and others providing information describing the site and its location. Each site's "unique identifying" property used in linking it to other entity levels, is the site number. There is also the potential for observing nonsite locational data for such applications as predictive modeling (Scholtz, 1980, 1981; Parker, chapter 8).

The provenience unit entity is identified uniquely by a *field serial number* (FSN) concatenated with an *accession number* which identifies the year of collection and the site. A number of provenience unit properties are recognized, including descriptive information about the type of unit, its physical characteristics, its relative locational data and its associational data. The associations are preserved by observing the provenience that the current provenience is a part of, superimposes, or is related to by one of the other associational types. Figure 4 illustrates the provenience unit entity properties. The provenience unit properties of the DELOS system are patterned largely after the work of Christopher Peebles with the Lubbub Creek Archæological Locality (C.S. Peebles, personal communication, October 15, 1979; Peebles & Galloway, 1981).

```
4-4-82                    ARKANSAS ARCHEOLOGICAL SURVEY
                             PROVENIENCE DATA FORM

  1) SITE #  [        ]   ACCESSION # [ 82 - ]   FSN # [        ]

  2) COLLECTION AREA _____ CONTROL UNIT [        ]  TRENCH # _____

  3) FSN CATEGORY [        ]  FEATURE # _____ SAMPLE ID# _____ MATRIX PROCESS [   ]
     (N x E) : (___ x ___)

  4) FEATURE SHAPE _____ FSN VOL. _____ m³  PERCENT FSN EXCAVATED _____

  5) A/B/E/ [   ]
            VERTICAL DATUM: _____ . ___ m

  6) COORDINATES OF CORNERS    N/S         E/W          N/S         E/W
                           (1) [   ]     [   ]     (3) [   ]     [   ]
                           (2) [   ]     [   ]     (4) [   ]     [   ]

  7) ARTIFACT CLUSTER/FEATURE DIAMETER _____ . ___ m

  8) ELEV/DEPTH
     SURFACE _____  (1) [  .  ] - [  .  ] m  (3) [  .  ] - [  .  ] m
                      (2) [  .  ] - [  .  ] m  (4) [  .  ] - [  .  ] m

  9) FEA. BASE      N/S          E/W                FEA. BASE
     COORDINATES  [   ] . ___ - [   ] . ___        ELEV./DEPTH _____ . ___ m

 10) STRATUM _____        TEXTURE _____

 11) MUNSELL COLOR _____ / _____ / _____

                                    ASSOCIATIONS
     This
 12) FSN contains: ...................... [   ] _____

 13) FSN is part of: .................... [   ] _____
 14) FSN lies adjacent to: .............. [   ] _____
 15) FSN is the same as: ................ [   ] _____
 16) FSN is within excavation unit: ..... [   ] _____

     SUPERPOSITION:
 17) FSN lies above: .................... [   ] _____
 18) FSN lies below: .................... [   ] _____

     CROSS-CUTTING
 19) FSN is intruded by FSN: ............ [   ] _____
 20) FSN intrudes FSN: .................. [   ] _____
 21) FSN has an intersection with FSN: .. [   ] _____

 22) COMMENTS _____

     RECORDER _____     DATE _____
```

Fig. 5.4. Form for observation of provenience unit entity properties.

The artifact entity level provides for the recognition of properties of an artifact or group of artifacts with similar properties from the same provenience unit (Fig. 5). Each entity at this level has as a unique identifier—a catalog number that is a concatenation of the accession number of the collection, the FSN of the provenience unit, a lab serial number (LSN), and sometimes an

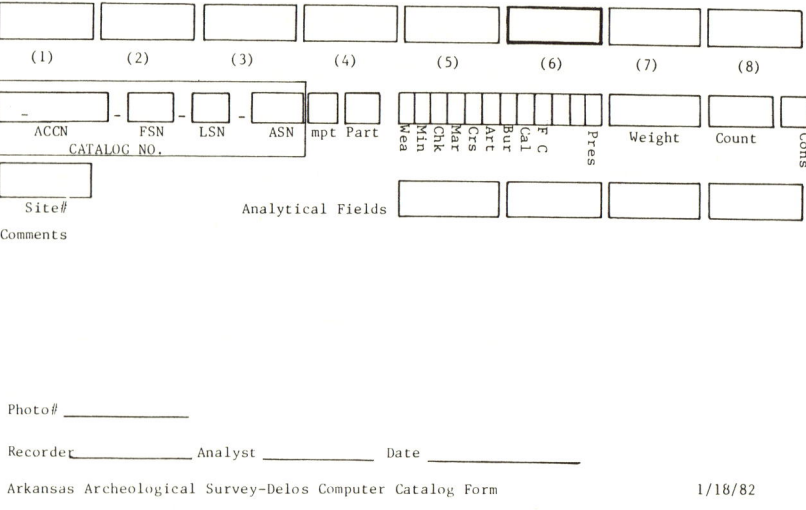

Fig. 5.5. Form for observation of artifact entity properties.

analytical serial number (ASN) linking it to more refined descriptive information than that standardly recorded. The properties standardly recognized are of both an object and attribute classificatory nature. They are preserved through a series of conventions for data documentation developed by Limp and Parker (1983) using a descriptive system for artifact and ecofact identification designed by Kaczor et al. (1983) and expanded by Lafferty (1983) and Lafferty and Lockwood (1983).

The classificatory properties of artifacts standardly recorded are included in a two-level hierarchical classification for identifying the artifact by morphological/functional characteristics and/or a type/variety identification for materials such as pottery and projectile points. Several attribute properties, as well as material, weight, or count data, and information relating to the preservation and condition of the object may be observed.

It is interesting to note that the conceptual model of data structure within entities (among properties) is somewhat analogous to that between entities. Some of the artifact properties themselves represent plex structures. This results from the intent to permit simultaneous object classification and classification based on attributes related to style, design, and manufacture. Figure 6 is a diagramatic representation of this approach for a subset of the ceramic data structure. On the left, the relationships between selected stylistic or design attributes and morphological elements are presented. On the right, similar plex relationships from the simultaneous description of ceramic morphology and temper type are displayed.

Completing the conceptual data structure model of AMASDA/DELOS and

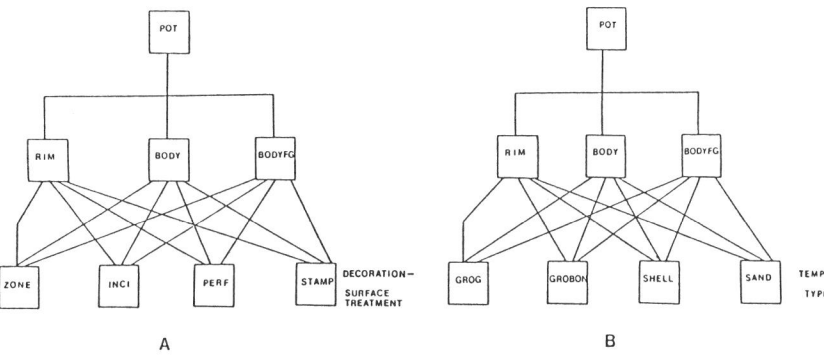

Fig. 5.6. Plex structure of ceramic data.

the process of data standardization is the DELOS dictionary of terms. This dictionary includes classification definitions for all object-clusters as proposed by Hodson (1982), and classificatory terms and attribute states which may be observed. The dictionary has the characteristic of open-endedness, in allowing new definitions to be added. DELOS currently recognizes over 120 attribute states for ceramics and some 90 raw material type for lithic items. Its dictionary provides a standard guideline to aid the analyst and helps to ensure a body of consistent, comparable information required for efficient data organization and subsequent analysis. The system is flexible (generalized) enough to meet diverse, expanding research needs, yet structured (standardized) enough to ensure continuity in data collection, providing a basis for subsequent analysis.

Physical Models and Physical Data Base Structure

Once a satisfactory conceptual model has been constructed, the problem of translating that model into a framework compatible with the physical structure of the computer remains. Whereas construction of a conceptual model requires the *recognition* of the data relationships necessary to address the problems under consideration, construction of a physical model and the realization of a physical data base structure requires the *transformation* of such relationships in a way that they can be efficiently stored, retrieved, and updated mechanically *with no loss of information*. This requires a consideration of the nature of data items, records, files, and their possible relationships within a data base, as defined by data base management principles and applied to the conceptual model's entities, sets of entities, and entity properties (Table 1).

Many possible physical data storage structures, reflecting many physical models, are available. Records may be stored in two-dimensional arrays, often called *flat files*, where the columns represent variables and the rows are observations. This physical data base structure has the capability of preserving all

Table 5.1.

Corresponding Elements of the Conceptual and Physical Models

Conceptual Model	Physical Model
Entity set	File of records
Entity	Stored records
Property of an entity	Data item

covariations within a conceived data structure. Its organization is the most direct reflection of the conceived data structure, and in this sense, is the most "natural" form of storage. Flat files have the primary disadvantage, however, of requiring the storage of all combinations of the observed properties of all entites. This implies that when archaeological data have a complex structure representable as a hierarchy or plex structure (as is typical), a flat file will contain many zero cells. Fully enumerated flat files, thus, are seldom a parsimonious physical data base structure.

Other physical storage structures are more complicated conceptually, but they can accommodate hierarchical and plex relationships without necessitating the storage of empty cells. One way of representing hierarchical or plex data relationships physically is with internally embedded *address pointers*. While potentially parimonious in their storage requirements and in preserving all currently known hierarchical relationships, files with pointers may be expensive to process. In addition, their rigidly defined data structure can make some queries difficult or impossible. Finally, such systems do not allow data independence. The GRIPHOS system (Heller, 1974) is an example. The data relationships between the root record and the lower-level nodes are maintained by up and down address pointers, allowing file searches to follow hierarchical data relationships within records. This type of data storage structure requires storage space for pointers and such processing data as field idenfitication and field length, reducing storage parsimony. If files are to be processed frequently in a sequential manner, considerable computer time may be required for identifying fields and following address pointers. Moreover, if the data records are reasonably consistent in data content, there is no savings in storage with such a hierarchical arrangement. In fact, there may even be a loss.

A second kind of physical data base structure that may be used to preserve hierarchical and plex data relationships without requiring the storage of empty cells is the *relational data base structure*. A relational data base structure is a series of two-dimensional tables where each record (row) contains all the property values associated with a single entity and each column is a group of data values relevant to a single property. The records among different tables or files—called relations—are linked to each other through the use of *keys* or common identifiers, which appear on each record. The FSN, LSN, and ASN identifiers within the AMASDA/DELOS system are examples. In this way, hierarchical and plex associations among entities may be reduced to relational files. The process by which this transformation is made is called *normalization*. Martin (1977) summarizes a number of logical operations that may be used by the data base manager to normalize a conceived data structure and define a relational data base structure.

Information from the several linked tables or relations of a relational data base structure can be accessed simultaneously, preserving the accurate relationships among entities and properties through three processes: SELECT, JOIN, and PROJECTION. A SELECT operation allows the selection of certain rows of a relation. When implementing a JOIN, relations can be merged. The process called PROJECTION allows the selection of certain columns, or data items, from one file or a number of JOINed files.

Relational data bases with keys for JOINing relations are designed to preserve relationships both within entities and between entities. For example, an encoded entity may represent a biface made of novaculite, expressing a within-entity relationship between form and material in this case. A relationship between entities is that exemplified by two artifacts which are related by having come from the same excavation unit. They have a similar value for the variable, excavation unit.

A complex, conceived data structure reduced to a set of relations is exemplified by the AMASDA/DELOS system. Figure 7 illustrates the normalized set of two-dimensional relations which retain the hierarchical data relationships illustrated in Figure 2, yet do not require a hierarchical physical storage structure with address pointers. The site data are maintained in one relation (AMASDA), in which each record is uniquely identified by its appropriate site number. The DELOS system consists of relations of provenience and artifact data. In the provenience relation, the site number is repeated, allowing JOINs between this relation and the site relation. In turn, the unique identifying number in a provenience record is a two-part number made up of an accession number and a field serial number (FSN). This identifying number is duplicated in the artifact relation, allowing JOINs between the provenience and artifact files.

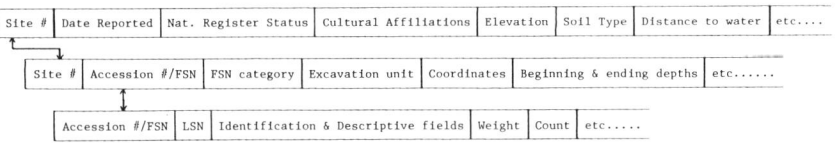

Fig. 5.7. Normalized two-dimensional files which retain hierarchical data relationships.

The cost of the reduction of complex structures to relational tables is the creation of the several redundant identifiers that must occur in each row in each relation. The practical result is that a complicated, multileveled structural model has been reduced to independent but related, easily investigated flat files. Additionally, a set of files has been created in which data relationships between data categories may be examined in all possible permutations between files. This is accomplished through JOIN operations. The increase in analytical power which is derived from this approach, in this case, easily justifies the redundancy which is introduced with the creation of the linking key variables.

Relational data bases represented as normalized two-dimensional flat files display a number of advantages as compared to data bases in which data are stored physically in a hierarchical or plex structure maintained with complex pointer linkages. These advantages, summarized by Martin (1977, pp. 255-226), include the following:

1. Ease of use. Two-dimensional tables provide an easy way to represent data to even those untrained in data processing techniques.

2. Flexibility. The researcher's needs for logical relations which do not exist physically can be satisfied by the "cutting and pasting" effects of such operations as SELECT, PROJECTION, and JOIN.

3. Security. Sensitive information can be in a separate relational table with additional security controls and only JOINed to other relations when needed. Archaeologists may consider site location information sensitive enough to require special precautions.

4. Relatability and precision. A system of relational two-dimensional tables gives the maximum flexibility in relating properties or entities from different relations in a nonmisleading, precise manner, protecting one from semantic disintegrity.

5. Ease of implementation. The simplification offered by normalization has major advantages over more complex physical techniques (e.g., storage hierarchies) in terms of ease of implementation. More rapid file searches are possible with physical storage techniques that avoid complex pointer linkages. Data represented as two-dimensional tables are easily interfaced with such systems as SPSS or SAS, lessening the need for specialized programming.

6. Data independence. This consideration is of extreme importance with any data base that needs to grow by adding new entities, attributes, and relationships. The cost of maintaining applications programs without data independence becomes problematic as the data base accumulates even the simplest changes. "Good data independence can probably be achieved more easily with normalized logical structures than with tree or plex structures" (Martin, 1977, p. 226).

CONCLUSION

The construction of a data base management system suitable for general archaeological applications requires a top-down strategy of development, involving the construction of the two models of the data to be managed. The first, the conceptual model, is oriented primarily towards refining the relationship between the data and the problem domain. The process of developing this model—data modeling—involves the selection of entities and nonredundant properties that accurately measure the greatest number of phenomena under consideration. The second model, the physical model, encompasses those general constructs of the subject of data base management by which relationships in the conceived data structure are accurately and easily translated into a physical data base structure compatible with computer hardware and software.

For a conceptual model to be flexible, parsimonious, and open-ended, it should permit 1) both assemblage and type-based analyses; 2) both object and attribute classification; 3) the investigation of relationships at the micro, semi-micro, and macro levels of spatial resolution; and 4) the occurrence of both hierarchical and plex relationships among entities.

Hierarchical and plex relationships within a conceptual model can be translated into a physical model implying a physical data base structure that is accurately and efficiently stored, retrieved, and updated when the data base structure is relational in nature. The process of translation, known as normalization, necessitates extensive consideration of mapping relationships to define path dependencies between entities and their properties in the conceptual model, and the removal of such dependencies between data items and records as the physical model and physical data base structure are created. The most common method associated with this process is the creation of multiple files linked by keys. In this case, limited redundancy is introduced into each record. However, the practical result of this redundancy is an absolute increase in the analytical power of the data base, realized in its potential to examine multiple permutations within and between the files composing the data base.

REFERENCES

Ashby, W. R. (1956). *An introduction to cybernetics*. London: Chapman and Hill.
Binford, L.R. (1982). The archaeology of place. *Journal of Anthropological Archaeology 1*, 5-31.
Binford, L.R., & Sahloff, J.A. (1982). Paradigms, systematics, and archaeology. *Journal of Anthropological Research 38*(2), 137-153.
Bordes, F. (1968). *The Old Stone Age*. New York: McGraw-Hill, Inc.
Brown, J.A. (1973). An application of a specialized data bank for analysis and information retrieval in the field. *Newsletter of Computer Archaeology 8*, 3-4.
Brown, J.A. (1982). On the structure of artifact typologies. In R. Whallon & J. Brown (Eds.), *Essays on archaeological typology*. Evanston, IL: Center for American Archeology Press.
Chenhall, R.G. (1965). *An investigation of taxonomic systems for the storage and retrieval of material culture data on computers*. Unpublished master's thesis, Arizona State University, Tempe.

Chenhall, R.G. (1967). The description of archaeological data in computer language. *American Antiquity 32*, 161-167.

Chenhall, R.G. (1971). The archaeological data bank: a progress report. *Computers and the Humanities 5*, 159-169.

Clarke, D.L. (1968). *Analytical archaeology.* London: Methuen.

Clarke, D.L. (1977). Spatial information in archaeology. In D.L. Clarke (Ed.), *Spatial archaeology.* New York: Academic Press.

Cowgill, G.L. (1973). The Teotihuacan data bank. *Newsletter of Computer Archaeology 8*, 6.

Cowgill, G.L. (1982). Clusters of objects and association between variables: Two approaches to archaeological classification. In R. Whallon & J. Brown (Eds.), *Essays on archaeological typology.* Evanston, IL: Center for American Archaeology Press.

Gaines, S.L. (Ed.). (1981). *Data bank applications in archaeology*. Tucson: The University of Arizona Press.

Heller, J. (1974). *On logical data organization, card catalogs, and the GRIPHOS management information system* (Museum Data Bank Research Report No. 3). Rochester: Museum Data Bank Committee.

Hodder, I.R. (1977). Some new directions in the spatial analysis of archaeological data at the regional scale. In D.L. Clarke (Ed.), *Spatial archaeology* (pp. 223-351). New York: Academic Press.

Hodson, F.R. (1982). Some aspects of archaeological classification. In R. Whallon and J. Brown (Eds.), *Essays on archaeological typology.* Evanston, IL: Center for American Archeology Press.

Irwin-Williams, C., & Clark, P. (1973). The development of data storage and retrieval systems in archaeology: The San Juan Valley archaeological program. *Newsletter of Computer Archaeology 8*, 4-5.

Kaczor, M., Rolingson, M.A., Limp, W.F., & Parker, S. (1983). DELOS artifact dictionary. In W.F. Limp & S. Parker (Eds.), *The DELOS System* (Technical Series No. 4). Fayetteville: University of Arkansas, Arkansas Archeological Survey.

Lafferty, R.H. (1983). Lithic resource exploitation and use in the Felsenthal uplands. In R.H. Lafferty & J.H. House (Eds.), *Final Phase II and Phase III investigations in the Sparta Mine Area* (Rep. submitted to the Shell Oil Company, Houston). Fayetteville: University of Arkansas, Arkansas Archeological Survey.

Lafferty, R.H., & Lockwood, R. (1983). Historic Sparta archeological materials. In R.H. Lafferty & J.H. House (Eds.), *Final Phase II and Phase III investigations in the Sparta Mine Area* (Rep. submitted to the Shell Oil Company, Houston). Fayetteville: University of Arkansas, Arkansas Archeological Survey.

Limp, W.F. (1978). *The ORACLE system users manual.* (Research Rep. No. 2). Bloomington: University of Indiana, Glenn Black Laboratory of Archaeology.

Limp, W.F., & Parker, S. (Eds). (1983). *The DELOS system* (Tech. Rep. No. 4). Fayetteville: University of Arkansas, Arkansas Archeological Survey.

Martin, J. (1977). *Computer data-base organization.* Englewood Cliffs, NJ: Prentice-Hall, Inc.

Moore-Jansen, P., Parker, S., & Million, M. (1981). *AMASDA site encoding manual* (Tech. Paper No. 1). Fayetteville: University of Arkansas, Arkansas Archeological Survey.

Newell, R.R., & Vroomans, A.P.J. (1972). *Automatic artifact registration and systems for archeological analysis.* Osterhout, The Netherlands: Anthropological Publications.

Peebles, C.S., & Galloway, P. (1981, May). *Notes from underground: Archaeological data management from excavation to curation.* Paper presented at the annual meeting of the Society for American Archaeology, San Diego.

Phillips, P. (1970). *Archaeological survey in the lower Yazoo Basin, Mississippi, 1949-1955* (Peabody Museum of Archaeology and Ethnology Papers No. 60). Cambridge: Harvard University.

Read, D.W. (1982). Toward a theory of archaeological classification. In R. Whallon & J. Brown (Eds.), *Essays on archaeological typology.* Evanston, IL: Center for American Archeology Press.

Scholtz, S., & Chenhall, R. (1976). Archeological data banks in theory and practice. *American Antiquity 41*, 89-96.

Spaulding, A.C. (1982). Structure in archaeological data: nominal variables. In R. Whallon & J. Brown (Eds.), *Essays on archaeological typology*. Evanston, IL: Center for American Archeology Press.

Struever, S. (1968). Woodland subsistence-settlement systems in the Lower Illinois Valley. In S. Binford & L.R. Binford (Eds.), *New perspectives in archeology*. New York: Aldine Publishing Co.

Voorrpis, A. (1982). Mambrino's helmet: A framework for structuring archaeological data. In R. Whallon & J. Brown (Eds.), *Essays on archaeological typology*. Evanston, IL: Center for American Archeology Press.

Whallon, R. (1972). The computer in archaeology: A critical survey. *Computers and the Humanities 7*, 29-45.

Whallon, R. (1982). Variables and dimensions: The critical step in quantitative typology. In R. Whallon & J. Brown (Eds.), *Essays on archaeological typology*. Evanston, IL: Center for American Archeology Press.

PART IV: REGIONAL ANALYSIS

6

Introductory Remarks on Regional Analysis

CHRISTOPHER CARR

The five chapters in this section discuss relevant structures of archaeological data on human settlement and subsistence at the regional scale. They also evaluate various analytic techniques (old and new) for their concordance with those structures.

The first three chapters, by Limp and Carr, Parker, and Kvamme, stand as a logically consistent unit. They present or employ a decision-making, theoretical framework for analyzing and explaining settlement or subsistence patterns. The authors assess several economic and statistical techniques (e.g., cost function analysis, statistical decision methods, kriging), which have previously been used in such analyses, for their congruence with the nature of the cognitive choice processes involved in settlement and subsistence behavior. They then present new methods (hierarchical choice analysis, multivariate logistic regression) that are often more concordant than the previous ones. The fourth chapter, by Keene, extends and qualifies these discussions by taking a partially Marxist viewpoint that stresses dialectics and the social domain. From this perspective, Keene critiques linear programming and other fine-grained analyses of subsistence that employ either a cognitive or evolutionary ecological framework. The final chapter, by Williams et al., is reprinted here in part to introduce the concept of the polythetic organization of behavior and archaeological entities, and one approach to the concept's methodological application. As a regional study, the work complements the use of the concept by Carr at the intrasite level (chapter 13).

THEORETICAL FOUNDATION

The chapter by Limp and Carr provides the primitive, conceptual foundation for this section. The authors present a highly generalized theory of rational choice. The alteration of several parameters in the theory allows the formulation of a continuum of more specific theories that range from a classical marginalist stance to set theoretic approaches that are useful in nonwestern situations. These theories vary in the particular assumptions that they make about three cognitive aspects of choice processes: 1) the level of detail of information that is assumed to be perceivable by or available to the decider (e.g., nominal or continuous scale distinctions), 2) the amount of information that is assumed to be processable by the decider, and 3) whether information is assumed to be processed sequentially or simultaneously.

The synthetic nature of the general theory of choice offers at least two benefits. First, by clarifying the three kinds of assumptions about choice processes that any specific economic theory or methodological application implicitly involves, it provides *dimensions* for evaluating the degree of logical concordance between theory, method, and phenomenon of interest/data. The authors summarize the relative restrictiveness of the assumptions of various theory-method pairings using these dimensions and discuss the approximate behavioral contexts in which such theory-method pairings are appropriate. Second, by defining the logical relationships among specific theories of rational choice, the general theory helps to resolve the apparent conflicts that are involved in the formalist-substantivist debate and the maximizer-satisficer debate. Through their explication of the general theory of choice, Limp and Carr show that in the first debate, marginalism (a specific form of choice process) has been confused with choice in general. In regard to the latter debate, the authors show that the concept of satisficing and its history of application have been misunderstood.

Two additional aspects of the chapter by Limp and Carr deserve to be highlighted. First, in considering how to evaluate an economic analysis, the authors distinguish between the logically concordant relationship that should exist between theory and method (what they term *etic coherence*) and that which should exist between a theory-method pairing and the phenomenon of interest (what they term *emic symmetry*). This distinction reiterates the two requirements for meaningful analysis that are discussed in the introduction of the volume. A second matter of importance that is discussed by the authors is the distinction between *physical properties* and *conditional preference aspects*. This distinction is critical to both developing a data base with a relevant subset structure and interpreting analytic results. When the variables that are used to describe observations are their physical properties, rather than their conditional preference aspects which were employed in the decision process, regularities in the decision process can be obscured. Moreover, it is inappropriate to conclude— solely on the basis of the predictability of a derived model of a decision process— that the variables that were chosen to describe observations capture their conditional preference aspects as envisioned by the deciders. The emic meaning of a set of variables requires rigorous validation with independent data, such as informant interviews. Finally, we may note that the distinction between physical properties and conditional preference aspects parallels Rappaport's (1979) distinction between *operational* and *cognized environments*, providing a natural bridge between economic and ecological theory.

METHODOLOGICAL ADVANCES

The chapters by Parker and Kvamme, in combination, present a new set of statistical procedures that allow the formulation of predictive models of settlement decision processes. Their approach offers three broad advantages over previous methods.

1) The approach takes the *land parcel* as the unit of analysis rather than the *site*, which has previously been used in settlement distributional studies (e.g., Struever, 1968) and catchment analysis (Vita-Finzi & Higgs, 1970). By considering all possible *alternative* locations of settlement—sites and nonsites—rather than simply settled locations, the method allows one to apply decision-making theoretical frameworks and techniques in evaluating settlement patterns. These techniques make it possible to (a) determine the relative importance of various biophysical attributes (and potential conditional preference aspects) of the landscape in determining settlement choice in a known area, (b) model the choice process, and thus (c) *generate* or predict settlement patterns in new landscapes rather than simply describe and *generalize* on the pattern of a known settlement distribution (Limp, 1981, p. 4). It allows the building of processual models and theory rather than rediscriptive ones.

2) The approach introduces the use of a statistical technique—*multivariate logistic regression (MLR)*—that concords reasonably well with settlement decision-making processes. (a) The familiar multivariate regression model involves a continuous dependent variable that ranges from $-\infty$ to $+\infty$. It thus is inappropriate for predicting the choice or nonchoice of a land parcel for settlement (site presence or absence), given the parcel's biophysical attributes as predictor variables. In contrast, a MLR model involves a dependent variable that is restricted in range from 0 to 1, and is therefore capable of representing the probability of choice or nonchoice of a land parcel. (b) The predictor variables in a MLR model can be nominal, ordinal, n-cotomized continuous, or continuous in nature. Thus, the *measurability* (Limp & Carr, chapter 7) of the biophysical attributes and potential conditional preference aspects of land parcels (predictor variables) can be controlled. This allows the formulation of a model that assumes a specified level of detail of the information available to and processable by the decider. (c) Also, in MLR, when working with nominal, ordinal, or n-cotomized continuous predictor variables, the number of distinct probability levels that is taken by the dependent variable can be controlled to some extent. This is achieved by specifying the number of predictor variables and number of states taken by each variable. In settlement analysis, the number of distinct probability levels represents the number of subsets of land parcels into which the global landscape set is divided and to which the decider is not

indifferent—the *k-fold partitioning parameter* (Limp & Carr, chapter 7) that represents the level of information accessible to and processable by the decider. Thus, the technique allows the formulation of a settlement selection model that assumes a choice structure and selection process that can range considerably in its degree of detail and determinism—from a set structure with a small number of partitions, which defines a highly stochastic selection process, to a continuously divisible structure, which defines a highly deterministic process in line with a marginalist stance. This flexibility is concordant with the general theory of choice that is presented in chapter 7 by Limp and Carr. (d) Unlike kriging and trend surface analysis, MLR makes no assumption about the *spatial continuity* (autocorrelation) of settlement. The predictor variables are landscape biophysical attributes, which may have patchy spatial distributions, rather than spatial coordinates which are autocorrelated. (e) One aspect of MLR that often may not be concordant with settlement decision processes—particularly in nonwestern contexts—is its *simultaneous* rather than *sequential hierarchical* consideration of multiple decision criteria (predictor variables). A hierarchical decision rule approach (Limp & Carr, chapter 7) may be more appropriate in this regard. However, this approach implies such a large calculation burden that it may not be feasible in most nontrivial archaeological applications (e.g., CRM projects). As a compromise between the conflicting needs for concordance and efficiency, a two-stage methodology can be used. This involves first using stepwise MLR to determine the approximate relative importance of various landscape attributes to the settlement choice process, and then incorporating only the more important attributes in alternative hierarchical decision tree models, which can be tested against each other in the manner illustrated by Limp and Carr (chapter 7).

3) The theoretical and methodological framework that is used by Parker and Kvamme allows a broad range of potential constraints on human settlement decisions to be evaluated for their importance: subsistence, constructional, psychological, social, and other factors (e.g., distance to plant food resources, soil drainage, locational exposure to natural hazards such as flooding or social hazards such as attack). In contrast, most previous decision-making analyses of prehistoric settlement choice (e.g., Jochim, 1976; Binford, 1980; Keene, 1981) have been limited to the investigation of potential causal factors in the subsistence domain. This limitation results from the fact that the settlement analyses have been *derived* from analyses and models of subsistence systems and their implications on the use of the environment and mobility.

The Multivariate Logistic Regression Approach in Total

The two chapters by Parker and Kvamme report or stress different aspects of the MLR approach in order to avoid redundancy. In total, the approach encompasses at least the following technical operations.

1) The sample of surveyed locations (sites and non-sites combined) is checked for its representativeness of the total range of environmental variation in the study area (or ecozone of interest; see below). This is done using K-S tests for continuous or ordinal variables and X^2 tests for discrete variables.
2) The significance of biophysical variables in determining settlement location is assessed. This is done in a stepwise manner, first with univariate (K-S and X^2) tests, then multivariate MPRR procedures, and finally MLR procedures.
3) Stepwise rather than simply static approaches to MLR procedures can be used.
4) The logistic regression model is validated statistically and tested in the field.
5) Probability surface maps of potential settlement locations can be generated with the MLR model.

Either random point location data or quadrat data on site presence/absence and environmental variation can be used to generate a MLR model. The model can be used simply as an aid for understanding settlement decision processes in an archaeologically known area, or it can be applied to biophysical data about an archaeologically unknown area for predictive purposes.

Comparison to Other Inductive Approaches to Predictive Modeling of Settlement Location

The framework for predictive modeling of settlement patterns that is used by Parker and Kvamme differs markedly from a variety of approaches that have been employed recently in CRM contexts in the western United States and have raised some controversy. These latter projects have used at least four methodologies (W. James Judge, personal communication, 1983).

1) *The density transfer method.* This approach involves the simple proportional transfer of site densities within an archaeologically known area to an unknown area of similar environment (e.g., Drager & Rice, 1983; Ebert & Gutierrez, 1979; Larralde & Nickens, 1980; Read & Nickens, 1980).

2) *The density regression method.* Here, site densities within *large* land units in an unknown area are predicted on the basis of a multiple regression between site density and biophysical features within large land units in a known area (e.g., Green, 1973; Kemrer, 1982; Nance et al., 1983). Large land parcels are defined here as those with dimensions greater than the minimum distance between sites and possibly including more than one site. Small land parcels are those of less area, not likely to include more than one site, as in Parker's and Kvamme's studies (chapters 8, 9, respectively). Either small quadrats or point locations fall in the latter class.

3) *The significance prediction method.* In this approach, an interval scale measure of the significance (CRM sense) of sites that are present within small land parcels in an unknown area is predicted. Zero significance is defined as site

absence. The prediction is made on the basis of a regression model that relates significance to biophysical predictors in small land parcels in a known area (James et al., 1983).

4) *Linear discriminant function analysis:* In this approach, site presence or absence in small or large land parcels in an unknown area is predicted. The prediction is based on a linear discriminant function analysis of the distribution of sites, nonsites, and biophysical attributes among land parcels in a known area (Holmer, 1979; Burgess et al., 1980; Larralde & Chandler, 1980; Peebles, 1981, 1983; Zier & Peebles, 1982).

Each of these approaches has one or more disadvantages that can be circumvented by using multivariate logistic regression in the manner of Parker and Kvamme.

The density transfer method allows the use of only categorical biophysical variables in predicting settlement location. It also does not allow one to determine which of the suite of biophysical attribute states that are shared in common by the known and unknown areas is responsible for site presence in a location; thus, it bring little understanding of the settlement decision *process*.

Neither the density transfer method nor the density regression method, in using large land parcels as the units of analysis, are concordant with settlement decision processes. Settlement decision processes involve locations of *restricted* area as logical alternatives as well as large ecotones. The importance of the idiosyncratic characteristics (e.g., shelter quality, view quality, slope) of small land parcels to the positioning of more permanent settlements is emphasized by Kvamme in his hierarchical spatial model of site selection. Also, in using large land parcels, neither method allows the prediction of *specific* locations that are likely to have or not have archaeological sites, which causes a problem for CRM planning. The use of large land parcels also poses operational problems in characterizing them for their biophysical attributes when they are internally heterogeneous (Lafferty et al., 1982, p. 66).

The significance prediction method represents an inappropriate application of multiple regression procedures. The model combines a dependent variable and independent variables that do not relate to each other as variables that define a single process. Biophysical attributes of a land parcel determine the preferability of the location for use in some manner and the presence or absence of a site type—not archaeological significance as an ad hoc polythetic composite index of site characteristics.

The linear discriminant function approach with small land parcels is closely related to the logistic regression method of Parker and Kvamme. It has the limiting assumptions, however, that the populations to be discriminated (e.g., sites and nonsites) are multivariate normal and have equal covariance matrices for the variables being investigated. It also does not allow the use of both continuous and discrete predictor variables in the same model (although discrete variables can be employed by themselves in kernel discriminant analysis).

Finally—and of greatest controversy in the use of predictive modeling—some studies of the above varieties (see Chandler & Nickens, 1983 for a summary of projects) have not taken into consideration the need to both statistically *validate* a predictive settlement model and to field *test* it prior to applying it to an unknown area for management purposes. This point is stressed by Parker. Also, some CRM studies, (e.g., Peebles, 1983, p. 9; Chandler & Nickens, 1983, p. 6-7) have suggested that predictive settlement models, alone—without field checks—be used to *determine* whether specific, archaeologically unknown locations can be cleared for development without significant impact on archaeological resources. This use is inappropriate, given the statistical rather than deterministic nature of both human settlement decision processes and the methods of analysis. A more appropriate role of predictive modeling in CRM would be as an aid, during the planning stages of compliance procedures, for *projecting* those areas of potential development that are less likely to include many significant sites. Berry (1984) and Ambler (1983) detail the abuses of predictive modeling of site location in CRM work.

Global vs. Local Analysis of Settlement Decision Process

The chapters by Parker and Kvamme differ in the geographic scales of the decision processes that the authors wish to consider and, thus, in certain aspects of the list of variables and the sample of location observations that they use. As Kvamme notes, a settlement process can be modeled as a hierarchy of decisions, with different levels pertaining to land units of different scales and to different kinds of preference aspects. The uppermost levels focus on broad alternative areas for settlement (e.g., ecozones) and the food and social advantages that they offer. The lowest levels are concerned with small alternative areas of actual occupation and their idiosyncratic characteristics that immediately affect occupation (e.g., slope, soil drainage, exposure). When a study area is moderately to strongly structured into geological and biophysical communities, such as the lifezones in Kvamme's study area or the various upland, terrace, and valley bottom ecozones in Parker's study area, it is possible to investigate at least two different levels of the settlement decision hierarchy for the area. One can ask, "What *ecozones* were more or less preferred for settlement for the food resources and social advantages that they offered?" Additionally, one can ask, "What specific locations *within* a given ecozone were more or less preferred for their characteristics that immediately affect occupation?"

The variables and observations (relevant subset structure) that are appropriate for a settlement decision analysis using MLR will vary, depending on whether one is interested in global, upper-level decision processes or local, lower-level decision processes. For a local analysis, variables that are concerned with local idiosyncratic characteristics that immediately affect occupation should be used. Only observations (locations) in the *same* ecozone should be included in the analyzed sample because only these represent logical *alternatives* to each other for exploitation or settlement. If local decision processes in multiple ecozones are of interest, a separate model should be built for each ecozone. In contrast, for a global analysis, variables that pertain to resource availability in broader catchments or to regional social advantages should be used. Locations from *multiple* ecozones, which are exploitation/settlement alternatives, should be included in the analyzed sample of observations, and one model that pertains to all ecozones should be built.

Kvamme is clearly interested in decision processes at the local level. The variables that he uses all pertain to local, idiosyncratic characteristics that immediately affect occupation (e.g., shelter, exposure, view, distance to water). Additionally, he discusses the preferability of formulating a separate model for each ecozone. In contrast, Parker is apparently interested primarily in global settlement decision processees. Most of the variables that she uses monitor biophysical community attributes (e.g., several soil characteristics, elevation, distance to upland/lowland ecotone, order of nearest stream). The positive or negative significance of these attributes in her model can be interpreted as the preferable or less preferable nature of various biophysical communities for use or settlement. Also, Parker builds one model pertaining to locations in all ecozones within her study area.

Both Kvamme's and Parker's analyses involve some incongruities between the variables or observations (subset data structure) that are used to model the decision processes of interest and the nature of the processes themselves. In each case, the problems arise from the small sample of site locations that is available for study and the necessity of lumping heterogeneous populations to proceed with analysis. In Kvamme's study, despite his interest in local decision processes within ecozones, and despite his use of a set of variables that monitor such processes, site and nonsite data from *multiple ecozones* were used to build a single MLR model. To keep this incongruence to a minimum, however, two steps were taken. 1) Analysis was restricted essentially to the more similar, lowland ecozones rather than allowed to include both lowland and mountain ecozones. This was done by weighting the sample of site and nonsite locations that were analyzed heavily toward the lowland ecozones, rather than proportional to the areas of each ecozone. 2) The relative proportion of sites and nonsites that were selected from each ecozone was held constant over zones (see Kvamme's chapter for a justification). In Parker's study, despite her interest in global decision processes that pertain to individual subsistence-settlement systems, site and nonsite data from *multiple systems* that reflect *different ecological adaptations* over time (hunter-gatherers and agriculturalists) were combined to build a single MLR model. In addition, a few of the variables that Parker used (e.g., soil depth to water, several measures of distance to water) pertain more to local decision processes than global ones.

In sum, Parker's and Kvamme's studies differ in whether the variables chosen for analysis pertain to global or local decision processes, whether observations from all portions of the environment or only some portions were selected for analysis, and whether environmental variation was sampled proportionally or disproportionally for those strata that were considered. These differences in the subset data structures that are assumed relevant by the authors reflect the different settlement decision processes of interest to them and the different analytic compromises that they had to make to study such processes.

The Future of Logistic Regression in Settlement Analysis

The chapters by Parker and Kvamme suggest several areas of concordance between method and data structure that need to be investigated more throughly and improved.

1) The method assumes that population density in the study area was great enough, or the study area was occupied long enough by peoples of a single settlement adaptation, that a high proportion of the locations in the most preferred attainable set were occupied. The method also assumes that the number of preferred but unsettled locations is small compared to the number of unpreferred, unsettled locations. These circumstances are necessary if the physical properties or potential conditional preference aspects that distinguish preferred from unpreferred settlement locations are to be determinable statistically. The robusticity of the approach in regard to these requirements needs investigation.

2) Related to the first point, it should not be expected that two environmentally similar areas, which are occupied by groups that had similar settlement decision frameworks, will be found in a MLR analysis to be characterized by a similar set of preference criteria. The results that are obtained will depend not only on the common decision framework that was used by the peoples in the two areas, but also on the relative population densities of the two areas and the degree to which less preferable locations of settlement had to be occupied in one area relative to the other. Different levels of the common decision tree hierarchy will possibly be evaluated if population densities differed much. This relationship between population density and decision analytic results needs to be investigated.

3) Both Parker's and Kvamme's studies use two kinds of variables: (a) *quadrat* characteristics that describe the nature of a particular land parcel or the immediate surroundings of a randomly chosen point (e.g., soil drainage within a unit), and (b) *absolute distance* characteristics that describe how far the land parcel lies from some desirable feature (e.g., distance to nearest permanent water). Settlement decisions among mobile and semimobile groups, however, often involve a third kind of variable, as well: *proportional distance* characteristics that describe the distance of a land parcel from one critical resource compared to its distance from another. Binford (1980) has documented the importance of this settlement characteristic among hunter-gatherers (collectors) in patchy to coarse-grained

environments in the mid to high latitudes. In these circumstances, settlements are often chosen so as to *equalize* the distances to critical resources relative to each other, rather than to minimize the absolute distance to any one resource. This aspect of settlement decision-making processes can be incorporated in a MLR analysis by including ratios of distances to critical resources among the list of variables that are analyzed. The ratios should be of the form:

$$\frac{\overline{XA} - \overline{XB}}{\overline{XA} + \overline{XB}}$$

where $\overline{XA}$ is the distance between location X and resource A and $\overline{XB}$ is the distance between location X and resource B. This form, rather than a simple ratio between absolute distances, is necessary for the variable to be definable in most cases (no division by zero, except when the two resources coincide at the site location) and a *linear* function of the absolute distance from either resource. In addition, the variable has a convenient restricted range, from -1 to $+1$.

Inasmuch as most environments have some resources with patchy or coarse grained distributions (e.g., lithic resources, animal migration routes, trade routes), the need for proportional distance characteristics of land parcels will have to be considered in most MLR applications.

4) Hunter-gatherer subsistence systems are characterized by reliance on diverse resources that are procured by multiple strategies in order to reduce the risk of not obtaining the food and raw material requirements of life at any one time (e.g., Lee, 1968, 1979; many citations in Jochim, 1976). Measures of food resource diversity within a one-day trip distance, two-day trip distance, etc., from a land parcel should therefore be considered for use in future MLR applications. The use of multiple measures of diversity, which consider multiple radii, is necessary to avoid the improbable assumption that hunter-gatherers exploit a catchment basin of one size for all resources (see next point).

5) As MLR applications become more sophisticated, involving measures of productivity of specific food resources as predictor variables (e.g., density of nut resources), care will have to be taken to avoid using a single size quadrat for measuring all resource potentials. Doing so would imply the erroneous assumption of a constant size catchment and constant production and transportation costs for all resources—a point stressed in chapter 7 by Limp and Carr. Other quadrat variables that do not involve a cost-production function (e.g., local drainage, susceptibility to attack) are not limited in this manner.

6) Future analysis will need to consider whether the prehistoric decision process that is to be modeled involved the *individual* natural characteristics of land parcels (e.g., nut productivity, soil drainage) or *constellations* of them that are regionally correlated (biophysical communities). Was settlement choice made in regard to individual landscape attributes or intercorrelating landscape attributes that define *dimensions* of variability? The answer to this issue will determine whether primary descriptions of the environment or their summary

dimensions (e.g., as obtained from a factor analysis; see Parker, 1981) should be used to build the decision model. Thus, the researcher is forced to consider how environmental variability was cognized at a *general* level.

As a means for solving this problem, it may be useful to consider ethnographic analogs that are selected on the basis of at least two criteria. These are: (a) whether the environment in the analogous circumstance has a *structure* similar to that of the landscape of interest (e.g., strong or weak dimensions of variability; many or few dimensions) and (b) whether the environment in the analog is similar in *content* to the landscape of interest (e.g., involves game animals and plant resources of similar sizes; behaviors; and habitats such as terrestrial, marine, or riverine).

7) Paralleling comments by Keene (chapter 10) on the limitations of linear programming models in subsistence analysis, we may note that the analysis of settlement decision processes using MLR makes it difficult to include social and political factors in the modeling process. In particular, it is difficult to relate site location choice to conditional preference aspects that pertain to the locations of other sites—as opposed to biophysical variables—unless the study area at large is well known archaeologically (W. James Judge, personal communication, 1983). Site clustering that results from dependence on central places (e.g., Cahokia, Pueblo Bonito), or voids in site distribution that result from the nucleation policies of central places (e.g., Teotihuacan) or border maintenance processes (e.g., Spencer, 1982) are some relevant factors that remain difficult to model.

This problem can be addressed to some minimal degree for complex societies by incorporating measures such as distances (absolute and proportional) to sites of various size classes and functions. It may be more difficult for simpler societies where the focal sites are less obvious, perhaps undiscovered, and possibly changed frequently over time with alliance structure. The problem can possibly be corrected to some degree in MLR applications that are concerned with modeling settlement decision processes in *known* study areas, but it does not seem solvable for CRM applications that are concerned with prediction in *unknown* areas. It is important that these two kinds of applications be distinguished in reference to this problem.

A more extensive discussion on some potential directions of development of MLR approaches to settlement decision modeling, and a critique of Parker's work, are provided by Carr (1981).

IN HISTORICAL PERSPECTIVE

The final chapter in this section, by Williams, Thomas, and Bettinger—though written ten years ago—is reprinted as a precocious effort to utilize several key concepts or methods that are discussed or qualified in other studies in the volume. 1) Williams et al. stress the *cyclical* nature of the scientific process, which Carr (chapter 2) discusses as a means for bringing concordance between theory, method, and data. This understanding of the scientific process stands in contrast to the more limited perspective—emphasizing the testing of hypotheses and explanation, through deduction—that preoccupied many archaeologists (e.g., Watson et al., 1971; Fritz & Plog, 1970) at the time that Williams et al. wrote their article. It should be noted, however, that the logical framework of Williams et al. oversimplifies the "deductive," hypothesis-testing phase of scientific logic, as have many other presentations. It does not acknowledge that the testing of a hypothesis through the analysis of complex data almost always requires inductive logic in addition to deductive logic, in order to successfully select relevant variables and cases and an appropriate analytic technique (see Carr, chapter 2).

2) The authors almost discover the appropriateness and the necessity of using the *land parcel*, rather than the site, as the unit of analysis in settlement pattern studies, as discussed by Parker and Kvamme. Williams et al. envision a fourfold contingency table that summarizes the environmental features of both site and nonsite locations. However, they are unable to realize an analysis in this format because they incompletely conceptualized the land parcel as a unit of analysis: they define preferable loci of settlement (locations that have more favorable biophysical characteristics) but not unpreferable loci. This mental framework, which is transitional between one that uses the site as the unit of analysis and one that uses the land parcel, clarifies how the former restricts one from applying a decision-making framework to the study of settlement patterns.

3) The chapter introduces the notion of *polythetic* organization—as opposed to monothetic organization—of entities. Following Clarke (1968, p. 35-38), the authors argue that envisioning and analyzing archaeological entities (e.g., archaeological cultures, settlement systems) as polythetic constructs has utility in two ways. (a) The real world—in this case, past human behavior—often operates in a polythetic rather than monothetic mode (chapter 11, p. 278). When such a condition holds, the analytic technique that is used should assume the polythetic organization of entities if it is to be concordant with the nature of the phenomenon of interest. This point is also made and emphasized by Carr in chapter 13, for intrasite analysis. (b) Regardless of whether a phenomenon of interest is organized polythetically or monothetically, envisioning it as polythetic can be helpful during early stages of analysis. It can allow the researcher to make explicit and operationalize intuitive impressions about the phenomenon until it becomes better known through analysis and perhaps becomes understandable in a monothetic framework (chapter 11, p. 279).

The approach to the study of archaeological entities as polythetic entities that is offered by Williams et al. differs in three ways from that presented by Carr in chapter 13. First, Carr stresses that polythetic or monothetic organization is a *natural aspect* of certain kinds of data, which results from the operation of specified *processes* under specifiable contexts. He explicitly seeks to enumerate the processes and contexts that determine those organizations for some kinds of artifact distributions within sites. In contrast, Williams et al. stress the utility of the polythetic concept as a *device* for operationalizing intuitions. They do not address the issue of whether settlement patterns and the behaviors and processes that generate them are polythetic in nature.

Second, Williams et al. employ the polythetic concept in its *fully* polythetic form (i.e., no attribute is necessary and sufficient for membership in a set), whereas Carr employs it as pertaining to any of a range of organizations that vary from fully polythetic through partially polythetic (some attributes may characterize all members of the set) to nearly monothetic. This difference stems from the different uses that the authors make of the concept, as previously mentioned. A fully polythetic organization can be used to define intuitive categories for which exceptions are anticipated across any attributes (Williams et al., chapter 11, p. 279), and thus is appropriate to Williams et al.'s concern for operationalizing intuitive classes. The definition of polythetic organization as any of a range of possible forms, on the other hand, allows the investigation of organizational variation as a function of variation in the kind and intensity of the processes that are responsible for organization—the intent of Carr's chapter.

Finally, Carr employs the concept of asymmetry as a fundamental organizational parameter that partially underlies the polythetic-monothetic continuum. This reflects Carr's interest in a continuum of organizational forms between the monothetic and fully polythetic extremes. In contrast, Williams et al., who have other purposes, do not use the concept of asymmetry.

REFERENCES

Amber, J.R. (1983). The use and abuse of predictive modeling in cultural resource management. *Contract Abstracts and CRM Archaeology 3*(3).

Berry, M.S. (1985). Sampling and predictive modeling on Federal lands in the West. *American Antiquity 49*(4), 842-852.

Binford, L.R. (1980). Willow smoke and dog's tails: Hunter-gatherer settlement systems and archaeological site formation. *American Antiquity 45*(1), 4-20.

Burgess, R.J., Kvamme, K.L., Nickens, P.R., Reed, A.D., & Tucker, G.C., Jr. (1980). *Class II cultural resource inventory of the Glenwood Springs resource area, Grand Junction district, Colorado* (Contract No. YA-512-CT9-222) submitted by Nickens and Associates. Grand Junction, CO: USDI Bureau of Land Management.

Carr, C. (1981). Review: Settlement prediction in Sparta. In R.H. Lafferty et al. Settlement prediction in Sparta [Monograph]. *Arkansas Archaeological Survey, Research Series, 14*, 263-278.

Clarke, D.L. (1968). *Analytical archaeology.* London: Methuen.

Chandler, S.M., & Nickens, P.R. (1983, April). *Regional sampling and predictive modeling in CRM: Some examples from the northern Colorado plateau.* Paper presented at the annual meetings of the Society for American Archaeology, Pittsburgh.

Drager, D.L., & Rice, P.M. (1983). *Environmental integration in archaeology.* Unpublished manuscript, National Park Service, Southwest Cultural Resource Center, Albuquerque, NM.

Ebert, J.I., & Gukierrez, A.A. (1979). Relationships between landscape and archaeological sites in Shenandoah National Park: A remote sensing approach. *APT, Bulletin of the Association for Preservation Technology 11*(4), 69-87.

Fritz, J., & Plog, F.T. (1970). The nature of archaeological explanation. *American Antiquity, 35*, 405-412.

Green, E.L. (1973). Location analysis of prehistoric Maya sites in northern British Honduras. *American Antiquity 38*, 279-293.

Homer, R.N. (1979). *Split Mountain cultural study tract* (Contract No. UT-080-CT9-003). Vernal District, UT: Bureau of Land Management.

James, S.A., Knudson, R., Kane, A.E. & Breternetz, D. (1983, April). *Predicting significance: A management application of high-resolution modeling.* Paper presented at the meetings of the Society for American Archaeology, Pittsburgh.

Jochim, M. (1976). *Hunter-gatherer subsistence and settlement: A predictive model.* New York: Academic Press.

Keene, A.S. (1981). *Prehistoric foraging in a temperate forest: A linear programming model.* New York: Academic Press.

Kemrer, M.F. (Ed.). (1982). *Archaeological variability within the Bisti-Star Lake Region, Northwest New Mexico.* Albuquerque: ESCA-Tech Corporation.

Larralde, S.L., & Chandler, S.M. (1981). *Archaeological inventory in the Seep Ridge cultural study tract, Uintah county, Utah, with a regional predictive model for site location* (Cultural Resource Series 11). Salt Lake City: Bureau of Land Management.

Larralde, S.L., & Nickens, P.R. (1980). *Archaeological inventory in the Red Wash cultural study track, Uintah County, Utah. In Sample inventories of oil and gas fields in eastern Utah, 1978-1979* (Cultural Resource Series, 5). Salt Lake City: Bureau of Land Management.

Lee, R.B. (1968). What do hunters do for a living, or, how to make out on scarce resources. In R.B. Lee & I. deVore (Eds.), *Man the hunter* (pp. 30-48). Chicago: Aldine Publishing Co.

Lee, R.B. (1979). *The !Kung San.* Cambridge: Cambridge University Press.

Limp, W.F. (1981). *Rational location choice and prehistoric settlement analysis.* Unpublished doctoral dissertation, Indiana University, Bloomington.

Nance, C.R., Holstein, H., & Hurst, D.C. (1983, April). *Evaluation of multiple regression models predicting archaeological site distributions at Fort McClellan, Alabama.* Paper presented at the annual meetings of the Society for American Archaeology, Pittsburgh.

Parker, S.C.S. (1981). Multivariate assessment. In R.H. Lafferty et al. Settlement prediction in Sparta [Monograph]. *Arkansas Archaeological Survey Research Series, 14*, 143-162.

Peebles, T.C., (1983, April). *Discriminant analysis in site predictive models: Problems and prospects.* Paper presented at the annual meetings of the Society for American Archaeology, Pittsburgh.

Peebles, T.C. (Ed.). (1981). *A Class II cultural resources inventory of the eastern Powder River Basin, Wyoming*, (Submitted by Metcalf-Zier Archaeologists, Inc.). Cheyenne: USDI Bureau of Land Management.

Rappaport, R.A. (1979). *Ecology, meaning, and religion.* Richmond, CA: North Atlantic Books.

Read, A.D., & Nickens, R.R. (1980). *The Cisco cultural resource study: A sample-oriented inventory, east-central Utah. In Sample inventories of oil and gas fields in eastern Utah, 1978-1979* (Cultural Resource Series, 5). Salt Lake City: Bureau of Land Management.

Struever, S. (1968). Woodland subsistence-settlement systems. In S.R. Binford & L.R. Binford (Eds.), *New perspectives in archaeology* (pp. 285-312). Chicago: Aldine Publishing Co.

Spencer, C. (1982). *The Cuicatlán Cañada and Monte Albán: A study of primary state formation.* New York: Academic Press.

Vita-Finzi, C., & Higgs, H.S. (1970). Prehistoric economy in the Mount Carmel area of Palestine: Site catchment analysis. *Proceedings of the Prehistoric Society, 36*, 1-37.

Watson, P.J., LeBlanc, S.A., & Redman, C.L. (1971). *Explanation in archaeology.* New York: Columbia University Press.

Zier, A.H., & Peebles, T.C. (1982). *Report on the Kemmerer resource area Class II cultural resource, inventory, Lincoln and Uinta counties, Wyoming* (Unpublished manuscript submitted by Metcalf-Zier Archaeologists, Inc.) Rock Spring, WY: USDI Bureau of Land Management.

7

The Analysis of Decision Making: Alternative Applications in Archaeology

W. FREDRICK LIMP
CHRISTOPHER CARR

> Anthropologists should study Economics and vice versa. I do agree with Gluckman that this should be done not to make the anthropologist an economist, but a better anthropologist. Given economic tools, he will improve anthropology. Give an economist the anthropological tools of sensitivity to what people say and of readiness to try to see order in different conceptual systems, and he may improve economics.
>
> Richard Salisbury

> Do I contradict myself? Very well then, I contradict myself. I am large, and I contain multitudes.
>
> Walt Whitman

Much archaeological investigation focuses on the discovery of patterning in archaeological evidence, and the explanation of such patterning as the result of human actions and site formation processes. Ultimately, however, this level of analysis serves only as an intermediary to larger, theoretical questions of the nature of the human actions that gave rise to the patterns.

The diversity of theories explaining human actions define a continuum with respect to the impact of human decisions on behavioral patterning. At one end are largely traditional theories, stressing the constraints placed on human action by social, cultural, or biological processes. In archaeology these have their most forceful expression in various classificatory or typological ap-

---

A large number of people gave willingly of their data and ideas. In particular, we would like to thank Andrew Christenson, Ray Druhot, James Denbow, Timothy Earle, Thomas Green, Cheryl Munson, Art Keene, and Sandra Parker. Special appreciation is extended to Patrick Munson, Harold Schneider, Paul Jamison, and Thomas Jacobson; and James Kellar of the Glenn Black Laboratory of Archeology who generously supported part of the research reported here. Van Reidhead made available important cost data and contributed significantly to the ideas developed.

proaches, to both archaeological materials and the behavior that generated them. At the other end are theories that focus on individual and group choice making.

In this chapter regularities in choice making are seen as the fundamental process underlying the regularities of human behavior, and thus, much of archaeological patterning. Unlike previous archaeological applications of economic theory, however, the approach taken here is more general, emphasizing a diversity of theoretical and methodological frameworks to be used in varying contexts, yet integrated within a single general theory of rational choice.

Many theories of human decision making, which previously have been applied in archaeology, derive largely from economic geography and/or marginalist economic literature. These theories often require major assumptions to be made about the information-processing ability and calculation capability of the prehistoric peoples being studied. Methodologies based on these theories commonly require data not obviously consistent with "non-market" economies. At the other extreme, many archaeologists, rightly dissatisfied with the magnitude and implications of these assumptions and data requirements, have proposed alternatives, such as the "satisficer" approach.

In this chapter an intermediate view is proposed: that previous problems in the application of economic theory to prehistoric (or nonwestern) situations result largely from the attempt to apply not a general theory of "rational economic man" but a specific theory of "marginal economic man." From this perspective, this chapter has four purposes:

1) The basic concepts and axioms of a truly general theory of rational choice will be introduced. It will be shown that this theory, with the variation of certain of its parameters, is capable of being transformed into a continuum of more specific economic theories: the marginalist stance, applicable to market economies at one end, and other approaches more appropriate to "non-market" economies at the other. The different theories posit different structures of the rational choice process, dependent on the information access and measurement capabilities of the decision units.

2) The concepts of marginalism, satisficing man, and least effort will be placed in a historic perspective within the literature of economics and anthropology. This will clarify where arguments for and against these frameworks currently being made by archaeologists—many of whom are apparently unaware of the history of these ideas—are misguided, too narrow, or out of date.

3) It will be shown that the inclusiveness and flexibility of general choice theory can be operationalized through a variety of analytical methods consistent with various structures of rational choice. This is one of the most powerful aspects of the economic approach.

4) Recent economic studies in archaeology illustrating the various analytical methods will be discussed and then evaluated for the logical consis-

tency between the methods used, the specific manifestation of rational choice theory assumed, and the nature of their data.

In viewing the history of development of economic theory and its adoption first in social and cultural anthropology and then in archaeology, the simple sequence of events clearly indicates the excellent future potential of rational choice theories in archaeology. In the same way that the precepts of logical positivism swept first through chemistry and physics, then through the social sciences, and inevitably led to the "new archaeology," a similar ordering pertains to rational choice. In the case of logical positivism, it is clear that archaeologists rushed to the polemic ramparts even as the physicists were realizing its weaknesses and attempting to develop a new synthesis, integrating positivist rigor and order with an almost metaphysical humility in the face of the awesome complexity of atomic particles. We as archaeologists should be particularly skilled at learning from hindsight and be cautious not to again grasp a falling standard of the intellectual battlefield. Rather, we can hope, as we view the potential of rational choice theories, that our desire for precision and rigor does not blind us to the even more troubling complexities of human behavior. It is in this context that the following is presented.

A PHILOSOPHICAL PERSPECTIVE: FUNDAMENTAL CHARACTERISTICS OF ANY THEORY RELEVANT TO ARCHAEOLOGY

To be parsimonious and testable with archaeological data, a theory of rational choice, like any theory, must have characteristics that are more restrictive than those of the theories of other scientific disciplines. This restriction results from certain limitations inherent in archaeological data. First, the archaeological context provides few, if any, possibilities for controlled experimentation to be used in testing the propositions deduced from a theory. It is difficult enough to isolate and estimate behavioral variables and parameters from archaeological measures, let alone hold them constant. For example, in most archaeological data sets, the variable, time, cannot be controlled well. Chronometric control sufficient to isolate data suitable for time-series or cross sectional analysis is rarely feasible (cf. Wolfman, 1983; Braun, chapter 16). Thus, an archaeologically relevant theory must be of a form that allows its testing in a manner different from controlled experimentation.

Second, because archaeological materials at a particular location may have derived from different activities at different times, yet cannot easily be assigned after the fact to different times, a few processes can generate a great diversity of site forms in various combinations. For example, from the two kinds of processes, settlement by nut processors and settlement by deer hunters, three kinds of sites can be produced: those indicating only nut processing, those indicating only deer hunting, and those indicating both as a result of alternate settlement of the same locations by nut processors and then deer hunters. The complexity increases exponentially with the number of disjoint activities considered. Thus, theories dealing with the *form* of archaeological remains are apt to be less parsimonious than those dealing with the *processes* by which archaeological remains are generated. An archaeologically relevant theory, then, should focus on behavioral process rather than archaeological form.

These two characteristics of an archaeologically relevant theory are met by the characteristics of Fredric Barth's "generative" theory:

> . . . form in social life is constituted by a series of regularities in a large body of individual items of behavior. Much effort in social anthropology has been concentrated on the necessary step of constructing models or patterns descriptive of such forms, whereby structural features of the society are exhibited. The kinds of models which I discuss here are of a different kind. They are not designed to be homologous with observed social regularities; instead they are designed so that they, by specific operations, can *generate* such regularities or forms. They should be constituted of a limited number of clearly abstracted parts, the magnitude or constellations of which can be varied, so that one model can be made to produce a *number of different forms*. Thus by a series of logical operations, forms can be generated, these forms may be compared to empirical forms of social systems, and where there is correspondence in formal feature between the two, the empirical form may be characterized as a particular constellation of the variables in the model (Barth, 1966, p. v).

Barth goes on to note that "the logical operations should mirror actual, empirical processes which can be identified in the reality being analyzed" (1966, p. v). Such theories permit explanation of forms because they deal with the generative processes underlying forms.

Moreover, a generative theory, in generating forms and thus implying what forms are "possible" and "impossible," defines a set of hypotheses that may be used to falsify the theory (or portions of it) with comparative data (1966, pp. v-vi). This process has the methodological equivalent of controlled experimentation, which is necessary for theory testing and modification.

Generative theories have additional assets. In generating multiple forms, the evaluation process can be based on the comparison of the degree of contradiction of two or more alternative hypotheses with the data, rather than a situation in which one either accepts or rejects the single alternative (Dean, 1978, p. 113). The existence of two or more alternatives can serve to remove the possibility of fixation on one approach which the researcher feels bound to support.

In addition to the properties proposed by Barth, an essential feature of an effective generative theory should include the ability to structure an axiomatic or algorithmic form (model). As von Bertalanffy has so cogently noted:

... an algorithm ... wins a life of its own as it were. It becomes a thinking machine, and once the proper instructions are fed in, the machine runs by itself, yielding unexpected results that surpass the initial amount of facts and given rules, and are thus unforeseeable by the limited intellect who originally has created the machine. (1955, p. 259).

The structuring of the generative theory as an axiom or algorithm has a number of significant implications, including precise stipulation of the parameters, variables, and relationships even when the solution generated lacks such precisions (Clarke, 1972, p. 35; Keene, chapter 10).

Like all theories, a generative theory should have several additional characteristics. First, it should produce "unpredictable" predictions. Second, the predictions should be capable of refutation. If the generative theory predicts circumstances which either must always exist by definition, or alternately, have no operationalizable means of refutation, then the theory is inappropriate. As Friedman (1953) has stressed, this refutability or capability of contradiction is essential. Third, the theory should be "explanatory" rather than "descriptive." As Clarke has cogently pointed out (though perhaps with another goal in mind) it would be possible to formulate a theory which, based on prior knowledge of the factors to be considered, "predicts" what is known (1972, p. 2). As a practical example, an archaeologist finding that sites in an area are often close to water sources might "predict" that all sites are close to water. Finally, the axiomatic or algorithmic representation of a generative theory must be a simplified analogy of reality, following Occam's Razor. Belief that the algorithmic representation of a generative theory is identical with the processual details of reality is "a methodological fallacy" (Machlup, 1967, p. 11). In the case of rational choice theory, it would be a mistake to equate a mathematical model of the decision-making process with the mental processes or group dynamics involved in such behavior (Arrow, 1951).

A GENERAL THEORY OF RATIONAL CHOICE

In this section, a general theory of rational choice, concordant with the characteristics of an effective generative theory as just described, will be introduced. The theory is essentially that derived by Arrow (1951) and discussed by Walsh (1970). The theory does not imply the constraints of the marginalist approach, though its parameters may be defined so as to generate this approach. To illustrate the concepts to be introduced, the process of settlement location selection will be used. Any decision area, however, could have been considered.

Preference, Ordering, and Selection

The basic proposition of a general theory of rational choice is that individuals and groups order or rank alternative courses of action into sets, termed *preference sets*. Selection of an alternative then is made from the highest ordered preference set that is *attainable*. This simple statement defines the essential features of "rational" choice: preference, ordering, and selection.

Sets

The set of all alternatives is termed the *global choice set*. Using the settlement selection process as an example, the global choice set would simply include all locations in the area of study.

All alternatives in the global set can be *partitioned* or divided into *attainable* and *unattainable* sets. These two sets are subsets of the global set, and membership in either is based on the *givens* or structural parameters of the situation. For example, consider the partitioning of a group of locations into attainable and unattainable sets on the basis of the attainability of the nut resources that they support. For a particular processing technique (e.g., hand cracking of nuts using nutting stones), we can propose that the time/effort involved in processing nuts, as well as transportation costs, cause only locations within 8 km of the nut groves to be within our example's attainable set. Clearly what is attainable is potentially alterable, as the givens change. If a new technology allowing more rapid processing of nuts or more rapid transportation became available, then our previous attainable set of locations would be substantially increased. This seemingly obvious idea has great potential for archaeology because, at any particular point in time, one of the primary elements in defining at least material attainable sets is available technology.

Because of this relationship between attainability and parameters such as technology, rational choice theory has the necessary concurrent aspects of synchrony and diachrony needed in an archaeologically relevant theory. When the parameters are held constant, the theory is primarily synchronic. As the parameters are permitted or caused to vary, the approach can become diachronic. For archaeology, which deals with both temporal and spatial variation, it is desirable to avoid theoretical frameworks in which a different theory is required in different situations—a diachronic theory versus a synchronic one. Rational choice theory subsumes both.

The formal notation of set theory can be used to organize these intuitive ideas. First, the set of all x in the choice set that are attainable can be indicated by

$$(x \in C / Ax)$$

where C is the global choice set. A is the property of attainability. Conversely, the unattainable x comprise the set

$$(x \in C / -Ax)$$

Using set notation, preference and indifference relationships can also be proposed. These are:

(1) $x_0 \, P \, x_1$
(2) $x_0 \, I \, x_2$

In the first case we state that x_0 is *preferred* to x_1. If given the choice between x_0 and x_1, the chooser always will take x_0. In the second case, the chooser is *indifferent* to either x_0 or x_2. He sees no differences between x_0 and x_2 or finds the differences between the two of no merit. Thus, he will take either x_0 or x_2, and does not care which one. Over a series of choices, he might choose either x_0, or x_2 randomly. Note that the indifference relationship does not imply that x_0 and x_2 are *identical* (though they may be), only that the chooser is *indifferent* to whatever differences may exist.

A further concept that should be introduced at this point is *transitivity*:

If $x_1 \, P \, x_2$ and $x_2 \, P \, x_3$
then $x_1 \, P \, x_3$

In short this concept indicates a logical consistency.

Much more elegant and extensive discussions of the properties of rational choice are available in Walsh (1970, pp. 77-87) and Newman (1965, pp. 10-45). However, the fundamental, essential ones are illustrated above. The remainder of the theory can logically be derived largely from such simple axioms.

With these primitive relationships we can return to the original concept of the attainable set. This set can now be subdivided—partitioned—into a series of subsets, which can be placed in a preference order. In our example, we could define subset N_1 as all locations within close proximity to the nut source (e.g., 1-3 km), N_2 as those intermediate (e.g., 3-6 km), and N_3 as those distant (e.g., more than 6 km). This partitioning is based on the physical properties of the locations.

The next step is to *induce an ordering* based on the relative preference of the sets of locations. One obvious order would be

$N_1 \, P \, N_2$ and $N_2 \, P \, N_3$

If this were the ordering, then any member of the subset N_1 would be selected, at random.

Physical Properties and Conditional Preference Aspects

Ordering of partitioned sets is based on the *conditional preference aspects* of the items in each set. A conditional preference aspect is a relevant choice-making characteristic of some physical property of an item; it is not isomorphic with the physical property. As an example, we can consider some potential, conditional preference aspects of the physical property, proximity to a permanent stream, for a location.

Physical Property	Potential Conditional Preference Aspects
Proximity to permanent stream	1) Access to domestic water 2) Access to transportation

3) Access to extensive aquatic food resources
4) Increased exposure to raiding parties

In short, a person does not prefer a location simply because of its physical properties. Rather a person prefers a location because of any single or combination of the conditional preference aspects of its physical properties.

A brief, intentionally simple example will illustrate the relevance of this distinction. If for a specific group of locations a significant preference aspect is access to transportation, then a number of physical properties might have the same choice-making aspects: nearness to a major overland trail, as well as proximity to a permanent stream. Conversely, locations near cut-off lakes with no outlets would be avoided. If we focus on only the physical property, nearness to permanent water, rather than the conditional preference aspect, access of transportation, then the fundamental choice-making *regularity* would be obscured. The apparently similar physical properties, proximity to a permanent stream and proximity to a cut-off lake with no outlet, have quite different conditional preference aspects. Again, we would be misled to focus on the physical properties.

Distinguishing a physical property from its conditional preference aspects emphasizes a further critical feature of the approach used here. The determination of a location's physical properties is essentially based on readily observable, *reproducible* physical referents. A physical feature of a location, such as number of meters from a water source, can be determined with equal facility by any individual. On the other hand, the assessment that, say, a high preference ordering is given to the conditional preference aspect, ease of access to domestic water, is not subject to similar easy evaluation.

Thus, reviewing the choice process, particular physical features are selected for partitioning the global choice set into subsets on the basis of their conditional preference aspects. The subsets are then ordered into a preference order based on the aspects defining them, and an alternative is selected from the highest attainable subset.

Dimensional and Primary Physical Properties

Some physical properties can be termed *dimensional* physical properties. A dimensional physical property is one in which the physical property is itself a complex variable including a number of *primary* physical properties. An example of a dimensional physical property is soil type.

Primary properties can, at least conceptually, be treated as isolated variables. It is possible to define all locations within, e.g., 100 meters of a domestic water supply, while concurrently holding the other primary variables constant, that is, controlling them independently. Dimensional variables, on the other hand, cannot be treated as isolated variables. A dimensional property can conceptually be decomposed into a number of primary physical variables, but these may not be controlled independently. This division of dimensional and primary physical properties to some extent parallels Plog et al.'s proposals for the separation of "intervening" and "independent" variables (1978, p. 183).

Production Frontiers and Trade-Offs

In our nut example, it might be preferable to choose either a location at which it is possible to produce the maximum nut harvest or one from which it is possible to achieve a desired level of harvest in the minimum time. Both preference aspects would give the same initial ordering of locations:

$$N_1 \, P \, N_2 \text{ and } N_2 \, P \, N_3$$

To create a more interesting example, we can propose that two features of a location are relevant to the decision process by adding a second resource, access to fish. With these two elements, it now becomes possible to make *trade-offs* in the preference ordering. Many locations near nut sources may be far from fish, and the converse. From a group of locations, production of various mixes of fish and nuts is possible. The production frontier (PF_1) shown on Figure 1 illustrates one array of possible combinations. From a subset of one or a group of locations, it may be possible to produce a maximum of 10 units of nuts but no fish (A), or 5 units of fish but no nuts (B), or various combinations such as at point C on PF_1, where eight units of nuts and one of fish are possible. All of the subsets of locations corresponding to the various production mixes along PF_1 are equally preferred with respect to the total production of calories they offer. For this conditional preference aspect, the decision unit would be indifferent to these alternatives. If additional aspects were involved, such as the preferable flavor of fish or nuts, then a new ordering would be appropriate.

A second group of locations, possibly at greater distances from the resources, have a lower production frontier, PF_2. At these locations, which again vary in the mix of nuts and fish they offer, a lower total caloric yield of nuts and fish may be produced. All the locations represented by PF_2 are less preferable than those represented by PF_1 with regard to the total production of calories they offer, but not necessarily in regard to the individual amounts of nuts or fish they offer.

Production of the mix of nuts and fish at point C on the production frontier may be attainable from *one* location or a *group* of locations, depending on the physical distributions of the resources. Thus, a number of different physical locations may correspond to a particular point on a curve. All the locations which correspond to a given point have the same conditional preference aspect for that combination of nuts and fish, though they, in fact, may be widely distributed across the landscape.

It is now possible to propose that certain constraints may be placed in the problem. Let us suppose that a particular level of protein is needed. Since both nuts and fish produce protein, though in differing proportions, a line can be drawn, DD_1, representing the various mixes of fish and nuts which have this

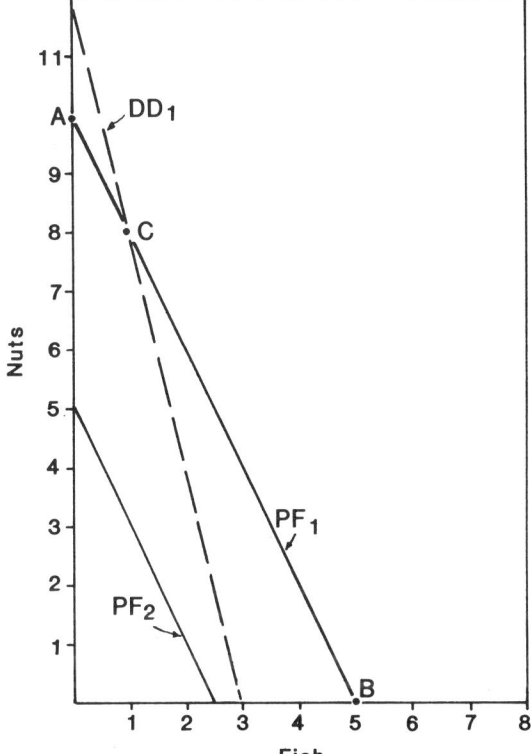

Fig. 7.1. Production frontiers and trade-offs for combinations of nuts and fish.

level of protein. All locations producing quantities to the left of the line have a lower preference order because they do not produce the appropriate level of protein. Locations represented by mix combinations to the right of the line are more preferred. Point A, for example, is on the higher production frontier for calories but falls lower in its preference ranking due to the reduced protein attainability.

Altering Production Parameters and Constraints

The attainability of any subset of locations depends on the *parameters of production*. In most archaeological problems, these parameters will include technology, environmental conditions, and the social organization of technology and labor. For example, continuing from the above illustration, suppose than an inefficient technology for nut gathering is used, requiring that a long time be spent in the gathering process. If a new technology improving the gathering time is then introduced, the production set frontier will be expanded. If the constraint on required protein remains the same, the attainable set will expand. Conversely, suppose a deterioration in the environment caused a reduction in the density of this food source. The attainable set would shrink. Similarly, changes in social organization, perhaps effecting the make-up of work groups and their productivity, could also alter the attainable set.

Alteration of system constraints, like alterations of production parameters, may change the attainability of subsets. For instance, a second constraint, such as group-spacing issues, might be added to the above case. This might have the effect of further reducing the attainable set.

Measurability and Marginality

In the most recent version of our example, we have suggested that very careful comparison between the units (locations) in terms of their productivity is possible. The ordering of *each* individual unit in relation to all others is possible, with the exception of exact ties, based on the exact same mix potential (e.g., exactly 5.0 units of nuts and 2.5 units of fish). In other words, it has been assumed that the *measurability* of the conditional preference aspects of items is great. For example, if there were 100 locations, then the chooser could distinguish among the conditional preference aspects of each of the 100 locations and rank them to form a preference order. If such an ordering were done, the theory would then predict that the highest ordered—optimal—location would be selected for a settlement.

In general, the degree to which any attainable subset of units may be partitioned into subsets of various preference is based on the measurability of the units' conditional preference aspects. If minor differences are measurable, then very subtle differences can be used to order the alternatives. As measurability decreases, the number of units that are "alike," i.e., to which the chooser is indifferent, increases. Detailed measurability is an assumption that typifies neoclassical, marginalist economic approaches.

As will be seen below, detailed measurability of the conditional preference aspects of a global set of units implies that great amounts of knowledge are accessible to the selector. Even in the very simple example just presented, we can see that complex and massive amounts of information would have to be examined to fully order the 100 locations. This circumstance would become even more overwhelming if we increased the number of conditional preference aspects considered for all locations. It is this type of information processing requirement, which is involved in the marginalist assumption of infinite measurability and in the assumptions behind the techniques used by marginalists, that has lead many to question the appropriateness of this approach in non-western situations.

Within the umbrella of general choice theory, however, it is not necessary to assume detailed measurability and ordering of *each* alternative. Rather, it is only necessary that each alternative be capable of being placed within an ordered *set*. These sets could simply be "good," "better," and "best" locations. *All* locations would have to be classifiable, but only into a subset; within the subset, no further ordering would be necessary. There might be ten locations in the "best" subset which are, in fact, *different*, but among which the differences are such that the chooser is indifferent.

When it is possible to order alternatives only among sets, not within them, the theory predicts that the alternative selected will be one from the most preferred set, the particular alternative chosen *at random* from those within it. In our settlement example, suppose that there are 100 locations, which can be ordered among three preference sets. The theory would predict that of the three subsets, a member of the highest ordered set will be selected. The *specific* location selected within that set cannot be predicted; this aspect of selection is a random process. The probability of any given member of the set being chosen is just the relative frequency of each location. If there were 10 locations within the most preferred set, then the theory would predict the probability of a given location being selected from it as $p = 0.1$, or one in ten. This compares to a probability of $p = .01$ of selecting a member of the global set without the ordering process. Thus, the theory allows the prediction of the alternative chosen with increasing probability as the choice process is better understood. Also, the theory specifies that as the chooser becomes more knowledgeable, choice may become more particular.

We can now see that a general theory of rational choice can have both deterministic and stochastic attributes. The theory predicts with $p = 1.0$ that a selection will be made from a specific partitioned set. Within that set, however, the probability of any specific unit being selected is a function of the number of units in the subset.

Implications of Variable Measurability

The measurability of the conditional preference aspects of a group of alternatives may be detailed or not, allowing their division and ordering into any number of subsets. In the example above, the number might range from 1 to 100. This fact may seem so obvious as to be trivial, but its implications on the process of ordering are of fundamental and overwhelming significance.

In particular, the measurability of conditional preference aspects and the degree to which a global set can thereby be partitioned has a behavioral or decision-making correlate. It represents the *information accessibility* and *processing capabilities* of the person(s) doing the ordering. Where much information about each alternative is available, and when the individual has the capability and desire to process this information, it becomes possible to make very subtle ranking variations.

This relationship between the measurability of conditional preference aspects and the nature of the decision-making process has methodological implications. Often, selection of an appropriate quantative methodology for analysis is seen as a function of the type of data available to the researcher. Certain methods, for example, are appropriate for interval data. What is perhaps not so obvious is that the selection of a methodology for the study of human decision making is inextricably interlinked to the nature of the emic choice process. As part of the decision process, the attainable choice set may have been partitioned into only a limited number of subsets. If this is the case, then, even though interval data may be available to the researcher, analysis using interval scale data and techniques may lead to spurious results. This circumstance has been demonstrated graphically in a study by H. Gladwin in his comparison of an additive vs. hierarchical decision rule (1975), as well as a number of other ethnographic studies (C. Gladwin, 1975, 1979, 1980; Johnson, 1978; Chibnik, 1980; H. Gladwin & Murtaugh, 1980).

Thus, the nature of the choice processes that generate an economic data set must be considered when assessing the methodologies appropriate for the analysis. When the measurability of conditional preference aspects is detailed and the global set can be partitioned minutely, methods requiring continuously divisible data, such as production function analysis, or linear programming are appropriate. As the selector's distinctions become more vague, techniques such as statistical decision analysis, decision trees, and hierarchical choice approaches become appropriate. This desirable relationship between choice process and analytic technique is one aspect of the concept of *emic symmetry*, to be discussed below.

K-fold Partitioning

It is possible to control the degree of measurability, information assessability, and processing capabilities assumed in a decision-making analyses by specifying the number of sets into which the global set is to be partitioned, that is, *k-fold partitioning* of the global set. The number of subsets k now becomes a measure of the continuity between the marginalist view of resources as factors having continuous, infinitely variable and perceptible properties, and that of binary choice. As the value of k approaches some small value, the character of choice moves from the marginalist position to a simple binary view.

We must be cautious in assuming for nonwestern contexts that detailed, k-fold decision processes do not occur because they are complex.

As Blumer has emphasized: "From the vantage point of the *particular human community*, living in a restricted geographical area, and over a restricted period of time there, there are very evident discontinuities in nature, that is, in living flora and fauna; and perception of certain of these is vital to human survival" (Blumer, 1970, p. 1083).

That the properties of any choice should be subject to a degree of discrimination greater than that resulting from a binary present/absent dichotomization is not, therefore, surprising. Even a cursory examination of the linguistic evidence illustrates this fact. In Byington's (1915) dictionary of the Choctaw language, for example, the following relative "frequency" terms may be noted:

ikshoka amohmi:	there is none at all
key uchohmi:	rare
ikchito:	scant; not great
achafoa:	a few and scattering, not many rare
apakna:	plenteous, abundant, copious
chitto:	less than chito
chito:	large, big, huge, immense, heavy, capacious, august, egregious, enormous, extensive

Thus, we should not automatically dismiss the emic capabilities of individuals to perform complex analysis.

In summary, by varying the number of sets into which the alternatives in the global set are classified, it is possible to generate, from the *general* theory of rational choice, more specific theories of the choice process. At the one end of the continuum (where k is large) stands neoclassical marginalist theory. At the other end (for small k) stands the set theoretic approach, or what will hereafter be termed axiomatic set theory.

Evaluation of the Relevance of the General Theory of Rational Choice to Archaeology

In the opening of this chapter, it was suggested that an archaeologically relevant theory should have the attributes of a generative theory, as well as additional features common to all theories. These characteristics include 1) being composed of a limited number of defined, measurable elements and interrelationships (e.g., axioms); 2) the ability to *generate* a diversity of possible archaeological forms and specify those that are possible and not possible under the theory, providing hypotheses that may be used to test the theory (as opposed to the experimental approach requiring the control of variables); 3) the ability to develop algorithms which are capable of modelling the theory, thus expediting the generation of alternative forms; 4) the prediction of "unpredictable" forms or relationships; 5) making refutable predictions; and 6) being explanatory, rather than redescriptive.

Each of these characteristics of an archaeologically relevant theory pertains to the general theory of rational choice outlined above. 1) The general theory of rational choice is well grounded and logically expanded from a limited number of axioms. Although only a limited number of axioms have been discussed here, readable and more complete discussions are provided by Walsh (1970) and Newman (1965). 2) The axiomatic formalizations focus on the process of decision making, as opposed to the forms generated by such processes. A variety of forms can be generated by adjusting the parameters of each empirical application of the theory (e.g., the number of partitions of the global set allowed). 3) Alternative algorithms allowing the generation of alternative forms are a natural outgrowth of the formal structure. As will be discussed below, a diversity of algorithmic formulations and analytical techniques may be used, implying differences in the information accessibility and processing capabilities of the selector, and other parameters of the decision-making process. 4) The unpredictability and 5) refutability of the predictions made by general choice theory will be illustrated in examples below. 6) The explicit, logical chain of derivations from axiom to prediction lends support to the explanatory power rather than rediscriptive nature of the approach, when the predictions concord with the evidence.

HISTORICAL PERSPECTIVE: DECISION ANALYSIS IN ARCHAEOLOGY, ANTHROPOLOGY, AND ECONOMICS

Since the mid 1970s there has been an increasing interest and application of a variety of economic theories and methodologies in archaeology. The increasing use of decision analysis models has engendered the beginnings of a lively debate. Unfortunately, the debate is largely a replay of those which arose in sociocultural anthropology in the 1960s, and/or in economics during the 1950s. There are two components to this debate: the formalist-substantivist arguments and the arguments for and against the view of "man, the satisficer."

The Formalist-Substantivist Debate

The essentials of the first argument will elicit a sense of *deja vu* among those familiar with the "formalist-substantivist" debates in anthropology in the 1960s and early 1970s (see Belshaw, 1965; Berliner, 1962; Bohannan & Dalton, 1962; Burling, 1962; Cancian, 1966; Dalton, 1961, 1963; LeClair, 1962; LeClair & Schneider, 1968; Sahlins, 1969; Schneider, 1970, 1974) because the arguments are essentially the same. The arguments of the 1960s fundamentally revolved around the appropriateness of a marginalist or formal approach applied in a "nonwestern" environment.

The essential point of origin for those arguing against the formalist view was the work of Polanyi (1957). As LeClair and Schneider have noted, Polanyi asserted that "in societies other than market-oriented societies, men in fact are not confronted with making choices in the sense of the formal meaning of economic" (1968, p. 10).

Substantivists pointed to the discrepancies between the powerful methodology of formal economics, requiring detailed measurability of conditional preference aspects, and the absence of easily evident nonwestern data sets consistent with those methods and assumptions. On this basis, they concluded, as they were philosophically inclined to do anyway, that use of choice theories was inappropriate in nonWestern situations. This conclusion, however, was erroneous; it was based on the false premise that formal applied economic theory is equivalent to economic theory in general. However, as has been repeatedly emphasized, marginalist theory can be seen as only one particular expression of general choice theory—that which is appropriate when preference partitioning is most subtle. When this circumstance is not true and when the attainable set cannot be minutely partitioned, it is still possible to employ axiomatic set approaches to choice. Thus, although in many nonwestern situations detailed measurability is not readily apparent, this does not imply, as the substantivist might, that theories of choice are not appropriate. Rather it indicates that care must be taken to apply the appropriate specific theory of choice and the methodologies consistent with it.

From a historical perspective it is not surprising that anthropologists of the 1960s drew upon marginalist concepts. Awareness of the different variations of economic theory and their subsumption under a general theory of choice is a relatively current one, even within economics. "Only recently have economists begun to understand consciously that the (general) theory of choice is the core of the pure science (as distinct from the engineering) in economics" (Walsh, 1970, p. 13). Within economics, it was only with the work of Arrow in the 1950s that the axiomatic formulations of the general theory of choice became influential and the proper role for marginalist approaches became clear. This position, however, was anticipated some 50 years earlier by Lionel Robbins (1935, p. 14), who has given perhaps the clearest definition of economics. Also, axiomatic choice concepts were proposed as early as 1926 by Frisch and later by Georgescu-Roegen (1935-36) and Wold (1943).

Malchup (1967) has emphasized that marginalism dominated economics perhaps as late as the early 1950s. This period saw a number of seminal articles and books, largely by Arrow and Debreu (see Newman, 1965, pp. 45-49 and Walsh 1970, pp. 14-60 for more details). Koopmans has described the impact of the then-newer axiomatic approaches to economics in his very influential *Three Essays* (1957):

> In recent years [these] mathematical tools of a more basic character have been introduced into economics, which permit us to perceive with greater clarity and express in simpler terms the logical structure of important parts of economic theory. Parallel with this change in tools, there has been a change in emphasis as between various aspects of the theories in which the tools are applied. Traditionally, mathematical economics has emphasized models that describe the formation of prices and quantities in competitive markets through unique, or at least locally determinate, solutions of equation systems. Such models have also been used to study how these solutions respond to changes in technological knowledge, in consumers' preferences, in governmental policies, or in "external conditions" such as weather or foreign demand. Calculus and the theory of implicit functions have formed the main mathematical tools for this type of analysis. The new tools allow us to shed new light on older and perhaps also more fundamental problems. The emphasis is shifted to the specification of conditions under which decentralization of economic decisions through a price system is compatible with efficient utilization of resources. It is not suggested that these classical problems were at any time lost out of sight. The "new

welfare economics" has made them its special concern. However, the tools referred to were inadequate for the purpose in question. In the first place, they did not permit recognition of restraints on choice that require expression by inequalities rather than by equations. Owing to this limitation of the tools in use, the literature of an entire period almost completely ignored such simple facts as the impossibility of consuming negative quantities of goods or of rendering negative quantities of labor, or the impossibility of running production processes in reverse. Secondly, the calculus, used in the way it was used to scan the (restricted) domain of the target function for a maximum position, is a myopic instrument. It served only to compare the would-be-maximum position with alternative positions in its immediate neighborhood. For this reason, the problem of formulating conditions under which a position could stand comparison with more distant rivals was not faced. (1957, pp. 5-6)

In anthropology, a well-developed application of concepts fundamentally similar to axiomatic set theory can be associated first with H. Gladwin (1975), C. Gladwin (1975, 1979), and Quinn (1975). The conceptual framework and methodologies used by these researchers are generally consistent with Arrow's axiomatic choice theory, though they do not emphasize the works of Arrow (1951), Debreu (1959), or others (e.g., Walsh, 1970; Newman, 1965) who had developed accessible axiomatic methodologies in economics.

At first, it may seem surprising that after twenty years, Arrow's work has not had a greater impact on anthropological analysis. However, upon further study, we can see why this is so. Even though Arrow won the Nobel Prize and his ideas, as well as those of similar thinkers, have had a fundamental impact on basic theory, they have had little effect on the "engineering" side of economics. Popular undergraduate and graduate texts in economics (e.g., Mainsfield, 1970; Henderson & Quandt, 1971) include, at best, only a superficial treatment of axiomatic choice theory. Even today, the overwhelming focus in economic teaching is on theory and method involving continuously divisible data.

To conclude, the basic issue of the appropriateness of choice and its scholarly study in nonwestern, nonmarket economies has been considered. The fundamental issues have only been superficially examined, the magnitude of the debate only fleetingly glimpsed, and the significant questions have by no means been answered. It should be clear, however, that there is substantial support for a rational choice approach in nonwestern situations, including archaeological contexts. Considerable force is added to its use when it is recognized that many of the substantivist criticisms of "economics" were actually directed to only the marginalist expressions of the basic processes of choice. Careful marginal perception of alternatives in a nonmarket environment may not be a universal nor even typical phenomenon as the substantivists have argued (we are not prepared to argue either for or against the matter here). However, with their polemic insistence on misidentifying marginalism with choice, the substantivists have insisted on throwing the baby out with the bath water. Fortunately, both modern economic theory and anthropological study have shown that, in theory and practice, there is a productive middle ground in the study of nonwestern decision processes.

The Unsatisfactory Satisficer

Paralleling the replay of the formalist-substantivist debate in archaeology is another dichotomy concerned with the general nature of choice-making theories: that between "satisficers" and "maximizers." In this dichotomy, the satisficers propose more than the inapplicability of "western" economics to nonwestern environments. They propose that humans *everywhere* do not order their alternatives and select the most preferred; rather, individuals choose the first acceptable alternative. Humans, accordingly, are not maximizers; they are satisficers.

Serving to illustrate the position of an archaeological satisficer is Sullivan and Schiffer's (1978) evaluation of the theoretical basis underlying the SARG (Southwestern Archeological Research Group) research design. Sullivan and Schiffer note that a

> . . . more fundamental question exists regarding the basic utility of "maximizing" economic models. In order for the minimax principal and the PLE (Principle of Least Effort) to operate, a number of significant preconditions are assumed to have been satisfied. The preconditions are that players (individuals or groups) can 1) process the requisite information within the constraints of prevailing conceptual schemes (providing the information is available); 2) correctly calculate the success probabilities of alternative strategies; 3) evaluate potential outcomes based on the computed probabilities and rationally select the most attractive outcome and 4) do not err in any of the above and 5) act in terms of the particular strategy which in probabilistic terms is the most maximizing or constitutes the "least average rate of probable work" . . . . (1978, p. 171)

They go on to suggest that "rational economic men" should be replaced with "satisficing men" who satisfice "because they have not the wits to maximize" and who instead pursue "a course of action which is simply good enough" (Sullivan & Schiffer, 1978, p. 171, quoting from an unpublished paper by McGuire, n.d.).

Zimmerman also advocates the satisficing man view in his book *Prehistoric Locational Behavior: A computer simulation* (1977). He is perhaps more forceful in his rejection of other alternatives when he argues:

> Major criticisms of economic man models in location theory focus on the logical consistency of assumptions of the motives ascribed to economic man, and reject the high level of knowledge and abilities attributed to him. Man often operates in less than optimal ways but usually in ways that

satisfy him in terms of needs. This satisficing behavior is both culturally and situationally defined. (p. 13)

Jochim (1976) also prefers the satisficer approach because

> ... it represents an attempt to be descriptive rather than normative, it may reflect real-world decision processes more faithfully. Second, some hunter-gather decisions involve the procurement of nonedible material items such as hides, antler, and bone; the usual high mobility of these groups, however, militates against the maximization of material acquisitions. Third, the presence of conflicting goals or objectives guiding the decisions would dictate the acceptance of submaximal levels of attainment, which might lead to the development of submaximal levels of aspiration. (p. 7)

The basis for all of these satisficer views is a series of articles and books written largely in the late 1950s by another Nobel Laureate in economics, H.A. Simon (e.g., 1955, 1957a, 1957b, 1959). Simon's early work can be seen as a *response to marginal utility theory* and to the then recently introduced game theory approach (Von Neuman & Morgenstern, 1947). Simon (1959) refers to the new experiments on "realistic" choice situations stating:

> In the few extensions that have been made, it is not at all clear that the subjects behave in accordance with the utility axioms. There is some indication that when the situation is very simple and transparent, *so that the subject can easily see and remember when he is being consistent,* [italics added] he behaves like a utility maximizer. But as the choices become a little more complicated—choices, for example, among phonograph records instead of sums of money—he becomes much less consistent. (1959, p. 258)

Based on evidence of this type (and one can only wonder at his categorization of phonograph record comparisons as only "a little more complicated" than comparisons of sums of money), Simon concluded that, in the face of an incredibly complex environment, most real-life choices lie beyond the reach of a maximizing mentality—unless the situations are heroically simplified by drastic approximations (1959, p. 259). This occurs because, among other factors, optimization "requires, of course, a complete ordering of pay-offs" (1955, p. 108).

Some essential features of Simon's work, relevant to this discussion, can be summarized as follows: 1) Simon was responding to (a) the introduction to economics of game theory, which requires utility functions and careful evaluation of alternative outcome probabilities (Simon, 1959, p. 257), and (b) marginal analysis theory, which necessitated the development of a continuous utility function (Simon, 1959, p. 256; 1955, pp. 104-105). 2) For Simon, the single overwhelming factor militating against rational choice is the complexity of the world, although "in simple, slow moving situations, where the actor has a single operational goal, a maximization or optimization approach may be appropriate" (Simon, 1959, pp. 255 & 279; see also Winter 1971, pp. 238-239). 3) The inability of individuals to determine a complete (total) ordering of the preferences made satisficing the only viable alternative (Simon, 1955, p. 108). 4) Thus, while the substantivists focused their attention on the ability of some nonwesterners to *perceive* detailed differences among items in their conditional preference aspects (information accessibility), Simon focused his attention on the ability of all humans to *process* large amounts of information having complicated relationships among the conditional preference aspects of items (calculation capability).

Examining these points, it becomes clear, paradoxically, that Simon appears to argue that rational choice is inappropriate in many western economic situations but *would probably be appropriate in many nonwestern ("simple") ones*. The important variable is not the inherent behavioral processes of perception and decision, but the impact of *information overload* on the individual decision maker, leading to an inability of the decision maker to order his preferences *completely*. If this view is correct, then the use of the satisficer model for prehistoric situations is not supported by the originator of the ideas.

Empirically, it is unclear as to the degree to which a satisficing approach to economic analysis of nonwestern systems is appropriate. Ortiz (1967) has noted that

> Rationality of behavior does not imply that there is a constant conscious awareness of having made a choice or even the ability to express it verbally in terms of quantities or factors . . . When a (Columbian Indian) farmer answered me, rather impatiently, that he really could not tell me how many items of manioc he was going to plant, because he stopped planting when he could see he had enough, he was quite clear as to the amount required. (pp. 195-196)

Similarly, Jochim, though accepting Simon's satisficer approach, documents an impressive number of reports of careful analysis, evaluation, and preference ordering of properties of various resources by various hunter-gathering peoples. As only one example, the G/Wi rate food sources "in order of importance" by the "thirst and hunger-allaying properties of the plant food, the ease with which it may be exploited, and last its flavor" (Silverbauer, 1972, p. 283, quoted in Jochim, 1976, p. 17). On the other hand, there concurrently is evidence that explicit, detailed analysis of the probabilities of alternatives and their costs does not occur in many specific situations (Shepard, 1964; C. Gladwin, 1975).

Clearly, what is needed is a single theory which can move through the continuum of decision making, not one theory for one situation and a second theory for another. Game theory is strictly applicable only where the perfect actor knows all the outcomes and can order *all* the alternatives. Simon's satisficer theory, developed especially in response to game theory, however, is pertinent only where information load far exceeds the processing capabilities of individuals and alternatives are ordered into only two sets: acceptable and unacceptable. In contrast to these two approaches, the generalized theory of rational choice is applicable to each of these extreme circumstances and the continuum of situations between, fulfilling the need for a unified theory. It allows for variation in the number of conditional preference aspects and the complexity of their interrelationships which a person considers, and in the number of preference sets which a person recognizes.

In conclusion, it can be argued that the application of a satisficing man model to the prehistoric past is both unnecessary and may, in fact, be in contradiction to the initial proposals of Simon. There are a number of further detailed criticisms of Simon's approach, but in this short overview, it is not possible to discuss them at length. Briefly, these 1) examine the general question of a descriptive versus normative or predictive theory (Malchup, 1967), 2) present extensive evidence that a "rule of thumb" (apparent satisficer mechanisms) may in fact be an excellent optimality rule (Baumol & Quandt, 1964), and 3) integrate satisficing and maximizing into a rational strategizing which is related to the social situation and structural position of the individual (Prattis, 1973). What has been a major set of questions in economics and anthropology has not been presented in its full flavor, but the discussion should be sufficient to demonstrate the considerable caution that should be placed on application of a satisficing man view to prehistoric questions.

Additional Disagreements

Literature on economic analysis within anthropology and archaeology indicate disagreement, not only with regard to measurability, information accessibility, and information processings capability, but also, to a lesser degree, with respect to two other subjects: 1) the concept of effort minimization, or *Zipf's Law*—the Principle of Least Effort (Zipf, 1949)—and 2) the role of normative constraints on choice.

In this chapter, the Principle of Least Effort is rejected as an assumption basic to any general theory of rational choice. Even a superficial examination of the economic literature, or even everyday life, indicates that *no one* rather than everyone, is engaged in true least effort activities.

The ready archaeological acceptance of Zipf's work, described by Kluckholm as "fertile and suggestive, mad, irrelevant" (1950, p. 20), comes as somewhat of a surprise. To emphasize this point, it is useful to contrast many of the current archaeological uses of Zipf's law with the following comments by Burling:

> Zipf believed that all of our behavior is oriented toward the minimization of effort. Now, taken literally, as a principle with no leeway for ambiguity, this is nonsense. Athletic events and taking a walk to work up an appetite are hardly understandable within this framework. This among other flights of fancy has lead most people who have stumbled upon his book to reject its principles, even while recognizing the fertile mind which pro-

duced them and the remarkable collection of data which he believed would support them . . . all this is rather neat, and it is reminiscent of the discussions of economists on how to maximize money income, except, of course, that it is so absurd to set up the minimization of effort as the overriding goal which guides all our behavior. . . . His lack of ambiguity, however, even though it may have led him to be rapidly rejected as a somewhat mad genius, allowed a more explicit formulation of the implications of a maximization theory. . . . Clearly the things we want are more complicated than expressed by any of these simple motivations. Certainly we are sometimes happy to avoid effort. . . . More significantly we often have to choose between these things. We must decide whether leisure (minimum effort) is more or less important to us at the moment than an increase in money income, or whether power is to be sought instead of either of these. (1968, pp. 181-182)

Regarding normative constraints on choice, it should be recognized that any application of rational choice theory to prehistoric peoples must address the criticism that such a theory is inappropriate in a nonwestern context because

The individual (and/or group) is constrained by normative/institutional factors. Although Duesenberry's famous axiom is applied to sociology and economics it is an appropriate example of this type of thinking. He has stated that "economics is all about how people make choices. Sociology is all about why they don't have any choices to make" (1960, p. 233). If there are, in fact, no choices, then any theory which deals with optimum choices is clearly inappropriate. However, individuals or groups can, and do, choose to violate a norm. If we, therefore, recognize that the violation of a norm is a "high cost" social choice, then the normative and decision approaches are not in contradistinction. In the short run, norms will serve to limit the alternative choices by "adding" a high cost to some alternatives, but the *process* of decision making remains the same. In the long run, and perhaps of more significance to archeology, is the clear evidence that norms/institutions are, themselves, subject to change through time as the norm's relative preference ranking is modified by other external forces (Limp, 1983b, p. 19).

The position proposed here as an appropriate and effective one for archaeology parallels that proposed by Barlett (1980, pp. 2-3) for the study of peasant farmer agricultural production:

We seek to understand the production system of peasant farmers—how they change, and what forces influence and inhibit change. We begin from the point that small farmers are neither irrational nor tradition bound and we assume that their agricultural patterns are the consequence of long- and short-term adaptations based on observation and experimentation. Determining first what agricultural decisions have been made, we can then pursue the impacts of those decisions.

EMPIRICAL APPLICATIONS AND THE CONCORDANCE OF THEORY, METHOD, AND DATA STRUCTURE

Emic Symmetry, Etic Coherence, and Data Accessibility

In the following section, we examine two couplings of economic theory, methodology, and data. Two examples serve to illustrate some typical problems in economic analysis, including the information processing capabilities of the decision maker implied, cost estimation, and the conformity between the theory and analytical methodology applied. One example will illustrate the use of economic methods in subsistence analysis; the second in settlement analysis.

To aid us in revealing these problems, we can formulate three measures of the effectiveness of theory and method, and their conformity to each other and the data at hand. These are: *emic symmetry, etic coherence*, and *data accessibility*.

Emic symmetry can be defined as the degree of similarity between the decision process as modeled in theory and as effected in practice. It can also refer to the concordance between the theory *implied* by the assumptions that a technique makes about the structure of the data to be analyzed, and the decision process that generated that data. For example, if a series of alternatives were subjected by a person or group to only a simple ordering among larger sets, then a theory requiring careful measurement of potentially continuously divisible data, such as cost curve analysis, would not have good emic symmetry with this circumstance. In such a situation, H. Gladwin's (1975) hierarchical model would have greater emic symmetry. *Etic coherence* is a measurement of the degree of coherence between a theory and an analytical method regardless of their applicability to any particular data. For example, if a decision model involves conditional preference aspects of a continuously divisible character, then methods such as partial differentiation may have a high degree of etic coherence. In contrast, for a hierarchical decision model, methodologies involving evaluation of set membership would be coherent. Finally, a particular analytical technique may require more or less detailed information on costs or productivity to be applied. This necessary level of information can be termed *data accessibility*.

Cost Function Analysis: Alternative Resource Choice

The following example illustrates the characteristics of economic theory applied to the analysis of costs, and the methods of cost function evaluation, in the context of archaeological catchment analysis. At the same time, it suggests generally productive insights that may be provided by such an approach, when applied to conventional catchment studies.

Cost function analysis permits the mathematical comparison of the costs of a series of different alternative strategies to achieving a particular goal. For example, if there are four different production techniques by which a particular good can be produced, then cost analysis would permit evaluation of the optimal mix of the alternatives for each level of output. Methodologically, the approach requires the determination of a *cost function* for each alternative production method. A cost function is simply the mathematical representation of the costs of the production method for each level of output. Evaluation of the optimal mix for a specific level of output is determined by a series of partial differentiations of the functions to assess the relative marginal costs of the methods at that output level (see Henderson & Quandt, 1971, pp. 70-79). As generally applied, cost function analysis requires an accurate representation of the costs in the form of a continuously divisible function. Earle (1980) has a useful discussion of an archaeological application of cost analysis.

The term *catchment analysis* was popularized in archaeological circles by Vita-Finzi and Higgs (1970; Higgs & Vita-Finzi, 1972). Paralleling their work was a comparable early effort by Munson et al. (1971). More recently, there has been a considerable growth in studies using catchment analysis (see Roper, 1979; Reidhead, 1976; Flannery, 1976; Rossman, 1976; Zarky, 1976; Higgs & Vita-Finzi, 1972). The methods and properties of the approach are well described in Higgs (1975: Appendix A) and Flannery (1976) and need not be repeated here.

While there is some moderate disagreement among the practitioners of catchment analysis over the size of the catchment that should be used, they are in general agreement that a catchment should be of a relatively small diameter. For example, Higgs and Vita-Finzi (1972) propose a 5 km diameter for the catchment of agricultural groups and a 10 km diameter for hunting-gathering territories. Rossman (1976) used 5 km, as did Zarky (1976); Munson et al. (1971) used ca 2.9 km, as did Smith (1975). Reidhead (1976) invoked a catchment with a 3.5 km diameter.

The substantial diversity in the above distances calls attention to the necessity of considering the basic assumptions underlying catchment analysis, including the economic, choice-making structure assumed. Catchment analysis and its assumptions have their roots in the work of von Thunen during the 1820s. Von Thunen was concerned with developing a theory that would predict the nature of land-use around an "isolated city." Von Thunen's study served as a basis for Chisholm's (1962) work, which provided the direct rationale for the development of catchment analysis in archaeology, as did the other important works of Hoover (1948), Isard (1956), and Dunn (1954). Von Thunen's work, and the economic assumptions involved in it, have been summarized by Haggett (1960, pp. 161-182), as follows: 1) There exists a single, large city, which 2) occurs in an "isolated state," surrounded by waste on all sides; 3) the city is located in the center of a featureless plain over which both *production costs* and *transport costs* are the same everywhere; 4) farmers supply the city in return for manufactured goods; 5) transport costs are exactly proportional to distance; and 6) profit is maximized by all farmers by automatic adjustments in the crops planted.

Of these assumptions pertaining to the structure of choice making, three are integrally a part of catchment analysis as applied archaeologically, yet are clearly violated in some, if not most, contexts. These are the assumptions of an isolated condition, and the assumptions concerning the nature of production and transport costs.

Regarding the assumption of isolation, even a superficial evaluation of subsistence behavior indicates that there is a complex matrix of variable production costs which significantly influences resource selection beyond the limits of the typical catchment. In the eastern United States, for example, there is extensive evidence in the ethnographic literature that exceptional distances were traveled routinely in hunting activities. Tooker reports travel of "200-300 leagues" (1964, p. 65). For many groups in the southeast, Hudson indicates that hunting groups ". . . sometimes ranged as far as two or three hundred miles away from their towns. These hunts were conducted by the men accompanied by their able-bodied women and some of the children" (1976, p. 271).

Likewise, the assumptions about production and transportation costs can be shown to be very restrictive. This can be done by example through an empirical evaluation of the production and transport costs of food resources available to the aboriginal inhabitants of the midwestern area of the United States. In the process, the impact on analytic results of violating the two assumptions of concern, which are intertwined, will become clear.

In the empirical approach to be used, production and transport costs are summarized as the *caloric* productivity of a resource. The use of calories are presented here only for exemplary purposes. For a discussion of the problems with caloric reductionism, see Keene (1979) and Limp (1983a).

It is possible to evaluate the productivity of a food resource both at its point of origin and at varying distances from this location so as to allow the computation of a cost function for the resource. The method of computation involves consideration of technical productivity, speed and distance of travel, and the necessity for overnight camps when the distances to be traveled increase (see Limp, 1983a for details).

Figure 2 illustrates the application of Limp's computations for hickory nuts (processed by mortar and boiling). It shows the net caloric output of hickory nuts at varying distances, taking into consideration the total costs of production and travel, in the form of an output/input ratio. A transport unit of 40 kg of unshelled nuts has been assumed. This unit represents approximately 62,000 calories at the point of origin, with only the cost of production (not transport) subtracted. The cost of production, approximately 3,300 calories, is based on experiments reported in Reidhead (1976). The output/input ratios, are shown for one-way travel distances from 0 to 200 km. The steps in the curve represent the effect of the cost of each overnight camp. The curvilinear nature reflects the increasing impact of the transport costs as a component of the total costs.

From these calculations, we discover that it is feasible to exploit hickories up

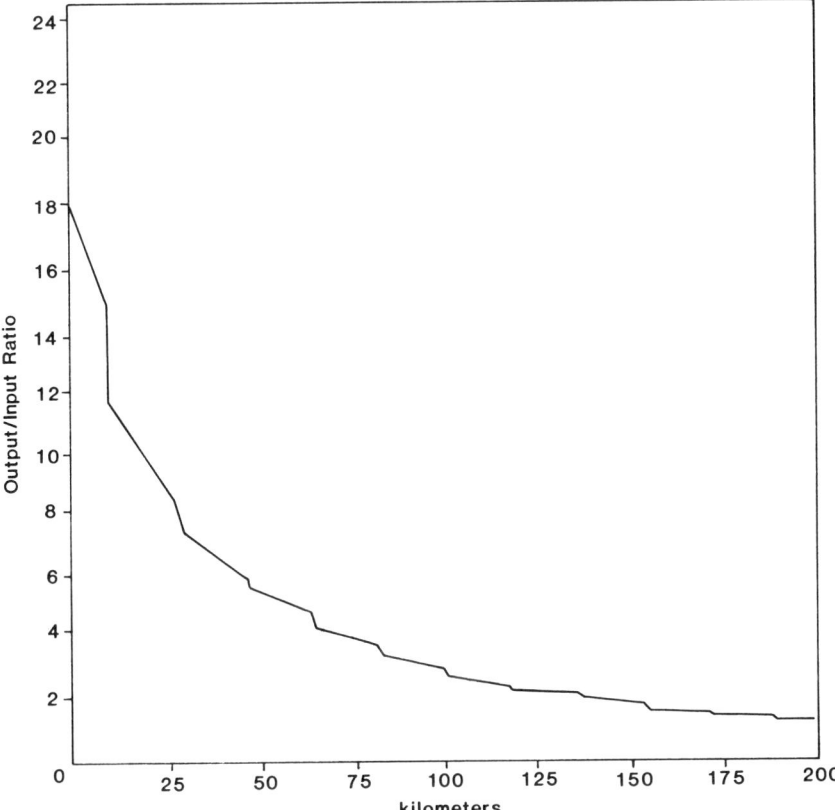

Fig. 7.2. Input/output ratios for various catchment distances for hickory nut production.

to 215 km away (one-way), with the calories produced still being greater than or equal to the calories required to obtain and process the resource. This "catchment" is considerably in excess of the 2 to 10 km circles often used in catchment studies. This is not to argue, however, that *any specific* catchment radius is correct or incorrect. Rather what is of significance is that a catchment basin is, in fact, a *variable* rather than a given, dependent on the cost analysis of a given resource and production technique. *To propose any single or even a limited number of catchment basins totally obscures the complex choice mechanisms and interrelationships which existed.*

Further suggestive of this circumstance are the data presented in Figure 3. In this figure, the distance dependent output/input ratios for four different resources are presented. Curve *A* illustrates the ratios for white-tailed deer using a stalking mode of hunting. Curve *B* indicates the relationship for hickory nut

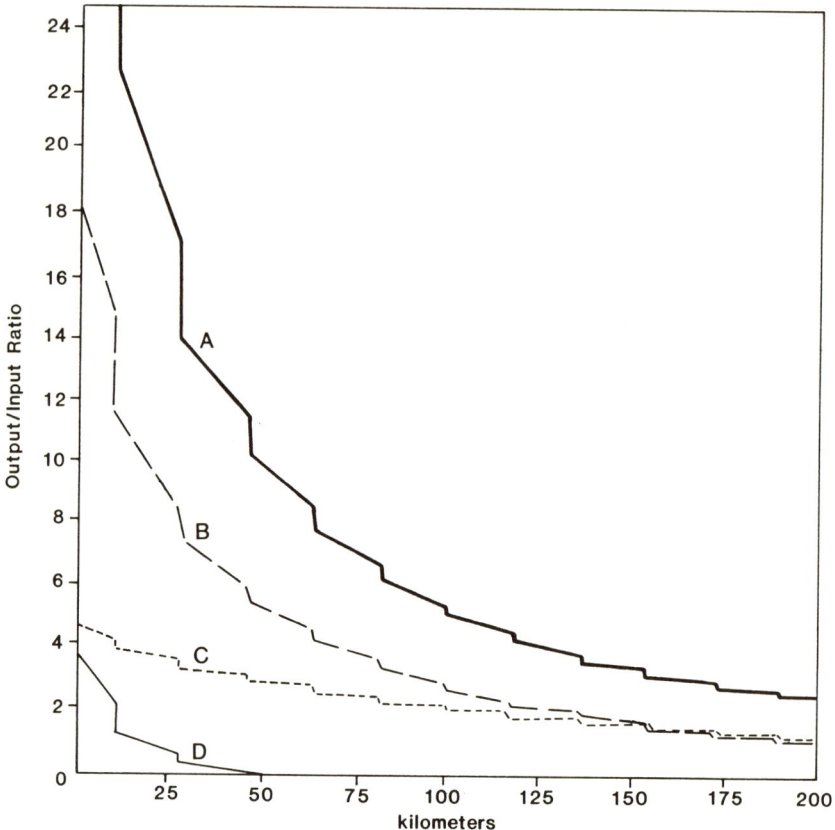

Fig. 7.3. Input/output ratios for various catchment distances for: (A) white-tailed deer, (B) hickory nuts, (C) white oak acorns, and (D) riverine mussels.

production discussed above. Curve C pertains to white oak acorns and D to riverine mussels. Again the original productive technique data were obtained from Reidhead (1976).

The figure shows that similar output/input ratios can be obtained for the several resources, but at varying one-way travel distances and for catchments of varying radii. Cost relationships are the same at 1 km for mussels, 20 km for white oak acorns, and 150 km for white-tailed deer. Again, this emphasizes that the catchment basins of different resources may vary in size, some being quite large, and that their size depends on the specific production and travel costs of the resources. It also emphasizes the fact that production and transportation costs need not be equal over all resources. Thus, we find that the two assumptions of isolation and uniform production and transportation costs involved in archaeological catchment analysis, as derived from von Thunen, are inappropriate to the example provided, and are probably inappropriate in most archaeological applications.

The impact of erroneously assuming a simple, restricted catchment basin and uniform production and transportation costs in a catchment analysis, as in traditional applications, has at least two facets. First, it may result in a decrease in the accuracy of the subsistence model-building process and associated predictions. Second, and perhaps more important, it may lead to a narrowing of the range of theoretical topics open for investigation. By making such assumptions, attention is drawn away from the choice-making process. If, instead, these assumptions are relaxed and the methods and theory of cost function evaluation are integrated into analysis, then the nature of decision process can be studied.

For example, in the case study presented above, we find that within a 25 km catchment basin, the unit productivity of deer is greater than any other resource (Fig. 3). Deer obtained at 26 km from a site are less productive, however, than hickories obtained in the immediate vicinity of the site. If these relationships are correct, then we might predict that a producer would choose to walk 20 km to obtain deer rather than produce hickory nuts at 5 km, if caloric productivity were the conditional preference aspect of primary importance. Of course, there may be a diversity of factors involved in any choice. It is by focusing on decisions of these kinds that cost function analysis can significantly augment and broaden the scope of traditional catchment analyses.

To take into consideration the diversity of factors involved in choices of the kind just discussed, and to evaluate when a producer should (optimally) shift from one resource to another, methodologically, cost function analysis employs a series of *normative decision rules*. The optimal mix of resources is determined by partially differentiating the cost functions of each resource in order to evaluate their marginal costs at each level of output, and then applying decision rules. The decision rules state that for any increase from a given output level, a producer should choose the alternative resource having the lowest marginal costs. Using our example, in behavioral terms, this would mean that a producer would evaluate the productive yield of *each* resource at *every* unit distance from the point of use. Considering the level of productive output desired to achieve compared to that already achieved, the producer would then ask at each such location, "Is it more productive to walk one more unit distance to obtain resource x (i.e., deer), or to remain within the current catchment and shift to some other resources, y or z (i.e., hickories). A series of decisions would be made accordingly. As long as the unit productivity of a particular resource is greater than any alternative resource, the producer will extend the catchment. At the point where the marginal cost of the first resource rises above that of an alternative for another unit extension of the catchment, the producer will hold the level of the first constant and shift his additional effort to the second.

Cost Function Analysis: Evaluation of the Concordance between Theory, Method, and Decision Process

Emic Symmetry

Emic symmetry for any specific case is, of course, impossible to determine confidently because it literally requires evaluation of the mental processes of the decision unit. As the above discussion intimates, however, complete cost function analysis does assume the *considerable* information processing capabilities of the decider and the decider's desire to make detailed evaluations. While it is impossible to say with assurance, it seems reasonable to conclude that this approach has a low emic symmetry in many applications, particularly those concerned with simpler societies. To avoid this problem of asymmetry between the structure of the phenomenon being examined and that assumed by the method and theory, others have proposed that the marginal evaluations be collapsed into a lower ordered ranking approach (see Hasdorf, 1980; Christenson, 1980). In these approaches it is assumed that the decision units simply rank order the alternatives. Such a solution would surely increase the emic symmetry, but it has significant consequences for the method, as we note below.

Etic Coherence

The type of data presented for the catchment problem is continuously divisible. It is possible to assume a theory of rational choice involving detailed measurability of conditional preference aspects and the ability of the decider to access and process continuously divisible information and calculate marginal costs in the manner described above. While we have not done so here, it would be correct and quite straightforward to actually compute the marginal costs as desired for the sample data, and the approach would have excellent etic coherence. Such an analysis would then yield optimal mixes of the resources for various desired levels of output.

As we have noted, however, in the discussion of emic symmetry, there is some potential question as to whether we should make the assumption of the necessary level of information processing capabilities. If, instead, we assume that these capabilities involved only rank ordering and that a set theoretic approach has emic symmetry, then the appropriate methodological equivalent would be found in either statistical decision analysis (Hillier & Liberman, 1974, p. 597ff) or the decision analysis methods proposed by C. Gladwin (1979).

Data Accessibility

Cost function analysis poses two problems in relation to data accessibility when applied in the context of catchment analysis of archaeological data. First, the methodology requires estimates of the production and transportation costs of particular resources on a *continuously divisible scale*. Estimates of this specificity are difficult and time-consuming to make. The production costs upon which the above discussions are based were derived only after extensive, replicative experimentation in prehistoric technology and/or extensive review of ethnohistoric literature (see Reidhead, 1976; Keene, 1981). These projects represented a major research commitment and expense. The value of any catchment analysis using a cost function approach must be considered in light of this expense.

A second, and related problem of using a cost function approach to catchment analysis is that it requires *accurate* estimates of production and transport costs. Cost function analysis is not a highly robust method. A small error in a particular cost estimate can have (though not always) a major effect on the optimal resources mix predicted, and its accuracy. The particular effect of an error on results depends on the shape of the cost functions. Unfortunately, the magnitude of the effect of any particular sets of errors on the accuracy of a solution is exceedingly difficult to estimate.

All archaeological studies are troubled to some degree by data accessibility. However, when the method employed requires continuously divisible data and the effects of errors on results may be substantial yet undeterminable, as in cost function analysis, then the appropriateness of the method must be carefully considered in relation to the nature of the data base.

Hierarchical Choice Models: An Application to Settlement Location Analysis

The second example of the use of economic methods in archaeology considers the subject of a decision maker selecting a locale for settlement. Axiomatic choice theory, operationalized within a hierarchical decision framework or methodology, will be employed.

Additive vs. Hierarchical Choice Models

Previously, we have considered the partitioning and the information processing capabilities of the decision unit. For choices involving more than one conditional preference aspect, yet another factor must be considered. Multiple conditional preference aspects may be evaluated either *simultaneously* or *sequentially* by the decision unit. For purposes of this discussion, a simultaneous decision can be modeled by the classical additive linear regression equation:

$$\text{choice } y = a + b_1 x_1 + b_2 x_2 + \ldots + b_n x_n$$

As Gladwin and Murtaugh have emphasized (1980, p. 133) this model implies that low values on one aspect can be "balanced off" against high values on another. The approach further assumes that it is possible to simultaneously evaluate a wide diversity of combinations of the aspects to achieve the optimal mix.

In contrast, a sequential decision process can be modeled using a hierarchical "decision rule" approach. A model of this approach might have the form discussed by Gladwin and Murtaugh (1980, p. 133):

$$\text{choice } y \,(1{:}\text{accept}, 0{:}\text{reject}) = x_1 \cdot x_2 \cdot \ldots \cdot x_n$$

This choice model

> ... differs from the additive choice model ("trade off" model) commonly assumed in discussions of indifference curves (the marginalist approach) .... The model that is actually used in this paper is hierarchical, in that it assumes decision makers consider aspects, dimensions, or criteria of objects separately and often sequentially. The consideration of later aspects takes place in a sequential process only if prior aspects have been considered and found to have the correct value. (H. Gladwin, 1975, p. 160)

A representative of the specific manifestation of general choice theory proposed here, as applied to settlement location selection, is shown in Figure 4 in primitive form. Each conditional preference aspect is evaluated sequentially and is accepted or rejected based on an evaluation of the specifics of the aspect.

H. Gladwin (1975) has shown that use of the additive model to analyze what was, in fact, a hierarchical decision process can yield statistically valid but totally erroneous estimators. In his study Gladwin used conventional regression techniques to investigate a data set that had been derived from a series of known hierarchical choices. The regression equation yielded apparently valid estimators but when these results were compared to the known choices they were found to have significant errors.

The development and application of a hierarchical decision model to a question of archaeological settlement analysis is exemplified by recent work by Limp (1983b), a small part of which is summarized here. In this example a

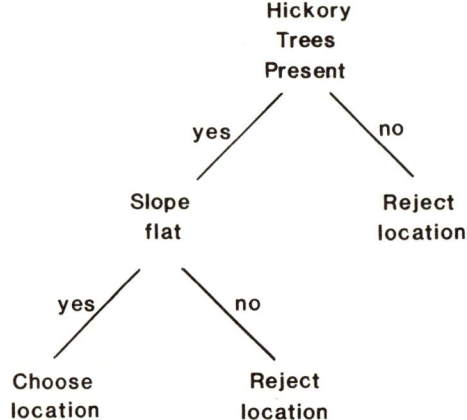

Fig. 7.4. A primitive hierarchical choice model of settlement location selection.

series of decision rules are evaluated for their capabilities in predicting site location.

The first step in applying the approach to archaeological data involved the selection of specific locational physical properties having potential importance in structuring the location choice process. Some 13 primary measurements were selected, based on an extensive review of archaeological and ethnographic literature (see Lafferty et al., 1982 for a further discussion).

In order to record the physical property information in the study area, a grid of hexagons was laid over the area. Each unit was constructed to a uniform size that would probably accommodate only one archaeological site (radius of 50 m) and was conceptualized as an alternative location for settlement. Each of the 13 physical properties was measured for the more than 21,000 units in the research unit. A suite of computer programs was developed to process the more than $\frac{1}{3}$ million observations that were generated. The software allowed the plotting of maps showing the distribution of selected properties. It further allowed the evaluation of each location as to whether it had been subjected to a modern intensive survey, whether a site was present, the type of site, and the characteristics of the artifact assemblage.

One hundred and forty-one combinations of the attribute states of the physical properties were evaluated for their potential in predicting site locations, the particular combinations having been chosen in relation to certain a priori hypotheses of interest (see below). This was done first by designating those units in the region having combinations of property states hypothesized to be preferable for settlement as *viable locales*. Then, for each combination of preferred states, the number and percentage of all viable locales having a site present in them was determined. This figure was taken as a measure of the ability of the combination of hypothetically preferable states to predict location choice, a higher value indicating greater predictive success.

Related combinations of attribute states can be combined into a *decision tree* (see C. Gladwin, 1979) on the basis of a priori considerations of the importance of the states as preference criteria so as to form an expected preference ordering of the items being considered for selection. This expected preference ordering can then be compared to that actually indicated by data in order to test the postulated relative importance of the attribute states.

The following discussion focuses on two decision trees dealing with the nature of location choice on the floodplain of the study area. Figure 5 graphically illustrates the first of these trees which involves the conditional preference aspects of soil permeability and flood risk for locations on the floodplain. The percentage of locations having each combination of the presence or absence of these preference aspects and also having sites in them is tabulated below the tree. As can be seen, the correspondence between the postulated preference ordering of locations and that indicated by the data is very good. Additionally, it can be noted that the postulated decision tree offered the best predictions of site

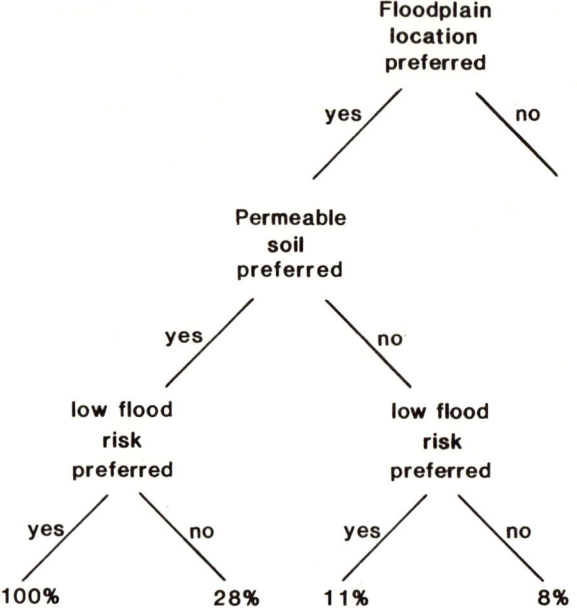

Fig. 7.5. Decision tree for floodplain locations including soil permeability and flood risk.

locations compared to others of the family of possible trees involving one or both of the floodplain locational attributes of concern. One alternative decision tree, which did not include low flood risk as a preferred aspect, was a good predictor of site location, but not as effective as the former. All decision trees which did not consider high soil permeability a preferred aspect were poorer predictors.

Figure 6 presents a second decision tree in which floodplain location, proximity to water, and low flood risk are the considered preference aspects. Again, the correspondence between the postulated preference ordering of locations and that indicated by site locational data is good. Compared to alternative decision trees within the same family, those trees that had proximity to water as a preferred locational aspect were uniformly superior to those which did not. Lower flood risk was also important but to a lesser degree.

In comparing Figure 5 and 6, it would appear that good soil permeability was a more preferred locational attribute than proximity to water. While this may be true, the situation cannot be assessed easily. Good soil permeability in the study area was associated with soil types which were only located near the largest stream. As a component of a dimensional physical property soil type, soil permeability does not yield itself to easy comparison to this other locational property for its importance.

Beyond the assessment of specific properties and location choice, it also is

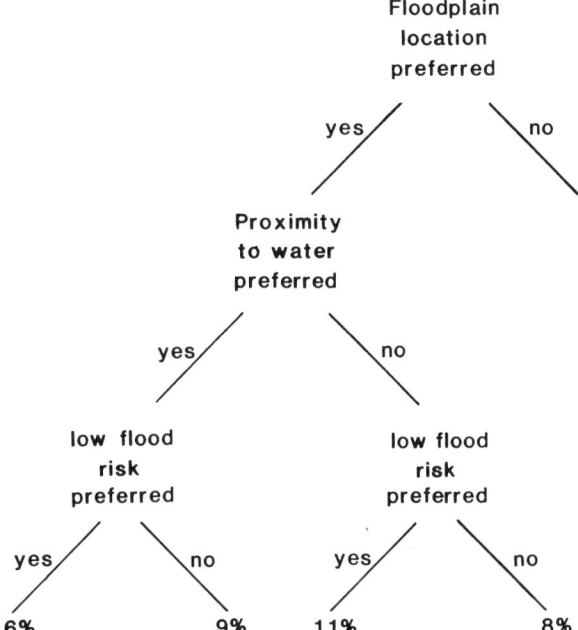

Fig. 7.6. Decision tree for floodplain locations including proximity to water and flood risk.

possible to apply this methodology to a more systematic evaluation of the differences of location decision processes among different cultural units. To illustrate the approach, evaluation of only two of the many hypotheses on cultural unit location choice that were considered will be summarized. These two hypotheses concerned four specific cultural units in the area: Early Archaic, Late Archaic, Early Woodland, and Late Woodland/Mississippian.

One area of interest was an evaluation of the differences in the decision process between Early and Late Archaic. Based on the characteristics of resource selection proposed for these periods (see Brown, 1977; Ford, 1974), it was posited, for example, that Late Archaic preferred locations could be more effectively predicted than Early Archaic preferred locations using the physical property, proximity to permanent water. To evaluate this prediction, decision trees in which variable distances to permanent water were included were constructed, and the observed results of these trees (e.g., the percentages in Figs. 5 & 6) were compared for locations with sites of the two cultural units. In ten of the decision trees involving units proximal to water, the relative density of Early Archaic sites was less than that for Late Archaic sites. In only six trees was the density of Early Archaic sites greater. Thus, the specific prediction that distance to water is a better predictor of Late Archaic sites than Early Archaic sites in the area of concern was evidently supported. Additionally, it was noted that Early Woodland and Late Woodland/Mississippian sites were distributed similar to the Late Archaic sites and unlike the Early Archaic sites. Thus, the Early Archaic occupations had a significantly less riverine focus than any of the other occupations.

There is at least one potential alternative explanation of this pattern, however, which would not require the hypothesis on decision making to be true. This is that the floodplain Early Archaic sites have been buried by alluviation. In at least two situations, deeply buried materials were observed eroding out of riverbank locations. As a result, even though the location choice modeling appeared to support the original prediction, it must remain unconfirmed.

A second prediction that was evaluated postulated that Late Woodland/ Mississippian groups should place a higher preference on high permeability soils than did earlier groups. The basis for this prediction lies in the assumption that the later prehistoric groups focused on agricultural products and would, therefore, prefer permeable soils (see Smith, 1978). Unexpectedly, it was found that all cultural units have a higher relative site density on the most permeable soil. This can be explained by the facts that soil permeability is strongly interlinked with a number of other soil and environmental variables as a dimensional physical property. Not only are permeable soils desirable for agriculture, but they also supported a vegetation type (cane) which, in turn, fostered a high faunal biomass. Such areas also could easily have been cleared to make way for any occupation. Furthermore, they were the highest locations on the floodplain yet relatively near the river course. They, therefore, were desirable for groups other than agriculturalists. In fact, considering sites of all time periods, the most permeable soil class was one of the best predictors of location choice.

Hierarchical Choice Analysis: Evaluation of the Concordance between Theory, Method, and Decision Process

Emic Symmetry

Within the original caveats about evaluation of emic symmetry, we can propose that the hierarchical choice theoretical approach and the decision tree methodology associated with it have a high degree of emic symmetry with the decision processes that probably occurred in the societies of the kinds examined. It would appear that the theory and the methodology do not place unreasonable requirements on the decision unit's information gathering or processing capabilities. In the example provided, all variables considered were simply ordered for their importance in the selection process, and locational units were ordered as sets rather than individually.

Although the hierarchical choice theoretical framework and the decision tree methodology employed in contexts of the kind illustrated here may have the greatest potential for symmetry between theory, methodology, and data structure, it is significantly constrained by the cumbersome methodology by which it is operationalized (see below). This problem characterizes not only the archaeological example presented here, but also ethnographic hierarchical decision studies (e.g., C. Gladwin, 1979). The archaeological application is limited further by the necessity of hypothesizing the potential decision trees without recourse to direct ethnographic data or observation.

Etic Coherence

There is a good degree of etic coherence in the approach presented here because the computer algorithm used to evaluate the permutations was designed specifically to mirror the decision trees under consideration, which in turn directly operationalize hierarchical choice theory. However, the methodology was limited by the absence of any simple statistical measurement for comparing the predictive strengths of alternative decision trees. This, compounded with the fact that the number of permutations of the 13 variables and the number of alternative decision trees was substantial, made evaluation of the importance of the chosen physical properties difficult. Even the 141 combinations studied were only a small fraction of the possible alternatives. Moreover, for this large number of variables and permutations, it was difficult to hold any single property constant while others varied. As a result of all of these problems, the potentially desirable goal of finding a single physical properties set predicting all site locales but only site locales (i.e., a site density of 100% and a site inclusiveness of 100%) was not feasible. It was not possible, therefore, to evaluate the success of a specific physical properties set in predicting location choice except on a series of competing, noncomplementary criteria.

Data Accessibility

The accessibility of the empirical data for each variable in this example was good. However, the massive task of gathering the mandated data must be noted as a restriction on feasibility. This task would have been necessary for any economic approach to locations prediction—hierarchical or nonhierarchical in design (see Parker, chapter 8). Fortunately, current remote sensing approaches indicate the potential for technological solution to the data-gathering encumbrance (see Kvamme, chapter 9).

Of greater concern, of course, is the conformity between the physical properties measured and the conditional preference aspects that operated prehistorically. This is not an issue of simple data accessibility, but clearly affects the structuring of observation and measurement. It is a problem that pertains not only to this example and the hierarchical framework used, but to any decision-making application in archaeology and sometimes ethnology.

There does not appear to be an easy solution for confidently assessing the conformity of the variables observed and the pertinent conditional preferences aspects in archaeological applications. It appears that only through careful ethnohistoric and ethnographic evaluations can we evaluate the first approximation of the conditional preference aspects. Further refinement must be derived from the consistency of the logic and degree of prediction support within the application.

A BRIEF INTRODUCTION TO AND ASSESSMENT OF OTHER SELECT METHODS OF ECONOMIC ANALYSIS FOR ARCHAEOLOGY

In this section we briefly consider a number of additional economic quantitative methods and associated theories which have or may have merit in application to archaeological data. Their potential in regard to their emic decision-making requirements and their data accessibility requirements is also mentioned. This discussion is meant only to suggest the diversity of economic literature on theory and method, rather than a systematic review.

Linear Programming

Linear programming is an exceptionally powerful methodology which has seen a wide diversity of applications in modern economic studies. Reidhead (1979) and Keene (1981; this volume, chapter 10) review the methodological and theoretical basis for the approach, as well as present specific archaeological applications (see Johnson, 1980 for a more pessimistic view).

Linear programming (LP), as normally applied, requires continuously divisible data; detailed linear cost functions based on analysis of a diversity of options; and a specifiable linear, algebraic, synchronic objective function which is the "targeted" relationship. Other variants of normal LP reduce some of these methodological limitations. Integer programming (Gaifinksel & Nemhauser, 1972) permits modeling with discrete, integer variables rather than requiring continuous variables. Separable programming, quadratic programming, and the sequential unconstrained minimization technique (Wagner, 1975, pp. 562-573; Hillier & Liberman, 1974, pp. 722-735) all reduce the necessity for linearity in the cost and/or objective functions, whereas dynamic linear programming (Throsby, 1962), in part, addresses the question of synchronic limitations. However, all these alternatives themselves have significant methodological constraints. For this reason, as well as the greater accessibility of computer algorithms for performing normal LP, we can anticipate that normal LP will be used for most archaeological studies.

Linear programming has a low potential for emic symmetry in most archaeological applications because it assumes major data gathering and processing capabilities for the modeled decision unit, including detailed measurability of conditional preference aspects and their simultaneous (as opposed to sequential) consideration. Also, etic coherence between LP and economic theory is troublesome because few cost functions actually are linear. The empirical data accessibility requirements of LP are massive, as both Keene (1981) and Reidhead (1976) demonstrate. Such data is primarily available through only modern experiment and/or inference from ethnographic or ethnohistoric accounts. In addition, in prehistoric situations, it is difficult to define the currency used to measure costs (see Keene, chapter 10).

The above assessment would seem to preclude LP from consideration by archaeologists, but there are aspects of LP which, while they do not eliminate these problems, certainly reduce them. These are parametric programming (or range analysis) and the analysis of the dual. Without giving technical details, it can be said that parametric programming can allow the researcher to determine the specific effect of changes or errors in the cost function and constraints on the optimal solution. The analysis gives precise values over which cost (or other variables) and constraints may range and not affect the solution. As a result, the researcher can assess the implications of potential inaccuracies in cost and constraint estimates, significantly reducing the impact of poor data accessibility and etic coherence.

The dual allows the researcher to evaluate the potential for emic asymmetry in his analysis. The dual quantitatively indicates the information accessibility and calculation capability that would have been needed by the decision unit if the modeled approach corresponds with the actual characteristics of the decision unit. This is done by stipulating the number of resources that constrain the solution (binding constraints). If the dual indicates that only one or a few resources constrained the solution, then this is clearly within the information gathering and processsing capabilities of the decision unit.

Thus, with the dual and parametric programming, LP may serve as an effective approach in a number of circumstances. Its actual emic symmetry, etic coherence, and data accessibility requirements are themselves a matter for case-by-case evaluation.

Statistical Decision Theory Using Decision Trees

This approach is similar in method to the hierarchical choice approach presented earlier, in that both employ decision trees. As commonly practiced, however, it differs from the hierarchial choice approach because it involves the assessment of numeric probabilities for various alternatives and a similar assessment of the "payoffs" (value) of each alternative.

Regarding the emic decision process assumed by the theory and the data accessibility requirement posed by the methods associated with it, statistical decision approaches may be restrictive. Statistical decision theory is characterized by the decision maker enumerating all the available courses of action, expressing the utilities, and quantifying his subjective probabilities. This approach also has limitations because the data required (the subjective probabilities, utilities, etc.) may be either impossible to obtain or heavily dependent upon the judgment of a single individual (Hillier & Liberman, 1974, p. 616).

However, when these data are available, decision analysis becomes a powerful tool in determining an optimal course of action.

Game Theory

Game theory concepts present an attractive structure from which to conduct analysis of prehistoric decision making. Such methods have been used, for example, in a number of anthropological studies (Barth, 1959; Davenport, 1960; Gould, 1963; Manch, 1971). The concepts underlying the initial SARG research design (Gummerman, 1971) used game theory nomenclature in presenting an analytical framework for the analysis of prehistoric site distributions.

Like statistical decision theory, game theory and its associated methodologies have a number of significant quantitative requirements for full application, increasing the likelihood of emic asymmetry when applied to prehistoric contexts. Objectively measurable and transferable "stakes of interest" (the expected gains) must be determined by the players. Alternative outcomes must be enumerated, as the probabilities for each alternative must be for each player.

The information accessibility requirements of game theory and its associated methodologies are high. In a specific empirical situation, it becomes quite difficult to obtain the level of information described above. Johnson (1980, p. 22) goes so far as to say that anthropologists "have had no success" with game theory. The economists, Dorfman, Samuelson, and Solow (1958), characterize the merits of the approach.

> What, in view of all these limitations, has game theory to contribute to economics? Oddly enough since game theory is an attempt to determine optimal strategies explicitly, the contribution seems to be qualitative rather than quantitative. The conceptual framework developed in game theory provides a useful set of constructs for the qualitative discussions of problems of opposing interest in economics (p. 445).

Appropriate Contexts of Use of the Diversity of Economic Theories and Methods

In our discussion of the formalist-substantivist debate it was proposed that the critical, theoretically relevant issue separating the two positions was the assessment of the amount of information that is *accessible* to a nonwestern decision unit. Methodologically, this degree of information accessibility can be modeled by the number of k-fold partitions into which the relevant decision information can be divided and whether the decider enumerates the probabilities of success and the payoffs offered by each set of alternatives. In the discussion of the satisficer-maximizer debate, it was further proposed that the key theoretical issue segregating these views was the information *processing* capabilities required of the decision unit. This requirement is represented methodologically by the sequential or simultaneous nature of information processing, the size of the matrix of variables simultaneously or sequentially considered, and the degrees to which the probabilities of success and the payoffs of alternatives are modeled into the decision process.

These two measures, information accessibility and information processing, can be used to display graphically (Fig. 7) the relationships between the various theoretical or methodological approaches discussed in this chapter, in regard to the nature of the decision-making process which they assume. In addition, a limited number of other approaches not discussed here are also displayed (see Bamoul, 1972 for discussions of these alternative approaches).

As Figure 7 clearly indicates, there is a diversity of economic approaches that are conceptually and methodologically appropriate across a wide range of combinations of circumstances. Previous applications of choice theory and method to archaeological problems have tended to focus on one or only a limited range of the alternatives, particularly at the more assuming end of the spectrum. This focusing has tended to obscure the range of choice analyses possible

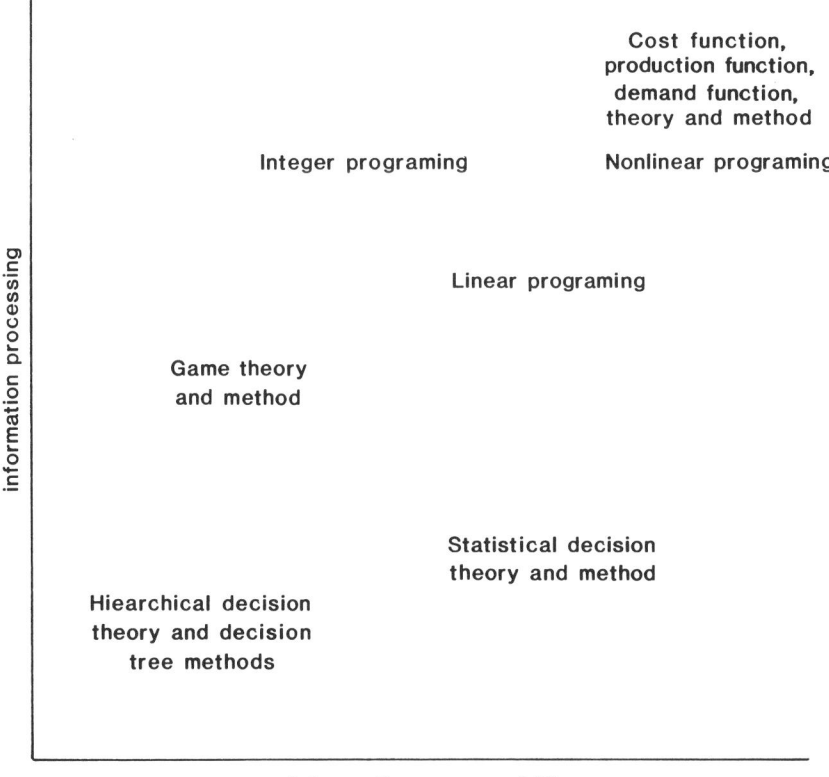

Fig. 7.7. Alternative economic approaches graphed along dimensions of information processing and accessibility.

and in many situations has led to an inappropriate rejection of choice analysis *generally*, when the correct conclusion to be drawn was that the *specific* pairing of theory and method was inappropriate. Additionally, the more focal view has not encouraged archaeologists to either consider the specific contexts in which one form of general choice theory might be more appropriate than another or to develop the proper bridging arguments between theory and data. It is hoped that this chapter has suggested the rich diversity of forms of choice analyses available, the work that still is necessary for us to be able to apply them appropriately, and the potential understanding of prehistoric behavior which may be gained by their appropriate application.

CONCLUSION

This chapter has only begun to present the complexity of the theoretical and methodological issues pertinent to the analysis of choice in an archaeological context. Furthermore, it should be emphasized that there is a wide diversity of theory-method couplings which have or could have merit in archaeological applications. It is appropriate, therefore, to close with two cautionary notes. First, it must be recognized that economics, perhaps more than any other social science, is ideological and intertwined with political implications. So, too, are any economic analyses, including those within archaeology.

> Every economic doctrine has a purpose. Economics is an ill developed branch of the biology of the human species; an economist is (presumably) a human being and cannot regard his fellowmen with the same detachment as his colleague in the laboratory regards a collection of fruit flies. Thus there is always an element of ideology in any discussion of social problems. (Robinson, 1980, p. 1x)

The presentation here has intentionally not addressed the subject of any of these ideological concerns, but an awareness of their existence and implications is critical to fully understanding and applying any economic theory. It is clear that neo-classical marginal analysis has, at least its roots in western "capitalist" economics, though this simple statement obscures a very real complexity. The ideological roots of axiomatic choice theory are more obscure. Axiomatic choice developed initialy out of fundamental disagreements between Arrow, who explicitly wished to include social factors generally and social welfare specifically in economic formulae, and neoclassical theoreticians, who were not so inclined.

It is far beyond the scope of this chapter to confidently place axiomatic choice within the diversity of economic ideology beyond these simple basic statements. Suffice it to say that the ideological and practical implications and assumptions of economic theories must be considered in any analysis, just as assumptions such as information processing capacity or the relation between physical properties and conditional preference aspects have been considered here.

A second consideration, only suggested here, is that economic models need not be restricted to the traditional arena of material provisioning. Blau (1964), Homans (1958), Heath (1976), Schneider (1974), and others have presented productive applications of choice theories to a diversity of processes, often collectively referred to as *social exchange*. Again, our discussion here has been restricted intentionally, in order to yield the clearest practical examples. However, we must emphasize that while, pragmatically, material provisioning may be initially the most productive area for economic theory in archaeology, it is by no means the only or the most important component.

Archaeologists have often been encouraged to consider the Indian behind the artifact. More recently the discipline has been invited to consider the system behind the Native American behind the artifact. The emphasis here has been on the decision process behind the system behind the Native American behind the artifact.

REFERENCES

Arrow, K. (1951). *Social choice and individual values*. New Haven: Yale University Press.
Barlett, P. (1980). Introduction: development issues and economic anthropology. In P. Barlett (Ed.), *Agricultural decision making* (pp. 1-16). New York: Academic Press.
Barth, F. (1964). Capital, investment and the social structure of a pastoral nomad group in South Persia. In R. Firth & B. Yamey (Eds.), *Capital, savings and credit in peasant societies*. Chicago: Aldine Publishing Co.
Barth, F. (1966). *Models of social organization*. London: Royal Anthropological Institute.
Baumol W., & Quandt, R. (1964). Rules of thumb and optimally imperfect decisions. *American Economic Review 65*, 23-46.
Belshaw, C. (1965). *Traditional exchange and modern markets*. Englewood Cliffs, NJ: Prentice-Hall.
Berliner, J.S. (1962). The feet of the natives are large: An essay on anthropology by an economist. *Current Anthropology 3*(1), 47-61.
Blau, P. (1964). *Exchange and power in social life*. New York: Wiley and Sons.
Blumer, R.N.H. (1970). Which came first, the chicken or the egghead? In J. Pouillon & P. Maranda (Eds.), *Exchanges et communications* (pp. 1069-1091). Der Hague: Mouton.
Bohannan, P., & Dalton, G. (Eds.). (1962). *Markets in Africa: Eight subsistence economics in transition*. Garden City, NY: Doubleday.
Bronitsky G. (Ed.). (1983). *Ecological models in economic prehistory* (Anthropological Research Papers No. 29). Tempe: Arizona State University.
Brown, J. (1977). Current directions in midwestern archaeology. *Annual Review of Anthropology 6*, 161-179.
Burling, R. (1968). Maximization theories and the study of economic anthropology. In E. LeClair & H. Schneider (Eds.), *Economic anthropology* (pp. 168-186). New York: Holt, Rinehart and Winston.
Byington, C. (1915). *A dictionary of the Choctaw language* (Bureau of American Ethnology Bulletin No. 46). Washington, DC: Smithsonian Institution.
Cancian, F. (1966). Maximization as norm, strategy, and theory. *American Anthropologist 68*, 465-470.
Chibnik, M. (1980). The statistical behavior approach: The choice between wage labor and cash cropping in rural Belize. In P. Barlett (Ed.), *Agricultural decision making* (pp. 87-114). New York: Academic Press.

Chisholm, M.D.I. (1962). *Rural settlement and land use: An essay in location.* London: Hutchinson.
Christenson, A. (1980). Change in the human niche in response to population growth. In T. Earle & A. Christenson (Eds.), *Modeling change in prehistoric subsistence economics* (pp. 31-72). New York: Academic Press.
Clarke, D.L. (Ed.). 1972. *Models in archaeology.* London: Methuen.
Clarke, D.L. (1977). *Spatial archaeology.* New York: Academic Press.
Dalton, G. (1961). Economic theory and primitive society. *American Anthropologist 63*, 1-25.
Dalton, G. (1963). Economic surplus, once again. *American Anthropologist 65*, 389-394.
Dean, J. (1978). An evaluation of the initial SARG research design. In R.C. Euler & G.J. Gumerman (Eds.), *Investigations of the Southwestern Anthropological Research Group: Proceedings of the 1976 conference* (pp. 103-117). Flagstaff: Museum of Northern Arizona.
Dunn, E.S. (1954). *The location of agricultural production.* Gainesville: University of Florida Press.
Earle, T. (1980). A model of subsistence change. In T. Earle & A. Christenson (Eds.), *Modeling change in prehistoric subsistence economics* (pp. 1-30). New York: Academic Press.
Epstein, T.J. (1967). The data of economics in anthropological analysis. In A.L. Epstein (Ed.), *The craft of social anthropology.* London: Tavistock.
Flannery, K.V. (Ed.). (1976). *The early Mesoamerican village.* New York: Academic Press.
Ford, R.I. (1974). Northeastern archeology: Past and future directions. *Annual Review of Anthropology 3*, 385-413.
Friedman, M. (1953). The methodology of positive economics. In M. Friedman (Ed.), *Essays in positive economics.* Chicago: University of Chicago Press.
Frisch, R. (1957). Sur un probleme d economie pure. *Metroeconomica 9*, 79-111. (From *Norsk Matematisk Forenings Skrifter*, 1926, Serie I, No. 16, pp. 1-40).
Georgescu-Roegen, N. (1936). The pure theory of consumer's behavior. *Quarterly Journal of Economics 50*, 545-593.
Gladwin, C. (1975). A model of smoked fish from Cape Coast to Kumasi. In S. Plattner (Ed.), *Formal methods in economic anthropology* (Special Publication No. 4) (pp. 77-128). Washington, DC: American Anthropological Association.
Gladwin, C. (1979). Production functions and decision models: Complementary models. *American Ethnologist 6*(4), 653-674.
Gladwin, C. (1980). A theory of real-life choice: Applications to agricultural decisions. In P. Barlett (Ed.), *Agricultural decision making* (pp. 45-86). New York: Academic Press.
Gladwin, H. (1975). Looking for an aggregate additive model in data from a hierarchical decision process. In S. Plattner (Ed.), *Formal methods in economic anthropology* (Special Publication No. 4) (pp. 159-196). Washington, DC: American Anthropological Association.
Gladwin, H., & Murtaugh, M. (1980). The attentive-preattentive distinction in agricultural decision making. In P. Barlett (Ed.), *Agricultural decision making* (pp. 115-136). New York: Academic Press.
Gumerman, G.J. (Ed.). (1971). *The distribution of prehistoric population aggregates* (Prescott College Anthropological Reports No. 1). Prescott, AZ: Prescott College.
Haggett, P. (1960). *Locational analysis in human geography.* New York: St. Martin's.
Hasdorf, C. (1980). Changing resource use in subsistence agricultural groups of the prehistoric Membres River Valley, New Mexico. In T. Earle & A. Christenson (Eds.), *Modeling change in prehistoric subsistence economics* (pp. 79-120). New York: Academic Press.
Heath, A. (1976). *Rational choice and social exchange.* Cambridge: Cambridge University Press.
Henderson, J., & Quandt, R. (1971). *Microeconomic theory: A mathematical approach.* New York: McGraw-Hill.
Higgs, E. (Ed.). (1975). *Paleoeconomy.* Cambridge: Cambridge University Press.
Higgs, E., & Vita-Finzi, C. (1972). Prehistoric economies: A territorial approach. In E.S. Higgs (Ed.), *Papers in Economic Prehistory* (pp. 27-36). Cambridge: Cambridge University Press.
Hillier, F.S., & Lieberman, G.J. (1974). *Introduction to operations research.* (2nd ed.). San Francisco: Holden-Day.
Homans, G.C. (1958). Social behavior as exchange. *American Journal of Sociology 63*, 597-606.

Hoover, E.M. (1948). *The location of economic activity.* New York: McGraw-Hill.
Hudson, C. (1976). *The Southeastern Indians.* Knoxville: University of Tennessee Press.
Isard, W. (1956). *Location and space economy.* Boston: MIT Press.
Jochim, M. (1976). *Hunter-gatherer subsistence and settlement: A predictive model.* New York: Academic Press.
Johnson, A. (1980). The limits of formalism in agricultural decision research. In P. Barlett (Ed.), *Agricultural decision making* (pp. 19-44). New York: Academic Press.
Keene, A. (1977). Nutrition and economy: Models for the study of prehistoric diet. In R.I. Gilbert & J. Meilke (Eds.), *Techniques for the analysis of prehistoric diets.* New York: Academic Press.
Keene, A. (1979). Economic optimization models and the study of hunter-gatherer subsistence settlement systems. In C. Renfrew & K. Cooke (Eds.), *Transformations: Mathematical approaches to culture change* (pp. 369-404). New York: Academic Press.
Keene, A. (1981). *Prehistoric foraging in a temperate forest.* New York: Academic Press.
Kluckholm, C. (1950). Review of *Human behavior and the principle of least effort. American Anthropologist 52,* 268-270.
Koopmans, T.C. (1957). *Three essays on the state of economic science.* New York: McGraw-Hill.
Lafferty, R.H. III, Ottinger, J.L., Scholtz, S.C., Limp, W.F., & Jones, R.D. (1981). *Settlement prediction in Sparta: A locational analysis and resource assessment in the uplands of Calhoun County, Arkansas* (Arkansas Archaeological Survey Research Series No. 14). Fayetteville: University of Arkansas, Arkansas Archaeological Survey.
LeClair, E. (1962). Economic theory and economic anthropology. *American Anthropologist 64,* 1179-1203.
LeClair, E., & Schneider, H. (Eds.). (1968). *Economic Anthropology.* New York: Holt, Rinehart and Winston.
Limp, W.F. (1983a). An economic model of settlement aggregation and dispersal. In G. Bronitsky (Ed.), *Ecological models in economic prehistory* (Anthropological Research Papers No. 29) (pp. 18-45). Tempe: Arizona State University.
Limp, W.F. (1983b). Rational location choice and prehistoric settlement analysis. University Microfilms, Ann Arbor.
Lipe, W., & Mason, R. (1971). Human settlement and resources in the Ceda Mesa Area, SE Utah. In G.J. Gumerman (Ed.), *The distribution of prehistoric population aggregates* (Anthropological Reports No. 1) (pp. 126-151). Prescott, AZ: Prescott College.
McGuire, T. (n.d.). *Choice and adaptation: The economic and ecological consequences of bounded rationality.* Unpublished written preliminary examination. University of Arizona, Tucson.
Machlup, F. (1967). Theories of the firm: Marginalist, behavioral, managerial. *American Economic Review 57*(1), 1-33.
Mainsfield, E. (1970). *Microeconomics.* New York: W.W. Norton.
Munson, P., Parmalee, P., & Yarnell, R. (1971). Subsistence ecology of Scovill, a terminal Middle Woodland village. *American Antiquity 36*(4), 410-431.
Newman, P. (1965). *The theory of exchange.* Englewood Cliffs, NJ: Prentice-Hall.
Ortiz, S. (1967). The structure of decision-making among Indians of Colombia, In R. Firth (Ed.), *Themes in economic anthropology* (Monograph 6). London: Association of Social Anthropologist.
Plattner, S. (Ed.). (1975). *Formal methods in economic anthropology* (Special Publication No. 4) (pp. 1-215). Washington, DC: The American Anthropological Association.
Plog, F., Effand, R., Dean, J., & Gaines, S. (1978). SARG, future research directions. In R.C. Euler & G.J. Gumerman (Eds.), *Investigations of the Southwestern Anthropological Group: Proceedings of the 1976 conference* (pp. 177-186). Flagstaff: Museum of Northern Arizona.
Polanyi, K. (1957). The economy as instituted process. In K. Polanyi, C.M. Arensberg, & H.W. Pearson (Eds.), *Trade and market in the early empires* (pp. 243-270). New York: Free Press.
Prattis, J.I. (1973). Strategising man. *Man 8*(1), 48-58.
Quinn, N. (1975). A natural system used in Mfantse litigation settlement. *American Ethnologist 3,* 331-351.
Reidhead, V. (1976). Optimization and food procurement at the prehistoric Leonard Haag Site,

southeastern Indiana. (University Microfilms, Ann Arbor; No. 77-10972).

Reidhead, V. (1979). Linear programming models in anthropology. *Annual Review of Anthropology 8*, 543-578.

Reidhead, V. (1980). The economics of subsistence change: A test of an optimization model. In T. Earle & A. Christenson (Eds.), *Modeling change in prehistoric subsistence economics* (pp. 141-186). New York: Academic Press.

Robbins, L. (1935). The subject matter of economics. In L. Robbins, *An essay on the nature and significance of economic science*. New York: St. Martins.

Robinson, J. (1980). Introduction. In V. Walsh & H. Gram, *Classical and neoclassical theories of general equilibrium* (pp. xi-xvi). New York: Oxford University Press.

Roper, D.C. (1979). The method and theory of catchment analysis: A review. In M.B. Schiffer (Ed.), *Advances in archaeological method and theory* (vol. 2) (pp. 119-140). New York: Academic Press.

Rossman, D. (1976). A site catchment analysis of San Lorenzo, Veracruz. In K.V. Flannery (Ed.), *The early Mesoamerican village* (pp. 95-102). New York: Academic Press.

Sahlins, M. (1969). Economic anthropology and anthropological economics. *Social Science Information 8*(5), 13-33.

Schneider, H. (1970). *The Wahi Wanyaturu: Economics in an African society.* Chicago: Aldine-Atherton.

Schneider, H. (1974). *Economic Man.* New York: Free Press.

Shepard, R. (1964). On subjectively optimum selections among multi-attribute alternatives. In M.N. Shelly & G.L. Bryan (Eds.), *Human judgements and optimality.* New York: John Wiley.

Silberbauer, G.B. (1971). The G/Wi bushmen. In M.G. Bicchieri (Ed.), *Hunters and gatherers today.* New York: Holt.

Simon, H. (1955). A behavioral model of rational choice. *Quarterly Journal of Economics 69*, 99-114.

Simon, H. (1957a). *Administrative Behavior* (2nd ed.). New York: Macmillan.

Simon, H. (1957b). *Models of Man.* New York: John Wiley & Sons.

Simon, H. (1959). Theories of decision-making in economics and behavioral science. *American Economic Review 49*, 253-283.

Smith, B.D. (1978). *Mississippian settlement patterns.* New York: Academic Press.

Sullivan, A., & Schiffer, M. (1978). A critical examination of SARG. In R.C. Euler & G.J. Gumerman (Eds.), *Investigations of the Southwestern Anthropological Research Group: Proceedings of the 1976 conference* (pp. 168-176). Flagstaff, AZ: Museum of Northern Arizona.

Tooker, E. (1964). *An ethnography of the Huron Indians, 1615-1649.* (Bulletin of the Bureau of American Ethnology No. 190.) Washington, DC: Smithsonian Institution.

Vita-Finzi, C., & Higgs, E. (1970). Prehistoric economy in the Mount Carmel area of Palestine: Site catchment analysis. *Proceedings of the Prehistoric Society 36*, 1-37.

von Bertalanffy, L. (1955). An essay on the relativity of categories. *Philosophy of Science 22*(4), 243-263.

von Newman, J., & Morgenstern, O. (1947). *Theory of games and economic behavior.* Princeton: Princeton University Press.

Walsh, V. (1970). *Introduction to contemporary microeconomics.* New York: McGraw-Hill.

Walsh, V., & Gram, H. (1980). *Classical and neoclassical theories of general equilibrium.* New York: Oxford University Press.

Winter, S. (1971). Satisficing, selection, and the innovating remnant. *Quarterly Journal of Economics 85*, 236-261.

Wold, H. (1943). A synthesis of pure demand analysis. *Skandinavisk Aktuariet-idskrift 26*, 85-118.

Wolfman, D. (in press). Geomagnetic dating techniques. In M.B. Schiffer (Ed.), *Advances in Archaeological method and theory.* New York: Academic Press.

Zarky, A. (1976). Statistical analysis of site catchments at Oco's Guatemala. In K. Flannery (Ed.), *The early Mesoamerican village* (pp. 117-121). New York: Academic Press.

Zimmerman, L. (1977). *Prehistoric locational behavior: A computer simulation.* (Office of the State Archaeologist Report No. 10). Ames: University of Iowa.

Zipf, G.K. (1949). *Human behavior and the Principle of Least Effort.* Cambridge: Addison-Wesley.

8

Predictive Modeling of Site Settlement Systems Using Multivariate Logistics

SANDRA PARKER

Archaeologists have long been intrigued by the patterning and regularity with which human groups distribute themselves across the available landscape, i.e., the manner in which the spatial dimension is utilized. David Clarke (1977, p. 1) made the claim that the study of various kinds of spatial relationships form ". . . a central aspect of the international discipline of archaeology and a major part of the theory of that discipline wherever it is practiced." Clarke's claim for the centrality of spatial concerns is exemplified by the action taken by the Southwestern Anthropological Research Group (SARG), which adopted at their organization meeting in 1970 the major research question of "why are population aggregates located where they are?" (Gumerman 1971, p. 4).

This interest in spatial relationships has manifested itself in the form of a variety of different approaches to the study of spatial archaeology, including settlement archaeology (Willey, 1953; Chang, 1958), the analyses of site settlement systems (Struever, 1968; Winters, 1969; Smith, 1978), regional studies (Phillips, 1970), locational analyses (Flannery, 1972; Crumley, 1976), catchment area studies (Roper, 1974, 1975, 1979; Peebles, 1978), and analyses of distribution maps and site densities. Further, the last three years have seen the development of predictive site locational modeling, a natural outgrowth of the theories and methodologies of spatial archaeology. Various models, which have been derived in a variety of environmental settings, have ranged from intuitive to statistical models based on probabilistic samples.

This chapter represents a continuation of such efforts, introducing and developing a formal, robust predictive modeling technique for studying archaeological site distributions. The discussion presents the relevant anthropological theory serving as a foundation and justification for the technique, its methodology, and additionally a large scale application.

Finally, the proposed method is compared to other approaches for modeling site distributions.

THEORETICAL FOUNDATION

The development of predictive models of site distribution has both practical and theoretical importance. The potential role of predictive settlement models in the management of cultural resources is obvious and is being realized with increasing frequency (e.g., Scholtz, 1980, 1981). Equally important, however, is the increased ability to predict site locations, which implies an increased *understanding* of the site settlement system which produced a particular site locational pattern in an area. Better predictive models are of value in developing a body of theory which attempts to explain the relationships between human groups and the biophysical and social characteristics of their environment. From a theoretical viewpoint, predictions and the evaluation of the predictions' correctness lie at the heart of the explanation of behavioral processes.

The basic axioms on which this analysis is based is that a given location is selected or rejected for the performance of an activity based on a complex assessment of the location's properties within a decision-making framework. This framework allows alternative locations to be ranked into groups of varying preference, the chosen locations coming from the most highly preferred group (see Limp, 1978, 1981; Limp & Carr, chapter 7 for a detailed discussion). These statements express the simplified but essential characteristics of axiomatic choice theory (Arrow, 1951; Walsh, 1970) as applied to activity and settlement location. This study attempts to mirror the proposed behavioral process of location selection with a multivariate logistic predictive model.

Previous archaeological analyses of the distribution of sites have focused on the distinction between a settlement pattern and a settlement system (cf. Winters, 1969; Parsons, 1972), the pattern being the empirical evidence of site distribution while the system is the behavioral abstraction of regularities in the processes which generated the pattern. This analysis proposes that the generating process is one of location assessment and choice, which in itself is sufficient to characterize the settlement system. The regularities defining a settlement pattern are seen as a reflection of underlying regularities in the settlement system.

The location selection decision-making process involves three basic components: the biophysical properties of location, the social subsystem, and the aggregated "cultural" or technical and structural information (Schneider, 1974). Ideally, all three of these components should be built into a location choice model. The most readily available information for an archaeological context, however, is data regarding the biophysical properties of locations, the social and cultural components of the location choice process usually being largely unknown except for well understood archaeological situations (e.g., protohistoric or ethnoarchaeological studies). The position taken in this research is that biophysical considerations constitute an important component in the location selection decision-making process and that the use of these data alone can provide sensitive and efficient locational models. This stance seems justifiable because the biophysical characteristics of an area provide a framework within which social and cultural subsystems function and with which they interact. In addition, certain settlement/environmental regularities have been demonstrated by a number of researchers in a diversity of environmental settings, giving support to the approach of the generation of biophysical settlement models (e.g., Jochim, 1976; Smith, 1978).

The results of the research presented here include a developed methodology for generating explanatory site locational models based on biophysical characteristics. The methodology produces an equation from which a probability for selection for settlement can be generated for each possible site location in an area under study. The equation, a logistic regression, is generated by a multivariate statistical procedure.

The use of a multivariate approach rather than a univariate one in this study is important. Multivariate analysis of a set of variables considers the effects of variables in combination, as a system, while univariate analysis does not. The choice of a multivariate model for predicting settlement locations is based on the assumption that settlement location choice involves a systemic treatment of biophysical variables.

The methodology to be described does not focus on the site as the unit of analysis; rather, it recognizes all possible site location choices—those without sites as well as those with. It predicts where sites are unlikely to occur as well as where they are likely to occur. If environmental information is known only for locations where sites are found, then it is impossible to use the proposed methodology and decision-making framework; locations where sites are not expected cannot be predicted. An effective predictive model must focus on *any* potential site location, not simply the locations where sites are known to exist.

The importance of modeling settlement systems with a data base that includes both site locations and nonsite locations can be illustrated with an example of a sample of locations in a research area. If only site locations are examined for some variable, such as distance to nearest water, interpretations could be erroneous if comparisons are made to the distribution of this variable for the total area with no consideration of the nonsite locations in the sample. Table 1 illustrates the hypothetical distribution of grid units over distance classes of the variable distance to nearest water for units which contain sites, all units in a total research area, and all surveyed units. If one compared the proportion of sites within 100 meters of a stream, 18.8%, with the proportion of grid units with equivalent distances to streams, 9.4%, the interpretation might be that sites are probably in close proximity to a stream. Consideration of the nonsite as well as the site locations in the sample, however, leads to a different interpretation. Examination of the distribution of this variable in the sampled units indicates that the sample was biased toward units in close proximity to water. Clearly, settlement models must take into account the characteristics of nonsite locations as well as those of site locations.

Table 8.1

Distribution for Variable Distance to Nearest Water

Distance (in meters)	Cumulative % of Sites in Sample (N=85)	Cumulative % of Grid Units in Entire Area (N=3854)	Cumulative % of Grid Units in Sampled Area (N=422)
0-100	18.8	9.4	17.5
100-200	30.6	26.2	35.8
200-300	49.4	44.5	57.1
300-400	64.7	58.0	72.8
400-500	74.1	69.9	82.7
500-600	81.2	79.5	88.9
600-700	85.9	86.4	92.4
700-800	94.1	91.7	95.7

THE MULTIVARIATE LOGISTIC APPROACH TO PREDICTIVE MODELING

For theoretical and practical reasons, then, the present research goal has been to develop an explanatory model relating site locations in an area to the biophysical characteristics of the area. To perform the desired functions, such a model must allow one to state the probability that a particular geographic unit in the area would have been selected for the location of a site. Such a model may be in the form of a prediction equation in which the dependent variable is site presence/absence and the independent or predictor variables are the biophysical variables.

The familiar multiple regression model, however, is not appropriate in this case where the dependent variable is a binomial response, i.e., coded as 0 or 1. The only possible attainable values for the site location variable are 0 (absence) and 1 (presence). The application of multiple regression to such data would produce a predictive equation which would predict dependent variable values over a range of values from $-\infty$ to $+\infty$. Such a predictive equation would not give interpretable results for data of this form.

The multivariate logistic model (Wrigley, 1976, 1977a, 1977b; Press & Wilson, 1978; Efron, 1975) is a regression model which does not predict values of the dependent variable; it predicts the probability, given a set of values for the independent variables, of a positive response for the dependent variable. As applied here, such a model will yield an equation for computing the probability of selection for settlement for each geographic unit in the research area. This equation is derived from data concerning site locations that are obtained from a surveyed sample of the area.

The theoretical basis for this approach to settlement location research is that location selection can be shown to depend significantly on environmental factors, expressed as multivariate combinations. The multivariate logistic technique of prediction focuses on the relationship between settlement locations and multiple biophysical characteristics to discriminate between geographic units in a surveyed area which are known to have been selected as site locations and those in which sites were not found. The logistic regression model (Table 2) uses this known environmental information from the surveyed area to derive an equation for predicting a probability of selection for each unsurveyed geographic unit in the research universe. One outcome of such an approach is the generation of a settlement probability surface for the study area. The target parameters in such an approach are not areal site frequencies or densities, but rather the quantitative associations of archaeological sites and biophysical properties.

This site settlement model application of logistic regression is the simplest form of a probability surface problem; the response or dependent variable has only two possible outcomes, site presence or absence. Probability surface models can, however, be extended to handle multinomial response variables for applications in which the response variable has more than two possible outcomes (Wrigley, 1977b, pp. 31-41; Kvamme, chapter 9). In the binomial case, the probability equation (shown in Table 2) yields the probability of a positive response for each unit of analysis, geographic units in the present application. The probability of a negative response is obtained by subtracting the positive probability from the quantity, one. Probabilities for the two possible outcomes sum to one. Similarly, in the multinomial application, a probability equation is generated for each possible outcome of the response variable, and the computed

Table 8.2

Logistic Regression Equation

$$\Pr\{E/\underline{x}\} = \frac{1}{1 + e^{-\{\alpha + \underline{\beta}\,\underline{x}\}}}$$

where $\Pr\{E/\underline{x}\}$ is the probability of the event, E, occurring given a vector of values for the explanatory variables,

and $e = 2.71828$ is the base of natural logarithms,

and $\alpha + \underline{\beta}\,\underline{x} = \alpha + \beta_1 x_1 + \beta_2 x_2 + \ldots + \beta_n x_n$,

and where α is a constant, and $\beta_1, \beta_2 \ldots \beta_n$ are weights or regression coefficients, and $x_1, x_2 \ldots x_n$ represent the explanatory variables.

probabilities for each analytical unit sum to the quantity one. The generalized probability surface model for multinomial response variables can be extended to any number of categories, although the site settlement probability surface problem is based on the two category response variable, site presence or absence.

There is a test of significance for the null hypothesis of no trend in a logistic regression, i.e., all the parameters in the equation are equal to zero (Wrigley, 1977b, p. 18). This test is not based on residual or regression sums of squares and the F ratio, but rather on the maximized log likelihood values of probability surfaces. The test statistic is

$$2 \log \lambda - 2 \log \lambda^* \text{ (g)}$$

where "log λ is the maximized log likelihood of a set of unrestricted probability surface models, and log λ^* is the maximized log likelihood of a set of restricted probability surface models embodying g constraints on the parameters of the set of unrestricted models." In other words, log λ^* pertains to the set of probability surface models containing only the intercept, and g is the number of parameters being estimated.

Data Requirements for Logistic Regression

The logistic regression model presents a methodology for discriminating between site locations and locations without sites. This discrimination is based on environmental characterizations of each of these kinds of locations. Therefore, the data requirements of the method include a data base describing the biophysical characteristics of both site and nonsite locations. The organization for such a data set can be either point based or quadrat data, but in either case the universe of analytical units is every possible site location in the research area.

A point based data set can be obtained by measuring the chosen biophysical variables at each site location and at a randomly selected sample of points where sites are not located (see Kvamme, chapter 9). The size of the sample of nonsite locations must be adequate for describing the environmental variations of the area. A data set of this nature is appropriate for the generation of a logistic regression equation; however, to produce a probability surface using this equation requires data from a large number of closely spaced points, gridded or not, if the surface is to accurately reflect the underlying biophysical variation.

An alternative to a point based data set is one based on quadrats. Using this approach to data collection, the research area is envisioned as a series of geographic units, each of which represents a possible site location. Measurements of biophysical variables are taken from the center of each unit, or observations are made for the unit as a whole. Units with a site within its boundaries are considered site locations. Obviously, the unit size must be of an appropriate scale relative to site size and density in the area to avoid multiple sites occurring in any one unit. Such a data base for a large area can conceivably become very large, although it does provide the basis for producing probability surfaces given a logistic regression equation.

The level of measurement required for independent variables in logistic regression is the same as that for multiple regression, and categorical responses may be included as dummy variables. As for any multivariate analysis, a reasonably large sample is desirable, and its size must exceed the number of variables in the equation.

SETTLEMENT MODEL IN THE SPARTA RESEARCH AREA

The generation of a multivariate logistic equation as a settlement model will be demonstrated by an application in the Sparta research area (Lafferty et al., 1981). This large area, about 14,170 hectares (35,000 acres) located in the Gulf Coastal Uplands near the Ouachita River Valley in southern Arkansas (Fig. 1), is to be developed as a lignite mine. The Ouachita River, a tributary of the Mississippi, is 16 km south of the mine area. This area is between the Ouachita Mountains, where extensive outcrops of such hard rock as chert and novaculite occur, and the rich farmlands of the Lower Mississippi alluvial valley.

The Sparta Environment

The area is characterized geologically by Eocene uplands in the northeastern corner of the research area; older terraces which are relict alluvial plains of the Arkansas, Ouachita, Red, and Mississippi rivers; and more recently formed terrace systems of the modern creeks such as Champagnolle, Taylor, Blann and Lloyd creeks (Fig. 2). The geological nature of the area is described by Saucier (1974) and Saucier and Fleetwood (1970).

Soils in the Sparta area range from well drained to poorly drained (Gill et al., 1980). The better drained upland soils in the northeastern section have been cultivated and terraced in the past, and some of these are presently in pastures (Lafferty, 1981, p. 14). The upland soils, Pikeville and Sacul, are the most severely sloped. The Savannah, Ruston, and Smithdale soils on the eroded edges of the Montgomery and Prairie terraces are more gently sloping. The more recently deposited soils of the area's southern portion, Amy and Pheba soils, are poorly drained and have little slope. Guyton, Ouachita, and Smithton soils have a high clay content and are poorly drained. The older terrace surfaces, Montgomery and Prairie terraces, are characterized in wet winter and spring months by standing water (Gill et al., 1980). Table 3 lists some characteristics of the soils in the Sparta research area.

The rivers and creeks in and around the Sparta area were probably important to the prehistoric inhabitants for a variety of reasons. Besides being sources of water and wildlife they also provided likely means of transportation (Lafferty, 1981, pp. 14-16). Water navigation in the research area, however, was probably

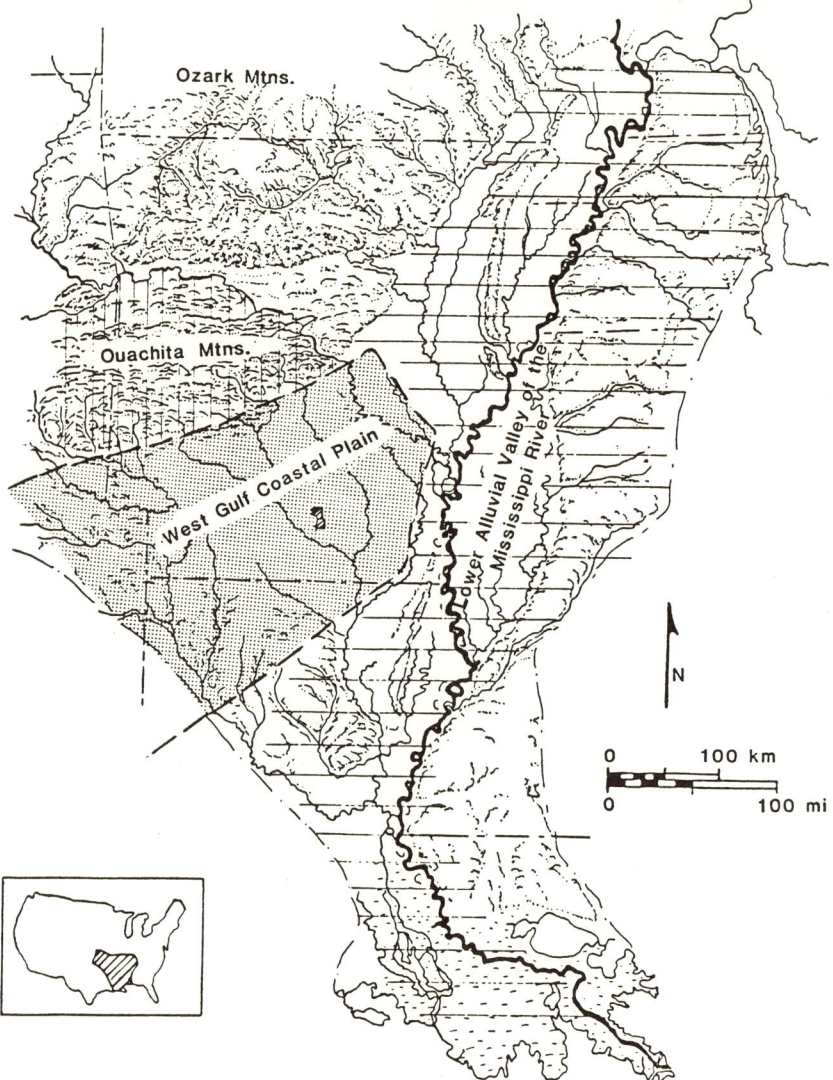

Fig. 8.1. The Sparta Mine area in the West Gulf Coastal Plain.

seasonal, since even the large creeks in the area are navigable by small boats in winter and spring only. One of the major east-west land routes in this section of Arkansas passes through the research area along the terrace edges above the Ouachita River (Lafferty, 1981, p. 16).

There is evidence for a number of fresh water springs in the area (Lafferty,

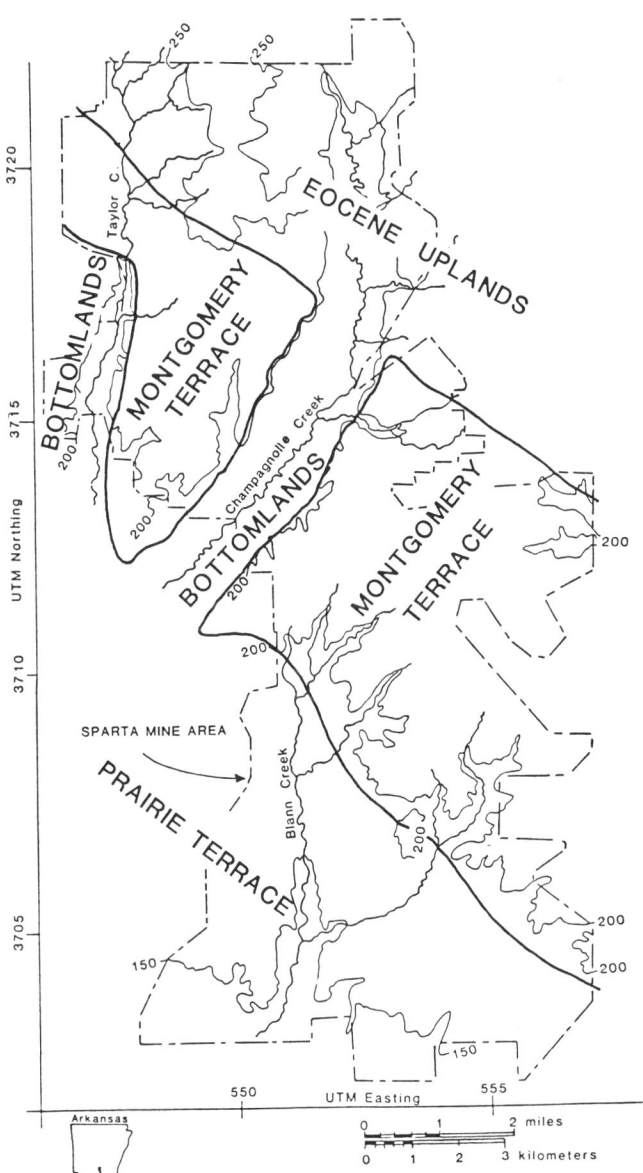

Fig. 8.2. Major surficial deposits in the Sparta Mine area (based on Fleetwood, 1969; Harris, 1892; and field observations).

1981, p. 18), which probably influenced prehistoric settlement in the vicinity, but all except a few of the spring locations are unknown.

The biotic zones of the research area are characterized by oak-hickory-pine

Table 8.3

Characteristics of the Soils in the Sparta Mine Area (after Gill et al., 1980)

	Guyton	*Ouachita*	*Amy*	*Pheba*	*Pikeville*	*Ruston*	*Sacul*	*Savannah*	*Smithdale*	*Smithton*
Animal unit months[1]	5.00	7.00	6.00	7.00	6.25	7.00	5.75	7.00	7.25	7.50
Loblolly pine index	90	100	90	90	80	80	84	81	80	90
Depth to available water in inches	0	33	0	8	80	18	80	27	80	4
Available water to 60 inches/square inch	11.67	11.70	10.10	7.83	5.90	10.20	7.42	6.57	11.72	10.79
Maximum liquid limit	27	30	30	25	30	20	20	25	20	—
Maximum plastic limit	7	12	5	8	4	3	3	4	5	—
Capability units	5	4	3	3	3	2	3	2	3	3

[1] Number of cows or horses that can be supported on one acre of Bermuda grass.

forest in the uplands and southern floodplain forest in the bottomlands (Fig. 3). The southern floodplain forest "has one of the richest biota and highest carrying capacity in North America" (Lafferty, 1981, p. 23) with a large number of both terrestrial and aquatic species. The upland forest is a relatively rich environment, providing sources of food for both humans and animals. The various nuts of the oak-hickory-pine forest provided food for humans as well as acorns for deer. The drier ground in the uplands attracts animals when the lowlands flood and, thus, would have provided increased hunting potential in wet winter and spring months.

Operationalizing the Logistics Model in Sparta: Choice of Units and Variables

The research approach of generating a multivariate logistics model to predict settlement locations in the Sparta area required two basic data collection efforts. These were the accumulation of a biophysical data base to provide the independent or predictor variables in the equation for the entire Sparta area, and a field survey of a portion of the area to provide information about site presence/absence, the dependent variable in the model.

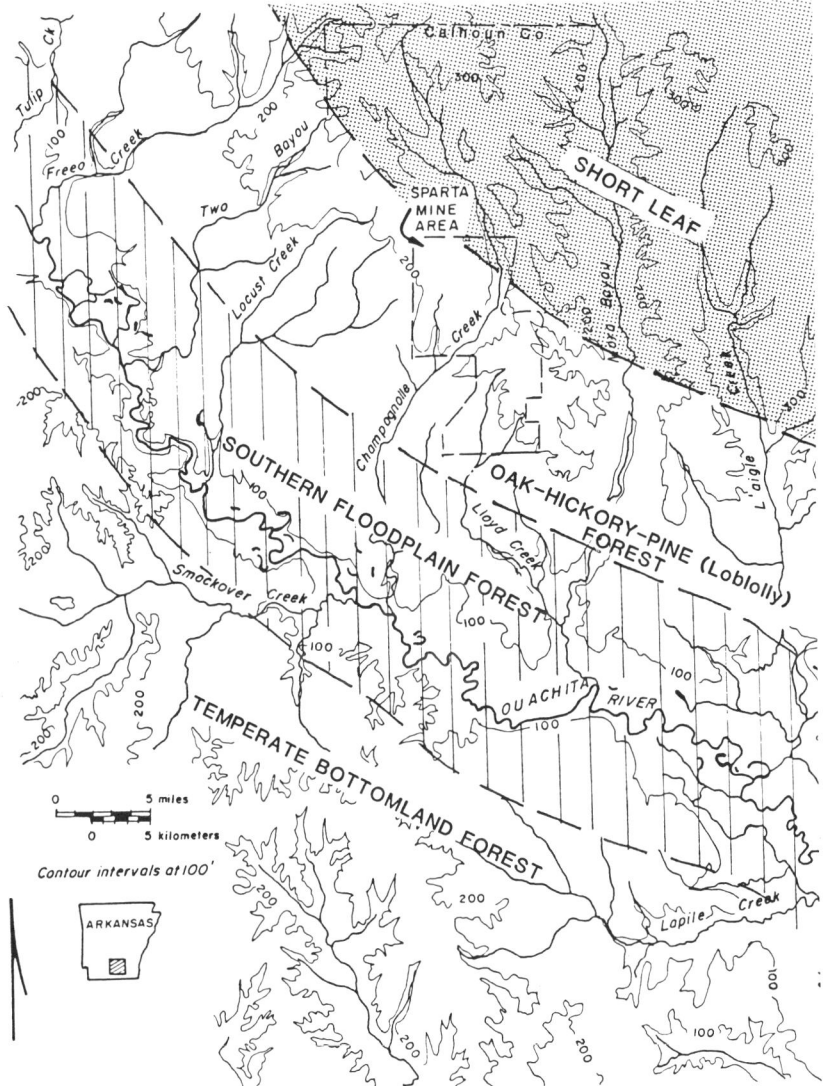

Fig. 8.3. Major biotic communities in the environs of the Sparta Mine area (based on Mase, 1979; Kuchler, 1964; and field observations).

The first of these efforts, the accumulation of a biophysical data base, was begun by overlaying on the Sparta area a grid, each unit of which represented a possible site location. Various grid methods are possible, e.g., rectangular or hexagonal. The fact that Sparta biophysical data were to be collected manually from maps influenced the selection in this case of a rectangular grid oriented to the Universal Transverse Mercator (UTM). For each grid unit, a number of observations of relevant environmental characteristics could then be recorded and manipulated.

A critical decision was the size of the grid unit. The number of units increases as the square of the unit size decreases. Halving the size of units would have quadrupled their number. An excessively small unit size would have made manual data collection prohibitively time-consuming and expensive. Also, it was desirable that units not be so small as to probably divide single sites among multiple units. On the other hand, an excessively large unit size would have yielded a "homogenized" picture of microenvironmental variability, making useful analysis impossible. Based on a careful evaluation of the geomorphic, pedological, and other environmental data, as well as anticipated site size and work force/time constraints, a grid unit of 4 hectares was chosen for the Sparta area. For the research area, this yielded 3,479 units.

Of equal importance to decisions regarding the unit of analysis in settlement modeling is the selection of variables for the model. In an archaeologically unknown region, the selection of variables for a model predicting settlement locations is based, by necessity, on a prior consideration of which characteristics of the environment might have been important to the people using that environment. Such evaluations may be based on known relationships between site locations and environmental variables in ethnographic or archaeological contexts thought to be similar to the area of study. Alternately, one may draw upon more generalized lists of fundamental physical properties of locations for human survival, which previous researchers (Lipe & Matson, 1971, pp. 133-134; Limp, 1981, pp. 62-63) have compiled from broader contexts. The latter approach was taken in the Sparta study. A portion of the generalized lists of basic life-support properties of locations thought important in the Sparta area served as the basis for selecting prediction variables for the model. These properties include:

1) Permanent water
2) Food resources
   (a) Floral, wild
   (b) Faunal, wild
   (c) Floral, domestic
3) Firewood
4) Construction materials
5) Location "comfort"
   (a) Location drainage
   (b) Slope
   (c) Exposure
      (i) Protection
6) Hazard

Representing most of the properties on this list, fifteen biophysical variables were chosen as independent variables in the Sparta modeling process (Table 4).

Most of the environmental information was taken from the United States Geological Survey 7.5 minute quadrangle maps of the area. These include five soil variables characterizing the predominant soil types, and ten nonsoil biophysical variables. All the variables are continuous in nature and appropriate for multiple regression (Kerlinger & Pedhazur, 1973). These variables are described as follows:

Permanent water. Water availability was reflected in variables which express the lineal distance to streams. It was not possible to assess "effective" distance to water in an area in which the nature of the virgin vegetation is unknown, although as Higgs and Vita Finzi (1972) note, the actual rate of travel, given different surface conditions, is a better estimate of the ease of access to a particular environmental feature than is lineal distance. In lieu of "effective" distance to water, the geographic units in the Sparta area were evaluated for distances to nearest stream and to second nearest stream. The latter measurement was made because of its potential importance, given the seasonally fluctuating nature of the water sources.

Stream order, computed using the Strahler method (Weide & Weide, 1973), was encoded for the nearest and the second nearest streams because the size of water sources could have had an effect on site locations.

Food availability. Several variables were encoded in an attempt to represent the availability of food resources in the absence of information about prehistoric vegetation for the area. Since some studies elsewhere have shown a consistent relationship between soil types and plant communities (Jones, 1969; Carmean, 1965, 1967), the predominant soil type within each grid unit was encoded using soil data from Gill et al. (1980). This made accessible information regarding soil characteristics, such as depth to available water, available water capacity, Loblolly pine index, soil capability class, and Bermuda grass index.

Biotic variation was also expressed in the variables by the encoding of distance to the upland/lowland ecotone, the location of presumably the most diverse kinds of plant communities in the research area. Studies in similar areas have shown that in such locations of upland/lowland community interaction, a large number of different kinds of plants and animals occur (Voigt & Mohlenbrock, 1964; Zawacki & Hausfater, 1969, pp. 31-40). Slope was considered also a determinant of possible plant communities and slope data was encoded from the soil type slope groupings (1-3%, 3-8%, 8-20%). Distance to and order of nearest stream junctions were encoded to represent the availability of a variety of aquatic food resources.

Location comfort. Some elements of location comfort are expressed by variables which reflect drainage and slope. Slope is encoded directly, and the soil variables are indirect measures of vegetation determinates that express some aspects of exposure and protection.

Flooding hazard. This property is expressed partially in the Sparta area by distance measures to the two nearest streams, distances to fourth order stream, and elevation above mean sea level. Exposure to attack is measured by distance to a fourth order stream.

Some of the general life-support properties of locations listed above are not reflected in the variables of the Sparta data set. This results from either the difficulty in obtaining accurate data on the properties or their probable lack of variation within the area. Topographic surface is a partial measure of exposure and protection, but this variable is not used in the Sparta settlement model because of the inappropriateness of the level of information available. Topographic features in this area, a terrace edge for example, frequently are not observable on the USGS topographic maps because of their subtlety with regard to the interval size of the map contours. Also not encoded are variables which measure the availability of firewood and construction materials. Such information is not available, but its lack is probably not significant because there was probably only minor variation of the accessibility of such resources in the research area. (For a more thorough discussion of variable selection for the Sparta settlement model, see Limp, Lafferty & Scholtz, 1981).

Operationalizing the Logistics Model: The Surveyed Sample

The second required collection effort was a field survey to provide information concerning site presence and absence. The nature of the survey, described in detail by Otinger, Lafferty, and Jones (1981, pp. 101-116), is briefly recapitulated here. The original survey strategy was planned to utilize the entire biophysical data base for the entire area to generate a stratified sample of the environment. Because of several constraints, including lack of access to some of the study area, this plan was abandoned in favor of one which was based on both random and stratified elements.

> The employed sampling strategy was to survey transects along two pipelines and one powerline route that run north to south across the project area. These were straight lines which had been randomly placed with respect to any particular environmental feature in the Sparta Mine area. The spacing of the lines approximately 3 to 5 km apart assured that there would be an even east-west dispersion. Since all three lines could not be completely surveyed within the time constraints of the fieldwork, choice had to be made about where the sampling transects would be placed along these north-south routes. For this purpose the project area was divided into macrotopographic units to assure that samples were taken from all areas of the project area. These were used as guides to make the sample representative. (Otinger, Lafferty, & Jones, 1981, p. 102)

After the survey sample of approximately 11% was taken, statistical tests were conducted to evaluate the representativeness of the sample. The cumulative percentage composition of each variable in the sample was compared with the percentage composition in the entire mine area. The two curves for each variable were plotted. A Kolmogorov-Smirnov test statistic was used to establish significant differences between curves for ordinal variables (Conover, 1971) and Chi-square tests were used for each nominal variable. The results of these tests (Lafferty, 1981, pp. 170-176) indicated that the sample was generally representative for the variables in the model; only two showed significant differences between the sample and the entire area—distance to a fourth order stream and soils. Locations at greater distances from a fourth order stream were relatively underrepresented in the sample as were Smithton soils. Guyton and Amy soils were overrepresented. These characteristics of the sample should be kept in mind when evaluating the model.

Predictive Model

Because we can presume that settlement patterns found in the Sparta area represent different settlement systems at different periods of time, the ideal approach would be to derive predictive equations for each different settlement system represented. Several factors, however, adversely affected attempts to subdivide the Sparta area sites into groups which might represent individual settlement systems. One of these factors is the low frequency of sites located in the surveyed sample. A much larger number of sites would have been required to represent adequately individual settlement systems. Also, the paucity of diagnostic artifacts recovered from the sites precluded refined cultural subdivision. For these reasons, all of the prehistoric sites, 30 in number, form the basis of the predictive model.

Undoubtedly there were some differences in site location selection processes throughout the entire prehistoric period. Hunting and gathering, as well as agricultural subsistence patterns, are probably represented in the sample of prehistoric sites. It is assumed, however, that there may be enough similarities in the biophysical characteristics of the chosen site locations to allow the derivation of a significant predictive model for prehistoric site location. Such similarities would represent *fundamental* physical properties of locations necessary for survival. The set of site locations used in building the predictive model, therefore, is concordant with the list of variables chosen.

All of the measured biophysical variables listed in Table 4 were included as predictor variables in the model. The derived equation was based on the entire surveyed sample of 414 geographic units, 30 of which were found to be the locations of prehistoric sites. The derived equation is seen in Table 5, in which the numbers in the first column represent the estimates for the parameters (α, $\beta_1, \beta_2, \ldots \beta_k$) of the multivariate logistic equation. This table also gives the Chi-square values and associated probabilities for each variable.

It is of interpretive value to examine the estimated coefficients in the model to determine how different variables affected location choices and which variables made the most contribution in determining the probabilities estimated by the model. Because the variables were standardized before analysis, the equation values estimated are standardized regression coefficients and therefore are

Table 8.4

Biophysical Variables

Soil Variables	Nonsoil Variables
Bermuda index	Slope
Loblolly pine index	Order of nearest stream
Available soil moisture	Order of second nearest stream
Depth to water	Order of nearest stream junction
Soil capability class	Distance to nearest stream
	Distance to second nearest stream
	Distance to nearest stream junction
	Distance to upland/lowland divide
	Distance to nearest fourth order stream
	Elevation AMSL

comparable between variables. The variable with the largest coefficient makes the largest contribution to an estimated probability, while those with coefficients near zero have minimal effect. The sign of the coefficients is also meaningful for interpreting the relationships between variables and estimated probabilities. For variables with positive coefficients, larger variable values produce larger probabilities, while an inverse relationship holds for those with negative coefficients. A comparative examination of the coefficients will provide behavioral interpretations concerning the process of location choice.

Table 5 indicates that the most significant variable in the prehistoric model is Bermuda index with a coefficient of −2.6529. The next three in order of significance are soil capability class (−1.6273), hectometers to fourth order stream (0.9838), and distance to nearest stream (−0.9662). The first two are both soil characteristics and are interpretable in behavioral terms. For the Bermuda index, low values are associated with higher estimated probabilities of location. This index probably is not measuring any one aspect of the environment of which the inhabitants were cognizant; instead, it represents a composite measurement expressing a number of environmental situations. The floodplains of the major creeks are composed largely of Guyton soils which have a low Bermuda index. There are fingers of better drained soils on the terrace edges where sites were located frequently, but these areas of better drained soils are often small, thus unmapped. The resulting situation is that sites tend to be located in areas where soil with a low Bermuda index was prominent.

Table 8.5

Alpha and Beta Coefficient Estimates for Prehistoric Logistic Equation

Parameter	Estimate	Chi-Square	p
Intercept α	−3.88351839	65.07	—
Slope	0.08348748	0.09	0.7686
Order of nearest stream	0.55842095	4.22	0.0399
Order of second nearest stream	0.85304633	12.10	0.0005
Order of nearest junction	−0.33082989	1.54	0.2147
Distance to nearest stream	−0.96615320	5.49	0.0192
Distance to second nearest stream	−0.34930253	0.61	0.4335
Distance to nearest stream junction	0.86718905	3.17	0.0750
Distance to upland/lowland divide	−0.80340604	5.88	0.0153
Distance to fourth order stream	0.98384191	10.94	0.0009
Elevation above mean sea level	0.01351760	0.00	0.9640
Bermuda index	−2.65285197	12.09	0.0005
Loblolly pine index	0.69048610	0.99	0.3185
Available soil moisture	−0.02505908	0.00	0.9595
Depth to water	0.87123864	2.57	0.1088
Soil capability class	−1.62725820	8.83	0.0030

There was a tendency for locations that were selected for settlement to be areas which have lower values for soil capability class. This means that for at least a portion of the sites there was a selective bias for areas which have more productive, more useful soils.

Additionally, the areas selected were usually on smaller tributaries, thereby accounting for the positive coefficient of the variable, hectometers to fourth order stream, for which large distances result in higher estimated probabilities. Champagnolle Creek is the only fourth order stream in the area, and a small portion of the southern part of the area is nearer to a fourth order stream outside the area than to Champagnolle. Greater distances from fourth order streams would have the effect of reducing flooding hazards as well as exposure to attack.

Most of the prehistoric sites are located near streams of second and third order rather than first order, thereby explaining the positive coefficients of order of nearest stream and order of second nearest stream. The smaller the value for order for these two variables, the smaller the estimated probability.

The negative coefficients for distance to nearest stream and distance to second nearest stream indicate that smaller distances result in larger estimated probabilities. This expresses the preference for settlement locations nearer to water sources rather than farther from water. This relationship reflects, not only the dependence of prehistoric peoples on streams for water, but probably also for aquatic food resources.

Availability of a variety of food resources is probably reflected in the relationship of site locations to the upland/lowland ecotone. Sites tended to be located near the divide, making food resources from both uplands and lowlands more accessible.

By defining a cutoff value between low and high probability, the model can be examined as to the number of site locations classified as nonsite locations. All except two of the geographic units with sites present were predicted with probabilities greater than 0.04; therefore, if 0.04 is accepted as the cutoff value, this allows the model to meet the criterion of misclassifying less than 10% of the site locations. The selection of a cutoff value is discussed further below. Figure 4 represents a probability surface of the Sparta area with low probability defined as below 0.04. This cutoff value results in 2,134 geographic units predicted with low probabilities and 1,345 high probability units.

Model Validation

It may be asked whether or not a logistic model with a significant fit is sufficient to allow interpretations of site probability for areas as yet unsurveyed. If predictive models are to contribute to a greater understanding of human settlement patterns and to the land-use decision-making process, it is imperative that a validation methodology be developed to allow for more rigorous model testing. Such procedures should allow the incorporation of further field tests. A several-stage validation procedure is outlined below.

Comparison of Predicted to Observed Site Frequencies

A first step in evaluating model validity is provided by a comparison of the observed frequencies of sites, considered by probability class, to the expected frequencies of sites predicted by the model. These are labeled observed probability and predicted probability in Table 6. The sample on which the model is based should have located sites in approximately equal numbers to that which the model predicts if the model is accurately representing the information in the sample. Expressed in another way, a line plotted through points representing observed versus expected site frequencies should approach a 45° angle. The closer the points fall to such a line, the better the fit of the model to the data. Figure 5 shows such a plot for the Sparta model and data. Examination of the points indicates that the observed and expected frequencies match quite well,

Fig. 8.4. Sparta probability surface. X = high probability.

with the exception of the very highest predicted probability class in which the number of observed sites falls short compared to model predictions. Considering, however, that there is low site density in the area, heavy ground cover affecting site visibility and relatively few units predicted with higher probabilities, it is reasonable to assume that chance factors could have resulted in the lower-than-expected site frequencies in the higher probability units. At any rate, over most of the probability classes these points do closely approximate a line at 45°.

Ideally, a logistic regression model should be tested by further survey. A field

Table 8.6

Probability Distribution of Site Presence and Absence for Grid Locations in Sample

Predicted Probability Classes	Midpoint	Geographic Units With Sites	Geographic Units Without Sites	Observed Probability
$p > .4$	0.7	5	5	0.500
$.22 < p \leq .4$	0.31	9	19	0.321
$.14 < p \leq .22$	0.18	6	24	0.200
$.10 < p \leq .14$	0.12	3	25	0.107
$.06 < p \leq .10$	0.08	2	46	0.041
$.02 < p \leq .06$	0.04	5	79	0.059
$p \leq .02$	0.01	0	186	0.000
		30	384	

survey designed as a test of the generated model can be designed to randomly sample the low probability units and observe whether sites are present in them. The model can then be rejected if more sites are found than are predicted by the cumulative Poisson distribution at a selected level of significance. Survey, however, is very time consuming, therefore expensive, and may be difficult to fund to a degree sufficient to test a settlement model in *low probability* areas where very few sites are expected. Instead of a random, low probability field test, a two-phase test can be designed to further validate the settlement model. One of these involves a cross-validation procedure using the data from which the model was derived and a cumulative Poisson assessment. The second phase of testing involves field survey. Both of these phases of model testing will be discussed relative to the Sparta project.

Cross-Validation Tests

The cross-validation procedure proposed here involves the selection of *portions* of the surveyed area for generating a model *approximating* the model to be tested. The unselected portions of the study area are then used to test the partial model as a reflection of the full model. This cross-validation procedure assumes that the reduced model being tested is approximately equivalent to the full model, an assumption that can also be tested statistically. If multiple reduced models, based on varying sized samples of the study area, are built, the validation procedure should also show that as the samples approach that of the full model, the fit of the equations to the data improves. This would be

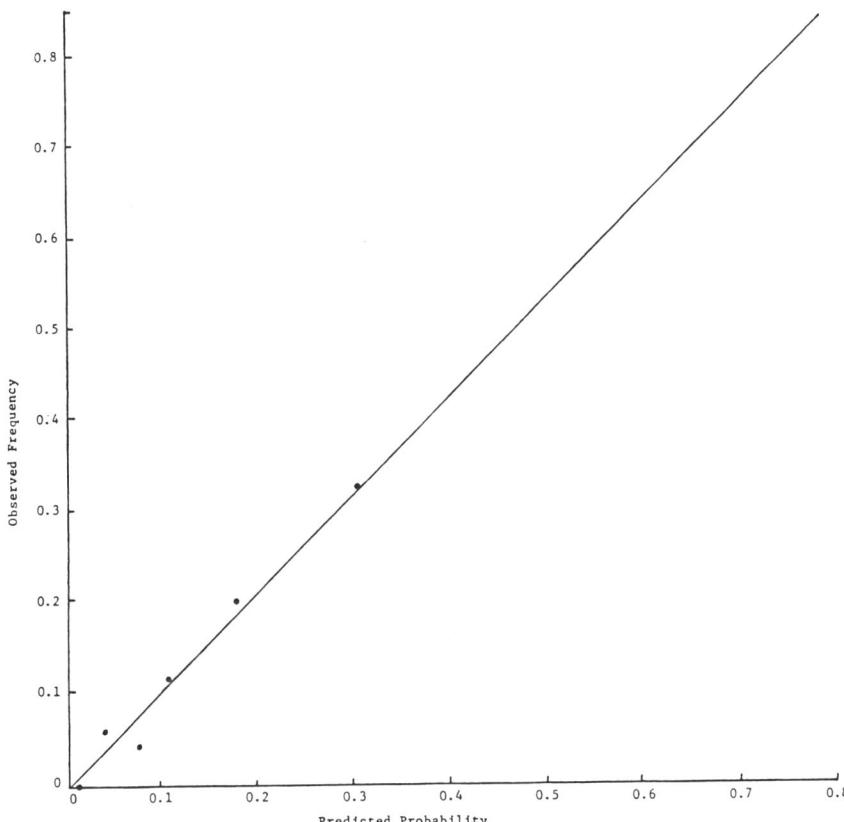

Fig. 8.5. Plot of expected vs. observed site frequencies for 1980 survey.

evidenced by the Chi-square values of the models and their associated probabilities.

In the case of the Sparta study, the entire sample—including 414 total units, of which 30 are sites—was divided at random into six groups. Two reduced models were generated and tested. The first of these was generated from four of the groups selected at random and tested with the remaining two groups. The second reduced model was generated from the four groups in the first reduced model, plus one of the remaining groups added at random and tested with the remaining one group. Admittedly, the two tested models are not identical to the full model because they are based on a somewhat different sample; the five-group sample more closely resembles the full model sample than does the four-group sample.

In order to use the proposed cross-validation procedures to assess logistic regression models, it is necessary first to recognize a cutoff point dividing low and high probability units. The definition of a cutoff value necessitates that a criterion be established. The criterion chosen in this case was derived by a careful consideration of the "loss level," given different values for the cutoff. If low probability units are to be evaluated as having such low site density as to make survey unproductive and impractical, then the cutoff value should be set such that the observed number of sites found in the defined low probability areas does not exceed an acceptable loss level. Establishing an acceptable loss level at less than 10% of the sites in the Sparta area yields a cutoff value of 0.04 because, with the logistic regression model, only two of the 30 sites (6.67%) were located in units with probabilities of less than 0.04.

Next, a reduced model was generated and tested. The four-group test, which included 22 sites and 254 nonsites, produced a logistic equation with a Chi-square value of 45.02 with 15 degrees of freedom. The critical value for a test at the 0.05 level of significance with 15 degrees of freedom is 25.00; therefore, the value of 45.02 indicates that the hypothesis that all parameters are equal to zero is rejected. Using this equation to generate probabilities for the sites in the remaining two groups and accepting 0.04 as the cutoff value between low and high probabilities produced one site probability below 0.04.

The cumulative Poisson distribution (Dixon & Massey, 1969, p. 533) was used to determine whether or not the model should be rejected, given the number of low probabilities generated for site locations, one in the case of the four-group model. To apply the cumulative Poisson test it is necessary to compute λ (Lamda), the parameter of the distribution. Lamda is equal to Np where N is the number of low probability units predicted in the test sample and p is the probability with which they are predicted. Thus, λ is the expected number of low probability sites in the sample. A cumulative Poisson table is then accessed to determine the maximum number of low probability sites allowed without rejecting the model, given the computed expected number and a chosen level of significance. Table 7 illustrates the computation of λ, which for the four-group model is 1.05. Because rejection of the null hypothesis indicates that the model is not a good fit, a confidence level of 90% was selected to decrease the chance of accepting a false hypothesis. Using a 90% confidence level, the model should be rejected if three or more sites in the test sample are predicted with low probabilities. The model predicted only one site with a low probability; therefore, it was not rejected.

The five-group model, including 26 sites and 319 nonsites, produced a logistic equation with a Chi-square value of 47.66 with 15 degrees of freedom. The critical value for a test at the 0.05 level of significance with 15 degrees of freedom is 25.00; therefore, the value of 47.66 indicates that the hypothesis that all parameters are equal to zero is rejected. The five-group equation predicted one site in the test sample with a probability below 0.04. Table 8 illustrates the computation of λ for this test. Using this value of 0.69 for the expected number of low probability sites and a 90% confidence level, the cumulative Poisson table

Table 8.7

Four-Group Test

In four-group subsample:

    22 positive site locations
       3 sites below 0.04 probability

    Test with remaining 2 groups:
       1 site below 0.04 probability

Probability Category	Average Probability (p)	Number of Units (N)	Expected Number of Sites (Np)
0-0.02	0.01	69	0.69
0.02-0.04	0.03	12	0.36
			1.05

$Np = \lambda = 1.05$

Accept model at 90% if there is one or fewer sites below 0.04 probability. There is one; therefore, model is not rejected.

Table 8.8

Five-Group Test

In five-group subsample:

    26 positive site locations
       2 sites below 0.04 probability

    Test with remaining 1 group:
       1 site below 0.04 probability

Probability Category	Average Probability (p)	Number of Units (N)	Expected Number of Sites (Np)
0-0.02	0.01	36	0.36
0.02-0.04	0.03	11	0.33
			0.69

$Np = \lambda = 0.69$

Accept model at 90% if there are two or fewer sites below 0.04 probability. There is one; therefore, model is not rejected.

indicates that the model should be rejected if it predicts 2 or more sites with low probabilities; therefore, the model was not rejected.

To enhance the evaluation of these reduced model tests in the determination of validity for the full logistic regression model, it is necessary to evaluate the degree to which the reduced models approximate the full. To do this, the stability of the reduced models can be compared to the full model. For example, do low probability units as determined by the full model remain low probability units in the four-group and the five-group models? To address this question, cross-tabulations can be performed for low and high probability classes between the three models. Table 9 illustrates these cross-tabulations and their respective phi coefficients for the Sparta data. Since a perfect correspondence would yield a phi coefficient equal to one, it is apparent that there is close agreement between the reduced models and the full model. It is also apparent that the probabilities predicted by the full model correspond more closely to those of the five-group model, as should be the case. Both the four- and five-group tests and the phi coefficients evaluating correspondence attest to the stability of the reduced models and goodness of fit of the full model to the data.

Field Test

The procedure for evaluating the validity of a logistic regression predictive model (described above) adds to the confidence with which such a model may be used. No validity tests are complete, however, without further field tests. The results of a second survey, not originally designed to test the model but judged useful for this purpose, therefore, are presented. This sample, collected in the spring of 1982, included the survey of all high probability units (those over 0.04 probability) in the first-five-year mine area, historic roadways, and "rare topographies" in the low probability units in the first-five-year mine area. The term *rare topography* indicates those areas in which a feature, such as a small terrace, appeared but was not reflected in the encoding due to the resolution of the USGS topographic maps from which biophysical data were taken. A screening step was undertaken to determine which of all surveyed units were examined in such a way that prehistoric sites stood an equal chance of being discovered. Units in historic roadways having heavy ground cover clearly did not meet this criterion. Units, which were judged to fulfill the requirement, numbered 196.

These units do not represent a probabilistic sample of the entire Sparta area—a type of sample which was desirable but not possible, given the plan for development of the mine. Given the nature of the sample, it is not defensible to test the model statistically; however, it is appropriate to ask how such a sample would be expected to behave if the model does have explanatory value.

Careful consideration has led to the following proposals regarding the expected behavior of any sample (not just a random sample) from the Sparta area. First, few sites should be found in the low probability areas if the model

Table 8.9

Cross-Tabulations between the Three Models

		Four-Group Model Probabilities		
		Low <0.04	High >0.04	
Full Model Probabilities	Low <0.04	2042	92	2134
	High >0.04	117	1228	1345
		2159	1320	3479

Phi coefficient = 0.873

		Five-Group Model Probabilities		
		Low <0.04	High >0.04	
Full Model Probabilities	Low <0.04	2048	86	2134
	High >0.04	34	1311	1345
		2082	1397	3479

Phi coefficient = 0.928

		Five-Group Model Probabilities		
		Low <0.04	High >0.04	
Four-Group Model Probabilities	Low <0.04	2023	136	2159
	High >0.04	59	1261	1320
		2082	1397	3479

Phi coefficient = 0.883

accurately locates these areas. Secondly, the observed proportion of high probability units containing sites should at least approximate and vary directly with the probabilities predicted by the model. That is, higher probability units should contain a larger proportion of sites than do lower probability units. More assurance can be placed in model validity if these characteristics are met by a sample of the area, regardless of how the sample was drawn.

An examination of a plot of expected versus observed site frequencies for the 1982 survey (Fig. 6) reveals that this sample does, in fact, behave as would be expected for any sample from the Sparta area. The surveyed units located in low probability areas, i.e., below 0.04, include no sites. Additionally, higher probability units contain a larger proportion of sites than do lower probability units.

Another characteristic of the 1982 sample, the survey energy expended per site compared to that of the 1980 survey, also serves to increase our confidence in validity of the model. The 1982 survey, which utilized the logistic model to

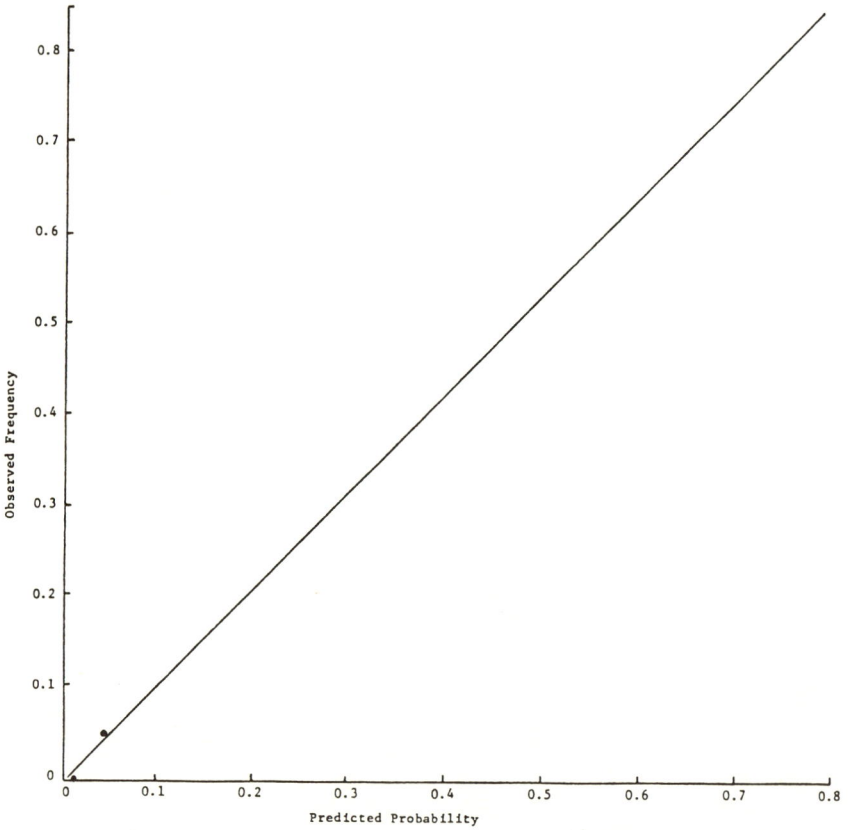

Fig. 8.6. Plot of expected vs. observed site frequencies for 1982 survey.

concentrate on high probability units (over 0.04), located four times as many sites per unit of time as did the 1980 survey.

It is of interest to note that the observed and predicted site frequencies do not match as well for the 1982 survey as for the 1980 survey, which did not benefit from such guidance. Fewer sites were found that were predicted. There are several possible explanations for this result. The 1982 survey was conducted in late spring when the ground cover was reaching its peak, as opposed to the 1980 survey, which was conducted in the winter. Also, it would seem that this result would be a logical outcome in any restricted area within the entire mine area simply because the environment is not represented totally in the sample, i.e., because of sampling error. Finally, sampling error could also have effected the higher probabilities disproportionately because they are predicted in such small numbers. Thus, the samples represent a very small sample of higher probability units.

COMPARISON OF MULTIVARIATE LOGISTICS TO OTHER PREDICTIVE METHODOLOGIES

Having demonstrated the multivariate logistics methodology with the Sparta data, we can make a more thorough comparison of this method of predicting archaeological site locations with other predictive methodologies. Discriminant function analysis is a statistical technique which can be applied like multivariate logistics to predict site locations. Two other less similar techniques that produce surface maps predicting values for a geographically distributed variable are trend surface analysis and Kriging. Each of these methodologies will be described briefly and compared to multivariate logistic models.

Discriminant Function Analysis

The multivariate statistical technique called discriminant function analysis is a classificatory methodology by which an item of given characteristics is classified into one of several alternative populations. In the present application, the item is a location with certain environmental characteristics, and the alternative populations are sites and nonsites. Estimated probabilities of inclusion of a location in these populations may be generated.

This technique represents a different problem from that of logistic regression and generally proposes a different solution, but the two methodologies are related. Linear discriminant analysis forms a linear combination of discriminating variables expressed as a discriminant function. The function is constructed so that the projections of the observations from the two populations onto the function are made as statistically distinct as possible, with the projections of the members of one group clustered at one end of the function and those of the other clustered at the opposite end. The discriminant function is of the form:

$$D_i = d_{i1}Z_1 + d_{i2}Z_2 + \ldots + d_{ik}Z_k$$

where D is the value of the projection (or score) of an observation on discriminant function i, each d is a weighing coefficient, and each Z is a standardized value of a discriminating variable used in the analysis. The coefficients may be interpreted similar to those in logistic regression, thus serving to identify the most discriminating variables. Because discriminant analysis and logistic regression seem to be alternatives for some applications, they will be compared in greater detail for their relative advantages.

Linear discriminant function analysis is based on the assumption that the populations being discriminated are multivariate normal with equal covariance matrices (Press & Wilson, 1978, p. 699). Multivariate normality of the predictor variables is a difficult assumption to satisfy in practice, as is complete equality of all of the underlying covariance matrices. Transformations inducing multivariate normality do not typically also induce equality of covariance matrices. The logistic formulation, on the other hand, can be derived with a wide variety of underlying assumptions (Anderson, 1972). These assumptions include not only those of discriminant analysis, but also the broader assumption that the predictor variables are independent and dichotomous zero-or-one variables, or that some are multivariate normal and some dichotomous. The logistic model is, therefore, relatively robust, i.e., many types of underlying assumptions lead to the same formulation. Thus, the technique is appropriate for analyzing a wider range of data structures.

With data that are strictly normal with equal covariance matrices, linear discriminant function estimators of parameters have been shown to be more efficient than logistic regression maximum likelihood estimators (Efron, 1975); however, the efficiency of estimators under nonnormality has not been compared. Because the maximum likelihood estimation of the logistic regression model is associated with sufficient statistics whereas the discriminant function is not, there is reason to suspect that the sufficient estimator of logistic regression would be superior in efficiency under nonnormality (Press & Wilson, 1978, p. 701). It has been shown, in fact, that under nonnormal conditions, logistic regression gives slightly better fits than linear discriminant functions (Halperin, Blackwelder, & Verter, 1971; Press & Wilson, 1978, pp. 702-705).

Further, in the absence of multivariate normality and equal covariance matrices, linear discriminant function estimators of coefficients will not be consistent (Halperin, Blackwelder, & Verter, 1971). Thus, with one or more binary predictor variables, accurate predictions cannot be expected, even with an infinite amount of data. Finally, under nonnormality, linear discriminant function estimators will tend to overestimate coefficients which are really zero, thereby erroneously including meaningless variables in the model (Press & Wilson, 1978, p. 701). Logistic regression gives both a consistent method of estimation and one which does not overestimate zero coefficients.

Given that archaeological data for predicting site locations will probably not have multivariate normal distributions with equal covariance matrices, logistic regression appears to be preferable to linear discriminant function analysis for making such predictions. Statistical tests for multivariate normality and equal covariance matrices should certainly be performed with positive results before the application of linear discriminant function analysis. In the event of multivariate normal distributions without equality of covariance matrices, quadratic discriminant function analysis using individual group covariance matrices can be substituted for the standard technique. The quadratic approach, however, does not generate a function with weighting coefficients for interpretation.

Trend Surface Analysis

Trend surface analysis was introduced into geography in the 1960s (Chorley & Haggett, 1965) and since that time has been applied to distributional studies of various archaeological variables (see Hodder & Orton, 1976, pp. 155-174 for a discussion of archaeological applications). A trend surface model is a linear regression in which the predictor variables are the geographical coordinates of each data point, site, or locality. For each of a series of i localities ($i = 1, \ldots N$) the generalized trend surface model can be written as

$$Z_i = f(U_i, V_i) + e_i$$

where Z_i is the response variable to be mapped (e.g., density of archaeological sites), U_i and V_i are the geographical coordinates of locality i, and e_i is the "local" as opposed to the "regional" component of the response variable. The most widely used form of the function $f(U_i, V_i)$ is the polynomial power series expansion (Wrigley, 1976, p. 9). Trend surfaces of different orders may be generated for the same data set, with order of the surface referring to the highest exponential power among the predictor variables.

Davis (1973, pp. 322-358) presents a thorough discussion of the methodology and potential problems associated with its use. Various aspects of the number and distribution of data points and shape of map area have been shown to create problems with the interpretation of trend surfaces:

1) The number and spacing of sample points influence the size of local deviations that can be detected.

2) The technique suffers from edge effects, i.e., distortions near the boundaries of the mapped area. Edge values are directly proportional to the order of the surface.

3) The shape of the map area can seriously affect the form of a polynomial fit.

4) Clustering of data points may have a deleterious effect on trend surfaces.

5) A severe limitation for archaeological site distribution applications is related to the assumed nature of the variables in the model. The response variable must be a continuous variable measured at a high level, at least an interval level of measurement. It has been argued by some researchers (Zubrow

& Harbaugh, 1978, p. 121) that site density may be treated as if it were a continuous variable. Indeed, in some instances such as colonization settlement patterns, there may be some justification for treating this archaeological variable as if it exhibits a degree of mathematical continuity. However, sparcely settled areas may be more meaningfully represented by observations of presence/absence of a site in each possible site location than by density within some arbitrarily larger area. Inasmuch as a methodology which handles a categorical response variable, such as multivariate logistic regression, can be applied in circumstances of both low and high site density, it is more powerful. Moreover, by operating on observations of site presence/absence rather than site density, such a method allows a study of settlement pattern that is of much finer resolution.

6) The nature of the predictor variables in trend surface models further limit the utility of the technique. Regardless of the particular form of the trend surface function $f(U_i, V_i)$ used, the information in the equation is based entirely on the coordinates of the sample data points. In other words, the predicted density value for an area is based entirely on the density values of nearby areas. Such an approach may represent efficiently a contagious or clustered distribution while not being appropriate for other distributions.

7) Even in the case of accurate representation of a distribution by a trend surface, this methodology gives no information for explaining why the distribution is in a particular form. Explication of site settlement systems is enhanced by methodologies which relate site presence to location characteristics, thereby allowing interpretations as to why sites are located where they are.

The multivariate logistics approach allows the incorporation of variables other than locational coordinates and identifies the variables which have greater influence on site location selection.

8) Finally, being based on spatial coordinates alone, a trend surface model cannot be applied in an area outside the region upon which it is based. In contrast, a logistic model can be applied to any area outside the sampled area, as long as the environmental milieu and cultural milieu were the same.

Kriging

In their article, entitled "Archaeological Prospecting: Kriging and Simulation," Zubrow & Harbaugh (1978) present a systematic method for predicting site densities. This method, called *Kriging*, is based on a methodology known as regionalized variable theory and is named for one of its developers, D.G. Krige of Johannesburg, South Africa, who used it to forecast values of gold-bearing deposits in the area.

Kriging involves the estimation by interpolation of the values of a spatially distributed variable (e.g., number of archaeological sites) per areal unit (e.g., square km) (see Blais & Carlier, 1968; Huijbregts & Matheron, 1971). The method assumes that the regionalized variable has values that are partially dependent upon geographic location, is spatially continuous, and has a random or stochastic component.

To employ the method, one must sample the regionalized variable at specific points. Through a special interpolation formula, values for the variable are estimated at intervening, nonsampled points. The assumption is that the value of the variable at any point is related to the values at other points, but that the influence of points in the immediate area is greater than that of more distant points. Thus, from a sample of either regularly or irregularly spaced grid squares, the predicted values of the variable are generated at the nodes of a regular grid, which makes up the surface. The surface is then mapped as optimal predictions. Thus, the method produces a result similar to that of trend surface analysis.

There are several disadvantages to Kriging that are not found to be problems with a multivariate logistic approach. Kriging requires the proper selection of several parameters. Zubrow & Harbaugh (1978, p. 14) assert, however, that even naive parameter estimates produce results no worse than those of other estimating techniques such as trend analysis. A multivariate logistics model, on the other hand, requires no arbitrary parameter estimates. The parameter estimates that maximize the fit of the model to the sample are derived from the sample itself.

Other disadvantages Kriging shares with trend surface analysis: 1) In order to use data for Kriging, one must assume that the regionalized variable—in this case the number of archaeological sites per grid unit—is a continuous variable, as the response variable in trend surface analysis is assumed to be. 2) The method, like most mathematical filtering approaches, suffers from a boundary problem. 3) Kriging uses the spatial coordinates of observations to model/predict their value, which may not be appropriate for other than clustered distributions. 4) In using only spatial coordinates to predict site densities, the approach does not facilitate an understanding of most of the processes structuring settlement patterns. 5) Being based on spatial coordinates, the results of a Kriging operation are not extendible beyond the surveyed area.

Multivariate logistic regression offers a number of advantages over trend surface analysis and Kriging in addition to those mentioned above. Both trend surface analysis and Kriging, as well as the multivariate logistics model, produce a surface map in which data obtained in an initial phase of site survey are used to interpolate or estimate site locational information concerning areas which have not as yet been examined. I would assert, however, that the estimated probabilities of a multivariate logistics model are more apt to be accurate than the Kriging or the trend surface results because the probabilities are based on the relationship of site locations to *biophysical characteristics*. The interpolated values of the regionalized variable in Kriging, on the other hand, are based on nothing but the *values of the variable at sampled points*, that is, the observed number of sites in the sampled grid units. Zubrow and Harbaugh admit that "one of the weaknesses of Kriging is that an experienced observer may be able to eyeball several variables interfering with the homogeneity and distance rules more efficiently and effectively than the technique" (1978, p. 114). This problem does not arise in multivariate logistic regression, where variables which may interfere in Kriging are among the independent variables employed in a logistics model and influencing the resulting surface.

A very real advantage to multivariate models over other predictive modeling techniques is that neither data point distributions nor size and shape of the mapped area are variables which influence the structure of the probability surface. The sample data points for a multivariate logistics model should be selected so that they represent the environmental variation in the area being modeled. Given this situation, the sample distribution and area shape are irrelevant.

It should be made clear, however, that the adage concerning not getting something for nothing certainly applies in the assessment of a multivariate logistics locational model. The data collection requirement for this approach is much greater than that of Kriging or trend surface methodologies. To allow the association of biophysical variables to the site location selection process, the logistic methodology requires the collection of biophysical data, presumably from maps and other sources, for nonsite as well as site locations. This extra data collection effort, however, produces results which make the effort worthwhile. There is a definite interpretive benefit from the logistic model. In addition to allowing the prediction of site locations, the multivariate logistics model enables one to elucidate site selection processes. Close examination of the estimated regression coefficients allows one a greater understanding of why certain locations were chosen over others, permits one to model site selection processes, and facilitates the linkage of decision-making theory and its broader implications with the data.

Finally, the multivariate predictive model considers all of the measured biophysical variables and their interaction simultaneously. Since the environment is, in fact, a multivariate interactive milieu, then such an approach gives a closer approximation to the situation in which site selection processes are enacted.

A word of caution is in order concerning spatial autocorrelation. Whereas Kriging and trend surface methodologies incorporate and capitalize on the assumption of spatial autocorrelation (lack of independence between contiguous geographic units), logistic methodology does not and its unknown effect must be recognized. It has been shown (Cliff & Ord, 1975) that in another multivariate technique, principal components analysis, if variables in a geographic data base are equicorrelated, the same results will be obtained as if successive observations were independent. Although it would be difficult to ascertain the relative levels of autocorrelation in a multivariate geographic data base, it is clear that all such variables are probably positively autocorrelated, i.e., a biophysical variable for a geographic unit is likely to be similar to that of surrounding units.

With this cautionary statement, multivariate logistics predictive methodology is recommended for further application and study of site settlement systems. Topics within the methodology which need further development are selection of variables on which to base models, validation of models including further survey and model refinement, assesesment of the effect of sparce as opposed to dense site settlements, and automated data collection procedures to allow efficient collection of large quantities of biophysical data. Multivariate logistics models have the potential of increasing our knowledge and understanding of location selection processes, both in a specific geographic area and in a general sense. As stated recently by Binford:

> Site patterning in both within-place and between-place contexts is a property of the archeological record. The accuracy with which we are able to give meaning to the record is dependent upon our understanding of the processes which operated in the past to bring into being the observed patterning. Put another way, our accuracy depends upon our ability to correctly infer causes from observed effects. (1982, p. 6)

REFERENCES

Anderson, J.A. (1972). Separate sample logistic discrimination, *Biometrika 59*, 19-35.
Arrow, K (1951). *Social choice and individual values*. New Haven: Yale University Press.
Binford, L.R. (1982). The archaeology of place. *Journal of Anthropological Archaeology 1*(1), 5-31.
Blais, R.A., & Carlier, P.O. (1968). *Applications of geostatistics on ore evaluation* (Ore Reserve Estimation and Grade Control, Special Volume 9). Montreal: Canadian Institute of Mining and Metallurgy.
Carmean, W.H. (1965). Black Oak site quality in relation to soil and topography. *Southeastern Ohio Soil Science Society Proceedings 29*, 308-310.
Carmean, W.H. (1967). Soil survey refinements for predicting Black Oak site quality in southeastern Ohio. *Southeastern Ohio Soil Science Society Proceedings 31*, 805-810.
Chang, K.C. (1958). Study of the Neolithic social groups: Examples from the New World. *American Anthropologist 60*, 298-399.
Chorley, R.J., & Hagget, P. (1965). Trend-surface mapping in geographical research. *Transactions, Institute of British Geographers 37*, 47-67.
Clarke, D.L. (Ed.). (1977). *Spatial archaeology*. New York: Academic Press, Inc.
Cliff, A.D., & Ord, J.K. (1975). Model building and the analysis of spatial pattern in human geography. *Journal of the Royal Statistical Society 37*, 297-348.
Conover, W.J. (1971). *Practical nonparametric statistics*. New York: John Wiley & Sons, Inc.
Crumley, C.L. (1976). Toward a locational definition of state systems of settlement. *American Anthropologist 78*, 59-73.
Davis, J.C. (1973). *Statistics and data analysis in geology*. New York: John Wiley & Sons, Inc.
Dixon, W., & Massey, F. (1969). *Introduction to statistical analysis*. New York: Irwin Co.
Efron, B. (1975). The efficiency of logistic regression compared to normal discriminant analysis. *Journal of American Statistical Association 70*, 892-898.
Flannery, K.V. (1972). The origins of the village as a settlement type in Mesoamerica and the Near East: A comparative study. In P.J. Ucko, R. Tringham, & G.W. Dimbleby (Eds.), *Man, settlement, and urbanism* (pp. 23-53). London: G. Duckworth.

Fleetwood, A.R. (1969). *Geological investigations of the Ouachita River area, Lower Mississippi Valley* (Mississippi River Commission Tech. Rep. 5). U.S. Army Corps of Engineers.

Gill, H.V., Larance, F.C., Faltz, C.L., & Avery, D.C. (1980). *Soil survey of Calhoun and Dallas counties, Arkansas.* Washington, DC: U.S. Department of Agriculture, Soil Conservation Service.

Gumerman, G.J. (1971). *The distribution of prehistoric population aggregates* (Prescott College Anthropological Reports 1). Prescott, AZ: Prescott College Press.

Halperin, M., Blackwelder, W.C., & Verter, J.I. (1971). Estimation of the multivariate logistic risk function: A comparison of the discriminant function and maximum likelihood approaches. *Journal of Chronic Diseases 24*, 125-158.

Harris, G.D. (1892). The tertiary geology of southwestern Arkansas. *Arkansas Geological Survey Annual Report for 1892 2*, 15.

Higgs, E., & Vita Finzi, C.V. (1972). Prehistoric economics: A territorial approach. In E. Higgs (Ed.), *Papers in economic prehistory* (pp. 27-36). Cambridge: Cambridge University Press.

Hodder, I., & Orton, C. (1976). *Spatial analysis in archaeology.* Cambridge: Cambridge University Press.

Huijbregts, C., & Matheron, G. (1971). *Universal Kriging (an optional method for estimating and contouring in trend surface analysis)* (Decision Making in the Mineral Industry, Special Volume 12). Montreal: Canadian Institute of Mining and Metallurgy.

Jochim, M.A. (1976). *Hunter-gatherer subsistance and settlement: A predictive model.* New York: Academic Press, Inc.

Jones, J.R. (1969). Review and comparison of project results. In R. Euler & G. Gumerman (Eds.), *Proceedings of the 1976 conference* (pp. 95-101). Flagstaff, AZ: Museum of Northern Arizona.

Kerlinger, F.N., & Pedhazur, E.J. (1973). *Multiple regression in behavioral research.* New York: Holt, Rinehart, & Winston, Inc.

Kuchler, A.W. (1964). *Potential natural vegetation of the U.S.* New York: American Geographical Society.

Lafferty, R. (1981). The environment. In R. Lafferty, J. Otinger, S. Scholtz, W.F. Limp, B. Watkins, & R. Jones, *Settlement predictions in Sparta* (Arkansas Archeological Survey Research Series 14). Fayetteville: University of Arkansas.

Lafferty, R., Otinger, J., Scholtz, S., Limp, W.F., Watkins, B., & Jones, R. (1981). *Settlement predictions in Sparta* (Arkansas Archeological Survey Research Series 14). Fayetteville: University of Arkansas.

Limp, W.F. (1978). *Optimization theory and subsistence change: Applications for prehistoric settlement location analysis.* Tucson, AZ: Society for American Archeology.

Limp, W.F. (1981). *Rational location choice and prehistoric settlement analysis.* Unpublished doctoral dissertation, Indiana University, Bloomington.

Limp, W.F., Lafferty, R., & Scholtz, S. (1981). Towards a model of location choice in Sparta. In R. Lafferty, J. Otinger, S. Scholtz, W.F. Limp, B. Watkins, & R. Jones, *Settlement predictions in Sparta* (Arkansas Archeological Survey Research Series 14). Fayetteville: University of Arkansas.

Lipe, W.D., & Matson, R.G. (1971). Human settlement and resources in the Cedar Mesa area, SE Utah. In G.J. Gumerman (Ed.), *The distribution of prehistoric population aggregates* (Prescott College Anthropological Reports 1) (pp. 126-151). Prescott, AZ: Prescott College.

Mase, R. (1979). *Environmental inventory and impact analysis, Sparta Mine, Calhoun County, Arkansas: Vegetation and wildlife draft report.* Austin, TX: Radian Corporation.

Otinger, J.L., Lafferty, R.H. III, & Jones, R.D. (1981). Field tactics and laboratory methods. In R. Lafferty, J. Otinger, S. Scholtz, W.F. Limp, B. Watkins, & R. Jones, *Settlement predictions in Sparta* (Arkansas Archeological Survey Research Series 14). Fayetteville: University of Arkansas.

Parsons, J. (1972). Archeological settlement patterns. *Annual Reviews 1*, 127-150.

Peebles, C.S. (1978). Determinants of settlement size and location in the Moundville Phase. In B.D. Smith (Ed.), *Mississippian settlement patterns* (pp. 369-416). New York: Academic Press, Inc.

Phillips, P. (1970). *Archaeological survey in the lower Yazoo River basin, Mississippi, 1944-1955* (Peabody Museum of Archaeology and Ethnology Papers No. 60). Cambridge: Harvard University.
Press, S.J., & Wilson, S. (1978). Choosing between logistic regression and discriminant analysis. *Journal of American Statistical Association 73*(364), 699-705.
Roper, D.C. (1974). *The distribution of Middle Woodland sites within the environment of the lower Sangamon River, Illinois* (Illinois State Museum Reports of Investigations 30). Springfield: Illinois State Museum.
Roper, D.C. (1975). *Archaeological survey and settlement pattern models in central Illinois.* Unpublished doctoral dissertation, University of Missouri, Columbia.
Roper, D.C. (1979). The method and theory of site catchment analysis: A review. In M.B. Schiffer (Ed.), *Advances in archaeological method and theory, Vol. 2* (pp. 119-140). New York: Academic Press, Inc.
Saucier, R.M. (1974). *Quaternary geology of the lower Mississippi valley* (Arkansas Archeological Survey Research Series 2). Fayetteville: University of Arkansas.
Saucier, R.I., & Fleetwood, A.R. (1970). Origin and chronological significance of late quarternary terraces, Ouachita River, Arkansas and Louisiana. *Bulletin of the Geological Society of America 81*, 869-890.
Scholtz, S.C. (1981). Location choice models in Sparta. In R. Lafferty, J. Otinger, S. Scholtz, W.F. Limp, B. Watkins, & R. Jones, *Settlement predictions in Sparta* (Arkansas Archeological Survey Research Series 14). Fayetteville: University of Arkansas.
Scholtz, S.C. (1980, November). *Predictive models and survey strategy in the Sparta Mine area.* Paper presented at the 37th Annual Southeastern Archaeological Conference, New Orleans, LA.
Schneider, H. (1974). *Economic man.* New York: Free Press.
Smith, B.D. (Ed.). (1978). *Mississippian settlement patterns.* New York: Academic Press, Inc.
Struever, S. (1968). Woodland subsistence-settlement systems in the Lower Illinois Valley. In L. Binford & S. Binford (Eds.), *New prespectives in archaeology.* Chicago: Aldine Publishing Co.
Voigt, J.W., & Mohlenbrock, R.H. (1964). *Plant communities of Southern Illinois.* Carbondale, IL: Southern Illinois University Press.
Walsh, V. (1970). *Introduction to contemporary microeconomics.* New York: McGraw-Hill, Inc.
Weide, D., & Weide, M.L. (1973). Applications of geomorphic data to Archeology: A comment. *American Antiquity 38*, 428-431.
Willey, G. (Ed.). (1953). Prehistoric settlement patterns in the Viru Valley, Peru. *Bureau of American Ethnology Bulletin 155*.
Winters, H. (1969). *The Riverton culture* (Illinois State Museum, Reports of Investigation 13). Springfield: Illinois State Museum.
Wrigley, N. (1976). An introduction to the use of logit models in geography. *Concepts and Techniques in Modern Geography 10*.
Wrigley, N. (1977a). Probability surface mapping: A new approach to trend surface mapping. *Transactions, Institute of British Geographers* (New Series), *2*(2), 129-140.
Wrigley, N. (1977b). Probability surface mapping: An introduction with examples and Fortran Programmes. *Concepts and Techniques in Modern Geography 16*.
Zawacki, A.A., & Hausfater, G. (1969). *Early vegetation of the Lower Illinois Valley* (Illinois State Museum Reports of Investigations 17). Springfield: Illinois State Museum.
Zubrow, E.G.W., & Harbaugh, J.W. (1978). Archaeological prospecting: Kriging and simulation. In I. Hodder (Ed.), *Simulation studies in archaeology* (pp. 109-122). Cambridge: Cambridge University Press.

9

Determining Empirical Relationships Between the Natural Environment and Prehistoric Site Locations: A Hunter-Gatherer Example

KENNETH L. KVAMME

The investigation of patterning in the spatial distributions of archæological sites within a region is an important element of modern archaeology. A major theme is the investigation of factors, both environmental and social, which might have influenced prehistoric groups' decisions concerning site placement. The central research question of the Southwestern Anthropological Research Group, for example, is "Why did prehistoric populations locate sites where they did?" (Plog & Hill, 1971, p. 8) Nevertheless, a clear research orientation for several decades and extensive borrowing of methods and theory from other disciplines have not led to the development of a reliable procedure for isolating determinants of site location from empirical data with accuracy or confidence. A wide range of environmental phenomena, including hydrographic, landform, soil, and vegetation characteristics, has been examined for possible relationships with the immediate locations of prehistoric sites (see Judge, 1973; Williams et al., 1973; Roper, 1979). These studies, however, have usually failed to offer objective evidence that the environmental phenomena examined are actually related to the presence or absence of sites (this is fully illustrated below). An important consequence of this has been the lack of development of a sound data base of archæological site location determinants, a foundation essential for the formulation of locational models or theories of settlement.

I would like to thank Christopher Carr for clarifying certain ideas; Michael A. Jochim, Albert C. Spaulding, and Michael A. Glassow of the University of California at Santa Barbara for many useful comments; Paul R. Nickens of Nickens and Associates, Montrose, Colorado, for allowing me to try some new ideas in the Glenwood survey; the Bureau of Land Management, Grand Junction District, Colorado, which has been supportive of this research; and Jo Ann Christein for a large amount of labor.

This chapter presents an approach designed to detect those particular environmental features in the immediate vicinity of archaeological sites that strongly influenced prehistoric peoples in selecting their site locations. Data obtained from the Glenwood Project, an archaeological reconnaissance performed in western Colorado (see Kvamme, 1980 for details), are used to illustrate the approach. Finally, an explanatory model of the site selection process is offered, based on the empirical findings of the application.

METHODOLOGICAL PERSPECTIVE

A central feature of this chapter is the use of basic pattern recognition principles. The pattern recognition concept is illustrated by quantitative psychologists who typically measure personality traits of a *control* group, a group selected randomly from the population, in order to have a comparative reference body of data with which the same traits of the group under study (such as suicide-prone individuals) can be contrasted (Overall & Klett, 1972, p. 257). Similarly, in remote sensing studies, spectral data are often measured from a variety of background settings in order to provide data with which spectral emissions from specific crop types, such as wheat, can be contrasted (Swain, 1978). Such control approaches are common in pattern recognition studies (see Duda & Hart, 1973).

In archaeology a similar approach could be undertaken: environmental data could be measured at archaeological site locations and contrasted with identical environmental measurements taken randomly in the environment where sites are known to be absent. By doing so, environmental features significantly related to the locations of sites could be determined. For example, if data are collected on some variable, such as the distance in meters to the nearest water source at a random sample of archaeological site locations within a study region, the distribution of the data might resemble Figure 1a. Because this distribution is strongly concentrated in the area of the graph representing short distances to water, the usual archaeological conclusion would be that water proximity is a factor important to site location. However, the too often unasked question is "How far is water from *any* location within the area under study?" By measuring the distance to water sources at a random sample of locations where sites do not occur, a nearly identical distribution could result (Fig. 1b). This comparative information would force the conclusion that water is generally close to any location within the area under study and that site proximity to water is not a constraining, significant factor in the area. On the other hand, if the comparative data were distributed as in Figure 1c, with a central tendency some distance from water, the archaeologist could safely arrive at the first conclusion. This example illustrates that the use of a comparative *negative* data set is essential for isolating environmental features selected by prehistoric groups in locating their sites with accuracy and confidence.

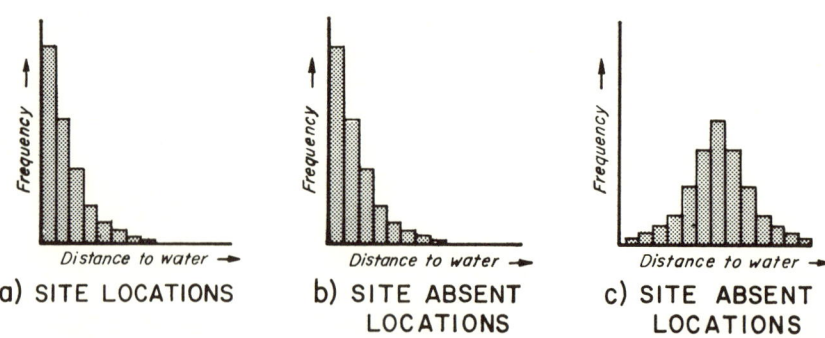

a) SITE LOCATIONS   **b) SITE ABSENT LOCATIONS**   **c) SITE ABSENT LOCATIONS**

Fig. 9.1. Distance to water in a hypothetical study area. Distribution *a* represents the empirical distribution measured at a random sample of archaeological site locations. If distance to water were measured at random locations where sites are absent and distribution *b* resulted, it could be concluded that proximity to water is not a significant locational factor. If distribution *c* resulted, the importance of water proximity would be indicated.

THE GLENWOOD PROJECT DATA BASE

The principles outlined above were incorporated into an archaeological site location study of lands administered by the U.S. Bureau of Land Management in the Glenwood Springs Resource Area of western Colorado. The BLM lands are a research universe of some 580,000 acres centered on the Colorado River (Fig. 2). In 1979, a 3% sample survey for archaeological resources in the Glenwood Area was performed under contract to the BLM. The archaeological data resulting from the Glenwood survey form the basis of this study (see Kvamme, 1980 for basic data and details).

Sampling Design

The U.S. Bureau of Land Management required an environmentally stratified random sampling design with sampling units conforming with the existing cadastral grid. Seven strata were defined by the locations of broad plant communities determined through vegetation maps, aerial photographs, and field inspection. With elevation in the study universe ranging from about 1,500 m to 3,000 m, the strata could be ranked from low to high as follows: riverine, sagebrush-grassland, pinyon-juniper forest, mountain brush, mountain grassland, aspen forest, and spruce-fir forest. Based on a consideration of travel costs, survey time, and the difficulty of locating survey units, the quarter-section (160 acres) was selected as the sampling unit. Three percent of the quarter-sections in each stratum was randomly selected for field inspection, resulting in a total survey of 109 sampling units, approximately 17,400 acres (Fig. 2).

The original intent of the project was to examine site location patterning

NATURAL ENVIRONMENT AND PREHISTORIC SITE LOCATIONS 211

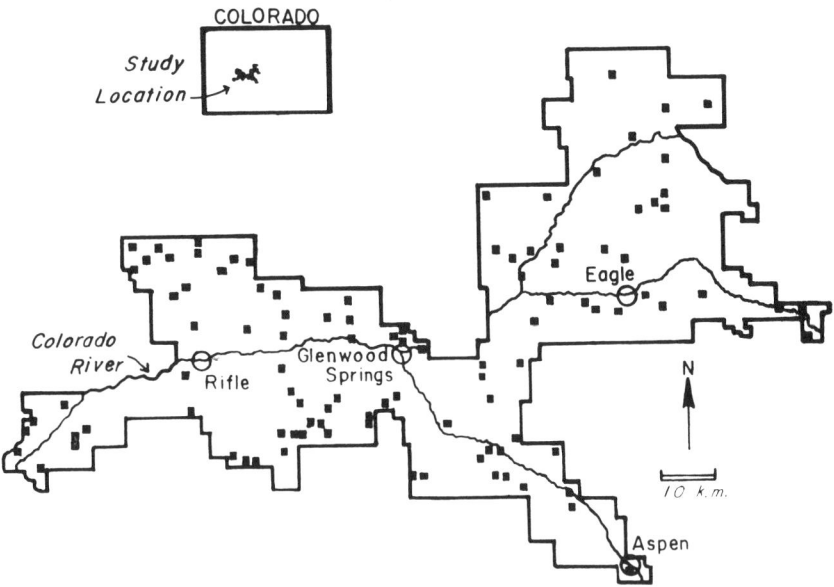

Fig. 9.2. Location of the Glenwood Springs Resource Area and sampling units.

within each environmental stratum, treating each as a separate research entity, using the methodological approach discussed above. Then, between-stratum patterns of site location would have been explored. Unfortunately, the site density in the resource area, which for the most part was previously unknown, turned out to be extremely low: only 58 lithic scatters representing sites of hunter-gatherer occupation (see below) and 72 finds of isolated artifacts were recorded. All of the sites occurred in only four lower-elevation strata: sagebrush-grassland (17 sites), pinyon-juniper forest (35 sites), mountain brush (3 sites), and mountain grassland (3 sites). (It is believed that nearly all of the surface sites existing in the sagebrush-grassland and pinyon-juniper communities were identified because of the high level of ground visibility they afforded. The infrequency of sites in the remaining communities is due in part to the dense vegetational cover occurring at high elevations.) Because of sample size problems stemming from the low number of sites discovered, the uneven distribution of sites per stratum, and the recognition of two site types to be used for analysis (see below), it was decided to abandon the goals of within- and between-stratum analysis and instead treat the sites as simply a sample of low-elevation occupations. The orientation of this study is, therefore, site patterning in these lower-elevation communities.

In order to search for patterns of association between archaeological site locations and environmental features, the Glenwood research design required a sample of locations lacking sites where comparative environmental measurements could be performed. (For convenience, the term *nonsite* will hereafter refer to any location in the study universe where archaeological materials are absent.) A random sample of nonsite locations was selected, distributed across each low-elevation community of interest *in the same proportion as the site locations within them*, in order to have a balanced and comparative data set.

The necessity of equivalent proportions of site and nonsite locations from each environmental stratum can be clarified by the following: Imagine a study universe with only two strata: 90% being a flat plain and 10% being mountainous. Only 10% of the sites (surface scatters) in the study area, however, occur in the plain; 90% are located in the mountains. The variable of interest is ground slope, and measurements of slope are obtained at each of the site locations, resulting in a distribution of slopes for all of the site locations (regardless of their zone of occurrence) showing a tendency for level ground (as we might expect because sites of occupation typically occur on level ground surfaces). In order to ascertain if a level ground surface was actually important in the site selection process, a control nonsite sample of slope measurements is needed.

One way to obtain such a nonsite sample would be in proportion to the area of each stratum (90% in the plain and 10% in the mountains), representative of the natural environment at large. In this nonsite sample, at least 90% of the slope measurements would be level, with only 10% or less being steep. (Some of the mountain nonsite location would fall randomly on level areas.) A comparison of slopes between all of the sites and all of the nonsites in this case would probably indicate that slope was *not* a constraining factor in the site selection process (because the majority of the nonsites are from the relatively level plain zone), even though the major portion of the site locations (the 90% in the mountains) might have been selected primarily on the basis of level ground surfaces.

If, on the other hand, the nonsite locations were selected from environmental strata in proportion to the occurrence of sites within them (with 90% in the mountains and 10% in the plain), the overall appearance of the nonsite slope data would be rather steep. A contrast with the site locations as a group would correctly show the importance of level ground to the locations of the majority of the sites. By weighting nonsite data proportional to the occurrence of sites within strata, we achieve a control data set that offers appropriate contrast when all of the sites are analyzed as a single group. Moreover, if an analysis by individual strata is still desired, a nonsite sample in each stratum is available.

Although it could be argued that the former nonsite sampling approach, sampling in proportion to stratum areas is desirable (e.g., to show a selection on the part of the prehistoric peoples for mountainous terrain), I argue that we already know this simply because 90% of the sites occur there.

In the Glenwood Project, nonsite locations were selected by first subdividing each of the 109 surveyed quarter sections into 64 units of 2½ acres (about the size of the largest archaeological site). A random sample of units was then selected within each vegetational stratum, proportional to the site sample size within it. As it turned out, the archaeological site density is so low in the Glenwood Area that none of the initially selected units contained archaeological materials. These nonsites, in essence could, therefore, be taken to reflect variation in the low altitude environment.

Because much more variation in environmental phenomena at nonsite locations was expected, a ratio of nonsites to sites of 2:1 was arbitrarily selected in order to better describe that variation. The nonsite data thus consist of a sample of 116 locations (2½ acre units) distributed in each environmental stratum in the same proportion as the archaeological sites. Data measured at these sites and nonsite locations form the basis of this study.

It should be noted that the six sites from the mountain brush and mountain grassland strata, and corresponding nonsite locations, are included in the study. From a hindsight perspective, it might have been more desirable to have excluded these locations for reasons similar to those for which the aspen forest and spruce-fir forest locations were excluded. By including the mountain brush and mountain grassland locations, the environmental variation of these communities was introduced in the analysis, thereby possibly decreasing the patterning to be found in the overall analysis, predominated by the lower elevation locations.

Site Types

Virtually all locational analyses assume that different types of archaeological sites are spatially located in different situations. Traditionally, the site types may be functional or chronological, where the different kinds of sites represent locations of different kinds of activities, different cultural adaptations, or both. In any case, different site types should be located with respect to different environmental features.

It was not possible, however, to type the sites within the Glenwood Project area into functional or adaptational types in the traditional manner, nor was it thought appropriate to do so, given the goals of the study. The archaeological sites encountered by the Glenwood Project are small hunter-gatherer lithic scatters consisting of chipped stone tools, debitage, and occasional ground stone. Chronological evidence (usually projectile point styles) occurred at only a limited number of the sites, preventing the examination of differences in site location strategies between various time periods. There was a high degree of variation in certain characteristics of the site assemblages suggesting functional differences among the sites, but it was not possible to consistently determine the specific activities carried out at each site for two reasons. First, the Glenwood

Project was conducted under a strict Bureau of Land Management no-collection policy, which precluded the possibility of in-depth artifact analyses. Second, it was difficult to interpret site functions from surface lithic scatters, especially when only a handful of artifacts occurred at many of the sites.

An alternative way of viewing site activities and of typing sites was taken, consistent with the overall aims of the project. The operational goal of this study is to examine the relationship between the *degree of use* of locations and their environmental characteristics. For example, do used locations (sites) have "favorable" environmental features when compared to unused (nonsite) locations? A related question is: do heavily used locations have "better" environmental features than little used locations? (The terms *favorable* and *better* are used in this chapter to refer to the suitability of the properties of a location for its extended use in meeting basic life and activity requirements [see Parker, chapter 8] rather than to imply culture-specific, emic assessments of location desirability.) It is clear that traditional functional and chronological site types are unsuitable for answering such questions; site types reflecting simply one dimension—the *amount of activity* that occurred at a location rather than the *kind of activity*—are needed.

In this regard, it was observed that the Glenwood sites ranged in size (indicated by the scatter of lithic debitage) from a few square meters to over 11,000 square meters. Also, the range in numbers and in the kind of chipped stone artifact types was similarly wide. It was then proposed that sites covering large areas, containing a large number of chipped or ground stone tools, and possessing a wide variety of tool types, reflect, on the average, more intense, extended, or possibly multiple occupations where a greater amount, number, or variety of activities occurred. This was based on the assumption that, in a general way, gross morphological types (e.g., projectile point, scraper, drill, biface, grinding stone) represent different classes of activities. On the other hand, sites covering a small area, containing few or no tools and few tool types were taken to probably reflect a more limited amount, number, and variety of activities.

Site types reflecting these extremes were defined through consideration of site size and an index of tool quantity and variety. The latter was calculated simply as the product of the number of stone tools found on a site times the number of tool type categories represented. A high index reflects a greater number and/or variety of tools, suggesting much activity prehistorically. Conversely, low index values suggest little activity. Utilizing the site area and tool index data in conjunction with field observations on occasional site features such as hearths, 15 *extended activity* sites (many activities/intense occupations) and 43 *limited activity* sites (few activities/short-term tasks) were defined (Fig. 3). These site-types allow a comparison of similarities and differences in the environmental characteristics of locations where much activity, little activity, or no activity (the nonsites) occurred.

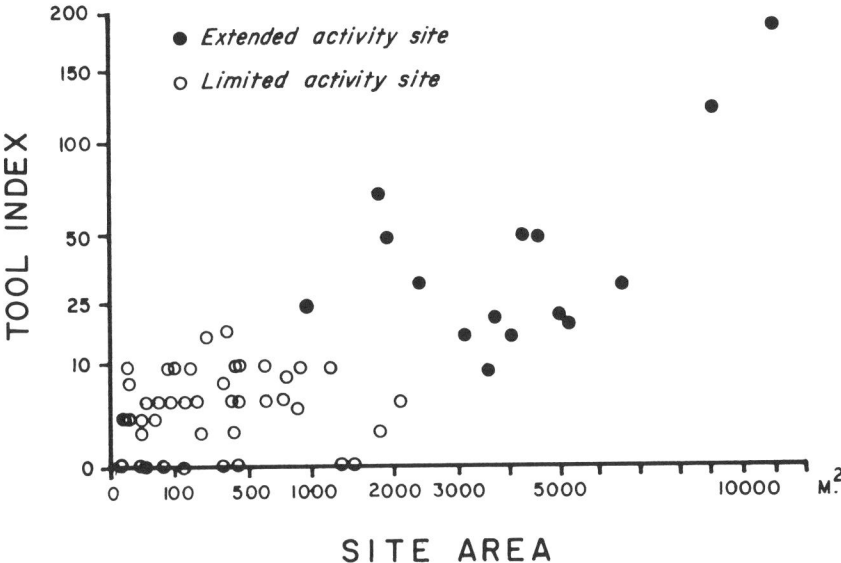

Fig. 9.3. Differences between extended activity and limited activity site types.

Environmental Data

A major concern in archaeological analyses which utilize environmental data is the correspondence of the modern environment with past conditions. In the Glenwood Project, most of the variables examined are related to landform, which may be assumed to be fairly constant over the time period under concern (there is presently no evidence of occupation prior to about 5,000 B.C.). Regarding variables related to vegetational cover, a series of paleoenvironmental studies within and adjacent to the project area (e.g., Reed & Nickens, 1980, p. 62; Scott & Seward, 1982, p. 54) suggest stability in both the compositions and locations of lower elevation pinyon-juniper and sagebrush communities over the past 5,000 years, the approximate period of interest here. Because of these stable environmental conditions and the homogeneous nature of the archaeological evidence (i.e., hunter-gatherer lithic scatters), it is assumed that there has been a similar adaptation to the environment through time by the prehistoric inhabitants of the Glenwood Area.

A number of environmental variables (Table 1) were defined and measured on USGS topographic or photographic maps at each site and nonsite location in the Glenwood Area. The variables consider several broad categories of environmental phenomena.

Water. That water resources are important to hunter-gatherer site location is widely accepted. In a cross-cultural study of criteria influencing hunter-gatherer site placement decisions, Jochim (1976, p. 55) assigns the proximity to water as a key factor determining the immediate locations of sites. Most often examined in settlement studies are distances to a variety of water sources, such as permanent rivers, semi-permanent streams, lakes, and springs (e.g., Brown, 1979; Judge, 1973, p. 120; Lafferty et al., 1981; Roper, 1979, p. 81; Parker, chapter 8). The arid nature of much of the Glenwood Area suggests that the placement of archaeological sites was probably influenced strongly by the locations of water sources.

Two types of water sources are defined by considering the factors of potential availability and relative proximity. Permanent water sources include rivers, streams, lakes, and springs where water is available year-round. Nearest water sources include the above plus other drainages where flow is seasonal or irregular. For a location adjacent to a river, the river would serve as both the nearest and permanent source of water. For a location near a ridge-top, however, the closest drainage would serve as the nearest water source, and if it were intermittent as is typical, rivers and lakes would then serve as the no-risk sources of water.

Two variables are measured in reference to each of these water sources: horizontal distance and, recognizing that the mountainous terrain of the region might play a role, vertical distance (Table 1).

View. It seems to be generally argued that opportunity for a good view of the surrounding terrain is important to hunter-gatherers in choosing the locations of their sites. The view might be needed to watch for game. Jochim (1976, pp. 51, 55) indicates that a good view is one of the chief objectives in the selection of the immediate site location. Both Brown (1979) and Judge (1973) used distance to an overview in their analyses of archaeological site location. The importance of view, of course, may vary with the size, herding, and visibility of the animal being hunted, and from region to region and season to season. For the Glenwood Area, view is considered to have been potentially significant in site location selection. Here, several species of large game were hunted prehistorically. Moreover, tremendous relief in the area offers numerous locations with expansive views. Two measures related to view are investigated (Table 1).

Shelter. The importance of shelter to site placement decisions among hunter-gatherers is recognized by Jochim (1976, p. 51) as being a central factor in the choice of location. Localities offering protection from wind, adverse weather, or sunshine (in desert regions) are sought for site placement.

Few archaeologists have dealt with shelter in locational analyses primarily because of the difficulty of developing a suitable measure of it. Euler and Chandler (1978), for example, were able to examine the shelter quality of sites in the Grand Canyon according to a series of situational categories only. In the Glenwood Project, a similar approach was undertaken by developing an ordinal scale describing different shelter situations (Table 1). The scale attempts to indicate how exposed a location is to atmospheric effects, such as wind or rain.

For example, an open hilltop is more exposed than a forested valley bottom. The reliability of application of this scale was examined by having three archaeologists familiar with the area independently rank the shelter situation categories. The resultant ranks were assessed with Spearman's *rho*. The coefficient values obtained (.90, .89, .83) indicate strong agreement among the archaeologists, suggesting that the assessment of shelter is a workable concept.

An additional facet of the sheltering effects offered by a location is its aspect or exposure, (Table 1). In cold climates, for example, south-facing exposures offer greater warmth from the sun.

Landform. The measurement of landform is a common practice in locational studies (e.g., Plog & Hill, 1971, pp. 16-17; Roper, 1979, pp. 77-78). Ground slope is widely investigated because settlements are typically located on level ground surfaces where steep slopes do not interfere with activities. Other landform measures also have been used, including a measure of relief that indicates the roughness or steepness of local terrain (Hurlbett, 1977, pp. 25-26). Extremely hilly or steep areas can be poorly suited for settlement because they increase energy and time expenditures in travel to food and water resources. Topographic diversity in the Glenwood Area is so great that slope and relief undoubtedly had a strong influence on prehistoric settlement decisions; they are included as variables in the analysis (Table 1).

Vegetation. Two variables related to vegetation patterns in the Glenwood Area are investigated (Table 1). One is the availability of firewood. Jochim (1976, pp. 51, 55) indicates that proximity to sources of fuel is generally a factor influencing the placement of hunter-gatherer camps. In the Glenwood Area it is not clear whether firewood was a constraint on site location. Firewood is readily available in most areas, represented by the oakbrush, pinyon-juniper, aspen, and spruce-fir communities. A second variable is taken from Gumerman and Johnson (1971), who discuss the contact or transition (the ecotone) between two biotic communities and its importance to prehistoric site occurrence. They argue that locating sites near an ecotone would allow easy access to both communities and their resources by prehistoric peoples

ENVIRONMENTAL FEATURES IMPORTANT TO HUNTER-GATHERER SITE LOCATIONS IN THE GLENWOOD AREA

Univariate Analysis

It was suggested earlier that much more environmental variation is expected to be encompassed by nonsite locations than site locations. This is expected because nonsite locations represent a weighted sample of essentially the total variation present in the environment. In contrast, prehistoric site locations should occupy only a limited portion of this total variation if the prehistoric hunter-gatherers were selecting particular environmental locations for use.

Table 9.1

Definition of Environmental Variables Measured in the Glenwood Project[1]

Water

1. *Horizontal distance to permanent water*
   The linear horizontal distance between the center of each site or nonsite and the nearest locus of permanent water (indicated by a solid blue-line feature).

2. *Vertical distance to permanent water*
   The vertical distance obtained by subtracting the elevation of the nearest locus of permanent water (indicated by the elevational contours) from the elevation of the center of each site or nonsite.

3. *Horizontal distance to nearest water*
   Defined as in (1) but measured to the nearest locus of any water source (indicated by a solid or dashed blue-line feature).

4. *Vertical distance to nearest water*
   Defined as in (2) but measured to the nearest locus of any water source (indicated by a solid or dashed blue-line feature).

View

5. *Distance to nearest vantage point*
   Vantage points are defined as hilltop or ridgecrest locations having at least 12 meters (the typical contour interval) of sharp relief over the surrounding terrain. The "tops" of hills or ridges were considered vantages to a point where the slope descended sharply, exceeding a 30% grade. The distance from the center of each site or nonsite to the nearest point of vantage was measured.

6. *View angle*
   Brown (1979, p. 197) defines this concept as the number of degrees of surrounding terrain visible from a site. It is measured by locating the contour line passing through the locus of interest (site or nonsite), extending an arc across that contour line in a *downhill* direction (with the vertex of the arc at the locus), and measuring the resulting angle. A hilltop provides a maximum amount of view, 360°, but the flank of a long ridge might provide a downhill view angle of only 180°.

Shelter

7. *Shelter quality*
   An ordinal rank of sheltering situations. Each site or nonsite was given the highest possible rank 0—unforested hilltop or ridgecrest; 1—flat (horizontal or sloping unforested area); 2—river valley floor (valleys are greater than 150 m wide); 3—below crest of ridge or hilltop (within 50 m) in unforested area; 4—near forest edge (within 50 m) but outside forest; 5—in topographic depression (ravine or drainage) in nonforested area; 6—clearing within forest (clearings have diameters greater than 50 m); 7—in forest on hilltop or flat area; 8—in forest in ravine or drainage depression; 9—in forest below (within 50 m of) hill or ridgetop; 10—base of vertical rockface/canyon wall.

Table 9.1 (cont.)

8. *Exposure*

   Measured at each site or nonsite by noting the prominent direction of sloping terrain indicated by a line drawn perpendicular to the elevational contours. The bearing (0-359°) of this exposure was recorded.

Landform

9. *Slope*

   Measured at each site or nonsite location as percent grade.

10. *Local relief*

    The maximum vertical elevation change (indicated by the elevational contours) within a 500 m radius of each site or nonsite.

Vegetation

11. *Distance to wooded (fuel source) area*

    Measured from each site or nonsite to the nearest wood-bearing plant community on USGS photographic quadrangles or to the green areas on USGS topographic maps.

12. *Distance to nearest ecotone*

    Measured from each site or nonsite to the "boundary" between major vegetational communities observed on USGS photographic quadrangles.

---

[1]The variables are measured on USGS 7.5′ topographic maps unless otherwise stated. All distances are in meters.

This should be true for each variable significant in the location selection process. For example, because nonsites were measured in virtually every kind of environmental situation, the whole range of possible ground slopes should be represented in this sample; a high level of variation should be present in the slope measurements. The archaeological sites, however, might possess slopes representing only a small portion of that range, and thus a lesser amount of variation.

Besides differences in *variation*, differences in *central tendency* between the site and nonsite locations should also exist. Using the above example, if the nonsite slopes range from 0 to 100%, the median slope might be 50%. However, if the prehistoric occupants were selecting mildly sloping ground surfaces on which to locate their sites, the slope at site locations might range from only 0 to 30%, requiring the median to be within that range. In this example, differences in both central tendency and variance exist between the site and nonsite groups.

The sample means, medians, variances, and coefficients of variation of the environmental variables measured at the Glenwood Project sites and nonsites are presented in Table 2. (The median in addition to the mean is presented because it often provides a better indication of central tendency for skewed distributions. Similarly, because the size of the sample variance is often related to the size of the sample mean, the coefficient of variation, which corrects for this effect [see Thomas, 1976, p. 83], is also presented.) In most cases, nonsites exhibit more variation in location than sites, as expected. Furthermore, differences in central tendency exist on many variables; e.g., site locations tend to be in closer proximity to permanent and primary water sources, vantages, and wooded (fuel) areas, be more sheltered, and have better views, less local relief, and more level ground surfaces than nonsites (Table 2).

These differences suggest the need for a more detailed statistical analysis. The Kolmogorov-Smirnov test was used on the Glenwood data to assess differences between site and nonsite distributions because it is sensitive to any kind of distributional differences which may occur: differences in means, variances, skewness, or kurtosis. The p-values associated with this statistic are presented with histograms of the data distributions in Figure 4. What follows summarizes these findings.

Water. Although the descriptive statistics indicate a tendency for site proximity to water sources (Table 2), it is only the vertical height above nearest sources of water that is strongly different from the nonsite locations ($p < .02$ in both extended and limited activity sites); sites tend to be located at shorter distances above nearest water sources than nonsites (Fig. 4). This might be explained by the fact that in the mountainous Glenwood Area, it is much more difficult to move up and down hill for water than it is to walk on level ground. Consequently, the vertical distance to water is a more important factor to the location of sites than horizontal distance. The sample medians also indicate a tendency for extended activity sites to be closer (in both dimensions) to nearest water sources than limited activity sites (Table 2).

View. The Glenwood data suggest a strong concern for view (perhaps to watch for game) on the part of the prehistoric inhabitants in selecting the locations of their sites. The data indicate (Table 2; Fig. 4) a distinct preference for all sites, regardless of type, to be located near or on points of vantage (with p-values < .01 in all cases). Additionally, the quality of view at locations, as measured by view angle, was an important consideration (Fig. 4). The distributions of view angles for all site categories are decidedldy oriented toward wider views ($p < .01$ in all cases) when compared to the nonsite distribution (Table 2).

Incidentally, the nonsite data, which approximate a normal curve with a central tendency of about 180° (Fig. 4), are supportive of the nonsite sampling program. Because the view angle can vary only from 1° to 360°, and because very wide or narrow views tend to be rare, whereas intermediate angles predominate, we would expect measurements of this variable at random locations over the landscape to produce a bell-shaped distribution with a central tendency mid-way between its extremes. A Lilliefors test for normality (Conover, 1971, p. 302) presents no strong evidence that these data are non-normal ($p = .10$).

Table 9.2

Sample Means, Medians, Variances, and Coefficients of Variation ($\sqrt{\text{Variance}}$/Mean) of the Glenwood Site/Nonsite Data

Variable	Extended Activity Sites				Limited Activity Sites				Nonsites			
	Mean	Median	Variance	CV*	Mean	Median	Variance	CV*	Mean	Median	Variance	CV*
Horizontal distance to permanent water	1493	1050	1439417	.80	1305	1125	817329	.69	1490	1300	1013524	.68
Vertical distance to permanent water	165	158	6514	.49	147	122	12398	.76	161	134	13297	.72
Horizontal distance to nearest water	122	100	4688	.56	163	125	14670	.74	180	150	30484	.97
Vertical distance to nearest water	20	15	142	.60	32	24	1097	1.04	50	37	2895	1.08
Vantage distance	36	0	2362	1.35	59	0	9348	1.64	164	150	22596	.92
View angle	243	260	6271	.33	251	260	3559	.24	183	180	4473	.37
Shelter quality	8	9	2.14	.18	6.9	7	4.28	.30	6.3	7	5.99	.39
Exposure (original)	180	170	5314	.40	165	160	5648	.46	162	160	10783	.64
Exposure (rescaled)	125	140	2112	.368	118	130	1957	.375	88	90	2551	.57
Slope	16.1	16	47	.43	18.8	16	73	.45	37	30	593	.66
Local relief	133	134	1550	.30	154	146	2540	.33	202	183	9672	.49
Distance to wooded (fuel) area	3.3	0	167	3.92	34	0	13866	3.46	39	0	11329	2.73
Distance to ecotone	865	450	1289268	1.31	752	600	413345	.85	860	575	6259346	2.91

*Coefficient of variance

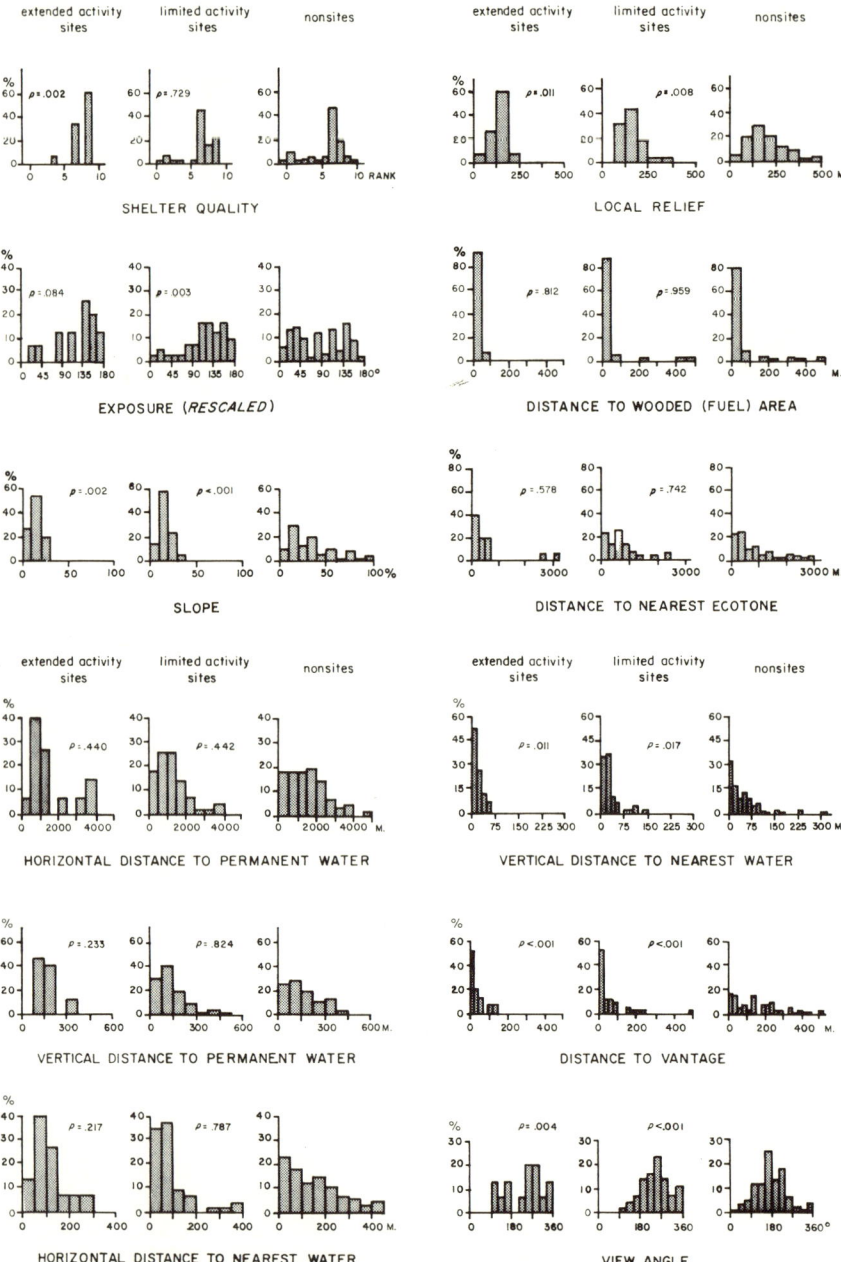

Fig. 9.4. Histograms of site and nonsite data for environmental variables defined in Table 1.

Shelter. The shelter quality of extended activity site locations is decidedly greater ($p = .02$) than that typically offered at nonsite locations (Table 2, Fig. 4). Limited activity sites, on the other hand, are located with no strong preference for sheltering effects ($p = .73$) (see below). This agrees with expectations concerning hunter-gatherer settlement locations (Jochim, 1976, p. 55): extended activity sites, which probably tend to represent the loci of more permanent settlement and should be sheltered, do indeed show a preference for good shelter.

Initial inspection of the site exposure data presented roughly normal curves centered about 180°, indicating decided preference for southerly exposures (perhaps in response to cold weather when warmth from the sun would be needed). The nonsite data, in contrast, produced an expected uniform distribution, indicating that each exposure bearing has about the same chance of occurring (which, again, is supportive of the nonsite sampling). When the Kolmogorov-Smirnov statistic was applied to these data, however, no strong differences between site locations of either kind and the nonsites were indicated. This arose, not because the contrast in exposures is insubstantial, but because the compass scale artifically constrains the average exposure for any uniform distribution of exposures to 180° (south). The average for the uniformly distributed exposures of nonsite locations, therefore, happened to correspond with the truely preferred southerly exposures of the site locations.

In order to side-step this difficulty and get at the apparent patterning, the data were rescaled. The west half of the compass was collapsed over the east half so that every bearing on the west half was given the bearing of its mirror image on the east half. The new scale, which now ranged from 0° to 180°, was easier to interpret: 0° is the least southerly exposure and 180° is the most. After this transformation, the median exposure for extended activity sites was found to be 140°, slightly more south than the median exposure for limited activity sites of 130°. The uniform nonsite distribution was still preserved, with the median of 90° at its center (Table 2; Fig. 4). The Kolmogorov-Smirnov statistic now indicated a strong difference in exposure between the limited activity sites and nonsites ($p = .003$), with a more moderate difference for the extended activity sites and nonsite ($p = .084$). The weaker significance of the latter contrast might reflect, in part, the smaller sample size of extended activity sites. Both the mean and median of the extended activity sites actually lay farther south than the corresponding statistics for the limited activity sites, with the variances being nearly identical (Table 2).

Landform. The importance of gently sloping surfaces to the prehistoric hunter-gatherers of the Glenwood Area is clearly indicated in the distributions of slope for all site-types ($p < .01$ in all cases). Slopes selected for site placement were always less than 40%, compared to slopes as steep at 100% in the nonsite distribution (Fig. 4).

Local relief was also found to be a significant determinant of site location for all site types ($p \leq .01$ in all cases). Sites tend to be situated at locations with much less local relief in comparison to the nonsite distribution (Fig. 4). Moreover, extended activity sites tend to occur in situations with less local relief than limited activity sites (Table 2). These relationships suggest that sites were located to reduce energy costs of movement, and that such optimizing was more important for repeatedly accessed extended activity sites than limited activity sites. At the extended activity sites, where movement might have included the daily procurement of food or water resources, relief is less and not as variable. At the limited activity sites, where repeated access was probably less frequent, relief is slightly greater and more variable (Table 2).

Vegetation. It is apparent that proximity to sources of fuel is not important to site location. In the Glenwood Area, wooded areas are extremely abundant and available within a short distance of almost anywhere, as indicated by the nonsite data (Fig. 4). Although Jochim (1976, p. 53) suggests that proximity to fuel sources is generally a factor influencing hunter-gatherer site placement, I found no clear evidence of its importance in the Glenwood Area ($p > .80$ for all site categories). Similarly, proximity to ecotones, which presumably would facilitate easy exploitation of adjoining plant communities (Gumerman & Johnson, 1971), was not a critical factor in the Glenwood Area for any of the site types ($p > 0.5$ in all cases, Fig. 4).

The absence of a relationship between sites and ecotones might be a result of the nature of plant communities in the study area. The vegetational strata generally parallel the major rivers in a series of linear belts and therefore do not possess great depth. As a result, the distance from any randomly located point to the boundary of the nearest ecotone is not great.

Multivariate Analysis

The use of comparative nonsite data in the previous section has demonstrated that multiple environmental factors are important to site presence on a univariate level. These factors include a concern for water, a good view of the surrounding terrain, good shelter, a south-facing exposure, a level ground surface, and a low amount of local relief. The question remains of the nature of overall locational differences between the sites and nonsites when all the environmental variables are considered jointly.

Multi-Response Permutation Procedures (MRPP) were used as a first step to assess the strength of overall environmental differences between the defined sites and nonsites and to illustrate a further application of this technique. MRPP were first introduced for intrasite spatial analysis (Berry, Kvamme, & Mielke, 1980, 1983), but are actually appropriate for assessing differences between predefined groups of observations (e.g., the sites and nonsites) in any body of multivariate data. The MRPP are analogous, in this sense, to one-way multivariate analysis of variance. They make, however, none of the usual normality and variance assumptions about the data and, like the univariate

Kolmogorov-Smirnov test, are sensitive to any kind of distributional differences. An MRPP analysis of the twelve environmental variables indicated appreciable environmental differences between the locations of Glenwood sites and nonsites. Comparing all the archaeological sites with the nonsites, the MRPP yielded a p value of $.26 \times 10^{-5}$.

Having confidence that strong differences exist between the site-present and site-absent locations, logit models (Wrigley, 1976, 1977) were used to explore those differences further and to identify the relative importance of the variables. Logit analysis is analogous to the well-known least-squares regression but differs in that the dependent variable consists of nominal-level categories; moreover, it is distribution independent. The logit model utilizes measurements on the independent "predictor" variables to estimate probabilities of membership in one of the dependent variable categories:

$$P_i = \frac{e^{\alpha + \beta_1 X_{1i} + \beta_2 X_{2i} + \cdots + \beta_n X_{ni}}}{1 + e^{\alpha + \beta_1 X_{1i} + \beta_2 X_{2i} + \cdots + \beta_n X_{ni}}} \quad (1)$$

where P_i is the probability that individual i belongs to group 1 (e.g., the site present group), the X_{ji} are the j independent variables for case i, and the β_j are weights. Significant non-zero coefficients on any variable indicate that the variable affects the presence/absence of sites, taking into account the simultaneous interaction of the other variables with the one of interest.

Two logit models were produced using maximum likelihood estimation: one model for the extended activity site/nonsite comparison and a second model for the limited activity site/nonsite comparison. A stepwise procedure for selecting variables for inclusion in the models was used. (Stepwise procedures select for inclusion in a model only a subset of the total number of variables available: those making a significant contribution to the model. Variables containing largely redundant information when considered with the other variables are not incorporated in the model.) It was necessary to use a stepwise approach, at least in the study of locations of extended activity sites, given that there were only 15 of these sites in the sample and there were 12 variables under examination. Forcing all 12 variables in a model with only 15 cases in one group would have caused highly unstable parameter estimates and greatly overestimated statistics of the model's performance (e.g., pseudo R^2 statistics near 1.00) (see below). Even though the limited activity site sample size (43) was large enough to have included all 12 variables in a model, stepwise selection procedures were also used in this study, in order to have comparability between models. The estimated standardized coefficients of the models and associated pseudo R^2 goodness of fit statistics, R_p^2 (Baxter & Cragg, 1970, p. 230), are presented in Table 3.

The logit models offer a number of insights about patterning in the data. First, the positive coefficients (β_j) of the models indicate that *increases* in the corresponding variables are associated with greater likelihoods of site presence.

Table 9.3

Logit Models with Standardized Coefficients for the Extended Activity Site/Nonsite Comparison and the Limited Activity Site/Nonsite Comparison

Extended Activity Site/Nonsite		*Limited Activity Site/Nonsite*	
Variable	β	Variable	β
water	−23.65	slope	−1.66
vantage	−12.18	vantage	−1.20
shelter	8.08	water	−1.06
slope	−5.55	shelter	0.84
exposure*	5.15	exposure*	0.76
		view	0.67
$R_p^2 = 0.891$		$R_p^2 = 0.581$	
Model significance: $p < .001$		Model significance: $p < .001$	
All variables are significant at: $p < .001$		All variables are significant at: $p < .02$	

*Rescaled values

Conversely, the negative coefficients indicate that *decreases* in the corresponding variables are associated with greater likelihoods of site presence. In other words, it is low values of slope, vantage distance, and water distance, and high values of exposure (rescaled), view angle, and shelter that are related to the presence of sites. This agrees completely with findings of the univariate analyses.

A second advantage of the multivariate models is that they consider the *interrelationships* of variables, and thus can produce findings not possible in univariate analyses. On a univariate level, view angle is related to the locations of extended activity sites, and relief is important to both extended activity and limited activity sites. The multivariate models, however, indicate that these variables do not contribute substantial information concerning site presence beyond that contained in the other variables. Similarly, although shelter does not strongly affect the locations of limited activity sites on a univariate level, it becomes a significant factor when considered with the other variables.

Finally, the usual interpretation of the estimated coefficients (β_j) are as rates of probability change. For example, increasing the distance to water by one standardized unit should decrease the logarithm of the likelihood ratio (P extended activity site/P nonsite) by 23.65 units if all other factors are held constant, causing a decrease in the probability of site presence (Table 3). Because the coefficients are standardized (removing the effect of different measurement scales) we see that, for the extended activity site model, a change of one standard unit of water distance (other factors held constant) has the most effect on the log-likelihood ratio (and the probability of occurrence of these sites), about twice that of a change of one standard unit of vantage distance; shelter, slope, and exposure follow in their effects (Table 3). Similarly, for the limited activity site model, it is slope that has the largest effect on the probability of occurrence of these sites, followed by vantage distance, water distance, shelter, exposure, and view.

It should be noted that the relative magnitudes and ranks of the β coefficients do not necessarily reflect the "importance" of the variables to site presence and the site selection process. Strictly speaking, such interpretations are valid only when the predictor variables are uncorrelated. When the predictor variables are correlated, as they are to some extent in the present analysis, adding a new variable to a model can drastically alter the "importance rankings" because new interrelationships between the predictor variables may be introduced. Caution should therefore be exercised in making such interpretations (see Darlington, 1968; Kerlinger & Pedhazar, 1973, p. 296).

Differences Between Site-Types in Locational Patterning

In the previous sections, a variety of differences were noted between the locational properties of extended and limited activity sites. Extended activity sites tend to be located closer to water sources, have better shelter, more southerly exposures, more level ground surfaces, and less local relief than the limited activity sites (see Table 2). In short, they appear to be located in "better" environmental circumstances. Similarly, for most of the variables examined, the locations of extended activity sites tend to be less variable than the locations of limited activity sites (indicated by the coefficients of variation and the sample variances in Table 2).

Admittedly, many of these differences are small, and few are statistically significant. This is not necessarily due to a lack of real differences; however, it is probably more a result of the small sample sizes of the two types of sites and the environmental differences between site types which should, in fact, be small compared to site/nonsite differences. If there were no patterning here, we would expect extended activity sites to be in better and less variable situations for roughly half of the variables. Instead, the differences are consistent in direction. The extended activity sites are "better" located than limited activity sites for 10 of the 12 variables in Table 2 (indicated by the sample medians or, if tied, the sample means) and are less variable for 8 out of 12 (indicated by the coefficients of variation), suggesting significant patterning. This is verified by an MRPP analysis. The MRPP are able to combine all the slight differences on each variable in a single test of difference (using all 12 variables simultaneously) between the site types. The result indicates that the site types are indeed located in different environmental circumstances ($p = .034$).

Because the extended activity sites probably represent, in many instances, the loci of extended habitations with multiple activities, one would expect that greater care and *consistent* planning went into the selection of their locations: they should be located consistently in "better" contexts because of the greater requirements of the environment demanded by longer occupation (e.g., proximity to water would reduce travel requirements for repeated trips to the water source). The limited activity sites, in contrast, were probably occupied for shorter periods, and therefore were placed with less planning and show less consistent concern for locational context.

This view is supported by the multivariate analysis in addition to the above statistics. The goodness of fit statistics of the logit models (R_p^2) indicate that the locations of extended activity sites are indeed more patterned (less variable) than the locations of limited activity sites (respective R_p^2's of .89 and .58, in Table 3). On the basis of all these statistics and arguments, therefore, it can be concluded that the locations of extended activity sites tend to possess more favorable and more patterned environmental characteristics than do the locations of sites where more limited activity occurred, although both types of sites were placed in broadly similar circumstances in comparison to the nonsites.

A MODEL FOR HUNTER-GATHERER SITE SELECTION

In looking for features of the physical environment determining the placement of prehistoric sites in the Glenwood Area, a number of patterns and tendencies in the data suggest some order in the site selection process. In this section, further patterning is described and a more systematic and coherent perspective for viewing the site selection process is developed. A profitable starting point is a model derived from ecology (Hutchinson, 1957) for examining the locations of organisms in space, and extended in geography (Hudson, 1969) to focus on the locations of human settlements in space. The model utilizes the concept of *ecological niche* in a locational perspective (Pianka, 1974, p. 185).

An ecological niche can be defined as the total range of conditions in the environment under which a population lives and replaces itself (Hutchinson, 1957). It can be determined empirically by actually measuring the living conditions of individuals of the population along a number of environmental dimensions. When graphed in multidimensional space, the empirical distribution of individuals defines an n-dimensional *hypervolume* which delimits the niche boundaries enclosing the complete range of conditions under which the particular organism can live and successfully replace itself (Hutchinson, 1957). The range of all possible values taken by the environment on each dimension (with or without individuals) can be viewed as defining the total environment; the niche may encompass only a limited portion or subset of all these conditions. Individuals near the centroid of the hypervolume are better located than individuals near the periphery.

Hudson (1969) extends this model to human settlement by examining the conditions near settlements along n dimensions of environment. The result is a *human settlement niche*, defined by the hypervolume of environmental characteristics permitting settlement. Recognizing that "there exist values that are too cold, too warm, too wet, too dry . . . for settlement to exist" (Hudson, 1969, p. 367), the human settlement niche, like the ecological niche, encompasses only a limited portion of the total environmental range.

Two aspects of the hypervolume model are of importance. First, environmental variation within the niche is a limited part or subset of the total range of variation in the whole environment. Second, certain settings within the niche itself may be more favorable than others. Thus, in a collection of potentially good site locations, some may be better suited for human use.

The ethnographic record provides a similar view. Site selection is viewed typically as a process of defining a narrow range of locations suitable for settlement within the total environmental variation of the region. As Rogers and Black (1976, p. 5) report of the Weagamow Ojibwa: "only certain locales were suitable for camping."

The selection or reduction process is viewed as hierarchically organized. In Jochim's (1976) generalized model of hunter-gatherer settlement, three levels or zones reflecting a hierarchical spatial organization are perceived. The widest zone is delimited by food resources of great mobility: large animals. A much narrower, intermediate zone encompasses resources of low or no mobility, such as small animals or plants. Finally, the immediate site location is determined by characteristics idiosyncratic to a specific locus such as shelter quality, view quality, and fuel and water proximity. Western and Dunne's (1979) work with the pastoral Maasai recognizes three levels or zones of selection that closely parallel the three zones outlined by Jochim for hunting-and-gathering groups. The outer zone delimits "an area to optimize food and water availability for adult livestock" (Western & Dunne, 1979, p. 94). An intermediate zone encompasses relatively local, nonmobile characteristics of the environment, such as the availability of wooded areas for building materials and soil characteristics which affect drainage patterns, dust conditions, and solar heat retention. Finally, the immediate site location is selected on the basis of specific attractions, such as a strategic view, the presence of shade trees, slope, etc. (Western & Dunne, 1979, pp. 94-95).

The process of site selection thus involves a narrowing of *subsets* of locations within the total environment, eventually resulting in a set of possible immediate site locations from which the actual site location is chosen (see Limp & Carr, chapter 7). This agrees with the idea of the niche as a subset of the total environment presented in the hypervolume model. The environment is stratified and organized hierarchically into subsets, each possessing more suitable environmental conditions for human settlement.

Site Selection Model

The concepts of the subsetted environment and niche, presented above, and the ethnographic data on site location parallelling it can be used to suggest a model of the site selection process. A study universe can be viewed as a *universal set* containing all possible locations (e.g., small area units). A smaller portion of this set includes only those locations which are accessible to humans: the *Accessible Space*. For example, locations on steep mountain slopes are inaccessible, thus narrowing down that portion of the total environment which can be reached. The size of the set of locations which are accessible is dependent on technological level. For example, with high levels of mountaineering technology, all slopes can be traversed. Similarly, the centers of lakes and large rivers can be reached only when the technology includes watercraft.

Within the Accessible Space is the smaller subset of loci suitable for the performance of activities: the *Activity Space*. An activity is defined here as the performance of a task at some location in space such as flint chipping, animal butchering, game viewing, and plant processing. Activities, as viewed here, are tied to locations; by definition, they exclude travel across a location (i.e., movement from one activity place to another). The Activity Space is thus a much narrower portion of the total environment than the Accessible Space; only a portion of the areas, which can be traversed, are suitable for the performance of activities. For example, a wide range of ground slopes can be traversed, but activities tend to be performed on level ground; thus, a deer might be killed on a steep slope, but it might be dragged to the nearest level location for butchering. Vantage points from which game might be viewed are necessarily located at the limited number of locations where a good view occurs.

Finally, the smallest set of space is *Settlement Space*, which is a subset of the Activity Space. The Settlement Space includes only those activity locations that are better suited for extended occupation and the performance of multiple activities required for such stays. Typically, activity loci might be determined with respect to a limited number of variables such as slope *or* view, the particular variables being dependent on the nature of the activity performed. In contrast, settlement loci might be selected for slope *and* view *and* shelter *and* water. Thus, Settlement Space is necessarily restricted to a smaller portion of the total environment because it is constrained by a greater number of environmental dimensions.

The relationships between the defined sets are portrayed with a Venn diagram in Figure 5. The progressive subdividing of the environment into areas with specialized characteristics (the subsets) reflects the increased narrowing of portions of the environment suitable for more extended use and agrees with the hierarchical organization of space seen ethnographically. The model addresses not only settlement behavior, but all locational behavior. In terms of the hypervolume model, the Accessible Space defines the actual niche of the human group in that it encompasses the total range of conditions in the environment under which the population lives and replaces itself (Hutchinson, 1957). The Settlement Space corresponds to Hudson's (1969) human settlement niche.

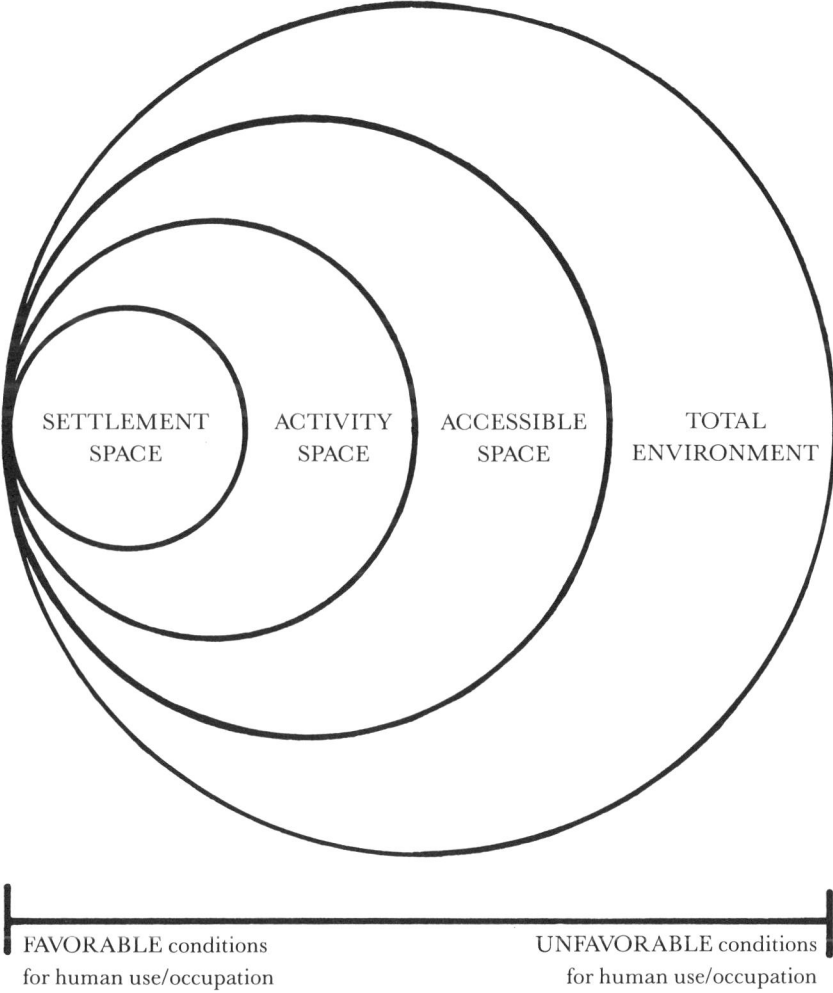

Fig. 9.5. Venn diagram illustrating environmental space as a series of increasingly specialized subsets.

Testing the Model

The Glenwood Project data base may be used to examine implications of this model. Utilizing concepts of the hypervolume model, the sets in Figure 5 can be defined empirically by measurements on n dimensions of the environment. The set including all possible locations in the environment corresponds to the Glenwood nonsites. As mentioned earlier, these locations essentially reflect variation in the environment as a whole. The set of accessible locations is represented by all locations where archaeological evidence is encountered. It includes places where projectile points were lost during a hunt or where items were discarded while moving camp, as well as the campsites themselves. In the Glenwood Project, Accessible Space is defined by the loci of the archaeological sites plus the loci of 72 finds of isolated artifacts. These isolated artifacts (many of them are projectile points) probably represent, for the most part, instances of extremely short-term activity when compared with the limited activity sites. The environmental variables discussed previously were measured at each isolated artifact location, and these data are now incorporated into the analysis. The archaeological correlates of the Activity Space are represented by all of the Glenwood sites, and the Settlement Space is represented by the extended activity sites only.

Differences in Variation

Since the site selection model focuses on the successive narrowing of portions of the environment used, there should be an ordering of variation on significant environmental variables:

$$\text{SETTLEMENT SPACE} < \text{ACTIVITY SPACE} < \text{ACCESSIBLE SPACE} < \text{TOTAL ENVIRONMENT}$$

(Relationship 1)

This pattern is portrayed in Table 4 where, in most cases, the postulated ranking is present.

Differences in Central Tendency

The successive narrowing of the environment, with each subset having "more favorable" situations, should cause an ordering in the central tendencies of each subset:

$$\text{SETTLEMENT SPACE} *\text{ ACTIVITY SPACE } * \text{ ACCESSIBLE SPACE } * \text{ TOTAL ENVIRONMENT}$$

(Relationship 2)

where * indicates that the set to the left has a more favorable median than the set to the right. (The medians can increase or decrease to the right or left depending on the direction of the measurement scale.) This relationship largely follows

Table 9.4

Comparison of Coefficients of Variation and Central Tendency Statistics for the Extended Activity Sites (EA), Limited Activity Site (LA), Isolated Artifact (IA), and Nonsite (NS) Groups on Significant Environmental Variables[1] An "*" indicates a correct relationship between two statistics according to site selection model.

	Comparison of Relative Variation				Comparison of Central Tendencies[2]			
Variable	EA Sites Settlement Space	LA Sites Activity Space	IA Accessible Space	NS Total Environment	EA Sites Settlement Space	LA Sites Activity Space	IA Accessible Space	NS Total Environment
Vertical distance to nearest water	.60	* 1.035	* 1.037	* 1.08	15(20) *	24(32) *	20(33) *	37(50)
Vantage distance	1.35	* 1.65	* 1.05	.92	0(36) *	0(59) *	100(101) *	150(164)
View angle	.33	.24	* .36	* .37	260(243)	260(251) *	200(191) *	180(183)
Shelter quality[3]	.18(2.14) *	.30(4.28) *	.32(4.70) *	.39(5.99)	9(8.0) *	7(6.9) *	7(6.7) *	7(6.3)
Exposure (original)	.40	* .46	* .48	* .64	NA	NA	NA	NA
Exposure (rescaled)	.368	* .375	* .49	* .57	140(125) *	130(118) *	100(95) *	90(88)
Slope	.43	* .45	* .70	* .66	16(16.1) *	16(18.8) *	16(19.1) *	30(37.0)
Local relief	.30	* .33	* .41	* .49	134(133) *	146(154) *	158(178) *	183(202)

[1]Although the site selection model indicates that the statistics in any column should be pooled with the statistics in all leftward columns, this is not done for simplicity and clarity of presentation. Note that pooling or not pooling will not change the nature of the relationship.
[2]The sample medium is followed by the sample mean in parentheses. If the medians are tied in any comparison, the mean is used instead.
[3]The variable shelter quality is an ordinal level variable. Since the coefficient of variation is a *ratio* of the standard deviation relative to the mean, a ratio level of measurement is technically required. For this reason, the sample variances are given in parentheses and are used for the comparisons.

from the variance argument and from arguments presented earlier. The results, presented in Table 4, are again largely in agreement.

Finally, an MRPP analysis between each of the four subset groups indicates substantial differences in the environmental characteristics of each subset. For example, the extended activity/limited activity site comparison yields $p = .03$, the limited activity site/isolated artifact comparison yields $p = .0003$, and the isolated artifact/nonsite comparison yields $p = .00004$.

These statistics present a strong argument for patterning in the Glenwood data base that is consistent with expectations of the site selection model. In order to more clearly illustrate the patterning in these results, a logit model can be used again, this time predicting the probability of membership of locations in each of the four environmental subsets, rather than simply site and nonsite sets. For this four-response category situation, the nonlinear probability model generalizes to the form

$$P_{r/i} = \frac{e^{\alpha_r + \beta_{1r}X_{1i} + \beta_{2r}X_{2i} + \cdots}}{\sum_{S=0}^{3} e^{\alpha_s + \beta_{1s}X_{1i} + \beta_{2s}X_{2i} + \cdots}} \quad r = 0,1,2,3 \quad (2)$$

where $P_{r/i}$ represents the probability of the rth response at location i with j environmental characteristics X_{ji}; and where the four responses, nonsite (NS), extended activity site (EA), limited activity site (LA), and isolated artifact (IA), are arbitrarily coded 0, 1, 2, 3 (see Wrigley, 1977, p. 31). Because the study sample proportions are calculated as weights within the r intercept terms α, the effect of the unequal sample sizes of each group may be removed by simply adding $ln (n_1/n_2)$ to the intercepts where the n_i are the group sample sizes (The slopes α_j, are unaffected because the intercept point is only changed on the discriminant plane [Maynard 1981, pp. 61-62]).

The probabilities of each of the four environmental categories can then be calculated conditional on only the environmental information. By treating each group as if its a prior chance of occurrence is equally likely (i.e., removing the effect that in nature there are far more locations in broader subsets than narrower subsets), we may examine the form of the probability distribution of each variable for each environmental subset, clarifying the prehistoric site selection process. The results for four of the more interesting variables are presented in Figure 6.

The graphs in Figure 6 summarize the two patterns discussed above, an ordering of variation and an ordering of central tendency, by providing a picture of the relationships. The rankings of the environmental spaces expected, given the relationship of ordered central tendencies, is strongly apparent: in "favorable" portions of the graph, Pr(EA) > Pr(LA) > Pr(IA) > Pr(NS), and in "unfavorable" portions of the graphs the opposite ranking occurs. This relationship is also suggested by the ordering of the highpoints in each graph. For example, in Figure 6c, from left to right, the extended activity curve peaks

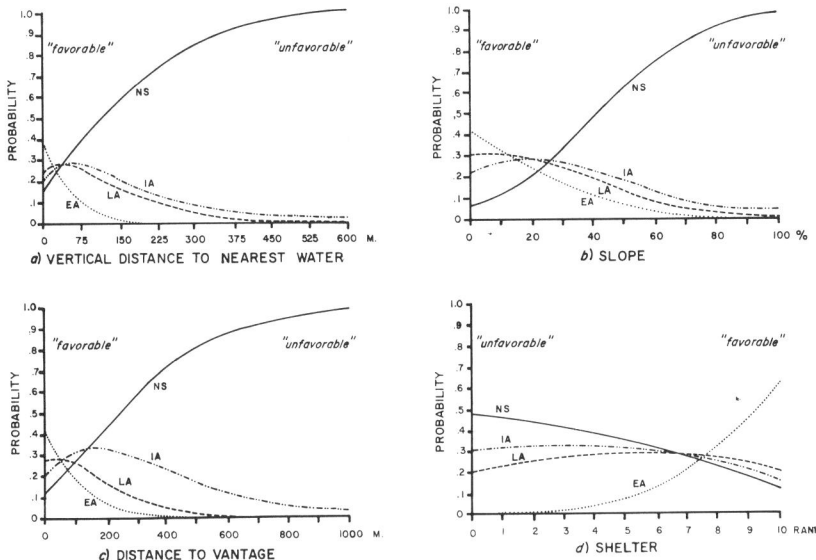

Fig. 9.6. Probability graphs of extended activity sites (EA), limited activity sites (LA), isolated artifacts (IA), and nonsites (NS) for selected variables. The probabilities are conditional on only the environmental measurements. Note that for a given value x of an explanatory variable: $\Pr(EA) + \Pr(LA) + \Pr(IA) + \Pr(NS) = 1$.

first, followed by peaks for the curves of the limited activity, isolated artifact, and nonsite locations. Second, the relationship of ordered variation is indicated in the graphs by the spread of each curve. The extended activity sites have the least variation on any variable, and accordingly, high probabilities of this group are restricted to a narrow range. The successively greater amounts of environmental variation encompassed by the limited activity sites and isolated artifacts are illustrated by successively wider probability curves. In ultimate contrast, the high variation of the nonsites is reflected by relatively high probabilities across each graph. Finally, the graphs facilitate the assessment of the "importance" of any variable in distinguishing each set. In Figure 6d we see that shelter readily distinguishes the extended activity sites but that the remaining groups are almost indistinguishable on this variable. This is consistent with the findings of the earlier, univariate analysis.

PROSPECTS AND PROBLEMS

The preceding sections have developed a logical view of the human use of space supported with real data. Beyond the theoretical level, the approach has practical uses. It was shown above that logit models can estimate the probability of occurrence of a site at a location, given the environmental characteristics of the locus. Such a model can actually be viewed as a predictive model of site location (see Parker, chapter 8). By measuring a number of environmental variables on a map at some locus, the probability of a site occurring at that locus can be estimated by utilizing a multivariate logit model similar to Equation 1.

In fact, such an approach is currently being used by the Bureau of Land Management cultural resource managers in the Glenwood Springs Resource Area. The strong patterning in the Glenwood data base has allowed highly useful predictive models to be formulated: approximately 75% of locations with sites and 85% of locations without sites (nonsites) can be correctly identified with the logit model (Kvamme, 1980, 1983).

When interest is in the locations of sites over wide regions involving many thousands of loci (small areal units), measuring many environmental variables at each locus under examination to obtain an estimated probability of a site being present becomes difficult and time consuming. To overcome this difficulty for the Glenwood Area, computer processing techniques are being used to systematically calculate 1) values for relevant environmental variables in each areal unit over a wide region, and 2) the corresponding probabilities of site presence (Kvamme, 1983). In short, the approaches presented here provide a workable method for federal agencies charged with managing cultural resources.

A major problem of all analyses dealing with spatial phenomena stems from the likelihood of spatial autocorrelation (Cliff & Ord, 1973), or what Tobler (1970, p. 234) refers to as "the first law of geography: everything is related to everything else, but near things are more related than distant things." Most statistical theory demands that observations be independent, but geographical data seldom have this characteristic (Haggett et al., 1977, p. 330). In the Glenwood area, the average distance between measured locations (the sites and nonsites) is only a few miles, and many of these locations occur much closer together; many of the Glenwood observations, then, are not truly independent.

At present, the effects of the lack of independence are largely unknown (see Cliff & Ord, 1975), although it is generally true that levels of statistical significance are overstated. This problem undoubtedly influences all statistical inferences of the type presented in this chapter, such as levels of significance, but in any case we still might focus on the mathematical relationships between means, variances, regression coefficients, etc.

CONCLUSION

The foregoing analyses have indicated a number of environmental factors related to the locations of sites in the Glenwood Area. By utilizing a comparative data set of environmental measurements obtained at locations where sites are known to be absent as a point of reference, it was possible to determine empirically those environmental features that actually influenced prehistoric inhabitants of the area in selecting the locations of their sites. These features included a concern for water, a good view of the surrounding terrain, good shelter, a south-facing exposure, a level ground surface, and gentle local relief. Because some confidence could be placed in these findings, a behavioral model of the site selection process was formulated and examined with the archaeological data. The model, based on observations in the ecological and ethnographic literature, views human uses of the environment as a reductionary or subsetting process. The widest subset includes all locations actually accessible to a human group. A narrower subset includes less favorable locations which are suitable for the practice of day-to-day activities. The narrowest environmental subset includes "more ideal" locations suitable for human settlement.

Environmental patterning in the Glenwood site types, which represent the archaeological correlates of these subsets, demonstrated that the model is a reasonable reflection of the prehistoric use of space in the Glenwood Area. Put simply, a strong relationship was found between the amount of activity that occurred at a location and how "favorable" that location is in its environmental characteristics. Locations where more activity occurred tend to have better and more patterned environmental circumstances than locations where less activity occurred. This pattern can be demonstrated archaeologically through quantitative analysis and is consistent with certain facets of the ethnographic record.

REFERENCES

Baxter, N.D., & Cragg, J.G (1970). Corporate choice among long-term financing instruments. *Review of Economics and Statistics 52*, 225-235.

Berry, K.J., Kvamme, K.L., & Mielke, P.W., Jr. (1980). A permutation test for the spatial analysis of the distribution of artifacts into classes. *American Antiquity 45*, 55-59.

Berry, K.J., Kvamme, K.L. & Mielke, P.W., Jr. (1983). Improvement in the permutation test for the spatial analysis of the distribution of artifacts into classes. *American Antiquity 48*, 547-553.

Brown, K.L. (1979). Late prehistoric settlement patterns in southwestern Kansas. *Plains Anthropologist 24*, 191-206.

Cliff, A.D., & Ord, J.K. (1973). *Spatial autocorrelation*. London: Pion.

Cliff, A.D., & Ord, J.K. (1975). The comparison of means when samples consist of spatially autocorrelated observations. *Environment and Planning A 7*, 725-734.

Darlington, R.B. (1968). Multiple regression in psychological research and practice. *Psychological Bulletin 69*, 161-182.

Duda, R.O., & Hart, P.E. (1973). *Pattern classification and scene analysis*. New York: John Wiley & Sons, Inc.

Euler, R.C., & Chandler, S.M. (1978). Aspects of prehistoric settlement patterns in Grand Canyon. In R.C. Euler & G.J. Gumerman (Eds.), *Investigations of the Southwestern Anthropological Research Group: an experiment in archaeological cooperation*. Flagstaff, AZ: Museum of Northern Arizona.

Gumerman, G.J., & Johnson, R.R. (1971). Prehistoric human population distribution in a biological transition zone. In G.J. Gumerman (Ed.), *The distribution of prehistoric population aggregates*. (Anthropological Rep. No. 1). Prescott, AZ: Prescott College Press.

Haggett, P., Cliff, A.D., & Frey, A. (1977). *Locational Methods* (2nd ed.) New York: John Wiley & Sons, Inc.

Hudson, J.C. (1969). A location theory for rural settlement. *Annals of the Association of American Geographers 59*, 365-381.

Hurlbett, R.E. (1977). *Environmental constraint and settlement predictability, northwestern Colorado.* (Cultural Resource Series No. 3). Denver: Bureau of Land Management, Colorado.

Hutchinson, G.E. (1957). Concluding remarks. *Cold Springs Harbor symposia on quantitative biology 22*(4), 5-427.

Jochim, M.A. (1976). *Hunter-gatherer subsistence and settlement: A predictive model.* New York: Academic Press, Inc.

Judge, J.W. (1973). *Paleoindian occupation of the central Rio Grande Valley, New Mexico.* Albuquerque: University of New Mexico Press.

Kerlinger, F.N., & Pedhazar, E.J. (1973). *Multiple regression in behavioral research.* New York: Holt, Rinehart & Winston.

Kvamme, K.L. (1980) Predictive model of archaeological site location in the Glenwood Springs Resource Area. In R.J. Burgess, K.L. Kvamme, P.R. Nickens, A.D. Reed, & G.C. Tucker Jr., *Class II cultural resource inventory of the Glenwood Springs Resource Area Grand Junction District, Colorado (Part II)* (Report submitted to the Bureau of Land Management. Montrose, CO: Nickens and Associates.

Kvamme, K.L. (1983). Computer processing techniques for regional modeling of archaeological site locations. *Advances in Computer Archaeology 1*, 26-52.

Lafferty, R.H., Otinger, J.L., Scholtz, S.C., Limp, W.F., Watkins, B., & Jones, R. (1981) *Settlement Prediction in Sparta* (Arkansas Archaeological Research Series, No. 14). Fayetteville: University of Arkansas.

Maynard, P.F. (1981) *The logit classifier a general maximum likelihood discriminant for remote sensing applications.* Unpublished master's theses, University of California, Santa Barbara.

Overall, J.E., & Klett, C.J. (1972). *Applied multivariate analysis.* New York: McGraw-Hill, Inc.

Pianka, E.R. (1974). *Evolutionary Ecology.* New York: Harper and Row.

Plog, F.T., & Hill, J.N. (1971). Explaining variability in the distribution of sites. In G.J. Gumerman (Ed.), *The distribution of prehistoric population aggregates* (Anthropological Reports No. 1) (pp. 7-36). Prescott, AZ: Prescott College Press.

Reed, A.D., & Nickens, P.R. (1980) *Archaeological investigations at the Debeque Rockshelter: A stratified Archaic site in west-central Colorado* (Report submitted to the Bureau of Land Management). Montrose, CO: Nickens and Associates.

Rogers, E.S. & Black, M.B. (1976). Subsistence strategy in the fish and hare period, Northern Ontario: The Weagamov Ojibwa, 1880-1920. *Journal of Anthropological Research 32*, 1-43.

Roper, D.C. (1979). *Archaeological survey and settlement pattern models in central Illinois* (Illinois State Museum Scientific Papers, Vol. XVI). Springfield, IL: Illinois State Museum.

Scott, L.J., & Seward, D.T. (1982). Pollen and macrofossil analysis of an Archaic site, 5EA484, in west-central Colorado (Appendix A). In A.D. Reed, *Archaeological investigations at 5EA484: An open archaic site in the Colorado Rockies* (Rep. submitted to the Bureau of Land Management). Montrose, CO: Nickens and Associates.

Swain, P.H. (1978). Fundamentals of pattern recognition in remote sensing. In P.H. Swain & S.M. Davis (Eds.), *Remote sensing: The quantitative approach.* New York: McGraw-Hill, Inc.

Thomas, D.H. (1976). *Figuring anthropology.* New York: Holt, Rinehart & Winston.

Tobler, W.R. (1970). A computer movie simulating urban growth in the Detroit region. *Economic Geography (Supplement) 46*, 234-240.

Western, D., & Dunne, T. (1979). Environmental aspects of settlement site decisions among pastoral Maasai. *Human Ecology 7*, 75-98.

Williams. L., Thomas, D.H. & Bettinger, R. (1973). Notions to numbers: Great Basin settlements as polythetic sets. In C.L. Redman (Ed.), *Research and Theory in Current Archaeology* (pp. 215-237). New York: John Wiley & Sons, Inc.

Wrigley, N. (1976). An introduction to the use of logit models in geography. *Concepts and Techniques in Modern Geography 10*.

Wrigley, N. (1977). Probability surface mapping. *Concepts and Techniques in Modern Geography 16*.

10

Constraints on Linear Programming Applications in Archaeology

ARTHUR S. KEENE

In a recent critique, James Moore and I argued that there is a tendency among archaeologists to confuse hard objects with hard data (Moore & Keene, 1983). While we as archaeologists are usually confident about inferring behavior from our analyses of the tangible products of archaeological practice—namely artifacts, features, and site distributions—we are considerably less comfortable when confronting those behaviors that are not so readily apparent in the archaeological record.

The advent of a modeling approach within archaeology has allowed us to redefine what we mean by hard data. Models, as conceptual tools, have enabled us to expand our investigations to areas where preservation is poor and to consider aspects of society that may not be readily apparent in cultural debris. Modeling has expanded our vision of the past and increased our ability to understand the past. Recently, we have realized a level of sophistication in our work where modeling is no longer regarded as a methodological buzzword, but rather a legitimate form of archaeological practice.

In Chapter 7, Limp and Carr make a strong argument for employing a particular family of models—mathematical decision-making models—in our investigations of prehistoric economy. This chapter continues Limp and Carr's exploration with a detailed and critical examination of the application in archaeology of Linear Programming (LP), a form of mathematical decision-making model frequently used by economists in problems of allocation. This discussion elaborates on a previous comprehensive review of the subject by Reidhead (1979) and differs in its critical outlook.

In this chapter I emphasize the technical and conceptual limitations of LP. My aim is to familiarize the reader with the potential benefits and pitfalls of

For assistance in the preparation of this paper I thank Dean Saitta, Bill Fawcett, John Curry, Bob Paynter, Martin Wobst, Dena Dincauze, John Cole, Maura Keene, Estelle Keene, Chris Carr, and Fred Limp.

240   REGIONAL ANALYSIS

using LP or similar optimization models in specific problem-solving contexts; and, more generally, to emphasize the benefits and hazards associated with any kind of modeling. I do so from the perspective that the precision and rigour of models, especially mathematical models, often imbue them with an elegance that is both mystifying and seductive. It is easy, therefore, to lose sight of the technical and conceptual limitations of such models and even the reasons for employing them in the first place. This is particularly true when the origin of our models lies outside our own discipline (Keene, 1983; Service, 1972).

Many of my criticisms of LP applications stem from my interest in theoretical questions of social power and social inequality. My critique is grounded in a paradigm that rejects the primacy of techno-environmental variables in the explanation of culture change and emphasizes social process, in an effort to create an understanding of past behaviors that does not simply mirror contemporary Western ideology (Keene, 1983, p. 148; Saitta, 1983; Moore & Keene, 1983; Bender, 1978).

ON THE NATURE OF MODELS

It is necessary to begin this chapter with a presentation of my views on what a model is and how it functions. A number of my criticisms of LP, as well as my disagreements with other researchers' criticisms of LP, are derived from these more general views.

Models are conceptual tools. They are employed by investigators who adhere to a variety of paradigms and who operate from different epistemological perspectives. Although both a logical positivist and a dialectical materialist may find a modeling approach helpful, it would not be surprising to find that such individuals might utilize models differently and bring to their use quite different expectations (contrast Harvey, 1969 with Harvey, 1973; Jochim, 1983 with Keene, 1981a; Low, 1974 with Palmer-Jones, 1979). Because models and the process of model building mean different things to different people, any discussion of models must begin with some clarification of philosophy, procedures, and expectations. In particular, I will address what I expect from a model and what I regard as legitimate criteria for evaluation. Detailed reviews of broader issues of the philosophy and mechanics of model building are discussed elsewhere (Lave & March, 1975; Harvey, 1969, 1973; Johnson, 1980; Levins, 1966; Clarke, 1967; Keene, 1979; 1983) and are not within the scope of this chapter.

Simply stated, models are representations of reality. They may be a substitute representation of some aspect of the real world, an idealization, a simplification, or a miniaturization. In any case, they offer us an image that enables us to visualize something that is not easily seen. We are intimately familiar with models in our daily lives: a map, a scale mock-up of the space shuttle, the wind tunnel in a Ford commercial, the physical representation of a DNA molecule, a video game. All of these allow us to see things that are not readily visible through a process of simplification. The value of models to the archaeologist is readily apparent. Phenomena that were seemingly intractable to the archaeologist of the 1960s—transgenerational change, population dynamics, mating networks, information flows, the simultaneous interaction among variables— become approachable through modeling techniques.

If we regard theory as a statement of variables significant to a given phenomenon and of the interactions that exist among those variables, then we may regard models as the embodiment or representation of theory. If theory establishes the rules for relationships among variables, models enable us to view the implications of changing the rules or to view the outcome of assigning specific values or conditions to those variables. Thus, models are not only manifestations of theory; they actually allow us to probe the limitations and sensitivities of theories. They give us an opportunity to shake up our ideas and our data and see what happens (Keene, 1979, 1981a). They encourage us to play with our conventional views of how the world works and they promote strong inference (Platt, 1964). Modeling, therefore, is an active part of theory building.

How do we evaluate models? The answer depends on what we wish to know and cannot be separated from paradigmatic and epistemological debates on validation, confirmation, and the nature of knowledge (cf. Brown, 1977; Mills, 1959; Rorty, 1979; Feyerabend, 1975; Hemple, 1966). The validity of a particular model is determined by the purpose of that model and must be evaluated relative to that purpose. For example, successful modeling for an archaeologist who wishes to predict location of sites to minimize construction impact may appear as failure to the archaeologist attempting to elucidate the processes that drive surplus production or accumulation.

I raise this point because models are criticized frequently for ignored variables or oversimplifications. Such criticism overlooks the paradox of models: their greatest strength, the ability to simplify reality and make problems tractable, is also a weakness. Such simplification sacrifices some aspects of reality (Levins, 1966; Keene, 1981a). Any individual modeling effort, therefore, is incomplete. Successful model applications generally result from approaching a problem with several different models or with several variations of a single model (Levins, 1966).

I want to emphasize that I am not advocating model relativism. Certainly one must examine whether a model does what is intended and whether it does this with any consistency and reliability. One must also evaluate whether the questions with which one is dealing are really worth asking or whether one's efforts simply represent fancy intellectual gymnastics.

In sum, I view models as heuristic devices, as means for examining the implications of theory, and as devices for shaking up our perceptions. Hence, I offer some simple criteria for evaluating models which I will apply to LP applications in archaeology. In evaluating models, I look for the following:

1. *Precise problem definition.* Mathematical methods can uncover patterning in data, but one must have some idea of what one is looking for and why (Moore & Keene, 1983; Mills, 1959; Parker et al., chapter 5).

2. *Justifiable assumptions.* While modeling usually involves the formulation of patently unrealistic simplifying assumptions, it is important to justify such assumptions (see Keene, 1981, pp. 9-14) and examine the implications of these simplifications. It is inappropriate to assume that this simplification eliminates the need to consider the variability that may result from factors not incorporated in the model.

3. *Significant insights.* Unfortunately, the literature abounds with elegant restatements of the obvious (e.g., as populations grow they require more food). A good model will reveal something that is worth knowing that we did not know previously. It will generate new hypotheses or provide some new way of perceiving relationships among variables.

4. *Robusticity.* A good model has broad applicability and allows obtained results to be linked with other research. Results should be insensitive to slight variations in input parameters or mechanical idiosyncracies of computation.

5. *Is the question worth asking?* The reader will note that I have not discussed validation procedures, tests of fit, or falsification criteria for evaluating models. This stems from my position that all models contain elements that are both true and false (Keene, 1981a, p. 224) and that they are most valuable when used heuristically. It also results from my rejection of a positivist approach to knowledge. My own feeling is that the value of models cannot be assessed except within a well-defined theoretical context, and that models, observations, and the relationship among them take on different heuristic characteristics when viewed through different theoretical lenses (Brown, 1977; Moore & Keene, 1983).

Too frequently, a good fit between model predictions and observations is taken as a confirmation of the model (cf. Keene, 1981a; Feyerabend, 1975; Hindess, 1973). It appears that the dominant epistemology of models in archaeology and the social sciences in general is to get the facts and the model to fit (e.g., Jochim, 1976, 1983; Reidhead, 1981). However, no model can account for all the facts, and several contradictory models can predict the same set of facts (Keene, 1981a; Levins, 1966; Palmer-Jones, 1979; Feyerabend, 1975). Too often neither the model nor the facts are properly theorized, and therefore alternative explanations are not rigorously considered or sought (Moore & Keene, 1983; Harvey, 1973; Hindess, 1973).

In the following pages I will provide a lengthy description of Linear Programming as a mathematical technique. I will then attempt to place the technique into a theoretical context. For further details on the mathematics of LP, the reader is referred to any of the LP manuals cited in this chapter.

INTRODUCTION TO LINEAR PROGRAMMING MODELS

Programming is the mathematics of allocating limited resources among competing activities in an optimal manner. A program is simply a plan or schedule of activities that best satisfies a specified goal among all feasible alternatives. Typically, the goal is defined in terms of maximizing or minimizing a function of several variables subject to certain constraints; for example, maximizing production or minimizing loss or risk, subject to the availability of labor, time, or raw materials. Programming is applicable to any problem in which one wishes to recognize the "best" choice or the range of feasible choices among several variables and several constraints.

Programming techniques are not statistical. They are mathematical operations for solving and analyzing a set of simultaneous equations and inequalities used to represent choice processes. They provide deterministic rather than statistical results and are not based on statistical theory.

Linear programming came into prominence during World War II as part of a field known as operations research, which today goes by the more familiar title of management science or scientific decision making (Wagner, 1975). Today, LP applications are common in several fields where decisions must be made among several variables subject to multiple constraints: economics, marketing, ecology, agriculture, and economic development-planning for predicting optimal crop mix (Delgado, 1979; Low, 1974; Johnson, 1980). LP has proven attractive because it is a powerful technique for manipulating complex data sets and is computationally simple. Applications to a range of problems in anthropology have become widespread since Joy's (1967) initial illustration (see Reidhead, 1979 for a review; Clarke, 1968; Dickson, 1980; Bettinger, 1980; Keene, 1981a; Behrens & Johnson, 1982; Hoffman, 1969; Selby & Hendrix, 1976; White, 1973). The two most comprehensive applications of linear programming in archaeology have been those of Keene (1981a) and Reidhead (1981). Both use linear programming to calculate optimum resource scheduling for prehistoric populations in the midwestern United States. Although the details of their studies vary, both attempt to define the production schedules which minimize the cost of resource procurement while satisfying an array of dietary and nonfood requirements. These two cases are summarized briefly below. First, however, I will illustrate how a linear programming model works.

Building a Linear Programming Model

A linear programming model is a representation of choices phrased as a series of linear algebraic equalities or inequalities that are solved simultaneously. In the simplest cases, LP models can be solved graphically, but for standard research they are solved with the assistance of a computer algorithm. Whereas assumptions of specific models may vary (cf. Keene, 1981a; Reidhead, 1981), all LP models must specify the following:

1. The conditions that must be satisfied (i.e., the constraints);
2. The alternative factors from which the decision maker can choose in trying to satisfy conditions (i.e., the variables);
3. The objective the decision maker desires to achieve (e.g., maximize output, minimize energy expenditure, maximize profit, minimize risk). The quantitative representation of this objective is known as the *objective function*.

The objective function and constraints must be stated in linear algebraic form. This requires that the variables of analysis be quantified at least at the ordinal scale. The justification and implications of these and other mechanical assumptions are discussed below (see Keene, 1981a, pp. 14-36; Reidhead, 1981, pp. 6-15).

The Diet Problem—A Graphic Solution to a LP Problem

In this section I will present a brief example of a static LP problem. The example, known as The Diet Problem, is the standard illustration found in LP literature (see Spivey & Thrall, 1970, p. 39; Dorfman et al., 1958, p. 9).

Simply stated, the problem is to select a sufficient diet for the least cost. Consider a diet that must satisfy at minimal cost (objective) m nutritional requirements (constraints) from n available foods (variables), each possessing a specific quantity of a given nutrient. The data to solve this problem can be visualized as a matrix (see Table 1). Let the columns represent available food resources and the rows their various nutrients. For example, element a_{ij} represents the amount of the ith nutrient in a standard unit of the jth food resource. Two additional vectors in the matrix must be considered. The column on the far right, known as the B vector, indicates the constraints—in this case, the minimum amount of each nutrient that must be acquired. The bottom row, or C vector, indicates the cost of acquisition of each resource. The problem can be stated algebraically as follows.

$$\text{minimize } z = \sum_{j=1}^{n} c_j x_j \qquad (1)$$

$$\text{subject to } b_i = \sum_{j=1}^{n} a_{ij} x_j \ (i = 1, 2, \ldots m) \qquad (2)$$

$$\text{and } x_j \geq 0 \ (j = 1, 2, 3 \ldots n) \qquad (3)$$

where z is the total cost of production, c_j is the cost of one unit of food j acquired, x_j is the number of units of food j acquired, b_i is the minimum requirement for nutrient i, and a_{ij} is the amount of nutrient i in the jth food. The equation to be minimized (e.g., 1) involving the C vector of costs is the objective function.

Table 10.1

Symbolic Notation in Sample Linear Programming Model—The Diet Problem

Nutritive Element (i)	Nutrients per Unit of Food (j)						Nutritional Requirement
	1	2	3	4	5	... n	
1	a_{11}	a_{12}	a_{13}	a_{14}	a_{15}	a_{1n}	b_1
2	a_{21}	a_{22}	a_{23}	a_{24}	a_{25}	a_{2n}	b_2
3	a_{31}	a_{32}	a_{33}	a_{34}	a_{35}	a_{3n}	b_3
m	a_{m1}	a_{m2}	a_{m3}	a_{m4}	a_{m5}	a_{mn}	b_m
Costs	c_1	c_2	c_3	c_4	c_5	c_n	$z = c_j x_j$

In order to simplify this explanation, I shall calculate an optimum diet of two hypothetical foods, I and II, while satisfying the minimum requirements for three nutritional elements, vitamins Q, R, and S. Numerical data for this model appear in Table 2. Each gram of Food I contains 2 mg of vitamin Q, 6 mg of R, and none of S. Food II contains 3 mg of Q, 4 mg of R, and 4 mg of S. One gram of Food I costs 8 arbitrary cost units, while one gram of Food II costs 4 units. We must satisfy the nutritional standards of at least 120 mg of vitamin Q, 120 mg of R and 40 mg of S with a diet of minimum cost. In other words, the problem is to minimize the objective function involving the costs associated with multiple variables (Foods I and II) subject to specific constraints (the dietary requirements). In algebraic terms:

variables: x_1 and x_2
cost: $z = 8x_1 + 4x_2 = $ minimum
constraints: $2x_1 + 3x_2 \geq 120$ (for Q)
$6x_1 + 4x_2 \geq 120$ (for R)
$4x_2 \geq 40$ (for S)

Because we cannot acquire a negative amount of a given food, we establish the additional constraints that:

$$x_1 \geq 0$$
$$x_2 \geq 0$$

Let us further assume that our resources are finite and that the maximum amount of each food accessible is:

$$x_1 \leq 70$$
$$x_2 \leq 30$$

Table 10.2

Numerical Data in Sample Linear Programming Model— The Diet Problem

Nutritive Element (Vitamin)	Nutrients per Unit of Food		Nutritional Requirement
	I	II	
Q	2	3	120
R	6	4	120
S	0	4	40
Cost	8	4	Minimum = ?
Amount of food available	70	30	

The process of minimizing the objective function under these constraints involves two steps. These are 1) defining those solutions to the inequalities involving the constraints that simultaneously satisfy all of them and 2) finding from among these solutions the optimal solution that minimizes the objective function. The first step is shown graphically (Fig. 1). Points on or above line A represent all possible combinations of Foods I and II that will satisfy the requirement of Vitamin Q. Points on or above line B represent combinations satisfying the constraint of R, and points on or above line C satisfy S. The shaded area on the graph represents all points (solutions) that will satisfy all constraints within the finite limitations of the resources. This area is called the area of *feasible solutions*.

The second step is finding the optimal solution. As in all static linear programming problems, the optimal solution will be found at one or more of the intersections of the lines that delineate the area of feasible solutions. In this example, the intersections occur at W, V, U, and Z on Figure 1, and one of them represents the optimal solution to the objective function—the diet of minimum cost. To determine which solution is optimal, it is necessary to compare only the costs of the diet at each corner of the area of feasible solutions. The optimum is found at point Z. At Z,

$$x_1 = 15$$
$$x_2 = 30$$

Thus, the optimum diet satisfying the hypothetical requirements consists of 15 gm of Food I and 30 gm of Food II. The cost of this diet would be 8(15) + 4(30) = 240 cost units.

The graphic method is applicable only to a two-variable problem. For three variables, a third dimension is needed, requiring a computer program to calculate the coordinates of the intersections of the equations of constraints and

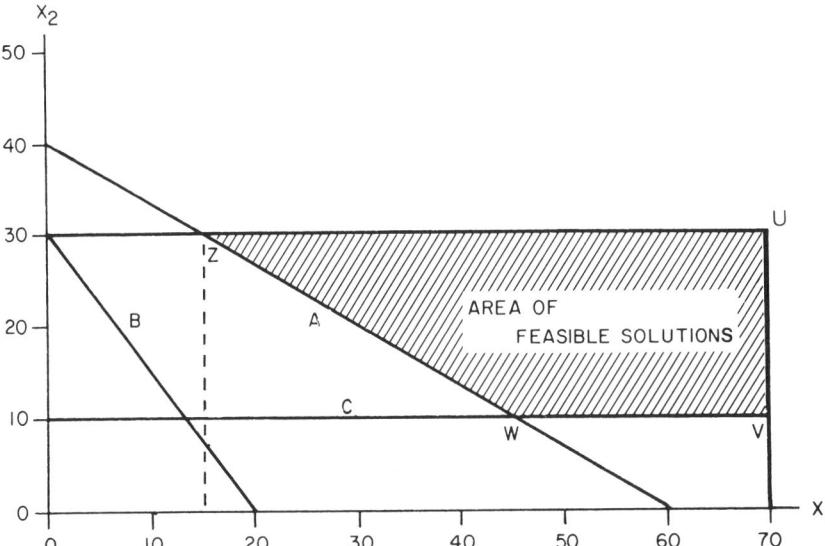

Fig. 10.1. Graphic solution to The Diet Problem. The equation of line A is $2x_1 + 3x_2 \geq 120$; of line b, $6x_1 + 4x_2 \geq 120$; of line C, $4x_2 \geq 40$. The minimum is given by $z = 8x_1 + 4x_2$, where $x_1 \geq 0$ and $x_2 \geq 0$ and $x_1 \leq 70$ and $x_2 \leq 30$.

to define the area of feasible solutions (Spivey & Thrall, 1970, p. 62; Cooper & Steinberg, 1974, p. 8).

The Simplex Method

The *simplex method* is the original algorithm developed to obtain an optimal solution to a LP problem and is still the most commonly used algorithm (see Wagner, 1975, pp. 91-118; Dantzig, 1963; Spivey & Thrall, 1970, for alternatives). The widespread availability of fine-tuned software has obviated the necessity for most users to learn how the algorithm works in detail.

Briefly, simplex is an iterative method that starts with an arbitrary, feasible solution (*basis* in LP terminology) and then seeks improved solutions (increasing or decreasing the objective function) until no further improvement is possible. In the graphic illustration, simplex begins by selecting a corner point in the feasible region and comparing it to adjacent corner points. If an adjacent corner point is better, the procedure continues by comparing that corner point with other adjacent points. When no improvement is possible, an optimal solution has been achieved. The procedure can be described geometrically as follows:

> Each basis corresponds to a vertex of the convex polyhedral set of feasible solutions. Going from one basis to the next represents going from one

extreme point to an adjacent one. Thus, the simplex method can be said to seek an optimal solution by climbing along the edges from one vertex of the convex polyhedral solution set to a neighboring one. (Wagner, 1975, p. 104)

Post Optimal Analysis

Calculating an optimal solution is just the beginning of a LP analysis. Most users of LP wish to consider additional questions: 1) What are the marginal costs associated with variables and constraints? 2) Which constraints are most influential in shaping the optimal solution? 3) What are the implications of altering the values of certain input variables, constraints, and cost coefficients or of adding new constraints or variables to a model? 4) How sensitive is the model to errors in the estimation of (changes in) input values? The answers to these questions are provided in the analysis of *post optimal data*, which constitutes the critical power of LP techniques.

Marginal Analysis. Calculation of the optimal solution to a LP problem with the simplex method is referred to as the *primal problem*. It involves the set of inequalities relating variables and constraints that are defined by the rows of a matrix structured as in Table 1, with an additional row of costs defining the objective function. These functional relations are known as the *primal*, and their solution as the *primal solution*. Every primal is accompanied by a mirror image of itself called the *dual*, the solution of which provides post optimal data. To solve the dual, the matrix defining the primal is essentially rotated to the left 90° so that the column of constraints (i.e., the b vector) becomes a row defining the objective function and the row of costs becomes a column defining the constraints. The inequities are also reversed from the primal to the dual formulation. While the goal of the primal in our example (Table 1) was to calculate the diet that would satisfy minimum nutritional requirements from an array of foods at lowest cost, the goal of the dual is to maximize nutrient production. The optimal solution to the dual, then, is found by applying the simplex algorithm to it.

Optimally solving the dual variables allows the calculation of *shadow prices* or *shadow costs*. Shadow prices are statements of marginal value, indicating the unit worth of each column vector (resource) or row vector (nutrient) as predicted in the optimal solution to the primal problem. To begin, let us consider the shadow prices of column vectors—resources. In our example, at the most basic level, a shadow price of a column vector indicates how much extra it will cost (i.e., how much it will alter the objective function) to increase production of a resource by a single increment. For resources unused in the optimal solution, shadow prices indicate the cost reduction necessary before the resource can enter the optimal solution. For resources that are expended, shadow prices suggest how much of an increase in their cost would be tolerated without altering the optimal solution if more of the expended resource became available (in consumer terms, how much more a decision maker would be willing to "pay" to acquire an additional unit of an expended resource).

In the diet problem example presented above, it might be useful to know how much the cost of Food II could increase and still remain in the optimal solution. Let us consider the problem in terms of the most limiting constraint (see below), vitamin Q. Food I provides 2 mg of vitamin Q at a cost of 8 units, for a cost/benefit ratio of 4. Food II has a cost/benefit ratio of 1.33. This indicates that Food II would be the optimal choice over Food I, even if the cost of Food II increased by as much as 300% (4.0/1.33). Thus, the maximum tolerable price for additional units of Food II is less than or equal to 12 (300% of the stated cost), and the shadow price is 8.0 (the maximum cost, 12 — the original cost, 4). The important conclusion is that if production of Food II could be increased, even at a higher cost, it would produce a net decrease in the total cost of production.

Shadow prices may be applied in the same way to the study of row vectors— here, nutrients. They have been used to consider a variety of questions in subsistence studies (see Keene, 1981a; Reidhead, 1981). In a diet problem we might wish to ask how the increase or decrease of a nutritional requirement will alter the objective function. For example, in the case presented above we might want to ask what the added cost of production would be if vitamin S requirements were increased by a single milligram. In this case, the cost would be zero because a surplus of this nutrient has been acquired in the optimal solution. The cost of increasing production of vitamin Q, on the other hand, is 4 cost units. Because the supply of Food II is depleted in obtaining the optimal solution the added intake of Q must come from Food I. This cost is 8 (the cost of 1 gm of Food I)/2 (the vitamin Q content of Food I) = 4 cost units per gram of Vitamin Q. Vitamin Q thus exhibits a shadow cost of 4.

Limiting Factors Shaping the Optimal Solution. A major concern of subsistence studies or any ecological analysis is the identification of limiting factors (Pianka, 1978). In LP models, limiting factors are referred to as the *binding constraints* of the model. A binding constraint is a constraint that has not yet been satisfied when all other constraints are satisfied. In the diet problem the binding constraints are those dietary requirements (nutrients) that are available in the least amounts or are the most costly to fulfill. I have argued elsewhere that binding constraints should be a major factor in determining subsistence decision (Keene, 1981a). Post optimal analysis identifies those nutrients that limit or bind the model under specified conditions.

An examination of the graphic solution in the example illustrated in Figure 1 allows us to identify vitamin Q as the binding constraint in this model. In satisfying the requirements for vitamins R and S at the least cost, the requirement for Q will not be fulfilled. The solution, therefore, must key on minimizing cost for the acquisition of vitamin Q. This is graphically evident by the fact that the optimal solution (point Z) falls on the production line for vitamin Q (line A). Any point below line A will result in a vitamin Q deficiency. At point Z, vitamins R and S are produced in surplus. (Note that any point above line B results in a vitamin R surplus, and any point above line C results in a surplus of vitamin S.)

Analysis of Errors in Input Values and Alterations or Additions to Them. Two final, closely related goals of post optimal analysis are the examination and modeling of specific system changes and the evaluation of effects of data errors. The first involves assessing the effects of changing the values of input parameters or adding new parameters upon the optimal solution. The second goal involves assessing the effects of changing the values of input parameters, but interpretation is in terms of the sensitivity of the optimal solution to error. All these operations fall under the heading of *sensitivity analysis*.

To begin, let us consider operations concerned with changes in the values of input parameters from the standpoint of error. In developing a data base for LP modeling, it is usually necessary to estimate some of the input data. Thus, one would like to know the range over which the data might vary without altering the optimal solution and whether the solution found is potentially an artifact of input errors.

For example, in my analysis of Late Archaic subsistence in Michigan, I argue that nuts were not part of an optimal diet. Such an inference is counterintuitive, given conventional scenarios for Late Archaic subsistence (e.g., Ford, 1977). However, it can be argued (if one accepts the cost framework I utilized; see below) that these results are not an artifact of errors in estimation of nut costs and model sensitivity; sensitivity analysis suggests that a cost reduction of more than 95% would be necessary before nuts would enter the optimal solution (Keene, 1979, p. 174). Calcium, on the other hand, is a limiting nutrient in all of my Late Archaic models. Several resources, such as turtle and fish, entered the optimal solution because they provide significant amounts of this limiting nutrient. However, human calcium requirements, calcium uptake and calcium content of foods are not well understood (Keene, 1981a), so one needs to know how sensitive the model is to minimal changes in calcium requirements. A reduction of 69% (800 mg to 250 mg per person per day) does not significantly alter the composition of the optimal diet. Therefore, the models are not especially sensitive to changes in calcium requirements and the potential errors in the calcium input data are not apt to have influenced the qualitative results. (The models are, however, sensitive to calculation of the calcium composition of foods—higher calcium content increasing the probability of entry into the optimal solution.)

This aspect of sensitivity analysis gives LP a considerable advantage over other mathematical models where the errors in estimates and implications of simplifications may not be readily apparent.

These same post optimal data can be used to examine the systemic interrelationships that shape the optimal solution and to consider the systemic implications of changes in input data. For example, in my Late Archaic analysis, it would have been possible to consider the effects of various technological innovations in the mode of processing different foods that reduce their exploitation costs (i.e., the effects of changes in the cost coefficients of the objective function) on the optimal balance of food resources. Similarly, the effect of variations in nutrient requirements (i.e., changes in constraints) with seasonal changes in weather on optimal diet could have been investigated.

Sensitivity analyses concerned with parameter value changes can be conducted with the aid of two mathematical operations: *parametric programming* and *ranging analysis* (see Wagner, 1975, Hillier & Lieberman, 1974 for details).

Parametric programming permits the systematic evaluation of simultaneous changes in several parameters (either cost coefficients or constraints) and hence permits a systematic sensitivity analysis (Wagner, 1975, p. 130; Hillier & Lieberman, 1974, p. 665).

Ranging analysis is similar to parametric programming but is not a simultaneous analysis. Rather, new values are substituted one at a time in the primal problem. The problem is then solved to determine if the solution has been altered. The results are essentially the same as those for parametric programming, with the exception that simultaneous changes in several coefficients cannot be examined. The approach is less efficient than parametric programming. Most software for the simplex method also provides a ranging analysis. Programs allowing parametric programming are not as readily available.

Another aspect of sensitivity analysis allows one to evaluate the effects of adding either new row vectors (constraints) or new column vectors (variables) to a model. Examining the effects of adding new constraints is more common and is achieved with the *dual simplex* method—a variant of the simplex algorithm.

Use of the dual simplex to add constraints to an optimal solution is also a means for feasibly analyzing data where the number of constraints to be considered is excessively large. When the simplex method is used to find an optimal solution, the number of computations increases roughly as a cubic function of the number of constraints (see below). When the number of constraints is large, it is sometimes advisable to focus on only a few of the constraints, eliminating those thought unlikely to be binding, based on a priori knowledge. The excluded constraints, sometimes referred to as secondary constraints, may then be examined for their effects on the model after solution of the primal problem using the dual simplex as part of post optimal analysis (see Wagner, 1975, pp. 145-150).

In summary, LP results are used in three broad ways: to define optimal solutions, to examine specified system changes, and to assess how inaccuracies in the input data affect results.

Linear Programming in Prehistoric Subsistence Studies

LP methods have been used to study a variety of subsistence problems, though most applications to archaeology to date have been formulated in terms of an optimal diet model (cf. Dickson, 1980). The first comprehensive applications of LP to questions of prehistoric subsistence by Reidhead (1976, rev. 1981) and Keene (1981a) focused on questions of optimal diet.

Reidhead set out to test the hypothesis that variability in prehistoric subsistence behavior was governed by the law of least effort (Zipf, 1949). Simply stated, Reidhead hoped to demonstrate that when choices existed among competing subsistence strategies, the one requiring the least labor input would be selected, all other things being equal. Reidhead developed an optimal diet model, much like the one illustrated above, in which he examined resources (the variables) in terms of nutritional benefits (the constraints) and varying cost (person-hours required to produce a specified amount). Resource values were modified to account for costs of and losses in storage, processing, and seasonal variation. Costs of alternative technologies (e.g., fishing with lines vs. traps) were also considered. Models were calculated for four discrete seasons in a "typical" year for two prehistoric adaptations in the Middle Ohio Valley, the Late Woodland foraging economy and the Fort Ancient corn agriculture economy.

Reidhead then tested his hypothesis of least effort by comparing the theoretically optimal resource schedule predicted by his models with data recovered from middens at the Leonard Haag site, a multicomponent occupation in Indiana with relatively good organic preservation. Reidhead found a high degree of congruence between his predictions and the data, and argued that subsistence strategies evident at Haag are those we would expect if minimization of labor was desired. Given that deviations between the theoretical optimum and the archaeological data exist, Reidhead concludes that a theory of least effort can explain a great deal, but by no means all of the variability in subsistence behavior in this case or in general. Reidhead's analysis also isolates limiting factors in the Woodland diet. As expected, protein was limiting in the Fort Ancient period, but not before. Less expected was the observation that energy was a limiting factor in at least one season (cf. Keene, 1979) and that calcium was limiting in general.

Another of Reidhead's objectives was to investigate the economics of subsistence change with reference to corn agriculture. He recognized energy as a binding constraint in the foraging, but not in the agricultural model. His suggestion that corn was incorporated into the prehistoric Ohio Valley economy because it increased the efficiency of production is a refreshing alternative to population pressure arguments.

In contrast to Reidhead, I used LP as a heuristic device to generate hypotheses rather than to test them. My objective was to generate insight into processes of adaptation to a benevolent environment—in this case the temperate forests—while avoiding the dependence on ethnographic analogy that dominated hunter-gatherer studies at the time (Keene, 1981a, 1981b; Wobst, 1978). I modeled the optimal diet for the Late Archaic population in the Saginaw Valley of Michigan for each month in a typical year. Model results were then compared with archaeological data revealing a high degree of congruence.

The model underscores the importance of gathered foods in the Late Archaic economy, an important insight given the poor preservation of plant foods throughout much of the study area and the hunting bias that pervades much of hunter-gatherer theory (Dahlberg, 1981). The model also points to the importance of clothing as a limiting factor in Late Archaic subsistence. The consideration of hides as a critical resource is a step away from the gastronomical determinism that dominates subsistence studies and suggests that other nonfood factors may also limit subsistence decisions (e.g., firewood, fuel [see Keene, 1979], raw materials, and social relations). The comparison between model and data suggests that winter and possibly fall encampments are not represented in the Saginaw Valley data base and that previous interpretations of year-round, sedentary occupations in that area are not easily supported.

The reader may wish to examine the primary reports for details, but this summary will at least provide a general picture of what LP models are, how they are used, and what kind of results can be derived. While Reidhead and I both examine questions of optimal diet, LP applications are by no means limited to this question (see Reidhead, 1979). I reiterate that LP may prove useful in any problem where selection or allocation must be made among several alternatives and where alternatives, constraints, and desired goals can be expressed quantitatively. For example, one might wish to examine strategies that would maximize nonsubsistence production while meeting basic subsistence needs. One might be interested in balancing production demands at the household level against the need to produce surplus for feasting at the village level (as in the case of Polynesian big-men). Or one might want to minimize distance traveled between extraction camps or nodes in an exchange, information, or tribute network. All of these problems could be examined with LP models.

BENEFITS OF LINEAR PROGRAMMING

When one's research questions can be phrased as a decision problem, LP may be an attractive technique for manipulating complex data sets. Some of its advantages are that it

1) is readily accessible to a novice user;
2) offers the modeler flexibility;
3) is computationally simple;
4) is a robust technique;

5) is computationally efficient;
6) is computationally consistent; and
7) has heuristic benefits.

Many of LP's advantages have been discussed elsewhere (Reidhead, 1979; Keene, 1981; Bettinger, 1980; Joy, 1967; Wagner, 1975). Here, I will consider only the last three.

Computational Burden

A concern of any modeler is the number of variables that can be (or should be) incorporated into the analysis. I was attracted to LP initially because it allows one to transcend the simple two-variable formulations that were prominent in ecology at the time (e.g., Loka-Volterra predator-prey models). In building simulations, one may have to keep the number of variables small so as to minimize the computational burden in regard to both programming and CPU time. However, this is not a problem with LP applications. It has been shown that using the simplex method, the computational burden increases roughly as the cube of the number of constraints increases. Thus, a 200-equation problem will require eight times as many calculations as a 100-equation problem. One-thousand-equation models are manageable (Wagner, 1975), though it is hard to imagine an archaeological problem of such magnitude (Keene's [1981a] model used twelve equations).

When the number of constraints becomes excessively large, alternative approaches are possible. The use of the dual simplex to add secondary constraints to a model, after having found the primal solution for a limited set of more primary constraints, has been discussed above. A second approach involves the use of the *upper bound technique*. This is a variant of the simplex algorithm for calculating the primal solution initially allowing the upper bounds of all variables to be excluded as constraints, thereby reducing calculation burden (Hillier & Lieberman, 1974).

In short, size and computational burden are not significant considerations in LP analysis.

Consistency

LP is an attractive technique in that results are replicable and consistent. The widespread availability of fine-tuned software obviates the need to confront programming idiosyncracies. Round-off error may be a problem when one is dealing with only a few significant digits, but most computer packages accommodate this problem. However, because the models are quantitative and because use of several significant digits is desirable to avoid round-off error, there may be a degree of false precision in the analysis (see below).

Heuristic Advantages

Perhaps the most important advantage of LP is that it, as all model building processes, offers significant heuristic benefits. In having to make explicit the activities of production, the constraints on production, and the interrelationships between activities and constraints, the researcher is forced to ask questions that might otherwise be neglected. Likewise, in having to quantify a matrix of coefficients for LP, the researcher must explore details he might otherwise not consider. For example, in his study of optimal diet in the prehistoric Ohio Valley, Reidhead (1981) was forced to assess the specific costs and benefits of resources (which he defined in terms of hourly labor and nutritional yield) in considerable detail. How abundant are hickory nuts, for instance? How reliable are they? How many can be harvested and with how much effort? Do they store well? Are they easily processed? What is their nutritional value? These questions take us beyond the simple qualitative and often inductive analyses that are prevalent in the study of prehistoric economy. As Johnson notes, model building "is at once a highly organizing experience and imaginatively stimulating one. It promotes clarity of thought, detailed attention to measurement and orderly exploration of alternative possibilities" (1980, p. 40).

LIMITATIONS OF LINEAR PROGRAMMING

Whenever a new method of analysis is introduced to a field, it is imperative to carefully examine its limitations. This is especially important with a proven and well-documented technique like LP, where one might assume that serious mechanical and conceptual problems have been worked out by previous practitioners. In this section, two kinds of limitations to LP will be discussed: 1) *mechanical limitations*—those constraints stemming from the computational mechanics of the technique; and 2) *conceptual limitations*—those based in assumptions, theory, and epistemology.

Mechanical Limitations

Linearity

A prerequisite of LP is that all mathematical functions in the model must be linear. For example, in the studies by Reidhead (1981) and Keene (1981a), it is assumed that cost is a linear function of production: that the total cost of production increases by the same increment for each successive item of the same kind added to the production schedule. This assumption of linearity may be somewhat unreasonable. In many cases, cost is more realistically represented by a curvilinear function with the nature of the curve varying with start-up or investment costs, group versus individual procurement (in the case of hunting), diminishing returns, territory size, and other factors (Keene, 1981a; Earle, 1980; Limp, 1977; Limp & Carr, chapter 7; Charnov, 1976). Lee, for instance, notes that among the San there is a significant inflection in the cost curve when a trip extends beyond one day because of the need to pack drinking water and other provisions (Lee, 1969, p. 61). Similarly, group procurement, such as the driving of bison into pounds or traps is not well represented by a linear cost function. There is a high investment cost in acquiring the first bison (resulting from the cost of building the pound, organizing the personnel, and driving the bison), but the marginal cost for each additional bison acquired in the same drive is minimal.

To accommodate curvilinear cost functions, it is possible to use a variant of LP called *separable programming*, a method in which a well-behaved curvilinear objective function is broken down into smaller linear segments, each of which is treated as a separate variable in the standard simplex solution (Wagner, 1975, p. 562; Hillier & Lieberman, 1974, pp. 171-180; Keene, 1981a, pp. 32-35). This approach greatly increases the size of the model, but will probably not present problems if the model contains only a few nonlinearities that need to be partitioned. But if the model is highly nonlinear, other programming methods may be needed. These include *convex programming* and *nonlinear programming* (see Wagner, 1975; Hillier & Lieberman, 1974). Convex programming is designed for the analysis of data where the relationship between cost and production is strictly convex. Nonlinear programming is a heterogeneous array of techniques, each useful for highly specific forms of relationships.

A more confounding problem in dealing with cost functions is not computational but operational. In archaeology, it is seldom possible to collect the empirical data necessary to develop accurate cost curves. Thus, while in most cases separable convex programming may be more concordant with the reality of the production process, it is not feasible to obtain the data required to employ such techniques (see below; Keene, 1981a, pp. 30-35). A more intractable problem concerning cost curves is conceptual. This is the definition of cost, which will vary depending on the theoretical orientation of the research (see below).

Dynamic Applications

The linear programming models discussed previously are essentially static models generating an optimal solution for a specific synchronic scenario. Most archaeologists, however, are interested in diachronic analyses. Diachronic modeling can be achieved technically within a mathematical programming format in at least four ways:

1) Information on binding constraints, marginal costs, and values derived in the postoptimal analysis of a static LP model for one time period can give insight into the effects of changing constraints and resource costs on optimal resource allocation over time. Examples of this approach (Reidhead, 1981; Keene, 1981a) have been summarized above.

2) The optimal solutions and post optimal analytic information from two static LP models pertaining to two different time periods and allocation systems can be compared to each other to reconstruct an evolutionary trajectory. This is exemplified by my (1979) examination of pre- and post-rifle economies among the Netsilik and by Reidhead's (1981) comparison of Late Woodland and Fort Ancient economies.

3) Dynamic linear programming approaches (see Throsby, 1962), in which the output from one time period is used as the input for the next, can be used. I am not familiar with any full applications of dynamic LP in anthropology, though the technique is used widely in agricultural economics (Throsby, 1962; Low, 1974). Perhaps applications in the anthropological literature are lacking because sufficient dynamic inferences can be generated using approaches 1 and 2. An archaeological study that begins to approach the dynamic LP method is Reidhead's Ohio Valley study. In this case, the modeling process involved using the output from one seasonal model to formulate the input for the next seasonal model in a subtractive fashion. However, the approach remained static in that the resource costs and availabilities used to build the model were long-term averages. An example of an archaeological question phrased fully as a dynamic LP problem would be one in which hunting affected the reproduction, density, and availability of a resource, and one in which the researcher wanted to model the feedback relationship between availability, productivity, and cost.

4) *Dynamic programming*, which requires formalization with differential equations, may be employed. Dynamic programming is applied typically in operations research on microdecision making, where optimality is time-staged, and where similar decision operations must be repeated frequently: for example, in establishing rules for inventory reordering that indicate when to replenish an item and by what amount.

Number of Variables vs. Number of Constraints

Typically, the number of variables investigated in an LP problem is greater than the number of constraints. This is not required mathematically, however. If the number of constraints exceeds the number of variables, an optimal solution can still be calculated by inserting slack variables—artificial variables that have a coefficient of zero in the optimal solution (Wagner, 1975).

The primary limitation of consequence is that the number of variables that can enter the optimal solution is no more than the number of constraints. For example, in subsistence studies, if it is possible to model only a few nutrient requirements (i.e., constraints) for a system, only a few food resources (variables) can enter into the optimal solution and the full range of resource decisions cannot be investigated. Moreover, the partial solution may be unstable and misleading—it may change significantly with the modeling of more constraints and the possibility of the model including more resources.

Conceptual Limitations

Up to this point, I have discussed the limitations of LP simply as a technique, free of any theoretical or epistemological context. LP is a fairly mechanical task, and its technological drawbacks are apparent. The conceptual limitations of LP, however, are less obvious. The predictive power of LP lies not in the technique itself, but in the theories on which LP models are based. Thus, any consideration of the benefits or limitations of LP analysis cannot be divorced from the limitations of the theory that LP is used to represent. Some of the conceptual problems associated with LP analysis are discussed below.

Emics vs. Etics

A question frequently encountered in using mathematical models is how much precision is *necessary*. Ideally, in building models one would like to maximize precision, generality, and realism (Levins, 1966), although obviously this cannot be done simultaneously. At the same time, one also must ask how much precision is *appropriate*.

LP models have been criticized for being too precise. Jochim (1983) argues that LP models often use decision-making criteria and detailed input that exceed the information processing capabilities of the actors (see Limp & Carr, chapter 7). Factors such as nutritional composition of foods, soil chemistry, and the logistical movements of game may indeed affect subsistence patterns, but most decision makers cannot track this information, nor are they capable of calculating differential payoffs (see Simon, 1957; Moore, 1983). Thus, subsistence decisions, Jochim argues, will tend to be based on simple axioms grounded in readily observed phenomena. He attempts to demonstrate that animal size and abundance are sufficient to predict most variability in subsistence decisions.

Jochim's argument that LP may not be the most appropriate method for tracking *emic decision processes* may be correct. At the same time, the method may be appropriate for the *etic evolutionary* analysis of decision strategies. For example, in my own work, I assumed that 1) there was selection over time in favor of groups that satisfied their basic needs, and 2) this occurred regardless of whether those desired outcomes were perceived by the actors themselves. Whether they perceive it or not, people are subject to the constraints of availability of food, dietary needs, climate, etc.; through selection, they must develop some means for coping with these constraints if they are to persist as a people. Inuit populations, for example, do not recognize the chemical, ascorbic acid, or the body's need for this vitamin; yet in an environment limited in ascorbic acid, they rarely suffer a deficiency. Therefore, in my work, I assumed that the process being tracked was a selective process rather than a cognitive one. These assumptions were grounded in evolutionary ecology and optimal foraging theory (Pianka, 1978; Winterhalder & Smith, 1981). (Editor's note: The precision of LP methods is concordant with the continuous scale nature of selective processes and the system equilibria determined by them.)

In sum, my models can be distinguished from those of Jochim (1976) and perhaps Reidhead (1981) by being etic rather than emic decision models. In various ways, I (1981a), Reidhead (1979), Selby and Hendrix (1976), and Johnson (1980) all make the distinction between the emics and etics of decision making, recognizing that the environment cognized by the actors is not totally congruent with the operational environment (Rappaport, 1968).

At another level, however, the precision in LP models may indeed be false, even from an evolutionary perspective. In my Late Archaic study (1981a), the model will choose the resource that provides 100 mg of calcium per 100g over that which provides 95 mg of calcium per 100g, all other things being equal. Clearly, by any practical standard, the resources should be considered equivalent. In this circumstance, what is called for is some sensitivity to possible effective ranges of variation in the evaluation of the solution and the post optimal data.

Finally, the inappropriateness of LP for modeling cognitive processes and its concordance in modeling evolutionary processes can be brought back to my discussion of the function of models. LP models are most useful when used to predict how people *should* make choices from an adaptive perspective rather than how people *do* make choices. LP models are normative models illustrating decision rules under tightly defined circumstances. Any well-formulated LP model should offer a theoretical baseline, or preferably, several theoretical baselines, against which one can examine behavior. Deviations from model predictions are to be expected, and it is these deviations from the modeled optimum which may prove to be of greatest interest. For example, if one were interested in food preferences, LP models, conscientiously formulated, might shed light on why scarce or expensive resources are utilized or why seemingly attractive resources are ignored.

Scale

Problems of scale abound in any kind of archaeological analysis. Social, political, and economic processes take on different appearances and have quite different implications when viewed over a variety of scales. Thus, when formulating an LP model, as in any cultural model, it is necessary to be sensitive to and make explicit the bounds of examination. Bounding a problem is an essential aspect of the modeling process.

Although LP analysis does not inherently impose scalar problems on our studies, the building of an LP model implies a choice of bounds. The choice of how one bounds a model may be a personal choice, a choice of convenience, or a choice grounded in theory. Although it is pointless to argue that one scale of analysis is preferable to another, neither can one dismiss scalar issues nor be indifferent to the implications of the bounds we impose on our models. In archaeological uses of optimization models, and perhaps in archaeological analysis in general to date, we have been less than sensitive to problems of temporal, spatial, and social scale (Wobst, 1978; Keene, 1983; Cross, 1983).

Temporal Scale. When one speaks of optimal behavior, one must ask, "optimal for whom and at what scale?" Behavior that is optimal in the short run may not be optimal in the long run and vice versa. Are we interested in optimal behaviors over a day, a month, a year, a generation? Would our models account for adaptations to a 100-year flood? Should they? Are we interested in possible responses to temporally local highs or lows, or averages or modes over time? At what scale do processes of adaptation operate and what are the mechanisms of adaptation?

A critical problem that I see in LP applications is that the scale of analysis is usually ambiguous and when specified is too small. LP applications are usually aimed at more proximate decision-making problems. On the other hand, archaeology's most noteworthy contribution to the social sciences is its ability to deal with large periods of time. Moreover, in using decision-making models and in our general discussions of biocultural change, the link between short-term decision making and long-term patterning, between local and global phenomena, and between micro- and macro-evolution is often unspecified and unexamined (Keene, 1983). Yet, if our goal is to understand process, if our goal is to use the past to build general theory that does not simply mirror the present, then this link which we typically ignore is the one which demands our closest attention.

Another problem inherent to past applications of LP is the use of temporally modal values in both short-term and long-term studies. Reidhead (1981), implying personal choice as the mechanism governing subsistence decisions, assumed optimization on a day-to-day basis. Keene, grounding his work in evolutionary ecology, assumed that selection operates to promote optimization, hence suggesting a longer interval. Both models, however, present "typical" years and employ modal values. The use of such modal values tends to homogenize environments temporally and spatially, and hence mask a good deal of the variability that conditions behavior and that we need to understand (Winterhalder, 1980; Root, 1980). My study of the Saginaw Valley of Michigan (1981a, 1981b) offers a general model for optimal resource selection in the Late Archaic period. But there is much variation with the Late Archaic period, even within the Saginaw Valley. Climatic fluctuations, continuous local plant succession, evolving social relations, and other variation argue against homogenizing the Late Archaic as a single entity. Can one really speak of a Late Archaic subsistence and settlement pattern, placing all sites from a 3,000-year range into a single pattern? Frequently one lacks the chronological control to do anything else (for an exception, see Braun, chapter 16), but in the process one combines data from multiple and probably contrasting patterns (see Read, chapter 3).

This problem of temporal scale is not implicit in LP methods, but rather in the way we have conducted our analyses. Post optimal data can show the implications of changes in modal conditions. One can, for example, examine the effects of variability in deer productivity, of forest succession, or of drought. One can look at highs and lows in resource cycles. All of this information is imbedded in the LP solutions. The models themselves elegantly organize our data, but one has to know what to ask of this organization and of the patterning revealed. The questions, of course, emanate not from methodological exactitude but from theory.

Spatial Scale. Few anthropologists today would argue that local behavior is solely or primarily determined by local conditions. The influence of world systems theory (Wallerstein, 1974) has forced anthropologists to place the behavior of prehistoric people—be they hunter-gatherers or citizens of archaic states—into a larger arena (Blanton, 1983; Paynter, 1982; Kristiansen, 1982). Extralocal sociopolitical relations affect local production options and vice versa. Spatial variation in resources affects extralocal relations and vice versa. Even our favorite ethnographic analogies of "band" level societies (like the San) suggest that local decisions cannot be understood outside of a larger spatial context (Lee, 1982; Weissner, 1982; Wobst, 1978).

However, in using LP models and optimal foraging approaches in general, Reidhead, I, and other archaeologists have homogenized space through the utilization of modal values, just as we have homogenized time. We recognize that the physical landscape is not homogeneous in terms of physiography or productivity, and we expect such variations at different scales to affect significantly how the landscape is used; yet our models tend to portray the landscape as uniform. As a result of not accounting for fluctuations in the spatial landscape, a number of significant questions could not be considered in the studies of Keene and Reidhead, mentioned above. For example, do local resource failures correlate with failures at a large spatial scale? How much space must be utilized to ensure buffers against local perturbations in productivity? In obscuring questions of spatial scale, we may simply be imposing our tendencies toward a parochial site-centered approach onto our behavioral models.

Social Scale and Social Interrelations. What is the appropriate unit of analysis in subsistence studies? Are subsistence strategies operationalized or selected on the level of the individual, the family, or the group? Most decision-making models are explicitly studies of individual decision making. I have argued elsewhere that in the study of social change, in contrast to biological change, the individual is neither an appropriate unit of analysis nor an appropriate unit of selection, and that society must be viewed as something more than the aggregate of individual behaviors and actions (Keene, 1983). What is optimal for one individual may constrain the options of another. Such contradictions that exist in any society—emanating initially from differences in ability, knowledge, and kinship, and ultimately from privileged access to information, resources, and power—have a significant impact on the shape of production and on society. But LP models have not, and probably cannot, account for dialectical relationships evident in human societies. Such models are imbued with an egalitarian ethic that assumes equal assessment of costs and equal distribution of benefits across society. Thus, they homogenize the interests of all members of society.

Production and distribution cannot be examined as simple man-land relationships. They are foremost social processes and cannot be separated from prevailing social and political relationships. In any society the organization of production, the extraction of surplus, the nature of distribution, and the quality of life are inextricably linked to questions of social power. Yet, LP applications impose such a separation, preventing the investigation of such relationships. It may be argued that knowledge of limiting factors in the physical environment is itself a useful piece of information, exclusive of social context, but it may also be argued that focus on such fine-grained questions has neither forced us nor allowed us to confront larger issues. What is the value of subsistence studies that remove production from its social context under the guise of simplifying assumptions? Research questions and analysis should not be so heavily shaped by methodology.

LP models not only do not deal well with problems of social scale, but tend to *obscure* them. This is not so much a problem of method but of theory and problem formulation. Consider, for example, White's (1973) LP analysis of subsistence production among the Kaupauku. White poses the problem as follows: What is the optimal mix of crops that will meet the minimum subsistence requirements of the Kaupauku? Selection must be made among three crops in two contrasting production zones. White's optimal solution is hardly congruent with actual Kaupauku behavior (see White, 1973, pp. 395-399 for details; Johnson, 1980). The problem is not in the analysis but in the formulation of the question. White's analysis ignores the productive demands engendered by a big-man political economy, necessitating, among other things, intensive surplus production at the local level for redistribution in competitive feasting at the regional level. In a big-man society, production is neither regulated at the household level nor conditioned by household needs. It is the big-man who drives production, maximizing surplus production at the household level without alienating his kin in order to surpass past redistributive efforts of his competitors without exceeding their ability to repay (Paynter & Cole, 1982; Root, 1983; cf. Pospisil, 1963). White's framework neutralizes these key political relations which condition behavior among the Kaupauku.

The optimal solution to the big-man's problem could also be calculated as a LP problem. The new constraints, suggested by an alternative theoretical framework, create a different picture than White's optimal solution. But even this reformulation would fail, I suspect, to predict Kaupauku behavior. The problem is that pigs (which are not even considered in White's analysis) are not simply food resources but a standard of exchange and a measure of social production. Root (1983) notes that the value of pigs is not simply nutritional. Pig production may be important compared to other modes of subsistence because it masks social contradictions in Kaupauku society. Because pigs typically are allowed to run loose in New Guinea villages, obvious differences in production and accumulation are not readily visible. Thus, an essential contradiction in this somewhat egalitarian society is ameliorated. This tendency to both mask and exaggerate (at different times) inequalities among the Kaupauku is not suggested by LP analysis, nor is it amenable to optimization analysis. An understanding of such behavior requires dialectical theory and models.

Finally, LP models obscure social scale in implicitly invoking an assumption of omniscience (Moore, 1983). Unlike game theory, which stimulates decision making under conditions of ignorance or partial information, LP applications assume an all-knowing, computationally perfect decision maker. Such models ignore the value of information as a critical resource and imply that all actors have *equal access* to information. By holding access to information constant, these models rob a decision maker of social context.

An omniscient decision maker may indeed be heuristically useful, but without the consideration of information as a socially mediated resource, these decision-making models obscure key social processes that we need to consider. For example, Moore (1981) has shown that among hunter-gatherers behavior is often limited by access to information rather than to food or raw materials, and that access to information is socially mediated. The disposition of information as a resource—its acquisition, dissemination, and manipulation—is a key variable in the formation and maintenance of social power.

Cost

Every optimization problem requires a currency, a measure of the goal to be optimized. In LP analysis, this currency must be a quantitative measure.

There has been considerable debate on the validity of various cost measures used in LP analysis and in optimization problems in general (e.g., Smith, 1979; Keene, 1981a, 1983; Reidhead, 1981; Jochim, 1983; Winterhalder & Smith, 1981; Earle, 1980; Durham, 1981). Some studies have favored simple currencies such as energy or time that are easily quantified and amenable to verification through experiment or observation. Others have opted for composite polythetic currencies that simultaneously examine several factors and hence more closely approximate the multiplicity of cost. I will not attempt to evaluate the various positions in the debate. Rather, I will suggest that different currencies are needed to examine different questions, and that in most cases, it will be useful to employ several currencies in successive modeling efforts.

Different currencies lend different insights into a problem. This was illustrated in a short study by Boy and Leatherman (1980). Using direct calorimetry, they conducted an input/output analysis of the time and energy involved in various aspects of collection and preparation of acorns. They demonstrated that if energetic efficiency is the desired objective, acorns represent an attractive resource, offering a high energy yield for a relatively low input. If, on the other hand, the desired objective is to minimize time input, acorns are quite expensive. Thus, acorns would be much more attractive in situations where energy was limiting, but time was not. This underscores the need to justify the use of any given currency and points to the necessity of employing multiple alternative currencies.

Unfortunately, multiple currencies and competing objectives are rarely examined in LP or other optimal foraging studies. One modeling effort that does consider alternative objectives is Redding's (1981) study of prehistoric sheep and goat herding in the Middle East. Redding simultaneously examines several different optimal strategies (e.g., maximizing meat production; maximizing milk yield; minimizing feed requirements while producing minimum satisfactory yields of milk, meat, and wool; and minimizing risk of loss). He also considers the implications of these strategies for herd composition (sheep and goat mix and demographic structure). While not formulated as an LP problem, Redding's study is amenable to LP analysis.

In formulating any optimization problem, we must first consider what kind of optimization we are looking for. We must then evaluate whether our measure of cost or currency actually portrays what it is intended to. Let us briefly consider some of the characteristics of currencies popularly used in optimization studies.

Energy. Energy is an attractive currency for several reasons. First, it is easily quantified and hence conducive to precise cost/benefit analysis. Methods for measuring energy expenditure directly are well developed (Passmore, 1964; Nydon & Thomas, 1983). When direct measurement is not possible, a growing data base exists on the energetics of work in foraging and agricultural societies (e.g., Winterhalder, 1977; Smith, 1980; Johnson, 1980: Thomas, 1973). Research in work physiology offers further analogies (Astrand & Rodahl, 1977). Second, work in evolutionary ecology suggests that there is a link between efficiency of energy acquisition and fitness (Pianka, 1978; Smith, 1979), though this position remains controversial (Vayda & McKay, 1975; Keene, 1983; Thomas & Nydon, n.d.). Third, it is generally agreed that energy offers an excellent measure for tracking the operation of systems (Adams, 1981; Smith, 1979; Thomas, 1973).

The most fundamental problem with energy as a currency is that research in energetics is so well developed that, as a matter of convenience, one may tend to avoid examining alternative currencies (see Vayda & McKay, 1975 for a more comprehensive critique of energy as a currency).

Labor Time. Like energy, labor time is an attractive currency, offering a quantitative measure of input for a given output that is easily calculated and conducive to empirical verification. As noted above, optimizing for time might yield different results than optimizing for energy (Boy & Leatherman, 1980; cf. Smith, 1979).

The primary problem with the use of labor time as a currency is in obtaining reliable estimates of time investment. Reidhead derived his time input estimates from historical accounts of hunting and gathering, ethnographic observations, and extensive experimentation (Reidhead, 1981, pp. 42-61; Limp & Reidhead, 1979). The array of information amassed by Reidhead is both informative and impressive, representing a considerable effort on his part. It is apparent, however, that there is not much literature available that would provide us with analogies for different environments and resources. Hence, any study similar to Reidhead's in a substantially different context would probably require a replication of his laborious experimental efforts.

Composite Currency. In my own optimal diet study (Keene, 1981a), I use as a currency an artificial measure designed to account for a composite of time invested, energy expended, and risk of failure or personal injury incurred in the procurement of individual resources. The cost of procuring each resource was calculated as follows:

$$C = (T_s + T_p + T_c) R$$

where T_s = search cost, T_p = pursuit cost, T_c = preparation cost, and R = risk. In addition:

$$T_s = k\,(m/d)$$
$$T_p = q/a$$
$$T_c = y$$

where m = resource mobility, d = resource density, q = distance at which a predator is perceived by a given prey less the distance at which a predator can strike, a = aggregation size of a resource, y = rank order of processing time, and k = a constant. Therefore,

$$C = [k\,(m/d) + (q/a) + y]\,R$$

A detailed basis for this equation is presented in Keene (1981a, pp. 24-36). The cost measure used is a simple extension of earlier formulations employed in geographic ecology (e.g., McArthur & Pianka, 1968; Schoener, 1970) and in archaeoloogy (Jochim, 1976).

The composite measure that I constructed appears attractive because it involves resource characteristics readily documented and quantified in wildlife literature. This obviates the need for extensive experiment and measurement each time the model is applied in a new setting. The composite measure also is probably more realistic than others in that it examines multiple axes of variability and, therefore, more closely approximates the complexity of cost.

At the same time, the composite cost measure has several disadvantages:

1) As a composite, polythetic measure of cost, it obscures the impact of individual cost factors. 2) The measure involves an implicit weighting of each of the factors of time, energy, and risk in a manner which is not explicitly justified in cognitive or evolutionary terms (Carr, personal communication, 1984). 3) The degree to which such a measure evaluates emic or etic decisions is open to question. 4) The composite coefficient may be unattractive because it estimates only relative cost and cannot be converted into any absolute, directly observable measure such as time or energy. Thus, the measure is not very amenable to empirical justification. 5) Search cost was approximated as an inverse function of density (Keene, 1981a; Schoener, 1970). This formulation is predicated on an assumption of random search—an assumption not justifiable in many instances of human foraging (cf. Marks, 1976; Winterhalder, 1977; Lee, 1979). 6) Durham (1981, p. 221) notes that the cost measure assumes a completely separate foray for each resource. Costs may, in fact, be diminished for those resources that can be procured through a mixed or multipurpose strategy. He suggests that the problem can be alleviated by averaging the calculated costs per resource over all the kinds of forrays in which it can be obtained. 7) Another problem is that of quantifying risk. Whereas risk may be a critical factor affecting decision making (Keene, 1979; Wiessner, 1982; Johnson, 1971), the measure I employed is not very satisfying. Resources are classified as low, medium, and high risk based on a subjective evaluation of predictability and risk of personal injury. The cost of medium risk resources are increased arbitrarily by 25%, and high risk by 50%. An examination of the model (see Keene, 1981a) shows that in most cases, elimination of the risk coefficient does not significantly alter the model solution.

In developing my LP model, I oversimplified how risk was perceived and acted upon. Acorns, for example, were regarded as high risk because a good crop is expected only one in four years and because there is intense competition with wildlife for this food. The actual risk involved in procuring acorns depends on the ability to predict a good or bad year, the availability of alternative strategies, the cost of sustaining multiple strategies and technologies, and the ability to outcompete wildlife. A number of questions are not addressed by my model: At what scale the environment is tracked (spatial and temporal information); at what scale selection for given resources takes place; to what degree and in what situations opportunism would be expected.

In sum, as Reidhead (1979) notes, we definitely need to do more work on the nature of cost.

Error Potential

Do the data used to build the model contain sufficient error to invalidate numerical results? Can one use, for example, studies of raccoon behavior in second growth forests in Minnesota to approximate raccoon behavior in climate associations in prehistoric Michigan? Some would argue that such analogies are inappropriate and impose a false precision on our analyses (Winterhalder, 1977).

Such criticisms miss the point of LP efforts. If one's goal were to recreate precisely the situation encountered by the prehistoric inhabitants at a given site, such criticism might have validity. However, as I stressed before, the benefits to be derived from LP modeling and modeling in general are more heuristic rather than predictive. The use of approximate values allows one to examine *relationships* among variables that we might otherwise ignore. It may also be argued that sensitivity and range analyses allow us to accommodate the imprecision in our models. If the imprecision of some model input is disconcerting, consider the alternative of using only inductive or qualitative analyses.

In sum, the danger is not in the false precision or imprecision of LP input and output. The danger arises when one takes these values too literally, when one views the LP analysis as a conclusion rather than one stage of an active, interactive process.

Social Costs

I have noted elsewhere (Keene, 1983) that economic behaviors or decisions entail not only a physical cost measurable in terms such as time and energy, but also in social cost. For instance, a strategy of streamlining decision making through the development of a regulating hierarchy may increase the fitness of the population by increasing the efficiency of resource utilization and production (Johnson, 1982). However, efficiency and equality may not be compatible (Keene, 1983; cf. Harvey, 1973). A shift in decision-making strategies can impose a social cost on the population. The cost may be manifest in a differential alteration of the quality of life for different segments of the population.

Such a cost is not amenable to analysis with conventional currencies; as I have noted before, LP does not deal well with dialectical relationships. Past LP analyses have avoided the issue of social cost. The tendency has been to hold social forces constant or to treat them as the dependent variables in a techno-environmental analysis (e.g., Earle, 1980; Schalk, 1981; Keene, 1981a; cf. Bender, 1978). While this is frequently justified as a first approximation, usually social process and social cost get approximated away. This circumstance arises partly because social cost is not very tractable and partly because frequently, our analyses were not explicitly informed by social theory. However, it is hard to imagine how one can discuss the evolution of social forms without considering social cost.

In sum, it should be quite clear that there is not a single, all purpose currency. Past LP studies show that societies are often faced with multiple conflicting objectives (Palmer-Jones, 1979; Selby & Hendrix, 1976). The differences between the cost measures that have been used is not solely a question of method, but rather is grounded in competing theoretical positions about what constitutes cost or why a certain kind of optimality is expected. LP models are simply representations of theory. We cannot evaluate the use of LP in archaeology without considering the theoretical underpinnings.

Epistemological Considerations

Most model builders recognize that any interpretation of model results is conditioned by or anchored to the assumptions and the theoretical heritage of that model. It is important, then, to consider the epistemological constraints that accompany a LP approach.

Like many methods used by archaeologists, the origins of LP lie outside of the discipline. As a result, LP, like any exogenous method, carries with it a good deal of conceptual baggage. A borrowing discipline tends to adopt not only the explicit agenda of the lending science, but also a hidden agenda that is an embedded set of well-defined notions of how the world is ordered (Keene, 1983). In the case of LP analysis, our problems are filtered through the lens of microeconomics. LP models are normative models. As Harvey (1973) notes, there is nothing wrong with normative models per se, but we need to think carefully about the kinds of norms they represent.

All scientific inquiry takes place in a social setting, expresses social ideas, and conveys social meaning. All methods applied in social science inevitably express ethical or ideological positions, whether we accept the responsibility or not (Mills, 1959; Harvey, 1973; Moore & Keene, 1983). The assumptions of microeconomics may appear value-free to some; however, such basic concepts as supply/demand, cost/benefit, marginality, and even rationality are not value-free technical terms. They are implicitly embedded in the ideology of the capitalist society in which we exist. These assumptions exemplify certain notions about natural processes that are not amenable to empirical falsification (Keene, 1983). As Meillassoux notes:

> Liberal economics was an historical and political attempt by the rising bourgeoisie to demonstrate that economics is ruled by natural and universal laws to which even the princes had to comply. The demonstration was supported by fairly accurate criticism of the feudal economy which prevented the free circulation of goods, money, and labor to the detriment of general prosperity, and by an abstract and more disputable description of what would happen in a state of free circulation and competition. Capitalism has dwelt since on the same doctrinal assumption, that is, that it is a natural and universal system and therefore immutable. This bias supports the same original purpose: to give the bourgeoisie apparent scientific ground for political domination. To accept this premise is to accept (willingly or not) the ideology of the domination of the capitalist class. (1972, p. 92)

Meillassoux adds that acceptance of universalist assumptions denies the economist the tools needed to recognize alternative economic systems. As social scientists and social theorists with a unique perspective on human behavior, it is essential that we ask what role our theory plays and whether we do more than simply create a reflection of the current dominant political and economic structure in our reconstructions of the past (Moore & Keene, 1983; Saitta, 1983).

The issue is not simply one of semantics or a resurrection of the substantivist-formalist debates (cf. Limp & Carr, chapter 7), but reflects fundamental differences in how we view the world. Consider the assumption of free choice that is imbedded in our decision-making models. Free choices, especially in kin-based societies are few. When they exist, they are constrained not so much by the characteristics of the physical environment as by the social actions of others. This is vividly apparent, even in our baseline studies of technologically and socially "simple" societies, such as the San (Lee, 1982; Wiessner, 1982). We can, of course, take power relations as a given and calculate optimal strategies under these constraints. We could, for example, calculate an optimal crop mix from which peasants could fulfill their primary obligations to rent, ritual, and replacement funds and still keep themselves fed (Wolf, 1966; Johnson, 1980; Thomas, 1978). But these models of proximate optimization create what Harvey (1973) calls status-quo theory—theory serving to maintain the status quo—which informs us little about how asymmetrical relations are established, how they are sustained, and how they may be altered. Those of us who have been using optimization models might want to pause and ask why we continue to generate theory that denies the importance of social power and which fails to inform us of its attendant processes.

How does this kind of theory mirror and legitimate social practice in the modern world? I do not expect to resolve the issue, for the questions posed are paradigmatic and mark a fundamental difference between a neo-classical and a radical view of economy. *What is disturbing is that in our use of models, such questions are rarely posed.*

It is not just our methods which carry a heritage, but the questions themselves. It is important for us to stop from time to time and consider whether the questions we are asking are what we really need to know. The focus on subsistence and settlement studies is understandable within the context of the Binfordian revolution and its proliferation of method aimed at unraveling patterns in data and reconstructing past lifeways (Keene, 1983). Two decades ago we needed to demonstrate that the past was knowable; subsistence settlement studies, aided by a range of new methods, proved a tractable problem. But years of resolving fine-grained questions (e.g., what did people eat?) have done little to enlighten us about the processes which shape and create societies. *The question, in closing, is not whether LP is appropriate for the analysis of subsistence data, but whether we want to ask subsistence questions which remove production from its social context.* LP can sort data and define patterns very well. The models discussed meet the criteria for what we expect from a good model. It remains for us to resolve whether we are asking important questions.

REFERENCES

Adams, R.N. (1981). Natural selection, energetics and cultural materialism. *Current Anthropology* 22, 603-624.
Astrand, P.O., & Rodahl, K. (1977). *A textbook of work physiology* (2nd ed.). New York: McGraw-Hill, Inc.
Behrens, C., & Johnson, A. (1982). Nutritional criteria in Machiguenga food production decisions: A linear programming analysis. *Human Ecology* 10(2), 167-190.
Bender, B. (1978). Gatherer-hunter to farmer: A social perspective. *World Archaeology* 10, 204-222.
Bettinger, R.L. (1980). Explanatory predictive models of hunter-gatherer adaptation. *Advances in Archaeological Method and Theory* 3, 189-255.
Blanton, R.E. (1983). The ecological perspective in highland Mesoamerican archaeology. In J.A. Moore & A.S. Keene (Eds.), *Archaeological hammers and theories* (pp. 221-231). New York: Academic Press, Inc.
Brown. H.I. (1977). *Perception, theory and commitment*. Chicago: University of Chicago Press.
Boy, D., & Leatherman, T. (1980, April). *Acorns in subsistence: An energetics approach*. Paper presented at the 20th annual meeting of the Northeastern Antoropological Association, Amherst, MA.
Charnov, E.L. (1976). Optimal foraging and the marginal value theorem. *Theoretical Population Biology* 9(2), 129-136.
Clarke, D.L. (1968). *Analytical archaeology*. London: Methuen.
Clarke, D.L. (Ed.). (1972). *Models in archaeology*. London: Methuen.
Cross, J. (1983). Twigs, branches, trees and forests: Problems of scale in lithic analysis. In J.A. Moore & A.S. Keene (Eds.), *Archaeological hammers and theories* (pp. 87-106). New York: Academic Press.
Cooper, L., & Steinberg, D. (1974). *Methods and applications of linear programming*. Philadelphia: Saunders.
Dantzig, G.B. (1963). *Linear programming and extensions*. Princeton: Princeton University Press.
Dahlberg, F. (Ed.). (1981). *Woman the gatherer*. New Haven: Yale University Press.
Dickson, D.B. (1980). Ancient agriculture and population at Tikal, Guatemala: An application of linear programming to the simulation of an archeological problem. *American Antiquity* 48, 697-712.
Dorfman, R., Samuelson, P.A., & Solow, R.M. (1958). *Linear programming and economic analysis*. New York: McGraw Hill, Inc.
Durham, W.H. (1981). Overview: Optimal foraging analysis in human ecology. In B.W. Winterhalder & E.A. Smith (Eds.), *Hunter-gatherer foraging strategies: ethnographic and archaeological analyses* (pp. 218-231). Chicago: University of Chicago Press.
Earle, T.K. (1980), A model of subsistence change. in T.K. Earle & A.L. Christensen (Eds.), *Modeling of change in prehistoric subsistence economics*. New York: Academic Press, Inc.
Feyerabend, P. (1975). *Against method*. London: Humanities Press.
Ford, R.I. (1979). Evolutionary ecology and the evolution of human ecosystems: A case study from the midwestern USA. In J.N. Hill (Ed.), *Explanation of prehistoric change* (pp. 153-184). Albuquerque: University of New Mexico Press.
Harris, M. (1979). *Cultural materialism: The struggle for a science of culture*. New York: Random House.
Harvey, D. (1969). *Explanation in geography*. London: Arnold.
Harvey, D. (1973). *Social justice and the city*. Baltimore, MD: Johns Hopkins University Press.
Hempel, C.G. (1966). *Philosophy of natural science*. Englewood Cliffs, NJ: Prentice Hall.
Hillier, F.S. & Lieberman, G.J. (1974). *Introduction to operations research* (2nd ed.) San Francisco: Holden-Day.
Hindess, B. (1973). *On the use of official statistics*. London: Macmillan.
Hoffman, H. (1969). A linear programming approach to cultural intensity. In I.R. Buchler & H.J.

Nutini (Eds.), *Game theory in the behavioral sciences* (pp. 179-190). Pittsburgh: University of Pittsburgh Press.
Jochim, M.A. (1976). *Hunter-gatherer subsistence and settlement: a predictive model.* New York: Academic Press, Inc.
Jochim, M.A. (1983). Optimization models in context. In J.A. Moore & A.S. Keene (Eds.), *Archaeological hammers and theories* (pp. 137-172). New York: Academic Press, Inc.
Johnson, A.W. (1971). Security and risk taking among poor peasants: A Brazilian case. In G. Dalton (Ed.), *Studies in economic anthropology* (Anthropological Studies series 7) (pp. 144-151). Washington, DC: American Anthropological Association.
Johnson, A.W. (1980). The limits of formalism in agricultural decision research. In P. Bartlett (Ed.), *Agricultural decision making* (pp. 19-43). New York: Academic Press, Inc.
Johnson, G.A. (1982). Organizational structure and scalar stress. In A.C. Renfrew, M.S. Rowland & B.A. Segraves (Eds.), *Theory and explanation in archaeology* (pp. 389-421). New York: Academic Press, Inc.
Joy, L. (1967). An economic homologue of Barth's presentation of economic spheres in Darfur. In R. Firth (Ed.), *Themes in economic anthropology* (pp. 175-190). London: Tavistock.
Keene, A.S. (1979). Economic optimization models and the study of hunter-gatherer subsistence settlement systems. In A.C. Renfrew & K. Cooke (Eds.), *Transformations: mathematical approaches to culture change* (pp. 369-404). New York: Academic Press, Inc.
Keene, A.S. (1981a). *Prehistoric foraging in a temperate forest.* New York; Academic Press, Inc.
Keene, A.S. (1981b). Optimal foraging in a non-marginal environment. In B.W. Winterhalder & E.A. Smith (Eds.), *Hunter-gatherer foraging strategies: Ethnographic and archaeological analyses* (pp. 171-193). Chicago: University of Chicago Press.
Keene, A.S. (1983). Biology, behavior and borrowing: A critical examination of optimal foraging theory in archaeology. In J.A. Moore & A.S. Keene (Eds.), *Archaeological hammers and theories* (pp. 137-155). New York: Academic Press, Inc.
Kristiansen, K. (1982). The formation of tribal systems in later European prehistory: Northern Europe 4000-5000 B.C. In A.C. Renfrew, M.S. Rowlands & B.A. Segraves (Eds.), *Theory and explanation in archaeology* (pp. 241-280). New York: Academic Press, Inc.
Lave, C.A., & March, J.G. (1975). *An introduction to models in the social sciences.* New York: Harper & Row.
Lee, R.B. (1969). !Kung Bushman subsistence: An input-output analysis. In A.P. Vayda (Ed.), *Environment and cultural behavior* (pp. 47-49). New York: Natural History Press.
Lee, R.B. (1982). Politics, sexual and non-sexual, in an egalitarian society. In E. Leacock & R.B. Lee (Eds.), *Political and history in band societies* (pp. 37-60). (New York: Cambridge University Press.
Levins, R. (1966). The strategy of model building in population biology. *American Scientist* 54(4), 421-430.
Limp, W.F. (1977, April). *The economics of agricultural dispersal.* Paper presented at the 42nd annual meeting of the Society for American Archaeology, New Orleans.
Limp, W.F., & Reidhead, V.A. (1979). An economic evaluation of the potential of fish utilization in riverine environments. *American Antiquity 44*, 70-78.
Low, A.R.C. (1974). Decision taking under uncertainty: A linear programming model of peasant farmer behaviour. *Journal of Agricultural Economics 25*, 311-320.
MacArthur, R.H., & Pianka, E.R. (1966). On the optimal use of a patchy environment. *American Naturalist 100*, 603-610.
Marks, S.A. (1976). *Large mammals and a brave people.* Seattle: University of Washington Press.
Meillassoux, C. (1972). From reproduction to production: A marxist approach to economic anthropology. *Economy and Society 1*, 93-105.
Mills, C.W. (1959). *The sociological imagination.* New York: Grove Press.

Moore, J.A. (1981). *Decision making and information among hunter-gatherer societies.* Unpublished doctoral dissertation, University of Massachusetts, Boston.
Moore, J.A. (1983). The trouble with know-it-alls: Information as a social and ecological resource. In J.A. Moore & A.S. Keene (Eds.), *Archaeological hammers and theories* (pp. 173-191). New York: Academic Press, Inc.
Moore, J.A. & Keene, A.S. (Eds.). (1983). *Archaeological hammers and theories.* New York: Academic Press, Inc.
Nydon, J., & Thomas, R.B. (in press). Methodological procedures for collecting and analyzing energy expenditure from a systems perspective. In L. Allen & G. Potto (Eds.), *Methodological issues in nutritional anthropology.* Cambridge: Cambridge University Press.
Palmer-Jones, R.W. (1979). Linear programming and the study of peasant farming: Rejoinder. *Journal of Agricultural Economics 30*(2), 190-204.
Paynter, R.W. (1981). Social complexity in peripheries. In S.E. Van Der Leeuw & Egges, A. (Eds.), *Archaeological approaches to the study of complexity* (pp. 118-134). Amsterdam, Netherlands: Van Giffen Instituut voor Prae-en Protohistorie.
Paynter, R.W., & Cole, J.W. (1980). Ethnographic overproduction, tribal political economy, and the Kapauku of Irian Jaya. In E. Ross (Ed.), *Beyond the myths of culture* (pp. 61-99). New York: Academic Press, Inc.
Pianka, E.R. (1978). *Evolutionary ecology* (2nd ed.). New York: Harper and Row.
Platt, J. (1964). Strong inference. *Science 146*, 347-353.
Pospisil, L. (1963). *Kaupauku-Papuan economy* (Yale University Publications in Anthropology No. 67). New Haven: Yale University Press.
Rappaport, R. (1968). *Pigs for the ancestors: Ritual in ecology of a New Guinea people.* New Haven: Yale University Press.
Redding, R.W. (1981). *Decision making in subsistence herding of sheep and goats in the Middle East.* Unpublished doctoral dissertation. University of Michigan, Ann Arbor.
Reidhead, V.A. (1976). *Optimizatioin and food procurement at the prehistoric Leonard Haag site, southeast Indiana: A linear programming approach.* Unpublished doctoral dissertation. Indiana University, Bloomington.
Reidhead, V.A. (1979). Linear programming models in anthropology. *Annual Review of Anthropology 8*, 534-578.
Reidhead, V.A. (1981). *A linear programming model of prehistoric subsistence optimization: A southeastern Indiana example.* (Prehistory Research Series 6:1). Indianapolis: Indiana Historical Society.
Root, D. (1980, May). *Tracking the archaeological record: Archaic site distributions in southern New England.* Paper presented at the 45th annual meeting of the Society for American Archaeology, Philadelphia.
Root, D. (1983). *Material dimensions of social inequality in nonstratified societies: An archaeological perspective.* Unpublished doctoral dissertation. University of Massachusetts, Amherst.
Rorty, R. (1979). *Philosophy and the mirror of nature.* Princeton: Princeton University Press.
Saitta, D.J. (1983). The poverty of philosophy in archaeology. In J.A. Moore & A.S. Keene (Eds.), *Archaeological hammers and theories* (pp. 299-304). New York: Academic Press, Inc.
Schalk, R. (1981). Land use and organizational complexity among foragers of northwestern North America. In S. Koyama & D.H. Thomas (Eds.), *Affluent foragers: Pacific coasts East and West* (Senri Ethnological Series, No. 9) (pp. 53-76). Osaka, Japan.
Schoener, T.W. (1971). Theory of feeding strategies. *Annual Review of Ecology and Systematics*, 366-404.
Selby, H., & Hendrix, C.A. (1976). Policy planning and poverty: Notes on a Mexican case. In P. Sanday (Ed.), *Anthropology and the public interest* (pp. 219-244). New York: Academic Press, Inc.
Service, E. (1969). Models for the methodology of mouthtalk. *Southwest Journal of Anthropology 25*, 68-80.
Simon, H.A. (1957). *Models of man: Social and rational.* New York: John Wiley & Sons, Inc.

Smith, E.A. (1979). Human adaptation and energetic efficiency. *Human Ecology 7*, 53-74.

Spivey, W.A., & Thrall, R.M. (1970). *Linear optimization*. New York: Holt, Rinehart & Winston.

Thomas, R.B. (1973). *Human adaptation to a high Andean energy flow system* (Occasional Papers in Anthropology No. 7). Pittsburgh: Pennsylvania State University.

Thomas, P.B. (1978). Effects of change on high mountain human adaptive patterns. In P.J. Webber (Ed.), *High altitude geoecology* (pp. 139-186). Boulder, CO: Westview Press.

Thomas, R.B., & Nydon, J. (n.d.). *Biological and social uses of human energetics*. Unpublished manuscript, University of Massachusetts, Amherst.

Throsby, C.D. (1962). Some notes on dynamic linear programming. *Review of Marketing and Agriculture Economics, 30*(2), 119-141.

Vayda, A.P., & B.J. McCay (1975). New directions in ecology and ecological anthropology. *Annual Review of Anthropology 8*, 293-306.

Wagner, H.M. (1975). *Principles of operations research* (2nd ed.). Englewood Cliffs, NJ: Prentice Hall.

Wallerstein, I. (1974). *The modern world system. (Vol. I)*. New York: Academic Press, Inc.

White, D.R. (1973). Mathematical anthropology. In J.J. Honigmann (Ed.), *Handbook of social and cultural Anthropology* (pp. 369-446). Chicago: Rand McNally.

Wiessner, P. (1982). Risk, reciprocity, and social influences on !Kung San economics. In E. Leacock & R.B. Lee (Eds.), *Politics and history in band societies* (pp. 61-84). New York: Cambridge University Press.

Winterhalder, B.P. (1977). *Foraging strategy adaptations of the Boreal forest Cree: An evaluation of theory and models from evolutionary ecology*. Unpublished doctoral dissertation. Cornell University, Ithaca.

Winterhalder, B.P. (1980). Environmental analysis and human adaptation. *Human Ecology 8*, 135-170.

Winterhalder, B.P., & Smith, E.A. (1981). *Hunter-gatherer foraging strategies: Ethnographic and archaeological analyses*. Chicago: University of Chicago Press.

Wobst, H.M. (1978). The archaeo-ethnology of hunter-gatherers, or the tyrany of the ethnographic record in archaeology. *American Antiquity 43*, 303-309.

Wolf, E. (1966). *Peasants*. Englewood Cliffs, NJ: Prentice-Hall.

Zipf, G.K. (1949). *Human behavior and the principle of least effort*. Reading, MA: Addison-Wesley.

11

Notions to Numbers: Great Basin Settlements as Polythetic Sets

LEONARD WILLIAMS
DAVID HURST THOMAS
ROBERT BETTINGER

1985 PREFACE

This chapter (excluding preface and references),* prepared well over a decade ago, evolved from the groping attempts of several field archaeologists to pin down concepts that previously had existed merely as "feel." The attempt to "operationalize" these field concepts did not, as Salmon (1982, p. 150) has recently suggested, arise as some misguided manifesto "to demand complete operational definition of all terms as a first step in the construction of an archaeological theory" nor "to perform reductions of the expressions in which these terms occur to expressions that contain only terms capable of operational definition." Rather, this and other attempts at operational definition (e.g., Thomas, 1970, 1981) arose because of a concrete problem facing all archaeologists who encounter real, empirical data: how are others to know what we are talking about? The problems of impressionistic data collection and analysis still remain with us, but at least archaeologists in general are beginning to realize the importance of defining what they do, rather then merely proceeding within a "trust me" framework.

In the following chapter, we attempt to take a bit of the mystery and uncertainty out of site survey. Experienced field workers tend to know, by feel, where the sites are. Similarly, those with experience in handling archaeological artifacts tend to know, once again by feel, how the various typologies work. Archaeology has been done this way for decades. But wouldn't it be better to *know why we know*?

We approached the matter of site location in two steps. First, we specified the

---

*Reprinted from *Research and Theory in Current Archaeology*, edited by C.L. Redman, 1973, pp. 215-237, John Wiley, New York, with permission of the publisher and the authors.

prior conditions under which sites would be expected to be found by employing polythetic criteria for potential site loci. Then, we tested this model by locating such potential loci with aerial photographs and by surveying in the field where sites actually occurred. The polythetic concept was not, of course, new to archaeology (see Clarke, 1968), and subsequent anthropological applications have demonstrated that the polythetic concept can still be of use in anthropological inquiry (e.g., Needham, 1975; Solheim, 1976; Carr, 1984; this volume, chapter 13).

More important than the operational definitions or the polythetic criteria employed in this modeling procedure, however, is its potential for application to the objectives of cultural resource management. Although some CRM projects have attempted such predictive modeling (e.g., Holmer, 1981), most regional plans still rely on the so-called "sensitivity map," a relatively crude percentagewise summation of site density per unit area (see Carr, chapter 6). We are surprised that so many of our management-oriented colleagues still ignore the simple model-building exercises such as those set out in this paper.

Conceptual aspects aside, the research reported here has been vastly expanded by over a decade of empirical fieldwork. A monograph-length treatment of the 1971 Reese River survey data has appeared (Thomas & Bettinger, 1976; Thomas, 1975). Bettinger has examined similar issues in his intensive fieldwork in Owens Valley, California (Bettinger, 1975, 1977, 1978). Thomas has just completed a large-scale program of survey and excavation in Monitor Valley, 15 km east of the Reese River Valley (Thomas, 1982a, 1982b, 1983a, 1983b).

In reading through this chapter, please keep the context in which it was written in mind. We have elected not to change the original 1973 manuscript at all; this is a statement of how we viewed archaeology over a decade ago. Our thinking was clearly the product of the early 1970s, reflecting the concern with building a theory of regional archaeology and a desire to supersede unsatisfactory impressionistic methods of fieldwork and analysis.

This chapter addresses two theoretical issues confronting modern American archeology: proper testing of hypothesis and operationalization of intuitive concepts. Based on earlier computer simulation models *(BASIN I)* and fieldwork in central Nevada, the authors derived hypotheses (integrated into the overall Reese River Subsistence-Settlement System) regarding winter village placement. Given the proper set of environmental conditions, we felt that we could successfully predict presence/absence of archeological sites, a hypothesis that required testing by independent data. But to conduct further field investigation, such intuitive concepts had to be quantified where possible. The relevant environmental variables were then defined into measurable quantities and these diverse criteria then welded into a single *polythetic definition*. In this manner, whenever at least five of the seven quantitative propositions were satisfied in nature, a site was predicted to occur. Subsequent fieldwork indicated the polythetic predictors to be accurate in approximately 95% of all cases in this area.

> Change from a qualitative to a quantitative approach is characteristic of the development of any branch of science. As some understanding is achieved of the broader aspects of phenomena, interest naturally turns to the finer detail of structure or behavior, in which the observable differences are smaller and can only be appreciated in terms of measurement [Greig-Smith 1964:ix].

In examining the literature of modern archeology, one cannot fail to notice the conscious and explicit trend toward rigorous quantification. While this is surely a laudable and in fact imperative bias, we feel that many quantitative studies tend to overstate their point; too often these products of numerical research are presented as something "brand-new," without traditional precedent. This approach ignores the many purely intuitive and qualitative constructs that serve archeology quite admirably—without objectivity. Much of the controversy between the traditionalist and the so-called new archeologist regards the proper role of intuition in archeological methods and theory. In the extreme, both positions fall far short of the mark. As we increase our knowledge of the past, we must continually refine and polish our definitions, a necessity due in part to the increasing importance of the computer. As Pelto (1970) has stressed, computers permit little room for ambiguity since machines take the worker at his word. In the rush to quantification, however, some have inadvertently lost sight of the true role of measurement in archeology. Instead of being an end in itself, quantification must always satisfy a nonquantitative need in pragmatic, problem-oriented research. Although a few quantitative techniques, such as factor analysis, can boast of being truly "new" (to archeology) and without analogic precursors, most methods of quantification have their epistemological ancestry in traditional archeological theory. We reject the adage seemingly implied in some recent studies: "If you can't measure it, you don't understand it." In fact, too often one gets the uncomfortable feeling that some recent papers can *measure* the phenomenon—often to several decimal places—but true understanding seems curiously lacking.

Our position is thus a middle-of-the-road stance, stressing that quantification in moderation is a logical and necessary step in the advancement of all sciences. Sometimes the early progress of a discipline can be gauged by its ascendency above the simple nominal (typological) level. And yet we cannot deny the overall utility and validity of what Phillips (1958) has called *feel*. As in *all* science, some of archeology's most significant breakthroughs come as the direct result of feel, through intuitive insight gained only from intimate familiarity with the primary data. Often such insights can be objectively framed as hypotheses and immediately tested; the recent success of archeological research in the American Southwest is largely the result of applying the quantitative approach to intuitive concepts. Hill's (1968) analysis of pueblo room patterning, for example, while providing an excellent model for archeological scholarship, did not produce startling results. Everyone familiar with the data already knew (intuitively) that the large rooms with hearths, mealing bins, and food remains were probably areas of habitation and that the deep, round features with the slab benches were the prehistoric analogs of kivas. The import of Hill's work is clearly not in providing us with penetrating new insights into Southwestern prehistory, but rather with the systematization and testing of notions that veteran archeologists have held implicitly for decades.

Although some of archeology's traditional techniques—such as seriation and dendrochronology—are relatively easy to quantify, the more diaphanous concepts have proven recalcitrant. The *type concept*, for example, plays a pivotal role in all archeological procedure, yet no investigator, to our knowledge, has succeeded in a truly objective treatment of typology. It is interesting that archeology's most sophisticated and quantitative analyses must still begin with an initial intuitive typology of artifacts, for example, Binford and Binford (1966), Longacre (1970), Hill (1970). This is not to belittle the work of these scholars—clearly this is the best set of treatments yet available—but rather to underscore the intuitive and subjective foundations of much of current archeological thought.

In exploring this topic further, we shall focus on a single aspect of modern archeology, the study of subsistence-settlement patterning. Despite the substantive progress in this area, most settlement studies remain at an intuitive, gut-level of analysis, for example, Willey (1956), Struever (1968). While intuitive assessment is sufficient for discussing a single ecosystem, large-scale comparisons and broad ecological studies are severely hampered by this lack of comparability and replicability. This chapter attempts, in a preliminary way, to add a measure of rigor to the analysis of prehistoric settlements.

THE NATURE OF POLYTHETIC ENTITIES

In his recent book *Analytical Archaeology* (1968), David L. Clarke repeatedly stressed that archeological entities are best analyzed within a polythetic framework. While agreeing with Clarke's position, we wish to consider the polythetic concept a bit further, in part to provide the proper background for our own research and also because we feel that the full import of polythetic description may have been somewhat obscured in Clarke's comprehensive monograph.

The biologist Morton Beckner (1959) outlined the basis of monothetic and polythetic entities in his book *The Biological Way of Thought*. Although Beckner originally coined the terms "monotypic" and "polytypic," Sneath (1962) suggested that since "polytypic" already has an established meaning in biology, Beckner's concepts, while perfectly valid, should be renamed *monothetic* and *polythetic* ("mono" means one; "poly," many; and "thetos," arrangement). In the following discussion, we have substituted Sneath's terms into Beckner's original exposition.

A monothetic criterion is one in which a set of propositions is considered both *necessary* and *sufficient* for group membership. Consider the following statement: all mammals have body hair, bear live offspring, and suckle their young. The assumption is that any creature satisfying these three criteria will be a mammal; furthermore, any individual without all three will *not* be a member of the class Mammalia. Following this reasoning, it is said that Clarence Darrow "established" that his opponent, William Jennings Bryan was not a mammal, since Bryan had never born offspring, had obviously never suckled his young, and was in fact quite bald.

It seems that nascent sciences often rely rather heavily on such definitions, while research remains concerned with finding gross divisions in long continua; monothetic statements are still frequent in preliminary archeological investigations:

> The cylinder jar with slab-shaped tripod legs is diagnostic of Teotihuacan III.
> All kivas have a *sipapu*.

In each case, a set of propositions is both necessary for membership in the class and sufficient for assigning an unidentified specimen to the previously designated category: all structures with a *sipapu* are kivas; no structure without a *sipapu* is a kiva.

Such all-embracing criteria are popular among some scientists—and despised by undergraduate students—because of the felicity with which new specimens may be classified, once one memorizes the rules. Yet as knowledge increases, these classifications invariably become oversimplistic: some kivas are found lacking a *sipapu* and Teotihuacan-like cylinder jars appear in Guatemala. The fault is not with the defining characteristics, for any such rigid set will eventually prove inaccurate, but rather with the monothetic approach to classification per se—the real world usually refuses to operate in a rigid, one-to-one fashion.

Beckner's remedy for this situation is the recommendation that the scientist explicitly recognize a more realistic mode of analysis, the polythetic framework. In Beckner's terminology, the classificatory problem is one of defining a group K in terms of a set G, comprised of the properties $f_1, f_2 \ldots f_n$; to consider K as a valid polythetic class, two basic properties must be satisfied:

1. Each individual must possess a large number of the f-properties in G.
2. Each f in G must be possessed by a large number of the individuals.

In addition, Beckner stipulated that for a class to be considered *fully polythetic*, no *f* in *G* is possessed by every individual in the aggregate. This definition is little more than a rigorous approach to the definition of intuitively valid categories, since no single criterion will adequately separate the given class—that is, exceptions are anticipated. Polythetic definition avoids the necessity for arbitrary delimitation of the K, non-K border since the polythetic sets are operational categories, adequately justified if only on the grounds of scientific economy. A de facto construct, the polythetic definition always allows for later redefinition in monothetic terms, should future research justify the more expeditious boundaries, such as all atoms have nuclei. We can thus define groups as *operationally* polythetic while recognizing that the entities may one day be proven as ultimately monothetic.

It must be stressed that the monothetic-polythetic dichotomy is not necessarily a division between good and bad, for each arrangement has its function in scientific research. Monothetic divisions are most useful in "classification from above," the sorting of specimens into progressively finer groupings. Excavators operate in this fashion by separating the grimy archeological specimens into rough field categories such as bone, sherds, chipped stones, ocher, and debitage. One experiences little difficulty in applying monothetic definitions at this point: all pottery sherds are expected to be made of clay and to be extremely hard or brittle. Monothetic divisions are also useful in classifying unknown artifacts into preexisting groups (identification): operational "keys" are becoming more important in the classification of archeological artifacts (see Thomas, 1970, for an example of an operational dichotomous key for identifying projectile points).

Polythetic groupings on the other hand offer the archeologist his best hope in quantifying intuitive feel. Archeological typology has never been bound by rigid adherence to specific rules, and archeologists are usually unable to agree on even a preliminary definition of *type*. The higher levels of classification suffer from this same problem, for although intuitive units usually seem to work in practice, scientific procedure requires that such categories be more efficiently defined and made repeatable between different investigators where possible.

To illustrate this point, let us consider the synthetic concept of the *Desert culture*, one of archeology's more prolific integrative concepts. As more data becomes available, however, it becomes clear that the Desert culture in its present form has nearly outlived its usefulness as a conceptual device. With Great Basin research largely beyond the typological level, the rubric of the Desert culture too often obscures rather than clarifies. Nevertheless, there remains that elusive essence, that flavor, that distinguishes Great Basin adaptations from those of nearby California, the Plateau, and the earlier Southwest. Why is it so difficult to put one's finger on precisely what makes the Desert culture distinctive? The problem is not in the subject matter, we feel, but rather in the theoretical framework in which the concept has been approached.

We shall argue that the Desert culture is a perfect example of a polythetic concept operating in archeology. In examining this question, let us use an indirect proof, assuming the opposite and demonstrating that this assumption leads us to an absurdity. The Desert culture has been variously defined by trait lists, such as that offered by Jennings:

> cave and overhang locations for settlement, bark or grass beds, seasonal gathering, intensive exploitation of resources, small seed harvesting and special cooking techniques, basketry (twining predominant), netting and matting, fur cloth, tumpline, sandals (moccasins rare), atlatl, pointed hardwood dart shafts, varied (relatively small) projectile points, preferential use of glassy textured stone, flat milling stone and mano, a high percentage of crude scraper and chopper tools, digging stick, firedrill and hearth, bunt points, wooden clubs, horn-shaft wrenches, tubular pipes, use of olivella and other shells, vegetable quids [1964:154].

This list, while not exhaustive, is sufficient to give the flavor of a Desert culture existence. In considering the Danger Cave assemblages, Jennings further synthesized this trait list into two basic components: "The twin hall marks [sic] of the Desert culture were the basket and the flat milling stone" (Jennings 1957:7). *Webster's Seventh New Collegiate Dictionary* defines *hallmark* as "a distinguishing characteristic, trait, or feature." If we assume that the Desert culture is monothetic, then these hallmarks must be both necessary and sufficient criteria of the concept. That is, the hallmarks must be present at all Desert culture sites and not present at any non-Desert culture sites. We know, of course, that both traits are quite frequent outside the Desert West, but let us restrict our gaze to the Desert West for the moment. Lovelock Cave, for example, is considered by Jennings (1964:153, 164) as a typical Desert culture site and as such, Lovelock can be expected to contain the hallmarks of the Desert culture. Yet in their report on the early excavations in Lovelock Cave, Loud and Harrington (1929:106) reported that out of hundreds of artifacts recovered, only two pieces of grinding stones were found—and those were both fragments of mortars, not flat milling stones! How can Lovelock Cave be said to represent the Desert culture if one of the two hallmarks is lacking? By our monothetic definition Lovelock Cave is not of the Desert culture, yet any archeologist familiar with the material would doubtless place Lovelock squarely in what Jennings called the Desert culture. The fault lies neither with the site nor with Jennings' definition, for he surely never intended his "hallmarks" as ironclad rules. The fault is to consider the Desert culture as monothetic. It is not.

We can thus see—if only through the process of elimination—that the Desert culture and many other archeological units have yet to establish any concrete examples of how such definitions will really help the practicing field archeologist. The rest of this chapter will demonstrate how the explicit use of a polythetic framework has aided us in clarifying the prehistoric settlement pattern relationships in the Reese River Valley of the central Great Basin.

THE REESE RIVER ECOLOGICAL PROJECT

The Reese River Ecological Project functions as a continuing program of paleoanthropology in the central Great Basin. The first phase of research was designed to test two hypotheses:

1. Julian Steward's (1938) theory of protohistoric patterns for the Great Basin Shoshoneans.
2. The applicability of this theory to the prehistoric periods of the same region.

Steward's excellent ethnographic data was translated into a computer simulation model *(BASIN I)* that generated over 100 quantitative propositions from the Steward theory (discussed in Thomas, 1971, 1972). In 1969 and 1970 field crews from the University of California (Davis) and the University of Nevada conducted a regional random sample of the Reese River Valley, gathering data relevant to the *BASIN I* predictions. The results of this phase of investigation seem to have adequately confirmed Steward's work at the protohistoric level and now permit archeologists to tentatively extend the Steward model from the historic period back to about 2500 B.C. in the Reese River area. In addition to testing Steward's theory, the field work generated new data that were synthesized into a new and more comprehensive theory describing the *Reese River Subsistence-Settlement System*.

> The Reese River Subsistence-Settlement System is defined for the Medithermal *Period* at the Reese River *Locality* . . . [and] is characterized by two types of settlements. The *Shoreline Settlement* consists of a series of sites located on a permanent water source within a lower sagebrush-grass lifezone . . . [and consisting] of massive linear scatters of artifacts, generally parallel to the flowing source of water. No consistent locus of habitation was re-occupied; apparently campsites were situated near scattered caches of seeds. . . . The *Piñon Ecotone* Settlement corresponds to Steward's winter village sites . . . [which] were located in stands of piñon and juniper trees, often on long, low ridges which fingered onto the valley floor . . . the precise locus of winter habitation varied from year to year; this fluctuating locus can perhaps be planned up to three years in advance . . . it is suggested that about five families lived on each ridge-top, but there might be several such ridge-top villages within a one mile radius . . . the Reese River system is really based upon a dual central base pattern, since habitation alternated between the two settlement types, depending upon the seasonal available resources . . . this adaptation, as "on the fence" compromise between wandering and sedentary life, seems to provide the flexibility required for success in a situation such as the central Great Basin [Thomas, 1973].

These habitation camps are complemented by a series of task-specific groupings, discussed by Thomas (1971).

ANOTHER LOOP IN THE CYCLE

The preceding operations can be viewed most profitably as the initial round in a generalized *scientific cycle* (Kemeny, 1959):

LOOP I

    i. FACTS: Steward's ethnographic field work (1935, 1936)

                                            INDUCTION ↓

    ii. THEORY: Steward's theory of Great Basin settlement patterns

                                            DEDUCTION ↓

    iii. PREDICTIONS: The BASIN I computer simulation model

                                            VERIFICATION ↓

    iv. FACTS: Reese River archeological field work (1969, 1970)

This initial cycle verified Steward's hypothesis and also produced a new set of untested facts, systematized into the Reese River Subsistence-Settlement System. As Kemeny has pointed out:

> These facts form a fourth stage for the old theory as well as the first stage of the new theory. Since we expect that Science consists of an endless chain of progress, we may expect this cyclical process to continue indefinitely [Kemeny, 1959:86].

The second round of the specific cycle requires a different research design and additional fieldwork in order to test the new theory.

LOOP II

    i. FACTS: Reese River archeological field work (1969, 1970)

                                            INDUCTION ↓

    ii. THEORY: The Reese River Subsistence-Settlement System

                                            DEDUCTION ↓

iii. PREDICTIONS: Specific site locations in the
 Reese River area
 |
 VERIFICATION
 ↓
iv. FACTS: Additional, independent field work
 (1971)

It is in this logical framework that we approached the 1971 field season at Reese River. Since economic necessities limited us to a single field session, we were forced to test only part of the total subsistence-settlement hypothesis. We elected to concentrate our resources on a quantitative test of the *Piñon Ecotone Settlement*. These sites are the prehistoric analog to the classic Shoshonean winter villages and seem to provide the mainstay in prehistoric settlement patterns.

OPERATIONAL AND POLYTHETIC DEFINITIONS

At the outset, we were faced with a situation common to many field archeologists—after years of working in an area, we gained an intuitive feeling of where unknown sites "ought to be." Given an archeologically unexplored area within the general region, we felt secure—perhaps arrogantly so—that our cumulative experience enabled us to predict where most of the sites would occur. In planning to test this intuition, we conferred with Julian Steward, experienced in both ethnographic and archeological research in the area:

> In my own fieldwork I made it a point to go over the root areas and the camping areas with my informant. It was commonly possible to verify the location of campsites and winter settlements by the presence of artifacts, particularly pottery which I believe implies some stability. . . . May I venture a couple of suggestions about the prehistoric settlement patterns . . . it would be most profitable to ascertain the specific factors determining winter settlement locations and then explore such places to see whether they were indeed utilized. I have always regretted that I did not have the time to do this to a much greater extent but what little I was able to do, I invariably found signs of occupation where the critical factors came together. These are reasonable access to pinenuts, a piñon-juniper belt which supplied firewood and preferably a stream for water or else higher altitudes where snow could be obtained [Julian Steward, personal communication, 1971].

Steward's feeling coincided with our own, that specific factors determined the winter village locality and where the factors co-occurred in nature, one could expect to find an archeological site.

The task then became one of *operationalizing* such variables into quantities directly observable in the field. We reviewed our previous survey data and found several common denominators that were present at most piñon ecotone settlements. The sites usually were located on long ridges that extended far onto the valley floor, although several sites were situated on gentle saddles between low piñon-covered knolls. Although access to the sites was often steep, the habitation areas themselves were generally quite flat and smooth. The winter sites were located in the low foothills, not far from the modern piñon-juniper ecotone, and finally, the sites generally had relatively easy access to either springs or flowing streams. As is true of many hunter-gatherer stations, however, the foragers preferred to camp a discreet distance from the water source. Unlike many modern campers, the Shoshoneans and their ancestors realized that in order to see and hunt game animals, they had to avoid the watering areas as much as possible. Experience told us that the piñon-ecotone settlements consistently clustered about these resource areas.

The first critical decision is to agree on what precisely constitutes a "site." In an ideal sense, we could have rigorously defined a site as a "scatter of prehistoric cultural debris that extends over a discernible extent (at least x square meters) and consists of a density of at least y cultural items per square meter." In practice, however, we lacked the quantitative survey data necessary for a serviceable definition of a site, so we elected to rely on our experience to tell us when we encountered a site in the field. We feel that this procedure, while haphazard and subject to later refinement, in no way hampered our work. We neglected no archeological sites in the area and, furthermore, we feel that any qualified visiting archeologist would be equally capable of locating these same sites in practice.

To some, our procedure may sound contradictory and perhaps even self-defeating. We have on the one hand called for precise definition of settlement patterns and then opted for a subjective assessment of our basic unit, the site. The first defense of this position was a pragmatic one, since we lacked suitable data to reach a workable definition prior to the 1971 season of field work. Yet there is another, more powerful justification for this position. Our acknowledged intent is to operationalize the definition of variables that condition Great Basin settlement patterns, that is, we wish to connect our intuitions to some measurable reality, as we felt it necessary to ensure that other investigators could test our hypothesis independently, and that our measurements were replicable. In dealing with operationism, one must continually balance empirical rigor against pragmatic necessity, for to demand precision in all definitions will lead one into the trap of an infinite regress, in which one's previous definition must be redefined continually. In practice, science simply accepts certain preliminary definitions as basic; mathematics, for example, considers certain premises that are accepted perforce—the "line," a "point," "the point lies on the line" and so forth—and these units become the foundation for a rigorous superstructure. We suggest a similar procedure for archeological entities; although we could define "site," we would still leave "cultural debris" and "cultural items" undefined. These terms could also be rigorously demarcated, but more undefined terms would arise until one is finally forced to accept some concept as given. Rather than chase the infinite regress, we have elected to simply accept "site" as our given and proceed from there (for further discussion of operationism in archeology, see Thomas, 1970). Perhaps David Hull has summarized our position most succinctly in his parable about early date farmers:

> To increase their yield they began to weed out the "sterile" trees. For a while they were successful until the last sterile male tree was cut down. Then all the other trees stopped producing. Theoretical terms are like the male tree. They are not completely operational, but they are necessary for the progress of science. Operationism is fruitful only when it is not total [Hull 1968:448].

With this hurdle of site definition suitably considered, we are free to operationally define the seven critical variables for site location:

f_1 The locus should be on a *ridge* or a *saddle*.

f_2 The ground should be *relatively flat*.
"relatively flat" $\leq$ 5% slope.

f_3 The locus should be in the *low foothills*.
"low foothills" $\leq$ 250 meters above the valley floor.

f_4 The locus should be within the modern piñon-juniper lifezone.

f_5 The locus should be *near* the extant piñon-juniper ecotone.
"near" $\leq$ 1000 meters.

f_6 The locus should be *near* a semipermanent water source.
"near" $\leq$ 1000 meters.

f_7 The locus should be *some minimal distance* from this source.
"some minimal distance" $\leq$ 100 meters

These figures are estimated from previous surveys and in a couple of cases, from our past field experience, without benefit of previous measurements. We have implied a few undefined terms such as *length, height, ridge, saddle*, and *ecotone*; we propose that each of these terms be accepted as given in the same sense as site.

To this point we have a set of partitive f-variables, operationally defined yet unrelated holistically. One could combine the seven variables into an inclusive definition of all potential piñon ecotone areas by simply requiring that all seven variables measure positively for all sites—yet this situation would suffer from all of the woes inherent in monothetic definition. We prefer to consider archeological sites as *operationally polythetic*, assuming no *sine qua non* variables. Accordingly, we define a *potential habitation locus*.

Group K (the set of all potential piñon ecotone habitation loci in the upper

Reese River Valley) is defined in terms of a set G of properties $f_1, f_2 \ldots f_7$ such that:

1. Each locus possesses a large ($n \geq 5$) number of the properties in G.
2. Each f-variable in G is possessed by large numbers of these loci.

Additionally, for the potential loci to be considered *fully polythetic*:

3. No f in G is possessed by every locus in the aggregation.

We have chosen the *five out of seven* as an arbitrary starting point, subject to verification and refinement by later field work.

In effect, this definition established two discrete populations. We have the population of all piñon-gathering sites in the Reese River Valley, which are defined by our intuitive notion of "site." The polythetic definition sets out a second population, the population of all potential habitation loci in the same area, defined by a polythetic combination of strictly topographic variables. The field work is designed to establish whether the population defined by cultural criteria is in fact isomorphic with the population defined by natural variables. That is, we wished to find whether the potential loci are acceptable predictors of archeological sites, and vice versa.

SURVEY RESULTS

To test the hypothesis of piñon ecotone locations, a 12-mile strip on the western slope of the Toiyabe Mountains was selected for intensive site survey (see Figure 1); this same area has been included in the stratified random sampling of previous years (see Thomas, 1969). Since hypothesis testing (verification) always necessitates data *independent* from those involved in the hypothesis formation (induction), the 13 randomly selected 500 square meter tracks were excluded from the 1971 survey. Thus no sites involved in forming the theory of Reese River settlement patterns were included in the sample selected to test this theory.*

As an initial step, stereographic pairs of United States Forest Service aerial photographs were studied in an attempt to find potential site loci—areas that

---

*Elsewhere in this volume, Professor Spaulding has disputed our stricture regarding independence of data used in hypothesis testing. It seems that Spaulding confuses LeBlanc's discussion of the logical structure of scientific explanation (chapter 13) with the specifics of statistical inference. Statistical inference is but a very specialized aspect of scientific explanation, and nowhere can we find a discussion of statistical hypothesis testing in LeBlanc's paper. We were making the simple point that when an investigator develops a *statistical hypothesis* on the basis of relationships observed in a set of data, he would be foolish to turn around and validate the hypothesis by "testing for statistical independence" on the same relationships in the same data. Let us hasten to add that there is nothing intrinsically wrong with formulating statistical hypotheses after examining the data, so long as these hypotheses are *tested on other* data. But when statistical hypotheses are "tested" on the same data that spawned them, a spurious impression of validity results, and the computed level of

satisfy at least five of the relevant topographic variables (the f_i). This preliminary scan enabled the field crews to efficiently plan the daily trek prior to survey of the area on foot. The survey itself was completed by teams of archeologists and students participating in the University of California (Davis) archeological field course. The 12-mile strip of piñon-juniper ecotone was completely examined and found to contain 65 archeological sites, each considered to be a member of the piñon ecotone settlement population.

The seven site variables were measured on each site in order to test the intuitive estimates already discussed. Table 1 indicates that the nominal attributes generally behaved as expected, with five characteristics falling within acceptable limits in over 90% of the sites measured. Variable f_6, the expectation that loci should be within 1000 meters of a semipermanent water source, agree with the expectation only about 77% of the time. Since no sites were over 1500 meters from water, this variable was perhaps too restrictive and a better estimate would probably be 1200 meters. The most inaccurate variable of all was f_2 the expectation that sites should be on ground with a slope no steeper than 5%. The 65 sample sites ranged from absolutely flat (0% slope) to a steep 20% slope; only about 35% of the sample sites proved as flat as expected. In previous fieldwork at Reese River, we never actually measured slope, so in considering the polythetic definition of site patterns, we had to guess at the operational figure of 5%, an estimate that was obviously too conservative. For future field work, the more suitable figure of 10% could be adopted.

Table 2 presents the tabulated findings of the metric expressions of these variables. The sample of 65 sites were analyzed to provide an estimate of the population parameter of all Reese River piñon sites—the 95% confidence limits. The figures for percentage of slope confirm that the f_2 variable limit should be changed to ≤ 10%.

Yet the operational definition and testing of site parameters was only the first part of this field experiment, for we were also concerned with the *holistic*

significance bears almost no relationship to the true value. We do not argue against the use of *a posteriori* statistical hypotheses, because rigorous *a priori* hypotheses are often hard to come by in archeology. But we do object to the improper use of statistical inference in archeology which results in unwarranted confidence in our (untested) hypotheses.

Spaulding also charges that our hypotheses "would have been forever unverifiable if it had happened that it was formulated after all of the Reese River sites had been inspected, a pretty pickle indeed." Apparently Spaulding uses an unusual definition of hypotheses. Spaulding suggests that had we first inspected *all* of the Reese River sites and *then* stated our "hypothesis," we would find ourselves in a logical pickle, since no independent data would be left for testing; our hypothesis would be "forever unverifiable." We see no pickle at all. Had we found *all* of the Reese River sites and then proceeded to frame a statement of our results, we would not be involved with hypothesis testing at all—we would be stating a *fact*. Hypotheses generalize from sample statistics to unknown population parameters, and hypotheses must be tested. Parameters, on the other hand, are invariant phenomena (facts) which describe the characteristics of the existing population. Facts are not tested, as Spaulding seems to imply.

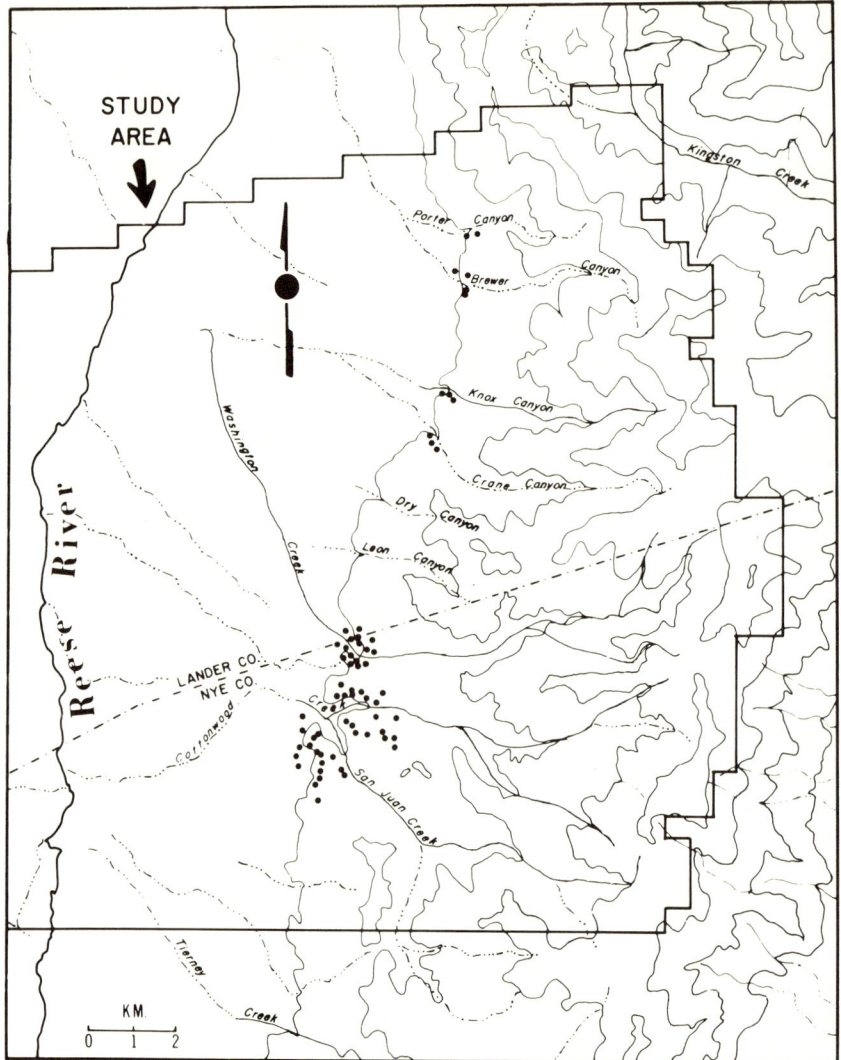

Fig. 11.1. Black dots indicate village sites located in the Toiyabe Mountains of the Reese River Valley, about 30 miles south of Austin, Nevada (see Thomas 1972 for details).

definition of site locations. This aspect of the fieldwork considered two hypotheses:
1. Null Hypothesis (H_0): Sites occur on potential loci with only random frequency.
2. Alternative Hypothesis (H_1): Sites occur on potential loci with a greater than random frequency in this case, defined as greater than the .05 level of statistical significance.

Table 11.1

Nominal Characteristics of Reese River Piñon Ecotone Sites

Variable	Nominal Totals			Agreement
	Ridge	Saddle	Other	96.9%
f_1 Topography	52	11	2	
	Yes (+)	No (−)	Range	
f_2 Ground flat?	24	41	0–20%	36.9%
f_3 In low foothills?	62	3	0–322 meters	95.4%
f_4 In modern piñon-juniper zone?	64	1	—	98.5%
f_5 Near piñon-juniper ecotone?	60	5	0–1400 meters	92.3%
f_6 Near water?	59	6	20–1500 meters	90.8%
f_7 Site not directly on water source?	61	4	20–1500 meters	93.9%

Table 11.2

Metric Characteristics of Reese River Piñon Sites

Variable	n	$\overline{X}$	S.D.	95% Confidence Interval
Percent slope	65	8.4%	4.2%	± 1.0%
Distance to ecotone	65	520.9 meters	357.1 meters	± 86.8 meters
Distance to valley floor	65	94.7 meters	63.5 meters	± 15.4 meters
Distance to water source	65	451.4 meters	354.7	± 86.2 meters

To test these competing propositions, field crews not only had to locate all archeological sites within the test region, but additionally, all potential loci of habitation had to be found and recorded. That is, in the 12-mile survey area, every time at least five of the f-variables were satisfied, the locus was recorded as an area of potential habitation, whether or not cultural material was present.

The survey results of holistic site definition are summarized in the following contingency table:

Table 11.3

Archeological Sites

		Present (+)	Absent (−)
Potential Loci	(+)	63	11
	(−)	2	∞

Of the 65 sites located, all but 2 were located on areas considered potential loci, areas that satisfied at least five of the seven critical environmental variables. The survey located only 11 potential loci that lacked archeological sites.

Obviously the polythetic definition is a highly successful predictor of site locations in this area; 97% of the sites are on potential loci. Additionally, 85% of the potential loci contained sites, accuracy that we feel is exceptional for most treatments of archeological survey material.

Yet simple percentages provide no measure of statistical probability of success, no statement of how often such results can be expected to occur through simple chance. Significance of contingency table results is usually assessed by the chi-square test of independence (Siegel 1956: 104). In this case, however, we cannot use the chi-square since the d box in Table 3 is undefined. Most association or correlation indices, such as Pearson's r, the phi coefficient, and Yule's Q consider common absence, the case in which both variables are negative or absent. In our experiment, we failed to derive a workable method of measuring the number of times sites did not appear where they should have; we lack significant information content in the d cell. To consider this factor, one would have to define a *minimal locus* as an arbitrary areal limit. Defining the spatial limit of sites is not difficult; one merely determines the extent of cultural debris. But the case of common absence requires the definition of an entirely synthetic unit, such as a 10- or 100- or 1000-meter grid. Consider the case of a steep hillside, an area that is predicted to not contain debris from the piñon ecotone sites (although it could perhaps contain lithic debris from task-specific activities such as hunting, root gathering, etc). If the habitation debris is absent from the hillside, how many times should we count this success? If the hillside itself is a natural unit, the case receives one count. But one could just as easily consider the hillside as a series of 25 discrete microtopographic features, each of them lacking cultural material. It should be clear that the d box could easily be inflated to infinity, invalidating any contingency statistic.

In order to properly assess the statistical probability of our results, we analyzed the data by the binomial theorem. Let us define the probability of finding a site at any given locus as p and the probability of not finding a site as q; p and q must sum to 1 since they are both mutually exclusive and exhaustive. The expected value of finding a site at any given locus is equal to

$$p = \frac{a_1}{a_2}$$

where a_1 = the total area occupied by archeological sites and a_2 = the total area surveyed. Unfortunately time did not permit the accurate measurement of a_1, so it is necessary to estimate the quantity. We feel that the value of $p = .01$ is a conservative and realistic estimate. The null hypothesis can now be refined to a point estimate.

$$H_0 : p = .01$$
$$H_1 : p > .01$$

The alternative hypothesis—that archeological sites should occur on areas of potential habitation with a greater than average frequency—is directional and hence one-tailed. The significance of our results can be computed by the z test of a binomial proportion (see Snedecor and Cochran, 1967: 211-213).

$$z = \frac{(|\hat{p} - p| - 1/2\, n)}{\sqrt{pq/n}}$$

where p and q are the expected probabilities and $\hat{p}$ is the observed value of a success (site corresponding to locus). The resulting z is 77.64, an astronomically high value, significant at much greater than the .001 level. These results permit us to reject the null hypothesis of no association and conclude that the polythetic definition of potential loci is a significant predictor of piñon village location. A similar case for the probability of a site at any given locus shows $z = 52.85$, again a highly significant outcome.

In addition to verifying the predictions of site location, data collected in the 1971 survey constitute further, and perhaps more refined, support for Steward's theory of Great Basin settlement and subsistence patterns and the *BASIN I* computer simulation of this same system (Thomas, 1972). This is based on three assumptions. First, as a basic premise we hold that site locations are affected in no small way by such considerations as the season of occupation, size of the occupying population, and the types of activities carried out at those locations. Individually, each of these and other variables probably exerts some demands in the logistics of site location. Second, no one of these variables by itself is sufficient to determine site location. This follows from earlier statements concerning the value of polythetic set criteria, and is evidenced by the fact that "winter-site" definition in the Reese River Valley is fully polythetic (see below). Third, in spite of the fact that a single locational criterion would not significantly restrict the spatial distributions of sites (e.g., the piñon-juniper lifezone comprises a vast portion of the Reese River Valley), combinations of two or more mildly restrictive criteria quickly reduce the number of possible locations that will fit the specified criteria. *If*, as we believe, site locations are sensitive to seasonality and resource procurement systems—among other things—and *if* combinations of several locational criteria (in this case five out of seven), delimit areas that are relatively small in comparison to the area denoted by any single criterion, *then* it follows that sites of a given type (here, type is defined on the basis of comparable social groups, season of occupation, and range of activities) should reveal a consistent polythetic set of locational criteria. On the other hand, shifts in subsistence, social units, or seasonality should be accompanied by concomitant—but not necessarily simple or direct changes in the polythetic set of locational criteria. The sites located in the Reese River Valley in 1971 did indeed display a consistent set of polythetic locational criteria even though they represented over 4000 years of occupation. This then can be taken as confirmation that these sites were all of a single type, described by Steward (1938) as "winter camps" and that the subsistence and settlement system described by Steward (1938) and modeled by Thomas (1972) can successfully account for the character and distribution of archeological materials deposited during this portion of the year.

SUMMARY

This experiment was designed to satisfy two purposes. The first was to provide an objective and independent test of part of the hypothesis of Reese River Subsistence-Settlement Systems that, it will be remembered, was the direct outcome of a previous test of Steward's theory. We wish to underscore the *cyclical* nature of such hypothesis testing, since every test produces a host of new hypotheses, which in turn must be verified. We feel that the results of the 1971 field season provided more than acceptable confirmation of the theory regarding the location of piñon ecotone settlements, and constitute additional support for Steward's discussion of settlement and subsistence in the Great Basin. It remains to test the rest of the propositions of the Reese River Subsistence-Settlement Systems, and finally, these results and new data must be synthesized into a new, more comprehensive hypothesis, subject again to verification. In theory at least, the inductive-deductive interplay should continue indefinitely.

Our second objective lay on a more generalized level, since the polythetic set has been shown to actually perform a valuable service in primary archeological contexts. In fact, without considering the sites in such polythetic fashion, we should have been unable to synthesize the partitive *f*-variables into a single holistic index of potential site location. As we have already pointed out, site definition is *fully* polythetic, since no *f*-variable was common to any of the 65 sites; we could not have chosen any monothetic criteria for none exists. Although Clarke (1968) has discussed the *logic* of polythetic sets and archeological entities, we feel that for the Reese River Valley at least, we have demonstrated the significant *utility* of the concept. Furthermore, the concept and application of polythetic procedures probably offers the archeologist his greatest hope in objectifying that elusive yet viable notion of *feel*.

In presenting the polythetic predictors of winter village sites, we harbor no illusions about having supplied a statement of absolute causality; we do not claim, for example, that the coincidence of at least five out of seven critical topographic variables *caused* archeological sites to be constructed on that spot. Absolute causality is a difficult matter indeed. A detailed discussion would be superficial at best, if not somewhat overbold at this point. Let us admit for clarity that we raise no cavil in applying the terms cause and effect to this or any similar archeological analysis so long as it is clearly understood in the Humean sense to imply no more and no less than A is always followed in a statistical sense by B. In the case at hand, A, the presence of a potential locus of habitation is a 97% efficient predictor—the cause if you wish—of B, the presence of an archeological site. To push causality further is to fall into the anthropomorphic trap of attempting to model behavioral laws in our own human image.

We also wish to disclaim any flirtation with passing off our settlement pattern predictors as anything like overt "ethnoecology"; in fact, we feel rather strongly that this research has very little to do with the prehistoric mind—no conscious mental templates or percepta are implied. The cognitive correlates of prehistoric settlement behavior remain a mystery. These data can perhaps be compared most closely to the results of the explicity etic ethnographic school, described by Pelto (1971). We can envision the case in which inhabitants of these ecotone sites—were they still alive—claim that such villages were moved due to purely ceremonial or religious circumstances, for example, death of a relative, omens of misfortune, or shamanistic visions. Yet as archeologists, we can be little concerned with emic causes, since these mentalistic configurations perished with the informants; students of archeology are free to deal exclusively with existential on-the-ground behavior of this and other past ecosystems. We feel that through a solid ecological approach to settlement pattern studies, the archeologist can produce etic data compatible with that obtained among living human societies.

ACKNOWLEDGMENTS

For most archeological field research programs, certain basic requirements will never change regardless of the trend toward sophisticated problem solving and methods of analysis. The notion of field work will continue to conjure up a certain feeling of romance and excitement no matter how experienced the field worker. However, upon completion of each archeological field season one thing always rings true: the work was hard and expensive. It is fitting at this point to extend our thanks to the various individuals, institutions, and students who provided the guidance, support, and labor necessary for a successful 1971 field season.

The 1971 field season was carried out under the auspices of the Department of Anthropology, University of California, Davis, California. We wish to acknowledge M.A. Baumhoff, D.L. True, and W.G. Davis of that department for their encouragement, interest, and cooperation concerning the Reese River Ecological Project in general and the 1971 University of California (Davis) Summer Field Course in particular.

We wish to acknowledge Julian H. Steward for his rigorous field work, which served as the framework for a series of hypotheses regarding winter village placement in the Reese River Valley area, and for his endorsement of the project.

For the countless blisters and sore feet encountered in the field, we acknowledge the students of the 1971 University of California (Davis) Summer Field Class.

We wish to thank the following people for their comments and suggestions in the final preparation of this manuscript: M.A. Baumhoff, James O'Connell, Jerry Moles, Rick Casteel, and Brian Hatoff.

The 1971 phase of the Reese River Ecological Project was supported by the National Science Foundation Traineeship and the Chancellor's Patent Fund (University of California, Davis), which we greatefully acknowledge.

Finally, to Liz Williams and Trudy Thomas go our deepest thanks and appreciation. Trudy served full time in the field from the very beginning of the Reese River Ecological Project in 1969. Liz, although serving only for brief periods during the three years, assumed the unenviable task of remaining at home and working. Their enthusiasm for the project and willingness to "carry their share of the load," made the project performance an easier task.

This chapter is Contribution Number 11 of the Reese River Ecological Project.

REFERENCES

Beckner. M. (1959). *The biological way of thought.* New York: Columbia University Press.

Bettinger, R.L. (1975). *The surface archaeology of Owens Valley, eastern California: Prehistoric man-land relationships in the Great Basin.* Unpublished doctoral dissertation, University of California, Riverside.

Bettinger, R.L. (1977). Aboriginal human ecology in Owens Valley, eastern California: Prehistoric culture change in the Great Basin. *American Antiquity 42*, 3-17.

Bettinger, R.L. (1978). Alternative adaptive strategies in the prehistoric Great Basin. *Journal of Anthropological Research 34*, 27-46.

Binford, L.W., & Binford, S.R., (1966). A preliminary analysis of functional variability in the Mousterian of Levallois facies. In J.D. Clark & F.C. Howell (Eds.), *Recent studies in paleoanthropology. American Anthropologist 68*(2), 238-295.
Carr C. (1984). The nature of organization of intrasite archaeological records and spatial analytic approaches to their investigation. In M.B. Schiffer (Ed.), *Advances in archaeological method and theory, Vol 7.* New York: Academic Press, Inc.
Clarke, D.L. (1968). *Analytical archaeology.* London: Methuen.
Greig-Smith, P. (1964). *Quantitative plant ecology* (2nd ed.). New York: Plenum Press.
Hill, J.N. (1968). Broken K Pueblo: Patterns of form and function. In S.R. Binford & L.R. Binford (Eds.), *New perspectives in archeology* (pp. 103-142). Chicago: Aldine Publishing Company.
Hill, J.N. (a1970). *Broken K Pueblo: Prehistoric social organization in the American Southwest.* (Anthropological Papers No. 18). Tucson: University of Arizona.
Holmer, R. (1981). 5. Predictive model. In J.C. Janetski (Ed.), *Prehistoric and historic settlement in the Escalante Desert* (Rep. of Investigations No. 81-10). Salt Lake City: University of Utah, Archeological Center.
Hull, D.L. (1968). The operational imperative: Sense and nonsense in operationalism. *Systematic Zoology 17*, 438-457.
Jennings, J.D. (1957). Danger Cave. *Society for American Archaeology, Memoir 14.*
Jennings, J.D. (1964). The Desert West. In J.D. Jennings & E. Norbeck (Eds.), *Prehistoric man in the New World* (pp. 149-174). Chicago: University of Chicago Press.
Kemeny, J.G. (1959). *A philosopher looks at science.* New York: Van Nostrand-Reinholdt.
LeBlanc, S.A. (1973). Two points of logic concerning data, hypotheses, general laws, and systems. In C.L. Redman (Ed.), *Research and theory in current archaeology* (pp. 199-214). New York: John Wiley & Sons, Inc.
Longacre, W.A. (1970). *Archaeology as anthropology: A case study.* (Anthropological Papers No. 17). Tucson: University of Arizona.
Loud, L.L., & Harrington, M.R. (1929). Lovelock Cave. *University of California Publications in American Archaeology and Ethnology 25*, vii-183.
Needham, R. (1975). Polythetic classification: Convergence and consequences. *Man 10*, 349-369.
Pelto, P.J. (1970). *Anthropological research: The structure of inquiry.* New York: Harper and Row.
Phillips, P. (1958). Application of the Wheat-Gifford-Wasley taxonomy to eastern ceramics. *American Antiquity 24*, 117-130.
Salmon, M.H. (1982). *Philosophy and archaeology.* New York: Academic Press, Inc.
Siegel, S. (1956). *Nonparametric statistics for the behavioral sciences.* New York: McGraw-Hill, Inc.
Solheim, W.G., II (1976). Correspondence: Polythetic classification. *Man 11*(2), 282-283.
Sneath, P.H.A. (1962). The construction of taxonomic groups. In G.C. Ainsworth, & P.H.A. Sneath (Eds.), *Microbial Classification* (pp. 289-332). Cambridge, Cambridge University Press.
Snedecor, G.W., & Cochran, W.G. (1967). *Statistical methods.* Ames IA: Iowa State University.
Spaulding, A.C. (1973). Archeology in the active voice; The new anthropology. In C.L. Redman (Ed.), *Research and theory in current archaeology* (pp. 337-354). New York: John Wiley & Sons, Inc.
Steward, J.H. (1938). Basin-plateau aboriginal sociopolitical grroups. *Bureau of American Ethnology, Bulletin 120.*
Struever, S. (1968). Flotation techniques for the recovery of small-scale archaeological remains. *American Antiquity 33*, 353-362.
Thomas. D.H. (1969). *Regional sampling in archaeology: A pilot Great Basin research design* (Archaeological Survey Annual Rep., 1968-1969, 11) (pp. 87-100). University of California.
Thomas, D.H. (1970). *Archaeology's operational imperative: Great Basin projectile points as a test case* (Archaeological Survey Annual Rep., 1969-1970, 12) (pp. 27-60). University of California.
Thomas, D.H. (1971). *Prehistoric subsistence-settlement patterns of the Reese River Valley, central Nevada.* Unpublished doctoral dissertation, University of California, Davis.
Thomas, D.H. (1972). A computer simulation model of Great Basin Shoshonean settlement patterns. In D.L. Clarke (Ed.), *Models in archaeology* (pp. 671-704). London: Methuen.

Thomas, D.H. (1973). An empirical test of Steward's model of Great Basin settlement patterns. *American Antiquity 38*, 155-176.

Thomas, D.H. (1975). Nonsite sampling in archaeology: Up the creek without a site? In J.W. Mueller (Ed.), *Sampling in archaeology* (pp. 61-81). Tucson: University of Arizona Press.

Thomas, D.H. (1981). How to classify the projectile points from Monitor Valley, Nevada. *Journal of California and Great Basin Anthropology 3*(1), 7-43.

Thomas, D.H. (1982a). The colonization of Monitor Valley, Nevada. *Nevada Historical Society Quarterly 25*(1), 2-27.

Thomas, D.H. (1982b). *The 1981 Alta Toquima Village project: a preliminary report* (Tech. Rep. Series, No. 27). Desert Research Institute, Social Sciences Center.

Thomas, D.H. (1983a). The Archaeology of Monitor Valley: 1. Epistemology. *Anthropological Papers of the American Museum of Natural History 58*(1), 1-194.

Thomas, D.H. (1983b). The Archaeology of Monitor Valley: 2. Gatecliff Shelter. *Anthropological Papers of the American Museum of Natural History 59*(1), 1-552.

Thomas, D.H., & Bettinger, R.L. (1976). Prehistoric piñon ecotone settlements in the upper Reese River Valley, central Nevada. *Anthropological Papers of the American Museum of Natural History 53*(3), 263-366.

Willey, G.R. (1956). Prehistoric settlement patterns in the New World. *Viking Fund Publications in Anthropology 23*.

PART V: INTRASITE SPATIAL ANALYSIS

12

Introductory Remarks on Intrasite Spatial Analysis

CHRISTOPHER CARR

Analysis of the spatial arrangement of artifacts within an archaeological site has two primary tasks. The first, which requires R-mode operations, aims at defining the degree of similar or dissimilar spatial arrangements of different artifact types or attributes over the site. Such patterning, with appropriate bridging arguments, can be used as evidence of the past operation of various activities, other cultural formation process, or natural formation processes. The second task, which requires Q-mode operations, aims at defining the spatial positions and limits of clusters, voids, or other interesting arrangements of artifacts that are of various types or that have certain attributes. This is done to document the different spatial distributions of different activities or other formation processes over the site, and the various relevant characteristics of their distributions. The results of both kinds of analyses can then be used to estimate the values taken by variables that comprise the behavioral-environmental system under study, of which the activities and formation processes are a part. Local population density, degree of mobility, and pattern of mobility are examples of such variables.

NEW TECHNIQUES

The two chapters by Carr, and Gladfelter and Tiedemann, respectively, introduce new techniques for achieving the R-mode and Q-mode operations previously described. Carr introduces four *similarity coefficients* (AVDISTGM, AVDISTLP1, AVDISTGP, AVDISTLP2) that can be used to define the degree of coarrangement of artifacts over an area. The different coefficients are appropriate under different conditions, depending on the form of organization of any depositional sets of similarly arranged types that may occur in the study area (i.e., relevant relational data structure), as determined by the processes of formation of the sets. The particular archaeological organizations and formation processes that are congruent with each coefficient are specified. All the coefficients require data in the form of item point locations.

Carr also introduces a new *clustering algorithm* (OVERCLUS), which is capable of grouping artifact types into multitype sets on the basis of the new similarity coefficients or other standard coefficients. Importantly, the algorithm allows, but does not require, the formed sets of types to overlap in membership. It thus accommodates typical variation in the relevant organization of depositional sets. The method is technically preferable to other algorithms that are currently available for defining overlapping sets in that it 1) does not require the specification of vital parameters of a data's relevant structure prior to analysis (e.g., number of types overlapping between groups), 2) allows control of the degree of inconsistency between pairwise relationships that is smoothed out of the data in arriving at a solution, 3) is efficient, and 4) is concordant with a wide diversity of similarity coefficients.

Finally, Carr evaluates other multivariate techniques that can be used to group types into depositional sets, including factor analysis, standard clustering procedures, and multidimensional scaling. These are evaluated for their degree of concordance with the potentially overlapping form of organization of depositional sets and the degree to which they are technically advantaged in the ways just mentioned. All of these considerations suggest the use of OVERCLUS, in conjunction with multidimensional scaling, as an optimal approach for defining multitype sets of artifacts.

The chapter by Gladfelter and Tiedemann introduces a new geographic technique—the continguity-anomaly (CA) method. This method, when used to analyze intrasite artifact distributions, is capable of determining the positions and spatial limits of clusters or voids of artifacts that are of a single type or that have certain attribute states. The method, which requires data in the form of grid cell counts of artifacts or other cell values, achieves this task through a systematic examination of the differences in cell counts or values among contiguous cells. This operation allows the identification of particular cells that are of a given level of similarity to or dissimilarity from surrounding cells. Such cells represent either whole clusters/voids, cells within gradations of change at the boundaries of such areas, or cells within such areas, depending on the mesh of the grid and the nature of the contiguity relations. Examination of cell value differences also allows the testing of such interesting cells for the statistical significance of their differences from neighboring cells and, thus, the significance of local autocorrelation or lack thereof.

Gladfelter and Tiedemann's general perspectives on spatial analysis, which led them to develop their contiguity-anomaly method, are similar to those that led Whallon (1984) to develop his productive methodology, *unconstrained clustering*. Both sets of researchers emphasize the importance of evaluating *local variation* in a spatial arrangement as opposed to its global, overall form of arrangement. In achieving this end, both sets of researchers have developed methods that *classify* cells/locales in accordance with their degrees of similarity to or dissimilarity from other cells/locales.

The two methods are equally advantageous compared to many other techniques in that they 1) do not assume any degree of spatial autocorrelation of cell values among cells; 2) are not plagued by a boundary problem; 3) do not assume that the global population of cell values conform to any well-known frequency distribution; 4) can accommodate data in either a grid cell format or an item point location format that has been transformed to a grid cell/local neighborhood format; and 5) allow the use of any of a broad range of variables in characterizing a cell, such as local densities or proportions of artifact types, or statistical moments of certain properties of the artifacts within cells/neighborhoods.

The two methods are complementary in two ways. The CA method allows assessment of the statistical significance of the departure or lack of departure of a cell's value from those of other cells, whereas unconstrained clustering does not. Unconstrained clustering allows multiple variables to be considered simultaneously in the evaluation of cell similarities and differences, whereas the CA method is essentially univariate in nature (although ratios of two variables and other multivariate summary measures can be accommodated).

Both methods are disadvantaged in that they employ a *single global* threshold, rather than locally variable thresholds, for defining significantly similar or different cells. This can imply erroneous assumptions about the nature of artifact organization and site formation. The single global threshold can imply, for example, an equivalent degree of internal homogeneity of all clusters in their artifact densities or compositions, and an equivalent degree of density or compositional contrast of all clusters from their backgrounds. A more detailed review of the advantages and disadvantages of both techniques, in relation to the nature of organization of intrasite archaeological records, is given by Carr (1984).

ENTRY MODELS AND POLYTHETIC ORGANIZATION OF DEPOSITIONAL SETS

Carr's chapter discusses a number of issues pertinent to the general volume themes, which need to be emphasized.

1) The use of *entry models* and *parallel data sets*, as one strategy for determining the relevant structure of a complex data set and for specifying the technique(s) appropriate for analyzing it (Carr, chapter 2), is exemplified. Data sets that are comprised of information on the spatial arrangements of various artifact types across a site are envisioned as complex data sets. Sets of information on the manner of formation of those arrangements are taken to represent parallel data sets that can give insight into the nature of relevant organization of the complex artifact arrangements.

2) Twelve models of possible organization of depositional sets in the archae-

ological domain are defined. These represent different *relevant relational data structures* that are generated under different conditions of formation, disturbance, excavation, and encoding of an intrasite archaeological record. These models, along with the processes that are responsible for them and the techniques of analysis that are concordant with them, represent entry models. The models can also be used to describe the organization of artifacts among and within activities in the behavioral domain, in ethnoarchaeological work.

3) The constructs of *polythetic and monothetic* organization, which are useful in modeling different kiinds of relevant structural relationships among archaeological entities in gcncral (Clarkc, 1968; Williams ct al., chapter 11), are linked to more basic, determinant dimensions of structural variation. These include local variation in the magnitude, direction, and completeness of *asymmetry relations* among entities. More detailed remarks on Carr's and Williams et al.'s discussions of monothetic and polythetic organization in this volume are given in chapter 6 (pp. 125-126).

4) Carr's chapter stresses and illustrates that the appropriateness of a technique for analyzing data cannot be judged in a *general*, a priori fashion, on the basis of the *number* of constraining assumptions that it makes about the nature of relevant data structure—a criterion for acceptance of analytic results that is in line with an exploratory data analysis approach to data examination (Carr, chapter 2). Rather, the *particular nature* of the assumptions and their degrees of congruence with the relevant form of organization of the *particular data* in hand is what matters.

Other points in Carr's paper that should be noted concern intrasite spatial analysis in general. These are the following:

5) It is proposed that the *inferential goals* of intrasite spatial analysis be widened to include not only the reconstruction of past activities, their frequencies, and spatial arrangements, but also various extra-activity cultural formation processes (e.g., curation rates, regional mobility patterns) and natural formation processes. All of these phenomena are useful as indicators or estimates of the states taken by variables that comprise past behavioral and environmental systems.

6) In regard to the *operational goals* of intrasite spatial analysis, it is argued that the search for supralocal (perhaps site-wide) relationships among artifact types, indicating supralocal depositional sets, can remain a valid goal. This is true so long as (a) the technique of analysis that is used is insensitive to any irrelevant local variation that may occur over space in the magnitude, direction, and/or completeness of asymmetry among coarranged types, and (b) the area that is examined does not include relevant localized relationships among artifact types that are contradictory (i.e., there is no pooling of relevant structures and populations). An opposing viewpoint on operational goals is taken by Whallon (1984).

FUTURE RESEARCH

The studies by Carr, and Gladfelter and Tiedemann, suggest some future lines of research that would be useful. These include 1) the specification of additional dimensions of variation of depositional set organization beyond those concerned with asymmetry and overlap, and the linkage of formation processes and concordant techniques to organizational variation along those dimensions, in the effort to develop more sophisticated entry models for getting into spatial data sets; 2) investigation of the optimal complementary uses of OVERCLUS and multidimensional scaling procedures in smoothing and representing spatial data; 3) extension of the CA method so as to make possible the statistical assessment of the form of arrangement of supralocal artifact distributions and their coarrangement; and 4) extension of the CA method so as to make possible the statistical assessment of local autocorrelation at varying geographic scales. The latter can currently be achieved cumbersomely by varying the mesh of the grid that is used. It also might be accomplished, however, by varying the number of k neighbor cells to which central cells are compared and the distance of neighbor cells from central cells, in a manner analogous to spatial filtering approaches (e.g., Scollar, 1969).

REFERENCES

Carr, C. (1984). The nature of organization of intrasite archaeological records and spatial analytic approaches to their investigation. In M.B. Schiffer (Ed.), *Advances in archaeological method and theory* (Vol. 7) (pp. 103-222). New York: Academic Press.

Clarke, D.L. (1968). *Analytical archaeology*. London: Methuen.

Scollar, I. (1969). Some techniques for the evaluation of archaeological magnetometer surveys. *World Archaeology* 1(1), 78-89.

Whallon, R. (1984). Unconstrained clustering for the analysis of spatial distributions in archaeology. In H.S. Hietala (Ed.), *Intrasite spatial analysis* (pp. 242-277). Cambridge: Cambridge University Press.

13

Alternative Models, Alternative Techniques: Variable Approaches to Intrasite Spatial Analysis

CHRISTOPHER CARR

Spatial patterns among artifacts over an archaeological site can be very important to the archaeologist. They can be used not only in traditional ways to reconstruct the activity areas, tool kits, and lifeways of past peoples, but also to formulate and test hypotheses on the state and organization of past cultural systems and natural environmental systems.

The potential of artifact patterns to serve in these manners has increased dramatically in the last ten years through advances in two areas. 1) Our better understanding of how archaeological records are formed and organized have provided a set of bridging principles and boundary conditions for assigning meaning to artifact patterns and for inferring the states taken by variables within past behavioral-environmental systems. 2) Advances in analytic procedures for recognizing spatial patterns among artifacts have broadened the range of forms of spatial variation that are "visible" to the archaeologist and available for interpretation.

If theory building and explanation in archaeology are to proceed efficiently and accurately, however, it is necessary to integrate these new insights into

---

The stimulation for this paper and much of its form derive from the conversations I have had with Robert Whallon and Michael Schiffer over the past several years. Robert Whallon taught me to ask a critical question: what techniques are most appropriate for analyzing a data set, in making assumptions consistent with its structure. I would not have answered this question in relation to spatial analysis in the way I have here, however, without the insight that Michael Schiffer has shared with me on the variable effects of formation processes from site to site. Larry Keeley helped me to broaden my understanding of the probable uses of Upper Paleolithic artifact classes and to interpret the Pincevent data. James Dunn and William Darden helped me to clarify my thoughts on the application of factor analysis and ITREG to similarity coefficients. Dan Puckett and David Waddell provided technical assistance in the computer digitizing and visual display of the Pincevent data. Funds for computing were provided by the Department of Anthropology, Fulbright College, at the University of Arkansas. To all of these persons and institutions I say thank you very much.

formation processes and analytic procedure. *It is necessary to develop a theoretical framework that allows the forms of organization of particular archaeological records to be described in terms that facilitate specification of the particular kinds of spatial analytic techniques that are appropriate for analyzing them.* In any given context, only some analytic methods are appropriate for revealing artifact spatial patterns within an archaeological record. These are methods that imply, by their algorithmic procedures, certain assumptions about the nature of formation and organization of the record that are compatible with those aspects of its actual mode of formation and organization that are of interest to the researcher. Only these methods will reveal generalized spatial patterns having behavioral or other relevant meaning. Thus, in more general terms, it is necessary to develop a theoretical framework facilitating *choice* of analytic technique so that logical consistency is maximized between technique and relevant aspects of data structure (see Carr, chapter 1).

One possible framework that can be developed for this purpose is a series of models of intrasite organization of artifacts and artifact types, where the models are components of *entry models* (see Carr, chapter 2) that link data to technique. In particular, the organizational models would have three characteristics. 1) In combination, the models would inventory all general forms of organization of artifacts and artifact types that might logically occur in various environmental and behavioral contexts (e.g., ratio-scale, ordinal-scale, nominal-scale, or polythetic forms of artifact type coarrangement) along various behavioral and formation-relevant dimensions of variability (e.g., form of coarrangement of types, overlapping vs. nonoverlapping artifact set structure). 2) They would be mathematical in nature, facilitating the linkage of each model to the assumptions made by particular analytic techniques and, thus, to techniques themselves. 3) Each model would be associated with a particular set of formation processes that could have generated the form of organization specified by it, thus linking each model to particular natural environmental and behavioral contexts and to specific data sets. Using models of this kind with some knowledge about the environmental and behavioral context of an archaeological site and the formation processes responsible for it, it would be possible to associate the site (or a portion of it) with one or a few mathematical models of its organization. This association, in turn, would suggest the one or several techniques most likely appropriate for its analysis.

The process of modeling various possible forms of organization of artifacts within sites and linking those models to analytic techniques and to formation processes will help the researcher maximize concordance between data structure and technique in particular circumstances. It also, however, should reveal general deficiencies in the techniques available for analysis and in our understanding of formation processes. Clarke (1968, pp. 32-34; 1972, pp. 1-10) and Haggett and Chorley (1967, pp. 19-26) have emphasized the importance of modeling for linking data to theory in a manner encouraging theory building;

modeling can also serve, however, to link data structures to techniques in a manner encouraging the development of analytic techniques in fruitful directions.

This chapter is the second of a series of three papers aimed at integrating recent advances in analytic procedure with our understanding of formation processes through the modeling of archaeological organization and the development of needed spatial techniques. The first paper (Carr, 1984) presents one mathematical model of organization of artifacts within archaeological sites— presumably that organization which is most common. Also, a model of the organization of artifacts within the "behavioral domain" of past events, and an enumeration of the formation processes transforming that behavioral organization into archaeological organization, are provided. Most quantitative spatial analytic methods currently used in intrasite archaeology are then assessed for their logical consistency with the model of archaeological organization, and thus, their appropriateness of application. In the course of the paper, procedures for the methods are summarized. Methods for assessing the form of arrangement of artifacts in space (clustered, random, aligned), for determining whether artifact types are coarranged, and for delimiting single and multitype clusters are considered. Finally, a new technique that allows assessment of whether artifact types are coarranged and that is more consistent with the model of archaeological organization is developed. This technique is *polythetic association*.

This paper develops a broader range of models of possible intrasite archaeological organizations. It then associates these organizations with some formation processes that might generate them and some analytic techniques most consistent with them. The technique of polythetic association is expanded to include several varieties concordant with the different models of archaeological organization. These models and techniques are illustrated using data from the Magdalenian reindeer hunting camp, Pincevent habitation no. 1, in the Paris basin, France (Leroi-Gorhan & Brézillon, 1966). The models and techniques pertain to the process of defining only the degree of coarrangement of artifact types over space, not the form of arrangement of artifacts or the boundaries of clusters.

To provide a context for these discussions and analyses, this paper also summarizes and evaluates the traditional goals of intrasite spatial analysis and calls for an expansion of their scope. It also evaluates the potential that three logical-operational frameworks for carrying out intrasite spatial analysis have for facilitating logical concordance between data and technique.

The final article of the series (Carr, 1986) discusses the necessity, in some cases, of screening intrasite arrangements of artifacts prior to their analysis with the techniques discussed here or other ones. In particular, it is argued that the spatial arrangement of an artifact class (especially ubiquitously distributed ones) can be a palimpsest which is attributable to multiple, overlaid but spatially nonparallel formation processes. In these circumstances, spectral analysis, Fourier analysis, and spatial filtering techniques can sometimes be used to dissect the palimpsest into subglobal component distributions, each of which is attributable to a more homogeneous range of formation processes. Each component can then be analyzed separately from the others, along with other artifact classes that are distributed in a similar fashion, using techniques that are more closely tailored to the particular nature of the distributions and their formation processes.

BASIC ASSUMPTIONS AND PHILOSOPHY OF ANALYSIS

Quantitative intrasite spatial analysis using modern methods of geography and mathematical ecology (Clark & Evans, 1954; Greig-Smith, 1952, 1964) had its beginnings (Peebles, 1971; Whallon, 1973) prior to the time of great concern over and documentation of archaeological formation processes. The subdiscipline is now in only the initial stages of integrating this new information on formation processes and modifying standard designs of intrasite research for concordance with them. As may be expected, a diversity of opinions occur in current literature as to the proper *goals* of and *logical-operational framework* for intrasite spatial analysis. The following section discusses these issues and attempts to resolve some of them.

Evaluation and Expansion of the Goals of Intrasite Spatial Analysis

Traditional Goals

In the early 1970s, two sets of goals of intrasite spatial analysis became formalized. One occurred at the operational level, concerned with defining relationships between artifacts in the archaeological domain. The second occurred at an inferential level, concerned with reconstructing past activities in the behavioral domain.

Operational goals. At the operational level, intrasite spatial analysis was undertaken in order to define four characteristics of artifact distributions. These are 1) the form of arrangement of artifacts of each functional type (scattered randomly over space, aggregated into clusters, or systematically aligned); 2) the spatial limits of single-type clusters, if they exist; 3) whether different artifact types are similarly or differently arranged (e.g., do their frequencies among grid cells covary), regardless of their form of arrangement; and 4) the spatial limits of multitype clusters, if the types exhibit both clustering and coarrangement (modified from Whallon, 1973).

Inferential goals. The operational goals of intrasite spatial analysis were designed to allow its inferential goals to be met. The four characteristics of artifact distributions were defined in order to allow the reconstruction of 1) the spatial limits of "activity areas," 2) the organization of artifact types into "tool kits," and thereby 3) the kinds, frequencies, and arrangement of activities that occurred within a site.

The focus of early spatial analyses on reconstructing the kinds of activities that occurred within a site and their frequencies and arrangements was a particular manifestation of a broader traditional goal of archaeology: to reconstruct past lifeways (Taylor, 1948). Activity and lifeway reconstructions as the endproduct of spatial analysis typified European studies in the 1960s and 1970s (e.g., Leroi-Gourhan & Brézillon, 1966, 1972; de Lumley, 1969a, 1969b) but were also apparent on the American side (e.g., Chang, 1967, pp. 231-232; Freeman & Butzer, 1966; see Kent, 1985 for a similar criticism of later ethnoarchaeological studies). The focus on activity reconstruction was also spurred on by the interest of New Archaeologists in documenting and analyzing phenomena at a level of inference higher than that of the event: the structure and dynamics of past *behavioral systems* (Binford, 1964; Struever, 1968, p. 287). Spatial analyses by Binford et al. (1970), Whallon (1973), Goodyear (1974), and Price (1975) clearly illustrate this concern.

Expansion of the Inferential Goals of Intrasite Spatial Analysis: Reconstruction of Formation Processes and Investigation of Behavioral-Environmental System States

Early quantitative studies of intrasite spatial organization focused on the reconstruction of only a portion of the phenomena that currently are within the potential scope of intrasite research. They also encompassed only a portion of its potential goals. An expansion of the range of intrasite spatial analysis is proposed in this section. In particular, it is suggested that *formation processes in general*, as opposed to only activities, can be the object of reconstruction efforts. It also is proposed that this broader range of processes can be used to document and analyze the structure and dynamics of *both* past *behavioral systems* and past *natural environmental systems*, as opposed to only the former. These potential aims of intrasite spatial analysis are implicit in the rationale for current ethnoarchaeological studies (e.g., Binford, 1977a, 1981a), but have not been explicitly considered or realized in archaeological spatial analyses drawing upon such studies.

To begin, it is necessary to clarify terms.

In this chapter, the term *formation process* is used to refer to both cultural and natural formation processes. Cultural formation processes are viewed, in the manner of Binford (1981, p. 200), as components of the behavioral system. They include not only specific *activities* leading to landscape modification, but also other organizational processes, such as mobility patterns or curation patterns, that comprise a behavioral system. To distinguish these other cultural formation processes from activities, per se, the term *extra-activity cultural formation processes* is used. Hopefully, this term will provide a means for resolving current ambiguity in the notion of cultural formation processes and clarify Binford's (1981a) and Schiffer's (1983, 1985) opposing viewpoints.

The broader range of processes and goals that potentially can be encompassed by an intrasite spatial analysis, and their placement within a chain of logical inferences, are shown in Figure 1. (Here, an inductive chain of inferences is shown; the deductive case would be similar.) This construct can be explained as follows. At the lowest level of abstraction are raw data in the form of artifact point locations or counts of artifacts within grid cells over the site. At a higher level are various generalizations about the data (test implications in deductive mode). These include measures of the degree of aggregation or dispersion of an artifact type, its degree of coarrangement with other types, and other kinds of patterns. These patterns can be derived from the data with visual or quantitative methods, but in either case, the search procedures should be made explicit and justified in ways to be described later (see Carr, chapter 2). Spatial patterns, in turn, can be used to infer information about *three* kinds of formation processes. This information includes 1) the occurrence, frequency of occurrence, and spatial organization of past *activities*, as evidenced by "activity areas" and "tool kits"; 2) the occurrence of *extra-activity cultural formation processes*, such as curation patterns that are definable by the polythetic organization of artifact types (see pp. 347-355); and 3) the occurrence, magnitude, and spatial organization of *natural formation and post-depositional processes*.

Correct inference of these nonobservables from spatial patterns involves the application of theoretically and empirically relevant bridging arguments—definitional assumptions (Binford, 1977b)—which allow behavioral or natural meaning to be assigned to them. Recent studies of archaeological formation processes in the fields of ethnoarchaeology, experimental archaeology, taphon-

Fig. 13.1. Inferential pathways leading to traditional and expanded goals and processes of interest in intrasite spatial analysis.

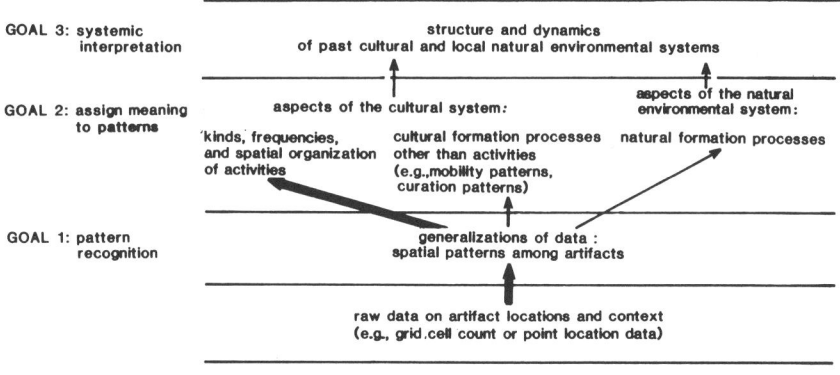

omy, and geoarchaeology, as well as formal deductive approaches to the subject matter, are useful in this regard. They document or suggest some of the kinds of arrangements of archaeological remains that different activities and formation processes can generate (Ascher, 1968; Binford, 1977a, 1977b, 1978, 1983; Schiffer, 1972, 1973, 1975a, 1975b, 1976, 1982; Schiffer & Rathje, 1973; Yellen, 1974, 1977; O'Connell, 1977, 1979; Gould, 1971, 1978; Gifford, 1978, 1981; Wood & Johnson, 1978; Butzer, 1982).

The activity areas, tool kits, activities, extra-cultural formation processes, and natural formation processes that are reconstructed for a site in turn represent or can be used to infer certain past behavioral and environmental *conditions* that are critical to formulating and testing hypotheses about the structure and dynamics of past behavioral systems (Binford, 1977) and natural environmental systems. Again, appropriate bridging principles provided by ethnoarchaeology and other fields are required. For example, the kinds, frequencies, and spatial organization of activities that occurred in a site can be used to infer its seasons of occupation (Binford, 1978), site functions (Styles, 1981), community population (Cook & Heizer, 1968; Yellen, 1977) household interaction patterns, community kinship, and social organization (Brose, 1968; Wiessner, 1982), etc. Extra-activity cultural formation processes can be used to infer community population size (Schiffer, 1972, pp. 161-162) or site seasonality (Binford, 1978a). The reconstructed processes may *directly represent* (as opposed to allow inference of) certain parameters of the behavioral system, such as pattern and degree of mobility. Natural formation processes can be used in a similar manner to reconstruct various conditions of the natural environment (Wood & Johnson, 1978).

These inferred or represented behavioral and natural environmental conditions constitute the states taken by variables comprising the behavioral-environmental system under examination. Thus, they can be used to suggest or test hypotheses pertaining to *relationships* among variables of that system, or cultural environmental systems in general. An example is the relationship between regional population densities and community organization or mobility within particular natural environmental contexts.

Therefore, extra-activity cultural formation processes and natural formation processes, as well as activities, can be integrated within intrasite spatial research. Their identification can be very useful, allowing hypotheses of anthropological interest within a behavioral-ecological-systems framework—as opposed to only a behavioral framework—to be formulated or tested. A broadening of both the processes and goals encompassed by intrasite spatial analysis beyond its traditional focus is possible, and has already been anticipated (e.g., Binford, 1983, chapter 6).

Events vs. processes. It is important to recognize, as Figure 1 shows, that using intrasite artifact distributions to estimate the states of variables that comprise a behavioral-environmental system does not require that specific behavioral *events* (activity episodes) or natural *events*, per se, be reconstructed. Inference need not proceed from spatial patterns to events to processes to system variable states, although it may. Rather, estimation of a behavioral or natural variable's state can be achieved more directly. Spatial patterns can be used to reconstruct formation processes themselves, directly, and these can serve as estimates of or can be used to infer estimates of the states of variables. That this is true can be argued both theoretically and by example.

From a theoretical standpoint, Binford (1981, p. 200) has emphasized that a cultural system is an open system, capturing and reorganizing matter and energy and relinquishing them through various cultural formation processes. Cultural formation processes are *components* of a cultural system that define its structural and dynamic properties. Those endproducts of cultural formation processes that indicate their past operation—various aspects of the organization of the archaeological record, such as intrasite artifact organization—thus *by definition* reflect the structure and dynamics of the cultural system. Similarly, natural formation processes are components of a local environmental system that define its organization properties. By definition, those effects of natural formation processes on intrasite artifact organization that indicate their past operation reflect the structure and dynamics of the natural environmental system.

Some examples of the use of intrasite distributional data to directly reconstruct cultural and natural formation processes, and the use of these as the states taken by variables within a behavioral-natural system or to infer such variable states, have briefly been alluded to, above. These can be clarified by focusing on less typically used extra-activity cultural formation processes and natural formation processes.

Among the variable states of a behavioral system that can be reconstructed in this manner are spatial and temporal pattern of regional mobility, degree of sedentism, and group size. Binford (1980, p. 9) has systematically linked the clarity of spatial structuring of use-areas within hunter-gatherer sites to the regional spatial pattern of their mobility (untethered residential, tethered residential, logistic) as determined by the grain of their natural environment (fine, patchy, coarse). For example, residential camps and extractive locations in some patchy environments, where the number of loci available for settlement and exploitation are limited, are likely to exhibit spatial patterns of artifacts that are considerably "blurred." This results from repeated reuse of the sites and spacing of activities in slightly different ways with each occupation. Ebert (1983) has extended Binford's framework so as to consider the organization of artifacts within "landscapes" (site and offsite areas as a continuum) as a function of various residential and logistic mobility options. Binford (1978) and Yellen (1974) have tied variation in the spatial configuration of hunter-gatherer camps to the season of their occupation, indicating temporal patterns of mobility. For example, Binford suggests that the more complex spatial patterning of winter camps than summer camps of Nunamiut Eskimo relates in part to the random loss of objects in the snow in winter sites, but not in summer sites. Finally, intrasite spatial patterning, as manifest in the degree to which refuse is deposited in formalized dumps as opposed to left within work areas, has been shown to be related to community population size (Schiffer, 1972, pp. 161-162) and degree of sedentism (Murray, 1980). As community population size increases, factors such as the need for unrestricted routes of access between principle work areas, sanitation, and scarcity of work space, place a premium on the discard of refuse in out-of-the-way places. Thus, a number of different variable states of a past behavioral system can be indicated by or inferred from extra-activity cultural formation processes that are directly reflected by different aspects of the spatial arrangement of artifacts within a site.

There are numerous examples of natural system variables, the states of which can be estimated through identification of natural formation processes directly from intrasite artifact distributional characteristics. These include various climatological variables; fluvial, aeolian, and other geomorphological variables; and vegetational variables. Butzer (1971, 1982) and Wood and Johnson (1978) describe these identification and estimation procedures in great detail.

Expansion of the scope of intrasite spatial analysis to include the reconstruction of extra-activity formation processes and natural formation processes in addition to activities provides several advantages.

Advantage 1. As mentioned above, it allows the researcher to investigate the structure and dynamics of both natural environmental and behavioral systems, not just the latter.

Advantage 2. It provides the archaeologist with a means for formulating or testing hypotheses about regional behavioral-environmental system organization with *intrasite* data that are *independent* of *regional* data. For example, hypotheses about mobility patterns can be tested with intrasite information on artifact arrangement as well as regional site distributional data. Thus, the archaeologist is placed in a better position for building and testing theory without circularity.

Advantage 3. Knowledge of the past occurrence of natural formation processes and extra-activity cultural formation processes within a site can give one an appreciation of the limitations of one's data. It can provide insight into those aspects of the data's structure that are relevant for making *behavioral* interpretations and those that are not (Schiffer, 1983).

This is especially true in regard to knowledge about natural formation processes. Natural formation processes do not always *reduce* patterning and increase entropy within the archaeological record (Ascher, 1968). They also can *produce* patterning which is not at all useful in reconstructing human behavior. The burrowing action of earthworms can produce novel arrangements of surficial debris (Ascher, 1968; Stein, 1983). Freeze-thaw cycles can produce "patterned ground" (surface stone aggregations in the shapes of rings, polygons, or stripes) or stone pavements. Expansion-contraction cycles in vertisols can form "linear gilgai" (Wood & Johnson, 1978). Water washing, wind, and soil creep can sort objects over space into different size, shape, and density classes (Shipman, 1981; Behrensmeyer & Hill, 1980; Gifford, 1980, 1981; Limbrey, 1975; Rick, 1976). The characteristic spatial patterns produced by these and other natural formation processes can be used to identify them within an assemblage, either visually or with the aid of quantification. At the very least, their approximate impact on the assemblage and their effect on its potential for behavioral reconstruction can then be assessed. In more favorable circumstances, their effects can be modeled and segregated from the data, leaving behind largely behaviorally significant variability to be studied (see Carr, 1982a, 1986 for appropriate quantitative techniques; also Villa, 1982).

Similarly, knowledge of the occurrence and effects of extra-activity cultural formation processes can be enlightening. For example, a researcher might come to an understanding that a site is a product of repeated, functionally similar, randomly overlaid occupations associated with a tethered mobility system, as evidenced by the ubiquitous distribution of most artifact types. This would suggest very strong limitations to intrasite spatial data for reconstructing community layout and organization.

In summary, the goals and processes encompassed by intrasite spatial analysis can be expanded to define a conceptual process involving minimally the four levels of abstraction and the three kinds of inferential pathways between levels shown in Figure 1. Whereas early studies of intrasite spatial patterning concentrated on reconstructing activities in order to document past lifeways or to monitor the organization and dynamics of past behavioral systems, current studies can be broader. They can involve the reconstruction of extra-activity cultural formation processes and natural formation processes as well as activities. And they can monitor both behavioral and natural environmental systems. This expansion of the scope of intrasite spatial analysis is advantageous in regard to the range of phenomena into which insight is afforded, the structure of archaeological reasoning, and the evaluation of data for their relevance.

It is necessary to qualify the above arguments. Although identification of formation processes through the spatial analysis of intrasite artifact patterns can be important, it should not be concluded that the proper position of such identification in the analytic process is only as the *outcome* of quantitative analysis. Some general knowledge about the formation processes that are responsible for a site is required if spatial analysis of its artifact distributions is to be relevant, accurate, and meaningful. This circumstance is addressed later (see pp. 316-328).

Evaluation of an Operational Goal of Intrasite Spatial Analysis

Current advances in understanding of the processes that generate archaeological records and their internal organization requires archaeologists to reassess not only the inferential goals of intrasite spatial analysis, but also its operational goals. Certain quantitative operations designed to search for certain kinds of spatial patterning among artifacts may or may not be concordant with the nature of artifact organization within sites. This section focuses on one operational goal: determining whether different artifact types are *arranged similarly or differently* over a site as a whole, that is, *globally*.

Whallon (1979, 1984) has stated that the search for global spatial patterns of coarrangement among artifact classes within sites is meaningless. He has implied that sitewide constructs such as tool kits, storage sets, etc., in the behavioral domain do not exist, or at least are impossible to reconstruct from archaeological remains. His new technique, unconstrained clustering, is designed explicitly to avoid the assessment of sitewide relationships between artifact types. It focuses on patterns of association or covariation of artifacts *within* clusters.

In discussing Whallon's position, I first would like to reiterate and expand on an argument that I have made previously (Carr, 1984). I then will qualify this argument and my previous conclusions.

The basis Whallon gives for his position is his correct observation of an erroneous assumption about formation processes that was implicit in early quantitative spatial analyses. Early analyses assumed that the *organization* of artifact types within the behavioral domain of past events was *transferred uniformly* into the archaeological domain, without variation over space. Thus, artifact types could be assumed to be organized in *one* manner across a site as a *whole*. Globally homogeneous structures—sets of artifact types showing spatially uniform patterns of coarrangement (e.g., covariation, association)—were sought. These structures were taken to indicate past activities and the organization of artifacts involved in them.

Current information on archaeological formation processes makes the assumption of spatially uniform transformation of artifact organization from the behavioral domain into the archaeological untenable. This position implies that *all* archaeological formation and disturbance processes responsible for a site's configuration were *spatially correlated* over the site as a whole (Carr, 1982a, 1986). In every site location where artifacts of a given type were manufactured, used, cached, or disposed of, the same processes of formation of deposits and post-depositional disturbance of them are presumed to have occurred to the same degree. For example, breakage rates, curation rates, degree of mining and recycling of artifacts, and rearrangement of artifacts by natural and agricultural disturbance processes are all assumed to have occurred in a uniform manner over the whole site. This assumption is not acceptable. Many formation and disturbance processes can occur in restricted portions of a site—different processes in different subareas.

The lack of spatially uniform transformation of artifact organization from the behavioral to the archaeological domain and the variability it introduces into spatial relationships in the archaeological domain does not necessarily imply, however, that such irrelevant variability cannot be isolated and *removed* from analysis statistically or overcome through the use of techniques *insensitive* to such forms of variation. It does not necessarily imply that global artifact organization pertaining to tool kits, storage sets, and related phenomena cannot be revealed (Carr 1982a, 1986, also below). Also, it does not necessarily imply that global organization of artifacts into such sets does not exist in the behavioral domain. These propositions remain to be demonstrated empirically.

Whallon (1984, pp. 251-258) gives some results of his analysis of the Mask site as empirical support of the proposition that global organization of artifacts into sets relevant to past behavior does not occur in most archaeological sites. He observes that at Mask, the same set of artifact types can show different patterns of covariation or association (positive, null, negative) over the site—that is, different forms of organization in different portions of it.

This datum, however, need not imply a lack of behaviorally relevant global structure. Variation over a site in patterns of local covariation or association of artifact types may indicate simply that correlation and association do not measure the strength of relationships between artifact types along scales that are pertinent to and concordant with the organization of tool kits, storage sets, etc.

The structure of any data set can be investigated from multiple angles using multiple techniques and different scales of measurement, implying different theoretical perspectives on what constitutes relevant data structure. This is a basic premise of exploratory data analysis (Tukey, 1977; Hartwig & Dearing, 1979). The lack of behaviorally relevant global organization that was found in the Mask data with correlation and association measures does not imply that relevant global organization does not exist in it relative to other techniques assuming other scales of measurement and implying other theoretical perspectives on the organizational nature for formation of archaeological records.

It can be argued that behaviorally relevant organization of artifact types into global sets reflecting tool kits, storage sets, refuse sets, etc., within sites often does occur. However, in this viewpoint, the nature of that organization is thought to vary among sites with the behavioral and environmental contexts of their formation, disturbance, and recovery. Moreover, the sets are thought in most circumstances—particularly those of hunter-gatherer sites such as Mask—to have a *polythetic* organization rather than a *monothetic* one, and to be *overlapping* rather than *nonoverlapping*. Under these conditions, correlation and simple association are not appropriate measures of the strength of relationship between types (Carr, 1984, below). They may not be capable of defining global sets of artifact types that accurately reflect tool kits, refuse sets, etc. Thus, from this perspective, Whallon's empirical results probably can be explained by an incompatibility between the analytic techniques he used to represent the Mask data set and those aspects of its structure relevant to tool kits and other sets. At minimum, no conclusions can be drawn as to whether artifacts exhibit global organization at Mask, and certainly no conclusions can be reached concerning whether they exhibit global organization within archaeological sites in general or within the behavioral domain in general.

Additionally, and more critical, the portion of the Mask data used by Whallon are insufficient to infer whether global structures such as archaeological tool kits, storage sets, etc., exist at the site. Each activity inferred by Whallon to have occurred at Mask is indicated primarily by *one* artifact type: rearmament by projectiles, wood working by wood scrap, butchering by large bones, final food processing and consumption by bone scrap, and multiple tasks by tools of unspecified function. Thus, the spatial variation in correlations between types observed at Mask do not document primarily the locally variable, *internal organization* of archaeological tool kits, refuse sets, etc. Rather, they document variable patterns of *spatial overlap* of activities and of the single artifact types representing them. They reflect relationships between artifact types in *different* artifact sets rather than *within* artifact sets. It is not possible with Whallon's selection of artifact types or in the way he has interpreted their meaning to conclude much about the degree of uniformity in the organization of archaeological "tool kits" over space.

The search for broad-scale patterning of artifact types within archaeological sites—in spite of the common difficulty of removing or overcoming a large percentage of the spatially differential effects of formation and disturbance processes—seems a reasonable goal, considering the probable existence of behavioral correlates for such patterns. Ethnography, ethnoarchaeology, and experimental approaches to the study of artifacts suggest that certain kinds of tools and debris do tend to be manufactured, used, curated, stored, and/or systematically disposed of together, constituting tool kits, manufacturing sets, cache sets, refuse sets, and other functional groups in the behavioral domain (see Carr, 1984, Table 1, for a long list of supporting references). Archaeologists need not give up the search for such sitewide entities. Rather, it is necessary to realize that 1) such sets—in both the behavioral and archaeological domains—can vary in structure from site to site, depending on environmental and behavioral contexts, and 2) the techniques used to search for them in any single case must be concordant with their particular structure and must remove or be insensitive to extraneous sources of variability. The various forms of polythetic association coefficients to be introduced later in this chapter are designed with these concerns in mind.

A qualification must be added to this argument. This pertains to the concepts of *pooled contradictory structures* and *subglobal components of artifact palimpsests*. Suppose two artifact types, *A* and *B*, sometimes are used together in the behavioral domain and deposited together on a site. At other times, *A* and *B* are systematically used in different activities and deposited separately. These two different relationships between *A* and *B* define different, contradictory artifact structures: one tool kit and depositional set in the first case, and two tool kits and depositional sets in the second case.

Contradictory artifact structures can be pooled within a site in two different ways. 1) They may be overlaid, one on top of the other, to greater or lesser degrees in various portions of the site. The result is what may be termed an artifact palimpsest (Carr, 1982a, 1986). 2) They may be segregated in different areas of a site.

If either of these conditions pertains, any attempt to define the degree of coarrangement among the two types using any coefficient of coarrangement applied to the *site as a whole* will give mixed results. The derived coefficient of coarrangement will measure the *average* strength of relationships among the two types considering *both* structures. It will also be affected by the relative frequency of the two structures. The coefficient will not accurately characterize the relationship between A and B for either structure. This is as true of polythetic measures of coarrangement as monothetic ones. It may be one unstated reason why Whallon finds meaningless the search for global patterns of coarrangement among artifact types within sites.

Nevertheless, useful results at a supralocal to sitewide scale of organization can often be obtained. To derive relevant estimates of the coarrangement of the two types at such scales, one must analyze the different structures separately and accept more than one estimate of the degree of coarrangement of the two types within the site. Separating the two structures for analysis can be achieved for either kind of pooling if the structures define clusters of different sizes and the artifacts of each type are fairly numerous. In this case, Fourier techniques can be used to resolve and isolate variation attributable to the two structures in the form of *subglobal components* of the artifact type distributions. Analysis of coarrangement then proceeds separately for the different structures using Fourier components within subglobal portions of the site (contiguously or noncontiguously distributed) rather than the original, undissected artifact type distributions. I have explained how to achieve such separation and analysis at length elsewhere (Carr 1982a, 1986).

In sum, previous discussions by Whallon (1979, 1984) and myself (1984) on searching for coarranged artifact classes within sites have been unclear in some respects. They have not taken into consideration the distinction between 1) *one* structure having a variable (e.g., polythetic) form of organization over a site (e.g., a polythetic depositional set), and 2) pooling of *multiple* different, contradictory structures. If this distinction is kept in mind and efforts are made to overcome both potential analytic problems, then it is clear that search for coarrangement among different artifact types can be meaningful, albeit sometimes subglobally rather than globally. The multiple polythetic coefficients of coarrangement that are designed in this chapter and the research designs using Fourier procedures that are specified in other papers (Carr, 1982a, 1986) are presented in this light.

Evaluation of Logical and Operational Frameworks for Intrasite Spatial Analysis

Several recent articles by Whallon (1979, 1984), Carr (1984), and Schiffer (1983) have discussed or implied stepwise approaches to intrasite spatial analysis that differ fundamentally in ways that can influence analytic results. These differences include 1) the degree to which it is necessary to *identify* the formation processes responsible for the study area (a site or portion of it) and to assess their impact on the organization of artifacts within it *prior* to quantitative analysis, rather than as the outcome of it; 2) the degree to which the search for patterning in artifact scatters should proceed *deductively*, in light of such knowledge, rather than *inductively*; and 3) the extent to which *multiple, generalized* analytic techniques should be used to search for spatial patterning in any given study area.

The differences among the researchers are of degree rather than kind. Each would probably acknowledge the usefulness of assessing formation processes before spatial analysis and through the outcome of such analyses; of using one's insight into the origin and organization of artifact distributions within a study area to design analyses congruent with them; and of viewing the data from multiple analytic perspectives that best concord with the data's structure. However, the researchers do have different tendencies, the consequences of the extremes of which should be recognized.

Also, the differences between the researchers' approaches to be discussed here pertain to the logic of analytic operation at only the lowest levels of inference within the scientific process—the manner in which recognition of patterns and assessment of their relevance should proceed. The differences do not concern their entire frameworks for scientific thought. All the researchers hold to a model of science having higher-level deductive and inductive elements.

Finally, the differences in inductive and deductive logic of concern, here, pertain to the manner of *routine application* of technique to data, rather than the logical process by which technique is *developed initially*.

An Approach Tending to Be Largely Inductive

The first approach to pattern recognition and evaluation, discussed by Whallon (1984), has the following characteristics:

1) Unnecessary preanalytic evaluation of formation processes and form of artifact organization. Identification of the formation processes responsible for a study area, evaluation of their impact on the organization of artifact distributions within it, and characterization of the relevant relational structure[1] of the data at hand—all prior to spatial analysis—are not seen as critical operations. Whallon recognizes that activities and other cultural formation processes within a single site or a portion of it can produce use-areas having extremely variable characteristics, and that consequently, spatial relationships among artifact types may change from locale to locale. He also notes that these variable products of a cultural system can be disturbed and made even more variable over space by post-depositional processes. However, to obtain an "accurate" analysis and representation of such variable data, Whallon does not advise a familiar statistical approach involving, first, determining the relevant structure of the data at hand, and then, choosing a particular technique of analysis concordant in its assumptions with the data's relevant structure. He does not suggest that the *specific formation processes* responsible for the study area and the *peculiar relevant form of organization* of artifact distributions within it be reconstructed prior to analysis and that technique be chosen accordingly. Rather, he encourages: (a) the development of new techniques that make as few as possible constraining assumptions about those characteristics of use-areas and artifact type relationships that tend to be variable *in general* over the archaeological record, and (b) the *general* application of such approaches.

Whallon's philosophy is evidenced in two ways. First, his technique of "unconstrained clustering" is designed for this purpose. It is said to assume only the constancy of proportions of artifacts within use-areas and is recommended for general use in place of more assuming methods. Second, in his example analysis using unconstrained clustering, he does not reconstruct the formation processses responsible for the site that is analyzed nor the nature of organization of its artifact distributions, even in sketch, prior to analysis and choice of technique. Rather, the nature of the formation processes peculiar to the site is one of the conclusions of the analysis (Whallon, 1984, p. 277). This may result partially from the experimental nature of the study, which focuses on technique development instead of total analytical design, though this is not made clear.

2) Use of multiple unassuming techniques. Whallon suggests (personal communication, 1983) that *multiple*, generalized pattern-searching techniques, each making equally few but different assumptions about the relevant form of organization of artifact distributions, should be applied to intrasite data. This should be done in order to determine what distortions of the data may occur in any given representation of them, as a result of the limiting assumptions of the techniques used to display them. A more complete and true representation of the data's relevant structure should then be assembled logically (rather than quantitatively) from the multiple representations. Whallon does not suggest that the researcher identify the formation processes responsible for a given study area, then postulate the particular nature of that aspect of its artifact organization that is relevant to the researcher's behavioral or environmental interests, and finally choose *one* or a few techniques most concordant with that specific relevant form of organization in order to represent the data.

3) Inductive pattern recognition. From both 1) and 2) above, it is clear that Whallon favors a more inductive approach to pattern-searching, involving multiple representations of the data from which patterns thought relevant are *generalized*. This stands in contrast to a more deductive approach. A deductive approach would involve identifying or postulating the formation processes responsible for a study area, deducing from those processes the relevant form of organization of artifacts within it, deducing from that organization the analytic technique(s) most appropriate for its analysis, and thus the *specification* of relevant artifact patterns.

In line with Whallon's more inductive approach, we find that unconstrained clustering "is hardly more than an elaborate approach to a descriptive summary or *display* of the data, or a series of such summaries and displays" (Whallon, 1984, p. 275). The precise borders of use-areas are not specified by the technique, but rather, are left for the researcher to generalize from one or more representations of the data.

The operational framework for spatial analysis that Whallon supports appears to be an expression of a more general philosophy and approach to analysis that Whallon references: *exploratory data analysis* (Tukey, 1977; Hartwig & Dearing, 1979). Exploratory data analysis (EDA) is an inductive approach to pattern recognition attributable to Tukey (1962, 1977, 1979). Unlike the statistical approach, which involves deductive testing of hypotheses and seeks to determine whether a particular expectable structure (test implication) occurs within the data set, EDA asks the question, "What *unanticipated* structures or relationships occur within the data, regardless of expectation?" (Tukey & Wilk, 1970, p. 371; Hartwig & Dearing, 1979, pp. 9-10). It is "exploratory" rather than "confirmatory": it has as its goal the searching for patterns that suggest new ideas and problem areas, leading to hypothesis formation rather than hypothesis testing (Tukey, 1979, p. 122; 1980, pp. 23-24; Hartwig & Dearing, 1979, p. 78).

Achievement of this goal of EDA is facilitated in three ways. First, analytic "flexibility" is stressed, involving the use of multiple techniques and reexpression of the data on various measurement scales (Tukey, 1980, p. 24; Hartwig & Dearing, 1979, p. 10). Multiple mathematical models are used to investigate the data from multiple perspectives rather than using data to evaluate models (Tukey & Wilk, 1970, pp. 376, 386). The various representations of the data created through the use of alternative techniques and models are then to be searched for patterning with a mind open to new ideas and skeptical of single interpretations (Tukey, 1970, p. 372; Hartwig & Dearing, 1979, p. 9). Second, graphic representation and visual display of the data is stressed (Tukey, 1980, p. 24). Finally, alternative representations of a data set are evaluated as more or less optimal based on the parsimony of the techniques that generated them and the simplicity (e.g., normality, linearity, smoothness) of the patterns that they reveal. This approach facilitates hypothesis generation (Tukey & Wilk, 1970, pp. 375-376, 378, 385). Correspondence between the assumptions of techniques and the relevant structure of data, as posited by a prior guiding hypotheses, is downplayed.

Clearly, many aspects of Whallon's approach to searching for patterning in intrasite spatial data correspond to characteristics of the more general philosophy of EDA and vice versa. We must ask whether such an approach, in its fullest expression, is generally appropriate to the analysis of intrasite spatial data.

The stress placed in EDA on viewing the data from multiple perspectives with least constraint, and the open mindedness it fosters, clearly is valuable in facilitating scientific progress and escaping the tyranny of theory and paradigm (Clarke, 1972, p. 8; Kuhn, 1970). This approach should be a part of analysis to the extent that the relevant structure of spatial data is represented in an unbiased and accurate manner.

Nevertheless, there are limits to the usefulness of a largely inductive pattern recognition approach like EDA in the context of intrasite spatial analysis, and in the analysis of complex data in general (see Carr, chapter 2). These are as follows:

Limitation 1. From a general perspective, given the alternative representations of a data set that are generated within an EDA approach yet the downplaying of a priori hypotheses in guiding analysis, it may not be clear which representation(s) of the data are truest to the relevant aspects of its structure and its manner of generation, and thus, can be accepted. Suppose that multiple representations of a data set are displayed by several methods, each making equally minimal assumptions about the data's structure. Certain strong aspects of the data's structure may be apparent from commonalities among all the representations. However, where differences between the representations occur, on what basis does one accept one expression of the data over another in filling out a characterization of the data? Tukey (1970, pp. 378, 385) suggests accepting that structure which is mathematically most simple. However, reality often is complex, and this criterion does not necessarily lead to relevance or interpretability. Whallon does not address this problem.

If one considers that the differences between the representations of a data set may arise from differences in the degrees to which the several techniques defining them make assumptions that are congruent with the relevant structure of the data, and that some representations may be more accurate displays of the data's relevant structure than are others, then two things become apparent. (a) Appropriate choice among alternatives is critical. (b) One cannot make an appropriate choice between alternatives without reference to knowledge about the relative degree to which the assumptions made by the techniques probably concord with the data's relevant structure. This, in turn, requires some minimal, *general knowledge*, in the form of guiding hypotheses, about the actual or probable nature of the relevant structure of the data in hand. By general knowledge I mean such things as whether phenomena of interest manifest themselves as nonoverlapping or overlapping relationships among observations, or again, whether they manifest themselves in the distributions of or relationships between ratio, interval, ordinal, nominal, or polythetic-scale measures. Such information stands in contrast to *specific knowledge* about particular relationships among particular observations and variables. General knowledge can be obtained inductively or deductively from information on the context of the data, its mode of generation, and/or theoretical expectation (see pp. 324-325; also Carr, chapter 2). Thus, a strictly inductive approach to pattern recognition, divorced from general knowledge in the form of guiding hypotheses about relevant structure, may prove impossible.

This general limitation to inductive pattern recognition seems characteristic of its specific application to intrasite spatial analysis. The use of this operational framework in intrasite spatial analysis, as Whallon tends to favor (though not his technique of unconstrained clustering) does not seem effective. In particular, relevant relationships between artifact types within sites may be of many different kinds (e.g., monothetic vs. polythetic, overlapping vs. nonoverlapping, covariational vs. associational, etc.; see below), depending on the formation processes responsible for them. In order to choose the one or few representation(s) of an intrasite data set that are most likely true to the relevant aspects of its structure and to justify that choice explicitly, it is necessary that one have, prior to analysis, general knowledge—guiding hypotheses—about (a) the nature of the formation processes responsible for that particular study area, (b) the nature of the relevant organization of artifacts within it, and thus (c) the relative degrees of concordance likely between relevant aspects of the data and the several techniques used to generate representations of it. How such insight can be gained is discussed below (see pp. 324-328).

Limitation 2. This limitation is closely related to the first. Without reference to some prior knowledge about the relevant structure of the data in hand, an inductive framework like EDA cannot use the *strongest criterion* to judge the appropriateness of alternative techniques in representing a data set: the relative degree of concordance of the techniques to the data's relevant structure. Less powerful criteria of evaluation must be used. These amount to three. Tukey suggests that the most appropriate methods are those that are most *simple* in operation or that produce results having the most *simple* mathematical structure (Tukey, 1970, pp. 378, 385). Whallon, in his similar framework, suggests the appropriateness of those techniques that make the *fewest* assumptions about the nature of the data's relevant structure.

None of these criteria for evaluating alternative techniques, alone or together, are sufficient to ensure the accuracy of analytic results.

(a) Simplicity of the algorithm says nothing about whether the algorithm violates the data's relevant structure.

(b) Simplicity of results is not a sound basis for judgement, given the complex patterning commonly found in archaeological records. Polythetic, overlapping depositional set organization, palimpsest structure to artifact distributions, and hierarchical organization of spatial relations among artifact types and use-areas are examples of such complexity (Carr, 1984). These result from equally complex formation processes, often spatially disuniform and overlaid.

(c) Methods making the *fewest* assumptions about the structure of a data set need not be the least *constraining*, if those particular assumptions violate the specific relevant structure of the data under study while assumptions of the alternative techniques do not. Under some circumstances, even a very assuming technique may be most appropriate. For example, use of correlation and factor analysis to define archaeological tool kits implies many restrictive assumptions about the nature of organization of artifact types within tool kits in the behavioral domain, artifact organization within corresponding depositional sets in the archaeological domain, and the formation processes responsible for the transformation of organization between the two domains. These assumptions include the monothetic, nonoverlapping organization of tool kits in both the behavioral and archaeological domains; an expedient technology; extended use of activity areas; minimal post-depositional disturbance; etc. (see Carr, 1984 for a further discussion). Tool types are assessed as coarranged or not, and members of the same depositional set or not, compared to very restrictive standards of organization. Nevertheless, this methodology is appropriate when such conditions are approximately the case, as in Schiffer's simulation (1975) and application (1976) of it; and it is *more* appropriate under these circumstances than other techniques would be which assess the degree of coarrangement of types against less restrictive standards of organization (e.g., association analysis). In this case, less assuming techniques could judge some types to be coarranged (members of the same depositional set) when they actually are not. Thus, *a technique cannot be judged as more or less appropriate on its own basis, according to the number and restrictiveness of the assumptions it makes. It can be judged for its appropriateness, in the strictest sense, only in the degree to which its assumptions concord with the relevant structure of the particular data to which it is to be applied.*

Limitation 3. A final limitation to an inductive pattern-searching framework that does not use prior information and hypotheses about the nature of the data to be analyzed is that only the data *as given*, or as reexpressed in *standard* ways, can be considered and manipulated. Likewise, patterns found within the data must be taken at face value. The possibility of *systematic* bias or distortion of the data and its patterns in certain uniform directions, or of the data representing a meaningless though patterned *composite* of multiple, unique patterns produced by diverse processes (i.e., a palimpsest; Carr, 1982) cannot be evaluated.

This general limitation of an inductive pattern recognition framework is especially true when the framework is applied to the study of intrasite patterning and a priori knowledge about formation processes is not used. An archaeological record is the product of multiple cultural formation processes. The effects of these are often spatially *overlaid* but not necessarily spatially *correlated*, resulting in a complex arrangement of artifacts (a palimpsest) that is not meaningful as a whole, as given. Also, the record can be distorted systematically in some manner by post-depositional disturbance processes (e.g., down-hill creep and elongation of artifact clusters). Without some prior knowledge and assessment of the nature of the formation processes responsible for the specific artifact arrangement under study, it is not possible to evaluate the degree to which the data represent a complex palimpsest or are systematically biased; nor is it possible to dissect the palimpsest into meaningful components for separate study or to correct for such bias, if this is the case. A strictly inductive pattern-searching approach to intrasite spatial analysis can yield various representations of patterns only *as expressed* within the data, and these patterns need not be relevant to understanding past behaviors or environmental conditions.

An Approach Tending to Be Largely Deductive

The second approach to pattern recognition and evaluation in intrasite spatial analysis is one implied by Carr (1984). It has the following characteristics:

1) Primarily deductive pattern recognition. The approach stresses the deductive selection of the analytic technique used to reveal patterning. A single model of archaeological organization, positing certain characteristics of depositional areas and depositional sets (e.g., hierarchically arranged depositional areas, areas of variable shape, globally polythetic and overlapping depositional sets) is presented as the most common form of archaeological organization relevant to behavioral reconstruction. This model is based on current understanding of site formation processes that has been derived from ethnoarchaeological and experimental archaeological studies. Various spatial analytic techniques available for archaeological application are then characterized, by deduction, as more or less constraining in general in their assumptions, compared to the one form of relevant organization.

It is then recommended that in most cases, the one or very few techniques having assumptions concordant with the modeled form of organization be applied to the study area at hand. Although Carr recognizes that it is preferable to choose analytic technique in relation to general knowledge about the actual or probable organization of the particular study area so as to maximize analytic concordance, he also argues that in many cases, this specific insight is not available. Thus, the researcher often must choose technique primarily deductively, using understanding of the organizational nature of archaeological records in general. The results that are derived in these instances are to be taken as the most behaviorally relevant representation of artifact distributional patterning that is possible for the area under current knowledge limitations.

2) Downplayed preanalytic evaluation of formation processes and form of artifact organization. As a consequence of the stress placed on deduction, the identification of formation processes responsible for any *particular* study area, evaluation of their impact on the organization of artifact distributions within it, and characterization of the relevant structure of the data at hand, are not emphasized. Techniques are assessed for the appropriateness of their assumptions primarily in relation to a general model of relevant organization rather than site-specific relevant organization.

3) Use of a few concordant techniques. It is suggested that intrasite analysis proceed with one or a very few specific techniques—those having assumptions most concordant with the study area's relevant organization, as expected from the general model of organization, or sometimes as known empirically. A unique solution which represents the data most accurately is sought. It is not recommended that the data be searched inductively with multiple techniques for multiple configurations.

Limitation. The more deductive approach to pattern recognition taken by Carr (1984) is just as tenuous as the inductive one discussed previously. Its primary drawback is that a technique's appropriateness is most often assessed relative to a *general model* of relevant archaeological organization, rather than the relevant organization of the *specific data* to be analyzed. To the extent that the data vary in structure from that proposed in the general model, a technique can be more appropriate or less appropriate for application to the data than its general assessment implies. Once again, a technique can be judged for the appropriateness of its assumptions, in the strictest sense, only in the degree to which its assumptions concord with the relevant structure of the particular data to which it is to be applied. Comparison of the assumptions of a technique to a general model of data structure—even if the model embodies the most commonly found kind of structure—will not do.

In summary, although the logical and operational frameworks used by Whallon and Carr differ in whether pattern recognition proceeds inductively or deductively, and in the degree to which multiple generalized techniques are employed, both frameworks share a critical flaw. They do not encourage the researcher to specify, prior to analysis, the nature of relevant organization of the particular archaeological record under investigation, and to choose analytic technique in relation to it. Although both frameworks express a concern for the tailoring of technique to relevant data structure, this tailoring is done at a *general level* that does not allow fine tuning of the relationship for specific data sets. Whallon proposes a *general technique* thought applicable to a diversity of intrasite data structures; Carr proposes a *general data structure* common to archaeological sites and suggests methods congruent with that structure.

In rightly trying to systematize methodology for the analysis of intrasite artifact distributions, both researchers have unfortunately downplayed the importance of evaluating the relationship between technique and data at the case-specific level. This is manifested in the lack of stress that either researcher places on identifying, prior to analysis, the formation processes responsible for the specific nature of the relevant organization of a study area.

A Pattern-Searching Framework Combining Inductive and Deductive Approaches: The Use of Entry Models and Parallel Data Sets

To overcome the problems associated with each of the two analytic frameworks previously discussed, and particularly to encourage evaluation of the relationship between technique and data at the case-specific level, an alternative framework can be used. This pattern recognition approach combines inductive and deductive relationships. It also emphasizes the importance of identifying the formation processes responsible for a study area's structure, and the specification of the general nature of that structure prior to analysis. The approach encompasses and expands upon a position on intrasite analysis taken by Schiffer (1983), and involves the use of entry models and parallel data sets, as discussed in chapter 2 by Carr. The steps of such a framework are summarized in Figure 2 and discussed as follows:

1) The formation processes—cultural and natural—responsible for a study area should be identified and assessed for their effects as much as possible. Identification of formation processes as a first step in intrasite analysis is Schiffer's primary contention. This can be done in an inductive manner using at least two approaches *not* involving the techniques and data to be used ultimately in defining depositional areas and depositional sets. (To not do so would be to invite circular reasoning into analysis). (a) A variety of *aspatial* measurements that are collected from multiple locales and deposits within a

Fig. 13.2. A pattern recognition framework that 1) combines inductive and deductive elements, 2) stresses "up front" identification of formation processes, and 3) uses the entry model approach to choosing an appropriate analytic technique. It is assumed in this schema that behavioral rather than natural formation processes are of interest.

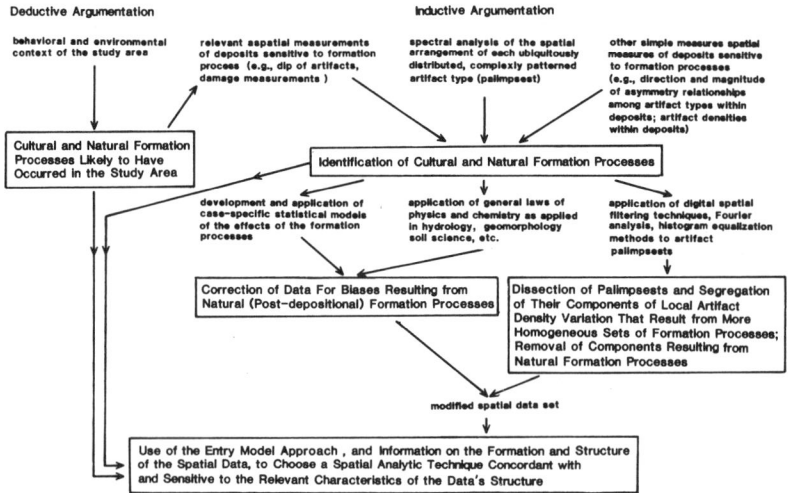

study area expressly for the purpose of identifying formation processes can be evoked. Such data might include frequency distributions of the size, specific density, orientation, or dip of artifacts or natural inclusions within various locales of the area; information on the use-lives, damage, and conjoinability of artifacts and their fragments within different deposits; and a large variety of sedimentological, geochemical, and ecological measures. Data of these kinds would constitute a simple, *parallel data set*, giving the researcher insight into relevant and irrelevant aspects of the structure of the *complex* artifact distribution data set of interest (to use the terminology presented in chapter 2). Schiffer (1983) does a very thorough job of inventorying and referencing discussions on these kinds of data and suggests their potential usefulness in reconstructing formation processes. (b) Distributions of artifact types appearing to be complex palimpsests can be investigated inductively for the possible occurrence of more meaningful components of local artifact density variation within them, using the technique of spectral analysis (Jenkins & Watt, 1968; Brillinger, 1975, chapter 5; Ontes & Enochson 1978, chapter 8). This method allows the predominant spatial scales and orientations of clusters of artifacts within such a distribution to be determined in spite of possibly complex patterns of overlap and post-depositional smearing of them. It can also be used to assess the spatial scale and orientation of smearing processes. Such information on the several scales and orientations of operation of cultural formation processes is invaluable in dissecting artifact palimpsests into more meaningful components, each due to a more homogeneous set of formation processes. Carr (1982a, 1986) summarizes the procedures by which this archaeological application can be made.

2) Using the knowledge gained on the nature and effects of specific formation processes on the structure of the artifact distributional data on hand, each artifact type distribution should be corrected as much as possible for post-depositional distortions (Schiffer, 1983). Where necessary, the distribution should be dissected into components, each representing a more homogeneous set of cultural or natural formation processes. If cultural formation processes are of interest, the components that are attributable to them can be analyzed separately in later steps of spatial analysis, free of interfering effects from each other and also from natural sources of distortion. If natural formation processes are of interest, their components can likewise be segregated and focused upon.

For the sake of explanation, let us consider isolating and analyzing behaviorally relevant aspects of the artifact distributional data. As in step 1, two means for achieving these ends are possible. (a) Schiffer (1983, pp. 677, 694) holds that because natural formation processes exhibit regularities, it is possible to build statistical or quantitative models of their effects on the particular deposits at hand. The models may be used to correct archaeological measurements of the deposits for biases resulting from the processes. A clear example of this approach is Rowlett and Robbin's (1982) quantitative method for reconstructing the original frequencies of artifacts deposited in strata prior to their post-depositional migration. Established physical and chemical laws also can be used to correct for biases. Application of the laws of movement of sedimentary particles within flowing water to water-rearranged artifact distributions is an example (Shackley, 1978; Gifford, 1980, 1981). (b) The methods of digital spatial filtering and Fourier analysis (Davis, 1973; Holloway, 1958; Robinson, 1970; Zurflueh, 1967; Gonzalez & Winz, 1977; Castleman, 1979) can be used to dissect each complex artifact distribution into component distributions of more homogeneous cause, allowing the isolation of behaviorally significant artifact density variations. This approach assumes that different kinds of activities, other cultural formation processes, and natural ones operate over areas of different spatial dimensions. Mathematical filters are designed to extract artifact density variations of particular scales or "frequencies" thought significant, based on previous spectral analysis of the data. The technique called histogram equalization (Gonzalez & Winz, 1977) can be used favorably to enhance the separation process. Carr (1982a, 1986). details a number of alternative concatenations of procedures for breaking apart an artifact palimpsest. The appropriate analytic design depends on the degree of density contrast between artifact clusters of the same or different sizes, the crispness of their borders, and whether high frequency noise due to unsystematic artifact recovery, unsystematic curation or recycling, or other causes is present in the data.

3) The spatial data set, which has been reduced to a group of behaviorally relevant component artifact density distributions and/or corrected for post-depositional disturbances, should be subsumed under one or a few alternative a priori models—*entry models*—that most likely represent the data's general relevant structure, that reflect its manner of formation, and that link it to an appropriate technique of analysis. Each entry model used for this purpose should involve three elements. (a) First is *a general organizational model of fundamental mathematical characteristics of artifact patterning*. Such characteristics might be whether artifact types occurring in the same depositional sets exhibit spatial asymmetry relations (Pielou, 1964); whether the direction of asymmetry is globally constant or reverses locally; whether the sets are likely monothetic or polythetic, overlapping or nonoverlapping; whether artifact clusters spatially overlap or not; etc. (b) The second element of an entry model is a list of the *formation processes* that might lead to the characteristics in the organizational model. (c) Finally, an entry model should specify the range of mathematical techniques having assumptions that are concordant with the organizational model's structure. By subsuming the spatial data set under one or a limited number of such entry models, linkage of the data (through the listed formation processes and the organizational model) to appropriate technique(s) for spatial analysis, and choice of such technique(s), is facilitated. Also, from a previous perspective (p. 319), the appropriate analytic technique(s) are specified using "general knowledge" of the relevant structure of the particular data in hand.

The subsumption of a data set under one or more entry models can be achieved by matching the formation processes responsible for the study area with those specified in the models. The formation processes which are enumerated as "responsible for the study area" and used for this purpose can be ones that have been documented *inductively* with information collected in Step 1, above. They also can be a set of hypothesized formation processes that are thought *likely* to have occurred in the study area and that have been suggested *deductively*. Deductive specification of such processes involves observing the general behavioral and environmental contexts of the site (e.g., approximate degree of regional mobility of the site occupants; the order-magnitude of site population; distance of the site from lithic resources as determinants of curation rates; geomorphic depositional setting), and then suggesting on the basis of theory or regional empirical generalizations whether particular formation processes operated on it (Schiffer, 1983, p. 692).

4) On the basis of the subsumption of the particular spatial data set under one or more general entry models (i.e., general knowledge of the data's relevant structure), one or more techniques most likely appropriate for analysis should be chosen (deduction). Where it is unclear which of several organizational models is most representative of the data and several techniques are used to analyze the data, a diversity of results may be generated. The alternative behaviors or other formation processes suggested by the alternative relationships in these solutions can be considered alternative hypotheses. They should be tested with independent information not used in associating the spatial data with the organizational models or techniques. Examples of such information would be use-wear data and conjoinable-pieces data, giving insight into the life histories, joint usage, and depositional patterns of artifact types (Van Noten et al., 1978; Cahen & Keeley, 1980; Villa, 1982).

Advantages of the entry-model approach. Using this pattern recognition framework, which combines both inductive and deductive elements, frees the researcher from the drawbacks of a strictly inductive or deductive search framework that were discussed preivously. Steps 1 and 2, involving correcting and dissecting the spatial data, ensure that the spatial data to be analyzed are both behaviorally significant and homogeneous in cause, as opposed to being distorted by post-depositional processes or a meaningless composite of patterning. In other words, the steps ensure that the data brought forward for analysis have a relevant relational and subset structure (see Note 1). Steps 3 and 4, concerned with positing those structural characteristics of the modified data that should or should not be assumed by the technique(s) to be used in analyzing the data, ensure that the method(s) chosen for analysis are those most concordant with the *specific* data in hand rather than those making the *least assumptions* or those *most commonly appropriate*, whether concordant or not with the specific case. All of the objectives of these steps must be realized if spatial data are to be represented in a meaningful way. Finally, by placing spatial analysis in the context of an understanding of the formation processes responsible for the data, it is possible to test alternative results for the likelihood of their accuracy in characterizing the data by evaluating whether the formation processes did, in fact, occur. This is not possible in the inductive approach described previously.

The keystone to this framework for pattern recognition is the premise long held by Schiffer (1972) and realized in a less systematic way by many archaeologists. This is that the *first order of business* of an archaeologist must be identification of the processes that generated the deposits to be studied, assessment of their relevance to the problem of interest, and correction for their inadequacies when possible. As he (1983, p. 697) has so strongly stated:

> The importance of identifying formation processes before behavioral or environmental inferences are offered can not be overemphasized. In far too many cases, the evidence used by an archaeologist owes many of its properties, not to the phenomena of interest, but to (other, irrelevant) formation processes. . . . If the latter are identified 'up-front', using the most sensitive lines of evidence, then the investigator will be able to establish which deposits are comparable and choose the most appropriate analytic strategies. On such a foundation are built credible inferences.

MODELS OF ORGANIZATION OF DEPOSITIONAL SETS AND ACTIVITY SETS

Having set forth a philosophy on how intrasite spatial analysis should proceed, a major task remains in developing alternative mathematical models of archaeological organization. These are essential components of the desired entry models that will facilitate the linkage of data having given structures and origins to techniques appropriate for their analysis. In this section, a first step is made in this direction. The organizational models to be discussed explore only two fundamental dimensions of artifact spatial organization, both concerned with only the *coarrangement* of artifact types. The models are useful in linking data to only those techniques that define sets of coarranged types. No attempt is made to model the alternative characteristics of use-areas and the conditions under which various methods are appropriate for delimiting them. A start in this direction, however, is provided in the first and last papers (Carr, 1984, 1986) of the series of which this one is a part

Basic Terminology

The models to be developed are concerned with linking fundamental organizational characteristics of archaeological deposits to formation processes and antecedent organization. Consequently, it is necessary to distinguish structures in the archaeological present from those from which they were derived in the behavioral past when referring to relationships among artifact types. Current terminology in archaeological literature does not permit this distinction, however. The terms "activity set" and "tool kit" are used to refer to structures in both domains: on the one hand, to those artifact types that were repeatedly used or produced together by the occupants of a site during the behavioral past; and on the other hand, to those artifact types that repeatedly occur together in the archaeological record when it is excavated.

To avoid ambiguities, these two different phenomena will be given separate terms here. The set of tool types that were used repeatedly in the past to perform a particular task and the debris which resulted from that task are called an *activity set*. In contrast, the tool and debris types that repeatedly are found together in the archaeological record today are termed, in the broadest sense (see below), *depositional sets*. Activity sets may be said to belong to a *behavioral domain* whereas depositional sets belong to an *archaeological domain*.

Depositional sets may be more diverse than activity sets in the processes responsible for their structure and content, and thus are more variable in meaning. In the behavioral domain, the tools and debris that are associated are those actually produced and/or used together. In the archaeological domain, the tools and debris that are found together could represent a number of behavioral phenomena. They might represent primary refuse bearing all the tools and debris produced and used together in one kind of task by the previous occupants of the site. Or they might include only a portion of those artifacts, if some were saved for use in other activities at a later time. An association of artifacts also could represent a cache—a special form of primary refuse containing items stored together for later use together in one or a diversity of tasks. Another possible kind of aggregation is tools and debris from many activities thrown away together in a formalized dumping location. Even more diverse, an aggregation of artifacts might not reflect past human behavioral processes at all, but rather, post-depositional processes of natural origin or contemporary human origin, such as fluvial transport or contemporary farming.

To refer in a precise way to the multiple kinds of depositional sets with different meanings, at the same time distinguishing them from activity sets, a hierarchy of terms can be used. At the most general level, the term *depositional set* can be used to describe associations of artifact types, without specifying the processes by which the associations were generated. Behavioral, geological, biological, or agricultural phenomena might be responsible for them. If natural or agricultural disturbances do not appear to have generated the associations and past behavioral processes appear responsible, the more specific term *anthropic depositional set* can be used for the associations. This implies that the associated types were repeatedly manufactured, used, stored, or disposed of together, but not specifying which of these. Finally, at the most specific level of designation, repeatedly associating artifact types might be *archaeological manufacturing sets, archaeological butchering sets, archaeological wood working sets, archaeological storage sets, archaeological refuse sets,* etc.

Mathematical Concepts and Dimensions of Organization

It is possible to view the structure of activity sets and depositional sets, and the formation and disturbance processes linking them, in mathematical, set-theoretic terms. A depositional set can be envisioned as a mathematical set, the organization of which is the end-product of structural transformations (archaeological formation and disturbance processes) operating on a previously structured set (activity sets organized by human behavior). In set theoretic terms, activity sets in the behavioral *domain* are *mapped* into depositional sets in an archaeological domain (or more precisely, *range*) through the operation of various *mapping relations* (Ammerman & Feldman, 1974).

Such an analogy of archaeological structures and processes to mathematical ones is useful. Through it, two fundamental dimensions of organization of artifacts within both the archaeological and behavioral domains are revealed. Importantly, these dimensions can be used not only to characterize the organization of particular configurations of artifact types in specific behavioral contexts or archaeological deposits, but also to determine the appropriateness of applying various spatial techniques to reveal such organization. Moreover, the effects of various formation and disturbance processes on artifact organization can be expressed vividly and succinctly in terms of the two dimensions. In brief, the analogy provides a productive mechanism for developing entry models of archaeological organization capable of linking specific data structures, formation processes, and techniques, as desired.

The two dimensions of organization identified are 1) a *nonoverlapping-overlapping organizational continuum* and 2) a *monothetic-polythetic organizational continuum.* These may be explained by reference to some basic concepts of set theory.

In set theory, an organization of entities can be described by using four basic concepts: 1) a *set*—a group of entities, 2) *members* or *elements of a set*—the entities that are grouped together, 3) *attributes*—the character states that the entities possess, and 4) the *list of attributes* that the entities in a set must share in part or in full to belong to it. To apply these concepts to the behavioral and archaeological domains for the purposes of describing the organization of activity sets and depositional sets and the organizational transformations linking them, untraditional referents are required. It is necessary to focus on sets of *events* and sets of *deposits* generated by them, rather than sets of artifact types (activity sets, depositional sets, tool kits). Suppose a group of past events at a site can be classified into several kinds according to the functional types of artifacts they involved. The several *events* (entities) that are of one kind comprise a *set*: they always or often entailed certain common artifact types (attributes). The several *artifact types* that were used in common comprise a *list of attributes* defining the set, or what has been termed above, an "activity set." Similarly, suppose that the archaeological *deposits* within a site can be classified into several kinds according to the functional types of artifacts they contain. The several deposits (entities) that are of one kind comprise a *set*; they always or often contain certain artifact types (attributes). The several *artifact types* held in common or tending to be held in common by the deposits comprise a *list of attributes*, or what has been termed above a "depositional set."

It is unfortunate that the term, activity set, occurs in archaeological literature, because in set-theoretic terms and within the framework presented here, it is a *list of attributes* required for membership in a set (of events) rather than a set, itself. Similarly, a depositional set is not a mathematical set, but rather a list of attributes required for membership in a set (of deposits). Since the term, activity set, is cemented in archaeological literature and depositional sets are analogous to them, I will continue to use these archaeological terms along with the mathematical.

The organization of sets, and by extension, the organization of lists of attributes that define their members, can be characterized as overlapping or nonoverlapping in nature, and monothetic or polythetic in nature. Although these concepts are introduced most easily as categorical descriptions of organization, it will be shown that they can be extended to refer to continuous dimensions of organization—a framework more useful for our purposes.

Nonoverlapping vs. overlapping sets. Different sets are said to be overlapping when their members share some of the character states required of them (partially or completely) for admittance into their respective sets. Different sets are said to be nonoverlapping when the members do not have in common any of the character states required of them for admittance to their sets (Jardine & Sibson, 1968; Sneath & Sokal, 1973, pp. 207-208). In the behavioral domain, two different functional categories of events—different sets of events—which are defined by the artifact types used in them, would be considered overlapping sets if some of the artifact types defining the sets were shared by them. The sets of events would be nonoverlapping if none of the artifact types defining them were shared by them. In the archaeological domain, two different functional classes of archaeological deposits—two different sets of deposits—would be considered overlapping if some of the artifact types defining the sets were the same. The different sets of deposits would be non-overlapping if none of the artifact types defining them were the same (Table 1).

Similarly, by extension, different lists of attributes required partially or completely of the members of different sets can be termed overlapping if some of the attributes in the lists are the same. They can be termed nonoverlapping if none of the attributes in the lists are the same. Two activity "sets" (two different lists of artifact types that always or often were entailed in the events falling in two different sets) would be considered overlapping if some of the artifact types comprising each activity set were the same. Two depositional "sets" (two different lists of artifact types that always or often are found among members of two different sets of deposits) would be considered overlapping if some of the

Table 13.1

Examples of Monothetic, Polythetic, Overlapping, and Non-Overlapping Sets of Archaeological Deposits

A Monothetic Set of Archaeological Deposits

Set 1. Member 1: deposit 1 with artifact types (attributes) A, B, C, D
Member 2: deposit 2 with artifact types (attributes) A, B, C, D
Member 3: deposit 3 with artifact types (attributes) A, B, C, D
Member 4: deposit 4 with artifact types (attributes) A, B, C, D

Two Monothetic Sets of Archaeological Deposits that are Non-overlapping

Set 1. Member 1: deposit 1 with artifact types (attributes) A, B, C, D
Member 2: deposit 2 with artifact types (attributes) A, B, C, D
Member 3: deposit 3 with artifact types (attributes) A, B, C, D
Member 4: deposit 4 with artifact types (attributes) A, B, C, D

Set 2. Member 1: deposit 5 with artifact types (attributes) E, F, G
Member 2: deposit 6 with artifact types (attributes) E, F, G
Member 3: deposit 7 with artifact types (attributes) E, F, G

No artifact type (attribute) is shared by the members of both Set 1 and Set 2, making them non-overlapping in nature.

Two Monothetic Sets of Archaeological Deposits That are Overlapping

Set 1. Member 1: deposit 1 with artifact types (attributes) A, B, C, D
Member 2: deposit 2 with artifact types (attributes) A, B, C, D
Member 3: deposit 3 with artifact types (attributes) A, B, C, D
Member 4: deposit 4 with artifact types (attributes) A, B, C, D

Set 2. Member 1: deposit 5 with artifact types (attributes) D, E, F
Member 2: deposit 6 with artifact types (attributes) D, E, F
Member 3: deposit 7 with artifact types (attributes) D, E, F

Artifact type D is shared as an attribute of the members of both Set 1 and Set 1, making them overlapping in nature.

A Polythetic Set of Archaeological Deposits

Set 1. Member 1: deposit 1 with artifact types (attributes) A, B, C, D
Member 2: deposit 2 with artifact types (attributes) A, B, C
Member 3: deposit 3 with artifact types (attributes)   B, C, D
Member 4: deposit 4 with artifact types (attribute) A
Member 5: deposit 5 with artifact types (attributes) A,   C, D

Two Polythetic Sets of Archaeological Deposits That Are Overlapping

Set 1. Member 1: deposit 1 with artifact types (attributes) A, B, C, D
Member 2: deposit 2 with artifact types (attributes) A, B, C
Member 3: deposit 3 with artifact types (attributes)   B, C, D
Member 4: deposit 4 with artifact types (attribute) A
Member 5: deposit 5 with artifact types (attributes) A,   C, D

Set 2. Member 1: deposit 6 with artifact types (attributes) D, E, F
Member 2: deposit 7 with artifact types (attributes)   E, F
Member 3: deposit 8 with artifact types (attributes) D, E
Member 4: deposit 9 with artifact types (attributes) D,   F

artifact types comprising each depositional set were the same. The depositional sets would be considered nonoverlapping if none of the artifact types comprising each depositional set were the same (Table 1).

Monothetic vs. polythetic sets. The distinction between overlapping and nonoverlapping sets and attribute lists refers to the *external* organization of sets. The distinction between monothetic and polythetic sets, and between monothetic and polythetic attribute lists, refers to the *internal* organization of sets. In a monothetic set, the elements of the set all share the same character states; all character states are essential to group membership. In a polythetic set, the elements share a large number of character states, but no single state is essential to group membership (Sneath & Sokal, 1973, p. 21; Clarke 1968, p. 37). In the behavioral domain, a functional set of events defined by the artifact types used in them would be monothetic if all the events used the same artifact types. The set of events would be polythetic if the events used a similar but not identical array of artifact types, and no one artifact type was essential to the occurrence of the events. In the archaeological domain, a set of functionally similar deposits would be monothetic if each deposit encompassed the same artifact types. The set of deposits would be polythetic if they shared many artifact types in common but no single artifact type were essential to the deposits' character.

By extension, if the attributes possessed by the members of a set as a whole are also possessed by *each* member, the list of attributes can be said to be monothetic. or *monothetically distributed* among members of the set. If *most* of the attributes possessed by the members of a set are shared in common by them, but no one attribute is required for membership in the set, then the list of attributes can be said to be polythetic, or *polythetically distributed* among members of the set. An activity "set" (list of artifact types characterizing a set of events) would be monothetically distributed among the events if all the artifact types in the activity set were used in each of the events. An activity set would be polythetically distributed among the events if the events involved in common most of the artifact types in the activity set, but no one artifact type were used in all the events. A depositional "set" (list of artifact types characterizing a set of deposits) would be monothetically distributed among the set of deposits if all the artifact types in the depositional set were contained in each of the deposits. A depositional set would be polythetically distributed among a set of deposits if the deposits held in common most of the artifact types in the depositional set, but no one artifact type were required of a deposit to be a member of the set of deposits (Table 1).

Continuous scale analogs. Nonoverlapping vs. overlapping and monothetic vs. polythetic characterizations of the organization of sets and attribute lists can be redefined on continuous scales. One can speak of sets and attribute lists that are more or less overlapping, or more or less polythetic/polythetically distributed. Two sets, and their defining attribute lists, become *more overlapping* as the number of attributes shared by the sets, compared to the total number of attributes involved, increases. Thus, the degree of overlap between two sets, A and B, can be expressed as

$$O_{ab} = \frac{C_{ab}}{C_a + C_{ab} + C_b} \times 100\% \qquad (1)$$

where O_{ab} is the percent overlap of the sets; C_{ab} is the number of attributes shared by sets A and B; and C_a and C_b are the number of attributes uniquely defining sets A and B, respectively.

A single set becomes *more polythetic* and its defining list of attributes becomes more *polythetically distributed* as smaller percentages of its attributes become shared by higher percentages of its members, on the average. Thus, the degree of polytheticness of a set can be expressed by a frequency distribution: each class of the distribution represents a range of percentages of attributes and the value of each class is the percentage of all possible pairs of members sharing given percentages of attributes (Fig. 3). It is possible to summarize the degree of polytheticness of a set in a single statistic using the mean or median of the distribution (see p. 345 & Table 3).

Building the Models

The defined monothetic-polythetic and nonoverlapping-overlapping dimensions can serve as a framework for developing alternative models of organization of artifact types. Such models might pertain to the distribution of artifact types among and within sets of behavioral events in the behavioral domain, or to their distribution and spatial arrangement among and within sets of archaeological deposits in the archaeological domain.

First Approximation of the Models, Using Variation along the Monothetic-Polythetic Dimension, Alone

Consider variation in the internal organization of sets along the monothetic-polythetic dimension, alone. Six models of organization can logically be defined along this dimension (although some may not occur in reality). These are shown in Figure 4.

The six models fall into two categories along the monothetic-polythetic dimension. Models 1 through 4 each illustrate a monothetic set of groups of artifacts, each group always possessing artifact types X and O. Models 5 and 6, by contrast, each illustrate a polythetic set of groups of artifacts; not all groups have both types of artifacts.

It is obvious, however, that there is more diversity among the models in their forms of organization than is indicated by the simple dichotomy of monothetic vs. polythetic structure. Nor is this diversity one of degree of polytheticness. To describe this variability, more basic mathematical concepts, defining a dimen-

Set: Member 1 has attributes A B C D
     Member 2 has attributes A B C
     Member 3 has attributes   B C D
     Member 4 has attribute   A
     Member 5 has attributes A   C

Data for Constructing Frequency Distribution

Pairs of members	Number of attributes shared
1 - 2	3
1 - 3	3
1 - 4	1
1 - 5	1
2 - 3	2
2 - 4	1
2 - 5	1
3 - 4	0
3 - 5	1
4 - 5	1

Number of members, n, = 5
Total number of pairs of members = $\frac{n!}{2[n-2]!}$ = 10

1 pair of members share no attributes (0% of the attributes) with other members
6 pairs of members share only 1 attribute (25% of the attributes) with other members
1 pair of members share only 2 attributes (50% of the attributes) with other members
2 pairs of members share 3 attributes (75% of the attributes) with other members
0 pair of members share 4 attributes (100% of the attributes) with other members

Degree of Polytheticness of the Set

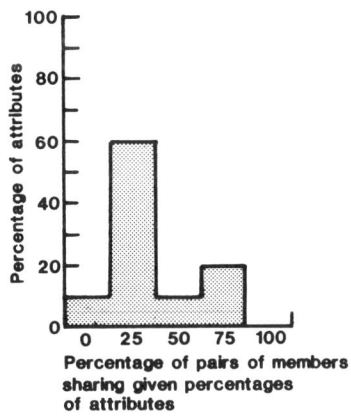

Mean polytheticness 35%

Fig. 13.3. The degree of polytheticness of a set can be defined by a frequency distribution that summarizes the percentage of the set's attributes shared by given percentages of pairs of members of the set.

sion both underlying and crosscutting the monothetic-polythetic one, must be explained.

Symmetrical vs. asymmetrical coarrangements (Pielou, 1964). These concepts are most easily explained in spatial terms pertinent to the domain of archaeological

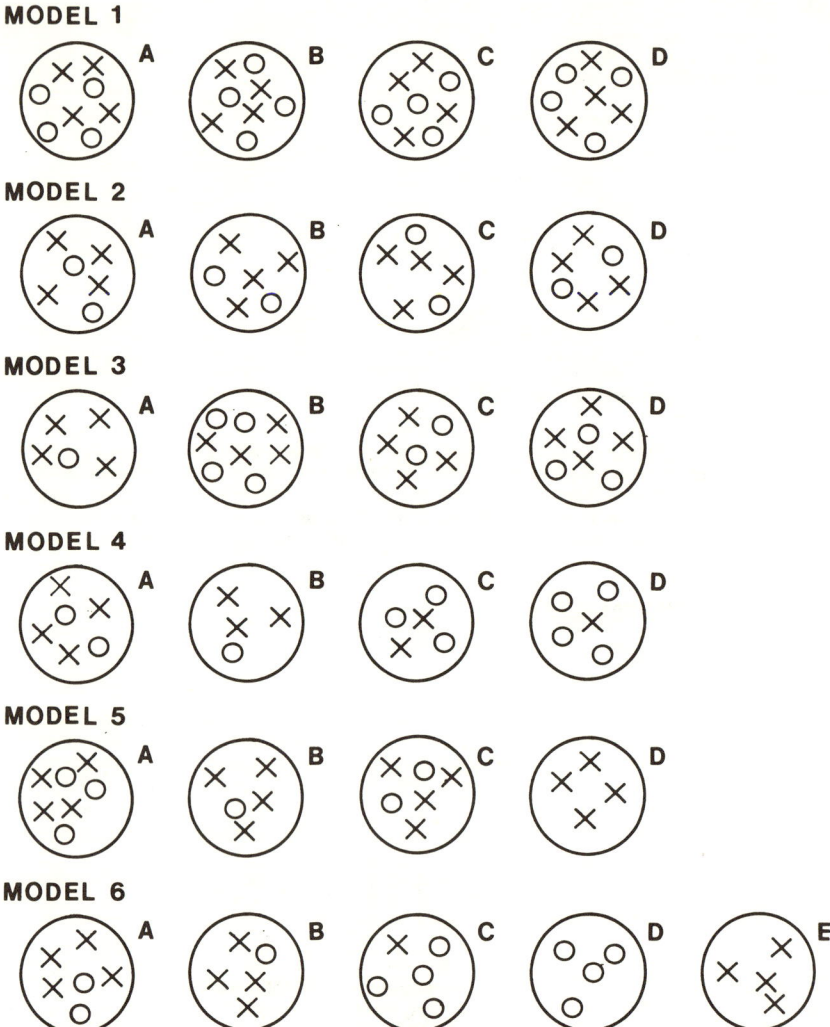

Fig. 13.4. Six models of organization of artifact types among archaeological deposits or behavioral events fall along a monothetic-polythetic continuum. Only one pair of types within the same set of deposits or events is shown; other types are assumed to have analogous forms of organization. The organizational characteristics of each model are described in Table 13.2.

deposits, but can be extended to the behavioral domain of events. Within a given area of reference, two types of entities are said to be symmetrically coarranged if wherever an item of one type occurs, an item of the other always occurs, and vice versa. In nearest-neighbor terms, this means that whenever one type of entity is a second's nearest neighbor, the second type of entity is always the first's nearest neighbor (Fig. 5a). A symmetrical coarrangement of two types of entities can occur only when they have equal densities and items of the two types *always can pair*, in addition to their having similar distributions. In contrast, asymmetrical coarrangements between two types of entities occur when they are scattered in a similar pattern over the same area, but in different densities. Items of the lower density type of entity always have items of the

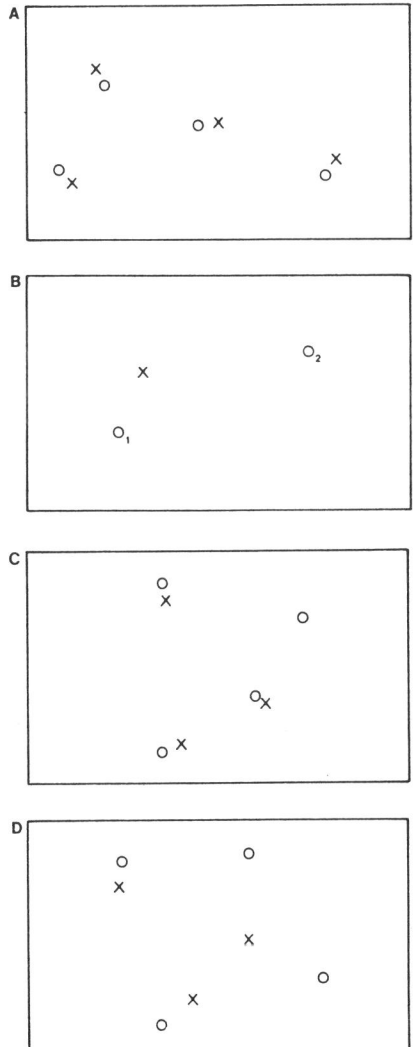

Fig. 13.5. Symmetry and asymmetry among artifact types. (A) A symmetrical coarrangement of two artifact types, X and O, defining a monothetic set. (B) Asymmetry in nearest neighbors. Artifact X is artifact O_2's nearest neighbor of the opposite kind, but O_2 is not X's nearest neighbor of the opposite kind. Artifact O_1 is artifact X's nearest neighbor of the opposite kind. (C) An asymmetrical coarrangement of two artifact types, X and O. (D) An asymmetrical arrangement of two artifact types, X and O, showing weaker coarrangement.

higher density type near them, but items of the higher density type only sometimes have items of the lower density type near them. Nearest neighbor relationships are not reciprocal (Fig. 5b-5d).

Magnitude and direction of asymmetry. Asymmetrical coarrangements of entities of two types can differ from one area of reference to another in two manners: the magnitude of their asymmetry and the direction of their asymmetry. The magnitude of asymmetry characterizing a coarrangement of types is equivalent to the *difference in the average areal densities* of items of the two types within the reference area. The direction of asymmetry refers to *which type* predominates in the reference area. For example, in Model 4, reference areas A and B exhibit asymmetrical coarrangements that differ in the magnitude of their asymmetries: the relative densities of types $X:O$ are 4:2 in area A and 3:1 in area B. Reference areas B and D have asymmetrical coarrangements that differ in the direction of their asymmetry: type X predominates in area B whereas type O predominates in area D.

Scale of asymmetry. It is also possible to distinguish the *scale* of the area of reference over which asymmetry is assessed. *Global* assessments over an area at large, more *local* assessments within a subarea of it, (e.g., within one cluster of items in an area having many clusters), and *very local* assessments pertaining to pairs of items, are possible. For example, in Model 3, entity types X and O are coarranged in an asymmetrical manner considering the global area containing $a, b, c,$ and d. They are arranged in a symmetrical manner if one considers only the more local area, B.

In a clustered coarrangement of two types where there exist several groups of items of the two types (e.g., Fig. 4), the symmetric-asymmetric dimension can crosscut or parallel the monothetic-polythetic dimension. The situation depends on the scale of the area over which each dimensional assessment is made and the size of the groupings of items.

1) If the area of reference for both dimensions is defined globally so as to include several groups of items, each with more than a pair of items (e.g., groups $A, B, C, D,$ and E in any of the models in Fig. 4), then the symmetric-asymmetric dimension will *crosscut* the monothetic-polythetic dimension; the relationship between them will be indeterminant. For example, all of Models 1 through 4 illustrate globally monothetic sets, yet Models 1 and 4 exhibit a globally symmetrical relationship between types X and O while Models 2 and 3 exhibit globally asymmetrical relationships between the types. Also, models illustrating globally monothetic sets (Numbers 2, 3, 4) as well as models illustrating globally polythetic sets (Numbers 5, 6) exhibit globally asymmetrical relationships between the two types.

2) If the area over which the monothetic-polythetic dimensional assessment is made is defined globally so as to include several groups ($A, B, C, D,$ and E), each with more than a pair of items, but the reference area for assessing symmetrical-asymmetrical relations is defined more locally, focusing on indi-

vidual groups, then the symmetrical-asymmetrical dimension will sometimes crosscut, sometimes parallel the monothetic-polythetic dimension, depending on the aspect of asymmetry considered. (a) Considering only whether asymmetry *occurs* and its *direction*, the two dimensions will *crosscut* each other, defining an indeterminant relationship between them. For example, all of Models 1 through 4 illustrate globally monothetic sets, yet Model 1 exhibits local (within group) symmetry between types X and O while Models 2 through 4 exhibit local asymmetry between the types. Also, models illustrating globally monothetic sets (Numbers 2, 3, 4) as well as models illustrating globally polythetic sets (Numbers 5, 6) exhibit locally asymmetric relationships between the two types. (b) On the other hand, considering the *magnitude* of asymmetry, and in particular whether asymmetry occurs to the extreme in some groups of items such that one type does not occur in them, then the symmetric-asymmetric dimension *parallels* and determines the monothetic-polythetic dimension. For example, in Models 5 and 6, the magnitude of local asymmetry is so large in one or two of the groups of items that one type is absent from them. In Models 1 through 4, this extreme amount of local asymmetry does not occur; each group of items includes items of both types. In these circumstances, *by definition*, Models 5 and 6 represent globally polythetic sets of groups while Models 1 through 4 represent globally monothetic sets of groups.

3) Finally, the scale of the area over which the monothetic-polythetic dimensional assessment is made can be global but the size of the groups of interest can be reduced to very local *pairings* of items rather than the multi-item groups considered before. Additionally, the scale of the area for assessing symmetric-asymmetric dimensional relations can be defined very locally so as to include only pairs of nearest neighbors. In these circumstances, the symmetry-asymmetry dimension will *parallel* and determine the monothetic-polythetic dimension. A very locally symmetrical coarrangement of items of two types *always* will define a monothetic set of pairs of items. In a symmetrical coarrangement, items of opposite types always are each other's nearest neighbors, implying that each pair of items in the global reference area (members of the set) is characterized by one item of each type, i.e., the set of pairs is monothetic. A very locally asymmetrical coarrangement of items of two types *always* will define a polythetic set of pairs of items. In an asymmetrical coarrangement, items of opposite types are not always nearest neighbors, implying that pairs of items in the global reference area (members of the set) sometimes but not always are characterized by one item of each type, i.e., the set of pairs is polythetic.

In developing models of organization of artifacts, it is important that the scales of the areas of assessment for the symmetric-asymmetric dimension and the monothetic-polythetic dimension, as well as the size of groups of items, be kept clear. This was not always done in the initial article (Carr, 1984) of the series that includes this one. The concept of polythetic sets of deposits or events was introduced using asymmetrical relationships between types at the *local* scale of *multi-item* groups, while the dependence of global polythetic organization on asymmetry was argued at the *very local* scale of *pairs* of items. The discussion just presented should allow modeling of artifact organization in a more consistent manner, as well as provide insight into organizational diversity not previously realized.

The six models. Using the distinction between symmetrical and asymmetrical coarrangements, as well as variation in the magnitude, direction, and scale of asymmetry, it is possible to construct the four globally monothetic models of artifact organization and the two globally polythetic ones in Figure 4, and to specify the organizational characteristics distinguishing them (Table 2). The six models differ in both global and local aspects of their organization. Model 1 differs from all the rest in that globally asymmetrical relations between artifact types, as well as locally asymmetrical relations between them (within groups of items), are not permitted. Models 2 through 6 differ from each other in various aspects of locally asymmetrical relations between types of items. For example, Model 2 does not permit local asymmetry to vary in magnitude from one group of items to the next, while Models 3 through 6 do. Models 3 and 5 do not permit local asymmetry to vary in direction from group to group, while Models 4 and 6 do.

The distinguishing characteristics of some of the models can also be summarized in terms of concepts that are more familiar than the various aspects of asymmetry, though less precise. In Model 1, artifacts of each type occur in 1:1 proportions, both globally, and locally within groups. In Model 2, the artifact types occur in the same proportion in each group of items, but the particular proportion is not specified. In Models 3 and 4, the organization of artifact types is more variable from group to group; the proportions of artifact types within groups can vary among groups. However, all types at least *occur* in each group. Models 5 and 6 have the most variable organization of artifact types among groups. Not only do the proportions of artifact types within groups vary from group to group, but some groups do not have occurrences of some kinds of artifacts.

The six models can be used to describe the organization of artifact types into sets within both the behavioral and archaeological domains. If the models are taken to describe archaeological organization, the groups of artifacts A through E in Figure 4 represent deposits forming either a globally monothetic or globally polythetic set. The two artifact types, X and O, are considered a depositional "set." If the models are taken to describe behavioral organization, the groups of artifacts represent events, again forming either a globally monothetic or globally polythetic set. The two artifact types, X and O, are considered an activity "set."

The several models can be viewed as simply *alternative* forms of organization of artifact types. However, as hinted above, they also can define a *sequence* of organizational forms. The sequence ranges from lower-numbered models hav-

Table 13.2

Mathematical Characteristics of the Six Models of Organization of Artifact Types in Figure 3

Characteristics	Models					
	1	2	3	4	5	6
Asymmetry within groups of artifacts allowed for one or more pairs of types	−	+	+	+	+	+
Differences between groups in the magnitudes of their asymmetries allowed for one or more pairs of types	−	−	+	+	+	+
Differences between groups in the directions of their asymmetries allowed for one or more pairs of types	−	−	−	+	−	+
Asymmetry within groups taken to the extreme, where one type, of one or more pairs of types, does not occur in some groups	−	−	−	−	+	+
Global monothetic or polythetic organization using A, B, C, D, E as groups of interest (Fig. 3)	monothetic	monothetic	monothetic	monothetic	polythetic	polythetic
Local monothetic or polythetic organization using pairs of items as groups of interest	monothetic	polythetic	polythetic	polythetic	polythetic	polythetic

ing very specific forms of organization of types among groups to higher-numbered models encompassing more variable organization.

It is also possible to view each model as more than just a *description* of the organizational relations that can occur between artifact types within sets of deposits or events. Rather, each can be seen as a *standard of organization*, which stipulates, for any given data set, the organizational relations among types that *minimally are required of them to be considered coarranged and interpreted as defining a set* of deposits or events. The sequence of models would then define an *ordered series of constraints* on the relationships among types, ranging from the most restrictive to the most permissive specifications necessary for the types to define a set.

It is advantageous, for several reasons, to view the models as a sequence and as standards of organization. 1) Site formation processes often are viewed as a series of actions cumulatively bringing increasing entropy (Ascher, 1968), bias (Cowgill, 1970), or distortion (Schiffer, 1972, 1976) to relationships among artifacts that once were more direct reflections of the behavioral system that produced them. By viewing the models as a sequence defining more and more variable organizational relations among types, it becomes possible to *link the models to a series of site formation processes* of cumulatively increasing number and disordering effects. Any of the models in the sequence can serve as the base-line organization initially produced by the behavioral system. The following, less constraining models then indicate organizational changes resulting from depositional and post-depositional formation processes.

2) Quantitative and statistical techniques vary in the degree to which their assumptions about a data set's structure are specific and constraining. In particular, techniques can vary in whether they assume ratio, interval, ordinal, or nominal scale relationships among entities to be significant, and whether they assume monothetic or polythetic relationships to be significant (Carr, 1984). They can be ranked in reference to these criteria, with ratio scale and monothetic organizational relations being most constraining. Since the models of artifact organization can be ordered into a parallel sequence, in which constraints on the relationships among types range from ratio to nominal scale specifications and monothetic to polythetic specifications, it becomes possible to *link each model to techniques* appropriate for describing its relevant structure.

3) As a consequence of the linkages described in points 1 and 2, it is possible to create a series of constructs, each of which relates a model of artifact organization to formation processes capable of generating such organization and to techniques appropriate for describing that organization. The combined process-model-technique constructs can serve as entry models that facilitate the linkage of an intrasite spatial data set to the techniques most appropriate for its analysis. This can be done in the following way. Suppose one knows something about the formation processes responsible for a study area and their effects on artifact organization, or can suggest some of the formation processes and their effects that likely occurred in the area on the basis of its behavioral and

environmental context. In this circumstance, the study area can be associated with and assumed to share in the artifact organizational characteristics of one or a few of the models of artifact organization, on account of the formation processes that the area and model(s) hold in common. Furthermore, the linkages between models and techniques allow the study area to be associated with one or a few appropriate analytic techniques.

Expansion of the Models to Include Variation along the Nonoverlapping-Overlapping Dimension

The six models of organization of artifact types constructed to this point are distinguished by characteristics along the monothetic-polythetic dimension of organization, alone. It is possible to elaborate them further from a set-theoretic perspective by introducing organizational diversity along the nonoverlapping-overlapping dimension. This can be achieved by duplicating the models in Table 2, resulting in twelve models: one set of six with the additional characteristic that sets of deposits or events are nonoverlapping, the other with the additional characteristic that sets of deposits or events are overlapping.

The variation in form of artifact organization that the models exhibit along the nonoverlapping-overlapping dimension, like that which they express along the monothetic-polythetic dimension, can be viewed as a *sequence*. The sequence ranges from an ordered form of organization not involving any overlap between sets of events or deposits to a highly variable form involving their overlap by up to all but one characteristic artifact type, each. Also, the nonoverlapping and overlapping models can be seen as *standards of organization*, stipulating for any given data the organizational relationships among sets of events or deposits that minimally are required for them to be interpreted as discrete sets. The advantage of these perspectives is the same as those just described: the organizational models can be linked to formation processes and analytic techniques and altered into entry models.

Complex Models

To present, it has been assumed that some single model of organization of artifact types is adequate for characterizing all the relationships among types that occur archaeologically or behaviorally within a study area. For example, if one pair of artifact types within an activity set or depositional set exhibits asymmetry with local variation in the direction of asymmetry, it has been assumed that all the other artifact pairs in that set and within other sets also exhibit that characteristic. Clearly, the situation can be more complex, with some type-pairs exhibiting one kind of organization and other type-pairs exhibiting others.

It is possible to specify all the permutations of the twelve forms of organization that might arise in the behavioral or archaeological domain within any single site encompassing multiple artifact types. And in some rare instances, it may be possible to classify a study area in relation to such permutations. However, considering the practical aim of this paper to provide models *facilitating linkage* of archaeological data structures to appropriate analytic techniques, such a detailed classification process does not seem pertinent. To classify a study area in such detail when attempting to determine the most appropriate technique for its analysis would require nearly as much knowledge about the area as that being sought through analysis.

In light of this practical limitation on classifying an archaeological data set, yet recognizing that a study area may exhibit multiple organizational relationships among different artifact pairs, some of which may be known, an alternative approach is suggested. If a study area is known or suspected to exhibit several different kinds of relationships between different pairs of artifact types, in concordance with several different models of organization, then the area should be characterized by those few models that represent the *most frequently occurring* organizational relationships in it. This will lead to the data set being examined by several different techniques that make different assumptions about the data's structure, and will possibly result in the definition of depositional sets that vary in composition. A composite picture of depositional set composition can then be constructed logically from the several solutions, bearing in mind the constraints under which they were derived, where those constraints conflict with formation processes, and where the constraints likely have produced erroneous representations. This kind of evaluation becomes possible only when working within a pattern-recognition framework involving knowledge about the formation processes responsible or probably responsible for the study area, as opposed to a completely inductive pattern-searching framework not involving this information.

Alternatively, one might think it appropriate to characterize the data by that *one* model requiring the *least constraining* relationships among artifact types, leading to the examination of the data set with one technique that assumes more variable organization of the data. However, this approach can lead to solutions just as erroneous as those obtained when using only one technique that assumes a more restrictive organization, depending on the actual forms of organization exhibited by the data. A technique that assumes the significance of only least constraining relationships among data items is as focused in its description of patterning as a technique that assumes the significance of only restrictive relationships; the difference is in only the *form* of patterning recognized, not the *range* of forms of patterns recognized. A "least constraining" method should not be confused with a "robust" one. Thus, this alternative seems inappropriate. An illustration of this point is made in the Pincevent example analysis, later.

Finally, it should be realized that the problem posed by study areas having depositional sets with multiple forms of organization is distinct from the problem of pooled *contradictory* structures. Moreover, the latter can be resolved under some conditions with Fourier and filtering methods, whereas the former cannot.

A Continuous-Scale Analog of the Twelve Models

Thus far, several discrete models of organization of artifact types in the behavioral and archaeological domains have been constructed, each model distinguished by nominal scale characteristics. Alternatively, it is possible to define a single hypervolume continuum of organizational variation using continuous scale, orthoganal dimensions analogous to the nominal scale characteristics.

Such a construct might be used to describe artifact organization within the behavioral or archaeological domains for theoretical purposes. It might also be used after an intrasite spatial analysis in order to specify precisely the organization of artifacts within a study area compared to that within other study areas. However, the construct would not be useful in characterizing the organization of artifacts within an area prior to spatial analysis and facilitating linkage of the data structure to an appropriate analytic technique; this would require more detailed information on the organization of artifacts within the site than would normally be available prior to analysis.

The dimensions that may be used to define the desired hypervolume are given in Table 3. Dimension 1 measures, over all deposits/events within a set, the average magnitude of local asymmetry exhibited by a type-pair defining that set, in turn averaged over all defining type-pairs for the set(s) of interest. It is analogous to the organizational characteristic listed in the second column of Table 2 for the discrete models. The measure is not affected by whether the magnitude or direction of asymmetry of types varies or is uniform among deposits/events (third, fourth columns of Table 2). Dimension 2 measures, over all deposits/events within a set, the variance among deposits/events in the magnitude of local asymmetry expressed by a type-pair defining the set, in turn averaged over all such type-pairs for the set(s) of interest. Since large variability among deposits/events in the magnitude of asymmetry between a type-pair can associate with a change in the direction of its asymmetry, dimension 2 also measures, over all deposits/events within a set, the variability or uniformity in the direction of asymmetry expressed by a type-pair defining the set, averaged over all such pairs for the set(s) of interest. The measure is analogous to the organizational characteristics listed in the third and fourth columns of Table 2 for the discrete models. Dimension 3 measures the percentage of deposits/events in a set having given percentages of the artifact types defining it (including deposits/events having 0% of some types), averaged over all depositional sets of interest within the study area. It is equivalent to the average degree of global polytheticness of the sets in the study area, where the global polytheticness of any single set is calculated as shown in Figure 3, and described pre-

Table 13.3

Dimensions for Defining a Continuous Scale Hypervolume of Intrasite Artifact Organization

Dimension 1. Average Magnitude of Local Asymmetry, A.

Let p = any pair of types within the same depositional set, for any of the sets defined by analysis

c_p = an artifact cluster or arbitrary analytical unit within the study area, having the pair of types, p

X_{pc_p} = the absolute value of the difference between the number of items of the two types in one pair, p, within cluster/unit c_p, divided by the total number of items of both types in the cluster/unit

n = the total number of clusters/units, c_p

m = the total number of pairs of types, p.

Then

$$A = \frac{\sum_{p=1}^{m} \left(\frac{\sum_{c_p=1}^{n} X_{pc_p}}{n} \right)}{m}$$

Dimension 2. Average Variability in Magnitude and Direction of Local Asymmetry, V.

Let p, c_p, n, and m be as before, and

X_{pc_p} = the difference between the number of items of the two types in the pair p within cluster/unit c_p, divided by the total number of items of both types in the cluster/unit

$var_{c_p}()$ = the variance of the measure in parenthesis over all clusters/units having the pair of types p.

Then

$$V = \frac{\sum_{p=1}^{m} var_{c_p}(X_{pc_p})}{m}$$

Dimension 3. Average Global Polytheticness of Sets, P.

Let d = any set of deposits characterized by a number of artifact types

p_d = any percentage of all the artifact types defining the set of deposits, d

X_{p_d} = the number of pairs of deposits sharing the given percentage, p_d, of all the artifact types defining the set of deposits, d

n_d = the total number of pairs of deposits with one or more of the artifact types defining the set of deposits, d

m = the total number of sets of deposits.

Table 13.3 (cont.)

Then

$$P = \frac{\sum_{d=1}^{m} \left(\frac{\sum_{p_d=1}^{100} (X_{p_d})(p_d)}{n_d} \right)}{m}$$

Dimension 4. Average Degree of Overlap among Sets, O.

Let a = one set of deposits/events defined by a certain list of artifact types
  b = another set of deposits/events defined by another list of artifact types
  C_{ab} = the number of artifact types shared by sets a and b
  C_a, C_b = the number of artifact types uniquely defining sets a and b, respectively
  n = the number of pairs of sets of deposits/events within the study area.

Then

$$O = \frac{\sum_{ab}^{n} \left(\frac{C_{ab}}{C_a + C_{ab} + C_b} \times 100\% \right)}{n}$$

viously (pp. 333-334). The measure is analogous to the nominal scale organizational characteristic listed in the fifth column of Table 2. Dimension 4 measures the average degree of overlap among all pairs of sets of deposits/events that are of interest within a study area. It is analogous to the nominal scale, nonoverlapping-overlapping dimension discussed previously.

The continuous dimensions of organization just established define the average conditions within a study area. The formulae may be modified in obvious ways to define the variance of such conditions around the norms.

LINKING THE MODELS OF ORGANIZATION WITH FORMATION PROCESSES

In this section, the twelve discrete models of organization of artifact types will be taken to represent structures within the archaeological domain. The aim is to link the models to various formation processes that can produce such structures. This linkage represents a critical step in formulating a series of entry models, each of which is composed of a model of artifact organization, an enumeration of the formation processes capable of generating that form of organization, and a list of mathematical techniques assuming that form of organization. The resulting entry models will facilitate the linkage of intrasite spatial data sets to techniques appropriate for their analysis.

The organization of artifacts within the archaeological record is the product of two phenomena: 1) their previous organization in the behavioral domain, and 2) the formation and disturbance processes transferring and transforming

Table 13.4

Processes Responsible for Absences of Artifact Types from Events or Deposits where they Might be Expected in the Behavioral or Archaeological Domains

Processes Responsible for Absences of Artifact Types from Events in Which Their Use Might Be Expected	*Processes Likely to Act Uniformly over All of Site?*
1. Several alternative tool types may be used to accomplish the same ends.	no
2. Some specific tasks within a general activity may be optional, making the use of some tool types optional.	no
Processes Responsible for Absences of Artifact Types from Deposits in Which They Might Be Expected	
1. The cultural formation processes in the behavioral domain stated above.	no
2. Artifact types comprising the same activity set may enter the archaeological domain as subsets separated in different locations of their manufacture, use, storage, or discard, none of which need coincide (Schiffer, 1972).	no
3. Large artifact types may be purposefully discarded in out-of-the-way, secondary trash deposits while smaller artifact types belonging to the same activity set may be discarded or lost anywhere without much annoyance (McKellar, 1973).	yes
4. Differential wear and breakage rates of different artifact types that belong to the same activity set and that are curated.	no

that organization from the behavioral to the archaeological domain. It is necessary to first consider the possible forms of organization of artifacts in the behavioral domain and their causes, as a baseline.

Processes Leading to Forms of Organization in the Behavioral Domain

Any of the twelve models of organization—encompassing monothetic and polythetic, nonoverlapping and overlapping forms—may describe the configuration of artifact types within and among sets of events in the behavioral domain. The basic processes responsible for variation along the monothetic-polythetic and nonoverlapping-overlapping dimensions are few. Monothetic-polythetic variation can result from the use or lack of use of *alternative* tool types for accomplishing the same ends in similar events, or of *optional* tool types for accomplishing optional subtasks within similar events. Nonoverlapping-overlapping variation can result from the use or lack of use of the same multipurpose tools in differing events (Tables 4, 5).

Table 13.4 (cont.)

5. A multipurpose artifact that is associated with more than one activity set can be deposited with artifacts from only one of the activity sets.	no
6. A multitype artifact that has several edges used for different purposes and is associated with more than one activity set can be deposited with artifacts from only one of the activity sets.	no
7. A broken artifact of one type may be recycled and made into an artifact of another type in a different activity set.	yes/no, depending on type
8. "Mining" of abandoned parts of a site or an abandoned site by prehistoric individuals or contemporary artifact collectors (Ascher, 1968; Reid, 1973; Schiffer, 1977, p. 26).	no
9. Effects of cultural and natural post-depositional processes that increase the entropy of the archaeological record.	
a. trampling by site occupants.	no
b. carnivore activity (Binford, 1977a, 1981b; Yellen, 1977b; Wandsnider & Binford, 1982).	no
c. plowing (Roper, 1976; Trubowitz, 1981; Lewarch & O'Brien, 1981).	yes
d. water washing, wind sorting (Shakley, 1978; Behrensmeyer & Hill, 1980; Limbrey, 1980).	no
e. biologically caused soil movements: pedoturbations caused by the burrowing actions of mammals, insects, and earthworms (Stein, 1980); treefalls.	no
f. meteorologically and geologically caused soil movements: soil creep, solifluction, cryoturbations, aquiturbations (Wood & Johnson, 1978).	no
10. Lack of preservation of bone items of a class.	no
11. Incomplete recovery of artifacts during excavation.	no
12. Misclassification of an artifact's function.	no
13. Use of an overly divisive functional classification scheme for typing artifacts.	yes
14. Use of a nonfunctional artifact classification scheme.	?

Variation along the nonoverlapping-overlapping dimension. It is easy to think of activity sets within primitive technologies that contain only single-purpose tools and that define nonoverlapping sets of events. However, a wide variety of activity sets that contain multipurpose tools and define overlapping sets of events are also known. Carr (1984, Table 1) and Cook (1976) reference many ethnographic, ethnoarchaeological, and tool experimental studies that document these two forms of organization. Microwear studies (e.g., Keeley, 1977, 1978; Odell, 1977) which document the use of prehistoric artifacts on single or multiple kinds of raw materials, provide further evidence of this kind of variation in tool use and organization in the past. For example, Keeley has shown

Table 13.5

Processes Responsible for Overlap among Sets in the Behavioral and Archaeological Domains

Processes Responsible for Overlap among Sets of Events in the Artifact Types Defining Them	*Processes Likely to Act Uniformly over All of Site?*
1. Single-type tools with one functional edge (e.g., prismatic blades) may have multiple purposes and be used in several different sets of events with different tool types (e.g., Cook, 1976).	yes
2. Multi-type tools with several edges used for different purposes (e.g., a Swiss Army knife) may be used in several different sets of events with different tool types.	yes
Processes Responsible for Overlap among Sets of Deposits in the Artifact Types Defining Them	
1. Cultural formation processes in the behavioral domain, stated above.	yes
2. *Systematic* spatial overlap of different kinds of activities, e.g., "agglomerated activity areas" (Speth & Johnson, 1976; Yellen, 1977a).	by definition
3. Redeposition of primary refuse generated by different kinds of activities in different areas *systematically* in the same formalized trash areas.	by definition
4. Extensive post-depositional smearing and blending of primary refuse from repeatedly neighboring activity areas of different kinds by natural processes of several kinds.	
a. plowing, if the artifact distribution comes from a surface survey (Roper, 1976; Trubowitz, 1981; Lewarch & O'Brien, 1981).	yes
b. trampling by the occupants of the site (Ascher, 1968).	no
c. carnivore action (Binford, 1981b; Yellen, 1977b; Wandsnider & Binford, 1982).	no
d. pedoturbations by the burrowing action of larger mammals.	no
e. soil creep, solifluction, cryoturbations, aquiturbations (Wood & Johnson, 1978).	no
f. water washing (Shackley, 1978; Behrensmeyer & Hill, 1980).	no
5. Misclassification of an artifact's function.	no
6. Use of a nonfunctional artifact classification scheme.	?

that endscrapers at the Epipaleolithic site of Meer II, Belgium, and possibly those of the later Paleolithic of Europe in general, were used almost exclusively on dry hide to cure or grain it (1978; Table 15, pp. 74-79). In contrast, knives at the site may have been used systematically on a diversity of materials (grasses, cane, mat; 1978, pp. 82-83), as were becs (bone or antler, hide; 1978, Table 19).

Variation along the monothetic-polythetic dimension. To see how organizational forms along this dimension might be created through the use of alternative tool types accomplishing the same ends in a set of events, one need only envision a set of carpentry events involving a hammer, nails, a screwdriver, screws, and a saw. A particular set of building tasks might always involve the use of all five artifact types, with both screws and nails being used to assemble cut pieces of wood (Model 2, 3, or 4). Or perhaps screws (and hence, the screwdriver) might be deleted from some of the operations (Model 5 or 6). For a set of tasks involving both screws and nails, screws might be used always in just a few critical positions, nails always predominating the tasks (Model 2 or 3); or the screws and nails might be used in widely varying proportions, neither one predominating in all the tasks (Model 4). In contrast, some kinds of activities always restrictively require certain tool types in a 1:1 ratio and do not permit the use of alternative tool types (Model 1). The use of mono and metate to grind grain or pound large seeds, roots, bulbs, or meat (Kraybill, 1977; Riddell & Pritchard, 1971; Driver, 1961, p. 93; Wheat, 1972, p. 117), mortar and pestle to crack nuts (Battle, 1922; Swanton, 1946; Waugh, 1916, p. 123) or maul and axe to fell trees (Swanton, 1946) are examples. Again, microwear studies document both single or multiple kinds of tools used for single kinds of tasks, illustrating variability in tool organization along the monothetic-polythetic dimension. For example, Keeley (1978, Table 19, pp. 79-80) concludes that becs and many forms of burins had equivalent functions (boring bone or antler) at Meer II, while he does not find any functional equivalent for endscrapers used in curing dry hides.

Processes Leading to Forms of Organization in the Archaeological Domain: The Monothetic-Polythetic Dimension

In the archaeological domain, the relationships that exist between artifact types within and among sets of deposits usually are no more constraining than the baseline organization of types in the behavioral domain from which they are derived. Generally, the net effect of formation processes is to increase the amount of *randomness and variety* in the relationships exhibited between artifact types as they are transferred from the behavioral to the archaeological domain and then altered within the archaeological domain (Ascher, 1968).

The models of organization along the monothetic-polythetic dimension are useful for describing these transformations. The models define a sequence of organizational configurations that range from those encompassing highly constrained relationships among types (Model 1) to those exhibiting more variable organization (Model 6). Differences between one or more successive models in the sequence can be used to define the changes that can occur among types as they are transferred to and within the archaeological domain. For example, suppose several types of artifacts form an activity set and are distributed among events within a site in the globally monothetic manner expressed in Model 3. It is expectable that they will usually become distributed among deposits in the archaeological domain in a manner that is equally or less constraining— perhaps monothetically (Model 3 or 4) or perhaps polythetically (Model 5 or 6).

Site formation processes can not only introduce randomness and variety into the relationships among artifact types; they also can cause *systematic biases*[2] in artifact type relationships away from the norm expressed in the behavioral domain (Cowgill, 1970; Schiffer, 1982). These changes, as well, can be described by the differences between some successive models in the sequence. For example, the change from Model 1 to Model 2 involves a change in the proportions of artifact types in the same magnitude and direction for *each* group of artifacts. The change from Model 1 or 2 to Model 3 involves a change in proportions only in the same direction for each group.

There are exceptions to the "increasing-entropy" characterization of the net effect of formation processes. Some of these pertain to natural processes that can lead to the spatial clustering of previously dispersed artifacts (e.g., through the action of earthworms (Ascher, 1968); freeze-thaw cycles; expansion-contraction cycles in vertisols, salinization and cracking of the soil; soil creep [Wood & Johnson, 1978]). Although most familiar, these processes are of less importance here because they usually do not operate *selectively* on *particular types* and the spatial relations among them (except when the types exhibit marked size or density differences). However, other formation processes—especially cultural ones—can operate selectively on certain artifact classes and the relationships among them, causing more constrained organization in the archaeological domain than the behavioral. 1) *Caching* can cause artifact types distributed polythetically among a set of events in the behavioral domain to enter the archaeological domain as a monothetic set. For example, consider screws and a screwdriver, nails and a hammer, which are used alternatively in different carpentry events by different carpenters along with a saw and file. This configuration of artifacts defines a polythetic set (Model 5 or 6). However, all the artifact types might be stored on each carpenter's workbench, defining a monothetic set (Model 3 or 4). 2) *Reuse of activity areas* for the same purposes can cause an increasingly constrained artifact organization. Suppose that functionally alternative artifact types are distributed polythetically among a set of events that occur in several different activity areas (Models 5 or 6). If events of that kind are performed repeatedly in those areas, with the particular alternative types used in each area varying randomly over time, and if artifacts are deposited relatively expediently, then over time, the inventory of artifact types found in each area will become more similar, ultimately defining a monothetic set of deposits (Models 2, 3, or 4) (Carr, 1984). 3) Similarly, if the refuse from each such activity area is repeatedly moved to *common refuse dumps* after each event, the inventories of artifact types in the refuse dumps will become more similar to each other, ultimately defining a monothetic set of refuse areas.

Considering the more common sequence in which greater net disorganization is introduced by site formation processes, it is possible to specify more precisely how formation processes can produce and be linked to variation in artifact organization like that exhibited by the several models along the monothetic-polythetic dimension. This can be achieved in part by using the concept of *unexpected absences*, which is defined as follows.

Assume that any of the five most constraining models in Figure 3 represent the organization of artifact types in the behavioral domain and that the lesser constraining models in the sequence represent artifact organization in the archaeological domain. It then may be said that "unexpected absences" of artifacts of some types in one or more groups (*A, B, C, D,* or *E*) occur in the less constraining models compared to the more constraining baseline models. For example, if Model 1 represents artifact organization in the behavioral domain while Model 2 represents artifact organization in the archaeological domain, then Model 2 exhibits "unexpected absences" of artifact type O: there is one item of type X for each item of type O in Model 1, but fewer items of type O in Model 2. In this context, unexpected absences represent the effects of formation processes that can increase the variability of relationships among artifact types. For example, in Model 1, each artifact of type X has a nearest neighbor of type O, whereas in Model 2, sometimes it has a nearest neighbor of type O, sometimes of type X.

The concept of unexpected absences and unexpected forms of organization of artifact types in the archaeological domain implies—in opposition to such forms—an ideal, expected form of organization of artifacts in the archaeological record. In this ideal, the organization of artifacts in the archaeological record *directly reflects* that in the behavioral domain, unaffected by extra-activity cultural formation processes (e.g., storage, curation) or natural formation processes—what Binford (1981) has termed a "Pompeii effect." However, the unexpected and expected forms of organization dealt with here differ in two ways from those described by Binford. 1) The "expected" form of organization of the archaeological record is not *absolute* in nature. It can be any of the *various* models of artifact organization presented above, thought of as a baseline organization of artifacts in the behavioral domain. 2) The concept of "unexpected" absences is used here simply as a *heuristic device* to clarify the differences in artifact organization that can distinguish the behavioral and archaeological domains. The reader is asked to view the archaeological record *as if* he were unaware of the effects of extra-activity cultural formation processes and natural formation processes and as if he thought archaeological artifact organization directly reflected behavioral artifact organization, in order to clarify the effects of those processes.

The unexpected absences in each of the five least constraining models (Models 2-6) in Figure 4 vary in their placement so as to produce five different organizational forms. The forms differ from each other and from Model 1 in whether they encompass global asymmetry, variation in the magnitude of local asymmetry, variation in the direction of local asymmetry, and/or whether some groups of artifacts totally lack some expected types (the four aspects of asymmetry variation listed in Table 2).

Now consider any two or more of the five least constraining models as representing archaeological records that have been derived from the behavioral domain as modeled by some less constraining model. The specific placements of unexpected absences in the models that represent the archaeological records, which define the specific differences between them in aspects of asymmetry, can then be attributed to and linked to the kinds, numbers, and intensities of the formation processes that generated them and that determine alterations between the behavioral and archaeological domains.

1) Kinds of formation processes. Assume a Model 1 or 2 form of organization of artifact types among events in the behavioral domain. If the formation processes responsible for a set of archaeological deposits within a site are of a kind likely to have acted *uniformly* over all events or deposits in the site, producing the same number of unexpected absences of the same kinds of artifacts in each locale, then asymmetry between the types will probably be of constant local magnitude and direction from deposit to deposit (Model 2). Table 4 lists several specific formation processes that tend to act in this manner. If the formation processes are apt to have acted *disuniformly* among events or deposits in the site, creating different numbers of unexpected absences of the same kinds of artifacts in different locales, then asymmetry between types among deposits will likely vary locally in magnitude, at least, and perhaps in direction (Models 3, 4, 5, or 6). Processes of this kind are much more common (see Table 4).

2) Number of formation processes. The greater the number of formation processes that are responsible for an archaeological record and that act differentially over space, the greater is the chance that some of the processes will not be spatially correlated. This will produce different numbers of unexpected absences of both the same and different kinds of artifacts in different locales, creating variation among deposits of a set in the direction as well as the magnitude of asymmetry between their artifact types (Model 4, 5, or 6).

3) Intensity of formation processes. The greater the intensity of a formation process that acts differentially over space, the greater is the likelihood that unexpected absences of the artifact type it affects will be taken to the extreme circumstance in which some deposits of a set lack the type completely (Model 5).

4) Number and intensity of formation processes, combined. As the number of formation processes that act differentially over space increases and their intensity increases, it becomes more probable that unexpected absences of several artifact types will be taken to the extreme circumstance in which some deposits of a set lack one or more of the types completely and the missing type(s) vary locally (Model 6).

In sum, systematic relationships can be found between the form of organization of artifact types within a set of archaeological deposits (as described by the models in Fig. 4 and Table 2) and the kinds, numbers, and intensities of the formation processes responsible for them.

In relating different kinds of formation processes to different models of artifact organization, the above framework considers only a general distinction: that between processes which tend to act uniformly over events or deposits vs. those which tend to act disuniformly. It also is possible, however, to associate *specific* kinds of formation processes (e.g., curation rates, various post-depositional processes, recovery bias, artifact classification bias) with specific models. Such linkages, however, are more easily expressed in mathematical terms and from the perspective of the techniques appropriate for analyzing data in the form of the models. Consequently, this discussion must await the introduction of such techniques and is given later (pp. 359-373).

Finally, it is possible to specify, to some extent, which models of archaeological organization are more likely to typify archaeological records in general. This can be done on the basis of the relative number of existing formation processes that act disuniformly as opposed to uniformly over events or deposits (Table 4). Given that most formation processes tend to act disuniformly over events or deposits, one can expect that many archaeological records will have artifact organizations similar to Models 3, 4, 5, or 6. This conclusion partially supports Carr's (1984) previous concern for the globally or locally polythetic organization of the archaeological record and the congruence of spatial analytic techniques to these forms of organization.

Processes Leading to Forms of Organization in the Archaeological Domain: The Nonoverlapping-Overlapping Dimension

The greater variation in relationships between artifact types that can arise, as they are transferred from the behavioral domain to the archaeological and then altered in the archaeological domain, can be described not only by the sequence of less and less constraining models of organization along the monothetic-polythetic dimension. A sequence of less constraining models of organization along the nonoverlapping-overlapping dimension also describes this transformation. Given either a nonoverlapping or overlapping baseline organization of artifact types between different sets of events in the behavioral domain, there will be a tendency for sets of deposits in the archaeological domain to be overlapping or to overlap more. This difference can result from the operation of any of several different kinds of cultural and natural formation processes (Table 5). The probability of occurrence of overlap or the increase in amount of overlap between sets of deposits will depend on the intensity with which those processes occur and/or the number of them that occur.

LINKING THE MODELS OF ORGANIZATION WITH SPATIAL ANALYTIC TECHNIQUES

In this section, quantitative techniques of spatial analysis that make assumptions that are congruent with the structure of the twelve models of artifact organization within the behavioral and archaeological domains will be specified and described. This linkage represents the final step in the development of a series of entry models, each of which is comprised of a model of artifact organization, the formation processes capable of generating that organization, and the spatial techniques assuming that form of organization.

Two broad approaches to defining the relationships between artifact types within a site are possible, only one of which is considered here. The first focuses on artifact types as pairs, and whether their arrangements are significantly similar or different in a statistical sense. Some procedures used in this manner include: significance tests for Pearson's correlation coefficient r (Olkin, 1967) and Kendall's rank correlation coefficient tau (Kendall, 1955), the X^2 test of independence using Yates continuity correction and mean or median split procedures (Dacey, 1973; Pielou, 1969), and segregation analysis (Pielou, 1964). Carr (1984) summarizes many of these procedures and their different assumptions, and references examples of their use on archaeological data.

The second approach to defining relationships between artifact types focuses on simultaneous relationships between multiple artifact types. It involves two steps. First, the degree of coarrangement of each artifact type with each other type is expressed with any of a number of "similarity coefficients," such as a Jaccard or correlation coefficient or an average intertype nearest neighbor distance. Then, a higher-level pattern-searching algorithm is applied to the matrix of coefficients for all possible artifact type-pairs in order to reveal groups of one to multiple artifact types that are more similar to each other in their spatial arrangement than they are to artifact types in other groups. The many varieties of factor analysis and cluster analysis are examples of such algorithms.

These two approaches can be used together to give a fuller understanding of one's data, the pairwise tests preceding the multitype analyses. However, in this chapter, only methods of multitype analysis will be discussed, with emphasis on similarity coefficients rather than higher-level algorithms.

General Perspective

The two steps of multitype spatial analysis—measurement of the degree of coarrangement of each pair of artifact types and definition of groups of similarly arranged types—require different sets of methods that make assumptions about different aspects of artifact organization. Measures of similarity, which are used in the first step, vary in their assumptions about form of organization along the monothetic-polythetic dimension (Table 6). Higher-level pattern-searching algorithms, which are used in the second step, vary in their assumptions about form of organization along the nonoverlapping-overlapping dimension (Table 7).

It is possible to order available coefficients for measuring similarity into a sequence according to the restrictiveness of their assumptions about artifact

Table 13.6

Similarity Coefficients Appropriate for Analyzing Spatial Arrangements of Artifact Types Having Various Forms of Organization along the Monothetic-Polythetic Dimension

Form of Organization	Appropriate Coefficient For Item Point Location Data	Appropriate Coefficient For Grid Cell Data
Model 1*	AVDISTM (this chapter; Carr, 1984)	—
2	—	Pearson's r
—	—	Kendall's tau and tau-b (Kendall, 1955), partially. Goodman and Kruskal's gamma (Goodman & Kruskal, 1963, p. 322), partially. Spearman's rho (Kendall, 1955), partially.
3	—	—
4	AVDISTLP1 (this chapter; Carr, 1984)	Jaccard similarity coefficient (Sneath & Sokal, 1973), Cole's C_7 (Cole, 1949), Hurlebert's C_8 (Hurlebert, 1969)
5	AVDISTGP (this chapter; Carr, 1984)	—
6	AVDISTLP2 (this chapter)	—

*Models shown in Fig. 3 and described in Table 2.

Table 13.7

Higher-Level Pattern-Searching Algorithms Appropriate for Analyzing the Spatial Arrangement of Artifact Types Having Nonoverlapping or Overlapping Set Organization*

Only Nonoverlapping Sets Constructed	Overlapping or Nonoverlapping Sets Constructed
1. standard polythetic agglomerative clustering routines (Sneath & Sokal, 1973; Anderberg, 1973; Hartigan, 1975)	1. R-mode or Q-mode factor analysis (Rummel, 1970; Davis, 1973)
2. interval scale matrix ordering (Hole & Shaw, 1967; Craytor & Johnson, 1968; Cowgill, 1972; Marquardt, 1978)	2. multidimensional scaling (Kruskal & Wish, 1978)
	3. cluster routines by Jardine and Sibson (1968); Cole and Wishart (1970); for small numbers of observations only
	4. ADCLUS least squares clustering procedures (Shepard & Arabe, 1979; Sarle, 1981; Arabie et al., 1981)
	5. ITREG (Darden, 1982)
	6. OVERCLUS (Carr, this volume)

*All algorithms may operate on each kind of similarity coefficient listed in Table 6, except factor analysis, which strictly must operate only on positive semidefinite matrices to obtain standard interpretations of generated statistics.

organization along the monothetic-polythetic dimension, i.e., according to the spatial relationships that are required to occur between two types for them to be considered coarranged by the measures. This sequence can be coupled with the sequence of organizational models, which similarly stipulate the relationships that are minimally required among types for them to be interpreted as a set. Thus, the models of organizational variation along the monothetic-polythetic dimension can be linked to mathematical measures appropriate for the analysis of data sets that are similar to the models (Table 6). Likewise, the several algorithms available for defining multitype groups can be ordered into two classes, according to whether they are restrictive and assume nonoverlapping structure or are more permissive and allow overlapping structure. This dichotomous sequence is paralleled by variation in the organizational models along the nonoverlapping-overlapping dimension, again allowing model data structures to be coupled with the techniques appropriate for the analysis of data of such forms (Table 7).

The coupling of a sequence of models of artifact organization and a sequence of techniques is helpful not only in meeting the aims of this chapter; it also makes clear certain areas of *technical deficiency* that require correction. First, only one of the models of organization along the monothetic-polythetic dimension has congruent measures of similarity allowing analysis of data in *either* item point location or grid cell format (Table 6). The fact that some models lack similarity measures useful in analyzing data of certain formats—particularly grid cell data—is critical. Most descriptions of archaeological sites record artifact proveniences in a grid cell format rather than a point location format. Often the mesh of the grid is too coarse for the data to be transformed into an approximate point location form that might be analyzed with point location similarity coefficients. Second, there appear to be no similarity coefficients, based on either grid cell or item-point location data, that are strictly concordant with the form of organization posed in Model 3.

The following sections detail the mathematical procedures of some of the measures and methods listed in Tables 6 and 7. They also expand upon the data organizational assumptions of the techniques in behavioral terms, and discuss the linkages between *particular* formation processes, models of organization, and techniques, which could not be presented earlier. The discussions of the similarity coefficients AVDISTM, AVDISTLP1, AVDISTGP, and AVDISTLP2 represent an elaboration and segmentation of the method called polythetic association (Carr, 1984) into several alternative techniques. Discussion will begin with the measures of similarity and proceed to the higher-level pattern-searching algorithms.

AVDISTM

A simple statistic that compares the arrangement of items of two artifact types is AVDISTM: the average absolute distance between items of one type and their nearest neighbors of the second type. A *base type* and *reference type* are chosen. For each item of the base type, the Euclidean distances at which surrounding items of the reference type occur are compared until the nearest neighbor of the reference type is found. The same procedure is then repeated, this time using the items of the reference type as base points and the items of the base type as the satellite reference points. The average intertype distance can be computed by

$$\text{AVDISTM}_{AB} = \frac{\sum_{1}^{n} \overline{AB} + \sum_{1}^{m} \overline{BA}}{n + m} \quad (2)$$

where n is the number of items of type A, m is the number of items of type B, $\overline{AB}$ is the distance from a given base item of type A to its nearest neighbor of type B, and $\overline{BA}$ is the distance from a given base item of type B to its nearest neighbor of type A. Note that the number of $\overline{AB}$ distances n and their sum need not be equal to the number of $\overline{BA}$ distances m and their sum. This depends on whether the number of items of type A and B over a site are equal and symmetrically arranged.

A computer program (POLYTHETIC1) for calculating AVDISTM and other coefficients for multiple pairs of artifact types is provided in Appendix A.

AVDISTM measures the degree of similar arrangement of artifacts of two types relative to the organizational standard characterized in Model 1 (Fig. 4, Table 2). Two artifact types are assumed to have a similar distribution only when they are arranged in a symmetric manner in a 1:1 proportion, both globally and locally. If two artifact types are coarranged such that items of one type are usually close to items of the second type and *vice versa*, both of the sums of distances, $\Sigma\overline{AB}$ and $\Sigma\overline{BA}$, will be small. AVDISTM will be small, indicating that the two types are coarranged. However, if two artifact types are coarranged, but in an asymmetrical manner (similar distributions, different densities; e.g., Model 2, Fig. 4) such that sometimes the less dense type is not close to the more dense type, then one of the sums of distances, $\Sigma\overline{AB}$ or $\Sigma\overline{BA}$, will be large—whichever represents the sum of distances from items of the more dense type to items of the less dense type. Consequently, AVDISTM will be inflated. The coefficient will erroneously indicate that the two types are less coarranged than they really are because it judges asymmetry between types, and "unexpected absences" of items of one type from the vicinity of items of another, as a form of dissociation.

Linkage of Model 1 and AVDISTM to behavior and site formation processes. Model 1 is an appropriate organizational standard and AVDISTM is a correspondingly appropriate measure of the coarrangement of types only when certain rigorous conditions, regarding past behavior and site formation processes, are met.

1) Usually, artifacts of types within the same activity set in the behavioral domain must have been distributed among events in the globally and locally symmetric manner shown in Model 1. Alternative tool types capable of accomplishing the same ends in different episodes of an activity type must not have been employed.

2) The artifacts must have been deposited expediently at their locations of use or in the same refuse dumps. If not deposited expediently, then artifact types in the same activity set must have had equivalent discard rates and all activity areas and refuse dumps within which they were deposited must have been used over an extended time, allowing the proportions of types within such locations to approach stable, 1:1 ratios over time.

3) The artifacts must have remained at their locations of deposition, unaffected by the numerous post-depositional processes that can cause "unexpected absences" of an artifact type (Table 4), until the time of excavation.

4) Artifacts must have been recovered completely and classified to function

correctly, again preventing "unexpected absences." Only if these conditions are true will the artifact types in the same depositional set, representing an activity set, be organized in the form that is stipulated by Model 1 and required by AVDISTM for them to be defined as one set.

Ratio and Rank-Scale Correlation Coefficients

Measures that assess the degree of similar arrangement of artifact type-pairs relative to organizational standards that are less constraining than Model 1 include a variety of ratio and rank scale correlation coefficients applicable to grid cell count data.

Pearson's product-moment correlation coefficient, r. This coefficient can be used to measure the degree of covariation among densities of two artifact types within grid cells. It obtains its highest value ($+1$), indicating perfect coarrangement of two types, when in every cell the *proportion* of artifacts of the two types is some constant; i.e., the data are consistent with Model 2.

Rank correlation coefficients. These measures include Kendall's *tau* and *tau-b* (Kendall, 1955; Nie et al., 1975, p. 227), Spearman's *rho* (Kendall, 1948), and Goodman and Kruskal's *gamma* (Goodman & Kruskal, 1963, p. 322; Nie et al., 1975, p. 228). They are somewhat more permissive than Pearson's *r*. They allow greater variation in the relationships between types within cells before their degree of coarrangement is judged less than perfect, but not to the extent implied by Models 3 or 4, where simply the co-occurrence of types is required. In particular, rank correlation coefficients measure the degree of concordance in two separate rank orderings of grid cells: one by their counts of one artifact type, and a second by their counts of a second type. The coefficients reach their greatest value, $+1$, which indicates perfect coarrangement of two types, when the concordance of the orderings is perfect, i.e., the cells with the first, second, and third highest counts for one artifact type also have the first, second, and third highest counts of the second type, and so on. The proportions of artifact types within cells can vary within restricted ranges without decreasing the value of the coefficients from that indicating perfect coarrangement. Minor local changes in the magnitude and direction of asymmetry between types from cell to cell are permitted, but not to the extent allowed in Models 3 and 4, which will result in discordances among the rank orderings (Fig. 6). Moreover, a monotonic relationship between the ranked number of items of each type within cells is still required, as in Model 2 and unlike in Models 3 and 4.

The different measures of rank correlation vary in how the degree of concordance between rank orderings of grid cells for two types is calculated. Kendall's *tau*, Spearman's *rho*, and Goodman and Kruskal's *gamma* do not discount the effect of tied cell rankings, which tends to inflate their values, whereas Kendall's *tau-b* reduces this distortion and seems preferable (Hietala & Stevens, 1977, p. 549). Also, Kendall's *tau* considers only the correct or incorrect *placements* of grid cells in the two ranked orderings of them, relative to perfect concordance; in contrast, Spearman's *rho* considers the *magnitude of displacements* of grid cells in the two orderings from a perfectly concordant order. Thus, Spearman's *rho* is more sensitive than Kendall's *tau* to large changes in the magnitude and direction of asymmetry between types from cell to cell which cause discrepancies in rank orderings (Fig. 6).

When using Pearson's *r* or any of the rank correlation coefficients, the size, shape, orientation, and placement of cells within the grid system must agree with the predominant size, shape, orientation, and placement of clusters of artifacts, if the values of these measures are to accurately represent the degree of coarrangement of types. The specific effects resulting from discrepancies between grid cell characteristics and cluster characteristics have been summarized by Carr (1984). To overcome these effects, *dimensional analysis of variance*

Fig. 13.6. Rank correlation coefficients allow minor local changes in the magnitude and direction of asymmetry between artifact types in a set to occur from grid cell to grid cell of a study area, without affecting the measures. Large variations in the magnitude and direction of asymmetry implied by Model 3 and Model 4 kinds of organizations are not permitted.

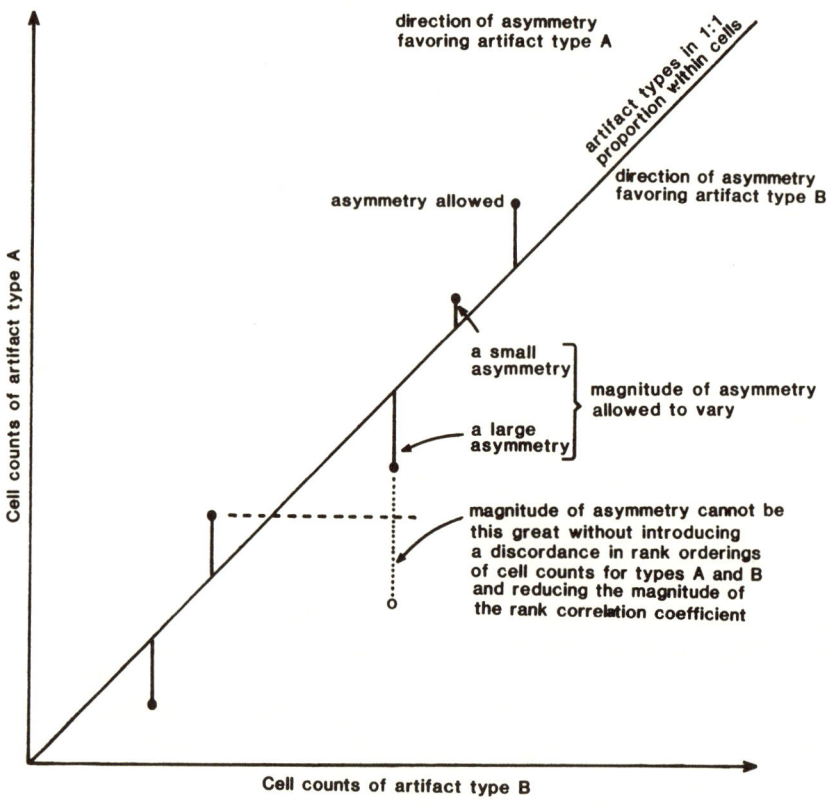

(Grieg-Smith, 1961, 1964; Kershaw, 1964) or *Morisita's method* (Morisita, 1959, 1962) can be used prior to correlation analysis. These methods allow counts within grid cells to be grouped into counts within blocks approximating the size, shape, and orientation of clusters. However, an approach preferable to using dimensional procedures followed by correlation on grouped data is *dimensional analysis of covariance* (Kershaw, 1960, 1961). The procedures for these methods and the limitations of their application to archaeological data are summarized by Carr (1984, pp. 144-154, 166-170) and Whallon (1973).

Linkage of Model 2 and Pearson's r to behavior and site formation processes. Model 2 is an appropriate standard of the relationships between coarranged artifact types, and Pearson's r is a correspondingly appropriate measure of coarrangement relative to that standard, under conditions almost as rigorous as those required of AVDISTM.

1) Artifact types used together as an activity set must have been used at all locations of activity in similar proportions, such that their frequencies covaried.

2) The artifacts must have been deposited expediently at their locations of use or in the same refuse dump.

Alternately, 1) artifact types in the same activity set must have had constant discard rates and 2) all areas of their deposition must have been used over an extended period of time, allowing the proportions of the types within such areas to approach some stable ratio over time.

3) In either case, post-depositional processes causing "unexpected absences" of an artifact type can have occurred, but are limited to those causing absences in equal frequency over all locations of deposition (Table 4, uniform processes). Only these processes will preserve some constant set of proportions between artifact types in the same activity set.

4) Incomplete recovery processes or misclassification processes causing unexpected absences of artifact types must have operated in such a way that absences are distributed in equal frequency over all locations of deposition (seldom true), for the same reason as in point 3.

Jaccard's and Cole's Similarity Coefficients

The degree of simple co-occurrence of two artifact types can be measured with a number of association coefficients that are based on grid cell distribution data organized in the form of a two-way contingency table. The two dimensions of the table represent the "presence" or "absence" of each type within any given grid cell. Presence and absence states can be defined in the usual manner for types occurring in sparse numbers in a few or moderate number of grid cells. Alternatively, they can be defined so as to represent a high-and-low cell count dichotomy made in reference to some count threshold value such as the mean (Dacey, 1973) or median (Pielou, 1969; Hietala & Stevens, 1977)—an approach useful for types having a greater range of cell counts and a more ubiquitous distribution. Among the most commonly used association coefficients calculated from data in this format are the *simple matching* coefficient, the *Jaccard* coefficient, and indices of *Dice, Bray,* and *Yule* (Sneath & Sokal, 1973).

The various association coefficients differ in the weights they attach to the a, b, c, and d cells of the contingency tables used in calculating them, and thus, are appropriate under different circumstances. Of relevance here is the weight given to the d cell in contributing to the association of the two dimensions. When the two levels of each dimension of the contingency table represent alternative attribute states of observations, one state of which *must occur* for each observation (e.g., dark hair/light hair; dark eyes/light eyes), then the matches of the d cell should count toward the association of the two dimensions. In contrast, when the two levels of each dimension represent the presence or absence of a characteristic which *need not or can not occur* for each observation, then a coefficient that omits consideration of negative matches is desirable: one is interested in the relative frequency of joint occurrences or single occurrences of the characteristics in only those observations that have one or more of them (Cole, 1949; Sneath & Sokal, 1973, p. 131).

Intrasite spatial data tabulating the presence or absence of artifact types within grid cells, where each type represents a characteristic that need not occur in all observations (cells), are of the latter form. Thus, they are appropriately analyzed only with coefficients that do not allow negative matches to contribute to association. One coefficient that accomplishes this requirement is the Jaccard coefficient

$$J_{xy} = \frac{a}{a+b+c} \quad (3)$$

where a, b, and c are the values of the a, b, and c cells in the contingency table for artifact types x and y. Other coefficients are Cole's C_7 (Cole, 1949, p. 423) and a more general and sometimes preferable form of it, Hurlbert's C_8 (Hurlbert, 1969).

Like the application of ratio and rank scale correlation coefficients, the application of association coefficients to archaeological data assumes that the size, shape, orientation, and placement of the grid cells within which the artifact distributions are framed are appropriate compared to these same spatial characteristics for artifact clusters. Deviation of grid cells from artifact clusters in these characteristics bias the association coefficients as measures of coarrangement in ways analogous to those in which the correlation coefficients are biased (Carr, 1984).

Jaccard's, Cole's, and Hurlbert's coefficients measure the degree of similar arrangement of artifacts of two types relative to the organizational standards characterized in Model 4. The measures obtain their highest value (+1), which indicates perfect coarrangement of two types, when both types simply *occur* jointly in the same grid cells and deposits, regardless of the magnitudes or directions of asymmetry between the types. The coefficients have less stringent requirements for assessing coarrangement than those stipulated by Model 3, which assumes that two types are coarranged only if they both occur together and maintain the same direction of asymmetry from cell to cell or deposit to deposit. There currently are no standard measures of association that assume the kind of organization expressed in Model 3, although this kind of data structure is not idiosyncratic to archaeology (Pielou, 1964).

Linkage of Model 4 and association coefficients to behavior and site formation processes. Association coefficients that are concordant with the form of organization in Model 4 are appropriate measures of the relationships between artifact types under conditions more typical of the archaeological record.

1) Even assuming that activity areas and their associated refuse dumps were used only a short period of time (an assumption leading to the most restrictive set of conditions to be discussed here), it is only necessary that artifact types in the same activity set were always used together; the proportions in which they were used need not have been constant.

2) The artifacts must have been deposited expediently in their locations of use or discard such that artifact types used together also occur together archaeologically. If the effects of differential breakage rates and curation rates or other formation processes have caused different subsets of the activity set to be deposited at different locations of its use, lower associations will be found between the artifact types; their membership in one activity set may not be apparent.

3) Only one representative of each artifact type that is deposited in the activity areas or associated dumps need have remained there and/or have been recovered and classified correctly. Whereas *any* amount of spatially nonuniform post-depositional disturbance, incomplete recovery, or misclassification of artifacts within deposits will distort the proportions of types within them—affecting the ratio scale correlation coefficient and the AVDISTM measure of coarrangement—these same processes can proceed in a nonuniform manner to a *considerable* degree without affecting the pattern of presence or absence states of types among deposits. The degree to which these processes can proceed for an artifact type is inversely related to its original frequency of deposition.

If activity areas and their associated refuse dumps were used over an extended period of time, even less constraining conditions are required for the appropriate application of association coefficients. As an alternative to condition 1, above, artifact types in an activity set can have been distributed in a globally polythetic manner among events and areas of use or deposition (i.e., as in Model 5 or 6). (This might result from some of the types having been alternative or optional tool forms.) In such conditions, the repeated use of the work areas or dumps will have caused the presence-absence states of each type in the activity set within each of the several locations to tend toward presence over time. This represents one circumstance in which the organization of artifact types in the behavioral domain is atypically *less constraining* than their organization in the archaeological domain.

As an alternative to condition 2, above, artifacts need not have been deposited expediently within activity areas or associated dumps, and types can have had variable discard rates. Again, repeated use of the locations will have increased the probability, over time, that all types within the activity set were deposited in each location and co-occur.

AVDISTLP1, AVDISTGP, AVDISTLP2

Measures of coarrangement that are concordant with Models 4, 5, or 6 and applicable to item point location data can be derived through modifications of the AVDISTM statistic. Central to each of the derivations is a key argument related to the goal of designing measures that are insensitive to *asymmetry* among artifact types or changes in its *magnitude* from place to place within a study area—the common denominators of the three models. The argument is as follows:

Suppose that two artifact types are coarranged within an area, but in an asymmetric manner. Items of the more densely distributed type will always occur in the neighborhoods of items of the less densely distributed type, but not vice versa; i.e., there will be "unexpected absences" of the less densely distributed type in certain locations of the more densely distributed type (Fig. 5c). Under these circumstances, the two sums of intertype distances $\Sigma \overline{AB}$ and $\Sigma \overline{BA}$, which were defined previously (pp. 359-360), will not be equal. The distances from items of the rarer type to items of the more common type will generally be small, as will their sum, because items of the rarer type usually are surrounded by items of the more common type. These distances and their sum will accurately indicate the degree of coarrangement of types under the assumption of permissible asymmetry relations, because they *ignore the "unexpected absences"* of the rarer type in some locations of the more common type. In contrast, the distances from items of the more densely distributed type to items of the less densely distributed type will sometimes be large, and their sum will be large, because items of the more common type are not necessarily surrounded by items of the rarer type. These distances and their sum will not accurately measure the degree of coarrangement of types under the assumption of permissible asymmetry relations, because they reflect the unexpected absences of items of the rarer type from the neighborhods of some items of the more common type. For example, in Figure 5c, type X and O are coarranged under the assumption of permissible asymmetry relations. The distances from type X (the rarer type) to type O (the common type) are all small, ignore the unexpected absence of an item of type X from the item of type O in the upper right hand corner, and accurately estimate the degree of coarrangement of the two types under the assumed form of organization. The distances from type O to type X, on the other hand, are sometimes small but sometimes large, consider any unexpected absences of type X from the vicinity of type O, and do not necessarily estimate the degree of coarrangement of the two types accurately.

To design a measure of coarrangement that is analogous to AVDISTM but unaffected by the asymmetrical form of arrangement of artifact types within a given area, it should be clear from the above that it is necessary to consider only those distances from items of the more common type to items of the rarer type. This can be achieved by calculating *two* average inter-item distances

$$\text{AVDIST1} = \frac{\sum_1^n \overline{AB}}{n} \qquad \text{AVDIST2} = \frac{\sum_1^m \overline{BA}}{m} \qquad (4)$$

and choosing the *minimum* of the two as the measure of coarrangement of the two types:

$$\text{AVDIST} = \min(\text{AVDIST1}, \text{AVDIST2}) \qquad (5)$$

High values of AVDIST, which indicate dissociation of two artifact types, will occur only when both types are *mutually distant* from each other.

By measuring the degree of coarrangement of two artifact types in this manner, it thus is possible to isolate two kinds of absences of an artifact of one type from the neighborhood of an artifact of another—the two kinds of absences having different *causes*. These are 1) *mutual* absences due to the *actual dissociation* of the types from each other and reflecting their belonging to different depositional sets, and 2) *unexpected asymmetrical* absences that indicate only the asymmetrical form of distribution of artifact types and that result from any of the *formation processes* listed in Table 4.

Note that the statistic, AVDIST, is insensitive not only to the asymmetrical form of coarrangement of two types, but also to local differences in the magnitude of the asymmetry. The average distance from items of the rarer type to items of the more common type—the chosen measure of coarrangement—is unaffected by whether items of the rarer type are missing from the vicinity of *few* or *many* items of the more common type in any given portion of the study area. Only the *ignored* average distance, from items of the common type to items of the rare type, is affected by the frequencies of unexpected absences and the magnitudes of asymmetry within subareas.

Three similarity coefficients—AVDISTLP1, AVDISTGP, and AVDISTLP2—which measure the degree of coarrangement of types relative to the different organizational standards posed in Models 4, 5, and 6, respectively, can be constructed. This can be achieved by 1) applying the procedure for partitioning intertype distances to areas of different scale, and 2) stipulating how the complete absence of a type from a cluster of artifacts should be handled.

Constructing AVDISTLP1. AVDISTLP1, a "locally polythetic average intertype nearest neighbor distance coefficient," is designed to be congruent in its assumptions with the organizational requirements for coarrangemnt that are specified by Model 4. Model 4 allows the asymmetry relations occurring between two coarranged artifact types to vary in direction and magnitude from artifact cluster to artifact cluster. However, it requires that each cluster contain at least one of the artifact types—that asymmetry in any cluster not be taken to the extreme case in which one of the types is completely absent from it (Table 2).

AVDISTLP1 allows the direction of asymmetry between two coarranged artifact types to vary from cluster to cluster by partitioning intertype distances locally, *within each cluster*. If AVDIST1$_j$ and AVDIST2$_j$ represent the partitioned average distances between items of two types A and B within cluster j having n_j items of type A and m_j items of type B, and if

$$\text{AVDIST1}_j = \frac{\sum_{1}^{n_j} \overline{AB}}{n_j} \qquad \text{AVDIST2}_j = \frac{\sum_{1}^{m_j} \overline{BA}}{m_j} \qquad (6)$$

then a measure of the asymmetrical coarrangement of the two types within cluster j can be defined as:

$$\text{AVDIST}_j = \min(\text{AVDIST1}_j, \text{AVDIST2}_j) \qquad (7)$$

The degree of coarrangement of the two types over the study area at large can be defined as the average of the AVDIST$_j$ statistics, weighted in accordance with the number of distances, x_j (either n_j or m_j), used to calculate them:

$$\text{AVDISTLP1} = \frac{\sum_{j=1}^{k} (x_j)(\text{AVDIST}_j)}{\sum_{j=1}^{k} (x_j)} \qquad (8)$$

By default, the statistic is congruent with Model 4's stipulation that the magnitude of asymmetry between coarranged artifact types be allowed to vary from artifact cluster to cluster; each intracluster measure of coarrangement, AVDIST$_j$ is insensitive to the magnitude of asymmetry within the cluster.

AVDISTLP1 is made congruent with the final requirement of Model 4—that each cluster contain at least one artifact of each type for two types to be considered perfectly coarranged—by adhering to a second stipulation in calculating the statistic. If within any cluster j only one of the two types under consideration is present, then the measure of coarrangement of the two types for that cluster, AVDIST$_j$, is defined as the average distance from items of the type present in the cluster to nearest items of the missing type in *any other cluster*. These *intercluster* distances, of course, will be large giving a large value to AVDIST$_j$ and increasing the value of AVDISTLP1 proportionally. As more and more clusters completely lack one of the two types, interpretable as less similar arrangement of the types under the assumptions of Model 4, more of the $AVDIST_j$ statistics will become large in value and AVDISTLP1 will appropriately become greater, indicating generally greater distances between items of the two types.

The procedures just presented assume three restrictive conditions of the data to be analyzed. 1) The spatial distribution of each artifact type exhibits clusters. 2) The clusters are spatially discrete and uniquely definable. 3) Clusters are the proper natural units between which asymmetries among artifact types should be allowed to vary in direction. The last assumption is valid if the processes responsible for local variation in the direction of asymmetry relations are the same cultural formation processes that were involved in artifact deposition and cluster generation. The assumption is invalid if the processes that caused asymmetry variation are post-depositional disturbance or recovery processes which could have operated on different spatial strata that crosscut clusters.

Some of these constraints can be relaxed if additional analytic steps are taken. 1) Suppose that clusters of artifacts are apparent within the distributions of each type but overlap mildly such that the cluster membership of relatively few items is uncertain (e.g., as in the Pincevent example, below). Also suppose that major changes in the direction of asymmetry between types do not occur within clusters, suggesting that clusters—rather than other strata crosscutting clusters—are reasonably proper units between which asymmetries among types should be allowed to vary in direction. In these circumstances, it is possible to draw *approximate* boundaries between the clusters and then to calculate within-cluster $AVDIST_j$ statistics that are nevertheless meaningful, using the following additional algorithmic procedure. If an item of type X has its nearest neighbor of the opposite type O *outside* the cluster j to which the item of type X is assigned (indicating a misdrawn boundary), then *that* nearest neighbor distance, rather than some spuriously larger one to a nearest neighbor of type O within the cluster, should be used to calculate the average distance from type X to type O in cluster j. In this way, the approximate method by which the boundaries between clusters are drawn and by which the item-membership of each cluster is determined does not artificially inflate the $AVDIST_j$ statistics and AVDISTLP1. Also, clusters can be retained as the natural units within which asymmetries between artifact types are allowed to vary, even though cluster boundaries are uncertain—a desirable circumstance.

2) An alternative approach can be taken if the data are more problematic in any of three ways: (a) if clusters are ill-defined, with wide artifact density gradients between the cores of clusters, making the cluster membership of many peripheral items unclear; (b) if clusters are not apparent at all; or (c) if clusters do not appear to be appropriate units between which artifact types should be allowed to vary in their asymmetries, based on knowledge of the formation and recovery processes for the site. The approach involves the following procedures. For any pair of types under consideration, the local relative densities of the two

types within the neighborhood of each item of either type is calculated. The radius of the neighborhood used to calculate local relative densities should be much less than that expected of any clusters that might occur in the data, but large enough to include at least several items of either type. A map of the local proportional densities of the two types then is made, which documents spatial variation in the direction of asymmetry between them (proportional densities greater than 1 or less than 1). This map can be used to define larger zones that are relatively homogeneous in the direction of local asymmetry between the types and within which $AVDIST_j$ statistics can be calculated meaningfully. AVDISTLP1 thus can be determined and the data can be analyzed in accordance with the stipulations of Model 4. Of course, if larger zones homogeneous in the asymmetry of the two artifact types are not defined by the resulting map, analysis of the data using Model 4 assumptions and the AVDISTLP1 coefficients is inappropriate.

A computer program for performing the operations of finding $AVDIST_j$ and AVDISTLP1 statistics for all pairs of types within a multitype spatial data set is provided in Appendix A. The program, POLYTHETIC2, requires the stratum assignments of each item of each type to have been determined in advance, whether the strata are clusters or zones defined on the basis of directions of asymmetries between types. It also assumes that the same strata are appropriate for each artifact type pair, though there may be instances in which this assumption is not desirable and program modification is warranted.

Constructing AVDISTGP. AVDISTGP, a "globally polythetic average intertype nearest neighbor distance coefficient," is designed to be congruent in its assumptions with the organizational requirements for coarrangement specified by Model 5. Model 5 allows the asymmetry relations between two coarranged types to vary in magnitude from cluster to cluster. It also allows asymmetry to be carried to the extreme where the rarer of the two types need not occur in some clusters, i.e., where depositional sets are globally polythetic. However, the model requires that the direction of asymmetry between the two types remain the same over all clusters—or over all locations if clusters do not exist.

All of these allowances and requirements of Model 5 can be operationalized by partitioning intertype distances into two sets globally, over the whole study area, rather than within clusters. Thus, if AVDIST1 and AVDIST2 represent the partitioned average distances between items of two types A and B within a study area having n items of type A and m items of type B, as in equation 4, then

$$\text{AVDISTGP} = \min(\text{AVDIST1}, \text{AVDIST2}) \tag{9}$$

defines the desired measure of coarrangement.

How AVDISTGP assumes the uniformity of asymmetry relations between two types over all clusters of artifacts or locales within a study area is apparent from the global manner of definition of the two kinds of average intertype distances, AVDIST1 and AVDIST2, and the choice of one of these global statistics as AVDISTGP. Suppose a study area is divided into strata representing clusters or areas of homogeneous asymmetry relations. The operation of calculating AVDISTGP for the study area at large is equivalent to 1) defining an $AVDIST1_j$ statistic and $AVDIST2_j$ statistic for each stratum j within the study area such that all the $AVDIST1_j$ imply distances from the same one kind of artifact to the same other kind and all the $AVDIST2_j$ imply distances in the reverse direction, 2) picking the same $AVDISTn_j$ statistic in all strata as if it were the minimum, and 3) averaging them. If an asymmetry reversal from the global norm occurs in any locale, the chosen $AVDISTn_j$ will *not* be the minimum of the two $AVDISTn_j$ statistics. The average of all the chosen $AVDISTn_j$ statistics, equivalent to AVDISTGP, will thus be inflated compared to that which would be obtained if the asymmetry reversal did not occur; this will indicate the less-than-perfect coarrangement of the two types by Model 5 standards.

How AVDISTGP assumes that the magnitude of asymmetry between two types can vary from locale to locale within a study area also is clear. Under the assumption that the data do not have local asymmetry reversals, the minimum $AVDISTn$ chosen to define AVDISTGP represents inter-item distances from the rarer to the more common artifact type in each locale. These distances are insensitive to the magnitude of asymmetry.

Finally, by extension, it can be shown that AVDISTGP does not require the rarer of two types to be present in each cluster or locale where the more common type occurs. Again, assume that the data do not have local asymmetry reversals and that the minimum $AVDISTn$ chosen to define AVDISTGP represents inter-item distances from the rarer to the more common artifact type in each locale. A locale will then contribute nothing to the value of AVDISTGP if the rarer type does not occur in it and the more common type does.

A computer program for calculating AVDISTGP statistics is provided in Appendix A. The program, POLYTHETIC1, does not require stratum assignments for each item of each type as does POLYTHETIC2.

Constructing AVDISTLP2. AVDISTLP2, another "locally polythetic average intertype nearest neighbor distance coefficient," is designed to be congruent with Model 6. Model 6, like Model 4, allows the asymmetry relations occurring between two coarranged types to vary in direction and magnitude from stratum to stratum. However, it also permits some strata to not have either one type or the other.

AVDISTLP2 allows the direction of asymmetry between two coarranged artifact types to vary from stratum to stratum using the same approach as AVDISTLP1, i.e., the partitioning of intertype distances into two sets locally, within each stratum (equations 6, 7, 8). This procedure also allows the magnitude of asymmetry relations between types to vary from stratum to stratum, as discussed above.

To allow some strata to not have one of the two types without increasing the value of AVDISTLP2—the point of departure of AVDISTLP2 from AVDISTLP1—it is necessary to make only a simple modification in the second procedural rule used in calculating AVDISTLP1. If within any stratum j only one of the two types under consideration is present, then the average intertype distance for the two types in that stratum, $AVDIST_j$, is set at 0 rather than at the average distance from items of the type present in the cluster to nearest items of the missing type that occur in other clusters. In this way, the absence of items of a type from a cluster does not cause any increase in the value of AVDISTLP2. The value of AVDISTLP2 depends entirely on the degree of coarrangement of the two types within only those strata where *both* are present.

Linkage of AVDISTLP1 to behavior and site formation processes. AVDISTLP1 is an appropriate measure of the coarrangement of types under the same behavioral and site formation conditions that were specified for Jaccard's and Cole's coefficient and that are congruent with the organizational properties of Model 4.

Linkage of Model 5 and AVDISTGP to behavior and site formation processes. Model 5 is an appropriate organizational standard and AVDISTGP is a correspondingly appropriate measure of the coarrangement of types under conditions that are both more and less restrictive than those appropriate for the application of Model 4, AVDISTLP1, and the association coefficients.

1) It is necessary that artifact types within the same activity set were always used together, with the more numerous types in one event always being the more numerous types in other events.

2) Artifact types must have been deposited expediently in their locations of use.

Alternatively, 1) artifact types in the same activity set must have had discard rates that varied within restricted ranges such that the ordinal relations among the rates did not vary over time, and 2) all areas of deposition must have been used over an extended period of time, allowing those ordinal relations between the frequencies of types to have stabilized over time.

3) Post-depositional disturbance processes and incomplete recovery or misclassification processes can have totally removed some artifact types from some depositional areas. However, if more than two artifact types exhibit eradication, the areas affected must be the same for all the eradicated types. The coincidence of the affected areas for the several eradicated types is necessary if a Model 5 type of organization rather than a Model 6 type of organization is to characterize the data. This requirement implies that the processes affecting the eradication of the several types must have been spatially correlated, which in some cases may be restrictive.

Linkage of Model 6 and AVDISTLP2 to behavior and site formation processes. Model 6 is an appropriate organizational standard and AVDISTLP2 is an appropriate measure of coarrangement of artifact types under behavioral and site formation conditions that are least restrictive.

1) Artifact types in an activity set can have been distributed in a globally polythetic manner among events and areas of use or deposition (Model 5 or 6 organization) as a result of some of them having been either alternative or optional tool forms.

2) Artifacts need not have been deposited expediently in their locations of use or discard, regardless of the length of time the areas were used. In some areas, some types within the same set can be unexpectedly absent as a result of the artifacts having been curated and the areas having been used over a limited amount of time.

3) Spatially nonuniform post-depositional disturbance, incomplete recovery, or misclassification of artifacts can have operated to a great degree in an uncorrelated manner, causing different artifact tyes within the same set to be completely missing in different areas where they might otherwise be expected on the basis of the types present in the areas.

At the same time, however, AVDISTLP2 requires the stringent condition that different activity sets (polythetically or monothetically organized) were deposited in areas that do not overlap to a *great* extent. Suppose that two different activity sets were deposited in many clusters, only a few of which overlap extensively. AVDISTLP2 will focus assessment of the degree of coarrangement of the artifact types on the few overlapping clusters where types from *both* sets are present and will ignore the larger number of areas where types from one or the other set are absent (Fig. 7). Artifact types that belong to the two different sets will spuriously be found to be similarly arranged. Slight amounts of overlap among many areas, however, will not produce such misleading results.

Higher-Level Pattern Searching Algorithms

Once the degree of coarrangement between each pair of artifact types has been measured with one of the similarity or dissimilarity measures previously described, it is possible to search for groups of multiple types having mutually similar arrangements. The algorithms in Table 7 can be used for this purpose. They essentially search for those relationships among type-pairs that are approximately *consistent* with and *reinforce* each other in suggesting that the multiple types belong to the same or different groups. The result is a matrix of *smoothed* relationships among types, which can be displayed visually as graphic representations having a *few* dimensions and in a way that the original matrix of complex relations cannot.

It is desirable that the algorithms used to find multitype sets have certain characteristics; consequently, some algorithms are preferable to others. These characteristics are as follows:

1) Control over smoothing. The degree of "inconsistency" between pairwise relationships that is ignored when "smoothing" them should be within the control of the researcher. Only some of the pattern-searching approaches in

374   INTRASITE SPATIAL ANALYSIS

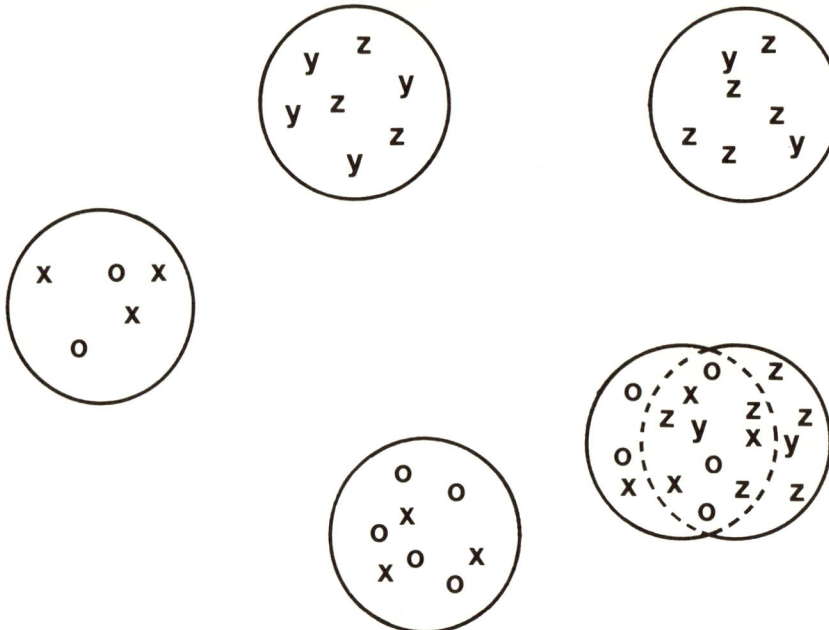

Fig. 13.7. Suppose artifact types *x* and *o* define one activity set and types *y* and *z* define another. If there is extensive spatial overlap in even just a few areas of their deposition, then AVDISTLP2 will take low values for artifact type-pairs in the different sets as well as for those in the same sets. It will spuriously indicate the similar arrangement of types in both sets. AVDISTM, AVDISTLP1, and AVDISTGP do not have this potential problem.

Table 7 allow this control. For example, when employing a polythetic agglomerative clustering approach, it is possible to choose whether a single, average, or complete linkage criterion is used to group types.[3] In an R-mode factor analytic or multidimensional scaling framework, one can choose the number of dimensions—and to some extent, the percentage of total variation in the data—to be included in displays of the data. The remaining algorithms in Table 7 do not have comparable mechanisms for controlling the degree of inconsistency that is ignored during analysis.

2) Permissible variation of structure along the nonoverlapping-overlapping dimension. The algorithm should allow groups of artifact types to be found that are overlapping, nonoverlapping, or a mixture of both forms of organization, depending entirely on the structure of the data. Table 7 lists the form of data organization, along the nonoverlapping-overlapping dimension, that is assumed by various algorithms.

3) Unnecessary a priori specification of structural parameters of the data. It should not be necessary to specify, before analysis, any vital parameters of the data's structure. The overlapping clustering approach of Jardine and Simpson (1968) and Cole and Wishart (1970) is less desirable in this manner. It requires the number of types in zones of overlap among groups to be specified (controlled by the parameter k). ADCLUS and ITREG require the number of groups of types to be known prior to analysis, and are also less preferable. The remaining algorithms in Table 7 are not constraining in this manner.

4) Concordance with similarity coefficients of many scales. The algorithm used to group types should be concordant with as wide a diversity of similarity coefficients as is possible. This trait becomes desirable when it is unclear which of a few models of archaeological organization along the monothetic-polythetic dimension is most congruent with the data at hand or when several models are congruent with different aspects of the data. Under these conditions, the data must be analyzed from several perspectives using different similarity coefficients. The several similarity matrices should be searched for multitype groups using the same pattern-searching algorithm, so that the several results are comparable.

All of the approaches in Table 7, except factor analytic ones, can be applied to matrices of any of the similarity measures described earlier. Factor analytic procedures require that the matrix to be operated on be *positive semidefinite*. This condition is met by variance-covariance matrices and correlation matrices, in relation to which principal components analysis and factor analysis were originally developed. It is also met by matrices of some other kinds of similarity measures, including the Jaccard coefficient, provided that there are no missing data (Gower, 1971, p. 860; 1966, p. 332).

Braun (1976, p. 52) has applied principal components analysis to a matrix of $\emptyset/\emptyset_{max}$ coefficients numerically identical to Cole's C_7 coefficient (Speth & Johnson, 1967, p. 42), in which case the matrix of coefficients apparently was not positive semidefinite. He notes that the technique correctly extracted the eigenvectors of the matrix, but the absolute sizes of the eigenvalues did not relate algebraically to the overall variance as in the normal use of principal components analysis. Braun argues, however, the the relative sizes of the eigenvalues properly indicated the relative importance of their associated eigenvectors in describing patterning in the matrix. The use of factor analysis with various similarity coefficients is an area that needs further investigation.

5) Efficiency. The algorithm should operate efficiently, such that similarities between a large number of types can be analyzed for multitype groups in a reasonable amount of computer time. The Jardine-Sibson and Cole-Wishart overlapping clustering routines are less useful in this way. The Cole-Wishart routine—the more efficient of the two—requires an impracticable amount of time when the number of artifact types to be grouped rises above approximately 16 (Cole & Wishart, 1970, p. 162).

The particular techniques that are most useful for defining multitype clusters can vary from instance to instance with the nature of the data being analyzed. However, considering all the desirable characteristics of a pattern-searching technique simultaneously, the most broadly applicable approach seems to be multidimensional scaling, sometimes coupled with OVERCLUS. These approaches are used on the Pincevent data set examined here, and require further exposition.

Multidimensional Scaling

Multidimensional scaling (MDS) includes a very wide diversity of alternative and complementary display techniques (Schiffman et al., 1980; Kruskal & Wish, 1978; Shepard et al., 1972; Romney et al., 1972). For the purposes of this chapter, it will be assumed that the reader is familiar with many of these approaches. Attention will be focused instead on the content of justifications and bridging arguments for choosing between the various procedures in relation to the nature of intrasite spatial data. Also, some of the problems likely to arise in the multidimensional scaling of intrasite data and appropriate solutions to them will be discussed.

1) Choice of regression methods. The objective functions used to obtain an MDS representation of similarity data can be determined with classical, monotonic, or categorical least squares regression techniques (Young & Lewychyj, 1980). The first approach leads to *classical* or *metric* MDS solutions, where a specific functional relation is assumed between the similarity coefficients in the unsmoothed matrix and distances between entities in the smoothed configuration. The latter two approaches lead to *nonmetric* solutions, where the function can be any rising, monotonic relation between dissimilarities and distances.

All the similarity coefficients described above for use in intrasite spatial analysis take ratio-scale values and are amenable to either classical or monotonic MDS procedures. It is advisable in most cases to begin analysis with monotonic procedures, in order to find the appropriate number of dimensions for representing the data. Representational accuracy in the chosen number of dimensions can then be refined with classical methods.

Monotonic procedures are more helpful than classical ones in determining the proper number of dimensions for displaying data, for two reasons. (a) Classical solutions are susceptible to inflation of stress values and to unstable representations when an objective function of the wrong form is used. These conditions make it difficult for the researcher to choose the appropriate number of dimensions for data-display using either of two common criteria: the stability of representations or their interpretability. Monotonic methods, which do not require the specification of an objective function of a particular form, are not so disadvantaged (Kruskal & Wish, 1978, pp. 76-78). (b) For monotonic methods, Monte Carlo studies are available, which suggest stress values that are and are not statistically significant (Kruskal & Wish, 1978, pp. 53-56).

For some intrasite data sets, however, classical methods are likely to be preferable from the start. This is true where groups of coarranged types are few in number and nonoverlapping, and where the differences in arrangement between groups is large compared to intragroup arrangement variation, i.e., where a few compact, distant groups characterize the data. Under these conditions, monotonic procedures can produce "degenerate" solutions (Kruskal & Wish, 1977, p. 30). The number of groups and their constituent types will be correctly identified, but the relationships among groups will not be accurately described, prohibiting analysis of hierarchical patterning. The problem of degeneracy and the necessity of using classical methods to overcome it are less likely for study areas where formation processes leading to overlapping sets of deposits have operated (Table 5).

2) Choice of approaches to interpreting configurations. Configurations that result from multidimensional scalings can be examined for relationships among entities in two ways. Most commonly, interpretable *dimensions* of variability within a configuration are sought by examining variation in the attributes of the scaled entities in different directions. Regression techniques are used to determine whether the attributes thought to explain the positioning of entities in certain directions actually have statistically significant explanatory power (Kruskal & Wish, 1978, pp. 35-43). An alternative approach is *neighborhood analysis*, in which local groups of entities with similar attributes are sought (Guttman, 1965; Kruskal & Wish, 1978, pp. 43-48). Clustering techniques can be applied to matrices of Euclidean distances between the stimulus coordinates of entities to locate potentially significant clusters (see pp. 380). A variety of standard statistical procedures can be used to test whether the distributions of attributes differ significantly from cluster to cluster.

For intrasite spatial analysis, where the goal is to define groups of similarly arranged types that represent depositional sets, the neighborhood analysis approach to configuration interpretation is more appropriate.

3) Methods for exploring local structures. In intrasite spatial analysis, both global and local structure are of interest. The researcher is concerned with hierarchical relationships among groups of artifact types representing depositional sets; these relationships indicate the overall organization of space-use within a site. He is also interested in the detailed relationship among pairs of types within depositional sets and shared by sets; these can indicate, for example, tool kit and technological organization. However, MDS typically provides more accurate representation of the general, global structure of a data set at the expense of details of local structure (Graef & Spence, 1976).

To obtain accurate information on the internal organization of depositional sets and their patterns of overlap, several procedures can be used. (a) A separate MDS can be made for the artifact types composing each group of each set of interrelated groups that is defined in the global configuration of all types within the data set. (b) In each such separate analysis, *jacknife* procedures, which involve the systematic elimination of alternative, single types from consideration, can be used to determine finer-scale dependencies (Mosteller & Tukey, 1977). (c) In each separate analysis, the matrix of residual distances also can be examined for this purpose (Kruskal & Wish, 1978, pp. 33, 45-48).

4) Compensating for unreliability in some similarity values. The values taken by a similarity coefficient for different pairs of artifact types can vary in their reliability, depending on the number of items of each type comprising the pairs. Coefficient values for type-pairs where one or both types are represented by only a few items have a greater likelihood of being biased as a result of either inadequate sampling of cultural formation processes or the effects of postdepositional disturbance processes.

Under these circumstances, it would be desirable to weight the contributions of various similarity values to the total configuration in accordance with their probable reliability, as a function of the number of observations on which they depend. However, this option is not available in standard scaling programs. As a less desirable alternative, a MDS analysis of only those frequent artifact types that have the most probably reliable similarity values can be performed first. This baseline analysis can then be followed by ones that introduce less probably reliable types into the solution, either sequentially or on a replacement basis. The reliability of the similarity values associated with such an introduced type, and of the configuration including it, can be approximately assessed by the degree to which the configuration of types remains essentially stable after the introduction of the questionable type, provided that the number of likely reliable types is much larger than the number of possibly biased ones.

5) Screening and analyzing data with ubiquitously distributed types. Artifact types that occur ubiquitously across a site in high densities should not be included initially in a MDS analysis; they can cause distortions in results. If the similarity coefficients used to summarize the degree of coarrangement of types are AVDISTGM, AVDISTLP1, or the similarity measures of Jaccard or Cole, the ubiquitous artifact types will be characterized as differing in their arrangement from all of the more spatially restricted types. This will lead to a *space-dilating* effect in the MDS solution. If the coefficients used are AVDISTGP or AVDISTLP2, the ubiquitous types will be characterized as very similar in their arrangement to all more spatially restricted types. This will produce a *space-contracting* effect. The scaling procedures of most MDS algorithms will compensate for the global average degree of dilation or contraction so as to produce a configuration of standard size and stimulus coordinates of similar range. However, any local variations in the degree of dilation or contraction from group to group of types will still be manifested in the final configuration. This distortion can involve either minor alterations in the distances among types and among groups of types within a configuration, causing no effect on the composition of defined groups, or more substantial shifts in the positions of types, leading to new group compositions. Additionally, the relationship between configuration stress and dimension over the various representations of the data can be altered, particularly at lower dimensions. All of these effects are noted in the analysis of the Pincevent data (see pp. 439-441).

To avoid these undesirable effects, two different strategies can be used. The one which is appropriate depends on the nature and probable causes of the ubiquitous distributions (Carr, 1984). (a) Suppose that a type has a ubiquitous, high density distribution which is fairly *uniform or random* in nature. The difference between the form of its distribution and that of other types in the data set which have clustered distributions (ubiquitous or restricted in space) indicates the different patterns of use, deposition, and possibly post-depositional disturbance of the type. The different form of its distribution, alone, suggests that it does not belong to depositional sets that might be definable among the types having clustered arrangements, and that it should be removed from analysis.

(b) If a type has a ubiquitous, high density distribution that exhibits local *clusters* of artifacts within it, this suggests that its distribution is a complex *palimpsest* (see p. 321) resulting from at least two different depositional or post-depositional processes: one leading to the ubiquity of artifacts, the other to their clustering. In this case, the artifact type's distribution should be dissected into its component distributions—one or more clustered distributions of restricted spatial extent and one or more ubiquitous distributions. This can be achieved using spatial filtering or Fourier procedures that are concordant with the formation processes thought responsible for the components. Similarity measures should then be calculated between all other types and those components that have spatially restricted, clustered distributions rather than the composite, ubiquitous distribution. These coefficients should be used in the MDS analysis. Carr (1982a, 1984, 1986) discusses the theory and methods for such dissection.

(c) A less complicated but also less precise alternative to the dissecting method for handling artifact types with ubiquitous, high-density, clustered distributions can be used. First, a multidimensional scaling of those artifact types that do not have ubiquitous distributions and that will not distort analysis should be performed in order to determine the stable relationships among these types. Then, the ubiquitous, high-density, clustered types can be brought into the analysis, one at a time, on a replacement basis, to determine their positions within groups of nonubiquitous types. The positioning of each ubiquitous type within the configuration will depend more on the relation of its *clustered* component(s) to the distributions of the other types than its ubiquitous component(s), the latter being more equally associated with all types. Of course, the ubiquitous component(s), will cause some distortion to the configuration.

Only one ubiquitous, high-density, clustered type should be brought into the analysis at a time. This is necessary to maintain the compositions of groups of nonubiquitous types as stable as possible so that they remain identifiable and so that the relationship of the ubiquitous type to the groups is clear. Moreover, there is no advantage to bringing several ubiquitous types into an analysis simultaneously. The resulting configuration will not suggest the proper degree of association of the clustered component(s) of the ubiquitous types to each other. The types will tend to associate strongly as a result of the common arrangement of their ubiquitous components, thus masking the degree of similarity in the arrangement of their clustered components. This tendency will increase as the *intensity* of patterning within the distributions of the ubiquitous, clustered types decreases, i.e., as the density differences between clusters and their ubiquitous background decreases. All of these phenomena were noted in the Pincevent data analysis.

A New Clustering Algorithm Allowing Cluster Overlap: OVERCLUS

Multidimensional scaling is useful for providing a representation of the multiple relationships between artifact types, which indicates groups of types that are more or less coarranged over a site. Used by itself, however, the method has drawbacks. 1) Visual representations of the data become more difficult to construct graphically in greater than two dimensions, ultimately requiring mental visualization (Kruskal & Wish, 1978), which is subject to distortion. This problem is typically met in archaeological data sets with larger numbers of artifact types, where overlap among even moderate numbers of multitype groups may define complex structures requiring three dimensions or more to be displayed with low stress. 2) The method presents simply a configuration of artifact types positioned relative to each other; it does not define groups of types having similar arrangements relative to some threshold level of similarity.

Additional analytic steps can be used to amend these problems. These involve calculating a matrix of Euclidean distances between the stimulus coordinates that have been produced for all types in a low-stress, low-dimensional scaling of the data, and then applying a new clustering algorithm introduced here—OVERCLUS—to the matrix. The OVERCLUS algorithm results in a list of types that are similarly arranged, at a specified level of similarity, on a complete or partial linkage basis.

Other clustering routines listed in Table 7 might also be used for this purpose (Kruskal & Wish, 1978, pp. 44-46). However, they are less desirable for one or more of the reasons enumerated earlier: they do not allow the user to control the amount of inconsistency between pairwise type relationships that is smoothed out of the data; they do not allow groups of types to overlap; they require a priori specification of certain parameters; and/or they are inefficient. Additionally, some of the routines (ADCLUS, ITREG) do not allow the researcher to control the level of dissimilarity used in defining groups, making it impossible to investigate hierarchical, nested relationships among groups. This limitation is critical in archaeological applications, for tools and tool kits often exhibit hierarchically nested relationships within sites (see Carr, 1984 for a detailed discussion).

In outline, OVERCLUS works as follows. 1) The dissimilarity coefficients (n total) for all pairs of types are ordered in a sequence, from those indicating greatest similarity to those indicating least similarity. The ordered values, D_i ($i = 1 \rightarrow n$), become the levels of dissimilarity to be used as linking criteria in each of a series of fusion steps to follow.

2) Starting with the first, lowest level of dissimilarity D_1 and proceeding to the final, greatest level of dissimilarity D_n, a series of fusion steps is initiated. At each step, all pairs of artifact types that have dissimilarity coefficients less than or equal to the given level of dissimilarity D_i are linked.

3) At each fusion step, a list of all linked pairs of types is generated. Under a complete linkage criterion, if three or more types are all mutually interlinked, then the *multitype* group is listed (e.g., *ABC*) in place of the multitype linkages among pairs (e.g., *AB, AC, BC*). A given type can be listed in more than one intra-linked group or linked pair, if it is so joined, which defines an overlapping set structure with the one type being shared among sets. Similarly, a linked pair or intra-linked group of several types can be listed in more than one more-encompassing intra-linked group, if the artifact types in the pair or group are so linked, which defines an overlapping set structure with more than one type shared among sets.

Linkage criteria less rigorous than the complete linkage one can be used. This can be achieved by allowing a multitype group to be listed when only a certain *percentage* of the pairwise relationships among the types comprising it (less than 100% and greater than 50%) are realized as linkages. By varying the percentage of realized linkages required for group definition, the researcher can control the degree of inconsistency between pairwise relationships among types that is ignored when constructing groups and defining a smoothed, summary configuration of the data at a given level of similarity. Using the complete linkage criterion (which requires 100% linkage of types within a group) results in a faithful, unsmoothed representation of the data, whereas using less stringent, partial linkage criteria produces smoother representations. Put in another, more standard perspective, the availability of both complete and partial linkage criteria allows the researcher to control whether groups are required to be hyperspherical in shape or permitted to be more amorphous, linear, or raggedy (Sneath & Sokal, 1973, pp. 216-245).

Caution must be used in specifying the degree of partial linkage required for group definition if a partial linkage approach is taken. Too liberal a criterion (low percentage requirement) can result in extensively overlapping groups and muddled results.

4) To determine the fusion step and degree of grouping most appropriate for displaying the data, two graphs are made: one of dissimilarity level vs. fusion step, and a second of the number of multitype groups or pairs listed vs. fusion

step. The graph of dissimilarity may rise slowly in some sections. This indicates that the artifact types being linked to others are joining them at relatively constant levels of similarity in arrangement, and that the groups being formed are relatively homogeneous internally in the degree of similar arrangement of their constituent types. In other places, the graph of dissimilarity may rise abruptly. This indicates that the artifact types being linked to others are increasingly more different in their spatial arrangements, and that the groups being formed are becoming less homogeneous in the degree of similar arrangement of their constituent types—an undesirable feature.

The graph of number of groups against fusion step will rise and fall repeatedly over its extent as different groups begin to form and then "crystallize" as the types within each group become more interlinked. Think of a multitype group that exists structurally within a data set (Fig. 8, step 0). As dissimilarity levels rise well below its threshold of definition, the number of discrete linked pairs and subgroups of types comprising the group-to-be at first increases. This occurs because not all of the pairwise linkages that are established among multiple types within the group-to-be are mutual ones (Fig. 8, step 2). Moreover, some types may link within one portion of the group, while separately, other types link within other portions of the group, forming various "seed" pairs and subgroups (Fig. 8, step 3). As dissimilarity levels continue to rise, however, linkages become more complete within multitype seed subgroups (Fig. 8, step 4); also, subgroups coalesce (Fig. 8, steps 6, 8). These "crystallization" processes lead ultimately to a reduction in the number of linked pairs and intralinked subgroups, until finally, the group-to-be emerges as one intrarelated structure (Fig. 8, step 10).

Fig. 13.8. As a potential group of artifact types becomes realized through the reduction of similarity thresholds and the creation of linkages between types, the number of linked pairs and subgroups at first increases and then decreases. Here, a complete linkage criterion is assumed.

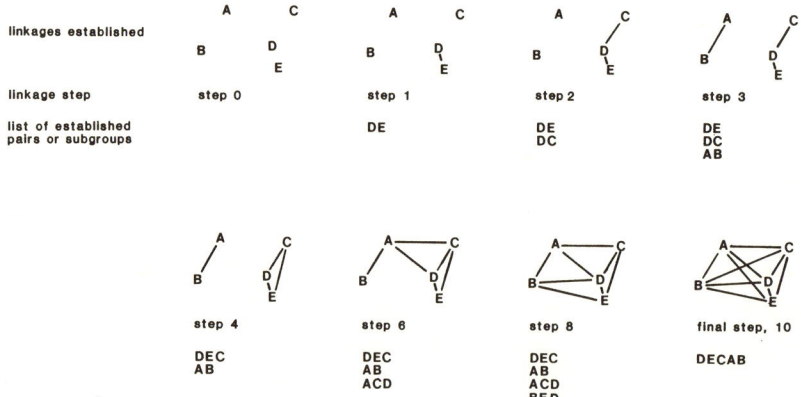

Fusion steps that are optimal for displaying a data set and that have preferred groupings of types can be identified by using a set of prioritized, preferred characteristics of the data representations at the different fusion steps. These characteristics can be determined from the two kinds of graphs. First, the steps should be those where the number of listed linked pairs or intra-linked groups is at a local minimum compared to that at neighboring fusion steps. This indicates the crystallization of groups and a simplification of organization (Fig. 8, steps 4, 10). Second, of these steps, more optimal ones will be those that also have been preceded by fusion steps where dissimilarity levels rose only slightly. This indicates that the groups that have crystallized are also relatively homogeneous internally in the degree of similar arrangement of many of their constituent types. Finally, from this reduced set of fusion steps, the ones most preferred for displaying the data will be those defining groups of types that are interpretable, whether from the perspective of the preferred hypothesis on spatial arrangement, or alternative or unexpected ones.

For intrasite data sets having several groups of artifact types that do not overlap extensively—as suggested by their undissected MDS solutions—the use of multiple, different dissimilarity thresholds for defining different groups of types may be preferable to using any one global threshold for defining all groups. (The application of one threshold implies that all use-areas of different kinds have similar artifact densities, and secondarily, are of similar size, which need not be true.) The distance thresholds used to define groups of artifact types in different portions of a MDS solution should be consistent with (i.e., less than) the expected artifact densities and scales of *potential* use-areas of different kinds which are suggested by the relationships among artifact types in the undissected MDS solution. Among the factors that should be considered when defining the expected nature of use-areas and appropriate maximum distance thresholds are: the kinds of activities suggested by the potential groupings of artifact types, the space requirements of those activities, whether sweeping and cleaning of activity areas probably occurred, whether depositional sets have been smeared by contemporary farming (in the case of surface collections), etc. When using this alternative approach to defining groups of types, the two kinds of diagnostic graphs described previously may be less helpful in determining pertinent dissimilarity thresholds than a systematic examination of: (a) the *sequence of linkages* created as dissimilarity rises and (b) the particular dissimilarity levels at which various *potential* groupings crystallize.

OVERCLUS can be applied to an *unsmoothed* original matrix of dissimilarity or similarity coefficients of any of the kinds discussed in this chapter, or to a *smoothed* matrix of Euclidean distances between stimulus coordinates produced by MDS procedures, in order to obtain groups of types. In the former approach, the percentage of realized pairwise linkages that is required for group definition must usually be kept at less than complete. This is necessary to allow some inconsistencies between multiple pairwise relationships to be smoothed out of the data, so that the predominant patterning among types can be represented more clearly. In the latter approach, where MDS procedures have already smoothed out many inconsistencies, more complete or absolutely complete linkage requirements can be used.

At the present time, it is unclear whether multidimensional scaling procedures or direct application of OVERCLUS is preferable for smoothing intrasite spatial data or other kinds of data.

ILLUSTRATION OF THE PROPOSED ANALYTIC FRAMEWORK AND NEW TECHNIQUES

In this section, the French Magdalenian site, Pincevent habitation no. 1 (Leroi-Gourhan & Brézillon, 1966) will be analyzed. This will be done to 1) exemplify the proposed inductive and deductive analytic framework for recognizing spatial patterning of artifacts within sites, involving the use of entry models, 2) illustrate some aspects of depositional set organization encompassed by the several models of intrasite artifact organization that have been presented, and 3) illustrate the use of the AVDIST coefficients, OVERCLUS, and MDS procedures that have been introduced.

It must be stressed that not all of the studies to be presented would normally be undertaken as part of a routine spatial analysis for the purpose of behavioral reconstruction; some are included simply for heuristic purposes. Also, many additional analyses, such as those concerned with decomposing artifact palimpsests and with delimiting artifact clusters/depositional areas, would normally be a part of a spatial analysis, but are not included here, given the topic of this chapter.

Pincevent was chosen as the site to be analyzed for several heuristic reasons. 1) Artifact distributional data are in the form of item point locations, which makes possible the illustration of the AVDIST statistics. 2) The list of tool and debris classes for which distributional data are available seemed on initial inspection to include groups of *multiple classes* which might be expected, on the bases of previous functional analyses of Paleolithic tools, to define *single* depositional sets or archaeological tool kits (e.g., burins, burin spalls, and becs used in working bone, antler, and/or wood). This characteristic of the data was required in order to illustrate variation in the *internal* forms of organization of depositional sets (along the monothetic-polythetic dimension) in addition to their external forms of organization (along the nonoverlapping-overlapping dimension), and the sensitivity of different algorithms to these forms. In this regard, the data stand in contrast to those from the Mask site analyzed by Whallon (1984), which document primarily the external organization of depositional sets. 3) The distributions of most artifact classes were not of a ubiquitous, clustered nature or of other forms suggesting a complex palimpsest, which would require decomposition with Fourier and spatial filtering methods. Thus, the analysis for defining depositional sets did not have to be preceded by complex screening operations that would have made the illustration less obvious, and to some, less believable. 4) The site represents the remains of a relatively short-term occupation (see below); it thus meets the assumption of approximate contemporaneity of depositional episodes, which is necessary in most intrasite spatial analysis.

Overview of Pincevent

Pincevent (Leroi-Gourhan & Brézillon, 1964, 1966, 1972) is located in the Paris basin of northern France, on the floodplain of the Seine river, between the confluences of the Yonne and Loigne rivers with the Seine. It includes a number of small occupations at various stratigraphic levels. One of these, habitation no. 1 (Leroi-Gourhan & Brézillon, 1966), is a reindeer hunting camp dating to the late Magdalenian. A 12,300 B.C. ± 400 uncorrected carbon date is preferred for the occupation over several dates in the 9,300-10,000 B.C. range on the basis of the context of the carbon samples and laboratory reports on processing difficulties (E. Gilot, 1966). The site is one of a series of known Magdalenian occupations within the Paris basin, which occur primarily within the main river valleys and less so in upland settings.

The time of occupation of habitation no. 1 corresponds to the Bölling or Alleröd period at the end of the second cold maximum of the Würm glacial. This was a period of rapid glacial retreat with some very cold oscillations (Butzer, 1971, p. 274; Flint, 1971, p. 626). Winters, rather than summers, are thought to have been colder than those currently, and the climate may also have been more arid as a result of the colder temperatures (Butzer, 1971, pp. 280-286). Vegetation in central and northern France at this time is reconstructed to have been still of a tundra-like form, on the plains, including pioneer and drought-resistant species such as Artemesia (like sage brush) and chenopods; and of a parkland composition in the foothills of the Massive Central, where juniper, spruce, alder, and/or birches were scattered among the former (Flint, 1971, p. 632; Butzer, 1971, pp. 287-289). The tundra vegetation may have been of a composition atypical of current tundras, and possibly resembled more a grassy steppe including herbs (Butzer, 1971, pp. 287-289; Hahn, 1977, p. 204).

Habitation no. 1 is comprised by a scatter of lithic artifacts and bone debris around three hearths that are aligned in the SW-NE orientation (Fig. 9). Several aspects of the remains suggest that each hearth occurred within a hut, which was possibly made of poles and skins, and that the three huts overlapped so as to form a larger building with a common central gallery and multiple entrances. 1) Within the distribution of flint and bone debris occur concentrations in the form of arcs. These are presumed to represent where rubbish, which were generated by activities in the more central parts of the structure, were swept to its *sides* (Leroi-Gourhan & Brézillon, 1966, pp. 332-336, 361). 2) Along one arc, there are several hummocks of soil with larger flint nodules on top. These occur

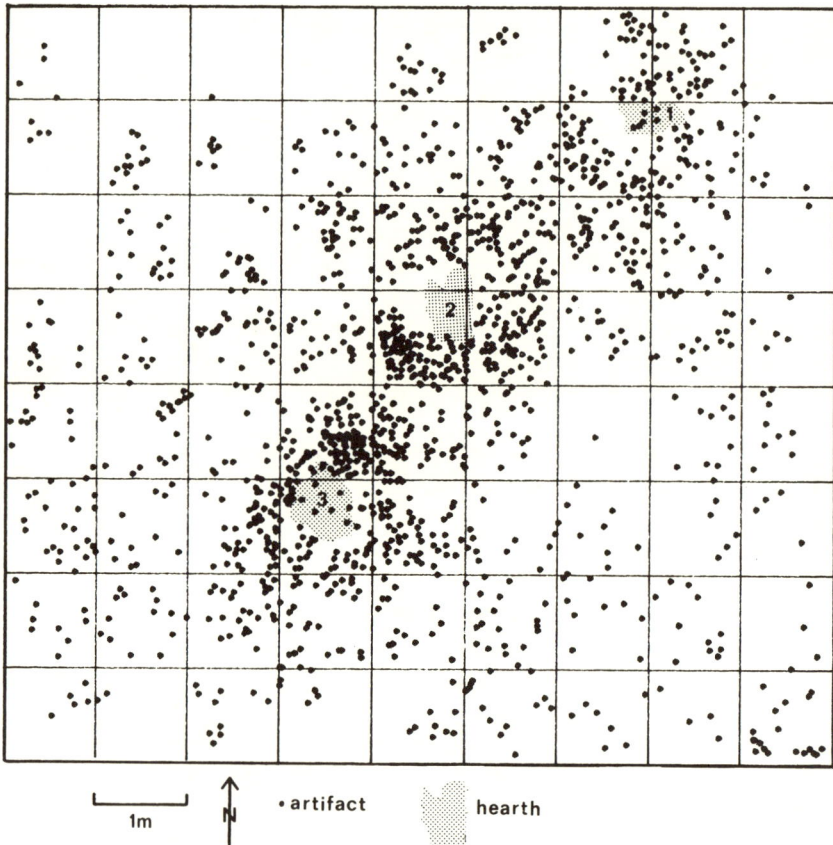

Fig. 13.9. Pincevent habitation no. 1.

on the prevailing upwind side of the structure and possibly represent positions at which tent poles were anchored (p. 362). 3) The concentrations of debris that define the hypothesized edges of the huts are not always delimited by a *sharp* boundary on their exteriors. This suggests that the huts were possibly of a tent structure in which swept debris was scattered under and somewhat beyond its skirt in places (p. 362). Tents of skin are a common form of housing among many mobile hunters of the arctic and subarctic, including the inland Eskimo and northern Athapascans of Canada (Speiss, 1979, p. 221). 4) Within much of the hypothesized building, and not anywhere outside it, a thin sprinkling of red ochre underlaid the artifacts, helping to define the building's outline (Leroi-Gourhan & Brézillon, 1966, pp. 330-332). The rationale for spreading ochre over the floor of the hut prior to its use is unclear. It was apparently swept, along with refuse generated within the huts, from several peripheral areas that were kept clean presumably for sleeping (pp. 331, 370).

The three huts and hearths seem to have been used contemporaneously rather than sequentially over the course of three separate occupations. This conclusion is based on several forms of evidence. 1) Most important, refitting studies of burins and burin spalls, cores and blades, and snapped blades indicate a rich network of joins among the three hearths and their surroundings (pp. 341-345, 349-350, 364). This might be seen, alternatively, as the product of recycling and mining behavior (Ascher, 1968; Reid, 1973) as the various huts were abandoned and occupied sequentially. However, some of the joins link items around a hearth of one hut to items against only the *walls* of *another* hut, suggesting activity around one hearth followed by the sweeping of debris from that activity against the walls of another hut which must have been standing at that time. 2) Some of the artifacts within habitation no. 1 are made of a red-brown flint, which is exotic to the Seine valley and which the occupants apparently brought with them to the site at its initial occupation. The latter is evidenced by the fact that all items of this flint are finished tools; no associated production debris or cores of red-brown flint for manufacturing these tools have been found at the site (Leroi-Gourhan & Brézillon, 1966, pp. 336-338). Importantly, the tools occur in *each* of the three huts and tool-refitting joins link pieces in the different huts. This suggests that the huts were contemporaneous components of a single structure used together during the initial occupation of the site, if mining was minimal. 3) The alignment and equi-spacing of the hearths suggests an integrated, organized use of the whole area rather than sequential, semi-randomly overlapping occupations. 4) Each of the three hearths is characterized by a similar stratigraphy. In each, the carbonaceous deposits are separated into two episodes of deposition by a thin, interbedded layer of sediment that possibly indicates a (brief?) period of site abandonment and water washing. This would suggest the contemporaneous use of all three hearths during both of two occupations, rather than their sequential use over two or three occupations. (For further evidence of two occupations, see below).

Binford (1983, pp. 158-159) has presented an alternative interpretation of habitation no. 1 that does not involve three interconnected huts. Rather, hearths 2 and 3 are envisioned as exterior hearths that were made and used sequentially in response to a change in wind direction during the course of a single occupation. Hearth 1 is thought possibly to have occurred inside a tent. The basis for Binford's interpretation is a supposed fit of the spatial arrangement of stone tool manufacturing debris around hearths 2 and 3 to his generalized model of a "men's outside hearth," which was developed using Nunamiut Eskimo data (Binford, 1978, pp. 348-350; 1983, pp. 149-156).

Binford's interpretation does not seem to be congruent with the Pincevent data in a number of ways, and thus is not preferred here to Leroi-Gourhan's reconstruction, which involves the three-hut structure.

1) Binford's model of a men's outside hearth specifies the accumulation of debris around one side of a hearth in two concentric arcs: an inner *drop zone* and

an outer *toss zone*. By the nature of the formation processes responsible for them, both zones—but especially the outer toss zone—should manifest themselves as gradients of debris density change rather than as sharply delimited arcs. In contrast, the exteriors of the arcs of debris at Pincevent (all artifacts considered) are sharply delimited in several areas (e.g., arcs IVb, c; VIa, b, c). It appears that debris had been moved—perhaps swept—up against some now-decomposed structure, such as the inside of a hut wall.

2) Binford's model specifies that the outer toss zone of debris should be wide, with 50-60 cm encompassing most artifacts in the Nunamiut case ($2\sigma = 48\text{-}58$ cm, depending on the artifact class; Binford, 1978, p. 349). In contrast, some of the arcs of debris around the hearths at Pincevent (e.g., VIa, b) are much narrower, as if debris had been moved *directly up against* some structure, such as the inside of a hut wall.

3) In addition to these two discrepancies between the *nature* of the arcs of debris at Pincevent and those in Binford's model, there is a discrepancy in the *positioning* of the arcs. Binford (1983, p. 158) states that the arrangement of debris from stone tool manufacture at Pincevent (Leroi-Gourhan & Brézillon, 1966, Fig. 56) "fits exactly" to the concentric arcs model of a men's outside hearth. I cannot find this positional resemblance for this debris class or any other artifact class, nor does Binford provide a statistical test of fit of the data to the model that might demonstrate such a resemblance. The manufacturing debris that constitute what Binford would apparently identify as a drop zone around the hearths concentrates immediately around them, within 0-.75 m of their edges, whereas the drop zone of Binford's model ranges from .4 to 1.0 m away from a hearth. The spatial arrangements of particular stone tool and debris classes (e.g., burins, burin spalls, backed bladelets, becs, cores) also show this discordance with the model. Rings of faunal artifact classes (e.g., ribs) around the hearths at Pincevent, which might be identified as toss zones, occur much too closely to the hearths (.1-1.5 m) to represent toss zones as defined by Binford's model (2-3.2 m away from a hearth's edge). In fact, most faunal elements ringing the hearths at Pincevent fall within essentially the same radius from the hearths as do the stone tools and manufacturing debris.

4) Perhaps most important, Binford's interpretation does not account for or is discordant with a number of data that are explained by Leroi-Gourhan and Brézillon's reconstruction. These data include the existence and placement of hummocks of soil with stones on top; the stratigraphy of the hearths; the systematic placement of the hearths; the spatial distribution of red ochre and its coarrangement with arcs of debris; the differences in the frequencies of various artifact types northwest and southeast of the hearths (see p. 447); and the similar frequencies of certain artifact types among all three hearths (see p. 449).

Thus, Leroi-Gourhan's reconstruction of three-interconnected huts is favored over Binford's outdoor hearth interpretation. The acceptance of Leroi-Gourhan's hut reconstruction, however, does not necessarily require acceptance of his conclusions on the residential as opposed to logistical nature of the site (Binford, 1978, p. 357), although the former interpretation is preferred for reasons given below.

Other habitations, presumably similar to no. 1, occur within a 2-hectare area of Pincevent, on the order of tens of meters apart. It was unclear at the time of publication of the site report whether these locations were occupied simultaneously with habitation no. 1 and represent an aggregation of social units, or indicate repeated reoccupation of the site, or both (Leroi-Gourhan & Brézillon, 1966, p. 371).

The approximate seasons of occupation of habitation no. 1 can be reconstructed from the age of kill of reindeer brought back to the site, the remains of which comprise nearly all of the faunal assemblage for the site. Leroi-Gourhan and Brézillon suggest, from the evidence, a late spring through November occupation that was probably continuous (ibid, p. 361). On the other hand, Guillien and Perpére (1966), the faunal analysts, find only a short period in late spring and a somewhat longer period during winter represented by the kills, there being no summer kills.

Reconstruction of the precise periods of occupation from the data at hand is difficult. The sample of ageable bones is small (18 pieces from 7 infants to juveniles). Moreover, the method that was used to determine age of kill was the degree of eruption of mandibular teeth, which can yield more variable results for incomplete specimens than was realized at the time of writing (Speiss, 1979, pp. 70-71). Nevertheless, the reconstruction of a discontinuous occupation, in winter and late spring, is consistent with at least two other data. First, as mentioned above, the stratigraphy within all three hearths suggests two episodes of occupation and deposition, with a period of waterwashing of sediments and possible site abandonment between them. Second, nearly all the tools in the habitation are found *within* the huts rather than outside, implying that most work took place inside. This would be expected in a winter context and less likely in a summer occupation of the kind suggested by Leroi-Gourhan and Brézillon.

Population estimates for habitation no. 1 are consistent with the numbers of persons typically found among winter microbands of artiodactyl hunters in the interior arctic and subarctic: a nuclear family of 5-7 persons to a group of 20 persons (Speiss, 1979, p. 221). The total floor area within the three huts in the site is ca. 30 m^2, corresponding to 6.4 persons using Narroll's (1962) regression and 2.6-7.4 persons using the data of Cook and Heizer (1968). The total floor space is typical of that of willow-frame/skin tents used by inland Eskimo and northern Athapascan hunters (20-33 m^2), which are occupied by 1 to 3 nuclear families (Speiss, 1979, p. 221). Leroi-Gourhan and Brézillon (1966, p. 370) estimate the probable population of habitation no 1. at 6 to 9 adults on the basis of the number of persons (2-3) that could have rested within each of three clearly debris-free areas, which are presumed to be sleeping areas within the huts, and a maximum of 10-15 persons considering two other possible resting places. The total population of Pincevent at the time of occupation of habitation no. 1 may or may not have included several such microbands in aggregation (ibid, p. 371).

It is possible to use these population estimates and other information to obtain a more precise estimate of the actual length of occupation of the site. Nearly all the bone debris in habitation no. 1 are of reindeer, which suggests the mainstay of the occupants' subsistence during the site's use. (Exceptions include: 1 bone of horse and several pieces of mammoth ivory, probably curated.) The estimated minimum number of reindeer of infant to juvenile age and adult age are 7 and 5, respectively (Guillien & Perpére, 1966, p. 377). These data can be used, along with nutritional data from Speiss (1979, pp. 28-29), to approximate the minimum (very conservative) number of man-days of food represented at the site. Taking into consideration nutritional variation with the age distribution and possible seasons of kill of the reindeer at habitation no. 1, a range of 101 to 227 minimum number of man-days of food are represented by the kill. If six adults occupied the site, this food supply would imply a minimum stay of 17 to 38 days; if nine adults, then 11 to 25 days. Thus, the actual length of occupation of habitation no. 1 appears to have been relatively brief. This result supports the suggestion of discontinuous use of the site rather than an extended late spring through November occupation, even considering the conservative nature of the estimated duration of stay. It also suggests a good context for spatial analysis, in which depositional areas are less likely to have been confused by their repeated relocation and overlap, with the growth of refuse.

The function of habitation no. 1 as a residential settlement or a more special purpose site (e.g., hunting stand, kill site) cannot be reconstructed with certainty from the data currently available. The interpretation of the site as a temporary residential settlement, however, seems preferable for several reasons. 1) The conservative minimum length of occupation of the site that has been estimated is more in line with a temporary residential settlement. 2) The range of activities that are reconstructed as possibly having occurred at the site (see pp. 423-428) includes *maintenance* tasks, such as making bone grease and working hide, (tacking, graining or sewing stages). 3) The location of the site in a floodplain rather than on some topographic rise with a good vista is not consistent with the interpretation of the site as a hunting stand.

The annual migratory and subsistence pattern of the occupants of habitation no. 1 is unclear, even by way of analogy to better-known regions and times. Three different patterns of human mobility have been reconstructed for regions to the southwest and northeast of Pincevent. In the Dordogne region to the southwest, during the Aurignacian, it appears that reindeer herds were followed from their summer pastures on the coastal plains to their wintering grounds in the sheltered valleys of the foothills of the Massif Central (Speiss, 1979, p. 234). To the northeast and east, Sturdy (1975, p. 74) has reconstructed that in the Late Glacial, herds were followed from their summer pastures in the foothills and mountains of central and southern Germany to their wintering grounds in the Flachland (coastal plain)—a pattern just opposite that to the southwest. Finally, Hahn (1977) has argued against Sturdy's reconstruction of long-distance migrations. He has assembled data that suggest a more localized exploitive strategy within southern Germany. The strategy involves tethered residential moves between large open-air winter sites in the foothills of the Alps and small spring and summer exploitive camps in both the valleys of the Jura mountains and the Jura plain.

Adaptations in the two areas adjacent to Pincevent may also have differed in the variety of animals that were used. Speiss (1979, p. 186) suggests the use of a variety of larger game animals in the Dordogne region. Sturdy (1975, pp. 79-94) describes a more focal, reindeer-based economy involving herd manipulation for the Flachland-German region, whereas Hahn (1977) suggests the use of a diversity of large and small terrestrial game and riverine resources in southern Germany.

Data Base

Choice of variables and observations. From the Pincevent assemblage, 23 artifact classes potentially reflecting specifiable activities or other formation processes were selected for distributional study. The artifact classes, abbreviations used for them in further analysis, and the activities and formation processes that they could indicate are shown in Table 8. The point location coordinates of items in the classes were recorded primarily from distribution maps given in the Pincevent site report (Leroi-Gourhan & Brézillon, 1966). Recording was done using a computerized digitizer that yielded item locations with a space dilating error of up to 4 cm over the 8 x 9 m grid, the error varying with the artifact class.

Items of four classes—piercers, micropiercers, notches, and lignite beads—were not plotted on maps within the site report; only their 1 m grid cell proveniences were mentioned in the text. The locations of each of these items were taken to be the centers of the grid cells in which they occurred, which produced locational errors of up to 71 cm (half the diagonal of the cells) for them. In a similar manner, a few items of some mapped classes were illustrated or mentioned in the text along with their grid cell proveniences, but not plotted on the class distribution maps (2 becs, 1 backed blade, 4 endscrapers). These items also were taken to be located at the center of their grid cells.

Endscrapers were divided into two classes: those with an approximately 60° edge angle (scrapa) and those with a bevel approaching 90° (scrapbc). This dichotomy was made on the basis of two a priori considerations. 1) It was thought that the dichotomy might distinguish those scrapers still usable and left in work areas from those exhausted and occurring in refuse areas. 2) It also was thought that the dichotomy might separate endscrapers used to deflesh hides from those used in graining hides (Carr, 1982b).

Table 13.8

Assignment of Functions to Artifact Classes within Pincevent

Artifact Class[1]	Possible or Probable (*) Functions/Activities Indicated	Supporting Evidence
V1. core (core)	*manufacture blades and bladelets (see below).	
V2. burin (burin)	*graving or boring primarily bone, antler, ivory.	Keeley (1978, p. 80; personal communication). Wear produced on stone tools used to work ivory is practically indistinguishable from that of bone or antler (Keeley, personal communication)
	*graving or boring wood less often.	Keeley (1978, p. 81)
	*groove-and-splinter technique.	local concentration of bone splinters with becs and burins between hearths 2 and 3 (Leroi-Gourhan & Brézillon, 1966, p. 364); (Clark, 1967, p. 64)
V3. burin spall (burinsp)	*see burin.	see burin
V4. bec and oblique truncations (bec)	*primarily boring, secondarily graving bone, antler, ivory.	Keeley (1978, p. 80; personal communication)
	*used for boring larger holes in contrast to those capable of being bored by piercers.	
	*groove-and-splinter technique on bone	Leroi-Gourhan and Brézillon (1966, pp. 320, 364), (Clark, 1967, p. 64), Semenov (1964), Clark and Thompson (1954), Keeley (1978, p. 80)
	pierce hides	Keeley (1978, p. 80)
	*rarely used on wood	Keeley (personal communication, on basis of evidence from Verberie, a site very similar in time and nature to Pincevent)
	truncations may be simply snapped blades, not used, or used for any of the purposes of utilized blades (see below).	Keeley (1978, p. 82)

Table 13.8 (cont.)

V5. piercers (pierce)	*bore bone, wood, deeper than micropiercers	tips snapped (Leroi-Gourhan & Brézillon, 1966, p. 293), Keeley (personal communication)
V6. micropiercers (microp)	*bore bone, less so wood, shallower than piercers; possibly decorative boring	Keeley (1978, p. 80; personal communication)
	*pierce hides	no snapped tips (Leroi-Gourhan & Brézillon, 1966, p. 293)
V7. notch (notch)	scrape wood or bone shafts	
	artifact of trampling	Keeley (personal communication)
V8, 9. endscraper, types A, BC (see text) (scrapa, scrapbc)	*primarily to grain dry hides, secondarily to scrape bone, wood, or deflesh hides	Keeley (1978, pp. 78-79), Semenov (1964, pp. 87-89), Barnes (1932, p. 53), Crabtree and Davis (1968), Gould et al., 1971; Hayden and Kamminga (1973), Mason (1889, 1899), Wilmsen (1970)
V10. backed bladelet (backbl)	*projectile point armatures/barbs set in grooved bone shaft or mastic.	2 backed bladelets stuck with mastic on an ungrooved bone splinter in another section of Pincevent; impact damage common on bladelets at the similar site, Verberie; any wear on Verberie specimens is from meat (Keeley, personal communication). Lithic analysis of Moss (1983).
	the multiple functions of utilized (backed or unbacked) blades (see utilized blade).	Some specimens are long enough (up to 4.2 cm; Leroi-Gourhan & Brézillon, 1966, p. 302) to have been used in this manner. Traces of wear usually on one side only (p. 304), indicating scraping, shaving, or whittling functions rather than cutting/puncture (Sollberger, 1969). Some burins, notches, made on backed bladelets (Leroi-Gourhan & Brézillon, 1966, pp. 302, 312) possibly indicating opportunistic tool manufacture during bone/wood working.
V11. utilized blade (utblade)	see backed blade	see backed blade. 41% of the blades in this category have natural backs (Leroi-Gourhan & Brézillon, 1966, p. 307)
	unused, trampled specimens	Keeley (personal communication)

Table 13.8 (cont.)

V12. lignite bead (bead)	*personal adornment	
V13. ivory (ivory)	*personal adornment	two pieces in association with a shell with two pearls; fossil shells pierced for wearing are found in other habitation sites within Pincevent (Leroi-Gourhan & Brézillon, 1966, p. 361)
V14. antler (antler)	*raw material for many antler items; worked by groove-and-splinter technique (see below)	Clark (1967, p. 64)
V15. phalanges (phal)	*preparation of broth by stone boiling foot minus hoof	partially articulated phalanges without terminal digits or hooves clustered around hearths with broken metapods (Leroi-Gourhan & Brézillon, 1966, pp. 352-353, 368)
	not used for making bone grease	although useful for this (Speiss, 1979, pp. 24-25), the phalanges are not broken up into small pieces as required (Leroi-Gourhan & Brézillon, 1966, pp. 352-353)
	not used as fuel	little bone within hearths (Leroi-Gourhan & Brézillon, 1966, p. 368)
V16. metapods (meta)	*preparation of broth by stone boiling foot minus hoof	see phalanges. Also, metapods of reindeer contain much marrow (Speiss, 1979, pp. 24-25). Those at Pincevent are broken at their extreme distal ends to free it to the broth (Leroi-Gourhan & Brézillon, 1966, p. 358)
V17. humerus, femur, radio-cubital (hfr)	*extraction of marrow	broken by percussion (Leroi-Gourhan & Brézillon (1966, p. 354); rich in marrow (Speiss, 1979, pp. 24-25)
	*raw material for many bone items (see below)	
V18. tibio-peroneal (tibio)	*extraction of marrow	see hfr
	*raw material for many bone items (see below)	
V19. scapula (scap)	*raw material for many bone items (see below)	Leroi-Gourhan & Brézillon (1966, p. 360)

Table 13.8 (cont.)

V20.	rib (rib)	eat meat	
		*not used for making bone grease	Although useful for this (Speiss, 1979, pp. 24-25), the ribs are not broken up into small pieces as required (Leroi-Gourhan & Brézillon, 1966, p. 356)
V21.	vertebrae (vert)	*refuse from butchering	Speiss (1979, pp. 21-25)
V22.	maxilla (maxill)	teeth used as beads for personal adornment	Clark (1967, p. 64). Teeth other than those of reindeer also were used. A fossil shark's tooth was found with 10 pierced pieces of shell in another habitation within Pincevent.
V23.	mandible (mandib)	teeth used as beads for personal adornment	see maxilla
		*extraction of marrow	rich in marrow (Speiss, 1979, pp. 24-25). Ascending ramus broken off of many specimens (Guillen & Perpère, 1966, pp. 374-377; site map)
V24.	pebbles of alluvial flint (flint)	*raw material for hammerstones, cores	Leroi-Gourhan & Brézillon (1966, p. 325)
V25.	sandstone and limestone (ssls)	*stone boiling, retain heat within hut	Leroi-Gourhan & Brézillon (1966, pp. 329, 367)

Supplement: Some Objects Made of Antler, Bone, and Wood during the Magdalenian in Southwest France and/or the Hamburgian-Ahrensburgian Region

Antler and/or Bone	lance heads, sometimes carved with motifs	(Bordes, 1968, p. 162)
	harpoon prototypes carved with motifs	(Bordes, 1968, pp. 162, 164)
	spear-throwers with ends carved with naturalistic representations of horse, ibex, birds, fish	(Clark, 1967, pp. 63-64)
	dart shafts	(Keeley, personal communication)
	clubs	(Clark, 1967, p. 65)
	bone wrenches ("pierced battons")	(Bordes, 1968, p. 163)
	needles	(Bordes, 1968, p. 163)
Wood	dart and arrow shafts	(Clark, 1967, p. 65)

[1]Standard abbreviations for the classes are in parentheses.

The chance of defining either of these distinctions by dichotomizing along edge angle was considered low to moderate from the outset. The total number of endscrapers is small (26); for such small populations of endscrapers, variation among individuals in tool manufacture and the timing of tool deposition often can mask functional and depositional distinctions of the kinds sought (Keeley, personal communication, 1983). Nevertheless, the dichotomization was made on the chance that it might prove significant, holding in mind the option of later lumping all scrapers into one class. In the end, it did prove useful (see pp. 426-427, 429).

Of the 26 endscrapers within the site, only 25 could be identified to edge angle class (Lerio-Gourhan & Brézillon, 1966, p. 283) and used in the analysis.

The Pincevent assemblage includes several kinds of long bones that were distinguished on the site report maps: humeri, femurs, radio-cubitals, and tibio-peroneals. All could have been exploited for their marrow (Speiss, 1979, pp. 24-25) or bone in similar ways, and might have been defined as one analytic class. Or they might have been defined as four separate analytic classes. However, for this analysis, the first three were included in one class (V17) while tibio-peroneals were segregated in a class by themselves (V18). The basis for this classification was a noticeable clustering of humeri, femurs, and radio-cubitals without tibio-peroneals in some locations (between hearths 2 and 3, northeast of hearth 2), and isolated groupings of tibio-peroneals in other locations (e.g., northwest of hearth 2, around hearth 3 in various locations). These patterns suggested differences in the mode of deposition and possibly use of the two classes of items.

Mandibles and maxilla were retained as separate classes in light of the possible exploitation of only mandibles for their marrow (Speiss, 1979, pp. 24-25). There also were some visible distributional differences between them.

Choice of research universe. The entire excavated area of habitation no. 1 was selected for distributional study. Visual inspection of artifact distributions over the area did not reveal pooled contradictory structures (see p. 314) of the kind where different artifact type relationships of association/dissociation occur in different sectors of the site—a circumstance that would have mandated subglobal analysis of separate portions of the site. The areal variations in type relationships that were noticeable seemed to fall within the realm of polythetic organization variation.

Choice of analytic strata. To study patterning in the magnitudes and directions of asymmetry among artifact classes from locale to locale, and to employ the AVDISTLP1 similarity coefficient, it was necessary to stratify habitation no. 1 into natural areas within which depositional and disturbance processes were most likely homogeneous. The hut walls and zones within the huts that are defined by Leroi-Gourhan and Brézillon (1966, p. 324, Fig. 50) are seemingly attractive for delimiting such strata. However, they were found inappropriate for these purposes in at least two ways. 1) Although it is probable that three huts did comprise habitation no 1, arranged approximately as reconstructed, the precise locations of their walls are unclear in some places; several concentric arcs of flint and/or faunal debris mark some sides (Leroi-Gourhan & Brézillon, Fig. 56) and a few sides are indicated by only a gradation in debris density (ibid, p. 362) or not at all. 2) The authors stratified space within the huts only partially, using debris density contours. Similarly, not all areas outside the huts were stratified. Thus, although the stratification devised by Leroi-Gourhan and Brézillon was adequate for their purposes, it was too approximate and incomplete to serve as a basis for the quantitative analyses to be made.

As an alternative approach to stratification, natural clusters of artifacts were defined. This was done primarily on the basis of artifact density contours and clear circumscribing arcs of artifact concentration within the composite distribution of all classes of artifacts (Fig. 10). The density contours that were used

Fig. 13.10. Analytic strata 1–15 in Pincevent habitation no. 1, which were used to study patterns in the magnitude and direction of asymmetry of various artifact classes and in calculating AVDISTLP1 coefficient values.

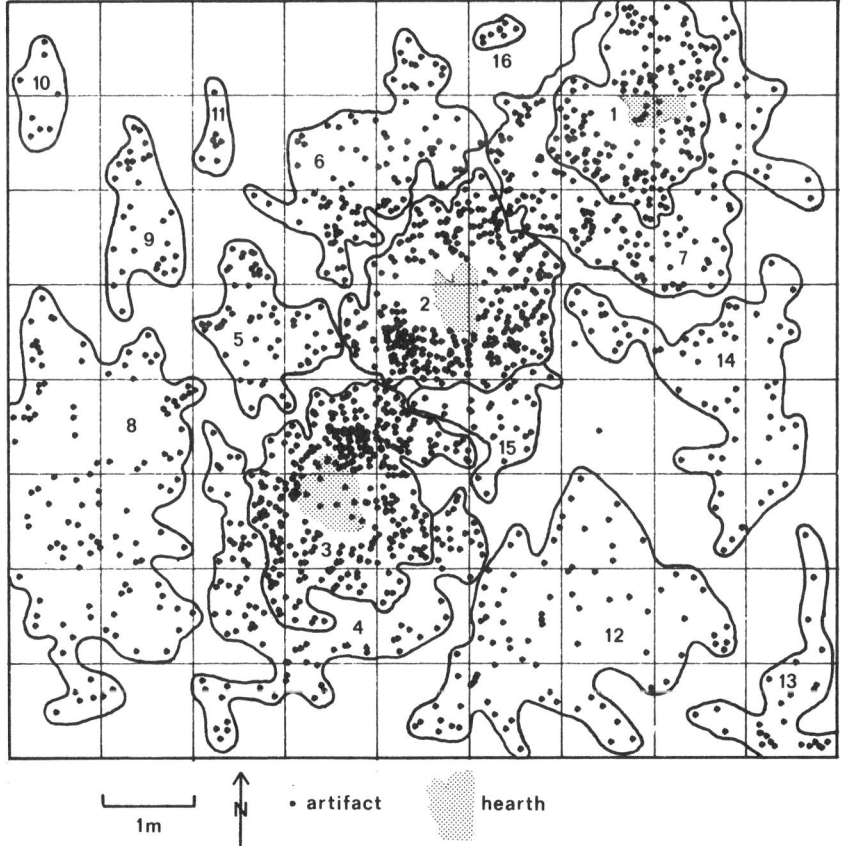

to define clusters were allowed to vary locally in level, so as to not constrain all clusters to equal densities. Most of the clusters are spatially discrete and were easily defined. A few clusters grade into each other in small areas, but seemed to be easily resolved by arcs of concentration that continue from the unshared perimeters of the clusters into their gray zones (e.g., separation of strata 7, 2, and 14). The distributions of some individual artifact classes also helped to resolve some ambiguities. Some clusters (12, 6, 4) which occur predominantly within the interior of a hut extend slightly beyond the hut walls as approximated by Leroi-Gourhan and Brézillon. However, this seems permissible, given the approximate nature of the wall reconstruction and also the possibility that debris that was swept to the sides of the huts scattered under and somewhat beyond the tent skirts.

Identification of Formation Processes and Their Effects on Artifact Organization

Beyond artifact classification and the assignment of probable meanings to classes, the first responsibility of an archaeologist who is attempting an intrasite spatial analysis is to reconstruct, as best as possible, those formation and recovery processes that probably determined or affected the general nature of spatial organization of the artifact classes. Processes responsible for artifact organization along the monothetic-polythetic and nonoverlapping-overlapping dimensions, as well as those determining the palimpsest or simple nature of artifact class distributions, are of concern. On the basis of this knowledge, the archaeologist should then try to correct the data at hand for any systematic, natural post-depositional distortions within it and to decompose any complex artifact distributions into simpler ones that represent more homogeneous sets of formation processes. In other words, the archaeologist should develop a behaviorally relevant data structure. Finally, one should use the information on the formation processes that are responsible or probably responsible for the site to subsume the spatial data under one or a few entry models that specify the kinds of organizational relationships that occur or probably occur most frequently among artifact classes in the corrected, dissected data. The models, in turn, would suggest the one or few techniques that are most congruent with the data and appropriate for its analysis.

Excavations and lab research can be designed for collecting various kinds of observations that can be used to determine the formation processes responsible for an assemblage and its organizational nature (Schiffer, 1983). However, even when using published archaeological data that was not collected or reported with such a purpose in mind, it may be possible to gain considerable insight into an assemblage's development and actual or probable structure. The information analyzed for this purpose will vary from site to site with the documentation that is available and the behavioral and geological context of the site. The analysis of habitation no. 1 is a typical example of research carried out under these constraints.

The formation, recovery, and analytical and reporting processes that determined the nature of organization of artifact classes in habitation no. 1 along the monothetic-polythetic dimension and nonoverlapping-overlapping dimension are summarized in Tables 9 and 10. The pieces of evidence that were used to identify their occurrences, also given in the tables, are all observations of kinds not used by the quantitative methods that were applied to define depositional sets: they do not include the spatial proximities of items of different artifact classes to each other. This operational constraint has been followed to avoid the circular reasoning that otherwise would occur when justifying the application of a technique with information approximating the results of its application.

Table 13.9

Identification of Formation Processes at Pincevent: Factors Leading to "Unexpected Absences" of Artifact Types from Deposits

Expected or Documented Process *	*Documentation*	*Organizational Model(s) along Monothetic-Polythetic Dimension (Fig. 3) likely Congruent with the Data*
1. Alternative tool types for same purpose	Large backed bladelets and utilized blades can be used for same tasks (Table 8), with possible exception of greater proficiency of backed blades in working harder materials. Also, many of the utilized blades (41%) have natural backs, making them functionally equivalent to the large, retouched backed bladelets.	Models 3, 4, 5, or 6
	Becs and burins are broadly functionally equivalent, used primarily to bore bone, antler (Keeley, 1978, p. 81), but may have slightly different uses.	
4. Differential discard rates	Burin; burin spall ratio of 130:206 (Leroi-Gourhan & Brézillon, 1966, p. 293; brown-	Models 2, 3, 4, 5, or 6

Table 13.9 (cont.)

	red artifacts brought to site partially used are not included).	
4. Non-expedient technology, curation	Several tool types (4 scrapers, 1 bec, 1 piercer, 5 burins, 18 utilized blades or truncations, 1 backed blade) of brown-red flint brought into site already manufactured (Leroi-Gourhan & Brézillon, 1966, p. 336). These same kinds of tools may have been removed from the site upon its abandonment.	Models 3, 4, 5, or 6
	Conjoined burins and burin spalls (ibid, p. 344) and conjoined pieces of cores (ibid, p. 341), linking different work areas around different hearths, indicate locations where the same curated item was used at different times.	
5. Multipurpose tools	Utilized blades and large backed bladelets for working with meat, hide, vegetable, wood, or bone materials possible.	Models 3, 4, 5, or 6
6. Multitype edged tool	6-7 endscraper-burins not included in burin inventory (6-7 burins "unexpectedly absent," 120 present).	Models 3, 4, 5, or 6
	One endscraper-piercer not included in piercer inventory (1 piercer "unexpectedly absent," 5 present).	
	One burin-notch not included in notch inventory (1 notch "unexpectedly absent," 19 present).	
7. Recycling of artifacts	Burins were frequently made from artifacts of other types serving other functions. Of 78 burin spalls having platform remnants identifying them as	Models 3, 4, 5, or 6

Table 13.9 (cont.)

	such, 27 (35%) carried edges with retouch typical of endscrapers (ibid, p. 296).	
9. Size sorting of artifacts by sweeping	Sweeping likely since site is a winter/late spring occupation and most tasks performed inside tents, where open work space is limited.	Models 3 or 5
	Sweeping indicated by debris-clear areas within the tents corresponding with areas lacking red ochre, which was sprinkled over the floor prior to use of the tents (ibid, pp. 330-332).	
	Sweeping of areas possibly indicated by conjoining of pieces of cores (ibid, p. 341), broken utilized blades (ibid, p. 337, 349), and burins or burin spalls (ibid, p. 337, 344) along the walls of the huts with pieces within work areas around the hearths.	
	Size sorting indicated by fact that of the conjoined burins and burin spalls separated between walls of the huts and work areas around the hearths, primarily burins (larger, sweepable) have been displaced to the walls while burin spalls (smaller, less sweepable) remain in the work areas.	
	Possible size sorting of artifacts swept beneath skirt of tent (ibid, p. 362).	
10. Lack of preservation of some items of a class	Vertebrae easily decompose in acid soils like those of Pincevent. Of the ca. 500 vertebrae expected within habitation no. 1, based on the minimum number of reindeer	Models 3, 4, 5, or 6

Table 13.9 (cont.)

	brought there, only ca. 100 were recovered (ibid, p. 360).	
14. Technological rather than functional classification of artifacts	Large backed bladelets and utilized blades may have been functionally equivalent, and thus be artifically segregated (see above).	Models 3, 4, 5, or 6
	Scraper classes A and B may have been functionally equivalent, and thus be artifically segregated (see text: Data Base).	
	Tibio-peroneals, may have been used for same purposes as humeri, femurs, and radiocubitals, and thus artifically segregated (see text: Data Base).	
Incomplete inventorying of some items on distribution maps	206 burin spalls were excavated (Leroi-Gourhan & Brézillon, 1966, p. 293), only 68 of which (those conjoinable with burins) are indicated on the distribution map (33%).	Models 3, 4, 5, or 6
	66 backed bladelets were excavated (ibid, p. 312), only 60 of which are indicated on the distribution map (91%).	

*Same number given to process as in Table 4, where a full description of it is given.

Table 13.10

Identification of Formation Processes at Pincevent: Factors Leading to Overlap Among Depositional Sets

Expected or Documented Processes*	Documentation	Organizational Model(s) along Nonoverlapping-Overlapping Dimension likely Congruent with Data
1. Multipurpose tools	Utilized blades and large backed bladelets for working	Overlapping

Table 13.10 (cont.)

	with meat, hide, vegetable, wood, or bone materials, possibly members or several kinds of tool kits.	
2. Multitype edged tools	2-3 endscraper-burins are included in both endscraper and burin inventories (2-3 out of 15 endscrapers = 13-20%; 2-3 out of 120 burins = 2-3%).	Overlapping
	1 endscraper-piercer may be included in endscraper inventory (1 out of 15 endscrapers = 7%).	
2. Agglomerated activity areas	A wide variety of activities (see Table 8) are represented by artifact types found in greater total numbers within the immediate hearth areas (Strata 1, 7; 2, 15; 3, 4) than peripheral areas (Strata 5, 6, 8, 9, 10, 11, 12, 13, 14, 16). These artifact classes include: core, burin, burin spall, bec, notch, backed bladelets, utilized blade, phalanges, metapods, ribs, (all > 2:1 ratio); hfr, mandibles (all > 1.5 and ≤ 2 ratio); endscrapers of classes A and B, ivory (all > 1 and ≤ 1.5 ratio).	Overlapping
3. Refuse from different kinds of activities deposited in same refuse areas through sweeping	See Table 9, entry 9, for evidence of sweeping.	Overlapping
	Conjoined burins and burin spalls (Leroi-Gourhan & Brézillon, 1966, pp. 337, 344) and conjoined pieces of cores (ibid, p. 341) indicate debris from different areas around a hearth or from different hearths were swept to common locations along the tent walls.	
4. Post-depositional smearing of primary refuse by trampling	Trampling likely, given a winter/late spring occupation where most tasks done within	Overlapping

Table 13.10 (cont.)

	tents, and given frequent socializing and movement between hearths. The latter is indicated by the conjoining of burins and burin spalls, and pieces of cores around different hearths with each other (ibid, pp. 341, 344).	
5. Typological rather than functional classification	Some utilized blades have natural backs (41% of the items in the class) and possibly functioned like large retouched backed bladelets.	Overlapping
	The larger of the backed bladelets may have functioned like utilized blades, while the smaller specimens may have served as projectile point armatures.	
	Many items in the class, becs, are simply obliquely truncated blades (19 of 45 items = 42%, ibid, p. 287), which may have been simply snapped blades used for any of the purposes of backed or utilized blades, but may also have been used like becs (ibid, pp. 287-288).	

*Same number given to process as in Table 5, where a full description of it is given.

Many of the observations also are of simple kinds that are available in many other published site reports. These data include 1) the probable functions of various tool forms based on previous studies of Paleolithic tool function, experimental studies in lithics, ethnographic analogy, and site-specific information; 2) the season(s) of occupation of the site as reconstructed from faunal remains; 3) patterns of lithic tool recycling and reuse evident from tool morphology; 4) spatial patterns for various individual artifact classes; 5) bone classes that have anomalously low numbers of elements compared to those expected on the basis of the estimated minimum number of individuals, in turn indicating differential preservation patterns; 6) various aspects of the composite distribution of all artifact types (e.g., arcs of artifact concentrations indicating tent wall locations; the density of cluster boundaries; the occurrence of most artifacts within the tents); 7) the diversity of tool classes found in various locations; and 8) the nature of the artifact classification scheme used by the researchers.

Processes affecting organization along the monothetic-polythetic dimension. Of the identified processes that can cause "unexpected absences" of artifacts and that determine depositional set organization along the monothetic-polythetic dimension (Table 9), almost all very probably acted *disuniformly* over habitation no. 1 (Table 4). Their effect would thus have been to make any depositional sets that do exist at the site to be organized in the form of model(s) 3, 4, 5, or 6 (Fig. 4). The specific form would depend on the particular actions of the processes and the organizational nature of the activity sets from which the depositional sets were derived. If it is also considered that the different processes were *not correlated* over space with each other, then the result of their combined effects would have been to make depositional sets organized more probably in the form of models 4 or 6.

It is necessary to determine whether the *strengths* of the processes that can cause unexpected absences and the *magnitudes* of their effects on depositional set organization were significant. If they were not, then depositional sets might have internal organizations essentially congruent with a different array of models, including more restrictive ones. Also, some estimate of the *range* of artifact types and depositional sets that were affected by the processes must be made. If only a few types or sets were affected, then the data as a whole might be approximately congruent in structure with a different array of models, again including more restrictive ones.

The magnitude of the effects of many of the formation processes that determine set organization along the monothetic-polythetic dimension and that have been identified for habitation no. 1 can be roughly estimated. This can be done using the number of unexpected absences of items in a class that have resulted from the action of the processes, expressed as a percentage of all items that *should* be in the class, present and absent. Measures of the monotheticness and polytheticness of depositional sets discussed at the beginning of this chapter cannot be used because such sets are not yet defined.

Formation, disturbance, and recording processes at Pincevent clearly had considerable effects on a number of artifact classes and their monothetic or polythetic organization into sets. 1) Incomplete documentation of the positions of 138 burin spalls and 6 backed bladelets on the distribution maps of these artifact classes has resulted in 67% and 9% of the items of these classes (respectively) being absent from locations where they might otherwise be expected. 2) Absences of the multitype edged tools—endscraper-burins, endscraper-piercers, and burin-notches—from the distribution maps of burins, piercers, and notches are 5% (6-7 items), 17% (1 item), and 5% (1 item), respectively. 3) Of the 500 minimum number of vertebrae of reindeer expected to occur within the habitation, only about 100 were found, probably as a result of decomposition processes or their use as fuel, yielding 80% of the items of this class unexpectedly absent. 4) Of the 73 utilized blades at the site, 41% have natural backs and functionally should have been classified with retouched backed bladelets (60 total, mapped), yielding 33% unexpected absences of items within the backed bladelet class. 5) Of 120 burins, 20 occur at the reconstructed perimeter of the huts, apparently swept there from more central work areas. This implies unexpected absences of burins from the work areas on the order of at least 18%. Similarly, of 68 burin spalls, 9 occur peripherally, implying 13% unexpected absences of items of this class from central work areas. These percentages pertain to burins and burin spalls in relation to *other* artifact types with which they might be coarranged. The percentages would be less for burins and burin spalls in relation to each other, given the parallel decrease in their numbers from work areas. 6) If endscraper types A and BC (7 and 18 items, each) were functionally equivalent and should not have been separated into two classes, their separation would imply unexpected absences of endscrapers from a composite class on the order of 28% (7 out of 25 items) and 72% (18 out of 25 items). 7) Similarly, if utilized blades (73 items) and the larger of the backed bladelets (perhaps half of the 60 specimens, with lengths approximately greater than the mean bladelet size of 3.3 cm) were functionally identical, their separation would imply unexpected absences of blades and larger bladelets from a composite class on the order of 71% (73 out of 103 items) and 29% (30 out of 103 items). 8) If tibio-peroneals and radio-cubitals (93 items, total) should have been kept together as a single class, their separation would imply 36% and 74% unexpected absences of long bones from the composite class (32 out of 122 items, 93 out of 122 items, respectively). Thus, the classes of artifact types at habitation no. 1 that are known or suspected to have been affected by formation, disturbance, recovery, reporting, and analytic processes that determine monothetic or polythetic depositional set organization were affected *substantially*.

The range of artifact classes that were possibly or definitely affected by formation and other processes to a significant degree is great. At least 10 of the 11 artifact classes, for which information was available on the magnitude of effects of formation processes on them, exhibit unexpected absences at the 15% level or larger. It is likely that additional artifact classes were affected to a similarly significant degree by one or more of the processes given in Table 9, but the magnitudes of the effects could not be assessed. Sweeping, for instance, is thought to have been spatially extensive, based on spatial patterns of conjoined artifacts. It probably affected the distributions of many kinds of artifacts additional to those just discussed. The effects of trampling, unknown for any artifact classes, probably were great, given that work was done within the confines of the living quarters.

Thus, *considering the diversity of formation, recovery, reporting and analytic processes causing unexpected absences, the magnitudes and range of their effects, and their lack of spatial correlation, it can be concluded that either Models 4 or 6 best typify the organization of depositional sets within habitation no. 1 along the monothetic-polythetic dimension. Similarity coefficients congruent with these models must be used to analyze the data.*

Processes affecting organization along the nonoverlapping-overlapping dimension. Overlap among at least some depositional sets in habitation no. 1 is likely, given the formation processes that have been identified for the site and that lead to this kind of organization (Table 10). The extent of overlap among sets and number of sets exhibiting overlap cannot be estimated at this stage. *It is necessary, therefore, that the higher-level techniques that are chosen for grouping artifact classes into depositional sets allow but not require the sets to be overlapping.*

Palimpsest organization. Two artifact classes at Pincevent—pebbles of alluvial flint (V24) and sandstone and limestone (V25)—have relatively ubiquitous distributions that also exhibit local clustering. These distributions are probably palimpsests. In a full spatial analysis, each would have to be dissected into their component distributions (at least two—a clustered and a ubiquitous component) of more homogeneous origin. Only the clustered components would be analyzed with the other artifact classes in defining depositional sets; the ubiquitous components would be analyzed separately. However, because dissection of palimpsests requires spatial filtering or Fourier procedures (Carr, 1982a, 1986) that are beyond the scope of this chapter, the distributions of alluvial pebbles and sandstone/limestone will not be dissected. An alternative approach will be taken, whereby first an analysis is made of the nonubiquitously distributed types and then the few ubiquitously distributed types are added to the study (see pp. 379-380, 423).

Formal Linkage of the Pincevent Spatial Data Set to Techniques Appropriate for Its Analysis

To this point, many of the steps in the pattern-searching framework that is shown in Figure 2, which combines inductive and deductive elements, have been addressed or carried out informally. These steps can be reiterated and the analysis can proceed in more formal terms using the concepts of entry models and parallel data sets, in order to deduce the particular mathematical techniques probably most appropriate for analyzing the Pincevent spatial data set.

1) A variety of forms of archaeological evidence not to be used in the spatial analysis of habitation no. 1, as well as information on the site's behavioral and environmental contexts, have been assembled. These constitute a "parallel data set" (Carr, chapter 2).

2) The parallel data set has been used *inductively* to reconstruct the cultural and natural formation processes that operated at the site. Recovery processes and documentation processes also have been identified.

3) The spatial data have been modified in reference to some of these processes and in preparation for analysis to the extent that artifact types with complex palimpsest distributions have been screened from initial analysis. Greater

modification of the data in order to correct for the effects of natural formation processes would have been desirable, had information on their operation been available.

4) On the basis of the formation processes, other processes, and relationships among them that have been reconstructed for the habitation no. 1 spatial data, and also considering whether these processes and relationships are similar to those specified by the various entry models developed previously, it is possible to *subsume* the spatial data set under either of two entry models. Both entry models enumerate kinds of formation processes and relationships among them that are similar to those reconstructed for habitation no. 1. One, however, specifies internal depositional set organization of the Model 4 type whereas the other specifies internal depositional set organization of the Model 6 type. Both entry models allow overlap among depositional sets.

5) Given the subsumption of the habitation no. 1 data under the two entry models and the fact that these models list mathematical techniques having assumptions that are congruent with the archaeological organization specified by the models, it is possible to *deduce* those techniques probably most appropriate for searching the data for depositional sets. These algorithms include the similarity coefficients, AVDISTLP1 and AVDISTLP2, coupled with some higher-level pattern-searching technique(s) allowing sets to overlap, such as MDS and/or OVERCLUS.

Depositional Sets at Habitation No. 1.

Method of Definition of Sets

For purposes of illustration, only AVDISTLP1, of the two coefficients thought congruent with the Pincevent data set, will be used to analyze it.

Measuring similarity and multidimensional scaling. Using the computer program POLYTHETIC2 (Appendix A), a 23 x 23 matrix of AVDISTLP1 dissimilarity coefficients among all the nonubiquitous artifact types was calculated (Table 11). From this matrix, scaled configurations of the types in spaces ranging from 6 dimensions to 1 were derived using nonmetric MDS procedures provided within the Statistical Analysis System (Proc ALSCAL, Level = Ordinal, Converge = .0001). Either nonmetric or metric MDS procedures might have been applied, given the ratio scale of the item-distance data; however, the former were preferred, for their greater usefulness in determining the optimal number of dimensions for displaying data (see pp. 376-377). Degeneracy of the nonmetric solution was not expected given the probable overlap among depositional sets, nor did it occur. Plots of configuration stress (Kruskal's formula 1; Kruskal & Wish, 1978, p. 24) against dimensionality, and an R^2 statistic (Young & Lewyckyj, 1980) against dimensionality, indicated an optimal compromise between low dimensionality and accurate representation of the data's dominant structure at 2-3 dimensions (Fig. 11, Table 12). The R^2 statistic, which indicates

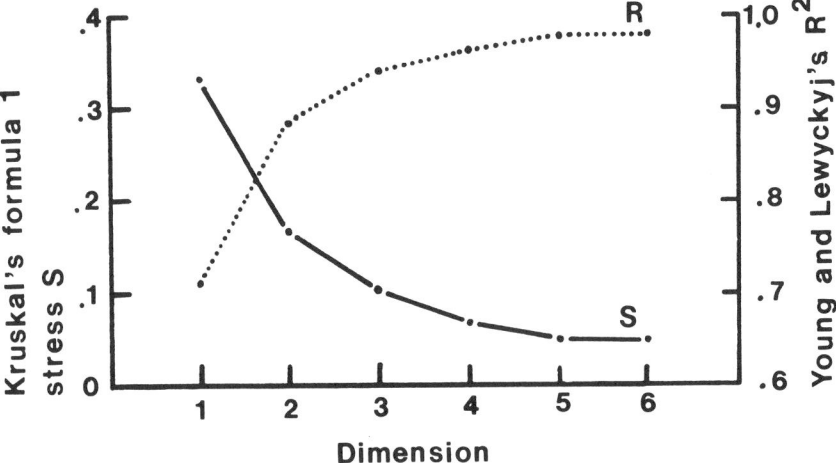

Fig. 13.11. Plots of configuration stress against dimensionality and of an R^2 statistic against dimensionality for a multidimensional scaling of 23 artifact classes from Pincevent. The AVDISTLP1 similarity coefficient was used. A 3 or 2 dimensional solution seems optimal.

the percentage of variation in the distances among types in full dimensional space that is encompassed by the distances among types in reduced space, is 94.2% for the 3-dimensional solution and 88.4% for the 2-dimensional solution. A plot of the distances among types in reduced space (disparities) against their distances in full dimensional space indicated that it was unlikely that classical scaling methods would facilitate much improvement in the representation of the data in 2- to 3-dimensional, reduced space. Several trial classical scalings also suggested this. The monotonic scalings were therefore accepted for further analysis. The configuration of types in 3-dimensional space, shown in Figure 12, was chosen for analysis.

Finer-scale multidimensional scaling. An examination of the 3-dimensional configuration indicated the possibility that the relationships within and between some clusters were distorted. Central to the configuration is a group of 11 artifact types (hereafter called *central types*), which probably is divisible into two or more subgroups. Central types include core, burin, burinsp, bec, notch, backbl, utblade, phal, meta, hfr, and rib. Surrounding this central cluster are 12 types (hereafter called *peripheral types*), some of which occur at great distances from the central group and comprise single or multitype "clusters." Because MDS usually reflects the global relationships among dispersed clusters more accurately and at the expense of local structural detail (Graef & Spence, 1976), it was concluded that the relationships among the 11 central artifact types and the composition of their subgroups might be distorted. Distortion of the rela-

Table 13.11

Matrix of AVDISTLP1 Statistics Defined for Habitation No. 1

	Core	Burin	Burinsp	Bec	Notch	Backbl	Utblade	Phal	Meta	Hfr	Pierce
Core	0.000	0.577	0.622	0.586	1.034	0.519	0.629	0.592	0.761	0.785	1.799
Burin	0.577	0.000	0.361	0.341	0.685	0.453	0.281	0.267	0.586	0.372	1.600
Burinsp	0.622	0.361	0.000	0.287	0.401	0.327	0.382	0.469	0.756	0.909	2.015
Bec	0.586	0.341	0.287	0.000	0.421	0.376	0.405	0.562	0.731	0.892	2.035
Notch	1.034	0.685	0.401	0.421	0.000	0.436	0.497	1.156	1.453	1.538	1.569
Backbl	0.519	0.453	0.327	0.376	0.436	0.000	0.380	0.552	0.823	0.998	0.804
Utblade	0.629	0.281	0.382	0.405	0.497	0.380	0.000	0.375	0.629	0.440	2.337
Phal	0.592	0.267	0.469	0.562	1.156	0.552	0.375	0.000	0.404	0.264	2.940
Meta	0.761	0.586	0.756	0.731	1.453	0.823	0.629	0.404	0.000	0.376	2.561
Hfr	0.785	0.372	0.909	0.892	1.538	0.998	0.440	0.264	0.376	0.000	2.326
Pierce	1.799	1.600	2.015	2.035	1.569	0.804	2.337	2.940	2.561	2.326	0.000
Microp	1.485	0.776	0.733	0.601	0.743	0.691	0.435	0.415	0.597	1.654	1.745
Scrapa	1.792	1.899	1.686	1.496	1.410	1.211	1.449	1.977	2.325	2.119	2.094
Scrapbc	0.793	0.990	0.999	0.647	0.563	0.465	0.725	1.037	1.179	1.118	1.609
Bead	2.553	2.234	2.012	2.020	2.116	2.109	2.537	3.087	3.512	3.002	1.047
Ivory	1.882	2.001	1.446	1.829	1.416	1.655	2.345	2.301	2.734	2.730	1.994
Antler	1.302	1.271	1.379	1.525	1.631	1.657	1.486	1.570	1.490	1.406	1.395
Tibio	0.445	0.622	1.108	0.998	1.208	0.912	0.647	0.570	0.535	0.532	2.221
Scap	1.418	1.585	1.885	1.783	1.851	1.838	1.619	1.432	1.542	1.651	2.019
Rib	0.661	0.443	0.717	0.601	1.104	0.738	0.375	0.379	0.400	0.319	2.694
Vert	1.883	1.828	1.607	1.744	1.856	1.671	2.325	2.393	2.904	2.674	1.757
Mandib	1.342	1.055	0.880	0.986	1.340	1.170	1.256	0.886	1.154	1.174	1.813
Maxill	0.953	0.776	0.876	0.782	1.079	0.979	0.945	1.034	1.031	1.291	1.479

	Microp	Scrapa	Scrapbc	Bead	Ivory	Antler	Tibio	Scap	Rib	Vert	Mandib	Maxill
Core	1.485	1.792	0.793	2.553	1.882	1.302	0.445	1.418	0.661	1.883	1.342	0.958
Burin	0.745	1.899	0.990	2.234	2.001	1.271	0.622	1.585	0.443	1.823	1.005	0.776
Burinsp	0.733	1.686	0.999	2.012	1.446	1.379	1.108	1.885	0.717	1.607	0.880	0.876
Bec	0.601	1.496	0.647	2.020	1.829	1.525	0.998	1.783	0.601	1.744	0.986	0.782
Notch	0.719	1.410	0.563	2.116	1.416	1.631	1.208	1.851	1.104	1.856	1.340	1.079
Backbl	0.691	1.211	0.465	2.109	1.655	1.657	0.912	1.838	0.738	1.671	1.170	0.979
Utblade	0.423	1.449	0.725	2.537	2.345	1.486	0.647	1.619	0.375	2.325	1.256	0.945
Phal	1.415	1.977	1.037	3.087	2.301	1.570	0.570	1.432	0.379	2.393	0.886	1.034
Meta	1.597	2.325	1.179	3.512	2.734	1.490	0.535	1.542	0.400	2.904	1.154	1.031
Hfr	1.615	2.119	1.118	3.002	2.730	1.406	0.532	1.651	0.319	2.674	1.174	1.291
Pierce	1.745	2.094	1.609	1.047	1.994	1.395	2.221	2.019	2.694	1.757	1.813	1.479
Microp	0.000	1.216	0.715	2.610	1.915	1.958	1.444	2.012	1.269	2.673	1.560	1.565
Scrapa	1.145	0.000	1.466	2.981	1.989	2.644	1.918	1.914	1.439	3.255	1.750	1.924
Scrapbc	0.715	1.466	0.000	2.621	2.439	1.829	0.893	1.626	1.040	2.641	1.790	1.589
Bead	2.610	2.981	2.621	0.000	1.735	1.849	2.876	2.983	3.365	1.171	2.722	2.056
Ivory	1.915	1.989	2.439	1.735	0.000	2.375	2.779	3.044	2.717	1.694	2.060	1.840
Antler	1.958	2.644	1.829	1.849	2.375	0.000	1.263	0.874	1.549	1.855	1.396	1.147
Tibio	1.444	1.918	0.893	2.876	2.779	1.263	0.000	1.432	0.509	2.738	1.698	1.318
Scap	2.012	1.914	1.626	2.983	3.044	0.874	1.432	0.000	1.691	3.341	1.610	1.572
Rib	1.269	1.439	1.040	3.365	2.717	1.549	0.509	1.691	0.000	2.987	1.513	1.466
Vert	2.673	3.255	2.641	1.171	1.694	1.855	2.738	3.341	2.987	0.000	2.143	1.709
Mandib	1.560	1.750	1.790	2.722	2.060	1.396	1.698	1.610	1.513	2.143	0.000	1.143
Maxill	1.565	1.924	1.589	2.056	1.840	1.147	1.318	1.572	1.466	1.709	1.143	0.000

Table 13.12

Stress of and Percent Variance of Data Explained by Configurations in Spaces of Different Dimensions

Number of Dimensions	Global Monothetic Algorithm (AVDISTGM)		Local Polythetic Algorithm (AVDISTLP1)		Global Polythetic Algorithm (AVDISTGP)	
	stress*	%σ^2	stress*	%σ^2	stress*	%σ^2
10 Type Study						
6	no solution possible		no solution possible		no solution possible	
5	no solution possible		no solution possible		no solution possible	
4	.009	99.9	.013	99.9	.052	96.0
3	.028	*99.5***	*.051*	98.1	*.094*	*89.7*
2	*.091*	*96.2*	*.123*	*93.3*	*.176*	*78.4*
1	.370	53.9	.260	79.8	.370	53.9
23 Type Study						
6	.041	98.9	.047	98.2	.088	91.6
5	.051	98.4	.055	97.8	.110	89.1
4	.067	97.5	.076	96.5	.134	85.9
3	.098	95.3	*.105*	*94.2*	.181	81.2
2	*.157*	*90.2*	*.170*	*88.4*	*.230*	*76.3*
1	.382	61.1	.333	71.5	.382	61.1
10 Type Study With 2 Ubiquitous Types						
6	no solution possible		no solution possible		no solution possible	
5	.010	99.9	.017	99.7	.036	97.2
4	.034	99.2	.045	98.3	.068	*92.9*
3	.046	98.7	*.060*	*97.5*	*.125*	*83.5*
2	*.089*	*96.2*	*.120*	*93.3*	.232	66.3
1	.426	44.9	.207	86.0	.426	44.9

*Kruskal's Stress formula 1. (Kruskal & Wish, 1978).
**Italics indicate that dimension for which an elbow in the graphs of stress vs. dimension or percent variance explained vs. dimension is observed.

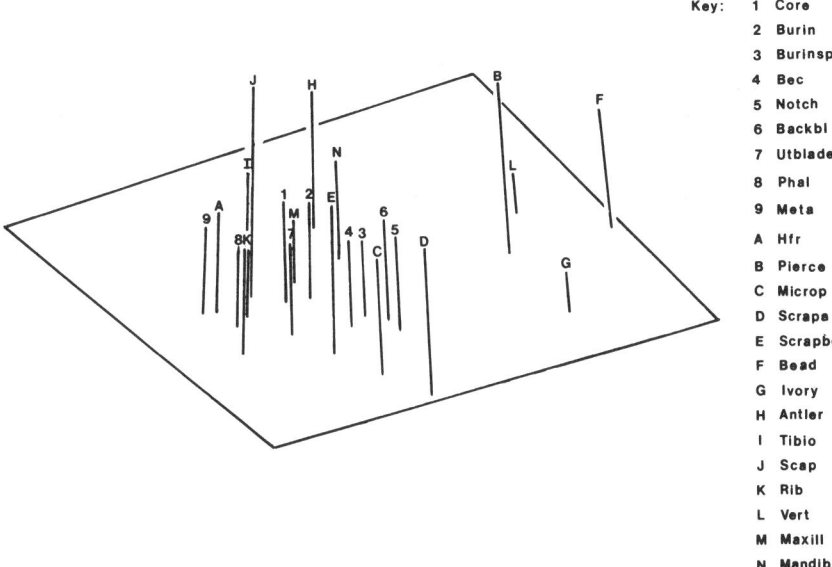

Fig. 13.12. A three-dimensional configuration of 23 artifact classes from Pincevent produced by their multidimensional scaling with the AVDISTLP1 similarity coefficient. The configuration is shown in perspective, using the same scaling factor for each dimension.

tionships among the central types also seemed likely, given that many of the peripheral types are infrequent (Table 22; 9 of the 12 types have less than 12 items) and the estimates of their relationships to the central types have a greater probability of being biased. To the extent that the relationships of the infrequent peripheral types to the central types are biased in complementary ways, the relationships of the central types to each other will be distorted more extensively. Thus, a more local MDS analysis, concentrating on the central group of 11 types, seemed appropriate before grouping types formally into depositional sets.

The choice of which particular types to include in the more local analysis was made entirely on the basis of the structure of the 3-dimensional configuration. The choice also, however, is meaningful: the 11 central artifact types are those that concentrate predominantly around the hearths of the site rather than in more peripheral strata (Table 13). Thus, the more local analysis can be viewed as a more detailed view of predominantly hearth-oriented depositional patterns.

A local MDS of 10 of the 11 central types was performed. (Rib unfortunately was deleted from analysis for reasons no longer felt justifiable but without ultimate consequences.) Those AVDISTLP1 coefficients within the larger matrix (Table 11) that are pertinent to the relationships among the 10 central

Table 13.13

Proportions of Artifacts of Given Types within Hearth Strata vs. Peripheral Strata*

$$\frac{\text{\#s within hearth strata}}{\text{\#s within peripheral strata}}$$

	More Hearth-Oriented Types			Less Hearth-Oriented Types
	>2	$2-1.51$	$1.5-1.01$	≤ 1
	core	hfr	scrapa	pierce
	burin	mandib	scrapbc	microp
	burinsp		ivory	bead
	bec			antler
	notch			tibio
	backbl			scapula
	utblade			vert
	phal			maxill
	meta			
	rib			

*Hearth strata include H1, H2, and H3. Peripheral strata include 8, 9, 10, 11, 5, 6, 16, 12, 13 and 14.

types were used to define monotonically scaled configurations of the types in spaces of 6 dimensions through 1, as before. Based on the stress and R^2 values for these solutions (Table 12), a 2 or 3-dimensional representation of the data seemed optimal. To maintain consistency with the previous analysis and also to gain "accuracy" in representation, the 3-dimensional solution, which encompasses 98.1% of the variation in the distances among the types in full dimensional space, was selected for further examination. The configuration (Fig. 13) exhibits a series of overlapping "clusters" or clinal relationships among types, without distant outliers. This feature, as well as the larger number of items upon which *all* AVDISTLP1 coefficients are based, suggests that the representation of the relationships among the types is probably more accurate than that for the 23 type solution. The larger R^2 statistic for the 10 type solution is consistent with this view.

Definition of depositional sets was achieved by a two-stage clustering design.

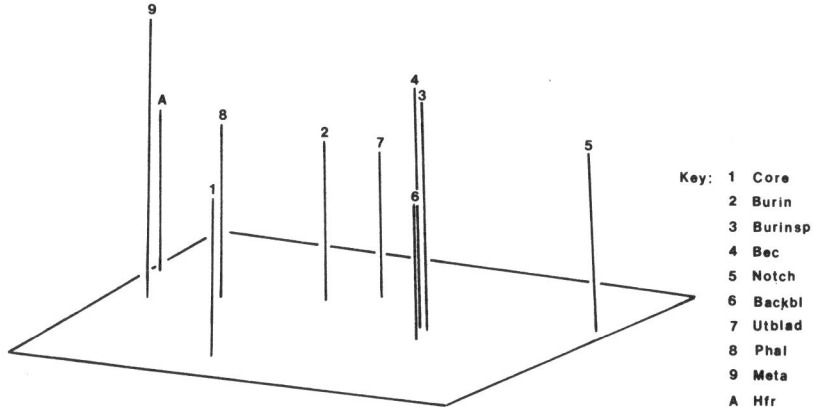

Fig. 13.13. A three-dimensional configuration of the 10 "central" artifact classes from Pincevent produced by their multidimensional scaling with the AVDISTLP1 similarity coefficient. The configuration is shown in perspective, using the same scaling factor for each dimension.

First, information from the 10-type MDS solution, which probably reflects the relationships among the central types more accurately, was used to cluster them. This result was then taken as a starting structure for clustering the remaining types with themselves and the clusters of central types, using information from the 23 type MDS solution.

Fine-scale clustering with OVERCLUS. The first stage of clustering, involving only the 10 central types, was achieved using the OVERCLUS approach. The stimulus coordinates for the 10 types in 3-dimensional scaled space (Table 14) were used to calculate a 10 x 10 matrix of Euclidean distances among all combinations of the types in that space (Table 15). This matrix is a "smoothed" representation of the matrix of average local polythetic distances among types (AVDISTLP1 coefficients; Table 11); those inconsistencies among the coefficients that are not expressible in 3 dimensions or less have been removed by the MDS operation. The amount of inconsistency smoothed from the matrix of AVDISTLP1 coefficients is $1 - R^2$, or 1.9% of the variation in the distances among all types in the full dimensional space. The matrix of Euclidean distances is also rescaled in mean and variance compared to the matrix of AVDISTLP1 coefficients, as a result of the MDS operations; thus the two cannot be compared directly.

The Euclidean distance coefficients in the smoothed matrix were used to link types sequentially in accord with OVERCLUS procedures involving a complete linkage criterion. Complete linkage was used because the data had already been smoothed by the MDS procedures and further smoothing using partial linkage was thought unnecessary. A list of types that link at each fusion step was

Table 13.14

Stimulus Coordinates for 10 "Central" Artifact Types in 3-Dimensional Scaled Space, Based on AVDISTLP1 Coefficients

	Dimension		
	1	2	3
Core	0.3020	−2.0773	−0.2606
Burin	0.3277	0.5162	−0.4198
Burinsp	−1.0527	−0.0667	0.5763
Bec	−0.9966	−0.1092	0.8210
Notch	−2.5571	0.5766	−0.0637
Backbl	−1.1592	−0.4322	−0.6820
Utblade	−0.1148	0.8271	−0.5814
Phal	1.2884	0.2359	−0.2551
Meta	1.8498	−0.1710	1.2654
Hfr	2.1124	0.7005	−0.4000

generated (partially reproduced in Table 16), as well as a graph of number of clusters vs. fusion (Fig. 14) and a plot of level of dissimilarity (Euclidean distance of fusion) vs. fusion step (Fig. 14).

It seemed appropriate to declare a *single* distance (artifact density) threshold for defining depositional sets. The relationships among the types reflected predominantly *one set of* hearth-oriented depositional patterns within the confines of an area approximately *uniformly constrained* in the availability of space, rather than multiple sets of depositional patterns in scattered areas of the habitation that have diverse spatial constraints. The threshold was determined using the previously discussed strategy involving prioritized, preferred characteristics of data representations at different fusion steps (p. 383). This strategy was realized as follows. 1) The plot of number of clusters vs. fusion step was made. This indicates several fusion steps/thresholds at which clusters inherent in the data crystallize and more simple organization is represented. These are the local minima or saddle points at steps 7, 14, 15, 16, 17, 18, 19, 20, 28, 29, and 30. 2) The plot of dissimilarity against fusion step was made. This plot indicates that of the fusion steps just mentioned, only some are preceded by

Table 13.15
Euclidean Distances among "Central" Artifact Types in 3-Dimensional Scaled Space, Based on AVDISTLP1 Coefficients

	Core	Burin	Burinsp	Bec	Notch	Backbl	Utblade	Phal	Meta	Hfr
Core	0.000	2.5985	2.5648	2.5942	3.9059	2.2403	2.9516	2.5147	2.8911	3.3186
Burin	2.5985	0.0000	1.7993	1.9195	2.9073	1.7830	0.5644	1.0142	2.3725	1.7943
Burinsp	2.5648	1.7993	0.0000	0.2546	1.7569	1.3146	1.7375	2.5027	2.9850	3.3999
Bec	2.5942	1.9195	0.2546	0.0000	1.9205	1.5459	1.9029	2.5492	2.8815	3.4369
Notch	3.9059	2.9073	1.7569	1.9205	0.0000	1.8314	2.5091	3.8653	4.6633	4.6832
Backbl	2.2403	1.7830	1.3146	1.5459	1.8314	0.0000	1.6391	2.5728	3.5937	3.4736
Utblade	2.9516	0.5644	1.7375	1.9029	2.5091	1.6391	0.0000	1.5572	2.8752	2.2382
Phal	2.5147	1.0142	2.5027	2.5492	3.8653	2.5728	1.5572	0.0000	1.6711	0.9570
Meta	2.8911	2.3725	2.9850	2.8815	4.6633	3.5937	2.8752	1.6711	0.0000	1.8979
Hfr	3.3186	1.7943	3.3999	3.4369	4.6832	3.4736	2.2382	0.9570	1.8979	0.0000

Table 13.16

List of Clusters of Artifact Types at Select Fusion Steps for the Analyis of "Central" Artifact Types, Based on AVDISTLP1 Coefficients

Fusion Step	Completely Linked Artifact Types	Dissimilarity
Step 14	1. burinsp-notch 2. burinsp-bec-backbl 3. burinsp-backbl-utblade-burin 4. burin-utblade-phal 5. burin-phal-hfr 6. phal-meta	1.7993
Step 15	1. notch-burinsp-backbl 2. burinsp-bec-backbl 3. burinsp-backbl-utblade-burin 4. burin-utblade-phal 5. burin-phal-hfr 6. phal-meta	1.8314
Step 16	1. notch-burinsp-backbl 2. burinsp-bec-backbl 3. burinsp-backbl-utblade-burin 4. burin-utblade-phal 5. burin-phal-hfr 6. phal-meta-hfr	1.8979
Step 17	1. notch-burinsp-backbl 2. bec-backbl-burinsp-utblade 3. burinsp-backbl-utblade-burin 4. burin-utblade-phal 5. burin-phal-hfr 6. phal-meta-hfr	1.9029
Step 18	1. notch-burinsp-backbl 2. bec-backbl-burinsp-utblade-burin 3. burin-utblade-phal 4. burin-phal-hfr 5. phal-meta-hfr	1.9195
Step 19	1. notch-burinsp-backbl-bec 2. bec-backbl-burinsp-utblade-burin 3. burin-utblade-phal 4. burin-phal-hfr 5. phal-meta-hfr	1.9205
Step 20	1. notch-burinsp-backbl-bec 2. bec-backbl-burinsp-utblade-burin 3. burin-utblade-phal-hfr 4. phal-meta-hfr	2.2382

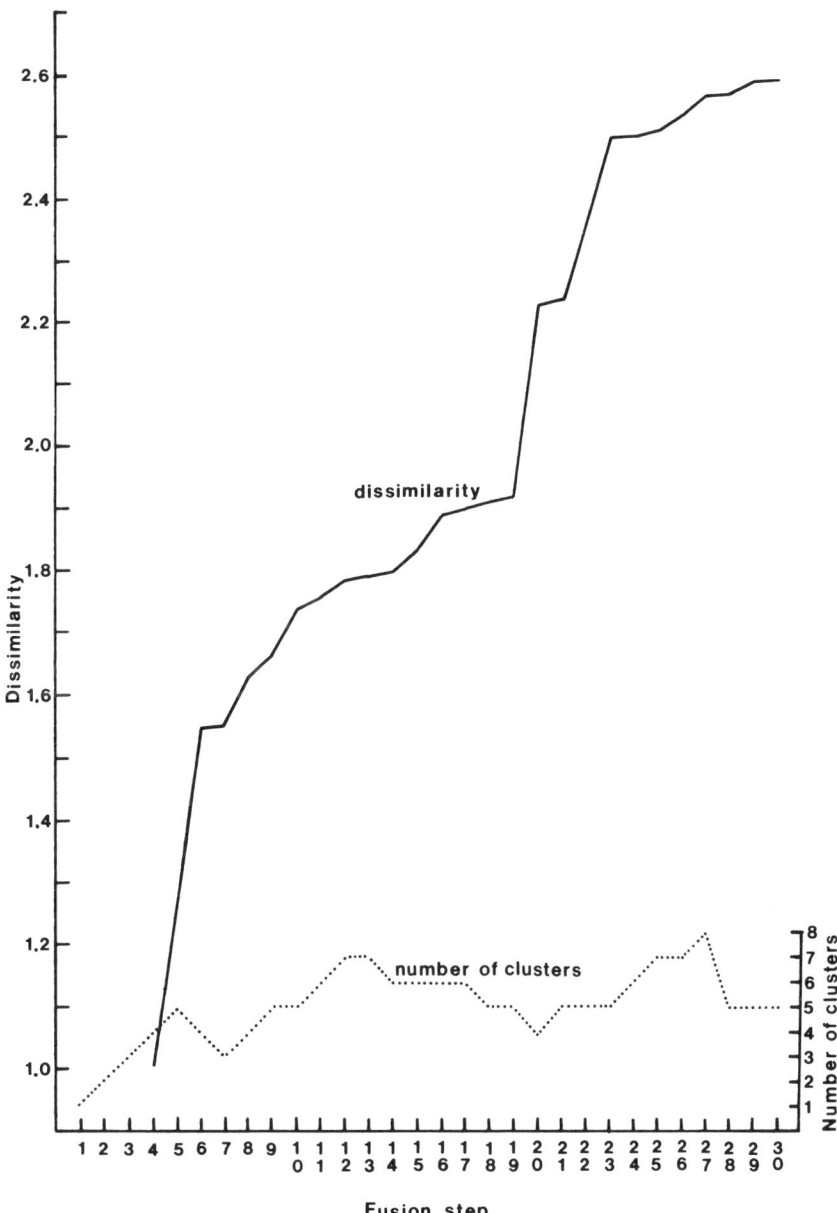

Fig. 13.14. Plots of number of clusters against fusion step and of dissimilarity against fusion step for an OVERCLUS analysis of the 10 "central" artifact types at Pincevent. The analysis is based on a matrix of Euclidean distances among the types that represents AVDISTLP1 coefficients smoothed by multidimensional scaling procedures.

the slight rises in dissimilarity which would suggest that the clusters that have crystallized are also relatively homogeneous. These steps include 14, 15, 16, 17, 18, 19, 28, 29, and 30. 3) Given the structural indeterminancy of the data set, the lists of grouped types for each of the latter array of fusion steps were inspected in order to determine stopping points that were preferable from an interpretive standpoint in two ways. (a) The stopping point generally defines and segregates groups of types that one might expect to be members of the same or different depositional sets, on the basis of the activities implied by the types (Table 8) and the context of deposition—here, possibly agglomerated or extremely overlapping activity areas (Speth & Johnson, 1976). (b) The stopping point defines groups that give insights into depositional set compositions and that imply activity organization or formation processes that, through plausible, might not otherwise have been discovered. These two criteria allowed the selection of a distance threshold of 1.8979 at fusion step 16. The resultant depositional sets for that step are shown in Table 16.

The clusters of types defined at fusion step 16 have two preferred characteristics in line with the criteria just cited. First, two certainly distinct activity sets become fully defined only by step 16. One set is suggestive of bone/antler/ivory/wood working, and more particularly, projectile point rearmament. It is composed of burin-burinsp-blackbl-utblade. The second set is suggestive of broth making and marrow boiling. It is composed of phal-meta-hfr. Although these groups also overlap at this step, some overlap is expectable, given their concentration around the hearths. (In fact, the degree to which they segregate at step 16 offers surprising resolution. This clarity decreases from step 20 onward.) Second, possibly subtle, unsuspected differences in the use of becs, notches, and burins—all broadly useful in working bone, antler, ivory, or wood—are indicated at step 16 by their membership in separate (though overlapping) sets. These distinctions fade in step 17 (where becs join burins) and again in step 19 (where notches join becs).

Broader-scale clustering. The second stage of clustering involved linking the 12 more peripheral types (and rib) to each other and the depositional sets formed previously. It was thought appropriate that the distance (artifact density) thresholds used to define depositional sets of these types be allowed to be higher and more variable than that applied to the central types. Many of the peripheral types (8 of 12) were most numerous in stata away from the hearths, where the availability of work space would have been less constrained and more variably constrained than work space around the hearths. The second stage of clustering was achieved as follows.

1) Potential groupings of peripheral artifact types with themselves and/or central artifact types were defined. This was done on the basis of their spatial relationships within the 23 type, 3-dimensional scaled configuration (Fig. 12) and the common activities that those relations might imply, and regardless of the magnitude of the distance threshold implied. These groups included scrapa-

microp-scrapbc (a potential hide working set); mandib-maxill-antler (all of the head region); scapula-hfr-antler (all sources of bone for making tools); rib-tibio-phal-meta-hfr (all involved in broth making, oil distilling, or eating); and bead-vert-ivory-pierce (all distant from the remaining artifacts).

2) A single distance threshold for the 23 type MDS solution, approximately analogous to that proposed in the 10-type solution, was defined by specifying a distance as large as the most distant intra-cluster relationships defined significant in the 10-type solution. This threshold was found to be 1.0966. It differs from the distance threshold for the 10-type solution (1.8979) largely because of the different scalings produced by the two MDS analyses.

3) To obtain a "first approximation" of clusters of peripheral types or peripheral and central types, the threshold of 1.0966 was applied to them. Those peripheral types that joined at or below this threshold with other peripheral or central types on a complete linkage basis were considered depositional sets for certain. Sets 4, 7, 8 through 15, and 17 listed in Table 17 were defined in this manner. These sets include a number of the relationships thought potentially significant and listed above (e.g., microp-scrapa; microp-scrapbc; maxill-mandib).

4) In line with the higher and more variable distance thresholds presumed appropriate for the peripheral types (above), the single threshold defining the tentative clusters was raised for some clusters, allowing the admittance of additional types to them on a complete linkage basis. Each new threshold was defined in accordance with certain strict stipulations. (a) As before, the threshold preferably should define and segregate groups of types that one might expect to be members of the same or different depositional sets, on the basis of the activities implied by the types (Table 8), e.g., the potential groups listed in point 1, above. (b) As before, the threshold might define groups that give insights into depositional set composition and that imply activity organization or formation processes which, though plausible, might not otherwise have been discovered. (c) A threshold chosen so as to define a logical group should not involve relationships among types that are inconsistent with the complete linkage criterion of the OVERCLUS procedures. For example, suppose type A is most closely related to type B, then C, and distantly related to D; type B is most closely related to A, then C, and distantly related to D; but C is most closely related to A, then D, then B. Although a linkage of A, B, and C might seem meaningful from an *interpretive* standpoint, it would also imply, assuming a complete linkage structure, linkages of A to D, B to D, and C to D—the first two relationships of which are not suggested *structurally* by the data and additionally might not be meaningful from an interpretive standpoint. Thus, the set ABC, though attractive from an interpretive standpoint, would not be defined; only the linkages of A to B, A to C, and C to D would be defined. In this way, the structural constraint of complete linkage on grouping proved very restrictive, preventing group definition that was oriented primarily toward creating interpretable sets

Table 13.17

Depositional Sets Defined Using the Dissimilarity Coefficient AVDISTLP1 with Multidimensional Scaling and OVERCLUS Algorithms

Set	Average Intertype Distance Threshold Used to Define Sets[1]
1. burin burinsp utblade backbl[2]	1.0966
2. burinsp backbl bec[2]	1.0966
3. burinsp backbl notch[2]	1.0966
4. phal meta hfr rib[2,3] ssls (clustered component)[4]	1.0966
5. utblade burin phal[2]	1.0966
6. hfr burin phal[2]	1.0966
7. rib utblade phal hfr[3]	1.0966
8. tibio hfr[3]	1.0966
8. core tibio[3]	1.0966
10. microp scrapa[3]	1.0966
11. microp scrapbc[3]	1.0966
12. microp notch[3]	1.0966
13. maxill mandib burin core[3]	1.0966
14. mandib antler[3]	1.0966
15. scapula[3]	1.0966
16. ivory bead vert[3]	2.4538
17. ivory notch backbl burinsp[3]	2.4538
18. bead pierce[3]	1.6005
19. vert mandib[3]	2.4538

[1] Relative to the 23-type multidimensional scaling solution as a standard.
[2] Group based on intertype relations in the 10-type multidimensional scaling solution.
[3] Group based on intertype relations in the 23-type multidimensional scaling solution.
[4] The undissected ubiquitous, high density, clustered distribution of ssls items, as a whole, was included in the 10 and 23-type multidimensional scaling solutions. The association presumably results primarily from the clustered component of this distribution.

and that might otherwise have occurred in an overly zealous manner. Table 18 is a list of the types to which given peripheral types are closest, which was used in defining structurally consistent thresholds and preventing overly zealous clustering. (d) The threshold should not be made so large—for the sake of linking types that would seem to define a meaningful group—that the group overlaps extensively with many surrounding groups. Again, this constraint proved to restrict over-zealous clustering. Table 18 was used to check for this restriction, as well.

On the basis of these criteria for defining thresholds, and considering the relationships among peripheral and central types that were thought potentially significant (step 1, above), the peripheral types were clustered with each other and with the central types. The resulting depositional sets, 19 in all, are shown in Table 17.

Consideration of ubiquitously distributed artifact types. To the 19 depositional sets found using MDS and OVERCLUS procedures, two final sets can be added: one comprised of the ubiquitously distributed artifact *class*, flint pebbles, and the second comprised of the ubiquitous *component* of the complex, widely-scattered artifact class, sandstone-limestone. These ubiquitous scatters are obviously different in their arrangement from the distributions of the other, nonubiquitous types. They also differ visibly from each other. The ubiquitous flint distribution has small, tight clusters of a few items each here and there; such minor clusters are not as common in the ubiquitous component of the ssls distribution.

Within the composite ssls distribution, there is a clearly clustered component composed of many items surrounding the hearths additional to the lighter-scatter, ubiquitous component. By introducing ssls, alone, into the 10-type, 3-dimensional MDS solution, it was found that the clustered component (presumably) of this type's distribution joined with only the types in set 4 below the 1.0966 threshold equivalent. The positions of the types other than ssls remained essentially stable in their positions with the introduction of ssls, which suggested the reliability of the new configuration. Diagnostic statistics for the augmented MDS solution are given in Table 12. No attempt was made to introduce flint into these solutions, given its more dispersed distribution over the site.

Interpretation of the Depositional Sets

In a routine spatial analysis, the process of interpreting the sets would involve considering both the activities implied by the artifact types defining the sets (Table 8) plus the spatial distributions of the sets. Because definition of multi-type spatial clusters of artifacts is beyond the scope of this chapter (see Carr, 1984 for applicable methods), the sets will be interpreted primarily on the former evidence. Spatial information will be limited to largely the hearth-oriented or nonhearth-oriented nature of the types (Table 13).

Table 13.18

List of Any Types to which Peripheral Types are Most Near in the 23-Type MDS Solution, Based on AVDISTLP1 Coefficients. Euclidean Distances between Types in 3-Dimensional Scaled Space are Shown

Tibio	Rib	Microp	Scrapa	Scrapbc	Mandib	Maxill	Antler	Scap	Ivory	Pierce	Bead	Vert
hfr 0.8650	utblade 0.6848	scrapbc 0.9940	microp 1.0188	microp 0.9940	burin 0.8337	core 0.8112	mandib 1.0683	tibio 1.3921	vert 2.1169	bead 1.6005	pierce 1.6005	bead 2.0252
core 1.0622	phal 0.7955	scrapa 1.0188	scrapbc 1.4845	utblade 1.2553	core 0.9627	burin 0.8875	burin 1.6601	antler 1.8651	notch 2.2353	antler 2.2883	vert 2.0252	ivory 2.1169
burin 1.1506	hfr 0.9252	notch 1.0698	notch 1.8885	rib 1.3499	maxill 1.0549	mandib 1.0549	core 1.7083	scap 2.1048	burinsp 2.3724	mandib 2.3939	ivory 2.4538	mandib 2.4444
meta 1.1561	meta 1.0416	backbl 1.2357	backbl 2.0434	backbl 1.3747	antler 1.0683	burinsp 1.1185	tibio 1.7842	hfr 2.2028	backbl 2.3957	backbl 2.4034	mandib 3.0371	burinsp 2.7222
utblade 1.1761	tibio 1.2051	bec 1.3120	bec 2.2700	tibio 1.4169	burinsp 1.3146	phal 1.2738	scap 1.8651	core 2.2979	bead 2.4538	notch 2.5723	backbl 3.0835	maxill 2.7563
rib 1.2057	core 1.3436	utblade 1.3802	utblade 2.3489	notch 1.4445	backbl 1.3728	bec 1.2770	maxill 1.9704	burin 2.3107	bec 2.6116	burin 2.8098	notch 3.1621	backbl 2.8761
phal 1.2936	scrapbc 1.3499	burinsp 1.5971	rib 2.4908	scrapa 1.4845	bec 1.4061	meta 1.3715	hfr 2.1985	maxill 2.3954	microp 2.9489	scrapbc 2.8618	antler 3.2169	pierce 2.8810
scap 1.3921	bec 1.4144	rib 1.6262	burinsp 2.5265	bec 1.4901	tibia 1.6344	hfr 1.4184	backbl 2.2038	meta 2.4714	mandib 3.0382	vert 2.8810	burinsp 3.3514	notch 2.9501
scrapbc 1.4169	burin 1.4397	burin 1.9064	burin 2.8092	burin 1.6678	notch 1.6564	utblade 1.4433	pierce 2.2883	rib 2.4822	pierce 3.0919	burinsp 2.8887	bec 3.5208	antler 2.9920
mandib 1.6344	microp 1.6262	phal 2.0609	tibio 2.8869	core 1.7848	utblade 1.6871	backbl 1.6045	burinsp 2.3239	utblade 2.4942	burin 3.1094	bec 2.8944	burin 3.5697	burin 3.0200
bec 1.6488	burinsp 1.7258	core 2.0649	core 2.9896	burinsp 1.8374	hfr 1.7455	notch 1.7682	bec 2.3265	phal 2.6822	maxill 3.1417	scap 2.9810	maxill 3.8093	bec 3.0422
backbl 1.7600	backbl 1.7524	tibio 2.1570	scrapa 3.0347	hfr 1.8677	phal 1.8447	tibio 1.8427	meta 2.3717	backbl 2.7167	scrapa 3.3048	core 3.0551	core 3.8261	core 3.1966

Set 1. Several interpretations of this association of artifact classes are possible. (a) All of the classes—burins, burin spalls, utilized blades, and backed bladelets—have in common their generalized possible use in or production in the graving, boring, or whittling of bone, antler, ivory, or wood (Table 8). In this case, their association would reflect the common activity in which they were used together or produced as refuse. (b) Alternatively, the association of backed bladelets which could have functioned as armatures on bone-splinter projectile points, with burins and utilized blades which are useful in the groove-and-splinter technique of bone working, could suggest the more particular activity of producing or rearming projectile points. The occurrence of this set around the hearths, where mastic for applying armatures to projectile points could have been melted, also supports this particular interpretation. As in the first interpretation, the association would reflect the common activity in which the artifact classes were used together or produced as refuse. (c) Burins are tools that sometimes were hafted for use (Keeley, personal communication, 1983). If burins were hafted using mastic just as backed bladelets would have been as armatures, the association of these two classes might in part represent the common hearth locations where tools were rehafted. In this case, the association would not represent tools used together in the same activity; rather, it would indicate only the common locations of their maintenance. This interpretation does not explain the association of utilized blades and burin spalls with burins and backed bladelets, and thus, can only supplement other interpretations of the set, at best. (d) Both utilized blades and some backed bladelets could have been used for a much wider range of tasks, such as cutting meat, hides, or plant material, as well as working wood, bone, antler or ivory. In this case, the association of the artifact classes in the set would represent the use of the same space for several kinds of activities. This is not unlikely, given the concentration of this set around the hearths, where lighted and heated work space presumably was valued and used for multiple purposes and where at least cooking tasks, in addition to the working of bone, antler, or wood, would have occurred.

All told, this depositional set could have been produced by one, several, or all of the processes just described. If one depositional process was involved, the production or rearmament of projectile points is most parsimonious and is thought most likely (Keeley, personal communication, 1983). The remains appear to represent primary refuse, given that the set includes burin spalls—small items that could comprise a drop zone (Binford, 1978, p. 345) and that would not easily be swept away.

Set 2. The common possible uses of the tools in this set include boring and whittling bone, antler, or ivory. Alternatively, the association could represent the spatial overlap of areas in which bone, antler, or ivory were worked using becs and burins, with areas in which projectile points were produced or rearmed. Again, the occurrence of burin spalls in this set suggests primary refuse. This interpretation is supported by the fact that heavy concentrations of becs, backed bladelets, burins, and burin spalls occur around two large stone blocks adjacent to hearths 2 and 3, which presumably were used for sitting while working (Leroi-Gourhan & Brézillon, 1966, p. 364) and around which debris and exhausted tools were dropped.

Set 3. The common possible functions of these tools include working bone, antler, ivory, or wood. More specifically, the occurrence of notches which are useful in shaving dart or arrow shafts, with backed bladelets which could have functioned as projectile point armatures, suggests the production of whole darts or arrows (shafts and points) rather than simply the rearmament of points. Alternatively, the set could represent the spatial overlap of areas of more generalized working of bone, antler, ivory, or wood, involving notches and burins, with areas where points were rearmed. Finally, given the location of the set primarily around the hearths, where foot traffic presumably was heavy, some notches might be simply blades that have been trampled and misidentified as notches. In this case, the set would represent a spurious manifestation of Set 1; all types within the set would occur in Set 1.

Set 4. All of the bones, save ribs, in this set are useful for making either broth or bone grease by stone boiling (citations and evidence in Table 8). This interpretation makes sense, given the concentration of items of these types around the hearths, as well as their association with sandstone and limestone rocks possibly used in stone boiling. Ribs were presumably eaten around the hearths, their occurrence within the set reflecting the spatial overlap of cooking and eating activities. It also is possible that the long bones, hfr, represent bone material used in making bone items, this activity having overlapped with eating and cooking around the hearths, as suggested by the next three sets.

Sets 5, 6, 7. These sets have members from both Sets 1 and 4 and represent their partial overlap.

Set 8. The long-bones in this group could have been used for making either bone grease around the hearths or bone artifacts in more peripheral strata, or both. The linking of tibio with hfr might suggest that the classification of tibio-peroneals separate from humeri, femurs, and radio-cubitals was a poor decision. The separation of tibio from hfr in Set 4, however, would suggest the opposite conclusion.

Set 9. The association of core and tibio could represent primary refuse from the manufacturing of blades to work bone, or more probably, the spatial overlap of knapping areas and bone grease preparation areas around the hearths. The use of tibia in the blade manufacturing process, itself, is not likely, given the usual manner of blade preparation by punch and hammer or pressure crutch techniques (Crabtree, 1968).

Sets 10, 11. The most parsimonious interpretation of this association is the common use of micropiercers and scrapers in working hide. The micropiercers would have been used to pierce holes in hides, either in the process of sewing them after their curing or to hold them in position during the final graining process. It is possible that some of the debris-free areas within the tents were areas where smaller pieces of hide were tacked and grained, rather than sleeping areas: many of the micropiercers and scrapers occur around the edges of the debris-free zones.

The fact that scraper types A and BC both associate with micropiercers but not with each other might be used to support the idea that these two kinds of scrapers, which differ in edge angle, were used for defleshing vs. graining hides, respectively. The two activities would have occurred in different locales but involved micropiercers in common. However, this does not seem likely, given the distribution of the possible defleshers *within* the huts and the messiness of defleshing hides, which normally would be done outdoors, weather permitting.

Alternatively and preferably, the two different distributions of scrapers and micropiercers might reflect a change in space-use over time. The scrapbc (high edge angle)-micropiercer distribution would indicate locations used earlier in the occupation and where exhausted scrapers were abandoned. The scrapa (low edge angle)-micropiercer distribution would indicate locations used later and where only partially depleted scrapers were left at site abandonment.

Finally, it might be argued that the association of micropiercers and scrapers of either kind reflects only the spatial overlap of two distinct activities: wood/bone boring (microp) and hide working (scrapers). Although this alternative cannot be negated, it does not seem as probable. Both types in the set tend to occur away from the hearths, where available work space was less constrained and overlap of activities was less likely.

Set 12. Micropiercers appear to have been used to work not only hide, but also bone, antler, ivory or wood, given their association in this set with notches. The micropiercers might have been used to obtain splinters of bone or wood from larger pieces of these raw materials, the splinters having then been rounded with notches. They might also, or alternatively, have been used to groove the lengths of dart shafts after the shafts were rounded with notches—a functional shaft design used by some American Indians (Winters, 1969, p. 54)—or to groove-decorate other items rounded with notches.

Set 13. This set is composed of artifact types that concentrate around the hearths: mandibles, burins, and cores. It might represent the spatial overlap of several unrelated activities around the hearths: bone grease making, bone/antler/ivory working, and knapping, respectively. The meaning of the occurrence of maxilla in the set is unclear.

Set 14. Both of the types in this set—antler and mandibles—are reindeer head parts that might have served as raw material sources. The association derives primarily from their coarrangement *outside* the huts (Strata 5, 9). Here, a few burins also occur, which might have been used to extract splinters of these raw materials. In this case, the association would be considered primary refuse left behind from an activity. However, the association could equally represent a secondary refuse deposit, dumped outside one of the hut entrances.

Set 15. Scapulae occur primarily outside the huts (Strata 12, 13, 5, 9), where they appear to have been deposited as refuse. Their location in areas separate from the head parts and appendages of the reindeer indicates that different reindeer parts were probably processed in different locales as well as deposited separately.

Set 16. The association of beads for personal adornment with ivory which might be made into similarly personal items is reminiscent of other such associations of personal belongings elsewhere in Pincevent (Leroi-Gourhan & Brézillon, 1966, p. 361). The occurrence of vertebrae in this set may represent a spurious association, given the small number of items (of each type) upon which the association is based.

Set 17. The association of notches, backed bladelets, and burin spalls with ivory—all hearth-concentrated types—suggests their common use in the working of ivory around the hearths. Alternatively, if the backed bladelets represent armatures on projectile points rather than tools for working ivory, the association could represent the spatial overlap of areas of ivory working—where notches, burins, and ivory were used—with areas of point armament. This interpretation is quite possible, given the locus of this set around the hearths, where work space was limited and probably used for multiple purposes. The remains would appear to represent primary refuse, given that the set includes burin spalls, which are harder to sweep.

Set 18. This set of beads and piercers may represent a spurious association produced by (a) the use of cell-centered positions for the items of both of the types, causing one item of each type to exactly coincide in one cell, and (b) the low number of items of both types (2 beads, 4 piercers). However, items of the two types do repeatedly occur in close proximity, and the piercers would have been appropriate in their tip diameters for drilling the holes in the carbon beads.

Set 19. This set is composed of reindeer vertebrae and mandibles that were dumped primarily outside of one of the hut's entrances (Strata 5 and 9), just as the head parts of Set 14 may have been. It is not known whether the vertebrae come from the neck region of the reindeer, but if so, then the two sets possibly represent a common depositional pattern for similar body parts.

Set 20. Alluvial flint pebbles, alone, comprise this set. Some of the items obviously were carried to the site and/or positioned within it by human forces, as evidenced by their size or clustering with artifacts. Many of the smaller items, however, may be natural alluvial inclusions (Leroi-Gourhan & Brézillon, 1966, p. 325), which gives the distribution of pebbles its ubiquitous characteristic.

Set 21. The ubiquitous component, alone, of the ssls distribution comprises this set. The clustered component was assigned to Set 4. Whereas the clustered component probably reflects primary deposition, around the hearths, of stones used in stone boiling (see Set 4), the ubiquitous component may represent secondary refuse deposition that involved the removal of heat-degraded stones from the hearth areas and the dumping of them in scattered locations away from the hearths and huts. Thus, we may see here an example of two components of the distribution of a single artifact class representing two different kinds of formation processes.

Broader Interpretations

The depositional patterns, formation processes, and activities reconstructed thus far would normally be explored further with plots of the spatial distributions of the several sets of artifact types. This would be done in order to infer patterns of interaction among social segments, population size and composition, site length of occupation, regional mobility patterns, and other states of variables of the behavioral-environmental system under examination.

Given the focus of this chapter, this step will not be taken. However, it is desirable to summarize some important conclusions and implications of the above analysis, which go beyond the reconstruction of depositional sets. Some of these approach this secondary level of synthesis. 1) The study of artifact class associations provides several kinds of information about artifact function not apparent from the list of types, their morphology, or their individual arrangements. (a) It helps resolve the ambiguity of the functions of several artifact classes and allows a more limited range of functions or a single function to be assigned to each class (e.g., scrapers for working hide rather than hide *or* wood/bone/antler). (b) It suggests functions that were not immediately suggested for some morphological classes. While burins are generally thought of as tools for boring or graving bone or antler (Keeley, 1978, p. 81; personal communication, 1983), the associations in Set 17 suggest their use on ivory, as well. [Use-wear from ivory is nearly indistinguishable from that from antler (Keeley, personal communication).] (c) The study suggests possible subtle differences in the uses of burins and becs, whereas recent interpretations of their function, based on use-wear analysis, have emphasized the equivalency of their use in boring bone or antler (Keeley, 1978, p. 81), albeit, to overcome traditional typological biases.

2) The analysis provides insight into the process of butchering and use of reindeer. Three different classes of animal parts have different depositional patterns, which suggests their different handling: appendages and abdomen (Set 4), shoulder girdle (Set 15), and head parts (Sets 13, 14, 19). The first class was used and deposited intensively around the hearths, in the process of cooking meat and making broth and bone grease. The latter two classes were deposited peripheral to the hearths and/or huts.

3) The analysis supports the conclusion (pp. 389-390) of a fairly short length of occupation. The clarity with which depositional sets from different activities around the hearths could be resolved (Sets 1, 2, 3, 4), yet their overlapping membership, suggests the operation of formation processes that would have led to a single, blurred palimpsest with an extensive length of stay.

EXPERIMENTAL INVESTIGATIONS OF THE BEHAVIORS OF THE NEW TECHNIQUES USING THE PINCEVENT DATA

To reach a better understanding of the behaviors of the several AVDIST coefficients and MDS procedures in response to data structures, the same distributional data were analyzed using the AVDISTGM and AVDISTGP coefficients and scaled in 6 dimensions through 1 using monotonic MDS procedures, as above. Both 10-type solutions for the central types, and 23-type solutions for the central and peripheral types combined, were calculated. An additional 10-type solution augmented with the two ubiquitous types (flint, ssls) was also calculated—a procedure not recommended for normal analytic investigations but having heuristic value. The distance matrices and statistics pertinent to these analyses are shown in Tables 19 through 22. On the basis of these results, several studies of the behavior of the coefficients and MDS procedures were made, as follows.

Effects of Incongruencies between Relevant Data Structure and the AVDIST Coefficients

It has been argued that the techniques used to analyze a spatial data set must be congruent with its relevant relational structure to obtain accurate results. Four AVDIST coefficients have consequently been proposed for analyzing four different relevant relational data structures, in which coarrangements among artifact types are organized in different ways along the monothetic-polythetic dimension (Models 1, 4, 5, 6 of Fig. 4). However, the particular effects of using the wrong coefficients to analyze data structures that are incongruent with them remain to be discussed and illustrated.

In preparation for this discussion, it must be noted that correct assessment of the organization of a number of artifact types into a depositional set, relative to other artifact types, depends on correct measurement of two kinds of relationships among types. These are 1) relationships between artifact types within the set, and 2) relationships of artifact types in the set to those not. In other words, both relationships of *internal cohesion* and those of *external isolation*, which help define a depositional set, must be correctly measured. If a coefficient underestimates or overestimates the strength of either of these two kinds of relationships, depositional set organization will not be accurately reflected, and the set may not be accurately determined in higher-level, multitype analysis.

In the following study, the accuracy of measurement of only the first kind of relationship is considered. It is asked how the accuracy of a coefficient in measuring the *degree of coarrangement* of two coarranged types is affected by the coefficient's assumptions about form of coarrangement compared to the types' actual form of coarrangement. Not considered is the accuracy of a coefficient in measuring the *degree of spatial segregation* of two dissimilarly arranged types, as a function of the assumptions it makes about form of spatial segregation (implied by its assumptions about form of coarrangement), compared to the types' actual manner of dissimilar arrangement. Thus, any conclusions drawn on the effects of incongruence between the assumed and actual forms of coarrangement of *two* types must be translated only with caution into conclusions on the accuracy of definition of depositional sets in higher-level, *multitype* analysis.

Predictable effects of inappropriate application of the AVDIST coefficients. From this perspective, several expectations can be posed about the effects of using the AVDIST coefficients to analyze data with which they are not congruent.

1) The AVDISTGM distance between two coarranged types will be excessively high if the types are coarranged in any of the forms of organization in Models 2 through 6. In these cases, the coefficient assumes more regularities in the magnitude and direction of asymmetry of the two types among strata than occur in the data. Depositional sets organized as in Models 2 through 6 consequently will not be defined as strongly by this coefficient as they might be by more congruent coefficients.

2) The AVDISTLP1 distance between two coarranged types will accurately reflect their degree of similar arrangement if the types are coarranged in any of the forms of organization in Models 1 through 4. In these circumstances, the coefficient assumes less constraining or equivalent characteristics of coarrangement than those expressed in the relationships among the types. This does not mean, however, that the coefficient will accurately measure the degree of segregation of types falling in different depositional sets that are organized like the more constrained Models 1, 2, and 3, or that it will lead to an accurate determination of such sets in higher-level, multitype analysis.

3) The AVDISTLP1 distance between two coarranged types organized in the form of Models 5 or 6 will be excessively high. In this case, the coefficient assumes the occurrence of both types in each stratum where one type occurs, whereas the coarranged types exhibit a less constrained organization, where some strata may have only one of the types. As a consequence, depositional sets organized as in Models 5 or 6 will not be defined as strongly by AVDISTLP1 as they might be by more congruent coefficients.

4) The degree of inflation of the AVDISTLP1 distance between types that are coarranged as in Models 5 or 6 may be either greater or less than the degree of inflation of the AVDISTGM distance between them, and thus, the AVDISTLP1 distance may be either greater or less than the AVDISTGM distance. This circumstance is not what one might initially expect from the relative degrees of discordance of the coefficients from the data.

Whether the AVDISTLP1 or AVDISTGM distance is more inflated and larger depends on the particular balance that occurs among several features of the data. The AVDISTLP1 distance will be more inflated and larger when (a) the number of strata having only one of the artifact types is high compared to the number of strata having both, (b) the number of items of the single type in the strata with only one type is high compared to the number of items in the

Table 13.19

Matrix of AVDISTGM Statistics Defined for Habitation No.1

	Core	Burin	Burinsp	Bec	Pierce	Microp	Notch	Scrapa	Scrapbc	Backbl	Utblade
Core	0.000	0.464	0.473	0.487	1.111	1.029	0.834	1.113	0.798	0.394	0.583
Burin	0.464	0.000	0.333	0.347	1.340	0.792	0.606	1.278	0.632	0.412	0.299
Burinsp	0.473	0.333	0.000	0.300	1.106	0.767	0.486	1.211	0.656	0.314	0.441
Bec	0.487	0.347	0.300	0.000	1.116	0.780	0.551	1.074	0.594	0.403	0.485
Pierce	1.111	1.340	1.106	1.116	0.000	1.548	1.439	1.873	1.656	0.922	1.439
Microp	1.029	0.792	0.767	0.780	1.548	0.000	0.784	1.043	0.706	0.759	0.755
Notch	0.834	0.606	0.486	0.551	1.439	0.784	0.000	1.361	0.561	0.513	0.693
Scrapa	1.113	1.278	1.211	1.074	1.873	1.043	1.361	0.000	1.416	1.018	1.176
Scrapbc	0.798	0.632	0.656	0.594	1.656	0.706	0.561	1.416	0.000	0.567	0.671
Backbl	0.394	0.412	0.314	0.403	0.922	0.759	0.513	1.018	0.567	0.000	0.437
Utblade	0.583	0.299	0.441	0.485	1.439	0.755	0.693	1.176	0.671	0.437	0.000
Bead	1.544	1.870	1.517	1.724	1.177	2.472	1.915	2.845	2.274	1.190	2.177
Ivory	1.701	1.479	1.219	1.339	1.648	1.642	1.242	1.877	2.207	1.444	1.897
Antler	1.280	1.176	1.262	1.341	1.409	1.791	1.260	2.238	1.449	1.420	1.289
Phal	0.542	0.298	0.448	0.493	1.877	0.946	0.815	1.334	0.728	0.531	0.402
Meta	0.700	0.489	0.648	0.648	2.355	1.173	1.058	1.682	0.925	0.793	0.575
Hfr	0.632	0.468	0.718	0.717	1.816	1.184	1.063	1.410	0.979	0.734	0.556
Tibio	0.565	0.602	0.695	0.806	1.765	1.102	0.972	1.564	0.880	0.624	0.647
Scap	1.101	1.305	1.387	1.471	1.780	1.802	1.750	1.718	1.455	1.211	1.350
Rib	0.631	0.439	0.631	0.606	1.901	0.814	0.939	1.121	0.828	0.737	0.441
Vert	1.762	1.789	1.607	1.744	1.757	2.673	1.758	3.255	2.641	1.671	2.325
Mandib	0.916	0.955	0.860	0.931	1.671	1.552	1.245	1.640	1.647	0.958	1.179
Maxill	0.665	0.669	0.802	0.665	1.373	1.325	0.886	1.698	1.266	0.745	0.826

	Bead	Ivory	Antler	Phal	Meta	Hfr	Tibio	Scap	Rib	Vert	Mandib	Maxill
Core	1.544	1.701	1.280	0.542	0.700	0.632	0.565	1.101	0.631	1.762	0.916	0.665
Burin	1.870	1.479	1.176	0.298	0.489	0.468	0.602	1.305	0.439	1.789	0.955	0.669
Burinsp	1.517	1.219	1.262	0.448	0.648	0.718	0.695	1.387	0.631	1.607	0.860	0.802
Bec	1.724	1.339	1.341	0.493	0.648	0.717	0.806	1.471	0.606	1.744	0.931	0.665
Pierce	1.177	1.648	1.409	1.877	2.355	1.816	1.765	1.780	1.901	1.757	1.671	1.373
Microp	2.472	1.642	1.791	0.946	1.173	1.184	1.102	1.802	0.814	2.673	1.552	1.325
Notch	1.915	1.242	1.260	0.815	1.058	1.063	0.972	1.750	0.939	1.758	1.245	0.886
Scrapa	2.845	1.877	2.238	1.334	1.682	1.410	1.564	1.718	1.121	3.255	1.640	1.698
Scrapbc	2.274	2.207	1.449	0.728	0.925	0.979	0.880	1.455	0.828	2.641	1.647	1.266
Backbl	1.190	1.444	1.420	0.531	0.793	0.734	0.624	1.211	0.737	1.671	0.958	0.745
Utblade	2.177	1.897	1.289	0.402	0.575	0.556	0.647	1.350	0.441	2.325	1.179	0.826
Bead	0.000	1.735	1.813	2.608	3.164	2.647	2.468	2.581	2.797	1.066	2.190	1.805
Ivory	1.735	0.000	2.242	1.906	2.476	2.328	2.503	3.044	2.416	1.694	1.927	1.531
Antler	1.813	2.242	0.000	1.240	1.318	1.234	1.186	0.856	1.335	1.532	1.368	1.035
Phal	2.608	1.906	1.240	0.000	0.355	0.368	0.664	1.220	0.377	2.393	0.968	0.716
Meta	3.164	2.476	1.318	0.355	0.000	0.399	0.645	1.255	0.437	2.855	0.922	0.762
Hfr	2.647	2.328	1.234	0.368	0.399	0.000	0.546	1.394	0.397	2.594	0.964	0.938
Tibio	2.468	2.503	1.186	0.664	0.645	0.546	0.000	1.276	0.593	2.634	1.316	1.134
Scap	2.581	3.044	0.856	1.220	1.255	1.394	1.276	0.000	1.187	2.447	1.590	1.370
Rib	2.797	2.416	1.335	0.377	0.437	0.397	0.593	1.187	0.000	2.952	1.286	1.074
Vert	1.066	1.694	1.532	2.393	2.855	2.594	2.634	2.447	2.952	0.000	1.932	1.525
Mandib	2.190	1.927	1.368	0.968	0.922	0.964	1.316	1.590	1.286	1.932	0.000	1.012
Maxill	1.805	1.531	1.035	0.716	0.762	0.938	1.134	1.370	1.074	1.525	1.012	0.000

Table 13.20
Matrix of AVDISTGP Statistics Defined for Habitation No. 1

	Core	Burin	Burinsp	Bec	Pierce	Microp	Notch	Scrapa	Scrapbc	Backbl	Utblade
Core	0.000	0.355	0.400	0.444	0.608	0.878	0.596	0.647	0.763	0.275	0.485
Burin	0.355	0.000	0.203	0.232	0.390	0.269	0.230	0.407	0.351	0.173	0.297
Burinsp	0.400	0.203	0.000	0.296	0.595	0.733	0.401	0.891	0.623	0.230	0.289
Bec	0.444	0.232	0.296	0.000	0.420	0.601	0.338	0.993	0.471	0.344	0.358
Pierce	0.608	0.390	0.595	0.420	0.000	1.000	1.212	1.518	1.194	0.861	0.548
Microp	0.878	0.269	0.733	0.601	1.000	0.000	0.693	0.985	0.700	0.701	0.302
Notch	0.596	0.230	0.401	0.338	1.212	0.693	0.000	1.327	0.550	0.505	0.240
Scrapa	0.647	0.407	0.891	0.993	1.518	0.985	1.327	0.000	1.293	0.871	0.445
Scrapbc	0.763	0.351	0.623	0.471	1.194	0.700	0.550	1.293	0.000	0.473	0.315
Backbl	0.275	0.173	0.230	0.344	0.861	0.701	0.505	0.871	0.473	0.000	0.235
Utblade	0.485	0.297	0.289	0.358	0.548	0.302	0.240	0.445	0.315	0.235	0.000
Bead	0.460	0.309	0.516	0.596	0.705	1.503	0.507	1.969	1.267	1.007	0.655
Ivory	0.902	0.329	0.531	0.383	1.302	0.785	0.607	1.223	1.148	0.808	0.441
Antler	0.881	0.606	1.236	1.284	1.062	1.552	1.093	1.881	1.145	1.394	1.122
Phal	0.377	0.281	0.233	0.281	0.603	0.508	0.258	0.423	0.408	0.251	0.340
Meta	0.384	0.441	0.397	0.393	0.674	0.618	0.394	0.452	0.457	0.416	0.501
Hfr	0.342	0.395	0.410	0.362	0.537	0.452	0.352	0.342	0.538	0.338	0.482
Tibio	0.466	0.592	0.482	0.665	0.806	0.760	0.546	1.178	0.489	0.443	0.619
Scap	0.791	0.628	1.345	1.415	1.292	1.549	1.617	1.623	1.247	1.131	1.254
Rib	0.393	0.420	0.348	0.314	0.729	0.278	0.320	0.255	0.348	0.369	0.356
Vert	1.076	0.855	1.561	1.625	1.621	2.473	1.617	3.098	2.619	1.629	1.607
Mandib	0.895	0.690	0.825	0.909	1.049	1.535	1.163	1.275	1.585	0.903	1.012
Maxill	0.542	0.349	0.781	0.662	1.058	1.175	0.728	1.170	1.245	0.693	0.632

	Bead	Ivory	Antler	Phal	Meta	Hfr	Tibio	Scap	Rib	Vert	Mandib	Maxill
Core	0.460	0.902	0.881	0.377	0.384	0.342	0.466	0.791	0.393	1.076	0.895	0.542
Burin	0.309	0.329	0.606	0.281	0.441	0.395	0.592	0.628	0.420	0.855	0.690	0.349
Burinsp	0.516	0.531	1.236	0.233	0.397	0.410	0.482	1.345	0.348	1.561	0.825	0.781
Bec	0.596	0.383	1.284	0.281	0.393	0.362	0.665	1.415	0.314	1.625	0.909	0.662
Pierce	0.705	1.302	1.062	0.603	0.674	0.537	0.806	1.292	0.729	1.621	1.049	1.058
Microp	1.503	0.785	1.552	0.508	0.618	0.452	0.760	1.549	0.278	2.473	1.535	1.175
Notch	0.507	0.607	1.093	0.258	0.394	0.352	0.546	1.617	0.320	1.617	1.163	0.728
Scrapa	1.969	1.223	1.881	0.423	0.452	0.342	1.178	1.623	0.255	3.098	1.275	1.170
Scrapbc	1.267	1.148	1.145	0.408	0.457	0.538	0.489	1.247	0.348	2.619	1.585	1.245
Backbl	1.007	0.808	1.394	0.251	0.416	0.338	0.443	1.131	0.369	1.629	0.903	0.693
Ublade	0.655	0.441	1.122	0.340	0.501	0.482	0.619	1.254	0.356	1.607	1.012	0.632
Bead	0.000	1.333	0.943	0.610	0.537	0.533	0.706	1.175	0.645	0.805	0.720	0.484
Ivory	1.333	0.000	1.497	0.517	0.648	0.524	0.811	2.106	0.420	1.373	0.990	0.496
Antler	0.943	1.497	0.000	0.722	0.775	0.625	0.999	0.752	1.125	0.747	1.353	1.031
Phal	0.610	0.517	0.722	0.000	0.342	0.334	0.616	0.509	0.365	0.954	0.426	0.540
Meta	0.537	0.648	0.775	0.342	0.000	0.366	0.617	0.876	0.420	0.589	0.477	0.434
Hfr	0.533	0.524	0.625	0.334	0.366	0.000	0.423	0.785	0.380	1.107	0.283	0.512
Tibio	0.706	0.811	0.999	0.616	0.617	0.423	0.000	0.798	0.398	1.677	0.817	0.722
Scap	1.175	2.106	0.752	0.509	0.876	0.785	0.798	0.000	0.714	0.839	1.517	1.174
Rib	0.645	0.420	1.125	0.365	0.420	0.380	0.398	0.714	0.000	1.731	0.791	0.649
Vert	0.805	1.373	0.747	0.954	0.589	1.107	1.677	0.839	1.731	0.000	1.179	0.602
Mandib	0.720	0.990	1.353	0.426	0.477	0.283	0.817	1.517	0.791	1.179	0.000	0.940
Maxill	0.484	0.496	1.031	0.540	0.434	0.512	0.722	1.174	0.649	0.602	0.940	0.000

Table 13.21

Partial Matrices of Distance Coefficients Relating Ubiquitous Types to Central Types

	AVDISTLP1 Coefficients			AVDISTGM Coefficients			AVDISTGP Coefficients	
	Flint	Ssls		Flint	Ssls		Flint	Ssls
Core	0.759	0.572	Core	0.735	0.509	Core	0.388	0.137
Burin	0.481	0.381	Burin	0.565	0.363	Burin	0.355	0.154
Burinsp	1.204	1.158	Burinsp	1.087	0.664	Burinsp	0.354	0.173
Bec	1.235	1.222	Bec	1.046	0.644	Bec	0.433	0.153
Notch	1.675	1.905	Notch	1.341	1.034	Notch	0.369	0.201
Backbl	1.236	1.080	Backbl	1.078	0.649	Backbl	0.379	0.137
Utblade	0.858	0.771	Utblade	0.743	0.456	Utblade	0.343	0.180
Phal	0.622	0.430	Phal	0.577	0.383	Phal	0.345	0.192
Meta	0.436	0.413	Meta	0.585	0.447	Meta	0.370	0.258
Hfr	0.518	0.434	Hfr	0.504	0.436	Hfr	0.356	0.261
Flint	0.000	0.255	Flint	0.000	0.326	Flint	0.000	0.271
Ssls	0.255	0.000	Ssls	0.326	0.000	Ssls	0.271	0.000

strata with both types, (c) the distances between strata having only one type and their nearest strata with both types is great, and (d) asymmetry between types within strata with both types is great. Figure 15 illustrates the effects of changes in two of these factors (b and c).

5) The AVDISTGP distance between two types that are coarranged as in Models 1, 2, 3, or 5 will accurately measure their degree of coarrangement. In these cases, the coefficient assumes less constraining or equivalent characteristics of coarrangement than those expressed in the organization of the types. Again, this does not mean, however, that the coefficient will accurately measure the degree of segregation of types falling in different depositional sets that are organized like the more constrained Models 1, 2, or 3, or that it will lead to an accurate determination of such sets in higher-level multitype analysis.

6) The AVDISTGP distance between two types coarranged as in Models 4 or 6 will be excessively high, given the more constraining characteristics of coarrangement assumed by this measure compared to those within the data. In particular, the coefficient overstringently requires that the direction of asymmetry between two types remain uniform over all strata. Depositional sets organized as in Models 4 or 6 will correspondingly be less strongly defined by AVDISTGP than they might be by more congruent coefficients. The AVDISTGP distance will not be as inflated as the AVDISTGM distance, which is more restrictive in its requirements for coarrangement.

7) When two types are coarranged as in Model 6, the AVDISTGP distance

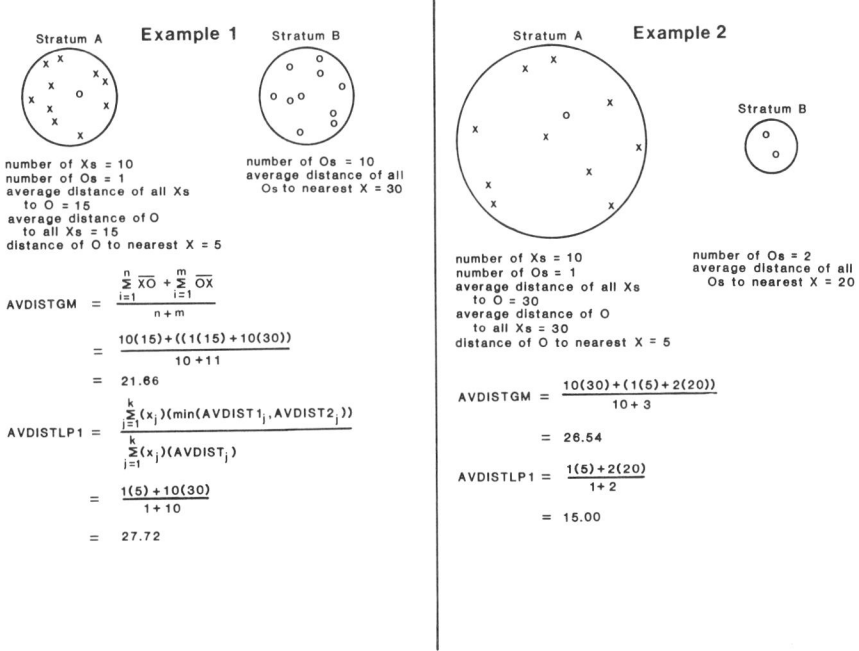

Fig. 13.15. AVDISTGM can be larger or smaller than AVDISTLP1 when both are discordantly applied to a Model 5 or 6 form of coarrangement of types. The magnitudes of the coefficients are not related to the degrees to which they are discordant from the data. Here, data examples 1 and 2 both illustrate two types that are coarranged in a Model 5 form. The coarrangements differ, however, in 1) the number of items of the type that sometimes occurs alone in clusters, for those clusters where it is alone, compared to the number of items of both types in strata having both types, and 2) the distances between strata having only one type and their nearest strata with both types. These factors affect the relative magnitudes of the two coefficients.

between them may be more inflated or less inflated than the AVDISTLP1 distance between them, and thus, the AVDISTGP coefficient may be larger or smaller than the AVDISTLP1 coefficient. Whether the AVDISTLP1 or AVDISTGP coefficient is more inflated and larger depends on the particular balance between several features of the data. A larger and more inflated AVDISTLP1 coefficient that AVDISTGP coefficient will be favored when conditions a-c (mentioned previously) occur, and when (d) among clusters, reversals in the direction of asymmetry between types are minimal.

8) The AVDISTLP2 distance between two types that are coarranged as in Models 1 through 6 will accurately reflect their degree of similar arrangement. However, the coefficient will not necessarily measure accurately the degree of

segregation of types falling in different depositional sets organized as in Models 1 through 5, nor will it necessarily lead to an accurate determination of such sets in higher-level, multi-type analysis.

Illustrating the effects of inappropriate application of the AVDIST coefficients. The effects of incongruency between a coefficient's assumptions and the form of a coarrangement can be illustrated with the Pincevent data. A number of artifact type-pairs having different patterns of asymmetry were chosen as *heuristic* examples of coarranged types organized as in Models 3 through 6, regardless of whether they were judged coarranged in the previous analysis (Tables 22, 23). All the pairs exhibit asymmetry of variable magnitude among strata, and vary in whether asymmetry changes in direction from stratum to stratum and

Table 13.22

Number of Items of Each Artifact Type within the Spatial Strata at Habitation No. 1

Artifact Type	Stratum Number												
	8	9	10	11	5	6	16	12	13	14	H3	H2	H1	Total
Core	2	1	0	0	4	0	0	2	1	0	24	9	5	48
Burin	7	1	0	0	1	12	1	1	0	7	31	43	16	120
Burinsp	0	0	0	0	0	9	0	0	0	1	28	21	9	68
Bec	2	0	0	0	0	4	0	0	0	1	14	19	5	45
Pierce	1	0	0	0	0	1	0	0	0	0	2	1	0	5
Microp	2	0	0	0	0	1	2	0	0	1	2	2	1	11
Notch	1	0	0	0	1	2	0	0	0	0	2	11	2	19
Scrapa	0	0	0	0	0	0	1	2	0	0	1	1	2	7
Scrapbc	5	0	0	0	0	0	0	0	0	1	5	6	1	18
Backbl	2	0	0	0	0	0	0	0	0	0	39	15	4	60
Utblade	6	0	0	0	0	8	1	1	0	2	26	20	9	73
Bead	0	0	0	0	1	0	0	0	0	0	1	0	0	2
Ivory	0	0	0	0	0	2	0	0	0	0	0	3	0	5
Antler	0	3	1	0	1	1	0	1	0	0	2	2	0	11
Phal	2	0	2	0	0	4	0	4	0	5	33	48	42	140
Meta	2	0	0	2	2	0	0	6	3	13	11	17	33	89
Hfr	6	0	1	0	4	3	1	20	0	8	13	23	14	93
Tibio	7	0	0	0	1	2	0	5	1	1	7	4	4	32
Scap	0	1	0	0	1	0	0	2	1	0	3	0	1	9
Rib	6	0	0	0	2	10	2	10	1	5	44	12	37	129
Vert	0	3	0	0	2	0	0	0	0	0	0	0	0	5
Maxill	0	0	1	0	1	1	0	1	0	2	2	0	1	9
Mandib	0	4	0	0	1	1	0	0	0	1	3	6	3	19

whether some strata have only one of the types, in accordance with the models. Minor exceptions of the arrangements of the pairs from the models of coarrangement they are taken to represent are shown in Table 23.

The values of AVDISTGM, AVDISTLP1, and AVDISTGP coefficients for the several pairs of types and the models they represent are shown in Table 24. The ordered relations among values of the different coefficients, for each pair representing each model of organization, all concord with the expectations discussed.

Some features in Table 24 that stress those behaviors of the coefficients that might not be expected initially from their design include the following. 1) The values of AVDISTLP1 and AVDISTGP for the pair representing Model 3 are exactly equivalent. Both coefficients accurately measure the degree of coarrangement of the types—despite the *different* assumptions they make about the organization of a coarrangement—because both make assumptions that are *less* restrictive than the data are constrained. This is not to say, however, that both coefficients would measure as equivalent the degree of segregation of types occurring in different depositional sets, or that such sets would be determined equally accurately using the two coefficients in a multi-type analysis.

2) The values of AVDISTLP1 (a more assuming coefficient) are sometimes larger, sometimes smaller than the values of AVDISTGM (a less assuming coefficient) for pairs representing Model 5, in accord with expectation 4, above. This illustrates that coefficients that are more constraining, in making greater numbers of restrictive assumptions about depositional set organization, do not necessarily give more inflated, inaccurate results than less constraining coefficients making fewer restrictive assumptions, when both are applied to data of an even less constrained form.

3) The values of AVDISTLP1 are all larger and more inflated than the values of AVDISTGM for the pairs representing Model 6 (though the reverse ordering also could have occurred). Again, this illustrates that the values taken by a coefficient and its accuracy are not necessarily a function of the number of constraining assumptions it makes, when applied to less constrained data.

The last two observations are very important in relation to the argument, which was made in the beginning of this chapter, about appropriate criteria for assessing the appropriateness of a technique for analyzing data. *An analytic technique can not be judged as appropriate or inappropriate, either generally or in relation to a specific data set, on the basis of the number of constraining assumptions about relevant data structure that it makes. The particular nature of the assumptions, and their degrees of congruence with the relevant form of organization of the data at hand, is what matters.*

Effects of Including Ubiquitous Types in Multidimensional Scalings Using Different AVDIST Coefficients

The effect of introducing ubiquitously, densely distributed artifact types into a multidimensional scaling of more spatially restricted types will vary with the distance coefficients that are used. AVDISTGM and AVDISTLP1 coefficients, which require both artifact types of a coarranged pair to always occur in strata where either one occurs, will tend to assess the ubiquitously distributed types as distantly related to the more spatially restricted types. When introduced in a scaling operation, the large coefficient values that relate the ubiquitous and spatially restricted types will produce a space-dilating effect in it. On the other hand, AVDISTGP and AVDISTLP2 coefficients, which allow artifact types to closely associate when they do not necessarily co-occur in every stratum where one of the types occurs, will tend to assess the ubiquitously distributed types as closely related to the spatially restricted types. When introduced in a scaling analysis, the small coefficient values that relate the ubiquitously and spatially restricted types will produce a space-contracting effect. The average, *global*, space-dilating effect or the average *global* space-contracting effect in any particular analysis will be scaled out of the final MDS configuration, but *local* variations in the degree of dilation or contraction from the global average will not.

The different space-dilating or space-contracting effects of adding ubiquitous types to a MDS analysis when using different AVDIST coefficients is suggested in Table 25. For each of the distance coefficients—AVDISTGM, AVDISTLP1, and AVDISTGP—the average of its values which relate each of the ten, spatially restricted, central artifact types to each other are shown. Contrasted with these values are averages of the distances of the ubiquitous types, flint and sandstone-limestone, to the central types, for the same coefficients. The average of the distances from the ubiquitous to the central types are higher than the average of the distances between only the central types for the AVDISTGM and AVDISTLP1 coefficients. Adding the former coefficient values to the latter when multidimensional scaling the data would produce a global, space-dilating effect with local ramifications. In contrast, for the AVDISTGP coefficient, the average of the distances from the ubiquitous to the central types is lower than the average of the distances between only the central types. Combining the former coefficients with the latter when scaling the data would produce a space-contracting effect, with local manifestations.

Multidimensional scalings of the 10 central types, and the 10 types augmented with the ubiquitous types, were made for each AVDIST coefficient. The relationships among types in optimal dimensional configurations (2 or 3-dimensions) for the original and augmented solutions were compared to each other for each of the three coefficients, in search of local ramifications of space dilation or contraction. Most relationships among the central types remained stable or changed only slightly with the addition of the ubiquitous types. However, for each of the three comparisons, repositioning of a few types proceeded to the point where the *composition* of sets was altered slightly.

For configurations having more than an optimal number of dimensions, introducing the ubiquitous types caused major repositionings of many central types. Most potential sets of central types within the original MDS solutions could not be recognized in the augmented solutions. This instability of the higher dimensional solutions is expectable. When data are configured in a space larger than that necessary to express their dimensions of variability, the configuration will express error in the data (Kruskal & Wish, 1978, p. 57), i.e., contradictions among the dissimilarities between entities. The AVDIST coefficients that describe the relationships of ubiquitous types to central, spatially restricted types imply relationships among the central types that are contradictory to (dilated or contracted compared to) those described by the coefficients that relate the central types to each other. In lower dimensions, these contradictions are smoothed considerably from the configuration, whereas in overly generous dimensions, they are not.

The practical conclusions to be drawn from this experiment are clear regarding the procedure of introducing artifact types with ubiquitous, clustered distributions into a MDS analysis in order to determine the relationships of their clustered components to other types. 1) It is not advisable to introduce more than one ubiquitous, clustered type at a time into a MDS analysis, particularly when the number of spatially restricted types in the original solution is small. 2) Determining the optimal number of dimensions for displaying a group of spatially-restricted types is crucial, particularly when one's purpose is then to introduce a ubiquitous type (and thus, coefficient contradiction) into the solution.

THE IMPORTANCE OF ACKNOWLEDGING ARTIFACT TYPE ASYMMETRIES AND POLYTHETIC ORGANIZATION IN SPATIAL ANALYSIS: ILLUSTRATION WITH THE PINCEVENT DATA

A key concept used in this chapter is asymmetry among artifact types within sets. By varying the direction, magnitude, and completeness of asymmetry relations allowed among artifact types within depositional sets over areas of different scales, it was possible to define the six models of depositional set organization along the monothetic-polythetic dimension (Table 2).

It is desirable to illustrate the extent to which spatial variation in the direction, magnitude, and completeness of asymmetry relations among types within sets can dominate the structure of an intrasite spatial data set. This will suggest the importance of acknowledging such variation when choosing techniques for analyzing intrasite data. Whallon's (1984) analysis of the Mask site, in which he documents vivid changes in the patterns of covariation among artifact types from areal stratum to stratum (Whallon, 1984, p. 257) possibly gives some indication of the extent to which changes in the magnitude and direction of asymmetry can occur among artifact types within sets from area to area of a site. However, most, if not all, of the artifact types included in that study appear to belong to *different* activity sets rather than the same (see p. 314). Consequently, the pattern of spatially variable correlations (and by implication, asymmetry relations) that were found among types appears pertinent to the

Table 13.23

Degree of Correspondence between the Characteristics of Arrangement of Pairs of Artifact Types and Characteristics of the Models of Coarrangement They are Taken to Represent

Model and Type Pair	Model Characteristics and Strata Corresponding to Them				Deviations from the Model
Model 3:	Both types must occur in each cluster	Asymmetry may be of different magnitudes in different clusters		Asymmetry must be in the same direction in each cluster	
bec-microp	strata 8,6,14,1,2,3	strata 6,1,2,3		strata 8,6,14,1,2,3	microp occurs alone in stratum 16
Model 4:	Both types must occur in each cluster	Asymmetry may be of different magnitudes in different clusters		Asymmetry may be of different directions in different clusters	
hfr-phal	strata 8,10,6,12,14,1,2,3	no strata with same magnitudes of asymmetry		strata 8,5,16,12,14 vs. 10,6,1,2,3,	hfr occurs alone in strata 5 (4 items) and 16 (1 item)
hfr-rib	strata 8,5,6,16,12,14,1,2,3	only strata 10 and 13 have the same magnitude of asymmetry		strata 10,5,12,14,2 vs. 6,16,13,1,3	hfr occurs alone in stratum 10 (1 item), rib occurs alone in stratum 13 (1 item)
Model 5:	Types may occur alone in some clusters	Asymmetry may be of different magnitudes in different clusters		Asymmetry must be in the same direction in each cluster	
burin-notch	burin alone in strata 9,16,12,14	only strata 9,12,16 have the same magnitude of asymmetry		strata 8,9,6,16,12,14,1,2,3	none

burin-bec	burin alone in strata 9,5,16,12	only strata 9,5,16,12 have the same magnitude of asymmetry	strata 8,9,5,6,16, 12,14,1,2,3	none
bead-maxill	maxill alone in strata 10,6,12,14,1	only strata 10,6,12,13 have the same magnitude of asymmetry	strata 10,6,12,14, 1,3	none
bead-mandib	mandib alone in strata 9,6,14,2,1	only strata 6 and 14 have the same magnitude of asymmetry	strata 9,6,14,1,2, 3	none
Model 6:	*Types may occur alone in some clusters*	*Asymmetry may be of different magnitudes in different clusters*	*Asymmetry may be in different directions in different clusters*	
burinsp-backbl	backbl alone in stratum 8, burinsp alone in strata 6,14	no strata with same magnitude of asymmetry	strata 6,14,2,1 vs. 8,3	none
scapula-antler	scapula alone in stratum 13, antler alone in strata 10,6	only strata 10,6,13 have the same magnitude of asymmetry	strata 12,13,1,3 vs. 9,10,6,2	none
scrapa-scrapbc	scrapbc alone in strata 8,14, scrapa alone in strata 16,12	only strata 16 and 14 have the same magnitude of asymmetry	strata 8,14,3,2 vs. 16,12,3	none
scrapa-microp	microp alone in strata 8,6,14, scrapa alone in stratum 12	only strata 8 and 12, and 6 and 14, have the same magnitude of asymmetry	strata 8,6,16,14,3,2 vs. 12,1	none

Table 13.24

Examples of Artifact Pairs Fitting Certain Models of Artifact Coarrangement and the Average Distance between Them Using Different Algorithms

Model and Type Pair	Algorithm		
	AVDISTGM	AVDISTLP1	AVDISTGP
Model 3			
bec-microp	.78	.601	.601
Model 4			
hfr-phal	.368	.264	.334
hfr-rib	.397	.319	.380
Model 5			
burin-notch	.606	.685	.230
burin-bec	.347	.341	.232
bead-maxill	1.190	2.722	.720
bead-mandib	1.805	2.056	.484
Model 6			
burinsp-backbl	.314	.327	.230
scap-antler	.856	.874	.752
scrapa-scrapbc	1.416	1.466	1.293
scrapa-microp	1.043	1.145	.985

external relationships (i.e., spatial overlap) among depositional sets more than to their internal organization. Moreover, covariation among types provides only an indirect measure of the magnitude and direction of asymmetry relations among types.

To more directly illustrate the internal organization of depositional sets in regard to asymmetry relations, the Pincevent data were examined for variation, among the defined spatial strata (Fig. 10), in the asymmetry occurring between those type-pairs which fall within the same depositional sets, as previously defined (Table 17). Analysis was focused on spatial variation in the *direction* of asymmetry among types and the magnitude of such asymmetry reversals, alone. The particular questions for which answers were sought are:

Table 13.25

Averages of AVDIST Coefficients Relating Central and Ubiquitous Artifact Types, Showing Space Dilating and Contracting Effects*

	AVDISTGM	AVDISTLP1	AVDISTGP
Average of distance coefficients relating central types.	.540 ± .183 (N = 45)	.592 ± .293 (N = 45)	.347 ± .091 (N = 45)
Average of distance coefficients relating ubiquitous types to central types.	.692 ± .278 (N = 20)	.870 ± .448 (N = 20)	.277 ± .101 (N = 20)

*Central types include: core, burin, burinsp, bec, notch, backbl, utblade, phal, meta, hfr. Peripheral types include: flint, ssls.

1) What is the *average magnitude of asymmetry reversals* between artifact types within the same depositional set?
2) How *common* are stratum-to-stratum reversals in the direction of asymmetry among types within the same depositional set?
3) Does spatial variation in the direction of asymmetry among types result from spatial variation in *formation processes*?

It is necessary to operationalize several terms to answer these questions. An *asymmetry reversal* can be said to occur between two types, for a given area composed of several strata, when some strata exhibit a predominance of one type and other strata exhibit a predominance of the other type. The *magnitudes* of asymmetry reversals within an area can be measured in the following way. First, the numbers of strata having a predominance of one type vs. the other are summed. The *"normal" direction* of asymmetry within the area is then defined as that direction which occurs between the type that predominates in most strata and the type that is found less frequently in those strata. For each stratum S not having this direction of asymmetry, the magnitude of its asymmetry reversal A_s between the two types i and j can be defined conservatively as:

$$A_s = \frac{|N_{is} - N_{js}|}{N_{is} + N_{js}} \times 100\% \qquad (10)$$

where N_i and N_j are the numbers of items of the two types in the stratum. The difference in counts of the two types has been adjusted by their total numbers within the stratum in order to make the measure comparable between strata or study areas having different densities of the two types, and between artifact type pairs having different densities. Note, also, that within any given study area, multiple measures of the magnitude of asymmetry reversal within it may be defined, one for each stratum exhibiting a reversal.

The *commonness* of asymmetry reversals within a study area can be measured in several ways: by the percentage of depositional sets within the area that have type-pairs showing asymmetry reversals; by the percentage of all pairwise combinations of types that fall within the same depositional sets and that exhibit asymmetry reversals; or by the percentage of types within the area that exhibit asymmetry reversals with other types in their depositional set.

These percentages, however, must be calculated in reference to total numbers of sets, combinations, or types that have the *potential* to express asymmetry reversals. In this study, a pairwise combination of types within a depositional set was not considered to have the potential for expressing asymmetry reversals over strata if both types did not occur together in at least two strata. In other words, the conservative position was taken that asymmetries taken to the extreme circumstance where one type or the other of a pair is missing from all but one stratum (where both occur) should not be considered in the analysis, less these indicate dissociation of the types rather than misjudged asymmetry in coarrangement. Thus, of the 41 pairwise combinations of different types within the depositional sets defined in Table 17, only 36 have the potential for asymmetry reversals. The pairs, ivory-bead, ivory-vert, ivory-backbl, and bead-pierce, do not co-occur in two or more strata (Table 22). Of the 19 depositional sets, two (Sets 16, 18) do not have the potential to show asymmetry reversals because none of the pairwise combinations among their defining types do, and one (Set 15) does not because it is composed of a single type. Of the 23 types, only 19 have the potential for showing asymmetry reversals with other types. Ivory, bead, and pierce occur in sets where none of the pairwise combinations among types have the potential to exhibit asymmetry reversals, for lack of spatial co-occurrence in two or more strata, and scapula belongs to a set by itself.

Additional sets and pairwise combinations of types were excluded from analysis because they probably pertain to the fortuitous spatial overlap of deposition of different kinds of activity sets from different kinds of activities, rather than to the deposition of single activity sets. Only the latter circumstances reflect the internal organization of depositional sets; the former reflect external relationships among depositional sets. Thus, depositional sets 5, 6, and 7, and the type combinations exclusive to them, were dropped from analysis. This resulted in the characterization of 31 pairwise combinations, 14 depositional sets, and 19 types as having the potential to exhibit asymmetry reversals.

Three contrasts among sets of strata thought to represent different behavioral or depositional contexts were defined in order to study the correspondence of spatial variation in the direction of asymmetry of types and spatial variation in formation processes. These are 1) hearth strata (H1, H2, H3) vs. peripheral strata (the remainder); 2) peripheral strata northwest of the hearths (8, 9, 10, 11, 5, 6, 16) vs. peripheral strata southeast of the hearths (12, 13, 14); and 3) the hearth strata among themselves.

The first contrast among strata clearly involves differences in their behavioral use, and probably in the patterns of deposition within them. Different artifact types and depositional sets tended to have been deposited in the peripheral strata compared to the hearth strata (Tables 13, 17). Moreover, the hearth strata represent areas of the site where work space was limited yet activity was focused—circumstances encouraging the cleaning of use-areas and type-sorting processes, as evidenced by conjoined pieces studies (see p. 387). In contrast, the peripheral strata—particularly those outside the huts—were zones of less intense activity where work space was more available and cleaning of use-areas was probably less frequent, if it occurred at all. It can be expected that these probable differences in the activities and processes responsible for artifact deposition in the hearth and peripheral strata resulted in variation in the magnitude and/or direction of asymmetry of types among the strata.

Contrasting patterns of use and deposition among the peripheral strata northwest and southeast of the hearths are suggested in Table 26. The northwest strata have much higher frequencies of artifact types that are tools (e.g., burins, becs) or raw materials that are useful for making tools (e.g., antler, tibio). The southeast strata have higher frequencies of types, most of which represent bone refuse from broth making and bone grease making in the hearth strata (phal, meta, hfr). If it is considered that the northwest strata correspond to areas immediately outside a main entrance of the hut, whereas the southeast strata occur within the back of the hut or behind it, these differences in artifact type frequencies become interpretable. The deposition of tools and raw materials around the entrance of the hut suggests the fabrication or maintenance of tools and goods in the daylight hours of warmer periods, outside, where light was better—a pattern similar to that found among the !Kung Bushmen (Yellen, 1974). The debris left from these activities, and perhaps others in the area, possibly represent primary refuse. In contrast, in the rear of the hut's interior and behind it, secondary refuse deposition is indicated by the presence, there, of debris that originated in the hearth strata during broth and bone grease making activities. Presumably, this material was swept to the rear of the huts or dumped behind them while cleaning the central hearth areas—a supposition supported by the conjoined pieces studies. This translocation of refuse, of course, would have allowed various sorting processes to have occurred and would have altered the pattern of asymmetry among artifact types. Thus, again, spatial variation in the magnitude and/or direction of asymmetry among types is expectable for two different sets of strata.

Contrasting patterns of use and deposition are also likely among the three hearth strata, particularly H2 and H3 vs. H1. It would appear that hearth 1 was used more for cooking (particularly broth making and bone grease making)

Table 13.26

Proportions of Artifact Types within Peripheral Strata Southeast vs. Northwest of the Hearths

Tool Type	Counts in Northwest Strata (8,9,10,11,5,6,16)	Counts in Southeast Strata (12,13,14)	Ratio of Counts, Southeast:Northwest Strata
*Less Hearth-Oriented Types**			
pierce	2	0	0.
microp	5	1	.2
bead	1	0	0.
antler	6	1	.16
tibio	10	7	.70
scapula	2	3	**1.50
vert	5	0	0.
maxill	3	3	1.00
More Hearth-Oriented Types			
core	7	3	.42
burin	22	8	.36
burinsp	9	1	.11
bec	6	1	.16
notch	4	0	0.
backbl	2	0	0.
utblade	15	3	.20
phal	8	9	**1.12
meta	6	22	**3.70
rib	20	16	.80
hfr	15	28	**1.80
mandib	6	1	.16
scrapa	1	2	**2.00
scrapbc	5	1	.20
ivory	2	0	0.

*Defined in Table 13.
**Indicates types having anomalously higher frequencies in strata southeast of hearths.

while hearths 2 and 3 were used more to supply heat to surrounding work areas (where tools were made and maintained and goods were fabricated) and sleeping areas. This difference is suggested in several ways. 1) Hearth strata 2 and 3 exhibit much higher frequencies of cores, burins, burin spalls, becs, scrapers (type bc), backed bladelets, and unbacked blades, than hearth stratum 1, whereas hearth stratum 1 has higher frequencies of metapods (from bone grease making) than strata 2 and 3. 2) Large blocks of stone useful for sitting and surrounded by concentrations of tools, indicating work areas, occur in hearth strata 2 and 3, but not 1. 3) The basin of hearth 1 is filled primarily with carbon deposits, indicating the major source of fire in the hut, whereas the basins of hearths 2 and 3 are filled more with fire-cracked rocks, indicating indirect heating (Leroi-Gourhan & Brézillon, 1966, p. 367). 4) Surrounding the hearths are debris-free areas which are 20-30 cm in diameter and in which there possibly stood racks that supported skins for stone boiling, broth making, and bone grease making. These are more frequent around hearth 1 (5 places) than hearth 2 (3 places) or hearth 3 (2 places) (ibid, p. 367).

Although it is clear that hearths 2 and 3 differ in their function from hearth 1, the difference appears to be largely one of degree rather than kind. Cooking and fabrication debris occur around all three hearths (Table 13), as do the debris-free areas that were possibly used in stone boiling. Moreover, the difference may pertain more to the frequency of tool manufacture and fabrication activities than to cooking activities. Some classes of debris from broth and bone grease making (phal, hfr) occur in more equal frequencies among all the hearths.

These differences among the hearths in their use, even if only quantitative, suggest that different patterns of deposition may characterize the strata in which they occur. The frequency with which the work areas that surround the hearths were cleaned, in particular, may have varied among them. These differences in formation processes, again, could have produced different magnitudes and directions of asymmetry among the artifact types in the different strata.

The three contrasts—among hearth and peripheral strata, northwest and southeast peripheral strata, and among hearth strata—allow one to examine whether asymmetry reversals over space correspond with spatial variation in formation processes. To show a correspondence for a given group of contrasting strata, it is necessary to show only that all or most strata having the "normal" direction of asymmetry fall in one contrast set (e.g., northwest peripheral strata) and the remaining strata having the reversed direction fall in the other contrast set (e.g., southeast peripheral strata). As the percentage of type-pairs that exhibit asymmetry reversals and show this correspondence increases for the group of contrasting strata, our confidence in a systematic relationship between asymmetry reversals and spatial variation in formation processes increases.

Having operationalized the three questions posed above, it now is possible to determine their answers with the Pincevent data.

1) Magnitude of asymmetry reversals. The average magnitude of asymmetry reversals among artifact types in the same depositional set, over all strata within the site, is significant: 4.32% ± 4.68%. Considering only the strata within the hearth-to-hearth contrast, where formation processes are known to have varied among hearths, the average magnitude of asymmetry reversals is more substantial: 10.96% ± 7.39%. Similarly, considering only the strata within the northwest-to-southeast peripheral strata contrast, again where spatial variation in formation processes is more certain, the average is high: 8.53% ± 5.25%.

2) Commonness of asymmetry reversals. Asymmetry reversals are very common in the Pincevent data. First, considering asymmetry reversals of any magnitude, it was found that of the 14 depositional sets having the potential for asymmetry reversals, 9 (64.3%) were composed of types, at least one of which exhibited asymmetry reversals with other types in its set. Of the 31 pairwise combinations of types having the potential for asymmetry reversals and occurring within the same depositional set, 20 (64.5%) involved asymmetry reversals over the strata in which the types occurred. Of the 19 types having the potential to show asymmetry reversals with other types in their depositional set, 17 (89.47%) exhibited such reversals.[4]

Considering only asymmetry reversals greater than 4% in magnitude, it was found that of 14 depositional sets having the potential for asymmetry reversals, 6 (42.9%) were composed of types, at least one of which exhibited asymmetry reversals with other types in its set. Of the 31 pairwise combinations of types having the potential for asymmetry reversals, 11 (35.5%) involved asymmetry reversals. Of the 19 types having the potential to show asymmetry reversals with other types in their depositional set, 14 (73.6%) exhibited reversals.[5]

Thus, asymmetry reversals among types within the depositional sets of Pincevent are quite common, and of significant magnitude. This is true even without counting those extreme cases of asymmetry, where one type is missing from the stratum in which another of the same depositional set occurs.

Of course, it must also be remembered that the statistics just discussed assume a particular mathematical method for defining which types comprise depositional sets. The types that comprise sets and the statistics that were calculated would differ somewhat if a different similarity coefficient or different distance thresholds for defining sets had been used. In particular, using AVDISTLP1 allowed the definition of sets having asymmetry reversals among types. At the same time, this coefficient seems more concordant with the relevant structure of the Pincevent data than do other coefficients, which gives support to at least the overall pattern of the statistics, if not their exact values.

3) Relation of asymmetry reversals to formation processes. Correspondences between spatial variation in the direction of asymmetry among types and spatial variation in formation processes were found to differ in strength for the three contrast studies. In the contrast between northwest and southeast peripheral strata, 2 pairs of types were found to have asymmetry reversals among the strata of interest. For both, *all* strata having the normal direction of asymmetry fell in one contrast set (either the northwest or southeast strata) and *all* strata having the reverse direction of asymmetry fell in the other. In the contrast between hearth and peripheral strata, 16 pairs of types were found to have asymmetry reversals among the strata of interest. For 3 of these type-pairs, all strata having the normal direction of asymmetry and all strata having the reverse direction of asymmetry fell into opposite contrast sets (either hearth or peripheral strata). For an additional 4 type-pairs, most strata having the normal direction of asymmetry and most having the reverse direction fell into opposite contrast sets. Thus, in the hearth-to-peripheral strata contrast, a total of 7 of 16 type-pairs (43.8%) exhibited full or partial correspondence between spatial variation in their direction of asymmetry and spatial variation in formation processes. In the hearth-to-hearth contrast, 11 pairs of types were found to express asymmetry reversals among the strata of interest. Only 3 of the 11 pairs (27.3%) exhibited the expected pattern, where reversals in the direction of asymmetry should distinguish hearth 1 from hearths 2 and 3. However, 6 of the 11 pairs (54.5%) did exhibit a pattern in which reversals in the direction of asymmetry distinguished hearth 3 from hearths 2 and 1. This stronger pattern, though unexpected, is nevertheless significant. It defines a more systematic variation in the direction of asymmetry among type-pairs over space. It also suggests that the formation processes distinguishing the three hearths from each other are not well enough understood, from the perspective of either Leroi-Gourhan and Brézillon's or Binford's interpretation of site use.

Thus, although there is some evidence in the Pincevent data for systematic relationships between spatial variation in the direction of asymmetry among artifact types in the same depositional set and spatial variation in formation processes, the evidence is not uniformly strong or conclusive. I would suggest that this probably relates more to oversimplification of the expectations posed compared to the complexity of the formation processes structuring the data, than to the validity of the general premise. The relationship between asymmetry and formation process should be investigated in other sites, where greater knowledge of their processes of formation is available through data of the kind suggested by Schiffer (1983).

In sum, the Pincevent data suggest that within a site, the magnitude and direction of asymmetry among artifact types within depositional sets can vary frequently, and to a great degree, from deposit to deposit. It is apparent that these forms of spatial variation—and the monothetic-polythetic dimension of organization that can be related to them—must be considered when choosing a similarity coefficient for defining site-wide depositional sets.

CONCLUSION

Scientific progress is marked not only by the development of models and theory allowing accurate prediction, but also an increase in logical congruence between techniques of analysis and the relevant structure of the data to be investigated. The latter can be achieved only by continuously developing and testing new methods, and by constructing models of relevant data structures that are suggested by current theory and empirical fact. It is hoped that the techniques and models for intrasite spatial analysis discussed in this chapter, as well as the example given, provide food for further thought and development.

NOTES

1. See Carr, chapter 2 for a general definition of relevant data structure, relevant relational data structure, and relevant subset data structure. In this context, a relevant data structure encompasses variables and observations and forms of relationships among them that are pertinent to the researcher's interest in past behavioral phenomena (e.g., tool kits, storage sets, activities) or natural environmental phenomena (e.g., geomorphological activity).

2. The changes that occur in relationships among artifact types as a result of formation processes can be called "biases" only from the perspective of their organization in the behavioral domain and our preconceptions that artifact organization in the archaeological domain should mirror that in the behavioral, as at Pompeii (Binford, 1981a).

3. The degree of *inconsistency* allowed between pairwise relationships among types when smoothing them should not be confused with the *levels of similarity* used in defining groups of types in polythetic agglomerative clustering routines or matrix ordering procedures after "smoothing" operations have been achieved.

4. The 17 types are burin, burinsp, backbl, utblade, bec, phal, meta, hfr, rib, tibio, core, microp, scrapa, notch, mandib, maxill, and vert.

5. The 14 types are burin, burinsp, backbl, utblade, bec, phal, hfr, rib, meta, microp, scrapa, core, mandib, vert.

REFERENCES

Statements on Philosophy of Science and Analysis

Binford, L.R. (1977b). General introduction. In L.R. Binford (Ed.), *For theory building in archaeology* (pp. 1-10). New York: Academic Press, Inc.

Binford, L.R. (1981a). Behavioral archaeology and the "Pompeii premise." *Journal of Anthropological Research 37*(3), 195-208.

Binford, L.R. (1983). *In pursuit of the past*. New York: Thames and Hudson, Inc.

Binford, L.W., & Sabloff, J.A. (1982). Paradigms, systematics, and archaeology. *Journal of Anthropological Research 38*(2), 137-153.

Cowgill, G.L. (1970). Some sampling and reliability problems in archaeology. In *Archeologie et calculateurs: Problemes semiologiques et methematiques* (Colloque Internationaux du Centre National de la Recherche Scientifique) (pp. 161-175). Paris: Editions du Centre National de la Recherche Scientifique.

Haggett, P., & Chorley, R.J. (1967). Models, paradigms and the new geography. In R.J. Chorley & P. Haggett (Eds.), *Models in geography* (pp. 20-41). London: Methuen.

Hartwig, F., & Dearing, B.E. (1979). *Exploratory data analysis*. Beverly Hills, CA: Sage Publications.

Kent, S. (in press). *Method and theory for activity area research: An ethnoarchaeological approach*. New York: Columbia University Press.

Kuhn, T.S. (1970). *The structure of scientific revolutions*. Chicago: University of Chicago Press.

Schiffer, M.B. (1983). Toward the identification of formation processes. *American Antiquity 48*(4), 675-706.
Schiffer, M.B. (1985). Review: *Working at Archaeology. American Antiquity 50*(1), 191-193.
Tukey, J.W. (1977). *Exploratory data analysis.* Reading, MA: Addison-Wesley.
Tukey, J.W. (1979). Comment to "Nonparametric statistical data modeling." *Journal of the American Statistical Association 74*, 121-122.
Tukey, J.W. (1980). We need both exploratory and confirmatory. *American Statistician 34*(1), 23-25.
Tukey, J.W., & Wilk, M.B. (1970). Data analysis and statistics: Techniques and approaches. In E.R. Tufte (Ed.), *The quantitative analysis of social problems* (pp. 370-390). Reading, MA: Addison-Wesley.
Whallon, R. (1979, April). *Unconstrained clustering in the analysis of spatial distributions on occupation floors.* Paper presented at the annual meeting of the Society for American Archaeology, Vancouver.
Whallon, R. (1984). Unconstrained clustering for the analysis of spatial distributions in archaeology. In H.J. Hietala (Ed.), *Intrasite spatial analysis* (pp. 242-277). Cambridge: Cambridge University Press.

Quantitative Methods of Spatial Analysis and General Statistics

Carr, C. (1982a, April). *Dissecting intrasite artifact distributions as palimpsests.* Paper presented at the annual meeting of the Society for American Archaeology, Minneapolis.
Carr, C. (1982b). *Handbook on soil resistivity surveying: Interpretation of data from earthen archaeological sites.* Evanston, IL: Center for American Archaeology.
Carr, C. (1984). The nature of organization of intrasite archaeological records and spatial analytic approaches to their investigation. In M.B. Schiffer (Ed.), *Advances in archaeological method and theory (Vol. 7*, 103-222). New York: Academic Press, Inc.
Carr, C. (1986). Dissecting intrasite artifact palimpsests using Fourier methods. In S. Kent (Ed.), *Method and theory for activity area research: An ethnoarchaeological approach* (Chapter 5). New York: Columbia University Press.
Castleman, K.R. (1979). *Digital image processing.* Englewood Cliffs, NJ: Prentice-Hall.
Clarke, D.L. (1968). *Analytical archaeology.* London: Methuen.
Clark, P.J., & Evans, F.C. (1954). Distance to nearest neighbor as a measure of spatial relationships in populations. *Ecology 35*, 445-453.
Cole, L.C. (1949), The measurement of interspecific association. *Ecology 30*, 411-424.
Dacey, M.F. (1973). Statistical tests of spatial association in the locations of tool types. *American Antiquity 38*, 320-328.
Davis, J.C. (1973). *Statistics and data analysis in geology.* New York: John Wiley & Sons., Inc.
Ebert, J. (1983). Distributional archaeology: Nonsite discovery, recording, and spatial analytical methods for application to the surface archaeological record. Dissertation proposal, University of New Mexico, Albuquerque.
Gonzalez, R.C., & Wintz, P. (1977). *Digital image processing.* Reading, MA: Addison-Wesley.
Goodman, L.A., & Kruskall, W.H. (1963). Measures of association for cross classifications III: Approximate sampling theory. *Journal of the American Statistical Association 58*, 310-364.
Gower, J.C. (1966). Some distance properties of latent root and vector methods used in multivariate analysis. *Biometrika 53*(3,4), 325-338.
Gower, J.C. (1971). A general coefficient of similarity and some of its properties. *Biometrics 27*, 857-874.
Greig-Smith, P. (1952). The use of random and contiguous quadrats in the study of the structure of plant communities. *Annals of Botany, London, N.S., 16*, 293-316.
Greig-Smith, P. (1961). Data on pattern within plant communities. *Journal of Ecology 49*, 695-702.
Greig-Smith, P. (1964). *Quantitative plant ecology.* London: Butterworth.

Hietala, H.J., & Stevens, D.S. (1977). Spatial analysis: Multiple procedures in pattern recognition. *American Antiquity 42*(4), 539-559.

Holloway, J.L. (1958). Smoothing and filtering of time series and space fields. *Advances in Geophysics 4*, 351-389.

Hurlbert, S.H. (1969). A coefficient of interspecific association. *Ecology 50*(1), 1-9.

Jenkins, G.M., & Watts, D.G. (1968). *Spectral analysis and its applications.* San Francisco: Holden Day.

Kendall, M.G. (1955). *Rank correlation methods* (2nd ed.). London: Charles Griffin.

Kershaw, K.Q. (1960). The detection of pattern and association. *Journal of Ecology 48*, 233-242.

Kershaw, K.Q. (1961). Association and covariance analysis of plant communities. *Journal of Ecology 49*, 643-654.

Kershaw, K.Q. (1964). *Quantitative and dynamic ecology.* New York: American Elsevier.

Morisita, M. (1959). Measuring the dispersion of individuals and analysis of the distributional patterns. *Memoires of the Faculty of Science, Kyushu University, Series E (Biology) 2*, 215-235.

Morisita, M. (1962). I_δ-index, a measure of dispersion of individuals. *Research in Population Ecology, IV*, 1-7. Fukuoka, Japan: Kyushu University.

Mosteller, F., & Tukey, J.W. (1977). *Data analysis and regression: A second course in statistics.* Reading, MA: Addison-Wesley.

Nie, N.H., et al. (1975). *SPSS* (2nd ed.). New York: McGraw-Hill.

Olkin, I (1967). Correlations revisited. In J. Sterley (Ed.), *Improving experimental design and statistical analysis.* Chicago: Rand McNally.

Peebles, C.S. (1971). Moundville and the surrounding sites: Some structural considerations of mortuary practices, II. In J.A. Brown (Ed.), *Approaches to the social dimensions of mortuary practices (Memoirs, 25)* (pp. 68-91). Washington, DC: Society for American Archaeology.

Pielou, E.C. (1964). Segregation and symmetry in two-species populations as studied by nearest neighbor relationships. In K.A. Kershaw (Ed.), *Quantitative and dynamic ecology* (pp. 255-269). New York: American Elsevier.

Pielou, E.C. (1969). *An Introduction to mathematical ecology.* London: Methuen.

Pielou, E.C. (1977). *Mathematical ecology.* New York: John Wiley & Sons, Inc.

Robinson, J.E. (1970). Spatial filtering of geological data. *International Statistical Institute, Review 38*, 21-32.

Speth, J.D., & Johnson, G.A. (1976). Problems in the use of correlation for investigation of tool kits and activity areas. In C. Cleland (Ed.), *Cultural change and continuity* (pp. 35-75), New York: Academic Press, Inc.

Whallon, R. (1973). Spatial analysis of occupation floors I: Application of dimensional analysis of variance. *American Antiquity 38*, 320-328.

Whallon, R. (1974). Spatial analysis of occupation floors II: The application of nearest neighbor analysis. *American Antiquity 39*, 16-34.

Zurflueh, E.G. (1967). Applications of two dimensional linear wavelength filtering. *Geophysics 32*, 1015-1035.

Higher-Level Pattern Searching and Clustering Algorithms

Anderberg, M.R. (1973). *Cluster analysis for applications.* New York: Academic Press, Inc.

Arabie, P., Carroll, J.D., DeSarbo, W., & Wind, J. (1981). Overlapping clustering: A new method for product positioning. *Journal of Marketing Research 18*, 310-317.

Cole, A.J., & Wishart, D. (1970). An improved algorithm for the Jardine-Sibson method of generating overlapping clusters. *Computer Journal 13*(2), 156-163.

Cowgill, G.L. (1972). Models, methods, and techniques for seriation. In D.L. Clarke (Ed.), *Models in archaeology* (pp. 381-424). London: Methuen.

Craytor, W.B., & Johnson, L.R. Jr. (1968). Refinements in computerized item seriation. *University of Oregon Museum of Natural History, Bulletin No. 10.*
Darden, W.C., Boatwright, E., & Hampton, R. (1982). ITREC: An iterative reclassification program that refines agglomerative hierarchical clustering solutions. *Journal of Marketing Research 19*, 600-601.
Graef, J., & Spence, I. (1976). *Using prior distance information in multidimensional scaling.* Paper presented at the joint meeting of the Psychometric Society and Mathematical Psychology Group, Bell Laboratories, Murray Hill, NJ.
Guttman, L. (1965). The structure of interrelations among intelligence tests. *Proceedings of the 1964 Invitational Conference on Testing Problems* (pp. 25-36). Princeton, NJ: Educational Testing Service.
Hartigan, J.A. (1975). *Clustering algorithms.* New York: John Wiley & Sons, Inc.
Hole, F., & Shaw, M. (1967). *Computer analysis of chronological seriation* (Monograph in Archaeology No. 53[4]) Houston: Rice University.
Jardine, N., & Sibson, R. (1968). The construction of hierarchic and non-hierarchic classifications. *Computer Journal 11*(2), 177-184.
Kruskal, J.B., & Wish, M. (1978). *Multidimensional scaling.* Beverly Hills, CA: Sage Publications.
Marquardt, W.H. (1978). Advances in archaeological seriation. In M.B. Schiffer (Ed.), *Advances in Archaeological Method and Theory (Vol. 1)* (pp. 257-314). New York: Academic Press.
Romney, A.K., Shepard, R.N., & Nerlove, S.B. (Eds.). (1972). *Multidimensional scaling: Theory and applications in the behavioral sciences, (Vol. 2).* New York: Seminar Press.
Rummel, R.J. (1970). *Applied factor analysis.* Evanston, IL: Northwestern University Press.
Sarle, W.S. (1981). The ADCLUS procedure. *SAS Technical Report S-124.* Cary, NC: SAS Institute.
Schiffman, S.S., Reynolds, M.L., & Young, F.W. (1980). *Handbook of Multidimensional Scaling.* New York: Academic Press, Inc.
Shepard, R.N., Romney, A.K., & Nerlove, S.B. (Eds.). (1972). *Multidimensional scaling: Theory and applications in the behavioral sciences (Vol. 1).* New York: Seminar Press.
Shepard, R.N., & Arabie, P. (1979). Additive clustering: Representation of similarities as combinations of discrete overlapping properties. *Psychological Review 86,* 87-123.
Sneath, P.H., & Sokal, R.R. (1973). *Numerical Taxonomy.* San Francisco: W.H. Freeman.
Young, F.W., & Lewychyj, R. (1980). *ALSCAL user's guide.* Chapel Hill, NC: Institute for Research in the Social Sciences.

Formation of the Archaeological Record

Ascher, R. (1968). Times arrow and the archaeology of a contemporary community. In K.C. Chang (Ed.), *Settlement Archaeology* (pp. 47-79). Palo Alto, CA: National Press Books.
Behrensmeyer, A.K., & Hill, A.P. (Eds.), (1980). *Fossils in the making: Vertebrate taphonomy and paleoecology.* Chicago: University of Chicago Press.
Binford, L.R. (1976). Forty-seven trips. In E.S. Hall, Jr. (Ed.), *Contributions to anthropology: The interior peoples of northern Alaska.* (Mercury Series paper 49). National Museum of Man, Archaeological Survey of Canada.
Binford, L.R. (1978a). *Nunamiut ethnoarchaeology.* New York: Academic Press, Inc.
Binford, L.R. (1978b). Dimensional analysis of behavior and site structure: Learning from an Eskimo hunting stand. *American Antiquity 43*(3), 330-361.
Binford, L.R. (1980). Willow smoke and dog's tails: Hunter-gatherer settlement systems and archaeological site formation. *American Antiquity 45*(1), 4-20.
Binford, L.R. (1981b). *Bones. Ancient men and modern myths.* New York: Academic Press, Inc.
Binford, L.R. (Ed.). (1977a). *For Theory Building in Archaeology.* New York: Academic Press, Inc.
Butzer, K.W. (1982). *Archaeology as human ecology.* Cambridge: Cambridge University Press.
Gifford, D.P. (1978). Ethnoarchaeological observations of natural processes affecting cultural materials. In R.A. Gould (Ed.), *Explorations in ethnoarchaeology* (pp. 77-101). Albuquerque, NM: University of New Mexico Press.

Gifford, D.P. (1980). Ethnoarchaeological contributions to the taphonomy of human sites. In A.K. Behrensmeyer & A.P. Hill (Eds.), *Fossils in the making: Vertebrate taphonomy and paleoecology* (pp. 93-106). Chicago: University of Chicago Press.

Gifford, D.P. (1981). Taphonomy and paleoecology: A critical review of archaeology's sister disciplines. In M.B. Schiffer, (Ed.), *Advances in Archaeological Method and Theory, (Vol. 4)* (pp. 365-438). New York: Academic Press, Inc.

Gould, R.A. (1971). The archaeologist as ethnographer: A case from the western desert of Australia. *World Archaeology 3*(2), 143-178.

Gould, R.A. (1978). *Explorations in ethnoarchaeology.* Albuquerque, NM: University of New Mexico Press.

Lewarch, D.E., & O'Brien, M.J., (1981). Effects of short term tillage on aggregate provenience surface pattern. In M.J. O'Brien & D.E. Lewarch (Eds.), *Plowzone archaeology: Contributions to theory and technique (Papers in Anthropology).* Nashville, TN: Vanderbilt University.

Limbrey, S. (1975). *Soil science and archaeology.* New York: Academic Press, Inc.

McKellar, J. (1973). *Correlations and the explanation of distributions.* Unpublished manuscript on file, Arizona State Museum Library.

O'Connell, J.E. (1977). *Room to move: Contemporary Alyawara settlement patterns and their implications for Aboriginal housing policy.* Unpublished manuscript on file, Australian Institute of Aboriginal Studies, Canberra.

O'Connell, J.E. (1979, April). *Site structures and dynamics among modern Alyawara hunters.* Paper presented at the annual meeting of the Society for American Archaeology, Vancouver.

Reid, J.J. (1973). *Growth and response to stress at Grasshopper pueblo, Arizona.* Unpublished doctoral dissertation. University of Arizona, Tucson.

Rick, J.W. (1976). Downslope movement and archaeological intrasite spatial analysis. *American Antiquity 41*, 133-144.

Roper, D.C. (1976). Lateral displacement of artifacts due to plowing. *American Antiquity 41*(3), 372-375.

Rowlett, R.M., & Robbins, M.C. (1982). Estimating original assemblage content to adjust for post-depositional vertical artifact movement. *World Archaeology 14*, 73-83.

Schiffer, M.B. (1972). Archaeological context and systemic context. *American Antiquity 37*(2), 156-165.

Schiffer, M.B. (1973). *Cultural formation processes of the archaeological record: Applications at the joint site, east central Arizona.* Unpublished doctoral dissertation, University of Arizona, Tucson.

Schiffer, M.B. (1975a). Behavioral chain analysis: Activities, organization, and analysis in archaeology. *Fieldiana 65*, 103-120.

Schiffer, M.B. (1975b). Factors and "tool kits:" Evaluating multivariate analysis in archaeology. *Plains Anthropologist 20*, 61-70.

Schiffer, M.B. (1975c). The effects of occupation span on site content. In M.B. Schiffer & J.H. House (Eds.), *The Cache River archaeological project* (Research Series No. 8) (pp. 265-269). Fayetteville: Arkansas Archaeological Survey.

Schiffer, M.B. (1976). *Behavioral archaeology.* New York: Academic Press, Inc.

Schiffer, M.B. (1977). Toward a unified science of the cultural past. In S. South (Ed.), *Research strategies in historical archaeology* (pp. 13-50). New York: Academic Press, Inc.

Schiffer, M.B., & Rathje, W.L. (1973). Efficient exploitation of the archaeological record: Penetrating problems. In C.L. Redman (Ed.), *Research and theory in current archaeology* (pp. 169-179). New York: John Wiley & Sons, Inc.

Shackley, M.L. (1978). The behavior of artifacts as sedimentary particles in a fluvial environment. *Archaeometry 20*, 55-61.

Shipman, P. (1981). *Life history of a fossil: An introduction to taphonomy and paleoecology.* Cambridge, MA: Harvard University Press.

Stein, J.K. (1983). Earthworm activity: A source of potential disturbance of archaeological sediments. *American Antiquity 48*(2), 277-289.

Trubowitz, N. (1981, May). *Settlement pattern survival on plowed northeastern sites*. Paper presented at the annual meeting of the Society for American Archaeology, San Diego.

Van Noten, F., Cahen, D., & Keeley, L. (1980). A Paleolithic campsite in Belgium. *Scientific American 242*(4), 48-55.

Van Noten, F., Cahen, D., Keeley, L.H. & Moeyersons, J. (1978). *Les Chasseurs de Meer* (Dissertationes Archaeologicae, 18). Brugge: De Tempel.

Villa, P. (1982). Conjoinable pieces and site formation processes. *American Antiquity 47*, 276-290.

Wandsnider, L.A., & Binford, L.R. (1982, April). *Discerning and interpreting the structure of Lazaret cave*. Paper presented at the annual meeting of the Society for American Archaeology, Minneapolis.

Wiessner, P. (1982). Beyond willow snake and dogs tails: A comment on Binford's analysis of hunter-gatherer settlement systems. *American Antiquity 47*(1), 171-178.

Wood, W.R., & Johnson, D.L. (1978). A survey of disturbance processes in archaeological site formation. In M.B. Schiffer (Ed.), *Advances in Archaeological Method and Theory (Vol. 4)* (pp. 315-381). New York: Academic Press, Inc.

Yellen, J.C. (1974). The !Kung settlement pattern: An archaeological perspective. Unpublished doctoral dissertation, Harvard University, Cambridge.

Yellen, J.C. (1977a) *Archaeological approaches to the present*. New York: Academic Press, Inc.

Yellen, J.C. (1977b). Cultural patterning in faunal remains: Evidence from the !Kung Bushman. In D.D. Ingersoll, J. Yellen, & W. MacDonald (Eds.), *Experimental archaeology* (pp. 271-331). New York: Columbia University Press.

Documentation of Artifact Function: Ethnographic and Experimental

Barnes, A.J. (1932). Modes of prehension of some forms of Upper Paleolithic implements. Prehistoric Society of East Anglia, *Proceedings 7*, 43-56.

Battle, H.B. (1922). The domestic use of oil among southern Aborigines. *American Anthropologist 24*, 171-182.

Bordes, F. (1968). *The old stone age*. New York: McGraw-Hill.

Clark, G. (1967). *The stone age hunters*. New York: McGraw-Hill.

Cahen, D., & Keeley, L.H. (1980). Not less than two, not more than three. *World Archaeology 12*(2), 166-180.

Clark, P.J., & Thompson, M.W. (1954). The groove and splinter technique of working antler in the Upper Paleolithic and Mesolithic, with special reference to the material from Starr Carr. *Prehistoric Society, Proceedings 19*, 148-160.

Cook, T.G. (1976). *Koster: An artifact analysis of two Archaic phases in west-central Illinois* (Prehistoric Records No. 1). Evanston, IL: Northwestern University Archaeological Program.

Crabtree, D.E. (1968). Mesoamerican polyhedral cores and prismatic blades. *American Antiquity 33*, 446-478.

Crabtree, D.E., & Davis, E.L. (1968). Experimental manufacture of wooden implements with tools of flaked stone. *Science 159*(3813), 426-428.

Driver, H.E. (1961). *Indians of North America*. Chicago: University of Chicago Press.

Gould, R.A., Koster, D.A., & Sonts, A.H.L. (1971). The lithic assemblage of the western desert Aborigines of Australia. *American Antiquity 36*(2), 149-169.

Hayden, B., & Kamminga, J. (1973). Gould, Koster, and Sontz on 'Microwear': A critical review. *Newsletter of Lithic Technology 2*, 3-14.

Keeley, L.H. (1977). The functions of Paleolithique flint tools. *Scientific American 237*, 108-126.

Keeley, L.H. (1978). Preliminary microwear analysis of the Meer assemblage. In F. Van Noten et al., *Les Chasseurs de Meer* (Dissertationes Archaeologicae, 18) (pp. 73-86). Brugge: De Tempel.

Kraybill, N. (1977). Pre-agricultural tools for the preparation of foods in the Old World. In C.A. Reed (Ed.), *Origins of agriculture* (pp. 485-522). The Hague, Netherlands: Mouton.

Mason, O.T. (1889). *Aboriginal skin-dressing: A study based on material in the U.S. National Museum* (Annual Report) (pp. 553-590). Washington, DC: U.S. National Museum.

Mason, O.T. (1899). *The man's knife among the North American Indians: A study in the collections of the U.S. National Museum.* (Annual Report for the Year 1897) (pp. 727-742). Washington, DC: Smithsonian Institution.

Odell, G.H. (1977). *The application of micro-ware analysis to the lithic component of an entire prehistoric settlement: Methods, problems, and functional reconstructions.* Unpublished doctoral dissertation, Harvard University, Cambridge, MA.

Riddell, F., & Pritchard, W. (1971). Archaeology of the Rainbow Point site (4-Plu-594), Bucks Lake, Pumas County, California. In C.M. Aikens (Ed.), *Great Basin anthropological conference 1970: Selected papers* (Anthropological Papers 1) (pp. 59-102). Eugene: University of Oregon.

Semenov, S.A. (1964). *Prehistoric technology: An experimental study of the oldest tools and artifacts from traces of manufacture and wear.* London: Cory, Adams, and MacKay.

Sollberger, J.B. (1969). The basic tool kit required to make and notch arrow shafts for stone points. *Texas Archaeological Society, Bulletin 40*, 231-240.

Swanton, J.R. (1946). Indians of the southeastern United States. *Bureau of American Ethnology, Bulletin 137.*

Waugh, F.W. (1916). Iroquois foods and food preparation. In *Geological Survey, Memoir 86* (Anthropological Series 12). Canada Department of Mines.

Wheat, J.B. (1972). The Olsen-Chubbuck site: A Paleo-Indian bison kill. *Society for American Archaeology, Memoirs 26.*

Wilmsen, E.N. (1970). Lithic analysis and cultural inference: A Paleo-Indian case. (Anthropological Papers 16). Tucson: University of Arizona.

Winters, H.D. (1969). *The Riverton culture.* Springfield: Illinois State Museum; Urbana: Illinois Archaeological Survey.

Paleolithic Archaeology

Adouze, F., Cahen, D., Keeley, L.H., & Schmider, B. (1981). Le site magdaléen de Buisson Campin, Verberie (Oise). *Gallia Prehistoire 24*(1).

Butzer, K.W., (1971). *Environment and archaeology* (2nd ed.). Chicago: Aldine Publishing Co.

Flint, R.F. (1971). *Glacial and quaternary geology.* New York: John Wiley & Sons, Inc.

Gilot, E. (1966). Mesures d'age par le carbone 14 d'echantillons provenant des foyers magdaléniens de Pincevent. In A. Leroi-Gourhan & M. Brézillon (Eds.), *L'habitation magdal*énienne no. 1 de Pincevent près Montereau (Seine-et-Marne), *Gallia Prehistoire 9*(2), 382.

Guillien, Y., & Perpère, M. (1966). Maxillaires de rennes et saisons de chasse (habitation 1 de Pincevent). In A. Leroi-Gourhan & M. Brézillon (Eds.), *L'habitation magdal*énienne no. 1 de Pincevent près Montereau (Seine-et-Marne), *Gallia Prehistoire 9*(2), 373-377.

Hahn, J. (1977). Essai sur l'ecologie du Magdalénien dans le Jura souabe. In *La fin des temps glaciares en Europe* (Colloques internationaux C.N.R.S. 271(1). Bordeaux, France: Universitè de Bordeaux.

Leroi-Gourhan, A. (1979) *Lascaux inconnu.* Paris: Centre National de la Recherche Scientifique.

Leroi-Gourhan, A., & Brézillon, M. (1964). Le site magdalénienne de Pincevent (Seine-et-Marne). *Bulletin de l'Associacion francais pour l'etude du Quaternaire 1*(1), 59-64.

Leroi-Gourhan, A., & Brézillon, M. (1966). L'habitation magdalénienne no. 1 de Pincevent près Montereau (Seine-et-Marne). *Gallia Prehistoire 9*(2), 263-385.

Leroi-Gourhan, A., & Brézillon, M. (1972). Fouilles de Pincevent. Essai d'analyse ethnographique d'un habitation magdalénien (La Section 36). *Gallia Prehistoire,* VIIeme Supplement.

Moss, E. (1983). *Pincevent et Pont d'Amdon* (British Archaeological Reports, International Series 177). Oxford, England.

Speiss, A. E. (1979). *Reindeer and caribou hunters: An archaeological study.* New York: Academic Press, Inc.

Sturdy, D.A. (1972). Some reindeer economies in prehistoric Europe. In E.S. Higgs (Ed.), *Papers in economic prehistory* (pp. 55-95). Cambridge: Cambridge University Press.

Miscellaneous

Binford, L.R. (1964). A consideration of archaeological research design. *American Antiquity 43*(2), 288-293.

Binford, L.R., Binford, S.R., Whallon, R., & Hardin, M.A., (1970). Archaeology at Hatchery West. *Society for American Archaeology, Memoirs 24.*

Brose, D. (1968). *The Archaeology of Summer Island: Changing settlement systems in northern Lake Michigan.* Unpublished doctoral dissertation, University of Michigan, Ann Arbor.

Chang, K.C. (1967). Major aspects of the interrelationship of archaeology and ethnology. *Current Anthropology 8*(3), 227-243.

Cook, S.F., & Heizer, R.F. (1965). *Chemical analysis of archaeological sites.* (Publications in Anthropology 2). University of California.

de Lumley, H. (1969a). A Paleolithic camp at Nice. *Scientific American 220*(5), 42-50.

de Lumley, H. (1969b). Une cabane acheuléenne dans la grotte du Lazaret. *La Société Préhistorique Francaise, Memoirs 7.*

Freeman, L., & Butzer, K.W. (1966). The Acheulean station of Torralba (Spain). A progress report. *Quarternaria 8*, 9-21.

Goodyear, A. (1974). *The Brand site: A techno-functional study of a Dalton site in northeast Arkansas* (Research Series 7). Fayetteville: Arkansas Archaeological Survey.

Naroll, R. (1962). Floor area and settlement population. *American Antiquity 27*(4), 587-589.

Price, T.D.H. (1975). *Mesolithic settlement systems in the Netherlands.* Unpublished doctoral dissertation. University of Michigan, Ann Arbor.

Struever, S. (1968). Woodland subsistence-settlement systems in the lower Illinois valley. In S.R. Binford & L.R. Binford (Eds.), *New Perspectives in Archaeology* (pp. 285-312). Chicago: Aldine Publishing Co.

Styles, B.W. (1981). *Faunal exploitation and resource selection: Early Late Woodland subsistence in the lower Illinois valley.* (Archaeological Program, Scientific Papers 3). Chicago: Northwestern University.

APPENDIX A: COMPUTER PROGRAMS FOR CALCULATING THE SIMILARITY COEFFICIENTS, AVDISTGM, AVDISTLP1, AND AVDISTGP

```
C***********************************************************************
C
C                         PROGRAM POLYTHETIC1
C
C***********************************************************************
C
C
C THIS PROGRAM CAN BE USED TO CALCULATE A MATRIX OF AVDISTM SIMILARITY
C COEFFICIENTS AND A MATRIX OF AVDISTGP SIMILARITY COEFFICIENTS AS
C DEFINED IN THE TEXT OF THIS PAPER.  THE TWO KINDS OF COEFFICIENTS DEFINE
C THE DEGREE OF SPATIAL COARRANGEMENT OF PAIRS OF ARTIFACT CLASSES ASSUMING
C DIFFERENT STANDARDS OF PERFECT COARRANGEMENT.  AVDISTM, A MONOTHETIC AVERAGE
C NEAREST NEIGHBOR DISTANCE BETWEEN ITEMS OF DIFFERENT ARTIFACT CLASSES,
C ASSUMES A MODEL 1 FORM OF COARRANGEMENT.  AVDISTGP, A GLOBALLY POLYTHETIC
C AVERAGE NEAREST NEIGHBOR DISTANCE BETWEEN ITEMS OF DIFFERENT ARTIFACT
C CLASSES, ASSUMES A MODEL 5 FORM OF COARRANGEMENT.
C
C IN SKETCH, THE PROGRAM INVOLVES SIX BASIC STEPS.  (1) IT READS THE X-Y
C COORDINATES OF ALL ITEMS IN EACH ARTIFACT CLASS TO BE USED IN CALCULATING
C THE AVDISTM AND AVDISTGP COEFFICIENTS.  (2) IT WRITES OUT VARIOUS INPUT
C VALUES AND STATISTICS THAT ALLOW THE USER TO CHECK WHETHER THE
C DATA HAVE BEEN READ CORRECTLY.  (3) IT CALCULATES THE AVERAGE NEAREST
C NEIGHBOR DISTANCE FROM ITEMS OF ONE ARTIFACT CLASS TO ITEMS OF ANOTHER, AND
C VICE VERSA, DEFINING AN ASYMMETRIC MATRIX OF AVDIST1 AND AVDIST2 COEF-
C FICIENTS, AS DESCRIBED IN THE TEXT.  (4) FOR EACH PAIR OF A BASE ARTIFACT
C CLASS AND A REFERENCE ARTIFACT CLASS TO WHICH A GIVEN AVDIST1 OR AVDIST2
C COEFFICIENT PERTAINS, THE PROGRAM OUTPUTS A LISTING OF ALL NEAREST NEIGHBOR
C DISTANCES FROM THE ITEMS OF THE BASE CLASS TO ITEMS OF THE REFERENCE CLASS
C THAT ARE USED IN CALCULATING THE AVDIST1 OR AVDIST2 COEFFICIENT.  THIS
C INFORMATION CAN BE USED TO GENERATE A HISTOGRAM OF NEAREST NEIGHBOR DISTANCES
C FOR EACH BASE CLASS/REFERENCE CLASS PAIR.  HISTOGRAMS OF THIS KIND CAN BE
C USED TO CHECK THE DATA FOR OUTLYING ITEMS OR FOR MULTIMODALITY IN DISTANCE
C RELATIONSHIPS, ALLOWING ONE TO ASSESS THE MEANINGFULNESS OF COMPUTING AN
C AVERAGE DISTANCE STATISTIC, AVDIST1 OR AVDIST2.  (5) THE PROGRAM CALCULATES
C A SYMMETRIC MATRIX OF AVDISTGP COEFFICIENTS FOR ALL ARTIFACT CLASS PAIRS AND
C A SYMMETRIC MATRIX OF AVDISTM COEFFICIENTS FOR ALL ARTIFACT CLASS PAIRS FROM
C THE ASYMMETRIC MATRIX OF AVDIST1 AND AVDIST2 COEFFICIENTS.  (6) THE PROGRAM
C OUTPUTS THE MATRIX OF AVDIST1 AND AVDIST2 COEFFICIENTS, THE MATRIX OF
C AVDISTGP COEFFICIENTS, AND THE MATRIX OF AVDISTM COEFFICIENTS, IN THAT ORDER.
C THE ASYMMETRIC MATRIX OF AVDIST1 AND AVDIST2 COEFFICIENTS GIVES THE
C RESEARCHER ONE MEANS FOR INVESTIGATING THE DIRECTION AND DEGREE OF
C ASYMMETRY BETWEEN VARIOUS PAIRS OF ARTIFACT CLASSES WITHIN THE STUDY AREA.
C
C SYSTEM UNITS AND FILES LINKED TO THEM, AS REQUIRED BY THE PROGRAM:
C
C UNIT 1.  THIS UNIT SHOULD BE LINKED TO A FILE CONTAINING A 1 COLUMN X N ROW
C MATRIX OF THE NUMBER OF ARTIFACT OBSERVATIONS IN EACH ARTIFACT CLASS, IN
C THE FORMAT (1X,I4).  THE NUMBER OF ROWS, N, SHOULD EQUAL THE NUMBER OF
C ARTIFACT CLASSES.
C
C UNIT 2.  THIS UNIT SHOULD BE LINKED TO A FILE CONTAINING A 2 COLUMN X N ROW
C MATRIX OF THE X-Y SPATIAL COORDINATES OF THE ITEMS OF ALL ARTIFACT CLASSES,
C IN THE FORMAT (F7.3,1X,F7.3).  THE NUMBER OF ROWS, N, SHOULD EQUAL THE
C NUMBER OF ALL ITEMS OF ALL ARTIFACT CLASSES.  THE X-Y COORDINATE PAIRS
C SHOULD BE ARRANGED SEQUENTIALLY BY THE ARTIFACT CLASS OF THE ITEMS
C THEY REPRESENT, WITH THE ORDER OF CLASSES BEING THE SAME AS THAT IN
C THE FILE LINKED TO UNIT 1.  FOR CONVENIENCE, THE USER MAY WISH TO KEEP
C THE COORDINATE PAIRS FOR EACH ARTIFACT CLASS IN A SEPARATE FILE AND
C THEN STACK THE FILES INTO ONE MASTER FILE OF THE REQUIRED FORMAT WHEN
```

```
C USING THE PROGRAM.
C UNIT 6.  THIS UNIT SHOULD BE LINKED TO A FILE OR DEVICE TO RECEIVE OUTPUT
C MONITORING THE PROGRESS OF THE PROGRAM AND WHETHER THE DATA ATTACHED TO
C UNITS 1 AND 2 HAVE BEEN READ CORRECTLY.  THE OUTPUT ROUTED TO THIS UNIT
C INCLUDES:  (A) A TOTAL OF THE NUMBER OF ARTIFACT CLASSES, (B) THE SEQUENTIAL
C ORDER NUMBER OF THOSE CLASSES OF ARTIFACTS THAT HAVE BEEN READ SUCCESSFULLY,
C AND (C) THE LAST X-Y COORDINATE PAIR OF EACH ARTIFACT CLASS THAT HAS BEEN
C READ SUCCESSFULLY.
C
C UNIT 3.  THIS UNIT SHOULD BE LINKED TO A FILE TO RECEIVE OUTPUT USEFUL IN
C GENERATING HISTOGRAMS OF NEAREST NEIGHBOR DISTANCES FOR EACH BASE CLASS/
C REFERENCE CLASS PAIR OF ARTIFACT CLASSES.  THE OUTPUT CONSISTS OF A SERIES
C OF MATRICES FOLLOWED BY AND SEPARATED BY THE WORD, "END," ONE MATRIX FOR
C EACH BASE CLASS.  EACH MATRIX HAS AS MANY ROWS AS THERE ARE ITEMS IN THE BASE
C CLASS (ONE ROW FOR EACH ITEM IN THE BASE CLASS) AND AS MANY COLUMNS AS THERE
C ARE ARTIFACT CLASSES (ONE COLUMN FOR EACH ARTIFACT CLASS, IN THE READ ORDER).
C THE ENTRIES DOWN ANY GIVEN COLUMN SPECIFY THE NEAREST NEIGHBOR DISTANCES
C FROM THE ITEMS OF THE BASE CLASS TO WHICH THE MATRIX PERTAINS TO ITEMS OF THE
C ARTIFACT CLASS (REFERENCE CLASS) ASSOCIATED WITH THAT COLUMN.  THE REFERENCE
C CLASS CAN BE THE BASE CLASS, ITSELF.  THE FORMAT OF ANY GIVEN ROW IS
C N(1X,F7.3), WHERE N IS THE NUMBER OF ARTIFACT CLASSES.
C
C UNIT 4.  THIS UNIT SHOULD BE LINKED TO A FILE TO RECEIVE THE OUTPUT MATRICES
C OF AVDIST1/AVDIST2 COEFFICIENTS, AVDISTGP COEFFICIENTS, AND AVDISTM COEF-
C FICIENTS, IN THAT ORDER.  THE THREE MATRICES ARE N X N IN DIMENSION, WHERE
C N IS THE NUMBER OF ARTIFACT CLASSES.  TO ALLOW THEM TO BE DISPLAYED ON AN
C 80-COLUMN PRINTER, EACH MATRIX GREATER THAN 10 COLUMNS X 10 ROWS IS BROKEN
C INTO TWO OR THREE SUBMATRICES OF 10 OR LESS COLUMNS X N ROWS, WHERE N IS THE
C NUMBER OF ARTIFACT CLASSES.  THE SUBMATRICES ARE OUTPUTTED SEQUENTIALLY,
C SEPARATED BY BLANK ROWS.  THE ELEMENTS IN EACH ROW OF A MATRIX OR SUBMATRIX
C HAVE THE FORMAT M(1X,F7.3), WHERE M IS THE NUMBER OF ELEMENTS PER ROW (10 OR
C LESS).  EACH MATRIX OR SUBMATRIX IS PRECEDED BY 5 BLANK ROWS.
C
C DEFINITION OF VARIABLES, ARRAYS, AND LIMITATIONS OF THE PROGRAM:
C
C NPOINT(26).  THE ARRAY OF NUMBERS OF ITEMS IN EACH ARTIFACT CLASS, FOR UP TO
C      26 CLASSES.  THE CONTENTS OF THIS ARRAY ARE READ FROM A FILE LINKED TO
C      UNIT 1.
C NCLASS.  THE NUMBER OF ARTIFACT CLASSES IN THE DATA SET.
C ART(2,381,26).  THE MATRIX OF 2 (X AND Y) SPATIAL COORDINATES FOR EACH OF
C      UP TO 381 ITEMS IN UP TO 26 ARTIFACT CLASSES.  THE CONTENTS OF THIS
C      MATRIX ARE READ FROM A FILE LINKED TO UNIT 2.
C AVDIST(26,26).  THE ASYMMETRIC MATRIX OF AVDIST1 AND AVDIST2 COEFFICIENTS FOR
C      UP TO 26 ARTIFACT CLASSES.  THE CONTENTS OF THIS MATRIX ARE OUTPUTTED TO
C      A FILE LINKED WITH UNIT 4.
C POLYD(26,26).  THE SYMMETRIC MATRIX OF AVDISTGM COEFFICIENTS FOR UP TO 26
C      ARTIFACT CLASSES.  THE CONTENTS OF THIS MATRIX ARE OUTPUTTED TO A FILE
C      LINKED WITH UNIT 4.
C XMONOD(26,26).  THE SYMMETRIC MATRIX OF AVDISTM COEFFICIENTS FOR UP TO 26
C      ARTIFACT CLASSES.  THE CONTENTS OF THIS MATRIX ARE OUTPUTTED TO A FILE
C      LINKED WITH UNIT 4.
C SUM(26,26).  AN ASYMMETRIC MATRIX OF SUMS OF NEAREST NEIGHBOR DISTANCES USED
C      IN CALCULATING THE MATRIX AVDIST.
C DST.  THE DISTANCE FROM AN ITEM OF A BASE CLASS TO AN ITEM OF A REFERENCE
C      CLASS.  THE TWO ITEMS ARE NOT NECESSARILY NEAREST NEIGHBORS.
C DIST(381,26).  A MATRIX OF NEAREST NEIGHBOR DISTANCES FROM THE ITEMS OF A
C      SPECIFIED BASE CLASS (WITH UP TO 381 ITEMS) TO ITEMS OF REFERENCE
C      CLASSES.  THE PROGRAM CALCULATES AS MANY DIST MATRICES AS THERE ARE
C      ARTIFACT CLASSES (I.E., BASE CLASSES).  THE CONTENTS OF THESE MATRICES
C      ARE OUTPUTTED TO A FILE LINKED WITH UNIT 3.
C IT IS POSSIBLE TO INCREASE THE PROGRAM'S LIMITS ON THE NUMBER OF ITEMS PER
C ARTIFACT CLASS TO 9999 AND THE NUMBER OF ARTIFACT CLASSES UP TO 30 BY
C ADJUSTING THE LIMITS SET IN THE DIMENSION STATEMENT (LINES 10, 20).  ANY
```

```
C FURTHER INCREASE IN THE NUMBER OF ITEMS PER CLASS OR NUMBER OF ARTIFACT
C CLASSES REQUIRES MORE BASIC PROGRAM MODIFICATION IN THE INPUT AND OUTPUT
C STATEMENTS (LINES 80, 110, 710-1170).
C
C IT IS ASSUMED THAT THE COORDINATES OF ITEMS RANGE BETWEEN -99.999 AND
C 999.999, THAT THE MAXIMUM DISTANCE SEPARATING ANY PAIR OF ITEMS IS 99999.,
C AND THAT THE MAXIMUM AVERAGE DISTANCE (AVDIST1, AVDIST2, AVDISTGP, OR
C AVDISTM) FROM ITEMS OF ONE CLASS TO ITEMS OF ANOTHER IS 999.999.
C
C THIS PROGRAM WAS WRITTEN AND IS SUPPORTED BY:
C
C                           CHRISTOPHER CARR
C                           DEPARTMENT OF ANTHROPOLOGY AND
C                           INSTITUTE FOR QUANTITATIVE ARCHAEOLOGY
C                           UNIVERSITY OF ARKANSAS
C                           FAYETTEVILLE, AR 72701
C
C
C************************************************************************
C
C
      DIMENSION ART(2,381,26),NPOINT(26),SUM(26,26),DIST(381,26)         INT00010
     1,AVDIST(26,26),POLYD(26,26),XMONOD(26,26)                          INT00020
C     READ IN ARRAY OF NUMBER OF OBSERVATIONS IN EACH ARTIFACT CLASS AND INT00030
C     CALCULATE NUMBER OF ARTIFACT CLASSES                               INT00040
      KOUNT=0                                                            INT00050
      DO 10 I=1,100                                                      INT00060
      READ(1,101,END=500)NPOINT(I)                                       INT00070
      KOUNT=KOUNT+1                                                      INT00080
      WRITE(6,101)NPOINT(I)                                              INT00090
   10 CONTINUE                                                           INT00100
  500 NCLASS=KOUNT                                                       INT00110
C READ IN ARRAY OF OBSERVED LOCATIONS OF ITEMS OF EACH CLASS             INT00120
      DO 11 KLASS=1,NCLASS                                               INT00130
      NPT=NPOINT(KLASS)                                                  INT00140
      DO 9 KPOINT=1,NPT                                                  INT00150
      READ(2,103)(ART(KCOOR,KPOINT,KLASS),KCOOR=1,2)                     INT00160
    9 CONTINUE                                                           INT00170
      WRITE(6,102)KLASS                                                  INT00180
      WRITE(6,107)(ART(KCOOR,KPOINT,KLASS),KCOOR=1,2)                    INT00190
   11 CONTINUE                                                           INT00200
C INITIATE DOS FOR OPERATING ON CLASS PAIRS OR A CLASS WITH ITSELF       INT00210
      DO 12 ICLASS=1,NCLASS                                              INT00220
      NPTB=NPOINT(ICLASS)                                                INT00230
      DO 13 JCLASS=1,NCLASS                                              INT00240
      SUM(JCLASS,ICLASS)=0.                                              INT00250
      NPTR=NPOINT(JCLASS)                                                INT00260
C INITIATE SEARCH FOR NEAREST NEIGHBOR OF SAME OR DIFFERENT CLASS        INT00270
      DO 14 KPNTB=1,NPTB                                                 INT00280
      DMIN=99999.                                                        INT00290
      DO 15 KPNTR=1,NPTR                                                 INT00300
      DST=SQRT((ART(1,KPNTB,ICLASS)-ART(1,KPNTR,JCLASS))**2+             INT00310
     1(ART(2,KPNTB,ICLASS)-ART(2,KPNTR,JCLASS))**2)                      INT00320
      IF(DST.LT.DMIN)DMIN=DST                                            INT00330
   15 CONTINUE                                                           INT00340
      DIST(KPNTB,JCLASS)=DMIN                                            INT00350
   14 CONTINUE                                                           INT00360
C FIND AVDIST FOR ITEMS OF 1 BASE CLASS TO ITEMS OF 1 REFERENCE CLASS    INT00370
      DO 27 KPOINT=1,NPTB                                                INT00380
      SUM(JCLASS,ICLASS)=SUM(JCLASS,ICLASS)+DIST(KPOINT,JCLASS)          INT00390
   27 CONTINUE                                                           INT00400
      AVDIST(JCLASS,ICLASS)=SUM(JCLASS,ICLASS)/NPOINT(ICLASS)            INT00410
   13 CONTINUE                                                           INT00420
```

ALTERNATIVE MODELS, ALTERNATIVE TECHNIQUES 463

```
C WRITE NEAREST NEIGHBOR DISTANCES FOR ALL ITEMS OF ONE BASE CLASS TO      INT00430
C ITEMS OF MULTIPLE REFERENCE CLASSES                                      INT00440
      DO 50 KPNTB=1,NPTB                                                   INT00450
      WRITE(3,104)(DIST(KPNTB,JCLASS),JCLASS=1,NCLASS)                     INT00460
   50 CONTINUE                                                             INT00470
      WRITE(3,108)                                                         INT00480
   12 CONTINUE                                                             INT00490
C FIND MINIMUM OF AVDIST1 AND AVDIST2, DEFINING AVDISTGP (POLYD)           INT00500
      DO 19 ICLASS=1,NCLASS                                                INT00510
      DO 20 JCLASS=1,NCLASS                                                INT00520
      POLYD(JCLASS,ICLASS)=AMIN1(AVDIST(JCLASS,ICLASS),AVDIST(ICLASS,      INT00530
     1JCLASS))                                                             INT00540
   20 CONTINUE                                                             INT00550
   19 CONTINUE                                                             INT00560
C CALCULATE AVDISTM (XMONOD)                                               INT00570
      DO 23 ICLASS=1,NCLASS                                                INT00580
      DO 24 JCLASS=1,NCLASS                                                INT00590
      XMONOD(JCLASS,ICLASS)=(SUM(JCLASS,ICLASS)+SUM(ICLASS,JCLASS))/       INT00600
     1(NPOINT(JCLASS)+NPOINT(ICLASS))                                      INT00610
   24 CONTINUE                                                             INT00620
   23 CONTINUE                                                             INT00630
C WRITE MATRICES OF AVDIST, POLYD, AND XMONOD VALUES TO UNIT4              INT00640
      WRITE(4,105)                                                         INT00650
      IF(NCLASS .LE. 10) GO TO 56                                          INT00660
      IF(NCLASS .LE. 20) GO TO 57                                          INT00670
      IF(NCLASS .LE. 30) GO TO 58                                          INT00680
   56 DO 30 ICLASS=1,NCLASS                                                INT00690
      WRITE(4,106)(AVDIST(JCLASS,ICLASS),JCLASS=1,NCLASS)                  INT00700
   30 CONTINUE                                                             INT00710
      GO TO 91                                                             INT00720
   57 DO 31 ICLASS=1,NCLASS                                                INT00730
      WRITE(4,106)(AVDIST(JCLASS,ICLASS),JCLASS=1,10)                      INT00740
   31 CONTINUE                                                             INT00750
      WRITE(4,105)                                                         INT00760
      DO 32 ICLASS=1,NCLASS                                                INT00770
      WRITE(4,106)(AVDIST(JCLASS,ICLASS),JCLASS=11,NCLASS)                 INT00780
   32 CONTINUE                                                             INT00790
      GO TO 91                                                             INT00800
   58 DO 33 ICLASS=1,NCLASS                                                INT00810
      WRITE(4,106)(AVDIST(JCLASS,ICLASS),JCLASS=1,10)                      INT00820
   33 CONTINUE                                                             INT00830
      WRITE(4,105)                                                         INT00840
      DO 34 ICLASS=1,NCLASS                                                INT00850
      WRITE(4,106)(AVDIST(JCLASS,ICLASS),JCLASS=11,20)                     INT00860
   34 CONTINUE                                                             INT00870
      WRITE(4,105)                                                         INT00880
      DO 35 ICLASS=1,NCLASS                                                INT00890
      WRITE(4,106)(AVDIST(JCLASS,ICLASS),JCLASS=21,NCLASS)                 INT00900
   35 CONTINUE                                                             INT00910
   91 CONTINUE                                                             INT00920
      WRITE(4,105)                                                         INT00930
      IF(NCLASS .LE. 10) GO TO 66                                          INT00940
      IF(NCLASS .LE. 20) GO TO 67                                          INT00950
      IF(NCLASS .LE. 30) GO TO 68                                          INT00960
   66 DO 36 ICLASS=1,NCLASS                                                INT00970
      WRITE(4,106)(POLYD(JCLASS,ICLASS),JCLASS=1,NCLASS)                   INT00980
   36 CONTINUE                                                             INT00990
      GO TO 92                                                             INT01000
   67 DO 37 ICLASS=1,NCLASS                                                INT01010
      WRITE(4,106)(POLYD(JCLASS,ICLASS),JCLASS=1,10)                       INT01020
   37 CONTINUE                                                             INT01030
      WRITE(4,105)                                                         INT01040
      DO 38 ICLASS=1,NCLASS                                                INT01050
```

```
      WRITE(4,106)(POLYD(JCLASS,ICLASS),JCLASS=11,NCLASS)         INT01060
   38 CONTINUE                                                    INT01070
      GO TO 92                                                    INT01080
   68 DO 39 ICLASS=1,NCLASS                                       INT01090
      WRITE(4,106)(POLYD(JCLASS,ICLASS),JCLASS=1,10)              INT01100
   39 CONTINUE                                                    INT01110
      WRITE(4,105)                                                INT01120
      DO 40 ICLASS=1,NCLASS                                       INT01130
      WRITE(4,106)(POLYD(JCLASS,ICLASS),JCLASS=11,20)             INT01140
   40 CONTINUE                                                    INT01150
      WRITE(4,105)                                                INT01160
      DO 41 ICLASS=1,NCLASS                                       INT01170
      WRITE(4,106)(POLYD(JCLASS,ICLASS),JCLASS=21,NCLASS)         INT01180
   41 CONTINUE                                                    INT01190
   92 CONTINUE                                                    INT01200
      WRITE(4,105)                                                INT01210
      IF(NCLASS .LE. 10) GO TO 76                                 INT01220
      IF(NCLASS .LE. 20) GO TO 77                                 INT01230
      IF(NCLASS .LE. 30) GO TO 78                                 INT01240
   76 DO 42 ICLASS=1,NCLASS                                       INT01250
      WRITE(4,106)(XMONOD(JCLASS,ICLASS),JCLASS=1,NCLASS)         INT01260
   42 CONTINUE                                                    INT01270
      GO TO 88                                                    INT01280
   77 DO 43 ICLASS=1,NCLASS                                       INT01290
      WRITE(4,106)(XMONOD(JCLASS,ICLASS),JCLASS=1,10)             INT01300
   43 CONTINUE                                                    INT01310
      WRITE(4,105)                                                INT01320
      DO 44 ICLASS=1,NCLASS                                       INT01330
      WRITE(4,106)(XMONOD(JCLASS,ICLASS),JCLASS=11,NCLASS)        INT01340
   44 CONTINUE                                                    INT01350
      GO TO 88                                                    INT01360
   78 DO 45 ICLASS=1,NCLASS                                       INT01370
      WRITE(4,106)(XMONOD(JCLASS,ICLASS),JCLASS=1,10)             INT01380
   45 CONTINUE                                                    INT01390
      WRITE(4,105)                                                INT01400
      DO 46 ICLASS=1,NCLASS                                       INT01410
      WRITE(4,106)(XMONOD(JCLASS,ICLASS),JCLASS=11,20)            INT01420
   46 CONTINUE                                                    INT01430
      WRITE(4,105)                                                INT01440
      DO 47 ICLASS=1,NCLASS                                       INT01450
      WRITE(4,106)(XMONOD(JCLASS,ICLASS),JCLASS=21,NCLASS)        INT01460
   47 CONTINUE                                                    INT01470
  101 FORMAT(1X,I4)                                               INT01480
  102 FORMAT(1X,I2)                                               INT01490
  103 FORMAT(F7.3,1X,F7.3)                                        INT01500
  104 FORMAT(100(1X,F7.3))                                        INT01510
  105 FORMAT(/////)                                               INT01520
  106 FORMAT(10(1X,F7.3))                                         INT01530
  107 FORMAT(1X,F7.3,1X,F7.3)                                     INT01540
  108 FORMAT(1X,'END')                                            INT01550
   88 STOP                                                        INT01560
      END                                                         INT01570

C***********************************************************************
C
C
C                         PROGRAM POLYTHETIC2
C
C
C***********************************************************************
C
C
C THIS PROGRAM CAN BE USED TO CALCULATE A MATRIX OF AVDISTLP1 SIMILARITY
```

```
C COEFFICIENTS, DEFINING THE DEGREE OF SPATIAL COARRANGEMENT OF PAIRS OF
C ARTIFACT CLASSES.  AS DISCUSSED IN THE TEXT OF THIS PAPER, AVDISTLP1
C IS A LOCALLY POLYTHETIC AVERAGE NEAREST NEIGHBOR DISTANCE BETWEEN
C ITEMS OF TWO DIFFERENT ARTIFACT CLASSES.  THE COEFFICIENT ASSUMES A
C MODEL 4 FORM OF PERFECT COARRANGEMENT.  IN THIS CASE, THE MAGNITUDE,
C AND DIRECTION OF ASYMMETRY BETWEEN ANY GIVEN PAIR OF ARTIFACT CLASSES
C CAN VARY FROM ARTIFACT CLUSTER TO ARTIFACT CLUSTER (OR ANY OTHER AREAL
C STRATUM HOMOGENEOUS IN THE FORMATION PROCESSES AFFECTING ASYMMETRY).
C HOWEVER, ASYMMETRY CAN NOT BE TAKEN TO THE EXTREME WHERE ONE ARTIFACT
C CLASS IS ABSENT FROM STRATA CONTAINING THE OTHER, AND VICE VERSA.
C
C IN CALCULATING AVDISTLP1 COEFFICIENTS, THIS PROGRAM REQUIRES THAT THE
C AREAL STRATUM AFFILIATION OF EACH ARTIFACT, AS WELL AS ITS X AND Y
C SPATIAL COORDINATES, BE KNOWN.  AREAL STRATA NEED NOT BE CLUSTERS OF
C ARTIFACTS THAT ARE SPATIALLY DISCRETE AND HAVE EASILY DEFINABLE
C BORDERS.  THEY CAN BE SOMEWHAT OVERLAPPING CLUSTERS, THE BOUNDARIES
C BETWEEN WHICH HAVE BEEN ONLY APPROXIMATED, OR MORE ILL-DEFINED ZONES
C THAT ARE RELATIVELY HOMOGENEOUS IN THE DIRECTION OF LOCAL ASYMMETRY
C AND THAT HAVE BEEN FOUND USING METHODS DESCRIBED IN THE TEXT OF THIS
C PAPER.  IN THE LATER TWO CASES, THE PROGRAM WILL COMPENSATE TO SOME
C EXTENT FOR THE MISDRAWING OF STRATUM BOUNDARIES AND THE EXCLUSION OF
C A NEAREST NEIGHBOR REFERENCE ITEM OF ONE CLASS FROM THE STRATUM OF A
C BASE ITEM OF ANOTHER CLASS.  THE PROGRAM ADDITIONALLY REQUIRES THE USE
C OF THE SAME SET OF AREAL STRATA FOR ALL PAIRS OF ARTIFACT TYPES, UNDER
C THE ASSUMPTION THAT EACH STRATUM IS RELATIVELY HOMOGENEOUS INTERNALLY
C IN THE DIRECTION OF ASYMMETRY FOR EACH ARTIFACT CLASS PAIR CONTAINED
C IN IT.  THIS ASSUMPTION SHOULD BE CHECKED BEFORE THE DATA ARE ANALYZED
C WITH THIS PROGRAM.
C
C IN SKETCH, THE PROGRAM INVOLVES SEVEN BASIC STEPS.  (1) IT READS THE
C X AND Y COORDINATES AND STRATUM ASSIGNMENTS OF ALL ITEMS IN EACH
C ARTIFACT CLASS TO BE USED IN CALCULATING THE AVDISTLP1 COEFFICIENTS.
C (2) IT WRITES OUT VARIOUS INPUT VALUES AND SUMMARY STATISTICS THAT
C ALLOW THE USER TO CHECK WHETHER THE DATA HAVE BEEN READ CORRECTLY.
C INCLUDED AMONG THESE ARE THE NUMBER OF ITEMS PER CLASS IN ALL STRATA
C COMBINED AND THE NUMBER OF ITEMS PER CLASS IN EACH INDIVIDUAL
C STRATUM.  THE LATTER STATISTICS ALSO ARE USEFUL IN EVALUATING THE
C DIRECTION AND DEGREE OF ASYMMETRY BETWEEN VARIOUS PAIRS OF ARTIFACT
C CLASSES IN EACH STRATUM AND HOW ASYMMETRY RELATIONS VARY OVER STRATA.
C (3) THE PROGRAM DETERMINES FOR EACH STRATUM HAVING ITEMS OF BOTH A
C GIVEN BASE CLASS AND A GIVEN REFERENCE CLASS WHETHER THE NEAREST
C NEIGHBOR ITEM OF THE REFERENCE CLASS FOR EACH ITEM OF THE BASE CLASS
C OCCURS WITHINTHE STRATUM.  THIS INFORMATION IS USED TO DETERMINE
C WHETHER THE STRATUM BOUNDARIES HAVE BEEN DEFINED APPROPRIATELY AND
C WHETHER ONLY INTRA-STRATUM DISTANCES BETWEEN ITEMS, OR BOTH INTRA-
C STRATUM AND INTER-STRATUM DISTANCES, SHOULD BE USED IN CALCULATING
C AVDISTLP1 COEFFICIENTS.  (4) TO HELP THE RESEARCHER ASSESS THE
C APPROPRIATENESS OF THE STRATA BOUNDARIES HE HAS DRAWN AND TO ALLOW
C STEPWISE IMPROVEMENT IN THEIR DEFINITION AND THE RESULTS OF ANALYSIS,
C THE PROGRAM OUTPUTS A SERIES OF MATRICES--ONE FOR EACH STRATUM--
C SHOWING THE NUMBER OF ITEMS OF EACH BASE CLASS THAT HAVE NEAREST
C NEIGHBORS OF A GIVEN REFERENCE CLASS IN OTHER STRATA, ALL REFERENCE
C CLASSES CONSIDERED.  (5) THE PROGRAM CALCULATES AND OUTPUTS A SERIES
C OF ASYMMETRIC MATRICES--ONE FOR EACH STRATUM--CONTAINING THE AVDIST1
C AND AVDIST2 COEFFICIENTS FOR EACH BASE CLASS/REFERENCE CLASS PAIR.  IF
C A BASE CLASS IS NOT PRESENT IN A STRATUM, THE VALUE, 999.000, IS OUT-
C PUTTED FOR THE COEFFICIENT VALUES OF THAT BASE CLASS IN THAT STRATUM.
C (6) THE PROGRAM CALCULATES AND OUTPUTS A SERIES OF SYMMETRIC MATRICES
C --ONE FOR EACH STRATUM--CONTAINING THE WEIGHTS, X(J), FOR EACH BASE
C CLASS/REFERENCE CLASS PAIR THAT ARE USED IN CALCULATING THE AVDISTLP1
C COEFFICIENT FOR THAT PAIR.  (7) THE PROGRAM CALCULATES AND OUTPUTS A
C SYMMETRIC MATRIX CONTAINING THE AVDISTLP1 COEFFICIENTS FOR ALL PAIRS
C OF ARTIFACT CLASSES.
```

```
C SYSTEM UNITS AND FILES LINKED TO THEM, AS REQUIRED BY THE PROGRAM:
C
C UNIT 1.  THIS UNIT SHOULD BE LINKED TO A FILE CONTAINING A 1 COLUMN X
C N ROW MATRIX OF THE NUMBER OF ARTIFACT OBSERVATIONS IN EACH ARTIFACT
C CLASS, IN THE FORMAT (1X,I4).  THE NUMBER OF ROWS, N, SHOULD EQUAL THE
C NUMBER OF ARTIFACT CLASSES.
C
C UNIT 2.  THIS UNIT SHOULD BE LINKED TO A FILE CONTAINING A 1 COLUMN X
C N ROW MATRIX OF THE NUMBER DESIGNATORS OF AREAL STRATA, IN THE FORMAT
C (1X,I4).  THE NUMBER OF ROWS, N, SHOULD EQUAL THE NUMBER OF AREAL
C STRATA.
C
C UNIT 3.  THIS UNIT SHOULD BE LINKED TO A FILE CONTAINING A 3 COLUMN X
C N ROW MATRIX OF THE X SPATIAL COORDINATES, Y SPATIAL COORDINATES, AND
C STRATUM AFFILIATIONS OF THE ITEMS OF ALL ARTIFACT CLASSES, IN THE
C FORMAT (F7.3,1X,F7.3,1X,F3.0).  THE NUMBER OF ROWS, N, SHOULD EQUAL
C THE NUMBER OF ALL ITEMS OF ALL ARTIFACT CLASSES.  THE ROWS OF
C COORDINATES AND STRATUM AFFILIATIONS SHOULD BE ARRANGED SEQUENTIALLY
C BY THE ARTIFACT CLASS OF THE ITEMS THEY REPRESENT, WITH THE ORDER OF
C CLASSES BEING THE SAME AS THAT IN THE FILE LINKED TO UNIT 1.  FOR
C CONVENIENCE, THE USER MAY WISH TO KEEP THE COORDINATES AND STRATUM
C AFFILIATIONS OF EACH ARTIFACT CLASS IN A SEPARATE FILE AND THEN STACK
C THE FILES INTO ONE MASTER FILE OF THE REQUIRED FORMAT.
C
C UNIT 6.  THIS UNIT SHOULD BE LINKED TO A FILE OR DEVICE TO RECEIVE
C OUTPUT MONITORING WHETHER THE NUMBERS OF ARTIFACT OBSERVATIONS IN EACH
C ARTIFACT CLASS, STORED IN A FILE ATTACHED TO UNIT 1, HAVE BEEN READ
C CORRECTLY.  THE OUTPUT ROUTED TO UNIT 6 IS THAT STORED IN THE FILE
C ATTACHED TO UNIT 1.
C
C UNIT 4.  THIS UNIT SHOULD BE LINKED TO A FILE OR DEVICE TO
C RECEIVE A NUMBER OF DIFFERENT KINDS OF MATRICES THAT:
C (A) MONITOR WHETHER THE DATA STORED IN THE FILE LINKED TO UNIT
C 3 HAVE BEEN READ CORRECTLY, (B) MONITOR THE PROGRESS OF THE
C PROGRAM, AND (C) ARE USED IN CALCULATING THE AVDISTLP1 COEFFICIENTS.
C THE FIRST MATRIX OUTPUTTED HAS N ROWS PERTAINING TO N AREAL
C STRATA AND M COLUMNS PERTAINING TO M ARTIFACT CLASSES (IN THE
C READ ORDER).  ITS ELEMENTS ARE THE NUMBER OF ITEMS OF EACH ARTIFACT
C CLASS IN EACH STRATUM.  TO ALLOW THE MATRIX TO BE DISPLAYED ON AN
C 80-COLUMN DEVICE, IF THE MATRIX IS GREATER THAN 10 COLUMNS, IT IS
C BROKEN INTO TWO OR THREE SUBMATRICES OF 10 OR LESS COLUMNS X N ROWS.
C THE SUBMATRICES ARE OUTPUTTED SEQUENTIALLY, SEPARATED BY BLANK ROWS.
C THE ELEMENTS IN EACH ROW OF THE MATRIX OR SUBMATRICES HAVE THE FORMAT
C J(1X,I4) WHERE J IS THE NUMBER OF ELEMENTS PER ROW (10 OR LESS).  THE
C MATRIX OR EACH SUBMATRIX IS PRECEDED BY 5 BLANK ROWS.
C
C NEXT ROUTED TO UNIT 4 ARE THREE SERIES OF MATRICES.  EACH SERIES
C CONTAINS AS MANY MATRICES AS THERE ARE AREAL STRATA--ONE FOR EACH
C STRATUM.  EACH MATRTIX OF EACH SERIES HAS N ROWS PERTAINING TO N BASE
C ARTIFACT CLASSES AND N COLUMNS PERTAINING TO N REFERENCE ARTIFACT
C CLASSES (IN THEIR READ ORDER).  EACH OF THE MATRICES IN THE FIRST
C SERIES HAS AS ELEMENTS THE NUMBER OF ITEMS OF A GIVEN BASE CLASS
C HAVING NEAREST NEIGHBORS OF A GIVEN REFERENCE CLASS OUTSIDE THE
C STRATUM TO WHICH THE MATRIX PERTAINS.  EACH MATRIX IN THE SECOND
C SERIES HAS AS ELEMENTS THE AVDIST1 AND AVDIST2 COEFFICIENTS FOR EACH
C BASE CLASS/REFERENCE CLASS PAIR, PERTINENT TO A GIVEN STRATUM.  EACH
C MATRIX IN THE THIRD SERIES HAS AS ELEMENTS THE X(J) WEIGHTS FOR EACH
C BASE CLASS/REFERENCE CLASS PAIR THAT ARE USED IN CALCULATING THE
C AVDISTLP1 COEFFICIENTS FOR THAT PAIR.  MATRICES PERTAINING TO STRATA
C IN WHICH A GIVEN ARTIFACT CLASS DOES NOT OCCUR, AND FOR WHICH AVDIST1
C COEFFICIENTS ARE UNDEFINED FOR BASE CLASS/REFERENCE CLASS PAIRS HAVING
C THAT ARTIFACT CLASS AS THE BASE CLASS, INCLUDE ELEMENTS WITH THE VALUE
C 999.000 FOR UNDEFINED AVDIST1 COEFFICIENTS.  TO ALLOW EACH MATRIX OF
```

ALTERNATIVE MODELS, ALTERNATIVE TECHNIQUES

```
C EACH SERIES TO BE DISPLAYED ON AN 80-COLUMN DEVICE, IF THE MATRIX HAS
C MORE THAN 10 COLUMNS, IT IS BROKEN INTO TWO OR THREE SUBMATRICES OF
C 10 OR LESS COLUMNS X N ROWS, WHICH ARE OUTPUTTED SEQUENTIALLY. THUS,
C THE THREE SERIES OF MATRICES ARE COMPOSED OF SEVERAL MATRICES--ONE FOR
C EACH STRATUM--WHICH IN TURN MAY BE COMPOSED OF TWO OR THREE SUB-
C MATRICES IN SEQUENCE. WHEN EACH MATRIX IN EACH OF THE THREE SERIES
C IS 10 COLUMNS OR LESS AND NOT BROKEN INTO SUBMATRICES, EACH MATRIX IS
C PRECEDED BY 5 BLANK ROWS AND THEN THE STRATUM DESIGNATOR PERTINENT TO
C IT. WHEN EACH MATRIX IN EACH SERIES IS BROKEN INTO SEQUENTIAL
C SUBMATRICES, ALL SUBMATRICES ARE PRECEDED BY 5 BLANK ROWS BUT ONLY THE
C LEAD SUBMATRIX IS PRECEDED BY A STRATUM DESIGNATOR, AS WELL. THE
C MATRICES OR SUBMATRICES IN THE FIRST SERIES, SECOND SERIES, AND THIRD
C SERIES HAVE ROWS WITH ELEMENTS IN THE RESPECTIVE FORMATS OF M(1X,I4),
C M(1X,F7.3), AND M(1X,F7.3), WHERE M IS THE NUMBER OF ELEMENTS PER ROW
C (10 OR LESS).
C
C THE FINAL MATRIX ROUTED TO UNIT 4 HAS AS ELEMENTS THE AVDISTLP1 COEF-
C FICIENTS FOR EACH PAIR OF ARTIFACT CLASSES. THE MATRIX HAS N ROWS
C AND N COLUMNS PERTAINING TO THE N ARTIFACT CLASSES, IN THE ORDER THEY
C WERE READ. IF THE MATRIX HAS MORE THAN 10 COLUMNS, IT IS BROKEN INTO
C TWO OR THREE SUBMATRICES OF 10 OR LESS COLUMNS X N ROWS, WHICH ARE
C OUTPUTTED SEQUENTIALLY. THE ELEMENTS IN EACH ROW OF THE MATRIX OR
C SUBMATRICES HAVE THE FORMAT M(1X,F7.3), WHERE M IS THE NUMBER OF
C ELEMENTS PER ROW (10 OR LESS). THE MATRIX (OR EACH SUBMATRIX) IS
C PRECEDED BY 5 BLANK ROWS.
C
C DEFINITION OF VARIABLES, ARRAYS, AND LIMITATIONS OF THE PROGRAM:
C
C NPOINT(23). THE ARRAY OF NUMBERS OF ITEMS IN EACH ARTIFACT CLASS, FOR
C       UP TO 23 CLASSES. THE CONTENTS OF THIS ARRAY ARE READ FROM A
C       FILE LINKED TO UNIT 1.
C NCLASS. THE NUMBER OF ARTIFACT CLASSES IN THE DATA SET.
C ISTRID(13).THE ARRAY OF NUMERIC IDENTIFIERS FOR EACH AREAL STRATUM,
C       FOR UP TO 13 STRATA. THE CONTENTS OF THIS ARRAY ARE READ FROM A
C       FILE LINKED TO UNIT 2.
C NSTRAT. THE NUMBER OF AREAL STRATA IN THE DATA SET.
C ART(3,140,23). THE MATRIX OF 2 (X AND Y) SPATIAL COORDINATES AND A
C       NUMERIC STRATUM IDENTIFIER FOR EACH OF UP TO 140 ITEMS IN UP TO
C       23 ARTIFACT CLASSES. THE CONTENT OF THIS MATRIX ARE READ FROM
C       A FILE LINKED TO UNIT 3.
C ISTRNM(23,13). THE MATRIX OF NUMBERS OF ITEMS OF EACH ARTIFACT CLASS
C       IN EACH STRATUM FOR UP TO 23 CLASSES AND 13 STRATA. THE
C       CONTENTS OF THIS MATRIX ARE OUTPUTTED TO A FILE LINKED TO UNIT
C       4.
C INDEX(140,23,23). THE MATRIX OF INDEX VALUES FOR EACH ITEM (AS A BASE
C       ITEM) INDICATING WHETHER ITS NEAREST NEIGHBOR OF EACH GIVEN
C       REFERENCE CLASS FALLS WITHIN ITS AREAL STRATUM. THE INDEX HAS
C       THE VALUE OF THE STRATUM DESIGNATOR OF THE ITEM IF THE NEAREST
C       NEIGHBOR OF THE GIVEN REFERENCE CLASS FALLS WITHIN THE ITEM'S
C       STRATUM. IT HAS THE VALUE, 77, IF THE NEAREST NEIGHBOR OF THE
C       GIVEN REFERENCE CLASS FALLS IN SOME OTHER STRATUM. UP TO 140
C       ITEMS PER CLASS FOR 23 CLASSES ARE PERMISSIBLE.
C NOUT(13,23,23). THE MATRIX OF THE NUMBER OF ITEMS OF A GIVEN BASE
C       CLASS WITHIN A GIVEN STRATUM HAVING NEAREST NEIGHBORS OF A
C       GIVEN REFERENCE CLASS OUTSIDE THE STRATUM.
C AVDIST(13,23,23). THE ASYMMETRIC MATRIX OF INTRA-STRATUM AVDIST1 AND
C       AVDIST2 COEFFICIENTS FOR UP TO 23 ARTIFACT CLASSES AND 13 AREAL
C       STRATA. THE COEFFICIENT IS UNDEFINED AND GIVEN THE VALUE
C       999.000 FOR EACH BASE CLASS/REFERENCE CLASS PAIR FOR WHICH THE
C       BASE CLASS DOES NOT OCCUR WITHIN THE STRATUM OF CONCERN. THE
C       CONTENTS OF THIS MATRIX ARE OUTPUTTED TO A FILE LINKED TO
C       UNIT 4.
C POLYD(13,23,23). THE SYMMETRIC MATRIX OF COEFFICIENTS, EACH DEFINED
```

```
C          AS THE MINIMUM OF THE AVDIST1-AVDIST2 COEFFICIENT-PAIR
C          PERTINENT TO A GIVEN PAIR OF ARTIFACT CLASSES WITHIN A GIVEN
C          STRATUM.  UP TO 23 CLASSES AND 13 STRATA ARE PERMISSIBLE.
C POLYT(23,23).  THE SYMMETRIC MATRIX OF AVDISTLP1 COEFFICIENTS FOR
C          EACH PAIR OF ARTIFACT CLASSES, WITH UP TO 23 CLASSES POSSIBLE.
C          THE CONTENTS OF THIS MATRIX ARE OUTPUTTED TO A FILE LINKED
C          WITH UNIT 4.
C
C IN THIS PROGRAM, STRATUM DESIGNATIONS MUST BE INTEGERS OF 3 DIGITS OR
C LESS, OTHER THAN 77.  IF THE USER WISHES TO USE THE STRATUM NUMBER,
C 77, THIS NUMBER IN LINE 960 OF THE PROGRAM MUST BE ALTERED TO SOME
C INTEGER OTHER THAN THE STRATUM NUMBERS USED.
C
C IT IS POSSIBLE TO INCREASE THE PROGRAM'S LIMITS ON THE NUMBER OF
C ITEMS PER ARTIFACT CLASS TO 9999, THE NUMBER OF ARTIFACT CLASSES
C UP TO 30, AND THE NUMBER OF STRATA UP TO 999.  THIS CAN BE DONE BY
C ADJUSTING THE LIMITS SET IN THE DIMENSION STATEMENT (LINES 10-30).
C ANY FURTHER INCREASE IN THESE PARAMETERS REQUIRES MORE BASIC PROGRAM
C MODIFICATIONS IN THE INPUT AND OUTPUT STATEMENTS (LINES 70, 90, 120,
C 180, 470-610, 1630-1800, 1820-2000, 2170-2340, 2490-2640).  IT IS
C ASSUMED THAT THE COORDINATES OF ITEMS RANGE BETWEEN -99.999 AND
C 999.999, THAT THE MINIMUM DISTANCE SEPARATING ANY PAIR OF ITEMS IS
C 100000, AND THAT THE MAXIMUM AVERAGE DISTANCE (AVDIST1, AVDIST2,
C AVDISTLP1) FROM ITEMS OF ONE CLASS TO ITEMS OF ANOTHER IS 999.
C
C THE EFFICIENCY OF THIS PROGRAM COULD BE INCREASED IN SEVERAL MANNERS
C TO ACCOMODATE LARGE NUMBERS OF ARTIFACTS PER CLASS AND/OR CLASSES,
C WITHIN SYSTEM-SPECIFIC CONSTRAINTS, IN SEVERAL WAYS.
C
C THIS PROGRAM WAS WRITTEN AND IS SUPPORTED BY:
C
C                         CHRISTOPHER CARR
C                         DEPARTMENT OF ANTHROPOLOGY AND
C                         INSTITUTE FOR QUANTITATIVE ARCHAEOLOGY
C                         UNIVERSITY OF ARKANSAS
C                         FAYETTEVILLE, AR 72701
C
C
C ***********************************************************************
C
C
      DIMENSION ART(3,140,23),NPOINT(23),ISTRID(13),ISTRNM(23,13),        INT00010
     1AVDIST(13,23,23),POLYD(13,23,23),XWEIGH(13,23,23),POLYT(23,23),     INT00020
     2INDEX(140,23,23),NOUT(13,23,23)                                     INT00030
C READ IN ARRAY OF NUMBER OF OBSERVATIONS IN EACH ARTIFACT CLASS          INT00040
C AND CALCULATE NUMBER OF ARTIFACT CLASSES                                INT00050
      KOUNT=0                                                             INT00060
      DO 10 I=1,9999                                                      INT00070
      READ(1,104,END=102)NPOINT(I)                                        INT00080
      KOUNT=KOUNT+1                                                       INT00090
      WRITE(6,104)NPOINT(I)                                               INT00100
   10 CONTINUE                                                            INT00110
  102 NCLASS=KOUNT                                                        INT00120
C READ IN ARRAY OF STRATUM NUMBER DESIGNATIONS AND CALCULATE NUMBER       INT00130
C OF STRATA                                                               INT00140
      KOUNT2=0                                                            INT00150
      DO 40 I=1,999                                                       INT00160
      READ(2,110,END=111)ISTRID(I)                                        INT00170
      KOUNT2=KOUNT2+1                                                     INT00180
   40 CONTINUE                                                            INT00190
  111 NSTRAT=KOUNT2                                                       INT00200
C READ IN ARRAY OF OBSERVED LOCATIONS OF ITEMS AND THEIR STRATUM          INT00210
C ASSIGNMENTS FOR EACH CLASS                                              INT00220
```

```
      DO 11 KLASS=1,NCLASS                                INT00230
      NPT=NPOINT(KLASS)                                   INT00240
      DO 9 KPOINT=1,NPT                                   INT00250
      READ(3,103)(ART(KCOOR,KPOINT,KLASS),KCOOR=1,3)      INT00260
    9 CONTINUE                                            INT00270
   11 CONTINUE                                            INT00280
C DETERMINE NUMBER OF ITEMS OF EACH CLASS IN EACH STRATUM INT00290
      DO 603 ISTRAT=1,NSTRAT                              INT00300
      ISTRT=ISTRID(ISTRAT)                                INT00310
      DO 604 KLASS=1,NCLASS                               INT00320
      KOUNT=0                                             INT00330
      ISTRNM(KLASS,ISTRAT)=0                              INT00340
      NPT=NPOINT(KLASS)                                   INT00350
      DO 605 KPOINT=1,NPT                                 INT00360
      IF(ART(3,KPOINT,KLASS) .EQ. ISTRT)KOUNT=KOUNT+1     INT00370
  605 CONTINUE                                            INT00380
      ISTRNM(KLASS,ISTRAT)=KOUNT                          INT00390
  604 CONTINUE                                            INT00400
  603 CONTINUE                                            INT00410
C WRITE NUMBER OF ITEMS OF EACH CLASS IN EACH STRATUM TO UNIT 4 INT00420
      IF(NCLASS .LE. 10) GO TO 201                        INT00430
      IF(NCLASS .LE. 20) GO TO 202                        INT00440
      IF(NCLASS .LE. 30) GO TO 203                        INT00450
  201 WRITE(4,105)                                        INT00460
      DO 680 ISTRAT=1,NSTRAT                              INT00470
      WRITE(4,109)(ISTRNM(KLASS,ISTRAT),KLASS=1,NCLASS)   INT00480
  680 CONTINUE                                            INT00490
      GO TO 41                                            INT00500
  202 WRITE(4,105)                                        INT00510
      DO 681 ISTRAT=1,NSTRAT                              INT00520
      WRITE(4,109)(ISTRNM(KLASS,ISTRAT),KLASS=1,10)       INT00530
  681 CONTINUE                                            INT00540
      WRITE(4,105)                                        INT00550
      DO 682 ISTRAT=1,NSTRAT                              INT00560
      WRITE(4,109)(ISTRNM(KLASS,ISTRAT),KLASS=11,NCLASS)  INT00570
  682 CONTINUE                                            INT00580
      GO TO 41                                            INT00590
  203 WRITE(4,105)                                        INT00600
      DO 683 ISTRAT=1,NSTRAT                              INT00610
      WRITE(4,109)(ISTRNM(KLASS,ISTRAT),KLASS=1,10)       INT00620
  683 CONTINUE                                            INT00630
      WRITE(4,105)                                        INT00640
      DO 684 ISTRAT=1,NSTRAT                              INT00650
      WRITE(4,109)(ISTRNM(KLASS,ISTRAT),KLASS=11,20)      INT00660
  684 CONTINUE                                            INT00670
      WRITE(4,105)                                        INT00680
      DO 685 ISTRAT=1,NSTRAT                              INT00690
      WRITE(4,109)(ISTRNM(KLASS,ISTRAT),KLASS=21,NCLASS)  INT00700
  685 CONTINUE                                            INT00710
   41 CONTINUE                                            INT00720
C CONSTRUCT INDICES FOR EACH ITEM INDICATING WHETHER ITS NEAREST INT00730
C NEIGHBORS OF GIVEN REFERENCE CLASSES FALL WITHIN ITS STRATUM.  INT00740
C INITIATE DOS FOR OPERATING ON CLASS PAIRS OR A CLASS WITH ITSELF INT00750
      DO 12 ICLASS=1,NCLASS                               INT00760
      NPTB=NPOINT(ICLASS)                                 INT00770
      DO 13 JCLASS=1,NCLASS                               INT00780
      NPTR=NPOINT(JCLASS)                                 INT00790
      DO 900 ISTRAT=1,NSTRAT                              INT00800
      ISTRT=ISTRID(ISTRAT)                                INT00810
C INITIATE SEARCH FOR NEAREST NEIGHBOR OF SAME OR DIFFERENT CLASS, INT00820
C IN A SPECIFIED STRATUM, IF POSSIBLE.                   INT00830
C CHECK IF BASE CLASS OCCURS IN THE STRATUM.             INT00840
      IF(ISTRNM(ICLASS,ISTRAT) .LE. 0) GO TO 900          INT00850
```

```
C INITIATE INCREMENTING OF ITEMS OF THE BASE CLASS AND CHECK IF THE      INT00860
C BASE ITEM OCCURS IN THE STRATUM OF INTEREST                            INT00870
      DO 14 KPNTB=1,NPTB                                                 INT00880
      IF(ART(3,KPNTB,ICLASS)-ISTRT)14,901,14                             INT00890
C CHECK IF THE REFERENCE CLASS OCCURS IN THE STRATUM                     INT00900
  901 IF(ISTRNM(JCLASS,ISTRAT) .LE. 0) GO TO 950                         INT00910
C INITIATE INCREMENTING ITEMS OF REFERENCE CLASS, AND FIND NEAREST       INT00920
C NEIGHBOR OF THAT CLASS IN ANY STRATUM (TO ACCOMODATE FOR INAPPRO-      INT00930
C PRIATELY DRAWN STRATUM BOUNDARIES).  IF BOUNDARIES ARE APPROX-         INT00940
C IMATELY APPROPRIATE, USUALLY THE NEAREST NEIGHBOR WILL BE IN THE       INT00950
C STRATUM OF THE BASE ITEM.  NOTE THE STRATUM OF THE NEAREST NEIGHBOR    INT00960
C OF THAT REFERENCE CLASS WITH AN INDEX VALUE EQUIVALENT TO THE STRATUM  INT00970
C NUMBER.                                                                INT00980
      DMIN=100000.                                                       INT00990
      DO 50 KPNTR=1,NPTR                                                 INT01000
      DST=SQRT((ART(1,KPNTB,ICLASS)-ART(1,KPNTR,JCLASS))**2+             INT01010
     1(ART(2,KPNTB,ICLASS)-ART(2,KPNTR,JCLASS))**2)                      INT01020
      IF(DST .LT. DMIN) GO TO 51                                         INT01030
      GO TO 50                                                           INT01040
   51 DMIN=DST                                                           INT01050
      INDX=ART(3,KPNTR,JCLASS)                                           INT01060
   50 CONTINUE                                                           INT01070
      INDEX(KPNTB,JCLASS,ICLASS)=INDX                                    INT01080
      GO TO 14                                                           INT01090
  950 INDEX(KPNTB,JCLASS,ICLASS)=77                                      INT01100
   14 CONTINUE                                                           INT01110
  900 CONTINUE                                                           INT01120
   13 CONTINUE                                                           INT01130
   12 CONTINUE                                                           INT01140
C INITIATE DOS FOR OPERATING ON CLASS PAIRS OR A CLASS WITH ITSELF       INT01150
      DO 112 ICLASS=1,NCLASS                                             INT01160
      NPTB=NPOINT(ICLASS)                                                INT01170
      DO 113 JCLASS=1,NCLASS                                             INT01180
      NPTR=NPOINT(JCLASS)                                                INT01190
      DO 1900 ISTRAT=1,NSTRAT                                            INT01200
      ISTRT=ISTRID(ISTRAT)                                               INT01210
C SET VALUE FOR INTRA-STRATUM AVDIST STATISTIC AT 999, SHOULD THE BASE   INT01220
C CLASS NOT OCCUR IN THE STRATUM.                                        INT01230
      AVDIST(ISTRAT,JCLASS,ICLASS)=999.                                  INT01240
      NOUT(ISTRAT,JCLASS,ICLASS)=0                                       INT01250
      KOUNT2=0                                                           INT01260
      SUM=0.                                                             INT01270
C INITIATE SEARCH FOR NEAREST NEIGHBOR OF SAME OR DIFFERENT CLASS        INT01280
C IN A SPECIFIED STRATUM, IF POSSIBLE.                                   INT01290
C CHECK IF BASE CLASS OCCURS IN THE STRATUM.                             INT01300
      IF(ISTRNM(ICLASS,ISTRAT) .LE. 0) GO TO 1900                        INT01310
C INITIATE INCREMENTING OF ITEMS OF THE BASE CLASS AND CHECK IF THE      INT01320
C BASE ITEM OCCURS IN THE STRATUM                                        INT01330
      DO 114 KPNTB=1,NPTB                                                INT01340
      IF(ART(3,KPNTB,ICLASS)-ISTRT)114,1901,114                          INT01350
C CHECK IF REFERENCE CLASS OCCURS IN THE STRATUM                         INT01360
 1901 IF(ISTRNM(JCLASS,ISTRAT) .LE. 0) GO TO 1950                        INT01370
C CHECK IF THE BASE ITEM HAS A NEAREST NEIGHBOR OF THE REFERENCE CLASS   INT01380
C IN ANOTHER STRATUM                                                     INT01390
      IF(INDEX(KPNTB,JCLASS,ICLASS) .NE. ISTRT) GO TO 1950               INT01400
C INITIATE INCREMENTING ITEMS OF REFERENCE CLASS AND CHECK IF            INT01410
C THE REFERENCE ITEM OCCURS IN THE STRATUM.                              INT01420
      DMIN2=100000.                                                      INT01430
      DO 115 KPNTR=1,NPTR                                                INT01440
      IF(ART(3,KPNTR,JCLASS)-ISTRT)115,1902,115                          INT01450
 1902 DST2=SQRT((ART(1,KPNTB,ICLASS)-ART(1,KPNTR,JCLASS))**2+            INT01460
     1(ART(2,KPNTB,ICLASS)-ART(2,KPNTR,JCLASS))**2)                      INT01470
      IF(DST2 .LT. DMIN2) DMIN2=DST2                                     INT01480
```

```
      115 CONTINUE                                                  INT01490
          SUM=SUM+DMIN2                                             INT01500
          GO TO 114                                                 INT01510
C IF THE REFERENCE CLASS OCCURS IN THE STRATUM, INCLUDE IN SUM THE  INT01520
C DISTANCES BETWEEN BASE ITEMS HAVING NEAREST NEIGHBOR REFERENCE ITEMS INT01530
C OUTSIDE THE STRATUM AND THOSE REFERENCE ITEMS. IF THE REFERENCE CLASS INT01540
C DOES NOT OCCUR IN THE STRATUM, FORM A SUM OF DISTANCES TO NEAREST INT01550
C NEIGHBORS IN ANY STRATUM                                          INT01560
     1950 KOUNT2=KOUNT2+1                                           INT01570
          DMIN3=100000.                                             INT01580
          DO 215 KPNTR=1,NPTR                                       INT01590
          DST3=SQRT((ART(1,KPNTB,ICLASS)-ART(1,KPNTR,JCLASS))**2+   INT01600
         1(ART(2,KPNTB,ICLASS)-ART(2,KPNTR,JCLASS))**2)             INT01610
          IF(DST3 .LT. DMIN3) DMIN3=DST3                            INT01620
      215 CONTINUE                                                  INT01630
          SUM=SUM+DMIN3                                             INT01640
      114 CONTINUE                                                  INT01650
          AVDIST(ISTRAT,JCLASS,ICLASS)=SUM/ISTRNM(ICLASS,ISTRAT)    INT01660
          NOUT(ISTRAT,JCLASS,ICLASS)=KOUNT2                         INT01670
     1900 CONTINUE                                                  INT01680
      113 CONTINUE                                                  INT01690
      112 CONTINUE                                                  INT01700
C WRITE NUMBER OF ITEMS OF GIVEN BASE CLASSES HAVING NEAREST NEIGHBORS INT01710
C OF GIVEN REFERENCE CLASSES OUTSIDE EACH STRATUM.                  INT01720
          DO 470 ISTRAT=1,NSTRAT                                    INT01730
          WRITE(4,105)                                              INT01740
          WRITE(4,107)ISTRID(ISTRAT)                                INT01750
          IF(NCLASS .LE. 10) GO TO 204                              INT01760
          IF(NCLASS .LE. 20) GO TO 205                              INT01770
          IF(NCLASS .LE. 30) GO TO 206                              INT01780
      204 DO 471 ICLASS=1,NCLASS                                    INT01790
          WRITE(4,109)(NOUT(ISTRAT,JCLASS,ICLASS),JCLASS=1,NCLASS)  INT01800
      471 CONTINUE                                                  INT01810
          GO TO 470                                                 INT01820
      205 DO 472 ICLASS=1,NCLASS                                    INT01830
          WRITE(4,109)(NOUT(ISTRAT,JCLASS,ICLASS),JCLASS=1,10)      INT01840
      472 CONTINUE                                                  INT01850
          WRITE(4,105)                                              INT01860
          DO 473 ICLASS=1,NCLASS                                    INT01870
          WRITE(4,109)(NOUT(ISTRAT,JCLASS,ICLASS),JCLASS=11,NCLASS) INT01880
      473 CONTINUE                                                  INT01890
          GO TO 470                                                 INT01900
      206 DO 474 ICLASS=1,NCLASS                                    INT01910
          WRITE(4,109)(NOUT(ISTRAT,JCLASS,ICLASS),JCLASS=1,10)      INT01920
      474 CONTINUE                                                  INT01930
          WRITE(4,105)                                              INT01940
          DO 475 ICLASS=1,NCLASS                                    INT01950
          WRITE(4,109)(NOUT(ISTRAT,JCLASS,ICLASS),JCLASS=11,20)     INT01960
      475 CONTINUE                                                  INT01970
          WRITE(4,105)                                              INT01980
          DO 476 ICLASS=1,NCLASS                                    INT01990
          WRITE(4,109)(NOUT(ISTRAT,JCLASS,ICLASS),JCLASS=21,NCLASS) INT02000
      476 CONTINUE                                                  INT02010
      470 CONTINUE                                                  INT02020
C WRITE INTRA-STRATUM AVDIST1 AND AVDIST2 COEFFICIENTS TO UNIT 4.   INT02030
          DO 615 ISTRAT=1,NSTRAT                                    INT02040
          WRITE(4,105)                                              INT02050
          WRITE(4,107)ISTRID(ISTRAT)                                INT02060
          IF(NCLASS .LE. 10) GO TO 207                              INT02070
          IF(NCLASS .LE. 20) GO TO 208                              INT02080
          IF(NCLASS .LE. 30) GO TO 209                              INT02090
      207 DO 616 ICLASS=1,NCLASS                                    INT02100
          WRITE(4,106)(AVDIST(ISTRAT,JCLASS,ICLASS),JCLASS=1,NCLASS) INT02110
```

```
      616 CONTINUE                                                      INT02120
          GO TO 615                                                     INT02130
      208 DO 617 ICLASS=1,NCLASS                                        INT02140
          WRITE(4,106)(AVDIST(ISTRAT,JCLASS,ICLASS),JCLASS=1,10)        INT02150
      617 CONTINUE                                                      INT02160
          WRITE(4,105)                                                  INT02170
          DO 618 ICLASS=1,NCLASS                                        INT02180
          WRITE(4,106)(AVDIST(ISTRAT,JCLASS,ICLASS),JCLASS=11,NCLASS)   INT02190
      618 CONTINUE                                                      INT02200
          GO TO 615                                                     INT02210
      209 DO 619 ICLASS=1,NCLASS                                        INT02220
          WRITE(4,106)(AVDIST(ISTRAT,JCLASS,ICLASS),JCLASS=1,10)        INT02230
      619 CONTINUE                                                      INT02240
          WRITE(4,105)                                                  INT02250
          DO 620 ICLASS=1,NCLASS                                        INT02260
          WRITE(4,106)(AVDIST(ISTRAT,JCLASS,ICLASS),JCLASS=11,20)       INT02270
      620 CONTINUE                                                      INT02280
          WRITE(4,105)                                                  INT02290
          DO 621 ICLASS=1,NCLASS                                        INT02300
          WRITE(4,106)(AVDIST(ISTRAT,JCLASS,ICLASS),JCLASS=21,NCLASS)   INT02310
      621 CONTINUE                                                      INT02320
      615 CONTINUE                                                      INT02330
    C FIND MINIMUM AVDIST STATISTIC FOR EACH STRATUM, FOR EACH BASE CLASS/ INT02340
    C REFERENCE CLASS PAIR.                                             INT02350
          DO 18 ICLASS=1,NCLASS                                         INT02360
          DO 19 JCLASS=1,NCLASS                                         INT02370
          DO 20 ISTRAT=1,NSTRAT                                         INT02380
          XWEIGH(ISTRAT,JCLASS,ICLASS)=0.                               INT02390
          POLYD(ISTRAT,JCLASS,ICLASS)=AMIN1(AVDIST(ISTRAT,JCLASS,ICLASS), INT02400
         1AVDIST(ISTRAT,ICLASS,JCLASS))                                 INT02410
          IF(POLYD(ISTRAT,JCLASS,ICLASS) .EQ. AVDIST(ISTRAT,JCLASS,ICLASS)) INT02420
         1XWEIGH(ISTRAT,JCLASS,ICLASS)=ISTRNM(ICLASS,ISTRAT)            INT02430
          IF(POLYD(ISTRAT,JCLASS,ICLASS) .EQ. AVDIST(ISTRAT,ICLASS,JCLASS)) INT02440
         1XWEIGH(ISTRAT,JCLASS,ICLASS)=ISTRNM(JCLASS,ISTRAT)            INT02450
       20 CONTINUE                                                      INT02460
       19 CONTINUE                                                      INT02470
       18 CONTINUE                                                      INT02480
    C WRITE WEIGHTS TO FILE                                             INT02490
          DO 630 ISTRAT=1,NSTRAT                                        INT02500
          WRITE(4,105)                                                  INT02510
          WRITE(4,107)ISTRID(ISTRAT)                                    INT02520
          IF(NCLASS .LE. 10) GO TO 210                                  INT02530
          IF(NCLASS .LE. 20) GO TO 211                                  INT02540
          IF(NCLASS .LE. 30) GO TO 212                                  INT02550
      210 DO 686 ICLASS=1,NCLASS                                        INT02560
          WRITE(4,108)(XWEIGH(ISTRAT,JCLASS,ICLASS),JCLASS=1,NCLASS)    INT02570
      686 CONTINUE                                                      INT02580
          GO TO 630                                                     INT02590
      211 DO 687 ICLASS=1,NCLASS                                        INT02600
          WRITE(4,108)(XWEIGH(ISTRAT,JCLASS,ICLASS),JCLASS=1,10)        INT02610
      687 CONTINUE                                                      INT02620
          WRITE(4,105)                                                  INT02630
          DO 688 ICLASS=1,NCLASS                                        INT02640
          WRITE(4,108)(XWEIGH(ISTRAT,JCLASS,ICLASS),JCLASS=11,NCLASS)   INT02650
      688 CONTINUE                                                      INT02660
          GO TO 630                                                     INT02670
      212 DO 689 ICLASS=1,NCLASS                                        INT02680
          WRITE(4,108)(XWEIGH(ISTRAT,JCLASS,ICLASS),JCLASS=1,10)        INT02690
      689 CONTINUE                                                      INT02700
          WRITE(4,105)                                                  INT02710
          DO 690 ICLASS=1,NCLASS                                        INT02720
          WRITE(4,108)(XWEIGH(ISTRAT,JCLASS,ICLASS),JCLASS=11,20)       INT02730
      690 CONTINUE                                                      INT02740
```

```
            WRITE(4,105)                                            INT02750
            DO 691 ICLASS=1,NCLASS                                  INT02760
            WRITE(4,108)(XWEIGH(ISTRAT,JCLASS,ICLASS),JCLASS=21,NCLASS) INT02770
        691 CONTINUE                                                INT02780
        630 CONTINUE                                                INT02790
      C FIND COMPOSITE AVDISTLP1 STATISTIC FOR ALL STRATA            INT02800
            DO 23 ICLASS=1,NCLASS                                   INT02810
            DO 24 JCLASS=1,NCLASS                                   INT02820
            SUM1=0.                                                 INT02830
            SUM2=0.                                                 INT02840
            DO 25 ISTRAT=1,NSTRAT                                   INT02850
            SUM1=SUM1+(XWEIGH(ISTRAT,JCLASS,ICLASS)*                INT02860
           1POLYD(ISTRAT,JCLASS,ICLASS))                            INT02870
            SUM2=SUM2+XWEIGH(ISTRAT,JCLASS,ICLASS)                  INT02880
         25 CONTINUE                                                INT02890
            POLYT(JCLASS,ICLASS)=SUM1/SUM2                          INT02900
         24 CONTINUE                                                INT02910
         23 CONTINUE                                                INT02920
      C WRITE MATRIX OF AVDISTLP1 VALUES TO UNIT 4                   INT02930
            WRITE(4,105)                                            INT02940
            IF(NCLASS .LE. 10) GO TO 213                            INT02950
            IF(NCLASS .LE. 20) GO TO 214                            INT02960
            IF(NCLASS .LE. 30) GO TO 216                            INT02970
        213 DO 30 ICLASS=1,NCLASS                                   INT02980
            WRITE(4,106)(POLYT(JCLASS,ICLASS),JCLASS=1,NCLASS)      INT02990
         30 CONTINUE                                                INT03000
            GO TO 38                                                INT03010
        214 DO 31 ICLASS=1,NCLASS                                   INT03020
            WRITE(4,106)(POLYT(JCLASS,ICLASS),JCLASS=1,10)          INT03030
         31 CONTINUE                                                INT03040
            WRITE(4,105)                                            INT03050
            DO 32 ICLASS=1,NCLASS                                   INT03060
            WRITE(4,106)(POLYT(JCLASS,ICLASS),JCLASS=11,NCLASS)     INT03070
         32 CONTINUE                                                INT03080
            GO TO 38                                                INT03090
        216 DO 33 ICLASS=1,NCLASS                                   INT03100
            WRITE(4,106)(POLYT(JCLASS,ICLASS),JCLASS=1,10)          INT03110
         33 CONTINUE                                                INT03120
            WRITE(4,105)                                            INT03130
            DO 34 ICLASS=1,NCLASS                                   INT03140
            WRITE(4,106)(POLYT(JCLASS,ICLASS),JCLASS=11,20)         INT03150
         34 CONTINUE                                                INT03160
            WRITE(4,105)                                            INT03170
            DO 35 ICLASS=1,NCLASS                                   INT03180
            WRITE(4,106)(POLYT(JCLASS,ICLASS),JCLASS=21,NCLASS)     INT03190
         35 CONTINUE                                                INT03200
         38 CONTINUE                                                INT03210
        103 FORMAT(F7.3,1X,F7.3,1X,F3.0)                            INT03220
        104 FORMAT(1X,I4)                                           INT03230
        105 FORMAT(/////)                                           INT03240
        106 FORMAT(10(1X,F7.3))                                     INT03250
        107 FORMAT(10X,I3)                                          INT03260
        108 FORMAT(10(1X,F4.0))                                     INT03270
        109 FORMAT(10(1X,I4))                                       INT03280
        110 FORMAT(1X,I4)                                           INT03290
         88 STOP                                                    INT03300
            END                                                     INT03310
```

14

The Contiguity-Anomaly Technique for Analysis of Spatial Variation

BRUCE G. GLADFELTER
CLIFFORD E. TIEDEMANN

Problems that arise in the mapping and interpretation of spatial data are not unique to geographers. The adoption of geographical methods by non-geographers, however, can involve the risk of inappropriate application of methodologies. The ensuing discussions stem from a sense that geographical work in the area of spatial statistics, especially measures of spatial autocorrelation, should have something to contribute to the solving of archaeological problems. In this chapter we are concerned with the recognition of spatial variability within an arrangement of data—variation that conventional analyses of spatial autocorrelation disguise.

Description and interpretation of intra-site spatial structure is a fundamental step in the analysis of data at both pre- and post-excavation stages of archaeological investigation. Many data are generated in choroplethic form, that is, they are gathered in a grid-cell format. Examples include pedestrian surveys that record artifact density, geophysical surveys (resistivity, magnetometry) that do not use continuous measurement and recording techniques, and chemical surveys such as phosphate testing. The spatial structure of excavated materials is also evaluated in choroplethic form, as in the case where the artifacts are recorded by number per unit area. Basic questions concern the recognition of pattern in the location of phenomena (clustering, randomness, uniformity, etc.) and the delimitation of boundaries of the components of the pattern.

The choroplethic structure readily supports the mapping of raw data and the

Certain aspects of this chapter were presented at the 1980 and 1981 annual meetings of the Society for American Archaeology. Bonnie Hole participated in the latter presentation and in many discussions of this material, particularly in regard to spatial autocorrelation computations and their comparability. Magnetometry data were generated with a grant from the Illinois Department of Conservation to Robert L. Hall and Bruce G. Gladfelter. Facilities and services of the Cartographic Laboratory, University of Illinois at Chicago, and the UIC Computer Center are gratefully acknowledged. The authors' names are listed alphabetically.

analyses of results, and allows the use of a variety of computerized analytical procedures aimed at providing an understanding of whatever patterns may be represented by the data. Imposing a Cartesian grid on data as one dimension of classification is accomplished easily and cheaply, does not counter data needs of other forms of processing, and perhaps most importantly, is compatible with long established archaeological practice.

The technique discussed in this chapter can be used to discern pattern in spatial arrangements and boundaries of the components of the pattern when data are presented in choroplethic form. The technique, the *Contiguity-Anomaly* (CA) method, is a procedure for analysis of spatial autocorrelation that does not require innovative forms or procedures of archaeological data collection. Because intra-site survey techniques conventionally generate information in grid-cell form (or, as in the case of piece-plotting, in Cartesian coordinates that are amenable to grid-cell treatment), the method can be used to reevaluate already existing information from previous surveys, as well as that from surveys yet to be conducted. In postexcavation contexts, use of the CA method may contribute to the recognition of "activity areas" (or more generally, areas of artifact deposition) by highlighting *foci* and/or *edges* within a spatial distribution of artifacts, and may distinguish between meaningful and meaningless, isolated finds. Sufficiently large areal features, in turn, may be subjected to separate examination of spatial structure in order to identify and delimit internal arrangements that can be masked when analysis includes widely ranging classes of depositional and nondepositional areas.

Whereas postexcavation analysis of the spatial arrangement of artifacts deals with matters of "where," pre-excavation analysis seems to address problems of "whether," particularly in the case of CRM mitigation projects. In this context, use of the CA method allows recognition of local spatial variation within a survey area and classification of locales as relatively "interesting" or "uninteresting," thereby permitting valuable work resources to be used most effectively.

When applied to archaeological problems, the spatial analytical methods emphasized herein imply certain assumptions about the nature of archaeological data and the preferred characteristics of analysis:

1) The size of cells comprising the observational grid, or the spacing of points at which observations are made, is presumed to be appropriate to (equivalent to or smaller than) the size of features being sought or delimited.
2) A high degree of spatial autocorrelation is not presumed. Observations are not assumed to be samplings drawn from a continuous surface, which is an underlying assumption of trend surface analysis, krigging, spatial filtering, and many other spatial techniques (see Parker, chapter 8). This seems appropriate because many archaeological features, such as wall trenches or hearths, possess properties that are very different

from their surroundings, and these differences are likely to be reflected in the data that are evaluated.
3) Spatial data are presumed to reflect meaningful arrangements. That is, anticipated clusters of like objects in or measurements of the archaeological record will appear as cluters, although perhaps only subtly.
4) The so-called *boundary problem*, which is critical in the evaluation of results from analyses of spatial autocorrelation, is to be neutralized insofar as that is possible. Only on rare occasions do competent cartographers have difficulty positioning contour lines near the edges of maps. Objective analysis of continuous surfaces does not, however, offer similar ease of manipulation or interpretation.
5) Characteristics of the statistics of the data are to be preserved and exploited whenever possible. Long or short tails of cell value distributions are to be incorporated into the analysis, rather than arbitrarily truncated or inappropriately transformed into statistical distributions having different qualities.

The ensuing discussion first summarizes and critiques cogent elements of spacing and autocorrelation methods. Because such methods provide a single-number summary statistic of global spatial pattern, we refer to them as being directed toward spatial autocorrelation "in the large." Second, an alternative approach—the Contiguity-Anomaly method—is developed for measuring spatial autocorrelation "in the small" allowing the classification of *individual* grid-cells or points in terms of their similarity to or dissimilarity from adjacent values. Third, we discuss the applicability of the CA method to identifying locationally anomalous cell values in pre- and post-excavation problems. Finally, the summary briefly includes some speculations regarding the appropriateness of the CA method for other important analytical problems dealing with spatial arrangements.

SPATIAL AUTOCORRELATION

Measures of spatial autocorrelation assess the locational variability of a phenomenon in two-dimensional space. In effect, the presence, absence, or measure of a variable at one location is compared (i.e., correlated) with the same property at one or more other locations. In practice, this translates to an assessment of the degree to which like objects are located near each other. This property can be measured in several ways, using some measure of the separation of places at which like objects are found, as with distance measures (i.e., first or nth order nearest neighbors), real numerical values for respective locations (i.e., numbers of artifacts in meter squares), or an accounting of the contiguousness of places with like properties (i.e., join-count statistics).

The outcomes of such analyses provide a statement of a spatial relatedness of a variable within a particular region. The presence of a high degree of positive spatial autocorrelation means that individual locations bear a strong similarity to those in their close proximity. That is, there is a pervasive structure within the region characterized by the spatial association of like things or measures of things. When a high degree of negative spatial autocorrelation occurs it indicates that the pervasive regional pattern is one of nearby locations having unlike things or measures of things.

Low degrees of positive or negative spatial autocorrelation indicate that observations gathered in close proximity are neither unusually like or unlike their neighbors, on the average compared to conditions that might be expected with random placement of the observations about the study area. It does not indicate the absence of very similar or dissimilar values gathered at nearby locations in some small subareas within the study area—pockets of locally high spatial autocorrelation—but *does* indicate, in a global sense, that locally high degrees of spatial autocorrelation are not so common as to dominate the outcome of an analysis.

Non-Contiguity Measures

Quantitative analysis of arrangements has been performed using a variety of methods, many of which explicitly or implicitly assess object spacing and only obliquely address the matter of spatial autocorrelation. Nearest neighbor analysis and analysis of distributions of distances separating higher order neighbors (Dacey, 1959, 1963; Thompson, 1956) are examples of techniques that draw on distance measurements, but do not directly assess the presence or nature of spatial autocorrelation. As with virtually all measures of areal pattern, *first* or higher order neighbor statistics indicate only *overall* conditions of arrangement of objects within a delimited study area.

It is possible to make procedural variations in such analyses and to compare the results in order to determine the presence and type of spatial autocorrelation within a data set. Typically, variations in analytic results within a particular site may be sought by redefining the membership or range of classes of objects subject to such analyses. And by systematically varying the size of study areas, internally homogeneous features may be isolated and bounded (Hsu & Tiedemann, 1968).

Repeated redefinition of classes, however, is a cumbersome and logically straining procedure when objects possess characteristics that resemble observations on a continuous distribution. Such problems lend themselves to regression analysis in which spacing is regressed against the continuous variable. However, the distance measurements must be transformed according to unique standardizing factors if the resultant regression parameters are to be tested using inferential methods (Tiedemann, 1978, 1979). In this context, significance tests of the regression coefficients may indicate the presence or absence of different degrees of spatial autocorrelation among the observations. Under the condition where the slope of the regression line is found to be not significantly different from zero, tests of the intercept value may reveal the overall arrangement characteristic of the objects under study in the same terms as traditional nearest neighbor analysis. Analysis of the standard error of the estimate yields insights as to the global qualities of such arrangements as well. Unlike other forms of distance analysis, though, the regression model preserves the identity of individual observations and permits further study of unaccounted-for variation, that is, residual analysis.

Assessment of object spacing is also implicit in *curve fitting* comparisons of observed frequency counts of occurrence for grid-cells to expectations based on assumptions of random placement of objects within study areas (Grieg-Smith, 1952; Getis & Boots, 1978). Obviously, higher cell frequencies indicate greater densities and closer spacing among those objects found within individual grid-cells. Classifying objects so as to include them or exclude them from the counting procedure can also become a major concern for this sort of spacing analysis because each object incorporated into the study is seen to possess no qualitative variation from all the others.

Methods for assessing neighbor distances are logical outgrowths of *quadrat counting* procedures, as can be seen in early derivations of nearest neighbor distance expectations (Clark & Evans, 1954; Dacey, 1959; Dacey & Tung, 1962). It is expectable, then, that the problem of requisite object classification is shared by traditional nearest neighbor and quadrat counting techniques. Quite different from traditional analytical methods that take into account the spacing of objects are those that account for spatial variations of qualitative characteristics, such as the sequence in which different sorts of observations may be encountered as an observer "moves about" a study area. These methods, because they focus on arrangements of like phenomena among contiguous cells, are commonly known as *contiguity measures* and are most frequently used to ascertain the degree of spatial autocorrelation present in a study area. As with methods focusing on spacing, the outcomes of most contiguity analyses are expressed in terms of comparison with an expectation reflecting a random placement process. Thus, conclusions are typically limited to statements containing key phrases such as ". . . more clustered than might be expected according to the assumption of random placement . . ." or ". . . more uniform than . . ."

Contiguity Measures

The variety of contiguity analysis which is conceptually the simplest is conducted using tallies of joins between cells containing data of a similar class. These analyses may involve two or a limited number of mutually exclusive data categories (Dacey, 1965; Cliff et al., 1975). In any case, an expectation based on the assumption of random placement can be computed using the observed proportions of cells within each category compared to the total number of cells. As with nearest and higher order neighbor distance analyses, manipulation of class and study area boundaries may be employed in order to detect subtle variations in spatial arrangements that can be linked to those observations or to cells marginally brought into or deleted from repetitive analyses. Of course, when studies involve reasonably large numbers of observations, the inclusion or exclusion of single or quite small numbers of cells in any category of cell is not likely to significantly alter the outcome.

Contiguity analysis of spatial arrangements may be carried out following methods which computationally resemble well-established inferrential statistical techniques and which allow reference to tables of the normal distribution (Moran, 1950; Geary, 1954; Cliff & Ord, 1969). These approaches yield ratios of summations of computations using pairs of observations to an appropriate factor of the population variance. In the case of Moran's I statistic, the numerator of the ratio is basically the sum, over each pair of contiguous cells, of cross-products of their deviations from the population mean (Appendix A). Geary's C statistic has as its numerator the sum of squared differences between values associated with adjacent cells (Appendix A). The two statistics are linearly related under conditions of random placement of values among cells within a study area (Appendix A).

Moran's I may be used to assess the degree of spatial autocorrelation among values assigned to arbitrarily placed points, as opposed to grid cells, by incorporating inverses of distances between observation points and summing over all possible pairings. However, the standardizing computations are considerably more complex for Geary's C statistic than with the case of grid-cells: indeed, they are so complex as to preclude such applications (Cliff & Ord, 1973). For gridded data, weighting schemes taking into account perimeter conditions of individual cells with respect to their adjacent neighbors, as well as the spacing of cell centers, has been suggested (Cliff & Ord, 1969). When dealing with square grids and symmetrical space, however, these terms reduce to constants and are safely ignored.

Limitations of the Statistics

Whether a measure of distance or of spatial autocorrelation, all of the statistics mentioned thus far have several traits in common. One is that most provide a single numerical parameter that categorizes the *overall* spatial pattern represented by objects or cells subjected to analysis. This statistic is then compared with a table of a well-known distribution. If its value lies in an extreme portion of the range of values reflecting a random generating process, the arrangement described by the statistic is judged to be significantly different from that which is apt to have been created by a random placement process.

A second common trait is that the range of possible results of all of the techniques mentioned above can be influenced by certain characteristics of the study area. Delimitation of spatial boundaries of the study area, for example, affects analysis of both spacing and cell adjacency. In point pattern analysis, the presence of boundaries forces recognition of neighbors at greater distances than might be identified if a search procedure extended uninhibitedly in all directions; orders of neighbors higher than the first are more seriously affected because their separations are necessarily greater. Join tallies are similarly impacted because cells along study area boundaries necessarily have fewer contiguous neighbors than interior cells, and corner cells are even more affected. Clearly, study areas with compact shapes are to be preferred over more sinuous shapes whenever a measure fails in the above ways.

Of the spacing methods mentioned, perhaps only one approach is not severely affected by the boundary problem. This approach involves the counting of points or objects within grid-cells and compares the frequencies of such tallies with an expectation based on the assumption of random placement of points among the cells. This approach, however, may lead to erroneous conclusions, for cell counts having a *frequency distribution* expectable under the assumption of random placement may be *arranged* spatially in a clustered manner (Hietala & Stevens, 1977). Moreover, these quadrat counting methods are severely affected by the size of cells into which objects are assigned. Excessively large cells will bias the result of an analysis toward the clustered end of the spectrum of possibilities, whereas excessively small cells will bias the outcome toward the regular or uniform end of the spectrum (Grieg-Smith, 1952, 1964). The effect of cell size on *join-count* statistics for noncontinuous data is somewhat more subtle; large cells cause a study area to be divided into a smaller number of cells, thus decreasing the proportion of interior cells and increasing the proportion of boundary cells, and biasing the analysis toward identifying more extreme arrangements—either more clustered or more regular than random.

Moran's I and Geary's C statistics are considerably less severely impacted by varying numbers of joins between adjacent cells. This is because the ratios upon which they depend include terms for numbers of joins in the region, not the number of joins per cell (Appendix A). Only in the standardizing computations is provision made for taking into account varying numbers of joins per cell, which in the instance of archaeological survey areas implies differentiation among interior, edge, and corner cells. However, the identity of an individual cell is lost in the computation of these two statistics (as well as for most of the others described above).

THE CONTIGUITY-ANOMALY METHOD

Because traditional spacing and spatial autocorrelation statistics offer little opportunity for identifying anomalous locations within a study area, an alternative method for studying spatial variation—one that focuses on detail rather than overall pattern—is proposed. This approach allows 1) the difference of a cell's value from the values of adjacent cells to be assessed for its significance and 2) the classification of a cell with regard to the relative magnitude of both its value and local differences. With these objectives as the bases for building such a method, the contributions of individual cell calculations to the computation of Moran's I and Geary's C—particularly to the numerators of these two ratios—are considered. The ratio proposed by Cliff and Ord (1969) is not considered here for reasons previously described.

The sums of cross-products of deviations from the mean in Moran's I does not seem appropriate for construction of the desired statistic because of potential ambiguities in the results. Summation of cross-products can yield divergent positive and negative numbers which usually indicate small and large differences between the observation for a central cell and those of adjacent units. But this is not always the case; for example, a moderate numerical observation surrounded by similar values yields a relatively high sum of cross-products, whereas the same value in the midst of dissimilar ones can produce a relatively low sum of cross-products. Even a very extreme numerical observation that is flanked on all sides by values slightly above and below the global mean may have its uniqueness dampened by the summing of nearly comparable positive and negative cross-products. Because all three of these conditions are not extraordinary, such insensitivity to extreme local variations compromises the worth of sums of cross-products for recognizing local variation.

The contribution of individual cells to the numerator of Geary's ratio provides somewhat more orderly results. All sums of squared differences (SSDs) are positive, of course, and the ambiguities arising from cross-product computations are not problematical. Similarity of values in adjacent cells is indicated by a low sum of squared differences, regardless of the positions of the numerical values in the total distribution of observations. Dissimilarity among values in adjacent cells is indicated by high sums of squared differences. Thus, sums of squared differences between values in adjacent cells, along with the cell values themselves, form the basis of Contiguity-Anomaly analysis.

It is desirable to compare the value of a sum of squared differences to that expected under the assumption of random placement. The distributional position of an SSD, along with that of the cell value, might then be used to classsify the individual cell with regard to its relative importance or interest. Under the assumption of random placement, the distribution of sums of squared differences somewhat resembles a $2\sigma^2 \chi^2$ distribution with the number of degrees of freedom being the number of adjacent cells—four, except for cells along the edges of the survey tract (Fig. 1). In the rare case where a central cell may have only a single neighbor, it is reasonable to accept values from a table of the χ^2 statistic reflecting one degree of freedom and an acceptable error level to be a prior criteria for identifying cells of interest. However, because the value for the central cell is fixed in the computation of sums of squared differences, the independency requirement of that distribution is violated and comparison of such sums over larger numbers of adjacent cells with values of the χ^2 statistic is invalid. Specially prepared tables for comparison are required even when values assigned to cells throughout a grid are randomly drawn samplings from a

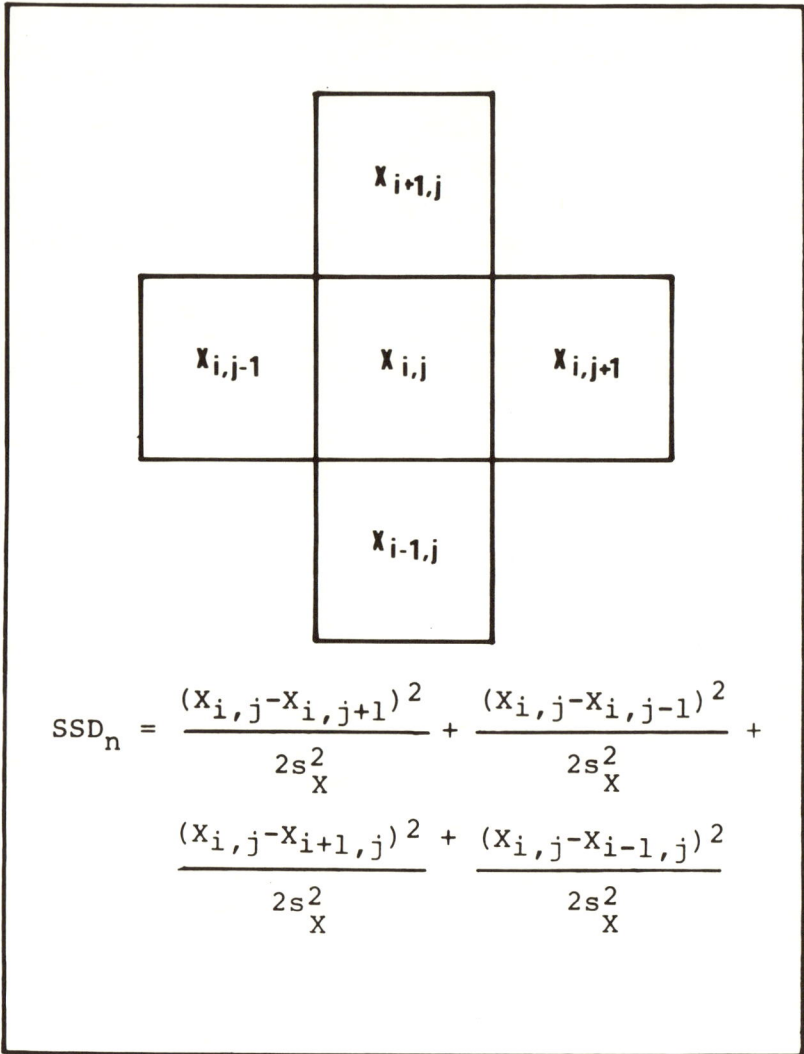

Fig. 14.1. Central and adjacent cells used in CA computations.

normal distribution with mean zero and unit variance (Table 1). Other statistical distributions—for instance the uniform distribution covering the range zero through one—require additional sets of figures, one set for each number of adjacent cells (Table 2).

Given the desirability of comparing a cell's SSD to a particular expectation, but the fact that cell values seldom conform to well-known statistical distributions, an alternative strategy is adopted. This approach views an observed

Table 14.1

Cumulative Probability Distributions of SSDs for Central Cells with K Adjacencies Estimated Using Monte Carlo Methods: Cell Values Drawn Randomly from a Normally Distributed Population with Mean Zero and Unit Variance

Percentile Rankings	Numbers of Adjacent Neighbors, K			
	1	2	3	4
	Sums of Squared Differences, SSDs			
99.0	6.5656	10.3994	14.2463	17.9811
97.5	4.9984	8.0909	11.1518	14.1568
95.0	3.8277	6.3781	8.8616	11.2950
90.0	2.6983	4.7427	6.6389	8.5413
85.0	2.0684	2.7869	5.4141	6.9840
80.0	1.6407	3.1489	4.5682	5.9364
75.0	1.3204	2.6822	3.9336	5.1561
70.0	1.0739	2.2939	3.4382	4.5355
60.0	0.7072	1.7023	2.6677	3.5937
50.0	0.4545	1.2675	2.0778	2.8812
40.0	0.2736	0.9187	1.6077	2.2878
30.0	0.1478	0.6331	1.1966	1.7816
25.0	0.1012	0.5055	1.0113	1.5426
20.0	0.0640	0.3935	0.8325	1.3051
15.0	0.0357	0.2864	0.6501	1.0707
10.0	0.0157	0.1802	0.4760	0.8257
5.0	0.0039	0.0893	0.2813	0.5449
2.5	0.0010	0.0451	0.1705	0.3646
1.0	0.0002	0.0179	0.0911	0.2211
	SSD Parameters[1]			
Mean	0.9980	2.0005	3.0025	3.9946
Variance	1.9960	5.0110	9.0824	14.0687
Skewness	2.7399	2.5117	2.4588	2.4469
Kurtosis	13.8397	13.2267	12.9694	12.7962
	Cell Value Parameters[1]			
Mean	−0.0020	−0.0026	−0.0010	−0.0017
Variance	0.9966	0.9943	0.9956	0.9973
Skewness	−0.0033	−0.0056	−0.0046	−0.0052
Kurtosis	2.9873	2.9911	2.9919	2.9993

[1] Parameters computed following Ebdon (1977)

Table 14.2

Cumulative Probability Distributions of SSDs for Central Cells with K Adjacencies Estimated Using Monte Carlo Methods: Cell Values Drawn Randomly from a Uniformly Distributed Population with a Range of Zero through One

Percentile Rankings	Numbers of Adjacent Neighbors, K			
	1	2	3	4
	Sums of Squared Differences, SSDs			
99.0	4.8259	7.7754	10.2581	12.7617
97.5	4.2342	6.6297	8.9556	11.1279
95.0	3.6028	5.5703	7.6894	9.6844
90.0	2.7957	4.5665	6.2749	8.0237
85.0	2.2468	3.8309	5.3805	6.9586
80.0	1.8277	3.3207	4.7082	6.1099
75.0	1.4905	2.8792	4.1476	5.7448
70.0	1.2169	2.5199	3.6835	4.8472
60.0	0.8053	1.9565	2.9569	3.9346
50.0	0.5101	1.4926	2.3958	3.2333
40.0	0.2990	1.1083	1.9034	2.6708
30.0	0.1582	0.7722	1.4737	2.1676
25.0	0.1066	0.6149	1.2623	1.9053
20.0	0.0657	0.4753	1.0512	1.6514
15.0	0.0357	0.3451	0.8356	1.3749
10.0	0.0157	0.2219	0.6073	1.0785
5.0	0.0037	0.1061	0.3580	0.7203
2.5	0.0009	0.0515	0.2164	0.4879
1.0	0.0002	0.0205	0.1137	0.2921
	SSD Parameters[1]			
Mean	0.9965	2.0006	2.9999	3.9932
Variance	1.4002	3.2040	5.4041	8.0107
Skewness	1.5161	1.3399	1.2675	1.2260
Kurtosis	4.7541	4.7887	4.6355	4.4896
	Cell Value Parameters[1]			
Mean	0.4994	0.4993	0.4997	0.4998
Variance	0.0822	0.0831	0.0832	0.0832
Skewness	0.0007	0.0014	0.0005	0.0001
Kurtosis	1.7994	1.7995	1.7990	1.7994

[1] Parameters computed following Ebdon (1977)

arrangement of data from grid-cells as being perhaps only one of a large number of spatial patterns that can be generated by random placement of values among cells in a study area. Monte Carlo simulation methods can be used to develop approximations to cumulative probability distributions of sums of squared differences, from which the necessary critical values for classification of individual cells can be determined. Specifically, by adopting the convention that the space over which the study is being conducted is symmetrical in all directions, the computation in the numerator of Geary's C may be modified to read as

$$SSD_n = \sum_{k=1}^{K} (x_k - x_n)^2 / 2\sigma^2$$

where n = an individual cell within a data matrix having I rows and J columns, and $I \cdot J = N$ cells; K = the number of contiguous cells: 4 for interior, 3 for edge, and 2 for corner locations; x = the observed value for a particular cell, as per Figure 1; and σ = the standard deviation of the cell observations.

For each cycle of the Monte Carlo simulation, then, this equation requires recording, for each cell n, the sum of squared differences between its value and those of K adjacent cells, the values of which have been randomly relocated throughout the study area, thus ensuring sampling without replacement. The entire cycle, random rearrangement followed by computation of the SSDs, is repeated so as to approximate a cumulative probability distribution with sufficient entries to accommodate decision-rule needs, so long as one does not risk repetitious sequences of n and its respective ks beyond a very small fraction of the summations dictated by chance alone. (Clearly, the chances of that happening are quite remote for all but the smallest archaeological grids.) Finally, the procedure is repeated for all possible values of K, two through four for grids with rectangular perimeters and square cells.

Under circumstances where inferential statistics are not demanded by the problem being analyzed, the complex Monte Carlo procedure for determining critical values for categorizing cell deviations may be by-passed (Fig. 2). Three examples come to mind. First, is the analysis of postexcavation data where the purpose is to identify and delimit features that are already known to exist, according to some rationale that allows subtle as well as obviously anomalous arrangements to be recognized. The same approach can be applied to pre-excavation survey data where it is certain that large cell deviations, relative to others, correspond to subsurface features. Under these conditions, it may be reasonable to simply identify as "interesting" the five or ten percentage point extremes of the data and sums of squared differences distributions, rather than specifying particular critical values.

Second, in instances were pre-excavation survey is to be expanded on a proven site or where it is to be shifted to locations of suspected sites having comparable environmental conditions and archaeological expectations, already

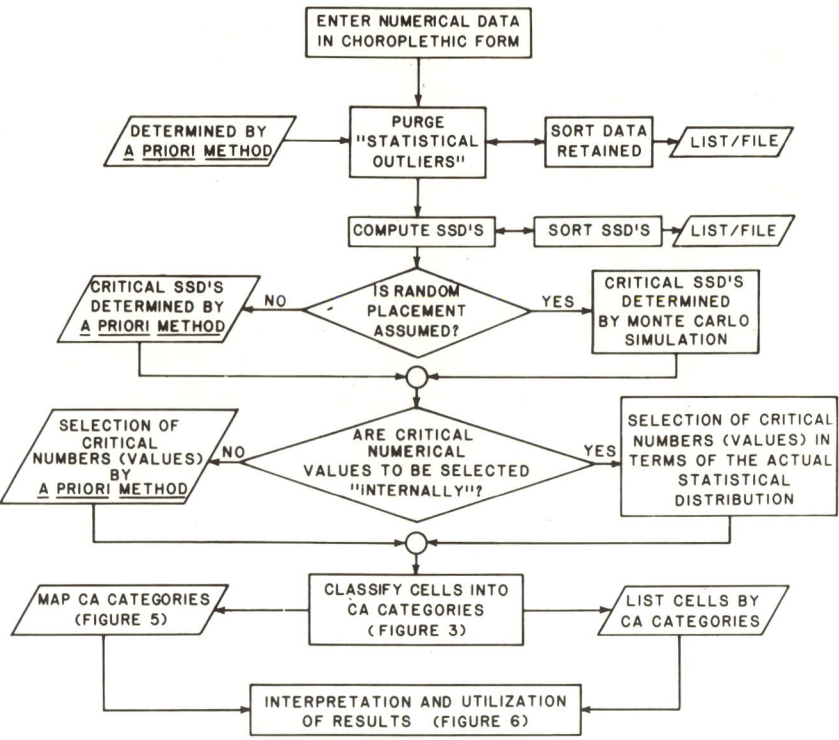

Fig. 14.2. Flow chart for CA application: *parallelograms* indicate computer inputs and outputs; *diamonds* indicate decision requirements; *rectangles* indicate computational procedures; *trapezoids* indicate manual operations; *lines* trace logical sequences of computations; and *circles* show junctions of alternate paths of computation.

successful critical values may be transferred as well. Third, in pre-excavation contexts, in addition to defining critical levels suitable for revealing the location and pattern of interesting cells, it is possible to tailor critical levels such that the percentage of cells and amount of area defined as "interesting" is adjusted to the work effort available for investigating them. In all these cases, the data at hand constitute the entire basis of categorization, without a need to consider whether or not an observed arrangement is one of a plethora of possibilities arising from a random placement process. Although this less involved procedure can save computational time, it leaves the status of edge cells, and especially corner cells, on somewhat less firm footing than interior cells simply because of their smaller numbers.

Statistical distributions of observations that include a small number of widely divergent values, *statistical outliers*, should be screened and such observations removed from consideration. In instances of identifying critical SSDs through

Monte Carlo simulation, a few excessively extreme values will produce larger variances than would otherwise be the case; because these sums are standardized using the variance, biased classifications may result. In instances where CA classes are determined on the basis of frequencies rather than critical values, central cells that otherwise are not particularly noteworthy may be inappropriately categorized as being significantly different from their neighbors because of the severe impact of the one wild value on the SSD.

Identification of statistical outliers can be accomplished in several ways; the procedure used in managing the sets of data discussed below is described in Appendix B. In that procedure, no effort is made to substitute "more acceptable" values for those that have been eliminated because the focus of CA analysis is on local variation and insertion of an inappropriate cell value may thwart the recognition of unusually small or great fluctuations among any or all of the neighboring cells. Furthermore, because the CA analysis is not at all dependent upon a particular number of adjacencies, such fabrications of data are unnecessary.

The definition of categories into which cells are to be classified for subsequent choroplethic display will be determined by the investigator, consistent with the task at hand. As one example, a matrix of nine categories has been defined in Figure 3, using the value of a central cell and its associated sum of squared differences from adjoining cells as the two dimensions of classification. Each illustration represents the numerical value of a real observation (n) with respect to the values of its adjoining observations (k). Diagram C-1 in Figure 3 represents an observation with a high value amid observations of considerably lower numerical values, box C-2 portrays an observation of moderate value among somewhat dissimilar numerical values, and so forth. These graphic representations highlight the ability of the CA method to evaluate spatial variation "in the small," and to yield nominal data for subsequent mapping. For ease of expression, CA categories are referenced by column and row (A-1, A-3, C-3, etc.) in the following discussion.

The Contiguity-Anomaly scheme of classification accomplishes several things. 1) The separate treatment of central cells having different numbers of adjacent cells, which we liken to numbers of degrees of freedom, ameliorates the boundary problem. 2) By taking into account sums of squared differences between values of central cells and those of their immediate neighbors, a means is provided for identifying cells of interest by themselves or as components of areally extensive features, without requiring measurement and analysis of additional variables. 3) Selection of critical values is accomplished on the basis of a priori determination of category frequencies reflecting predilections toward either theoretical statistical, pragmatic operational, or economic concerns. 4) Because Monte Carlo simulation of random placement is used to develop cumulative probability distributions of sums of squared differences, the critical values used in categorization decision rules are internalized and reflect the data

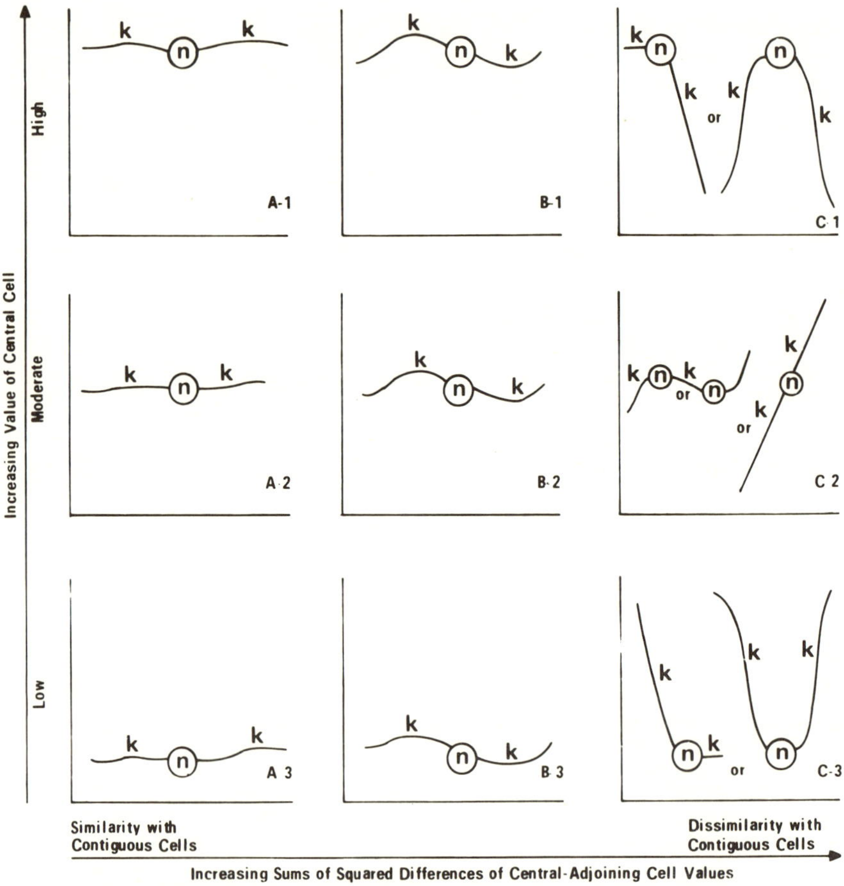

Fig. 14.3. Diagramatic representation of CA categories. The curve(s) in each of the categories, labelled A-1 through C-3 as referenced in the text, represent(s) the field of numbered values (*k*) adjacent to the central cell (*n*). The sets in categories C-1, C-2, and C-3 illustrate two types of numerical fields within which a central cell might be located.

that are being used, rather than some other presumed or assumed statistical distribution.

POTENTIAL APPLICATION IN ARCHAEOLOGY

Because traditional, spatial autocorrelation analytic methods yield only one-number descriptors of overall arrangement, these methods have not been used to interpret internal arrangements of spatial patterns. Generally, grid networks are interpreted using isoplethic (contouring) procedures (e.g., SYMAP), with or without spatial filtering techniques such as trend surface analysis. These approaches have limitations. Valid use of trend surface analysis presumes an underlying spatial autocorrelation, the isolation of interestingly anomalous cells being very dependent upon the order of the polynomial used to specify the generalized surface. Implicit in the use of isoplethic treatments, such as the SYMAP algorithm, is the assumption that the observer can recognize the signatures of causal phenomena within the spatial array and that supplemental filtering can remove large scale, regional trends so that smaller scale features may be recognized. Choroplethic maps, by contrast, are more naive constructs of data collected in a Cartesian grid format; they are not subject to imputed confusion caused by interpolation of surface configurations.

Pre-excavation Spatial Distributions

Because the CA method is conceptually based on choroplethic mapping of cell data, it is well suited to evaluation of magnetometry surveys: obviously aberrant readings are easily screened from the statistical distribution (Appendix B); cellular values along the edges of the grid can be evaluated unencumbered by the boundary problem; and less obvious magnetic anomalies can be disclosed in addition to strong ones. We evaluated some of the results of a proton magnetometry survey (gradiometric mode) conducted as part of a larger project designed to document the occurrence of subsurface archaeological features at the Cahokia site (Gladfelter et al., 1979). The CA method was used to compare its objective analytical results with the subjective assessments made earlier by an archaeologist. The four survey units examined consisted of a total of 4,029 points each centered in a meter square. A few cells within the grid had been shovel probed or tested by excavation.

Large magnetic anomalies isolated by the CA analysis were found to correspond with locations that had been selected for test-probing using raw magnetic data. Eight cells, several of which were identified as statistical outliers prior to CA analysis, contained nails, horseshoes, cans, wire and the like. When tested, seven different clusters of anomalous cell values produced cultural material (a celt, flakes, scrapers, ceramics, a possible hearth).

More interesting than the identifications of these obviously anomalous cells are the other, more subtle choices made by the analysis. Some 80 cells (roughly 5% of the total number) were identified with magnetic values which were less extreme ($+3$ through -8) but quite different from their contiguous cells. These included dipolar anomalies of varying strengths. Moreover, these locations were in different magnetic environments: a survey unit with a generally negative field; a unit that was highly diverse magnetically; and a unit with little magnetic variability. In each case, the cells identified by the computer program had not previously attracted the attention of the archaeologist and, therefore, were not tested by excavation. Analysis of local variations in these data by the CA method showed that appreciably more of the area surveyed is of potential importance than was recognized by subjective criteria. The CA method may be sensitive to the same sorts of variations as a subjective interpreter, but because its computations are preformed blindly and a single a priori classification scheme is used, it is not overwhelmed by the presence of a few, very conspicuous cell values or local variations.

In Figure 4, magnetometric values obtained for another portion of the same areal survey are presented in choroplethic form. This network consisted of 728 cells in a 26x28 matrix; cell values are gamma differences between two simultaneous magnetometric readings in a gradiometric mode. The choropleth map of cell values depicts ten quantiles of values that include varying percentages of the total numerical distribution, from the lowest 2.0% to the highest 0.5% of the values (i.e., quantiles 2.0, 7.0, 18.5, 37.4, 18.3, 7.6, 3.3, 2.6, 1.8, and

Fig. 14.4. Choropleth map of raw data from magnetometry.

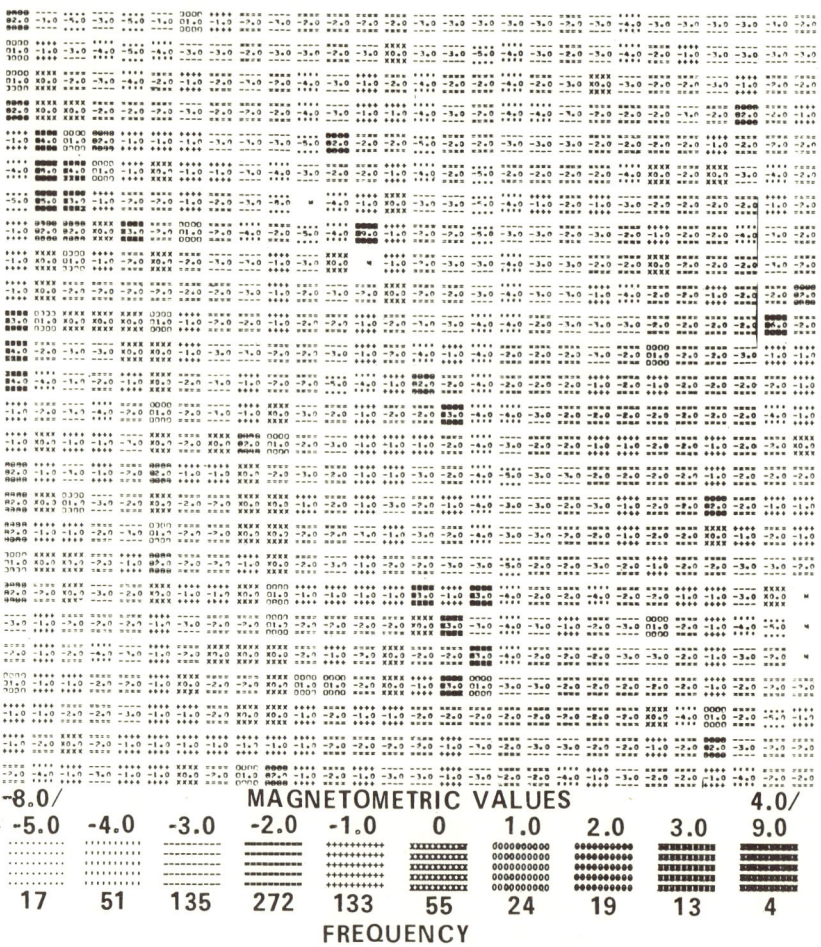

0.5%, respectively, subject to rounding error). This procedure for defining categories of values was selected because the data are treated as integers and because the range of observed values is small compared to the intervals separating them—there are many observations of certain values (272 −2s, 135 −3s, etc.).

Fig. 14.5. CA classification of choropleth map of magnetometry data.

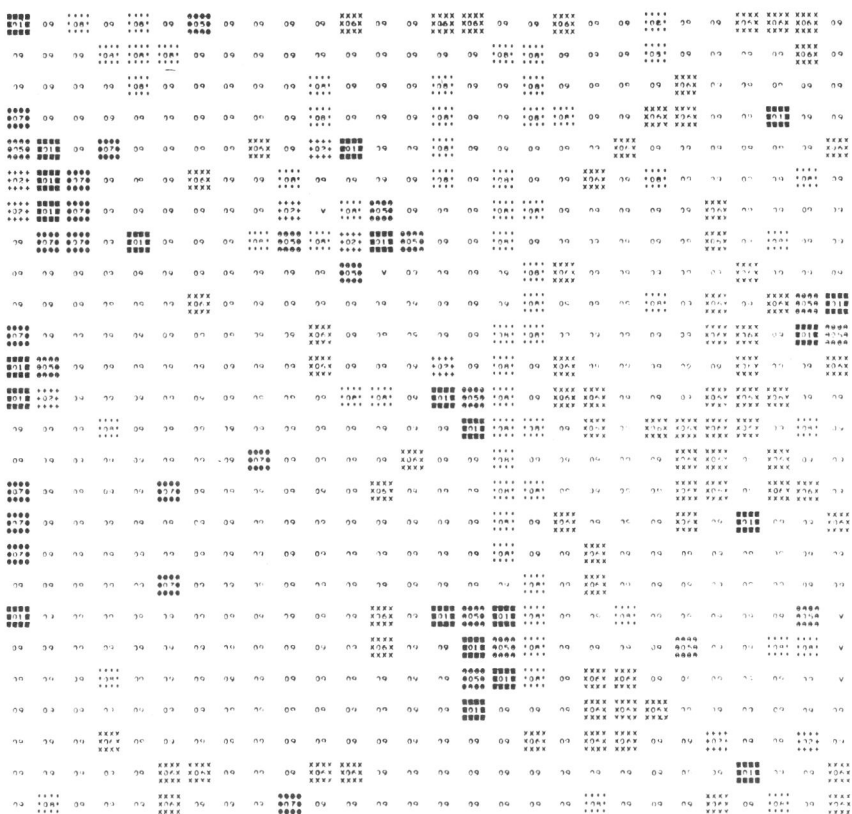

In preparation for applying the CA method, extreme magnetometric values were eliminated from the distribution. Elimination of the cells does affect the mean and variance of cell values included in the analysis, but to considerable advantage because the precision of statistical analysis is enhanced. In pragmatic terms, the eliminated cells intuitively would have attracted attention in any case. Cells adjacent to those containing aberrant values were treated similarly to the manner in which cells along the edge of the study area were handled. That is, if they were originally adjacent to four cells, one of which contained a wildly different value, they were treated as being adjacent to three cells with the actual values observed.

A choropleth map of CA categories for the magnetometric data clarifies significantly the spatial arrangement (Fig. 5). There is some similarity with the choropleth map of the raw data, mostly in the coincidence of general areas of extreme values. The CA map additionally, however, isolates particular cells in terms of their degree of difference from adjoining cells. In evaluating magnetometric results, the locations of such abrupt changes in values and their sign are of interest and these are identified by the CA technique, whether moderate or extreme observations are involved (CA categories C-2, and C-1 or C-3, respectively; Fig. 3). The intermediate or "gray" areas of the distribution (CA category B-2) have been suppressed; these cells comprise 81% of the distribution in our example and hold little interest. Thus, the CA method allows for the identification of cells which have values very different from adjoining cells and which, because they may not be extreme values, would not otherwise be selected for investigation. In other words, weak local variations within a spatial array can be isolated, and the positions of these variations in the cumulative probability distribution of all cell values may be used to denote whether or not it merits investigation within the time and cost constraints of the investigator.

Excavated Spatial Distributions

An arrangement of artifacts at a site is the material legacy of many activities. It can include elements of occupational activity and of postoccupational disturbances, but in either case, it represents only those things that were recovered. Pattern recognition and isolation of spatial components can be accomplished by Contiguity-Anomaly analysis, perhaps initially using the total recovered assemblage (distribution map of all artifacts) and subsequently using distributions of selected artifact types. In addition, spatial structures of certain measurements of the artifactual population (measures of artifact attributes, statistical moments of certain properties of artifacts for cells, ratios of artifact types, etc.) can be evaluated in terms of locational contiguity, and as a result, boundaries of spatial distributions can be recognized. The CA method is amenable to treatments of all of these things.

For the simplest case, consider a hypothetical map of the total distribution of artifacts excavated from a particular surface which, although point-plotted, can be easily transformed to grid-cell units. The results of a CA analysis can be interpreted in terms of the simplified matrix shown in Figure 6. The archaeological meaning of contiguity association is, of course, a matter of personal inference, and interpretations will vary with the cultural affinity of the site as well as among investigators. However, patterns referenced in Figure 6 might be interpreted as (A) represents a depositional (work or disposal) area; (B) an area originally not used, an area the use of which produced no artifacts, an area swept clean, or an area postoccupationally disturbed; (C) part of an area of concentrated use or uses; (D) an area of limited utilization or from which artifacts have been collected; (E) an area not used intensively or having had uses that produced few recoverable material traces.

These possibilities and other notions may be refined by CA treatment of subsets of the total artifact distribution. At this simplest level, the CA method goes beyond locating cells with high or low artifact density; it can isolate artifact concentrations, regardless of the density level, that are different from surrounding cells or, conversely and unlike other applications, density concentrations that are like adjoining cells. These determinations are more than intuitive or subjective appreciations because the cell values are assessed in terms of significance with respect to the total array of cell density differences represented by the data.

Areal boundaries may be erected for differently classified zones, the efficacy of which will be largely a function of the spatial and nonspatial data structure of the cell values. If, for example, it is assumed that the classification scheme in Figure 5 represents numbers of artifacts per cell rather than magnetometric values as is actually the case, areas of different artifact aggradation can be bounded rather neatly. Much of the area in Figure 5 is of little interest (CA category B-2), whereas concentrations are highlighted. Furthermore, the nature

Fig. 14.6. CA classification of hypothetical map of artifact densities.

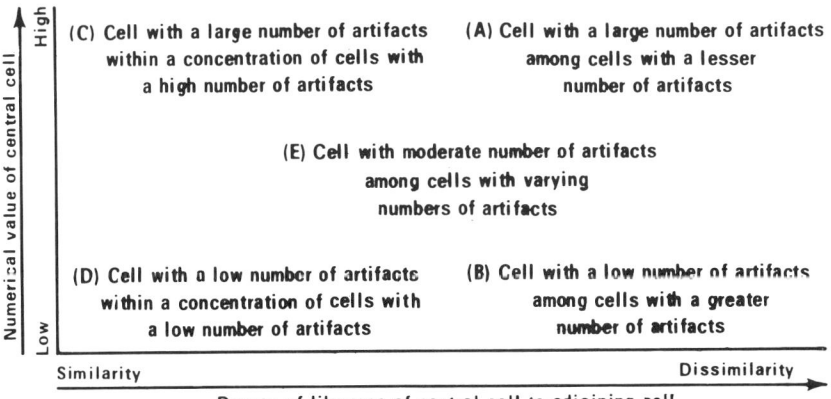

of the spatial boundaries is indicated—abrupt changes in values of contiguous cells or gradual changes.

SUMMARIZING REMARKS AND CONTINUING RESEARCH

The CA method complies with the five implicit assumptions about the nature of archaeological data and preferred characteristics of analysis that are noted in the introduction of this chapter. The innovation of this approach is that by using Monte Carlo simulation, the technique can be applied to any grid-cell data set; the numerical population does not have to conform to a well-known distribution. The technique ameliorates concern over the boundary problem that compromises certain methods of spatial autocorrelation analysis. The ease of computation provides a rapid approach, with flexibility in defining critical values within the numerical distribution that are of interest to the user. Rather than indicating only the degree of clustering, randomness, or regularity in a spatial structure, as do some coefficients of spatial autocorrelation, the CA method assesses additional aspects of spatial form—the varying degrees of similarity among adjacent cell values. Elements of pattern can be recognized and delineated.

Ancillary uses of CA computations can be anticipated. First, the global character of arrangement of values among the cells can be assessed. A Monte Carlo simulation of sums of squared differences can be performed so as to yield N values, and the results sorted to create a cumulative probability distribution reflecting random placement of cell values. The sums of squared differences computed for an observed arrangement of N cell values, sorted to form a second cumulative probability distribution, may be compared to that of the first using the Kolmogorov-Smirnov test. If the cumulative probability distribution of sums of squared differences from observations strays beyond the upper bound of the K-S test, greater regularity than that expected under the assumption of random placement of values among cells is indicated. Should the cumulative probability distribution of sums of squared differences from the observed cell values dip below the lower bound, greater clustering than that expected under the assumption of random placement is indicated at the significance level adopted for specifying the test limits. It must be noted, however, that the boundary problem is not avoided here, since only cells with specific numbers of adjacencies can be used in the Kolmogorov-Smirnov test, thus forcing differentiation among interior, edge, and corner cells.

Second, by determining CA categories for cells in a study area for two different types of items of interest, such as cores and flakes, a crude measure of co-occurrence of these two types can be computed based on the X^2 statistic. A two-way table of CA categories, one dimension for cores and the other for flakes, is developed, and each cell is tallied according to its nominal classification in both dimensions. Expectancies are determined for all table entries in the usual manner and a summary statistic is computed. The computed statistic is then compared to entries in a table of X^2 values for 64 degrees of freedom (assuming all nine CA categories depicted in Fig. 3 are used). Should the computed value be less than expected for the specified σ error level, a high degree of co-occurrence is indicated. If the computed value is greater than expectation for a $1-\sigma$ level, a high degree of negative co-occurrence is suggested. Computed summary statistics between the critical values do not support a working hypothesis to the effect that co-occurrence between the two types of artifacts is stronger than merely coincidental at the time of observation. For the example given, the first outcome supports interpretations that core locations in the survey grid are associated with the locations of flakes; the second, that core locations are distinctly not associated with those of flakes; and the third, that there is no conclusive support for either of the first two hypotheses.

Failure to verify either of the first two hypotheses when intuition suggests their validity should not necessarily be seen as giving support to the notion that one or both of the locational patterns of the two artifact types are based on random placement processes relative to the other. Nor should such an outcome be seen as a repudiation of the idea that the spatial arrangement of the two artifacts has a significant joint probability element. Rather, it may suggest that the original depositional processes were very much interlinked, but subject to either different stochastic processes during the time of deposition or to different modification processes following deposition. Indeed, using Monte Carlo simulation to model such random depositional or postdepositional disturbances in multitype arrangements hypothesized to have had high joint probabilities, along with the CA based procedure outlined above, may permit investigators to break the shackles of the usual null hypothesis that permits distinguishing between only random coarrangement and associations or dissociations that are found to be significant. Ideally, such methods might lead to the possibility of discriminating between truly interlinked depositional events subject to disorganizing processes and unlinked events.

The CA method can be used in locational analyses that do not presume spatial autocorrelation as well as in situations that must assume some degree of spatial autocorrelation. In the first case, the observed spatial arrangement is accepted as a given, and one is interested only in the identification of points or cells that are of a certain degree of similarity or dissimilarity as defined by the user. Analytical procedures in this instance do not require Monte Carlo simulation and the selected cells on a map simply represent high, low, or intermediate values of likeness with respect to adjacent cells. In the second case, on the other hand, using Monte Carlo simulation, the observed spatial distribution is viewed as but one of many that may occur through random placement, and the user determines whether or not spatial autocorrelation "in the small" is significantly different from that arising from random placement. In this case, autocorrelation can be demonstrated and levels of statistical significance of central cell values with respect to adjacent ones can be assessed.

APPENDIX A

The basis of the Contiguity-Anomaly technique for analysis of spatial variation is spatial autocorrelation analysis. In acquiring an appreciation of how SSDs are distributed for varying numbers of adjacencies and under varying conditions of arrangement, much was learned about measures of spatial autocorrelation as well. Below are presented some observations on two statistics of autocorrelation, as well as their formulations using a symbolism allowing comparison of contributing and standardizing terms.

Comments on Moran's I and Geary's C Statistics

Under conditions of random placement of values among cells in a study area, it has been demonstrated that I and C, and their normalized transforms, are linearly related (Fig. 7). One thousand trials involving the placement of 728 randomly selected, normally distributed values (mean zero, unit variance) about a 26x28 cell matrix yielded means for Z_I and Z_C of 0.0622 and 0.0821, respectively, and variances of 0.9942 and 1.0030. Paired by simulation cycle number (1 through 1000), the normalized deviates produced the following parameters of regression (Z_I on Z_C) and correlation: $b = 0.9923$, $a = 0.0204$, $s_{yx} = 0.1551$, and $r = 0.9879$. For experiments using uniformly distributed values with a range of zero through one, the resulting parameters were as follows: mean and variance for estimates of Z_I, 0.0570 and 0.9870; mean and variance for Z_C, 0.0779 and 0.9893; from the regression and correlation analysis of paired observations $b = 0.9961$, $a = 0.0211$, $s_{yx} = 0.1006$, and $r = 0.9949$.

Experience gained during the simulation studies of the CA method also indicates that I and C are fairly tolerant of a wide range of numerical distributions from which cell values may be drawn; that is, both seem to consistently give results that are approximately normally distributed regardless of the statistical distribution of cell values. However, both are fairly intolerant of "statistical outliers." Instances of fewer than one-half of one percent of observed cell values that are several deviations more remote from the mean of the overall numerical distribution have been found to completely reverse the outcome of these computations, resulting in indices higher than expected under the assumption of random placement, suggesting regularity, whereas exclusion of wildly deviating values yields the opposite conclusion (Tiedemann & Gladfelter, 1980). In this last regard, Geary's C appears to be less severely impacted than Moran's I.

THE CONTIGUITY-ANOMALY TECHNIQUE

NORMALLY DISTRIBUTED CELL VALUES

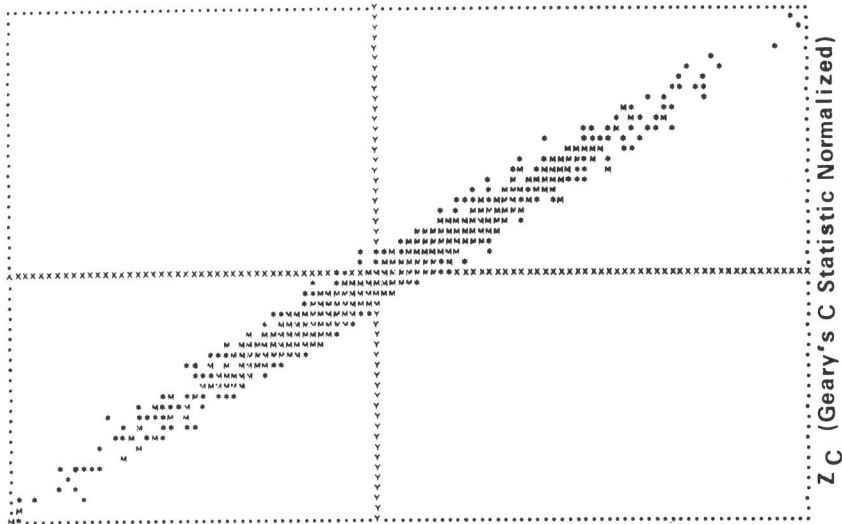

UNIFORMLY DISTRIBUTED VALUES

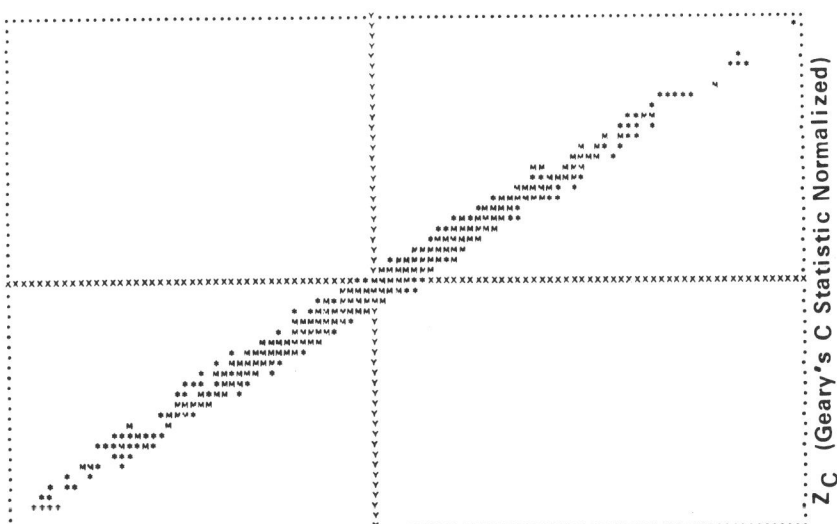

Fig. 14.7. Scatter diagrams of standardized transformations of Moran's I and Geary's C statistics for normally and uniformly distributed cell values.

Moran's I and Geary's C Statistics

Simplified computational forms for Moran's I and Geary's C spatial autocorrelation statistics are presented below. These versions are compatible with the assumptions used throughout this paper. They are expressed using comparable symbols and terminology to facilitate comparison.

Computation of Moran's I Statistic

The following equations and variable descriptions have been adapted from Ebdon (1977) and from Cliff and Ord (1973).

$$I = [N \sum_{i=1}^{N} \sum_{j>i}^{N} (x_i - \bar{X})(x_j - \bar{X})]/J \sum_{i=1}^{N} (x_i - \bar{X})^2$$

$$\sigma_n^2 = \{(N^2 J + 3J^2 - N \sum_{i=1}^{N} L^2)/[J^2(N^2 - 1)]\} - E_I^2$$

$$\sigma_r^2 = \left(\{N[J(N^2 + 3 - 3N) + 3J^2 - N \sum_{i=1}^{N} L^2] - k[J(N^2 - N) + 6J^2 - 2N \sum_{i=1}^{N} L^2]\}/[J^2(N-1)(N-2)(N-3)]\right) - E_I^2$$

$E_I = -1/(N-1)$

$Z_I = (I - E_I)/\sigma_n$ (for normally distributed data)

$Z_I = (I - E_I)/\sigma_r$ (for randomly distributed data)

I = Moran's spatial autocorrelation coefficient
Z_I = I standardized to approximate a normal (0,1) deviate
E_I = expectation for I under the assumption of random placement
σ_n and σ_r = standard deviates for estimates of E_I
N = number of cells in the study area
J = number of joins between adjacent pairs of cells
k = kurtosis of the observations

$\sum_{i=1}^{N} \sum_{j>i}^{N} (x_i - \bar{X})(x_j - \bar{X})$ = cross-products of deviations from the mean summed over all cells i, for each cell i summed over all cells j, j contiguous to i, and $j > i$ (that is, no double counting)

$\sum_{i=1}^{N} L^2$ = squared number of joins per cell, summed over all cells

Computation of Geary's C Statistic

The following equations and variable descriptions have been adapted from Geary (1954).

$$C = [(N-1)/2(2J)][\sum_{i=1}^{N}\sum_{j=1}^{N}(x_i - x_j)^2 / \sum_{i=1}^{N}(x_i - \bar{X})^2]$$

$$\sigma_n^2 = \left(\{N^2(2J/N)^2 + 2N[(2J/N) + (\sum_{i=1}^{N}L^2/N)]\}(N-1)/[N^2(N+1)(2J/N)^2]\right) - E_C^2$$

$$\sigma_r^2 = \left[(\sum_{i=1}^{N}L^2\{[N(N^2 - N + 2)k] - [N(N^2 + 3N - 6)(\sigma_X^2)^2]\} + 2J(2J+2)\{[N(N^2 - 3N + 3)(\sigma_X^2)^2] - [N(N-1)k]\})\cdot\{1/[(N-1)(N-2)(N-3)]\}\{(N-1)^2/[N^2(2J)^2(\sigma^2)^2]\}\right] - E_C^2$$

$E_C = 1.0$

$Z_C = (E_C - C)/\sigma_n$ (for normally distributed data)

$Z_C = (E_C - C)/\sigma_r$ (for randomly distributed data)

C = Geary's spatial autocorrelation coefficient
Z_C = C standardized to approximate a normal (0,1) deviate
E_C = expectation for C under the assumption of random placement
σ_n and σ_r = standard deviates for estimates of E_C
N = number of cells in the study area
J = number of joins between adjacent pairs of cells
σ_X^2 = variance of the observations
k = kurtosis of the observations

$\sum_{i=1}^{N}\sum_{j=1}^{N}(x_i - x_j)^2$ = squares of differences summed over all cells i, for each cell i summed over all cells j, j contiguous to i

$\sum_{i=1}^{N}L^2$ = squared number of joins per cell, summed over all cells

APPENDIX B

Extracting Statistical Outliers

It can be demonstrated that extreme values, or "statistical outliers" severely impact the computation of contiguity measures of entire arrangements and confuse the identification of individual cells that are interestingly different from or similar to their neighbors. It is appropriate, then, that they be eliminated prior to CA analysis. Elimination of extreme values will affect both the parameters of the observations and the sums of the squared differences. The consequence of removing extreme values from consideration is only a minor degradation of precision if the values are validly a part of the population, but a significant increase in estimation power if the eliminated values derive from inaccurate measurement. Also, their elimination from the computations can be justified on the basis that merely their great deviations from the mean of the observations are sufficient to attract attention.

Usual means for eliminating statistical outliers, however, either are intended for sample sizes much smaller than is typical of the number of cells in many archaeology surveys, or require parameter estimates derived independently of the data at hand. To avoid these restrictions screening for outliers has been accomplished by treating the observations as if they possessed a normal distribution, and by searching the tails of their real distribution for gaps between sequential observations in excess of six times the standard deviation of the most extreme value in repeated samplings of size N from a theoretical normal distribution. Calculation of the standard deviation for these particular values in a sample from a normal distribution requires that the percentile rankings of individual values are known:

$$s_p = [p(1-p)] / \{N[(1/\sqrt{2\pi})e^{z_p^2/2}]^2\}^{1/2}$$

in which p is the percentile rank of the highest value in a sample of size N (expressed as the decimal fraction), $p = (N-0.5)/N$, and z_p is the theoretical normal deviate associated with that rank (Hald, 1952). Finally, this screening criterion is rescaled through multiplication by the standard deviation of the observations. All values in, say, the five- or ten percent tails of the distribution of observations that are separated from a value closer to the mean by a gap between sequential values wider than the screening criterion, are dropped from consideration in the analysis for spatial uniqueness. Their removal, of course, changes the number of values included in the analysis, as well as the mean and variance of the remaining observations. The search for statistical outliers is repeated using the new value of N, the new variance of the observations, and a recomputed standard deviation for the highest value in which case p and z_p are adjusted to reflect the smaller sample size. Attempts to recognize and discard outliers are repeated until none are identified.

REFERENCES

Clark, P.J., & Evans, F.C. (1954). Distance to nearest neighbor as a measure of spatial relationships in populations. *Ecology 35*, 445-453.

Cliff, A.D., Martin, R.L., & Ord, J.K. (1975). A test for spatial autocorrelation in choropleth maps based upon a modified X^2 statistic. *Transactions, Institute of British Geographers 65*, 109-129.

Cliff, A.D., & Ord, J.K. (1969). The problem of spatial autocorrelation. In A.J. Scott (Ed.), *Studies in regional science, London papers in regional science 1*, (pp. 25-55). London: Pion.

Cliff, A.D., & Ord, J.K. (1973). *Spatial autocorrelation*. London: Pion.

Dacey, M.F. (1959). A note on the derivation of nearest neighbor distance. *Journal of Regional Science 2*, 81-87.

Dacey, M.F. (1962). Analysis of central place and point patterns by a nearest neighbor method. In K. Norborg (Ed.), *Proceedings of the I.G.U. symposium on urban geography, Lund studies in geography, series B, human geography 24*, (pp. 55-76). Lund, Sweden: Royal University of Lund.

Dacey, M.F. (1963). Order neighbor statistics for a class of random patterns in multidimensional space. *Annals, Association of American Geographers 53*, 505-515.

Dacey, M.F. (1965). *A review on measures of contiguity for two and k-color maps*, (Tech. Rep. No. 2). Chicago: Northwestern University, Department of Geography.

Dacey, M.F., & Tung, T. (1962). The identification of randomness in point patterns, I. *Journal of Regional Science 4*, 83-96.

Ebdon, D. (1977). *Statistics in geography: A practical approach*. Oxford: Basil Blackwell.

Geary, R.C. (1954). The contiguity ratio and statistical mapping. *The Incorporated Statistician 5*, 115-145.

Getis, A., & Boots, B. (1978). *Models of spatial processes*. Cambridge: Cambridge University Press.

Gladfelter, B.G., Nashold, B.W., & Hall, R.L. (1979). *A geomorphic, magnetic, and archaeological investigation of the Dunham tract, Cahokia Mounds Historic Site, July-August 1976* (Rep. to the Illinois Department of Conservation relating to an archaeological study on the location of proposed interpretation center for Cahokia Mounds Historic Site). Springfield, IL: Illinois Department of Conservation.

Grieg-Smith, P. (1952). The use of random and contiguous quadrats in the study of the structure of plant communities. *Annals of Botany, London 16*, 293-316.

Grieg-Smith, P. (1964). *Quantitative plant ecology*. London: Methuen.

Hald, A. (1952). *Statistical theory with engineering applications*. (G. Seidelin, Trans.). New York: John Wiley & Sons, Inc.

Hietala, H.J., & Stevens, D.S. (1977). Spatial analysis: Multiple procedures in pattern recognition. *American Antiquity 42*, 539-559.

Hsu, S., & Tiedemann, C.E. (1968). A rational method of delimiting study areas for unevenly distributed point phenomena. *Professional Geographer 6*, 376-381.

Moran, P.A.P. (1950). Notes on continuous stochastic phenomena. *Biometrika 37*, 17-23.

Thompson, H.R. (1956). Distribution of distance to nth neighbor in a population of randomly distributed individuals. *Ecology 37*, 391-394.

Tiedemann, C.E. (1978). *Searching for an orderly size-spacing relationship: 100,000 glimpses of settlement pattern*. Paper presented at the meeting of the Association of American Geographers, West Lakes Division, Mankato, MN.

Tiedemann, C.E. (1979). *Distance to nearest larger neighbor as a measure of spatial autocorrelation: Tests of sensitivity*. Paper presented at the meeting of the Association of American Geographers, Philadelphia.

Tiedemann, C.E., & Gladfelter, B.G. (1980). *A computer program for evaluating spatial archaeological data*. Paper presented at the meeting of the Society for American Archaeology, Philadelphia.

Tiedemann, C.E., & Gladfelter, B.G. (1981). *Statistical distributions of between-cell-differences estimated using Monte Carlo methods*. Paper presented at the meeting of the Association of American Geographers, Los Angeles.

Tiedemann, C.E., Gladfelter, B.G. & Hole, B. (1981). *The contiguity-anomaly method: A nonstandard approach to spatial autocorrelation*. Paper presented at the meeting of the Society for American Archaeology, San Diego.

PART VI: ARTIFACT ANALYSIS

15

Introductory Remarks on Artifact Analysis

CHRISTOPHER CARR

This section discusses quantitative approaches to artifact seriation (Braun, chapter 16; Jones, chapter 17) and artifact classification (Hoffman, chapter 18). Each chapter illustrates in detail some of the logical processes involved in defining a data set with a relevant subset structure and specifying its relevant relational structure in preparation for choosing an appropriate analytic technique, as discussed by Carr (chapter 2) and Read (chapter 3). Additionally, Braun introduces a new set of techniques for achieving seriation, and Hoffman introduces a stepwise analytic design for selecting variables to develop a classification scheme.

In regard to the logic involved in developing a seriation, Braun and Jones each use deductive and CEDA strategies to specify variables and observations that are relevant. Braun's orientation, however, is toward deductive argumentation, whereas Jones relies primarily on the CEDA approach.

DEDUCTIVE SPECIFICATION OF SERIATION CRITERIA

Braun argues that the one or several variables (ordering criteria) that are chosen to develop an artifact seriation should not only change their states monotonically over time (a standard minimal requirement of seriation variables), but also have three other characteristics. 1) They should be sensitive to a *single* biophysical or cultural process over time. This characteristic is necessary to avoid the blurring or distortion of the true chronological relationships between archaeological entities that can occur when multiple processes with different rates of change are tracked by the individual or multiple variables. It is also necessary for establishing the relevance of the constructed seriation model to new observations that remain to be ordered. 2) The variable(s) should be insensitive to the behavioral phenomenon that is ultimately of interest. This is necessary to avoid circular reasoning in documenting and studying the process of interest. 3) The variable(s) should vary on an interval or ratio scale. This requirement derives from the nature of the evolution of cultural-environmental systems and systems in general. Individual components or subsystems of a cultural-environmental system sometimes change in a punctuated fashion, from quasi-steady state to quasi-steady state, rather than slowly and uniformly over time (von Bertalanffy, 1968; Rappaport, 1979). Also, different components can change at different times, sequentially or dialectically, rather than simultaneously (Slobodkin & Rapoport, 1974; Braun & Plog, 1982; Leach, 1954). To monitor such diagnostic patterns of change *within* an evolutionary trajectory, rather than simply the initial and final states of the system, it is necessary that the time of events be determined on a scale as close to continuous as possible.

In line with these principles, and given Braun's general commitment to documenting and explaining patterns of social organizational change (Braun, 1977; Braun & Plog, 1982), he selects certain technological characteristics of ceramic cooking vessels (e.g., their wall thickness, tempering characteristics) to develop a seriation model for west central Illinois. These variables are sensitive to a single process (changing subsistence and cooking practices), are insensitive to the social phenomena of interest, and vary meaningfully on a ratio scale. Elsewhere, Braun (1982) outlines additional principles of ceramic technology that he uses to deduce tempering variables relevant to tracking the single subsistence process.

The observations that Braun uses to develop a seriation model for west central Illinois are selected primarily deductively, on the basis of several arguments. These pertain to the relevance of datable carbon samples and pottery samples to their proveniences of deposition, the relevance of the assayed ages of carbon samples to their dates of burning, and the cultural contexts of deposition. Some observations, however, are eliminated from analysis on the basis of criteria arrived at within a CEDA framework. These criteria pertain to the probable girth of the vessel from which a sherd was derived, the disuniformity of a sherd in its thickness, and the geographic area/subsistence system in which the observation occurs.

INDUCTIVE SPECIFICATION OF SERIATION CRITERIA

Jones, like Braun, is concerned with developing seriation models that use continuous variables and that track a single process through time. The approach she uses to select relevant variables and observations, however, is largely an inductive, CEDA approach rather than a deductive one. She starts with a range of lithic technological indices (variables) that are currently thought to vary *among* Levantine Mousterian assemblages over time for all chipped stone artifact classes or that are potentially of interest. She then determines whether such indices also vary significantly over space, depth, or artifact classes *within* assemblages. Significant variation of an index along any of these intrasite dimensions is used to infer that it varies with phenomena/processes other than some single process in time to which artifact manufacturing methods were sensitive, and that it defines multiple intrasite artifact populations. These other phenomena/processes include variation in artifact function, and whether the artifacts represent the endproducts (tools) or byproducts (debitage) of artifact manufacture. Both of these extraneous processes can be controlled for, in part, by calculating indices within artifact classes. For a given class, indices that still vary over space or depth within an assemblage are eliminated as candidates for developing a seriation model. In this way, Jones sorts through the particular processes (reflected in particular indices) and particular populations (artifact classes) to find those that are relevant for developing a time seriation.

In most cases, Jones is unable to state the specific nature of the processes and populations to which inappropriate or appropriate indices are sensitive. She does, however, identify variation in the length:width ratio for Levallois points— an index relevant for developing a time seriation—as being related to changes in core preparation techniques and reduction strategies over time.

NEW METHODS FOR SERIATION: TIME SERIES APPROACHES

Braun's chapter introduces the use of certain new techniques for constructing seriations. These fall within the field of time series analysis. Time series analysis is a diverse set of alternative methods used to describe, partition, and/or predict variation in a series of observations over time (Rich, 1973) or space (Holloway, 1958; Castleman, 1979). It includes the methods of autocorrelation analysis, spectral analysis, Fourier analysis, and a wide diversity of filtering procedures. Archaeologically, many of these methods have been or are being applied to the analysis of spatial series and distributions of soil resistivity, magnetometry, and soil chemistry observations within sites (Scollar, 1970; Carr, 1977, 1982a; Gladfelter & Tiedemann, chapter 14); intrasite artifact distributions (Carr, 1982b; 1983; 1984; in press, this volume, chapter 13); and regional artifact distributions (Hodder & Orton, 1976, pp. 174-183; Ebert, 1983). The methods have not, however, been used previously in archaeology to analyze observations in a time series for seriation purposes, although the parallel to geological stratigraphic applications (Davis, 1973, pp. 222-256) is clear.

Of the many methods that are encompassed by time series analysis, those that Braun has chosen for developing a seriation model include 1) a PROBNORM running filter (smoothing) function, which is used to segregate a trend from stochastic and local variation in the values of the seriation variable over time, and 2) inverse-prediction regression procedures, which are used to model the smoothed time series, with age as a function of the seriation variable.

These methods are concordant with several aspects of the relevant relational structure that probably characterize seriation data of the kind that meets Braun's requirements (above) and that involves absolute carbon dates. 1) The methods accommodate one variable or dimension as a function of time—that seriation variable which presumably monitors a single process. 2) They assume that the seriation variable has a ratio scale, which is in line with the aim of developing a continuous seriation model. 3) The filtering methods take into consideration error in the measurement of the time variable. 4) They also accommodate uneven spacing of observations along the time scale, as is characteristic of datable carbon samples from a region. 5) The use of an inverse prediction approach for defining a final regression with age as a function of the seriation variable acknowledges that archaeological samples for developing a seriation model are usually collected not as if age were the dependent variable and the seriation criterion were the predictor variable, but rather vice versa. The values of the predictor seriation variable are not selected in accord with an appropriate regression design, but rather by the availability of observations of the dependent time variable. This situation results from the limited number of independently datable samples from uncontrolled times that are offered by the archaeological record.

Finally, an additional advantage of Braun's time series approach must be mentioned. The regression methods that he uses allow one to calculate an estimate of the error of the predicted date of a new observation to which the seriation model is applied. This feature is not currently available in other seriation methods.

DEDUCTIVE SPECIFICATION OF CLASSIFICATION CRITERIA

Hoffman's chapter on artifact classification contributes to the areas of both analytic process and technical development. Considering analytic process first, his chapter, like Braun's, illustrates the use of primarily deductive argumentation to specify the relevant variables and observations to be used in an analysis. Hoffman's orientation toward this mode of defining a relevant subset structure is evident in three ways.

1) At a general level, Hoffman argues against the normative-empiricist stand that artifact classes are naturally inherent in a population of artifacts. Instead, following Dunnell (1971) and Vierra (1982), he stresses that artifact classes are arbitrary groupings, created by the typologist through his act of selecting a particular set of variables that are used as a basis for classification. Under these circumstances, for classification to be a purposeful endeavor, the typologist must select classification variables carefully and deductively. They must be selected in concordance with his research goals, the nature of organization and content of the phenomena of interest as expected theoretically or known, and the meaning and relevance of the variables in relation to those goals and phenomena.

2) At a more specific level, Hoffman suggests that morphological variation in chipped stone artifacts (particularly points) can reflect several sources of varia-

tion: (a) variation in their function, (b) the ethnic affiliation and norms of their manufacturers, (c) the individual motor habits of their manufacturers, and (d) their stage of maintenance/recycling. He stresses that to build a classification of chipped stone artifacts that directly reflects one of these phenomena of interest, it is necessary to determine the meaning of the different kinds of morphological variation that the artifacts encompass—in terms of function, ethnicity, motor habits, and maintenance—and to select variables for classification accordingly.

3) In practice, Hoffman differentiates various point forms using a variable (a dimension defined by blade edge angle and blade size) that he takes to indicate the stage of maintenance of a point on the basis of a deductive argument. To deduce the meaning of the variable, he uses a principle of lithic technology. This principle is concerned with (a) pressure flaking as a means for resharpening points when efficient utilization of lithic raw materials and minimization of risk of damaging the point are important and (b) the effects of pressure flaking on point form. Also, Hoffman concludes from his analysis the different meanings that morphological variation in the stems, as opposed to the blades, of points can have in relation to ethnicity and tool maintenance, respectively. He notes the importance of this difference in deductively selecting variables for building classifications that reflect ethnicity or tool maintenance.

NEW METHODS FOR ARTIFACT CLASSIFICATION

In regard to technical development, Hoffman's chapter makes two contributions.

1) It distinguishes the kinds of analytic tasks to which factor analysis and canonical correlation are suited, and then proposes the integration of both techniques in a CEDA stepwise analytic design for selecting appropriate variables for constructing artifact classification schemes. The proposed design involves (a) the initial exploratory use of factor analysis to determine the basic dimensions of variability in an artifact data set, (b) the assignment of probable behavioral meanings to those dimensions using the principles of lithic technology, (c) the testing and refinement of those meanings using canonical correlation to document the relationships among variables that pertain to different dimensions, and (d) the selection of classification variables that are relevant to the phenomena of interest on the basis of the several multivariate analyses. It should be made clear that although Hoffman proposes for the initial use of factor analysis as an inductive *pattern-searching* device, following Christenson and Read's (1977) use of it for this purpose, Hoffman's experimental analytic work, which leads to this recommendation, does not employ the method in this manner. Instead, Hoffman uses the technique primarily as a devise to *summarize* multiple morphological measures as single dimensions that are already known to exist in the input data set.

2) Hoffman enumerates the advantages and disadvantages of using polar or Cartesian coordinate measures of point morphology. Among the issues he discusses is the degree of concordance between the assumptions that the measures make about point form and the formal attributes that the researcher wishes to analyze. Many Cartesian coordinate measures of points assume that the points have a symmetrical outline and well defined junctures between blade, haft, and other elements. When this is not true, polar coordinate measures are to be preferred.

Hoffman's chapter also provides a good illustration of the argumentation that is appropriate when selecting and justifying the selection of one factor analytic method relative to another: principal components analysis, factor analysis with orthoganal rotation, or factor analysis with oblique rotation. His logic (a) allows for either inductive or deductive uses of these methods, (b) expresses concern over representing the structure of a data set in its own terms, and (c) recognizes alternative philosophies about whether fundamental processes can correlate. His analysis of a point morphology data set using all three factor approaches vividly illustrates how different factor approaches can vary in their appropriateness for analyzing a particular data set, given the data's relevant structure and the philosophical perspective of the researcher.

Finally, Hoffman's chapter makes two contributions at the levels of middle range theory and the substantive. It documents a significant negative relationship between the edge angle and size of point blades, but not hafts. This supports studies of a number of other researchers on the nature of point maintenance. Also, the chapter clearly documents the need for reassessment of traditional point typologies in the eastern United States, a conclusion foreshadowed in an earlier work by Binford (1965).

REFERENCES

Binford, L.R. (1965). Archaeological systematics and the study of culture process. *American Antiquity 31*, 203-210.

Braun, D.P. (1977). *Middle Woodland-early Late Woodland social change in the prehistoric midwestern U.S.* Unpublished doctoral dissertation, University of Michigan, Ann Arbor.

Braun, D.P. (1982). Radiographic analysis of temper in ceramic vessels: Goals and initial methods. *Journal of Field Archaeology 9*(2), 183-192.

Braun, D.P., & Plog, S. (1982). Evolution of "tribal" social networks: Theory and prehistoric North American evidence. *American Antiquity 47*(3), 504-525.

Carr, C. (1977). A new role and analytical design for the use of resistivity surveying in archaeology. *Mid-Continental Journal of Archaeology 2*(2), 161-193. Evanston, IL: Center for American Archaeology.

Carr, C. (1982a). *Soil resistivity surveying*. Evanston, IL: Center for American Archaeology.

Carr, C. (1982b, April). *Dissecting intrasite artifact distributions as palimpsests*. Paper presented at the annual meeting of the Society for American Archaeology, Minneapolis, MN.

Carr, C. (1983, June). *A design for intrasite research*. Paper presented at the National Park Service Research Seminar in Archaeology, Fort Collins, CO.

Carr, C. (1984). The nature of organization of intrasite archaeological records and spatial analytic approaches to their investigation. In M.B. Schiffer (Ed.), *Advances in Archaeological Method and Theory (Vol. 7)*. New York: Academic Press, Inc.

Carr, C. (in press). Dissecting intrasite artifact palimpsests using Fourier methods. In S. Kent (Ed.), *Method and theory for activity area research: An ethnoarchaeological approach* (Chap. 5). New York: Columbia University Press.

Castlemen, K.R. (1979). *Digital image processing*. Englewood Cliffs, NJ: Prentice-Hall.

Christenson, A.L., & Read, D.W. (1977). Numerical taxonomy, R-mode factor analysis, and archaeological classification. *American Antiquity 42*(2), 163-179.

Davis, J.C. (1973). *Statistics and data analysis in geology*. New York: John Wiley & Sons, Inc.

Dunnell, R.C. (1971). *Systematics in prehistory*. New York: Free Press.

Ebert, J. (1983). *Distributional archaeology: Nonsite discovery, recording, and spatial analytical methods for application to the surface archaeological record*. Unpublished dissertation proposal, University of New Mexico, Albuquerque.

Hodder, I., & Orton, C. (1976). *Spatial analysis in archaeology*. Cambridge: Cambridge University Press.

Holloway, J. L. (1958). Smoothing and filtering of time series and space fields. *Advances in Geophysics 4*, 351-389.

Leach, E.R. (1954). *Political systems of highland Burma*. Boston: Beacon Press.

Rappaport, R.A. (1979). *Ecology, meaning, and religion*. Richmond, CA: North Atlantic Books.

Rich, L.G. (1973). *Environmental systems engineering*. New York: McGraw-Hill, Inc.

Scollar, I. (1970). Fourier transform methods for the evaluation of magnetic maps. *Prospezioni archeologiche 5*, 9-40. Rome: Fondazione Lerchi.

Slobodkin, L.B., & Rapoport, A. (1974). An optimal strategy of evolution. The *Quarterly Review of Biology 49*(3), 181-200.

Vierra, R.K. (1982). Typology, classification, and theory building. In R. Whallon & J. Brown (Eds.), *Essays on archaeological typology* (pp. 162-175). Evanston, IL: Center for American Archaeology.

von Bertalanffy, L. (1968). *General system theory*. New York: George Braziller.

16

Absolute Seriation: A Time-Series Approach

DAVID P. BRAUN

Traditional archaeological seriation asks the question, "Can we order this set of objects or places according to their relative ages, based on their physical characteristics?" The study of cultural processes with archaeological data, however, demands far greater temporal control: estimates of the absolute ages or contemporaneity among objects or places. Such control can come from physico-chemical methods of independent dating, but the costs and other limitations of these methods preclude independent dating of all the objects and places we may need to study. Thus, we should be asking instead, "How well can we estimate the absolute ages of objects or places, based on their physical characteristics, without the aid of case-by-case independent dating?"

We are left, that is, with the task of calibrating our seriation models with independent dating controls with two goals in mind: 1) Ideally, our method of calibration should produce a continuous, *accurate* estimate of absolute age along the seriation scale. 2) Ideally, we should have some means of determining the *precision* of our temporal estimates.

The importance of these two goals for processual archaeology is clear. Cultural change only rarely consists of discrete events that occur simultaneously across the entire system. Different aspects of cultural systems are far more likely

Michael L. Hargrave and M. Denise Hutto aided greatly in the early stages of this work. Samples were obtained from the Center for Archaeological Investigations of Southern Illinois University at Carbondale; the Center for American Archaeology at Kampsville, Illinois; the Illinois State Museum; the Museum of Anthropology of the University of Michigan; and one private collection. I thank all of the following for their assistance with records and collections: David Asch, Charles Bentz, Brian Butler, Ken Farnsworth, James Griffin, Pete May, David Morgan, William Parry, Frank Rackerby, Tom Rocek, Mark Sant, John Speth, Stuart Struever, Bonnie Styles, and Michael Wiant. Material support has come from the Southern Illinois University, Office of Research Development and Administration, Department of Anthropology, and Center for Archaeological Investigations; and from the Northwestern University 1980 Summer Field School. Jim Brown, Gordon Bronitsky, Chris Carr, Jeff Hantman, Michael Schiffer, Vin Steponaitis, and Robert Whallon provided useful comments on the original draft, for all of which I am grateful.

to change at different times and rates and to follow different patterns of change, depending on the form and strength of the triggering factors. In turn, it is the very sequencing and patterns of change within a system that reveal to us how and why the system is changing. The explanation of cultural change thus requires the ability to analyze conditions not only before and after, but also during any periods of change (or stability), and to deal with time on as close to a continuous scale as possible (e.g., F. Plog, 1973, 1977, 1979).

The calibration of seriation models to meet the two suggested goals poses problems of both method and theory. My purpose here is to discuss both classes of problems and to suggest areas for further research. I also present an example from my current work on midwestern U.S. Woodland ceramic chronometry. This work has stimulated much of my thinking on the subject, as have Dean's (1978) preliminary general model of the archaeological dating process and S. Plog and Hantman's (1980) exploration of similar analytical problems for northeastern Arizona.

SOME PROBLEMS IN ABSOLUTE DATING AND SERIATION

The absolute ages of most archaeological remains are determined from the spatial association of materials with each other by following two approaches: The less common but more direct approach involves analysis of the depositional association between objects and places, on the one hand, and independently dated events, on the other. The more common approach, seriation, involves analysis of the attributes of objects or places, or of objects in association with them, which have been compared only elsewhere against independently dated events.

The first approach has received some methodological interest, most recently by Dean (1978). In briefest form, the approach requires an analysis of the relevance of a dated event (the age of formation or death of some directly datable material) to a target event (the age of construction of a place or set of objects, the remains of which are preserved in depositional association with the directly dated material). Such analyses involve a consideration of, for example, the possible magnitude of any difference in age between the dated and target events, as well as the cultural and depositional processes linking them (Dean, 1978).

The second approach, seriation, combines all the steps and problems of independent dating with a myriad of additional ones involved in the building and application of a seriation model. The building of a standard seriation model begins with an attempt to identify "primarily temporally sensitive" types or, more recently attributes for inclusion in the model (Marquardt, 1978). All presumably temporally sensitive criteria satisfying various statistical prerequisites are then combined to produce the model. This model consists of an ordering based on a measure of similarity or dissimilarity among the objects in the original data set. That is, it consists of an empirical generalization based on the original set. The ordering may be continuous or, more commonly, may define only a series of discrete phases or temporal increments. The ordered phases are then generally assigned to specific time spans, based on independent dates for any of the attributes, types, or deposits included in the original data set. In use, the model is then applied to cases not included in the original data set, under the assumption that the directional changes observed among the original cases hold true for all objects of the same types or possessing the same set of attributes.

There are four major problems with this approach:

1) The approach assumes that artifacts involved in any one aspect of cultural life will always change in the same way from one location to the next within a single cultural province. Thus, by always selecting contexts of deposition representing the same aspects of cultural life we should be able to obtain temporally consistent results in applying the seriation model. Notice, however, that the seriation criteria are usually selected not because they informed us about some specific variable of cultural life, but only because they showed monotonic change over time. How, then, do we know how to control for context of deposition in our application?

2) Seriation criteria are selected solely because they are apparently temporally sensitive, without regard to the cultural or bio-physical constraints to which they respond. This makes it unlikely that the seriation model will duplicate the actual temporal relationship among the ordered units in any consistent way. Even if each criterion changes monotonically over time, the criteria and the different underlying constraints to which they respond will not necessarily change at the same rate or follow the same pattern of variation in their rate of change (e.g., F. Plog, 1979). A seriation model that combines attributes of different cultural meanings, therefore, cannot be presumed to avoid blurring and distorting the true chronological relationships present. This danger holds even if depositional-contextual variation among the ordered units has been controlled (cf. Marquardt, 1978).

Ceramic seriation models, for example, commonly include attributes of vessel composition, shape, and decoration. These attributes each respond to a different range of constraints: from the availability of raw materials, to the demands for particular functional characteristics, to the social and symbolic environments of manufacture and use (e.g., Braun, 1982, 1983; Graves, 1981; Hally, 1983; S. Plog, 1980; Rye, 1981; Steponaitis, 1982a, 1982b; Smith, 1981). If we combine such diverse attributes in a single model, how can we be sure of the instrument's applicability?

3) By combining attributes sensitive to a variety of cultural constraints, a seriation model becomes inappropriate for ordering material to study any one of

those constraints. For example, as S. Plog and I have noted (Braun & Plog, 1982, p. 522), a ceramic seriation analysis based in part on decorative criteria cannot be used to order units for a study of social networks based on a decorative-stylistic analysis if the same decorative criteria apply to both analyses. We need, instead, to be able to build our seriation models so that the ordering criteria are not also sensitive to the cultural phenomena we wish to study among the ordered units. This is necessary to avoid circular reasoning.

4) Given the essentially inductive nature of the seriation modeling process, how can we assume that the model will accurately describe the temporal relationships among cases not included in the original data set? That is, by what criteria do we establish the relevance of the original data set and model for new cases to be ordered? Also, beyond the questions of relevance and accuracy, how do we know how precise our estimates of temporal position are? Few methods of seriation consider, even mathematically, the problem of the potential error of estimate in applying a seriation model to new cases.

The calibration of seriation models with independent dates, then, compounds several problems. With the independent dates, we face the problems of arguing relevance and dealing with the measurement error present in most laboratory methods. With the seriation models, when they are applied to cases other than those in the original data set, we face additional problems of arguing relevance, justifying accuracy, and estimating precision.

One possible approach for dealing with these problems is presented below. This approach is not offered as a panacea, but only as one which, under certain broad circumstances, can help us around the problems just discussed. It should be considered as a potential complement to, rather than as a replacement for, more traditional approaches to seriation.

A TIME-SERIES APPROACH FOR SOLVING THE PROBLEMS

We can tackle the forementioned problems first on the issue of the relevance of a seriation model. Clearly, we need to select criteria for inclusion in a seriation model not because they are simply temporally sensitive, but because they also inform us about change in some specific aspect of cultural life.

The problem we face is analogous to the problem of monitoring or tracking the output of a black box. Consider how the output of a system is tracked in real-time: Different properties of the system are monitored directly against an external chronometric standard (Fig. 1). Each property is selected for what it is thought to indicate about the internal workings of the whole. Such control is also necessary in processual archaeology, except that, as mentioned earlier, it is impractical to use an external standard on our scale. In the example illustrated, full use of an external archaeological standard would entail at least twenty-four individual assays; and this is only a trivial example of the combination of long

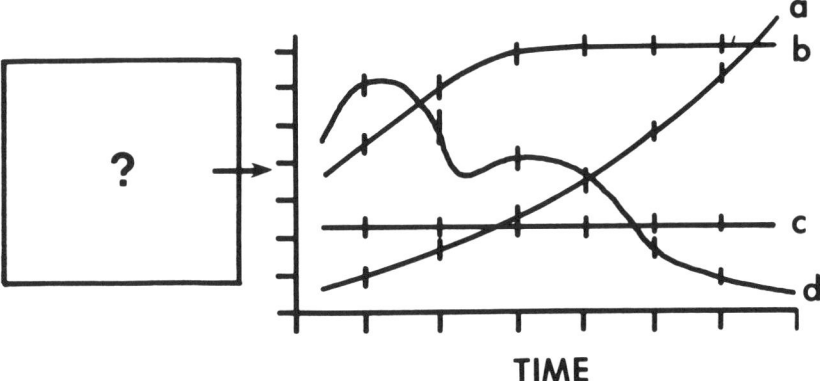

Fig. 16.1. Black box model of how a system's performance is monitored over time.

sampling spans and short dating intervals required of processual research (e.g., F. Plog, 1979).

An alternative approach for archaeology, however, is also suggested by the illustration. If one of the four variables, variable *a* for example, could be tracked alone against an external chronometric standard, the values of the other three variables need only be plotted *against a* to achieve full temporal control. That is, a description of change in any one variable, if that variable consistently changes value over time, can serve as a chronometric standard for the rest of the system.

What might we use as our cultural reference variable(s)? 1. A potential cultural reference variable could be any property of a cultural system that changes state consistently over time, the changes in which can be explained by reference to underlying cultural or bio-physical processes. If we select our seriation criteria based on such a *prior* consideration of what they indicate about past cultural life, we can more easily argue their relevance for providing a primarily temporal ordering of cultural traces. Having selected our criteria based on their inferred cultural meaning, we will also be able to build an appropriate model of what, if any, contingent effects and depositional processes need to be controlled.

2. A potential cultural reference variable must also have material correlates that are relatively widespread in the archaeological record. This is necessary if the material correlates of other variables are to be ordered in comparison to them.

We could construct a seriation model, for example, using only continuous, small-scale characteristics of decorative elements present on pottery from settlements in a restricted region. Such characteristics could be argued to be subject only to some drift within each localized community because they have no effect on the symbolic content of design (e.g., Friedrich, 1970; Graves, 1981; S. Plog, 1980). Differences in the decorative treatments accorded to different morphological/functional classes of vessels would of course require analytical control (S. Plog, 1980, pp. 77-98). The "cultural variable" being treated would be, then, in theory, a form of culturally neutral, aesthetic variation. Those characteristics showing a consistent directional drift over time could then be isolated, and a description of their change through time constructed and calibrated by means of independent dating. Deposits containing remains of decorated pottery of the morphological/functional class specified could then be "dated" through comparison of their pottery's decorative elements against the calibrated reference. Such an approach has been advocated and carried out successfully by S. Plog and Hantman (1980), using data from Black Mesa, northeastern Arizona. Other examples include Binford's (1962) regression method for using kaolin pipestem diameters as a seriation criterion for seventeenth- and eighteenth-century American sites and, although using a geochemical rather than a cultural variable, the construction of archaeomagnetic dating curves (e.g., Bucha, 1971).

The research reported below is presented as a further example. In this instance, characteristics of domestic ceramic cooking technology sensitive to changes in cooking and dietary practices in the central midwestern United States (e.g., Braun 1982, 1983) are used as the criteria for seriating Woodland-period domestic deposits.

The approach taken here may be termed a time-series approach, as opposed to the more straightforward regression approach of Binford (1962) or Plog and Hantman (1980). Time-series analysis, like factor or cluster analysis, consists of a body of interrelated and often alternative algorithms rather than a single algorithm. The purpose of time-series analysis is to take a sequence of observations of some variable over time and partition the observed variation into several possible sources: linear and nonlinear trends; cyclical variation at different underlying frequencies; autocorrelation or autoregressive effects; interruption (stimulus-response) effects; and a random or "noise" component. The analyses may be conducted either to evaluate the structure of a past sequence of events or to extend the evaluation into a forecast of the near future (e.g., Rich, 1973, pp. 214-253).

Consider, for example, the possibilities for evaluating the structure of variation in mean hourly temperature at some weather station. Our primary interest might be to determine whether there has been a 10-year cooling or warming *trend*, or alternately, to identify *cyclical* variations resulting from diurnal or annual positioning of the earth, or from sunspots. In either case, non-cyclical trends must first be detected, generally through some form of regression analysis, and their variation removed from the data statistically. Periodic variation can then be examined in the residual data set using either a moving average technique or Fourier series analysis. Moving-average filters mathematically smooth-out and allow the extraction of short-term variation, both cyclical and random. Fourier analysis allows the removal of variation attributable to only cyclical components of specified frequencies.

To continue the example, we also might want to know the extent to which the earth at the weather station acts as a heat sink, with one day's temperatures partially "led" by, i.e., autocorrelated with, the preceding day's or week's temperatures. Or we also might want to know if the arrival of a cloud of volcanic ash in the upper atmosphere had any effect at ground-level—an example of a possible interruption effect. Detection of either autocorrelation or interruption effects require the prior detection and filtering-out of first trend and then cyclical effects.

Time-series analysis, then, is a way to ask a variety of statistical questions concerning change over time of a given sequence of observations. The application in this chapter is extremely simple. More complex aspects of the field are covered in numerous texts—some specifically directed toward the social sciences (e.g., Gottman, 1981; McCleary & Hay, 1980).

The time-series problem posed here is to describe the long-term trend of aspects of Woodland domestic ceramic cooking technology and to measure the size of all other variation as an indicator of the potential error of estimation in that description. This modeling presents few problems in theory. By definition, what we seek is a description of the trend of a criterion X against time T, such that, upon inversion of the relationship, T can be estimated from the value of X. Construction of a model thus requires the collection of independent dates for samples of X distributed across X's full range of variation. Superficially, we seem to have a simple problem of regression.

As Dean (1978, pp. 226-229) demonstrates, however, independent dating in archaeology involves two sources of inherent error: First, all independent dating techniques carry some form of *measurement error*, e.g., the published standard deviations for radioisotopic techniques (Browman, 1981). Second, the potential for a disparity between the dated and target events, due to the depositional processes responsible for their archaeological association, also demands recognition. This second source of error may be termed *associational error*, although it can be broken down into several possible components (Dean, 1978).

On the other side of the equation, our observations of X, the ordering criterion, also involve several types of error. Laboratory measurement error must always be acknowledged. In addition, we must allow for stochastic variation due to the idiosyncracies of raw materials, deposition, preservation, and the motor skills of the manufacturer(s) of the objects we study. Finally, we must recognize that several sources of systematic non-temporal variation in X may also have existed. Those that we recognize, we can control analytically, but we can never assume we have identified all. Our time-series model, after inversion, can thus be expressed minimally as:

$$T + E_{mt} + E_a = f(X) + E_{mx} + E_s + E_o \qquad (1)$$

where T = age

X = seriation criterion

E_{mt} = measurement error of T

E_a = associational error of T

E_{mx} = measurement error of X

E_s = stochastic error of X

E_o = error of X due to systematic sources of variation.

Calibration thus requires not only the observation of X and T and the description of $f(X)$, but also the estimation of all the error terms. The term E_s, of course, would be routinely estimated as part of calculating a least-squares estimate of $f(X)$; but what about the other error terms?

A measure of E_{mt} should be recorded for every value of T used in the initial data. Its value can then be pooled across all observations of X. Control of E_{mx} can be obtained through the collection of multiple measurements of X for each observation of T, and multiple replication measurements for each observation of X. The term E_o can be controlled by identifying sources of systematic variation with our bridging arguments of relevance and then eliminating their effects either by controlling the selection of samples or by partial regression. Unidentified sources of systematic variation will simply contribute to the estimate of E_s. We are left only with E_a as a headache for building theory. The bridging relationship between dated and target events must be argued on a case-by-case basis (Dean, 1978, pp. 229, 249; e.g., Schiffer, 1982).

The calculation of $f(x)$ has its own problems. First, in most archaeological cases, our choice of the values of X to include in our data base will be dictated not by a proper regression design, but by the availability of observations of T. We are at the mercy of the archaeological record, most commonly, for obtaining samples of independently datable material. Only in rare instances, where our dating method applies to the same material that holds the prospective seriation criterion, are we spared of this. In effect, we most often will have collected our data as if T were the independent variable and X the dependent one. Consequently, we must proceed using the technique of inverse prediction (Sokal & Rohlf, 1982, pp. 496-498): we first calculate $X = f(T)$, and then "invert" or solve the equation for $T = f(X)$. For linear functions $f(T)$, this is a simple matter. For curvilinear functions, the job becomes quite complex. The process of inversion is shown graphically in Figure 2.

Second, our model identifies the presence of error terms for both X and T. Thus, we may need to use a Model II regression method that controls for the

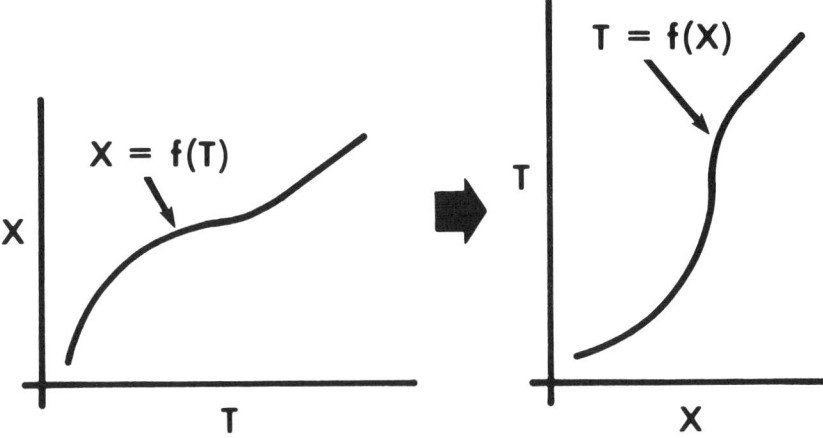

Fig. 16.2. Graphic illustration of the inversion of the relationship $X = f(T)$ to the form $T = f(X)$.

resulting bias of standard techniques for estimating the parameters of $f(T)$ (Sokal & Rohlf, 1982, pp. 547-555). The method for controlling bias in Model II regression is not difficult for first-order equations, but is potentially difficult for higher-order equations.

Third, the "noise" resulting from the compounding of several error terms could produce a graph in which the overall trend is partially masked by apparent short-term or high-frequency variation. Thus, the problem of describing the overall trend is equivalent to the problem of choosing the order of the polynomial function to be used for algebraic curve-fitting or designing a filter of the appropriate frequency-response in time-series analysis (e.g., Gottman, 1981, pp. 53-102; Sokal & Rohlf 1982, pp. 671-683). How much of the variation we observe is only "noise" and how much of it is "signal"?

Further, in time-series analysis, the smallest frequency of variation detectable (the *Nyquist frequency*) is one with a period twice as long as the time-sampling interval (Gottman, 1981, pp. 15-16). To detect true oscillations of a 25-year duration, for example, we would need a sampling interval of 12.5 years. Such a sampling density could be impractical over long spans.

Finally, many curve-describing techniques require equidistant time-sampling points. In choosing our data in archaeology, we can rarely control our time-sampling that accurately. We must therefore employ an integrative or interpolative technique on our raw data (e.g., Davis, 1973, pp. 176-181) to generate the input data structure we need.

Given all of the above considerations, it is clear that there can be no statistical cookbook for the approach advocated here. Rather, the approach defines a family of analytical principles, the implications of which will differ for different kinds of data. The problems of calibrating an archaeomagnetic curve, a pottery microstyle seriation curve, or, as below, a ceramic technological curve, or the problems of calibrating with radiocarbon versus tree-ring dates, for example, are analogous but not identical. Each requires its own set of solutions; the midwestern research presented below illustrates but one possible solution.

A MIDWESTERN WOODLAND EXAMPLE

Routine methods of ceramic temporal seriation for the midwestern Woodland period, ca. 500 BC - AD 900, exemplify the problems of seriation methods in general. The standard seriation (e.g., Griffin, 1952; Griffin et al., 1970, pp. 1-10) relies on a typology that combines a wide range of both decorative and technological criteria. In use, it does not permit control of the cultural meaning of the attributes employed or the kinds of proveniences used to establish the descriptive model. Also, it handles time in discrete phases rather than as a continuous variable. The user cannot estimate the statistical reliability of any application, or presume that the discrete phases identified represent real units of cultural stability, or use the ordering as a means of control in sociological studies of decorative variation (Braun, 1977, pp. 136-138; 1981a; Hargrave, 1981; Hargrave & Braun, 1981).

A search for a better method for ordering Woodland pottery-bearing deposits, however, has led to the recognition that several of the ordering criteria in the standard seriation model probably related to changing patterns of vessel use. Woodland ceramic assemblages in the midwest consisted almost exclusively of a proportionately wide-mouthed form of jar. The shape of this jar form varied somewhat with vessel size and changed gradually over time. Its wide, unrestricted orifice relative to its overall height and width identifies the Woodland jar form as a generalized mixing/cooking container. Variation in its physical characteristics, therefore, can be viewed in the context of changes in the Woodland diet.

In this context, changes in temper size, density, and composition; in vessel wall thicknesses; and in overall vessel shape all could be argued to have occurred in reponse to changing cooking and dietary practices. The most important of these latter changes was an increasing use of cultivated edible seeds, increasingly including certain more starchy varieties within a diversifying, broad-spectrum subsistence regime. The ethnobotanical record amply documents this overall trend. The ceramic-technological evidence and interpretations, and the ethnobotanical evidence for this trend are presented elsewhere (Braun, 1982, 1983).

The ceramic technological changes provided an opportunity to study changing subsistence practices during the transition to a food-producing economy through a medium far less subject to problems of preservation than the ethnobotanical record. In addition, the changes suggested a better method of ceramic temporal seriation: a method involving the tracking of a *single cultural process* that also relied on a ubiquitous class of domestic cultural refuse. If the ceramic technical changes could be shown to be consistent across a wide geographic area and predictable over time, our seriation needs would be met.

The data base for the research was determined by the availability of independently dated pottery-bearing deposits. This has led, to date, to the selection of 56 proveniences with associated radiocarbon dates from the lower Big Muddy, lower Kaskaskia, lower Illinois, and central Mississippi drainages in western Illinois (Fig. 3).

The American Bottom of the Mississippi valley has not been included for two reasons. First, only a handful of Woodland-period, radiocarbon-dated proveniences (all from the end of the period) are yet available for general study. Second, whereas most Woodland pottery in Illinois was tempered with mixtures of sand and/or crushed rock, the American Bottom pottery more often received crushed ceramic fragments as temper. These two classes of nonplastic inclusions could have had different effects on the mechanical performance characteristics of the finished vessels (e.g., Rye, 1976; Steponaitis, 1982), affecting both vessel shapes and wall thicknesses. Such potential, non-temporal sources of ceramic variation required control in the research (see below), and in this case it was simpler to exclude the few samples in question.

The criteria for selecting the 56 sample proveniences and the means used for obtaining information on each of the parameters for Equation 1 (above) are presented below.

Sample Age, T. The independent datings came entirely from radiocarbon assays run on charcoal in depositional association with pottery remains in the four contiguous drainages. Aside from several samples not relocated, all reported samples meeting the criteria set forth below and available as of August, 1982, have been examined for possible inclusion.

The ages of the 56 sample assays were corrected using the dendrochronological calibration curve of Damon et al. (1974). Radiocarbon ages range from 2170 RCBP to 1030 RCBP; corrected ages range from 2216 to 1017 BP. This 1,200-year span covers the Early-Middle Woodland transition and all of the Middle and Late Woodland periods. Earlier samples exist, but are too widely spaced in time to be usable; yielded no pottery fragments appropriate for analysis; or could not be relocated (Table 1). The Late Woodland period ends with the widespread adoption of a very different ceramic industry, the Mississippian. Table 1 lists the samples included, or examined but eventually excluded, in the research.

Measurement Error for Sample Age, E_{mt}. This parameter is estimated for each sample by the published radiocarbon error. Radiocarbon laboratories, of course, differ in the way they calculate the error terms they publish. However, in the absence of data for adjusting between-laboratory differences, the published figures were taken at face value. Samples with published error terms

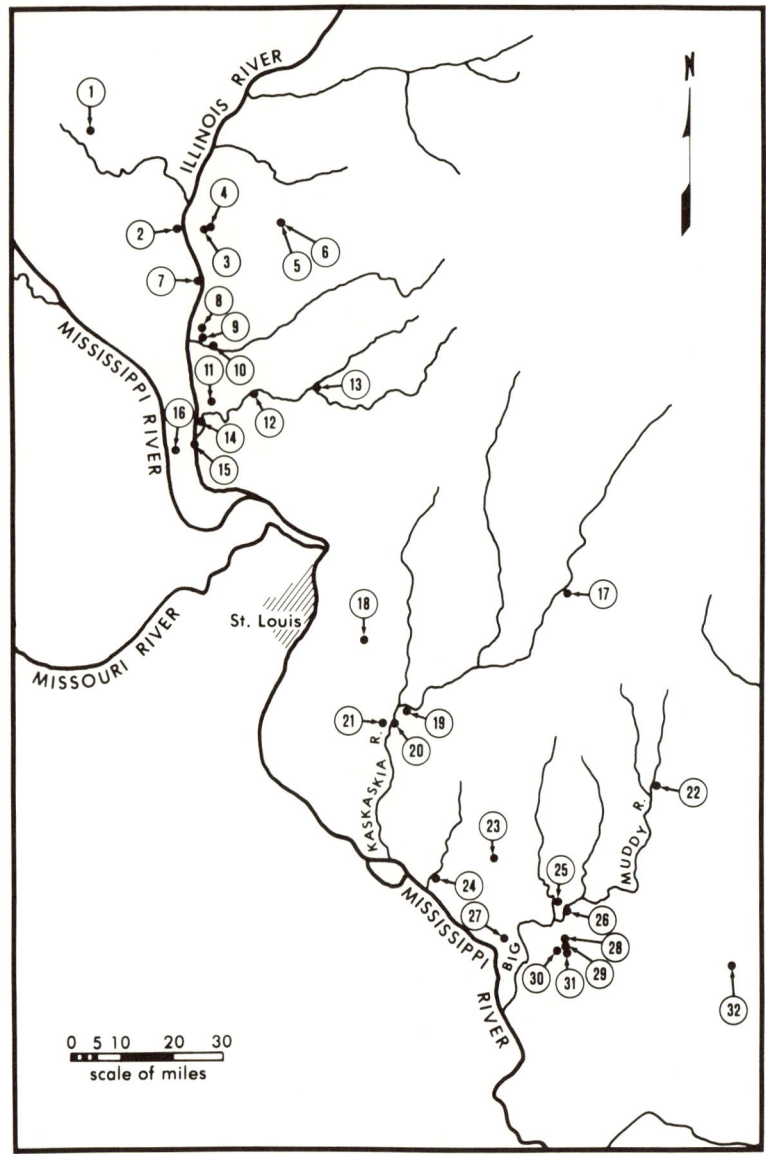

Fig. 16.3. Map of central midwest showing Woodland sample locations. *Key:* 1—John Roy; 2—Napoleon Hollow; 3—Campbell Hollow; 4—Smiling Dan; 5—Archie; 6—Massey; 7—Stillwell; 8—Newbridge; 9—Bridgewater; 10—Apple Creek; 11—Koster-East Field; 12—Crane; 13—Loy; 14—Macoupin; 15—Peisker; 16—Snyders; 17—Texas #1; 18—Rosewood; 19—Kingfish; 20—Emge; 21—Marty Coolidge; 22—Fry #1; 23—Burning Star; 24—24A1-30; 25—Consol; 26—Raymond; 27—Twenhafel; 28—Grammar Shelter; 29—Cedar; 30—Throgmorton; 31—Landreth #1; 32—Carrier Mills.

ABSOLUTE SERIATION: A TIME-SERIES APPROACH 521

Table 16.1

Samples Examined for Time-Trend Analysis

Prov[1]	Sample RCBP	Age BP[2]	Lab. No.	Reference[3]	Sample Size[4] N	N_i	Comments
10:fea.17A	2660 ± 130	—	M-1408	RC8:266	—	—	anomalous
2:sq.216	2590 ± 70	—	ISGS-890	(A)	0	0	no sherds
15:fea.Q	2514 ± 84	—	0-2266(1,2)	(K)	10	—	too isol
31:fea.26	2490 ± 60	—	Dicar-125	(B)	23	—	too isol
14:fea.31	2410 ± 210	—	M-2226	RC14:207	—	—	anomalous
15:fea.4	2275 ± 130	—	M-1404	RC8:265	—	—	not loc.
17:fea.17	2230 ± 110	—	GX-0361	(C)	—	—	anomalous
15:fea.A-G	2200 ± 110	—	0-2270(1)	(K)	—	—	not loc.
15:fea.20	2180 ± 130	—	M-1403	RC8:265	—	—	not loc.
31:fea.91	2170 ± 65	2216 ± 116	Dicar-124	(B)	15	8	ok
25:fea.15	2140 ± 50	2181 ± 108	Dicar-?	(D)	23	14	ok
22:fea.2	2100 ± 290	2138 ± 305	Dicar-122	(E)	5	2	ok
30:fea.84	2080 ± 65	—	Dicar-128	(B)	1	0	small n
12:fea.104F4	2050 ± 70	2078 ± 119	ISGS-898	(A)	22	16	ok
4:sq.39	2020 ± 75	—	ISGS-854	(A)	0	0	no sherds
14:fea.23	2020 ± 200	2044 ± 203	M-2225	RC14:207	15	4	ok
13:fea.72	2010 ± 85	—	ISGS-181	RC17:168	—	—	not loc.
31:fea.1	2005 ± 80	—	ISGS-178	(B)	0	0	no sherds
2:fea.45	2000 ± 70	—	ISGS-916	(A)	2	0	small n
15:fea.M	1900 ± 160	2009 ± 164	M-1155(2)	(K)	12	8	ok
2:Block I	1970 ± 70	—	ISGS-935	(A)	3	0	small n
13:#4-31c	1970 ± 75	—	ISGS-171	RC17:168	—	—	not loc.
14:fea.127	1950 ± 200	1964 ± 203	M-2229	RC14:207	15	6	ok
31:fea.82	1940 ± 70	1953 ± 79	Dicar-130	(B)	48	18	ok
6:fea.11	1930 ± 70	1942 ± 79	ISGS-963	(A)	16	12	ok
31:fea.19	1920 ± 70	1931 ± 79	ISGS-245	(B)	5	1	ok
30:fea.99	1910 ± 130	1919 ± 135	Dicar-127	(B)	10	3	ok
5:fea.4	1900 ± 70	1908 ± 79	ISGS-966	(A)	20	15	ok
29:fea.5	1900 ± 75	1908 ± 83	ISGS-246	(B)	7	2	ok
14:fea.173	1900 ± 140	1908 ± 145	M-2243	RC14:207	50	6	ok
16:fea.8c	1890 ± 75	1897 ± 83	M-1154	RC5:231	60	28	ok
2:sq.237	1880 ± 70	—	ISGS-931	(A)	1	0	small n
15:fea.2	1880 ± 120	—	M-1570	RC10:70	—	—	not loc.
15:fea.5	1860 ± 140	—	M-2223	RC14:207	—	—	not loc.
16:fea.C	1850 ± 120	1853 ± 125	M-1487	RC7:131	16	7	ok
15:fea.W	1850 ± 105	—	0-2269(1)	(K)	5	0	small n.
2:sq.237	1840 ± 75	1842 ± 83	ISGS-834	(A)	36	26	ok
4:p.m.86	1830 ± 50	—	Beta 4534	(A)	0	0	no sherds
30:fea.73	1820 ± 410	—	Dicar-129	(B)	—	—	large sd
15:fea.V	1820 ± 160	—	0-2269(2)	(K)	4	0	small n
2:fea.42	1810 ± 70	—	ISGS-929	(A)	0	0	no sherds
4:sq.954	1805 ± 95	—	Beta-4980	(A)	—	—	anomalous
5:fea.5	1800 ± 70	1798 ± 79	ISGS-964	(A)	8	7	ok

Table 16.1 (cont.)

Prov[1]	Sample RCBP	Age BP[2]	Lab. No.	Reference[3]	Sample Size[4] N	N_i	Comments
2:Block I	1800 ± 70	1798 ± 79	ISGS-904	(A)	56	34	ok
17:fea.17	1800 ± 90	—	GX-0362	(C)	—	—	anomalous
4:Trench F	1708 ± 75	1777 ± 80	ISGS-841	(A)	9	4	ok
15:fea.7	1770 ± 130	—	M-1405	RC8:265	—	—	not loc.
6:fea.1	1750 ± 70	1744 ± 75	ISGS-965	(A)	12	6	ok
12:fea.25F2	1750 ± 70	1744 ± 75	ISGS-951	(A)	29	14	ok
26:no prov.	1745 ± 200	—	M-891	RC2:35	—	—	not loc.
14:fea.215	1730 ± 130	1721 ± 133	M-2245	RC14:208	3	1	ok
16:fea.8d	1720 ± 75	1710 ± 80	M-1155	RC5:231	81	25	ok
4:fea.61	1700 ± 70	1689 ± 75	ISGS-958	(A)	9	5	ok
15:fea.1	1700 ± 120	—	M-1569	RC10:70	—	—	not loc.
18:fea.62	1670 ± 75	1658 ± 80	ISGS-754	(F)	10	1	ok
11:fea.1070	1650 ± 100	—	GX-2400	(A)	—	—	not loc.
18:fea.87	1630 ± 75	1616 ± 80	ISGS-743	(F)	22	17	ok
4:sq.954	1630 ± 80	—	Beta-4981	(A)	—	—	anomalous
7:fea.14	1550 ± 120	1531 ± 123	M-1263	RC6:4	55	24	ok
1:fea.1	1530 ± 70	1511 ± 73	ISGS-978	(A)	33	26	ok
18:fea.121	1530 ± 75	1511 ± 78	ISGS-728	(F)	15	9	ok
17:str.6	1510 ± 55	1490 ± 59	GX-0366	(C)	31	16	ok
14:fea.44	1500 ± 130	—	M-2244	RC14:207	—	—	anomalous
10:fea.367	1490 ± 104	1470 ± 106	M-1721 & OWU-105B	RC10:76 RC9:326	7	3	ok
9:fea.2	1470 ± 130	1449 ± 132	M-1998	RC12:168	10	1	ok
12:fea.61F1	1410 ± 70	1388 ± 73	ISGS-861	(A)	50	42	ok
1:fea.5	1400 ± 70	1378 ± 73	ISGS-971	(A)	46	35	ok
14:fea.1026	1390 ± 70	1368 ± 73	ISGS-918	(A)	31	21	ok
19:fea.18	1380 ± 80	1357 ± 83	Beta-3911	(G)	20	13	ok
17:str.5	1355 ± 110	1333 ± 112	GX-0363	(C)	19	12	ok
11:fea.1133	1330 ± 100	—	GX-2399	(A)	—	—	not loc.
7:fea.9	1330 ± 120	1307 ± 122	M-1262	RC6:4	60	36	ok
8:fea.2	1330 ± 400	—	M-2002	RC12:169	—	—	large sd
20:fea.7	1325 ± 135	1302 ± 137	GX-2683	(H)	19	12	ok
10:fea.84	1310 ± 100	—	M-1406	RC8:266	—	—	anomalous
16:no #	1310 ± 150	1287 ± 158	M-714	RC4:187	50	24	ok
8:fea.6	1290 ± 130	1268 ± 140	M-2000	RC12:169	18	6	ok
3:fea.2	1240 ± 70	—	ISGS-899	(A)	2	0	small n
3:fea.3	1250 ± 70	—	ISGS-947	(A)	3	0	small n
19:fea.17	1230 ± 60	1209 ± 79	Beta-3912	(G)	22	12	ok
21:fea.150	1205 ± 100	1185 ± 112	GX-2681	(H)	47	28	ok
10:fea.215	1200 ± 130	1180 ± 140	M-2001	RC12:168	63	35	ok
23:fea.31	1200 ± 220	1180 ± 226	Dicar-144	(I)	21	16	ok
10:fea.203c	1160 ± 120	1141 ± 130	M-1407	RC8:266	59	33	ok
27:fea.13	1150 ± 150	1131 ± 159	M-1190	RC14:204	54	25	ok
19:fea.3	1120 ± 70	1102 ± 87	Beta-3910	(G)	47	22	ok
19:fea.31	1120 ± 80	1102 ± 95	Beta-3913	(G)	16	7	ok

Table 16.1 (cont.)

Prov[1]	Sample RCBP	Age BP[2]	Lab. No.	Reference[3]	N	N_i	Comments
21:fea.164	1120 ± 100	1102 ± 112	GX-2682	(H)	6	3	ok
28:fea.4	1115 ± 75	1097 ± 91	ISGS-183	(B)	20	8	ok
4:fea.87	1110 ± 75	—	ISGS-956	(A)	0	0	no sherds
24:fea.2	1090 ± 75	1074 ± 91	UGA-3994	(J)	19	15	ok
4:fea.28	1050 ± 75	1035 ± 81	ISGS-843	(A)	16	9	ok
9:fea.1	1050 ± 200	1035 ± 202	M-1999	$RC$12:168	24	11	ok
10:fea.451	1030 ± 120	1017 ± 124	M-1997	$RC$12:168	50	14	ok

[1] First number identifies site, following key for Figure 3.
[2] Corrections following Damon et al. 1974
[3] RC = Radiocarbon
(A) = Center for American Archaeology, Kampsville, Illinois, Records on File.
(B) = McNerney (1975, p. 407)
(C) = Morrell (1965, p. 64)
(D) = Southern Illinois University, Center for Archaeological Investigations, Records on File.
(E) = Hall and Elliston (1974, p. 23)
(F) = Charles Bentz, personal communication, September 9, 1982.
(G) = Lupinot et al. (1982, pp. 87-88)
(H) = Kuttruff (1974, p. 234)
(I) = McNerney (1974, p. 109)
(J) = Hutto and Butler (1981, p. 27)
(K) = Struever (1968)
[4] N = number of sherds measured.
N_i = number of sherds measured which were used in calculations after application of all selection criteria.

greater than ± 300 were excluded, as this was considered an intolerable level of uncertainty. Solid-carbon assays also were excluded.

The measured error value was adjusted for dendrochronological calibration error, after Damon et al. (1974, p. 365). Because C^{13} values were available only for the most recently assayed samples, no additional isotopic corrections were applied to any sample values. Most of the samples of charcoal assayed had contained only wood charcoal or nut hull fragments. Thus, correction for isotopic fractionation effects probably would have had little effect on the results; and the ± 120 correction factor suggested by Damon et al. (1974, p. 365) for samples lacking a C^{13} assay has been omitted (cf. Browman, 1981).

Associational Error for Sample Age, E_a. Four aspects of this required control: 1) the relevance of the charcoal to the provenience of deposition, 2) the relevance of the assayed age to the date of burning of the raw material, 3) the relevance of the pottery to the provenience of deposition (and hence to the date itself), and 4) the cultural context of the activities that could have produced the deposit (see Schiffer, 1982 for a discussion of similar problems in Hohokam chronological studies).

The midwestern Woodland period witnessed frequent reoccupation of settlement locations. Components representing brief occupations or lacking postdepositional disturbance from a later occupation consequently are rare. Domestic sites also generally yield not occupation surfaces, but zones of accretion of midden and soil disturbed by and overlaid by similar deposits of later occupations. Deposits resulting from probably single events—e.g., a broken, charred pot and its charred contents lying amidst charcoal and ash *in situ* in a hearth—consequently are also rare.

Pottery placed with the dead has always been regarded as a good candidate for independent dating and for building seriation models. However, such pottery may have had little in common with vessels made for actual use during the midwestern Woodland period (e.g., Griffin et al., 1970). Such pottery also would not necessarily have entered the archaeological record as soon after its manufacture as more probably would have been the case for everyday utility wares (e.g., David, 1972; DeBoer, 1974; DeBoer & Lathrop, 1979).

In view of these problems, dated proveniences were selected using the following criteria:

1) Burials and burial facilities were excluded from consideration. The intent here was to construct a model for use with domestic contexts and sensitive to dietary changes whether or not pottery commonly included with burials could also thereby be ordered.

2) Analysis was restricted to deposits in pit features or, in the cases of the samples from Grammar Shelter and Napoleon Hollow-Block I, to deposits of apparently brief origin and sealed context. Use of stratigraphic records for pit features allowed the further exclusion of those pits where very slow accumulation or the possibility of later disturbance of the fill could not be ruled out. For all other cases, the fill was assumed to have originated in trash dumping after use of the pit for some specific activity. In no case were the records sufficient to indicate either that the charcoal resulted from burning *in situ*, or that the pottery was made or used with the fire that produced the charcoal. All that could be argued was that the pottery and charcoal entered the pit fill at approximately the same time.

3) To be as conservative as possible, samples containing fewer than ten sherds, of $1/2$-inch minimum diameter, also were excluded. It was assumed that sherds smaller than this arbitrary criterion were more likely to have been moved about easily in the formation of deposits, and thus could not be trusted as indicators of technology during any one narrow span of time.

4) Archaeological charcoal can often represent the incompletely oxidized heart of an originally larger log. The radiocarbon date can thus pertain to the average age of inner rings rather than to the desired reference age of death of the tree or limb. Conversely, the earthen fill of a pit can often contain older material disturbed by the intrusion of that pit (or a neighbor) into earlier deposits. The radiocarbon date could then pertain to either the younger or older constituents

of the fill. Therefore, where use of the traditional seriation method for the region (e.g., Griffin et al., 1970, pp. 1-10) suggested a significant discrepancy between artifact styles and radiocarbon date as estimators of the pottery's age, the entire sample was excluded. However, given the uncertainties of the traditional seriation method, only apparent discrepancies on the order of hundreds of years could be safely identified without biasing the entire study's results.

In sum, given the large number of depositional events and processes affecting the relationship between the charcoal-based date and the age of manufacture of any pottery present in the same provenience, associational error was assumed to be Normally distributed among the included samples, in accord with the Central Limit theorem.

Dating Criterion, X. As noted earlier, domestic ceramic technological attributes that changed during the Woodland period include: temper size, density, and composition; wall thicknesses; and whole vessel shape. As I discuss elsewhere (1982, 1983; see also Rye, 1976; Steponaitis, 1982a, 1982b), these technical changes would have directly affected the thermal and mechanical performance characteristics of vessels in use. Overall, for the Middle-Late Woodland sequence, temper particle size and density decreased, as did average vessel wall thickness. Vessel shapes also became increasingly globular. This sequence would be expected as a consequence of increasing demand for vessels of greater thermal conductivity and greater resistance to fracture from thermal shock. Such changes in demand, in turn, are precisely what we would expect for the use of a cooking container increasingly devoted to the processing of masses of seeds, particularly starchy seeds, for food (see Hargrave, 1981).

In the present research, efforts eventually concentrated on the analysis of only vessel wall thickness, controlling for several other technological variables (see below). This restriction arose for two reasons. First, experiments with an X-ray photographic technique for assessing tempering characteristics rapidly for large numbers of sherds (Braun, 1982) were only partially successful. Refinements of the technique, in order to decrease measurement error and control for the effects of sherd thickness on particle visibility, are necessary before the technique fulfills all its promise. Second, whole vessel shape could not be assessed consistently from sherds and had to be dropped from consideration.

Measurement Error for Sherd Thickness, E_{mx}. Each sherd from a sample deposit, meeting the minimum size criterion mentioned earlier, was considered for analysis. Thickness measurements were recorded if the sherd appeared regular enough to also allow the recording of curvatures (see below). Thickness was recorded to the nearest 0.1 mm at four points spaced equally around the sherd margin, beginning at a point chosen at random. Areas affected by stamped or noded decoration were avoided. Sherd widths, unfortunately, were not recorded, so that variation in thickness could not then be controlled for sherd area—a shortcoming to be corrected in future applications.

The recording of four measurements allowed assessment of intra-sherd variability, E_{mx}. The standard deviation of intra-sherd thicknesses averaged 0.4436 mm across all samples, but did not vary consistently with intra-sherd average thickness or with sample age. Such consistency suggests that the potters sought to control the absolute variability of vessel walls, rather than allowing more variability for thicker walls.

Any sherd with a standard deviation $(s_{(n-1)})$ greater than 1.0 mm among its four measurements of thickness was excluded from further analysis. This criterion was chosen because it is easily replicable in future applications and appeared to exclude only the more obviously irregular sherds from analysis. Application of the criterion excluded 4% of all sherds otherwise includable in the analysis.

Sources of Systematic Non-Temporal Variation in Sherd Thickness, E_o. The thickness of a ceramic vessel's walls negatively affects the wall's thermal conductivity and resistance to fracture from thermal shock. However, it positively affects the wall's resistance to fracture from mechanical forces. This latter relationship is affected further by vessel shape. The smaller the diameter of curvature (girth) of a wall, the higher its breakage loading strength for a given value of thickness. A skilled potter can control breakage loading strength also by varying temper composition and manufacturing technique, and by varying vessel height more than girth to achieve differences in vessel capacity. Consequently, a potter faced with changing demands on the final product must balance these several factors of mechanical need against each other and against manufacturing cost in order to achieve a desired product. Changes in particular properties of vessel construction, e.g., in vessel wall thicknesses, thus will indicate changing demands on performance, but only if viewed against other vessel properties.

Initial investigations (Braun, 1983) showed that sherd thickness during the Middle Woodland period varied positively with wall girth. Girth was measured using a gauge held perpendicular to each sherd's approximate center. The axis of minimum diameter was taken as the indicator of the original vessel's girth at the sherd's point of origin. During the Late Woodland period, wall girth was found to hold less and less influence on thickness, until by about A.D. 800 thickness actually tended to decline slightly with increasing girth—another sign of increasing demand for thermal conductivity and shock resistance.

Due to the changes in the girth:thickness relationship, sherds from small-diameter vessels showed little variation in wall thickness regardless of age of manufacture. At the other extreme, sherds from apparently very large-diameter vessels proved highly variable. This latter tendency suggests either that the sherds actually came from smaller but irregularly shaped vessels, or that they came from bowls (as opposed to jars) not recognized during analysis (see below). Experiments showed that when sherds with girth measurement values of exterior diameter less than 20 cm or greater than 45 cm were excluded, the remaining sherds showed strong and consistent variation with sample age. Thus, the analysis focused in effect on only one size class of vessel. It is interesting to note that because vessels interred with Woodland burials almost always were small ones (e.g., Griffin et al., 1970), the 20 cm-girth criterion alone would have excluded most burial proveniences from inclusion in this analysis.

Analysis also focused on only one gross shape class and excluded all sherds from the basal portions of vessels. Consistency in tracking a single set of technological demands on pottery required exclusion of all except the dominant jar form of vessel. Bowls are only a rare constituent of Middle Woodland and later Late Woodland assemblages, and no other vessel forms other than unique specimens are known.

Basal sherds were excluded because vertical loading stresses concentrate in that region of vessels. Compensation for this pattern of loading commonly leads to the retention of basal walls thicker than those of the main vessel body. Sherds were coded according to their probable position of origin on the parent vessel, from rim to base, so that the effects of overall position could be studied. However, the vast majority of sherds could be classified only as "position-indeterminate," thus limiting further study.

In practice, sherds were assessed at one sitting for curvature, thickness, and position, or excluded as not falling in the jar category. All further sorting occurred during statistical analysis of the coded data.

The final systematic factor controlled in the analysis was space. When dealing with such a potentially ecologically and demographically sensitive phenomenon as cooking and dietary practices, spatial variation in subsistence systems must be considered. Samples from various areas were included in this study only if published reports on both ceramic technology and ethnobotanical remains from those areas indicated consistency with the other sample areas.

Rather than directly testing the model's spatial integrity, analysis was restricted to areas for which the published reports appeared to indicate consistency already. In a parallel study, Hargrave (1981) has found that the next drainage to the southeast of those studied, the Saline Valley of Illinois (Fig. 2), contained a more conservative ceramic assemblage. Based on six dated samples from the Carrier Mills Archaeological District, spanning the same 1,200 years of the Woodland sequence, Hargrave (1981, pp. 92-101) found average thicknesses to be consistently over 5 mm greater than those found for contemporary samples in the neighboring lower Big Muddy drainage. This technological difference parallels evidence for a much lower importance of edible seeds in the Carrier Mills diet throughout the Woodland sequence (Lopinot, 1982, pp. 804-806). Eventually, of course, it will be important to determine the wider geographic applicability of the present findings through direct investigation.

Stochastic Error of Sherd Thickness, E_s. In theory, this parameter is estimated as the residual variance after the removal of all other error terms and systematic effects, including the temporal trend. In practice, because a numerical value cannot be assigned to associational error or to unidentified systematic effects, this parameter's measurement takes in much more. I will return to this problem after discussing the estimation of $f(X)$, the trend of sherd thickness over time.

One small source of stochastic variation, however, could be partly controlled. Sherds identifiable as originating from the same broken vessel were not all measured; instead, sherds that fit together were treated together as a single case. On the other hand, sherds of the same vessel of origin that did not fit together could not be easily identified as such, due to the variation in firing color and surface texture common within even single Woodland vessels. How much the variation in thickness for a single vessel may depart from or follow the variation among multiple vessels should be determined in any future applications.

In summary, the final data set consisted of pottery from 56 pit features of acceptable integrity, from a restricted region, with each sherd satisfying five criteria: 1) a standard deviation of thickness less than or equal to 1.00 mm, 2) origin from a jar vessel form, 3) origin from any portion of a vessel other than the base, 4) a girth value greater than or equal to 20 cm but less than or equal to 45 cm, and 5) failure to match up with any other sherd from the same provenience.

Time-Trend of Sherd Thickness, $f(X)$. The data for this analysis were collectable, clearly, only with sample date as the independent variable and sherd thickness as the dependent variable—an uninverted form of the model that is needed, as opposed to the inverted form described previously. We have multiple measurements of sherd thickness for each sample date, but did not choose the samples because they fell into specific increments of mean sherd thickness per sample. Consequently, our task is to calculate a description of thickness as it varies dependent on sample age $f(T)$, and then to invert the equation, yielding $f(X)$.

The initial step in this process is to convert the raw thickness data, which are sampled irregularly in time, to interpolated values spaced regularly in time. Equidistant values of the independent variable are required by all trend-describing techniques.

The interpolation requires two considerations. First, which raw samples should we include in the estimation of X for each value of T? Second, how far apart should we set our values of T, i.e., how wide should we set our interpolative increments? The issue of sample inclusion arises because, in the most common form of interpolation known as rectangular integration (e.g., Davis, 1973, pp. 176-181), only those samples falling within some fixed span of each estimated value of T would be used. In the present instance, however, such a procedure would not take into account the fact that the sample ages themselves are estimates, with an associated error estimate. Further, such a procedure would not weight the samples differentially according to the magnitude of their associated temporal errors.

Consider, for example, how we would use the information on three pottery samples dated 1730 ± 50, 1710 ± 50, and 1685 ± 150 for estimating mean sherd thickness X, for the interval 1675-1725. Under most procedures, only sherds from the 1685 and 1710 samples would be used to estimate X for the given interval, and they would be treated equally. The 1730 sample, however, actually has a higher probability of truly dating within the given interval than does the 1685 sample; not only should its sherds be used in estimating X for the interval, but they perhaps should be given more weight than the sherds from the 1685 sample.

It is necessary, therefore, to use the dating error of each sample to assess the relevance of each sample for each interpolative increment and to assign a weight to its sherds in estimating X for that increment. This has two effects. First, it provides a more realistic estimate of X for each interval through the differential weighting. Second, it provides a smoothing filter for removing some of the error of $f(T)$ arising from dating measurement error. That is, unlike many time-series methods, it *simultaneously* both interpolates equivalent temporal increments and acts as a filter for noise arising from measurement error in T.

The second consideration in interpolation, that of the width of the interpolative increment, arises because the apparent shape of the trend in X is affected by this parameter. Clearly, our object is to use increments as narrow as possible to ensure sensitivity to the details of the trend, but not so narrow that they introduce a false precision to the calculations. Given the Nyquist frequency limitations of time-series analysis mentioned earlier, we also need increments at most half as wide as the smallest fluctuation in T we wish to resolve. To pick out true fluctuations of at least 100 years in duration, for example, we would need an increment width of 50 years.

The method chosen here for simultaneously interpolating equivalent temporal increments and smoothing (or filtering) the estimates of mean X (by increment of T) can be called a *PROBNORM* method, after the probability function within the SAS statistical computing package which I have used in its construction (SAS Institute, 1982, pp. 179-180). As a first step, the estimated age and dating error of each sample are used to estimate the probability that that sample actually dates to some given interval. The resulting probabilities define the weights of the desired filtering function. Each estimate of probability assumes only that the dating error for a radiocarbon assay is Normally distributed about the stated sample mean age with a standard deviation equal to the published error value and an infinitely large sample size, following Long and Rippeteau (1974).

To calculate this probability, the beginning and ending dates for the interval in question are converted to Z scores for each of the sample dates, based on the sample dates and dating errors. The probabilities of occurrence of each Z score are then determined from a table or, as in the case of the SAS PROBNORM function, from a mathematical integration of the cumulative area under the Normal distribution. The probability W_i, that a radiocarbon sample truly dates within a given interval is then given as the absolute value of the difference between the two cumulative probabilities for that sample and that interval's beginning and ending points. Thus,

$$W_i = P\left(\frac{D_i - (\hat{T} + m)}{sd_i}\right) - P\left(\frac{D_i - (\hat{T} - m)}{sd_i}\right) \quad (2)$$

where W_i = probablity that sample i falls within the interval $\hat{T} \pm m$

D_i = mean age estimate for sample i

sd_i = standard deviation of D_i

$\hat{T}$ = interval centerpoint

m = 1/2 interval span or increment

P = cumulative probability that the observed Z score could be obtained from an infinitely large sample with distribution Normal (O,1).

The second and final step of the PROBNORM method generates the desired interpolation and smoothing of the data. It uses the values of W_i, for each interval as weighting factors for the observations of X from each sample in order to calculate for that interval an estimated mean value of X, labelled $\hat{X}$, as follows:

$$\hat{X} = \frac{\sum\limits^{i}(W_i \sum\limits^{j} X_{ij})}{\sum\limits^{i} W_i J_i} \quad (3)$$

where $\hat{X}$ = estimated mean value of X for the interval of study

W_i = probability that sample i falls within the interval of study

X_{ij} = value of X for case $j = 1$ to J from sample $i = 1$ to I.

J_i = total number of cases of X in sample i

This filter function weights each sample differentially for each increment of $\hat{T}$, according to both the sample's dating error and the number of cases (e.g., sherds in our example) contained in that sample.

The filter function can be adjusted according to how much importance one wishes to give to the published dating error values and, consequently, how smooth a curve one seeks. Samples can be selected for inclusion in the calculation of $\hat{X}$ for a given interval according to their values of W_i. At the extreme, using W_i greater than zero as the criterion for inclusion, every sample theoretically will contribute something to the calculation of every $\hat{X}$. The resulting curve of $\hat{X}$ will be relatively smooth. A more conservative approach, however, would be to consider for each interval's calculations only those samples for which W_i exceeds, for example, .05 or .10. For $W_i > .05$, we would end up using only samples lying within a much narrower range of sample dates than for $W_i > 0$, producing a curve more sensitive to the true variation in X. With a 50-year interpolative increment, for example, a sample with a standard deviation of 100 years would achieve a value of $W_i > .05$ only if the sample date fell within 168 years of the increment's midpoint.

Application of the PROBNORM method to the Woodland samples, therefore, required the selection of an appropriate interpolative increment width, and the assessment of $\hat{X}$ for several cut-off values of W_i. The increment width was calculated from the observed mean interval between raw sample dates (22 years) and its standard deviation ($s_n = 21.8$ years), so that at least 90% of the raw intervals would be smaller than the interpolative increment width. This calculation produced a figure of $(22 + (z_{.90} \times 21.8)) = 49.9$ years, here rounded to 50. The raw data consisted of measurements of mean thickness *per sherd* for 791 sherds which satisfied the five criteria for selection discussed earlier and came from 56 dated proveniences. $\hat{X}$ was calculated using values of $W_i > 0$, $W_i > .05$, and $W_i > .10$.

Figure 4 presents the results of the application of the PROBNORM interpolative/filtering method to the 56 dated samples of pottery, with $\hat{X}$ measured as the estimated mean thickness of pottery and controlling for the several factors

Fig. 16.4. Time-trend of mean vessel wall thickness $\hat{X}$, using PROBNORM method and controlling for wall girth, position, and intra-sherd variability.

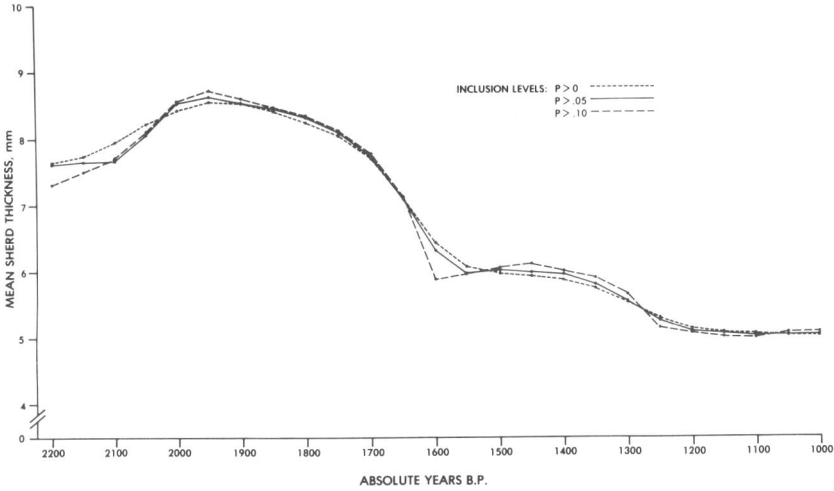

discussed above. The end-points of the graph are defined so that no increment's midpoint is either higher or lower, respectively, than the highest or lowest raw sample date. Also note (see Table 1) that few raw dates fall between 1700 and 1550 BP. Few substantial components from this period, the Middle-Late Woodland transition, have yet been investigated.

Figure 4 shows $\hat{X}$ estimated with the three cut-off values for W_i. In this example, $W_i > .05$ appears a good compromise between the over- and under-sensitivity of the .10 and 0-level criteria, respectively, and is used as the basis for all further discussion.

Figure 4 graphically defines the uninverted relationship $\hat{X} = f(\hat{T})$. I have not yet attempted an algebraic description of $f(\hat{T})$ overall. Such a description would unnecessarily complicate matters at the present stage of research by raising the problem of how to invert the overall equation to the form $\hat{T} = f(\hat{X})$. When I do attempt it, fortunately, it will not be necessary to use a Model II procedure for describing the entire curve, for two reasons. First, use of the PROBNORM interpolative/filtering method has already removed an unmeasured but substantial portion of the error term E_{mt}. Second, Model II procedures are necessary only if one expects a systematic relationship between T and E_{mt}, or between X and E_{mx} or E_s or E_a (Sokal & Rohlf, 1982, pp. 547-555). No such systematic relationships are expected or observable in the present example. At present, a graphical solution serves our purposes well enough.

The shape of the time-trend for $\hat{X}$ in Figure 4 provides much information on changes in cooking and dietary practices. In earlier considerations of the changes between only 1950 and 1000 BP, I have argued that changes in the importance of thermal stresses, arising from an increasing importance of starchy seeds as food, determined the overall shape of the curve (Braun, 1982, 1983). The increase in thickness leading up to the conditions at 1950 BP does not fit this overall interpretation. A possible reason for this, however, is suggested by the list of systematic constraints on wall thickness. The one factor not controllable using single sherds is vessel height. Taller vessels would contain higher stresses from vertical loading than would shorter vessels and, consequently, would be built with stronger walls. Thus, at least some of the variation in wall thicknesses along the entire sequence could be proposed as a consequence of varying average vessel height and, hence, average volume. The shape of the entire curve, in fact, parallels a curve of increasing and then decreasing average housefloor area (Braun, 1981b), supporting the idea that the ceramic curve partially reflects variation in average household size as well as in dietary constitution. I am exploring this idea with further research.

Prediction of Sample Date from Sherd Thickness. Sample date is predicted for a collection of sherds by calculating the mean sherd thickness for all sherds in the collection satisfying the five selection criteria discussed earlier. The graphical solution of this step requires only identifying the date value $\hat{T}$ at which the observed mean thickness value intersects the trend line. However, two problems arise.

First, the trend reverses itself between 2100 and 1700 BP. Values of $\hat{X}$ between 7.3 and 8.6 mm predict two dates. Additional information on the context or other aspects of a sample being dated along the trend will always be needed to distinguish the two parts of the Middle Woodland period, if a continuous-scale date is to be predicted. For this purpose, the traditional seriation model will serve adequately. Stylistic attributes, stratigraphic position, ceramic tempering characteristics, chipped stone characteristics, or the presence of certain stylistic markers among any sherds from small jars and bowls present, all allow for a gross separation of the sort needed (e.g., Cantwell, 1980; Griffin, 1952; Griffin et al., 1970, pp. 1-10; White, 1968). The need for such markers, however, makes it far easier to date *collections* of sherds found in a meaningful provenience than to date, for example, single sherds removed from context. (I will return to this point shortly.) In the present example, it is assumed that the researcher can distinguish features as dating either earlier than 1900 BP or later than 2000 BP, allowing an overlap.

The second problem in using the trend line is: What do we do when a sample of pottery falls outside the range of the graph, i.e., exceeds ca. 8.6 mm or falls below 4.9 mm? The trend line plots average thickness only; hence, the simplest response to this problem is to define a sample's estimated date based on its point of closest approach to the trend line.

Error of Prediction of $\hat{T}$ from $\hat{X}$. The error of prediction is most easily determined empirically. A linear equation for $\hat{X} = f(\hat{T})$, in this case *Thickness = a + b(Date)*, is easily definable *for each 50-year interval* between the interpolated midpoints. This equation is inverted to the form $\hat{T} = f(\hat{X})$ as: *Date = (Thickness-a)/b*. The standard error of estimate of *Date* for each of these short lines is then calculated empirically for all pieces of pottery with observed mean thicknesses between the maximum and minimum values of thickness predicted by the uninverted equation $f(\hat{T})$ for that interval.

For example, for the interval 2100 to 2050 BP, the predicted minimum and maximum mean thickness values are 7.76 and 8.05 mm, respectively. The slope of the equation for $f(\hat{T})$ for that interval is $(7.76-8.05)/50 = -.0058$ with an intercept of $8.05 - (-.0058 \times 2050) = 19.94$. The equation for predicting date from thickness, from this interval, then, is $f(\hat{X}) = (X - 19.94)/-.0058 = \hat{T}$. Table 2 presents values rounded to two decimal places for all variables. The actual calculations for $f(\hat{X})$, for each interval, used unrounded values.

To avoid reintroducing dating measurement error in calculating the standard error terms, the importance of each piece of pottery has to be weighted inversely according to the dating measurement error for its sample-of-origin. This weighting, following the reasoning of Long and Rippeteau (1974, pp. 208) is the inverse square of the published dating error.

The standard error thus is calculated, *for each interval*, as

$$s.e. = \sqrt{\frac{\sum_{}^{ij} d_i^2 (T_{ij} - \hat{T})^2}{\sum_{}^{ij} d_i \times \sum_{}^{ij} d_i - min(d_i)}} \qquad (4)$$

where d_i = inverse square of the standard deviation for the date of sample i.

$min(d_i)$ = smallest value of d_i obtained among the sample contributing observations to this interval, and

j = 1 to j = number of sherds from sample i contributing to the calculations for this interval.

The values of the standard error terms for successive increments of thickness and predicted date are given in Table 2. Use of the table is straightforward: For a sample of n sherds of unknown age but presumably assignable to one side or the other of the curve-reversal, the mean date of the sample is predicted graphically from mean sherd thickness. The error of estimate is given as $\pm (t_\sigma (n-1))$ × (standard error for the interval containing the estimated mean). It is because of this formula for assessing precision that the method works best for collections rather than for single sherds.

For example, a sample of 25 sherds with mean thickness 7.5 mm would have a predicted age of 1685 BP, with a 95% confidence interval of (1.711)(41.25) = ±71 years. If the sample size were 60 sherds, the 95% error would be (1.67) × (41.25) = ±69 years.

As noted earlier, these estimated errors arise from several sources other than stochastic variation. Error due to dating error cannot be ruled out, nor can error due to unrecognized systematic effects. More importantly, what I referred to earlier as associational error probably accounts for some immeasurable portion of the unexplained variation. Not surprisingly, the standard errors are largest for those periods during which the rates of change in $\hat{X}$ are relatively low. Other criteria will be needed to provide greater precision during these periods.

Nevertheless, as intended, the curve of $\hat{X}$ provides far greater accuracy than any previous temporal seriation for the region, with two further advantages: We can estimate the precision (probable error) of any predicted date, and we know in advance to what contexts it may be reliably applied.

PROBLEMS AND PROSPECTS

The work needed to improve the specific Woodland model seems clear; to improve the general method, less so.

The specific Woodland model could benefit from changes in measurement technique, the inclusion of additional samples more evenly distributed over

Table 16.2

Standard Errors of Estimate for $\hat{T} = f(\hat{X})$
Based on Probnorm Curve with $W_i > .05$

Thickness Range, mm. Early	Late (rounded)	Date, BP Range	SE[1]	N
7.60	7.64	2200-2150	37.01	49
7.64	7.76	2150-2100	36.66	3
7.76	8.05	2100-2050	50.18	8
8.05	8.52	2050-2000	48.24	4
8.52	8.52	2000-1900	14.70[2]	132
8.52	8.43	1900-1850	41.86	7
8.43	8.29	1850-1800	61.46	6
8.29	8.07	1800-1750	68.83	7
8.07	7.70	1750-1700	47.17	27
7.70	7.06	1700-1650	41.25	48
7.06	6.31	1650-1600	25.14	106
6.31	5.95	1600-1550	32.09	61
5.95	5.94	1550-1400	75.64	4
5.94	5.78	1400-1350	38.32	30
5.78	5.54	1350-1300	34.38	49
5.54	5.25	1300-1250	27.88	62
5.25	5.07	1250-1200	55.62	24
5.07	5.02	1200-1000	32.16	214

[1] Calculations of SE assume that the researcher can divide collections into pre-1900 and post-2000 BP populations, except for collections with mean thickness of 8.52 mm or greater. These latter samples are all estimated to date to 1950 BP. Early collections averaging less than 7.60 mm are assumed to date to 2200 BP; late collections averaging less than 5.02 mm are assumed to date to 1000 BP.

[2] This figure applies to the estimation of a sample's age as lying within 50 years of 1950 BP. No greater accuracy is yet possible.

time, and expansion of the spatial range of the data base. The changes in measurement technique have already been mentioned.

The inclusion of additional samples will have several effects. Radiocarbon assays now routinely provide error values between only ± 50 and ± 100, and C^{13} assays have become inexpensive and readily available. As such increasingly precisely dated samples become available, both the accuracy and precision of the curve $f(\hat{X})$ will improve. Similarly, the potential size of associational error could be reduced by restricting the analysis to radiocarbon assays of only charred annuals, as they become available. Assuming control of fractionation effects, for example, charred nut shells would be a better dating medium than the uncontrolled range of charred woods and annuals commonly used.

As Tables 1 and 2 show, the present data base is not evenly distributed over either time or $\hat{X}$. With a greater number and more even distribution of samples, it will become possible to reduce the width of the interpolative increment. All of these effects will contribute to the ultimate goal, reducing the standard errors of prediction along the curve.

Expansion of the spatial range of the data base is necessary to directly establish the spatial limits of applicability of the specific model. Such information will be useful to studies of variation in cooking and dietary practices as well.

Finally, the use of a second seriation curve to complement the curve based on pottery wall thicknesses also warrants exploration. A second curve, which gives more precise estimates where the thickness curve reverses or lies level, would compensate for the deficiencies of the single-variable model.

On the more general level, questions remain primarily about the possible quantification of associational error, the possible need for a Model II curve-fitting regression technique, the possibility for testing for temporal mixing in provenience contents based on the *variance* in values of the seriation criterion for a given sample provenience, and the possibility of designing research so that the ordering criterion X can be collected as the independent rather than the dependent variable. The identification of appropriate cultural variables must remain a case-specific problem, although the idea of "cultural variables" itself poses serious theoretical challenges. None of these issues, however, prohibits further applications.

Finally, it may not necessarily be the case that associational error will be Normally distributed across a population of site-formational events. Although this may be debated abstractly, it would be more appropriate to evaluate the shape of associational error empirically for a given problem set by examining the distribution of large numbers of samples of criterion values from relatively narrow temporal intervals. Appropriate statistical steps could then be taken if the distributions proved significantly non-Normal.

Clearly, the applicability of the suggested time series approach has limits. To construct a predictive model, the approach requires variables that can accept a continuous, ratio scaling, and also requires relatively unmixed proveniences for simultaneous scaling and independent dating. Beyond this, constructing a model requires either already dated proveniences (or objects) or the resources to collect the necessary chronometric data. These may be only mechanical limitations, but they can still be significant according to circumstances. A final limit holds even if the preceding requirements can be met: One can end up with a curve with too little directionality to allow any predictive use.

I would, therefore, answer the question posed at the beginning of this chapter with this: in theory, we can indeed estimate the absolute ages of objects or places just as accurately and precisely from their physical characteristics as from case-by-case independent dating. In practice, we may only lack the necessary data.

REFERENCES

Binford, L.R. (1962). A new method of calculating dates from kaolin pipe stem samples. *Southeastern Archaeological Conference Newsletter 9*, 19-21.

Braun, D.P. (1977). *Middle Woodland-early Late Woodland social change in the prehistoric central midwestern U.S.* Doctoral dissertation No. 77-26210, University of Michigan, Ann Arbor.

Braun, D.P. (1981a). Ceramic decorative diversity and Illinois Woodland regional integration. In B.A. Nelson (Ed.), *Decoding Prehistoric Ceramics* (in press). Carbondale, IL: Southern Illinois University Press.

Braun, D.P. (1981b, May). *Illinois Woodland social change as organizational transformation*. Paper presented at the annual meeting of the Society for American Archaeology, San Diego.

Braun, D.P. (1982). Radiographic analysis of temper in ceramic vessels: Goals and initial methods. *Journal of Field Archaeology 9*, 183-192.

Braun, D.P. (1983). Pots as tools. In J. Moore & A. Keene (Eds.). *Archaeological hammers and theories*. New York: Academic Press, Inc.

Braun, D.P., & Plog, S. (1982). Evolution of 'tribal' social networks: Theory and prehistoric North American evidence. *American Antiquity 47*, 504-525.

Browman, D.L. (1981). Isotopic discrimination and correction factors in radiocarbon dating. In M.B. Schiffer (Ed.), *Advances in archaeological method and theory, Volume 4* (pp. 241-295). New York: Academic Press, Inc.

Bucha, V. (1971). Archaeomagnetic dating. In H.N. Michael & E.K. Ralph (Eds.), *Dating techniques for the archaeologist* (pp. 57-117). Cambridge: MIT Press.

Cantwell, A. (1980). Dickson Camp and Pond: *Two early Havana tradition sites in the central Illinois valley*. (Reports of Investigations 36). Springfield: Illinois State Museum.

Damon, P.E., Ferguson, C.W., Long, A., & Wallick, E.I. (1974). Dendrochronologic calibration of the radiocarbon time scale. *American Antiquity 39*, 350-366.

David, N. (1972). On the life span of pottery, type frequencies, and archaeological inference. *American Antiquity 37*, 141-142.

David, J.C. (1973). *Statistics and data analysis in geology*. New York: John Wiley & Sons, Inc.

Dean, J.S. (1978). Independent dating in archaeological analysis. In M.B. Schiffer, (Ed.), *Advances in archaeological method and theory, (Vol. 1)* (pp. 223-255). New York; Academic Press, Inc.

DeBoer, W.R. (1974). Ceramic longevity and archaeological interpretation: An example from the upper Ucayali, Peru. *American Antiquity 39*, 335-343.

DeBoer, W.R., & Lathrap, D.W. (1979). The making and breaking of Shipibo-Conibo ceramics. In C.C. Kramer (Ed.), *Ethnoarchaeology: implications of ethnography for archaeology* (pp. 102-183). New York: Columbia University Press.

Friedrich, M.H. (1970). Design structure and social interaction: Archaeological implications of an ethnographic analysis. *American Antiquity 35*, 332-343.

Gottman, J.M. (1981). *Time-Series analysis: A comprehensive introduction for social scientists.* New York: Cambridge University Press.

Graves, M.W. (1981). *Ethnoarchaeology of Kalinga ceramic design.* Doctoral dissertation, University of Arizona, Tucson. (University Microfilms, Ann Arbor, MI).

Griffin, J.B. (1952). Some early and middle Woodland pottery types in Illinois. In T. Deuel (Ed.), *Hopewellian communities in Illinois* (Scientific Papers No. 5) (pp. 93-130). Springfield: Illinois State Museum.

Griffin, J.B., Flanders, R.E., & Titterington, P.F. (1970). *The burial complexes of the Knight and Norton mounds in Illinois and Michigan* (Memoir 2). University of Michigan, Museum of Anthropology, Ann Arbor.

Hall, E., & Elliston, J. (1974). *A report of an archaeological excavation at the Fry Number One Site (SIU 22C3-38), Jefferson County, Illinois, 1972.* Ina, IL: Rend Lake College.

Hally, D.J. (1983). Use alteration of pottery vessel surfaces: An important source for the identification of vessel function. *North American Archaeologist 4*, 1-25.

Hargrave, M.L. (1981). *Woodland ceramic chronometry and occupational intensity at the Carrier Mills Archaeological District, Saline County, Illinois.* Unpublished master's thesis, Southern Illinois University, Carbondale.

Hargrave, M.L., & Braun, D.P. (1981, May). *Chronometry of mechanical performance characteristics of Woodland ceramics: Methods, results, applications.* Paper presented at the annual meeting of the Society for American Archaeology, San Diego.

Hutto, M.D., & Butler, B.M. (1981). *Archaeological investigations for the Mary's River scenic overlook, Randolph County, Illinois (Research Paper No. 26).* Southern Illinois University at Carbondale, Center for Archaeological Investigations, Carbondale.

Kuttruff, L.C. (1974). *Late Woodland settlement and subsistence in the Lower Kaskaskia River Valley.* Doctoral dissertation, Southern Illinois University, Carbondale. (University Microfilms, Ann Arbor, MI).

Long, A. & Rippeteau, B. (1974). Testing contemporaneity and averaging radiocarbon dates. *American Antiquity 39*, 205-215.

Lopinot, N.H. (1982). Summary of the botanical analysis. In R.W. Jefferies & B.M. Butler *The Carrier Mills archaeological project: Human adaptation in the Saline Valley, Illinois* (Research Paper No. 33) (pp. 797-806). Southern Illinois University at Carbondale, Center for Archaeological Investigations, Carbondale.

Lopinot, N.H., Hutto, M.D., & Braun, D.P. (1982). *Archaeological investigations at the Kingfish site, St. Clair County, Illinois* (Research Paper No. 25). Southern Illinois University at Carbondale, Center for Archaeological Investigations, Carbondale.

Marquardt, W.H. (1978). Advances in archaeological seriation. In M.B. Schiffer (Ed.), *Advances in archaeological method and theory, Vol. 1* (pp. 257-314). New York: Academic Press, Inc.

McCleary, R., & Hay, R.A. Jr. (1980). *Applied time series analysis for the social sciences.* Beverly Hills, CA: Sage Publications.

McNerney, M.J., (Ed.). (1974). *Archaeological investigations at the Burning Star No. 4 Mine, Perry County, Illinois* (Archaeological Salvage Report 39). Southern Illinois University Museum.

McNerney, M.J. (1975). *Archaeological investigations in the Cedar Creek Reservoir, Jackson County, Illinois* (Southern Illinois Studies 12). Southern Illinois University Museum.

Morrell, L.R. (1965). *The Texas site, Carlyle Reservoir, Clinton County, Illinois* (Archaeological Salvage Report 23). Southern Illinois University Museum.

Plog, F.T. (1973). Diachronic anthropology. In C. Redman (Ed.), *Research and theory in current archaeology* (pp. 181-198). New York: John Wiley & Sons, Inc.

Plog, F.T. (1977). Explaining change. In J.N. Hill (Ed.), *The explanation of prehistoric change* (pp. 17-57). Albuquerque: University of New Mexico Press.

Plog, F.T. (1979). Alternative models of prehistoric change. In C. Renfrew & K.L. Cooke

Transformations: mathematical approaches to culture change (pp. 221-236). New York: Academic Press, Inc.

Plog, S. (1980). *Stylistic variation in prehistoric ceramics*. Cambridge, England: Cambridge University Press.

Plog, S., & Hantman, J.L. (1980). Multiple regression analysis as a dating method in the American Southwest. In S. Plog (Ed.), *Spatial Organization and Exchange: Archaeological Survey on Northern Black Mesa, Arizona* (in press). Carbondale: Southern Illinois University Press.

Rich, L.G. (1973). *Environmental systems engineering*. New York: McGraw-Hill, Inc.

Rye, O.S. (1976). Keeping your temper under control: Materials and the manufacture of Papuan pottery. *Archaeology and Physical Anthropology in Oceania 11*, 106-137.

Rye, O.S. (1981). Pottery technology. In *Taraxacum Manuals in Archaeology, 4*. Washington, DC: Taraxacum.

SAS Institute (1982). *SAS user's guide: Basics*. Cary, NC: SAS Institute.

Schiffer, M.B. (1982). Hohokam chronology: An essay on history and method. In R.H. McGuire & M.B. Schiffer (Eds.), *Hohokam and Patayan: prehistory of southeastern Arizona* (pp. 299-344). New York: Academic Press, Inc.

Smith, M.F., Jr. (in press) Toward an economic interpretation of ceramics: Relating vessel size and shape to use. In B.A. Nelson (Ed.). *Decoding Prehistoric Ceramics*. Carbondale: Southern Illinois University Press.

Sokal, R.R., & Rohlf, F.J. (1982). *Biometry* (2nd ed.). San Francisco: W.H. Freeman.

Steponaitis, V.P. (1982a). *Ceramics, chronology, and community patterns: An Archaeological study at Moundville*. New York: Academic Press, Inc.

Steponaitis, V.P. (1982b, March). *Technological studies of prehistoric pottery from Alabama: Physical properties and vessel function*. Paper presented at the Wenner-Gren symposium, "Multidimensional approaches to the study of ancient ceramics," Lhee, Netherlands.

Struever, S. (1968). *A re-examination of Hopewell in eastern North America*. Unpublished doctoral dissertation, University of Chicago.

White, A.M. (1968). *The lithic industries of the Illinois valley in the Early and Middle Woodland period* (Anthropological Papers No. 35). University of Michigan, Museum of Anthropology.

17

The Use of Technological Indices: A Case Study for the Levantine Mousterian

MARCIA L. JONES

The process of structuring techno-typological variability observed among lithic assemblages into a spatio-temporal framework of industries is frequently a very problematic stage of Paleolithic research. The definition of lithic industries depends upon successfully sifting out activity-specific, spatial bias within specific assemblages in order to arrive at temporally significant patterns for a region. Only after defining and chronologically ordering lithic industries can one address more complex problems concerning change in prehistoric adaptive strategies.

Acknowledging that the composition of a lithic assemblage recovered from a site is influenced, in part, by the types of activities undertaken during occupation of the site (Binford & Binford, 1966; Binford, 1982), the focus of lithic chronological analyses has shifted increasingly away from the functional aspects of lithic assemblages to their technological characteristics. Inter-assemblage, stratigraphic trends in these technological characteristics have been quantified using various indices, and the index values have then been used to characterize specific lithic assemblages in terms of their industrial affiliation and chronological placement (Jelinek, 1981; Close, 1977; Lubell, 1974).

To utilize technological indices in this manner, however, one must first determine whether the amount of variation in a particular index is sufficiently small *within* an assemblage to reasonably allow the determination of an index

I would like to express my sincere appreciation to Dr. Harold Hietala for his counsel and encouragement throughout the course of this research and for his assistance in editing earlier drafts of this manuscript. I would also like to thank Dr. Arthur Jelinek for providing additional information on results of his analyses of the Rosh Ein Mor material and Dr. Anthony Marks for providing access to the lithic material from Rosh Ein Mor and Nahal Aqev. The initial recovery of lithic material from these two sites was made possible through grants from the National Science Foundation (GS42680, GS28602x, GS28602x1) awarded to Dr. Marks.

value *representative* of the assemblage. Only if intra-assemblage variation in the values of an index over space, depth, and artifact class is small compared to inter-assemblage variations can the index be used to seriate assemblages.

Two technological indices defined for use in analyzing Levantine Mousterian assemblages merit particular examination. These are, Jelinek's width/thickness ratio and Munday's index of artifact elongation (Jelinek, 1977; Munday, 1979). Both indices seem to exhibit temporal significance and possibly can serve as general chronological indicators in seriating Levantine Mousterian assemblages.

Using the sequence of Levantine Mousterian assemblages from Tabun Cave, Israel, Jelinek suggests that the relationship between the width and thickness of artifacts changes through time. Specifically, among assemblages from Tabun, the width/thickness index and variance in this index increase with time (Jelinek, 1981). Other Levantine Mousterian assemblages from Israel were analyzed and seemed to follow this trend as well, regardless of the geographic location of the site or typological composition of the assemblage. Therefore, he concludes that this technological trend transcends typological variability, and thus, would be useful in seriating Levantine Mousterian assemblages (Jelinek, 1981).

Munday's (1979) intra-site analysis of lithic assemblages from the Central Negev site, Nahal Aqev, investigates localized technological change. Based on the premise that artifact elongation is a measure of production efficiency, diachronic change in the relationship of length to width of artifacts at Nahal Aqev is attributed to a shift in core reduction strategies. This shift is related by Munday to a deterioration of environmental conditions. The environmental record indicates that the climate became increasingly warm in the northern Levant (thus increasingly arid in the southern Levant) during the course of the Mousterian occupation (Jelinek, 1981). Consequently, an index measuring artifact elongation would have temporal implications (Munday, 1979).

In reviewing these studies, it is apparent that considerable effort has been directed toward detecting diachronic patterning in technological index variation. More often than not, these patterns are detected by graphically plotting the index values of assemblages thought to have relatively certain chronological placements. If index values change in a similar direction, a "trend" is defined. Rarely, however, are these "trends" tested to see if the differences are indeed statistically significant, or merely a result of fortuitous intra-assemblage sampling.

In this chapter, three sources of intra-assemblage variability in technological index values are examined for their significance and potential in leading to unrepresentative characterization of the technological attributes of assemblages. These are: variability in index values among the *artifact classes* within an assemblage, variability over the *spatial* extent of the assemblage, and variability over the *depth* of the assemblage. One-way ANOVA procedures will be used to test the significance of these possible sources of variation. By definition, an index will be considered *stable* in regard to one of these sources of variation if an insignificant F-statistic value is found with an ANOVA test. The archaeological implication of this stability varies according to the source of variation considered in the ANOVA model (Table 1). Only indices that are stable in regard to all three sources of intra-site variation can be considered potentially useful for seriating assemblages (Fig. 1).

Table 17.1

The Sources of Variation Examined in this Study Using ANOVA Models and the Archaeological Implications

Possible Outcomes of the F-Statistic	Archaeological Implications Given the Specified Source of Variation:				
	Statistical Implications	Artifact Classes	Areas within an Assemblage	Levels of an Assemblage	Assemblages
Between group variation ≤ within group variation	lack of statistically significant differences	stable index; insignificant artifact-specific variation	stable index; insignificant activity-specific variation	stable index; insignificant temporal variation	stable index; insignificant temporal variation between sites
Between group variation > within group variation	statistically significant differences	significant artifact-class specific variation	significant activity-specific variation	significant intra-assemblage temporal variation	significant inter-assemblage temporal variation

An index exhibiting statistically significant variation (as opposed to stability) over artifact samples from diverse stratigraphic or spatial units within an assemblage can have an additional property. The values of an index may vary systematically among stratigraphic units so as to form a *trend* over them. Similarly, the values of an index may vary systematically over space, with samples having like values aggregating spatially and segregating spatially, from samples having different values. In this case, the index values can be said to form a spatial *pattern*.

In the present study, assemblages from two Levantine Mousterian sites in the Central Negev, Israel were analyzed for intra-assemblage and inter-assemblage variability in six technological indices of artifact morphology: length; width; thickness; size—expressed as a product of length, width, and thickness; length/width ratio as an expression of Munday's attribute of elongation; and Jelinek's width/thickness ratio. The analyses focused on five problems:

1. Which indices vary across artifact classes within an assemblage, indicating that the proportional occurrence of artifacts of different types within an assemblage influence index values, making the indices less useful for inter-assemblage chronometric studies?

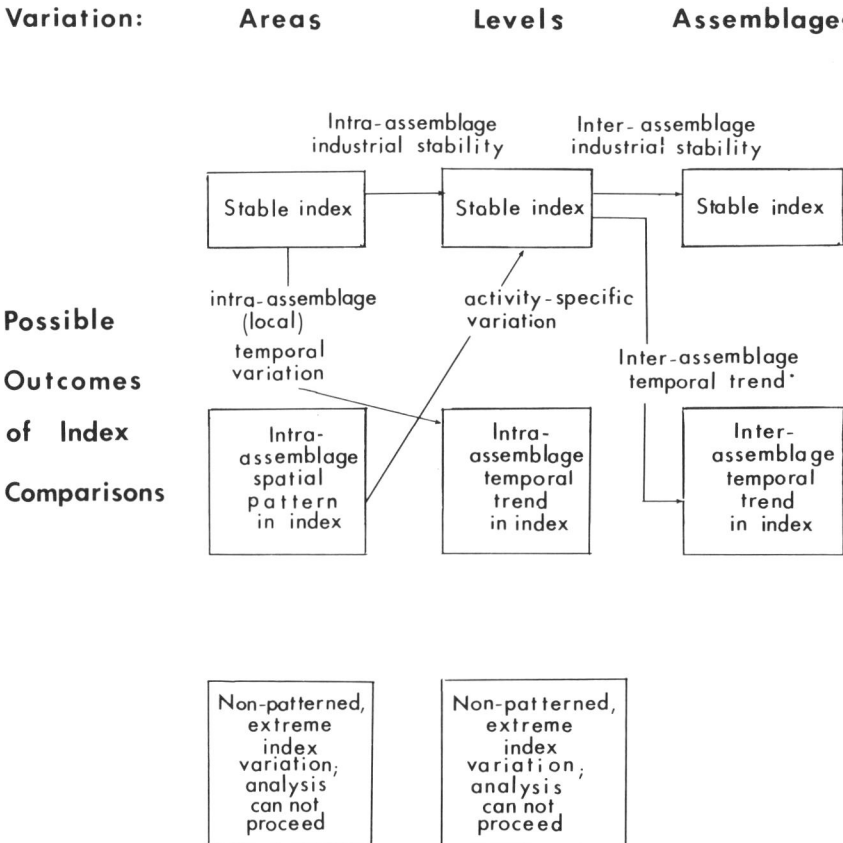

Fig. 17.1. Hierarchical organization of analyses at Rosh Ein Mor and Nahal Aqev and their archaeological implications. This implication is applicable in this study only because other variables (geographic location, mode of occupation, and distance to resources) are controlled.

2. Which indices exhibit patterns over space within an assemblage for individual artifact classes, indicating that *functional* or activity-specific variation affects technological index values, making the indices less useful for inter-assemblage chronometric studies?
3. Which indices exhibit trends through levels of an assemblage, indicating *localized temporal trends*, making the indices less useful for inter-assemblage chronometric studies?
4. Which indices exhibit spatial stability within each assemblage, yet a trend over time between assemblages such that the index could be used

as an aid in seriating assemblages? For each index having these properties, does each artifact class participate equally in the trend?
5. How does the variability of indices observed over artifact classes, space, and time affect published interpretations of inter-assemblage variability?

The sites serving as a basis for the analyses are Rosh Ein Mor and Nahal Aqev, both in the Central Negev of Israel. Both have been classified as early Levantine Mousterian based on general typological characteristics, pollen data, and Thorium/Uranium dating of travertines from a fossil spring adjacent to Nahal Aqev (Crew, 1976; Munday, 1977; Schwartz et al., 1979).

THE SITES

Both Rosh Ein Mor and Nahal Aqev are attractive for intra-site analyses, as both occur in open-air settings and contain thick cultural deposits with relatively high densities of artifacts occurring throughout the deposits. To date, the major Levantine Mousterian sites are located in cave settings, where the barriers established by the cave walls impose artificial spatial restrictions on the distribution and organization of the inhabitants' activities. Furthermore, the slow rate of sedimentation in caves makes differentiation of occupation levels difficult. In contrast, Nahal Aqev and Rosh Ein Mor are extremely large, open-air sites. The estimated area of *in situ* deposits at Nahal Aqev is about 1,200 sq m, and that of Rosh Ein Mor is about 3,000 sq m (Marks, 1977). Due to the limited excavation of Nahal Aqev, horizontal spatial information is available only from Rosh Ein Mor. However, vertical variability can be reliably monitored at both sites; cultural deposits exceed 50 cm in thickness in both.

Rosh Ein Mor

The 45 square-meter block excavated at Rosh Ein Mor incorporates three contiguous areas corresponding to two artifact concentrations (A and B) and an intermediate area (C) (Fig. 2). An extremely high density of lithic material occurs throughout the cultural deposit (ca. 1600 artifacts/ m^3). Excavations were carried out in 5 cm levels (Marks, 1977).

Lack of stratification in either sediments or cultural material suggests continuous occupation (Marks, 1977). This notion was tested by Hietala and Stevens (1977) by examining the spatial distribution of major tool classes. The spatial analyses revealed that certain tool classes—endscrapers, burins, notches, Levallois points, and possibly perforators—tend to aggregate in areas A and B throughout the six contiguous 5 cm levels analyzed. Also, this "tool-kit" was found to segregate consistently from Levallois blades and Levallois flakes throughout the six levels. Levallois blades, Lavallois flakes, sidescrapers, and ostrich egg shells exhibited other spatial patterns over the six levels. These

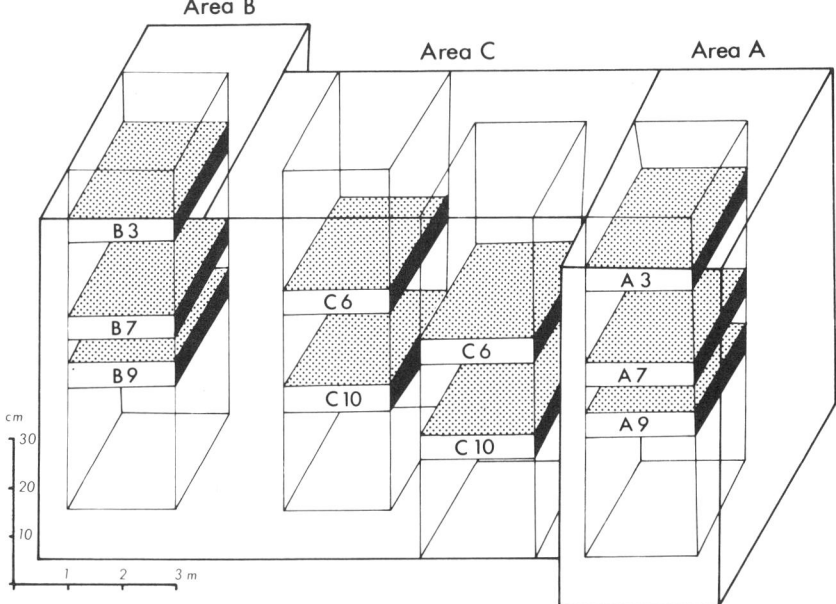

Fig. 17.2. Map of Rosh Ein Mor showing the excavation block and sample units used in the current study.

observations support the hypothesis that the occupation was continuous, if not semi-sedentary (Marks, 1977; Hietala & Stevens, 1977).

In the current re-analysis of Rosh Ein Mor material, a sample of the units in each of the three areas of the site was used to test for horizontal and vertical variability in technological indices. Due to curatorial arrangements with the Israeli Department of Antiquities, only material from alternate excavation levels of Rosh Ein Mor were available for re-analysis (Crew, 1976, p. 76). Samples were drawn from Level 3, areas A and B; Level 6, area C; Level 7, areas A and B; Level 9, areas A and B; and Level 10, area C (Fig. 2). Debitage from A7 was analyzed, but tools were not available from this unit at the time of this study.

Nahal Aqev

Excavations at Nahal Aqev were restricted to a 1 x 8 m main trench that cuts into the terrace in which the site is situated, and an adjoining trench, perpendicular to the first, along the western terrace slope (Munday, 1977, pp. 37-39) (Fig. 3). The maximum area excavated from any individual excavation level at Nahal Aqev was 13 sq m. Horizontal spatial comparisons could not be profitably undertaken at this site, given these limited excavations.

To ensure stratigraphic control, all sample units for this study are located in the main 1 x 8 m trench that cuts through the terrace; excavation units from the trench running along the terrace slope were avoided to reduce the possibility of mixture resulting from erosion. Four adjacent quarter-square meter quadrats from the main trench were selected as sample units (Fig. 3).

Three main levels of occupation were defined at Nahal Aqev. The lowest, Level 3, is 70 cm thick. Level 3 was excavated in 5 cm intervals, which later were collapsed into 10 cm strata (3a-3g) for analysis. Samples for this study were drawn only from Level 3, as the potential for disturbance was less here than in Levels 1 and 2 (Munday, 1977, p. 40). In addition, strata of Level 3 are most pertinent in examining technological change. In Munday's analyses of intra-site variability at Nahal Aqev, a shift in core reduction strategies, as reflected in a shift in the frequency of complex dorsal scar patterns and facetted platforms, was found to occur through the strata of Level 3 (Munday, 1979, p. 94). Munday found that coincident with this change in core reduction strategies, artifacts diminish in size and in laminarity (Munday, 1979, p. 94).

MEASUREMENT TECHNIQUES AND METHODS OF ANALYSIS

Two distinct measuring techniques have been employed in recent analyses of Levantine Mousterian lithic assemblages (Jelinek, 1977; Munday, 1976a) making comparison of published results difficult. At Tabun (Jelinek, 1977), length measurements were made relative to the line between the bulb of percussion and the point where the flake finally separated from the core. Width was measured perpendicular to and at the midpoint of length. Thickness was measured at the midpoint of the width (Fig. 4). Hereafter, this measuring

Fig. 17.3. Map of Nahal Aqev showing the excavation block and sample units used in the current study.

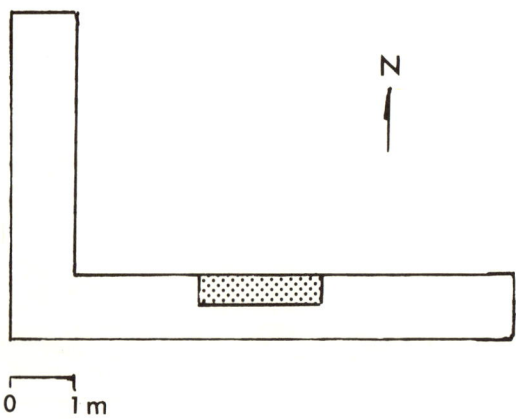

technique will be referred to as the J method. On the other hand, the M method will refer to the measuring technique employed by Munday in his analysis of the Central Negev material. In this case, the artifact is oriented along the axis of detachment and the maximum dimensions are recorded (Fig. 4). To control for methodological differences, all indices were recorded using both techniques.

Given the differences in artifact orientation, the J method consistently gives larger length values, whereas the M method consistently gives larger width and thickness values. Despite differences in mean values, judgments of the statistical significance of between-group variation using ANOVA procedures are generally in agreement for any given index, as are intra- and inter-assemblage trends. To simplify the presentation of results in the text, trends will be described only in terms of the J method observations, except where circumstances dictate illustration of M method measurements.

STATISTICAL ANALYSES

Testing the Significance of Index Variation among Artifact Classes

Consistent with both the M and J methodologies, all complete pieces greater than 25 mm in diameter were included in all analyses presented here. In contrast to the M and J methodologies, however, samples of artifacts and the index variability they encompass were partitioned by *artifact class* for analysis. In the M and J methods, all tools and debitage are lumped into a composite artifact sample in formulating the various technological indices, presumably because an attempt is being made to monitor the *total industrial package* presented in the assemblage. For this study, samples were partitioned into the following classes: flake debitage, blade debitage, Levallois flakes, Levallois blades, Levallois points, and retouched tools. Index values were calculated for each of these classes, separately.

Fig. 17.4. Comparison of the J method and M method of measuring artifact dimensions.

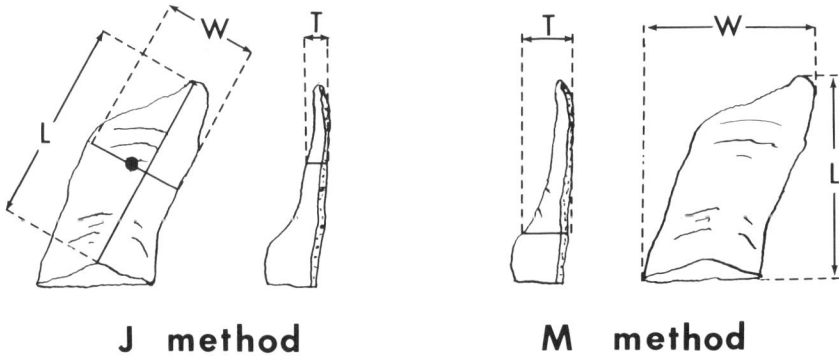

J method   M method

The rationale for partitioning samples into artifact classes rather than collapsing across classes when calculating index values is that the latter approach confounds the information content of a technological index, masking some of the sources of its variation. By partitioning an assemblage into specific artifact classes, it becomes possible to observe whether inter-assemblage trends in an index's value occur over all artifact classes or only some, and whether different classes exhibit different trends. It is intuitively reasonable to think that tools, representing the *end products* of lithic reduction, may exhibit diachronic patterns of variation in their technological index values that differ from those of debitage, representing the *byproducts*. Also, Levallois flakes and blades, differing definitionally in their size, shape, and mode of manufacture from each other and from non-Levallois pieces, might reasonably be hypothesized to exhibit different patterns of diachronic variation in their index values.

Importantly, if differences in the diachronic patterning of index values do occur by artifact class, then one cannot assume, as Jelinek and Munday do, that index values *transcend typological variation* and are unaffected by variation in the specific properties of different artifact classes within assemblages. It becomes necessary to control for the artifact classes comprising assemblages when searching for or applying technological indices having chronometric value.

To examine whether the values of each of the six technological indices of interest vary significantly among artifact classes at Rosh Ein Mor and Nahal Aqev, one-way ANOVA tests were performed for each index and each assemblage, using samples from all the areas and strata available for consideration (see above). Variation among artifact classes is statistically significant for each index in each assemblage (Table 2, Fig. 5). This suggests that, at least for the

Table 17.2

ANOVA Comparison of Index Variation among Artifact Classes

Index	*Rosh Ein Mor*	*Nahal Aqev*
Length	$p = 0$	$p = 0$
Width	$p = .0000$	$p = .0000$
Thickness	$p = .0037$	$p = .0060$
Size (L × W × T/1000)	$p = .0000$	$p = .0440$
Length/Width	$p = 0$	$p = 0$
Width/Thickness	$p = .0000$	$p = .0008$
	($n = 1019$)	($n = 245$)

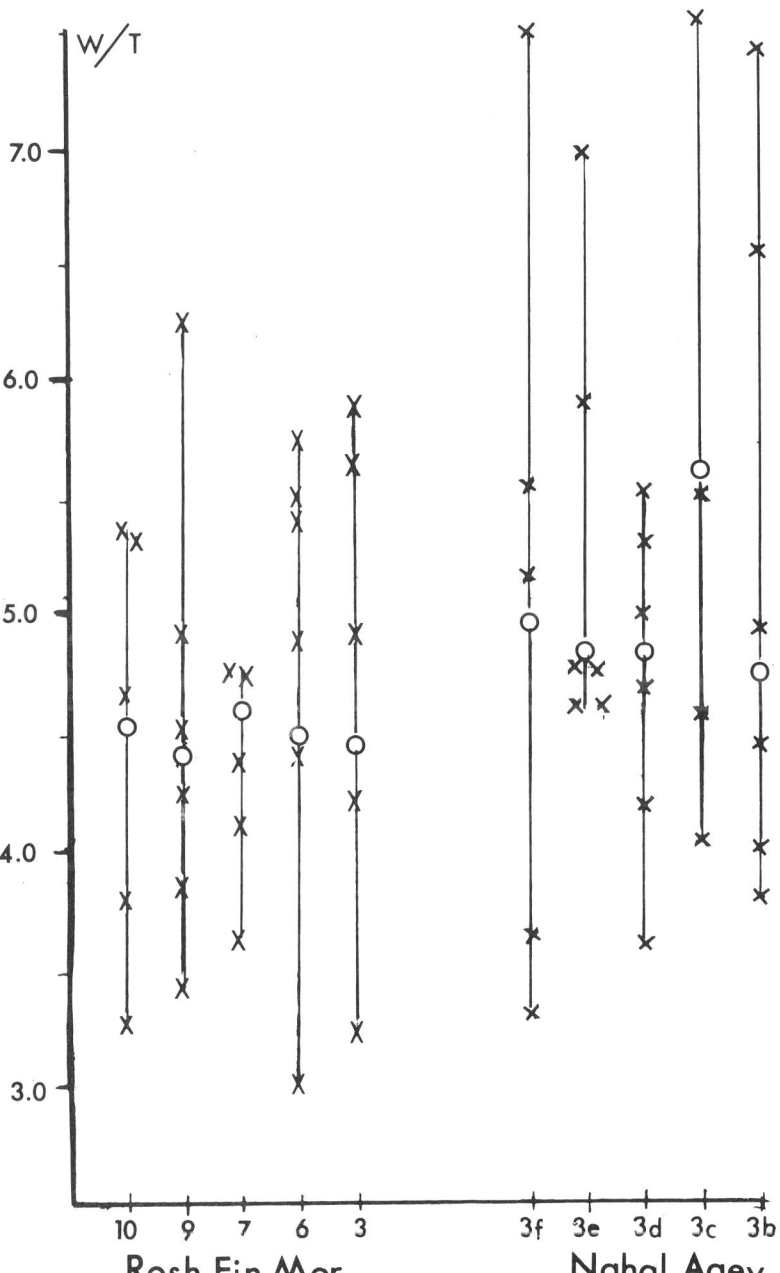

Fig. 17.5. Variation in the width/thickness index among artifact classes at Rosh Ein Mor and Nahal Aqev. o—Mean for the level over all artifact classes. x—Mean for individual artifact classes within that level.

assemblages examined, search for diachronic trends in the values of the indices must take into consideration the artifact classes comprising the assemblages.

Intra-Assemblage Analyses

Before examining *inter-assemblage* variation in the technological index values of individual artifact classes, it is necessary to determine if the index values exhibit significant variation *within* each assemblage, over either space or depth. As mentioned previously, differences between archaeological entities are statistically significant only if the amount of variation between them exceeds that found within them. In the past, determination of the amount of intra-assemblage variation encompassed by the values of technological indices has largely been ignored in inter-assemblage analyses.

The necessity of examining intra-assemblage *spatial* variation in technological index values prior to inter-assemblage analysis, in general and in regard to this study, is suggested by the recent work of Binford (1982). Binford postulates that activity-specific factors and variation in site formation dynamics may account for much of the variation among Mousterian assemblages in southern France.

In this study, information on index value variation over space within sites is available from Rosh Ein Mor alone. There, the two "toolkit localities," areas A and B, and the intermediate area, C, are recognized (Hietala & Stevens, 1977). On the basis of this patterning, technological indices can be examined across the site to see if artifacts occurring within the toolkit localities are significantly different in morphology from those in the intermediate area. Index value variation over depth can be examined at both Nahal Aqev and Rosh Ein Mor. Finally, because we are able to control for variability due to typological differences by partitioning assemblages into artifact classes, it is possible to determine *which artifact classes* exhibit stable indices across space or over the stratigraphic levels within the assemblages, and alternatively, which exhibit spatial patterns or stratagraphic trends within assemblages. Two of the problems outlined in the introduction (2 and 3) can thereby be examined through intra-assemblage analyses at Rosh Ein Mor and Nahal Aqev.

Variation in the values of each of the six indices was first examined across space at Rosh Ein Mor, partitioning the set of artifacts by class. For each index and each artifact class, a one-way ANOVA was performed using samples from all levels. The only class that simultaneously exhibits statistically significant variation in index values among samples from different parts of the site *and* spatial patterning of the values in relation to the depositional areas A, B, and C is blade debitage (Table 3). In regard to the patterning of index values, blade debitage from the intermediate area C was found to be significantly larger and more elongate than blade debitage from the toolkit localities of A and B (Fig. 6). Thus, only blade debitage exhibits an activity-specific pattern for the technological indices considered. Retouched tools were found to exhibit statistically

Table 17.3

Intra-Assemblage Comparison of Artifact Dimensions at Rosh Ein Mor

Characteristics of Intra-assemblage Variation		Artifact Classes					
		Flake Debitage	Blade Debitage	Levallois Flakes	Levallois Blades	Levallois Points	Retouched Tools
Significance of variation across space, all levels combined (F prob for Areas A,B vs. Area C)	L	.9729	.0001*	.4482	.4343	.7458	.4620
	W	.6208	.0026*	.6631	.3159	.5756	.0424*
	T	.2698	.0299*	.5024	.6704	.7552	.1011*
	Size	.5522	.0030*	.7132	.7468	.7120	.0955*
	L/W	.7120	.0977*	.2678	.8476	.9476	.1051*
	W/T	.5452	.4756	.5634	.6731	.2417	.0005*
Pattern in index among areas, all levels combined	L	—	longer in C	—	—	—	—
	W	—	wider in C	—	—	—	wider in C
	T	—	thicker in C	—	—	—	thinner in C
	Size	—	larger in C	—	—	—	larger in C
	L/W	—	more elongate in C	—	—	—	less elongate in C
	W/T	—	lower W/T in C	—	—	—	higher in C
Significance of index variation among levels, combined (F prob values)	L	.4328	.0030*	.5573	.8394	.6135	.8436
	W	.0032*	.0339*	.9858	.5968	.5375	.0462*
	T	.0427*	.1682	.9767	.8302	.4250	.3621
	Size	.2480	.0226*	.9379	.8166	.3917	.7997
	L/W	.6968	.2944	.1578	.6586	.9965	.3125
	W/T	.3406	.8303	.8108	.3090	.7359	.0313*
Trend in index over depth, all areas combined	L	—	no trend	—	—	—	—
	W	no trend	no trend	—	—	—	no trend
	T	no trend	—	—	—	—	—
	Size	—	no trend	—	—	—	—
	L/W	—	—	—	—	—	—
	W/T	—	—	—	—	—	no trend
Individual areas exhibiting significant variation over depth (F prob with area in parentheses)	L	—	—	—	—	—	—
	W	(A).0000*	—	(B).0980*	—	—	—
	T	(A).0080*	—	—	—	—	—
	L/W	(A).0940*	—	(B).0611*	—	—	—
	W/T	—	—	—	—	—	—

*Significant at the .11 level or better

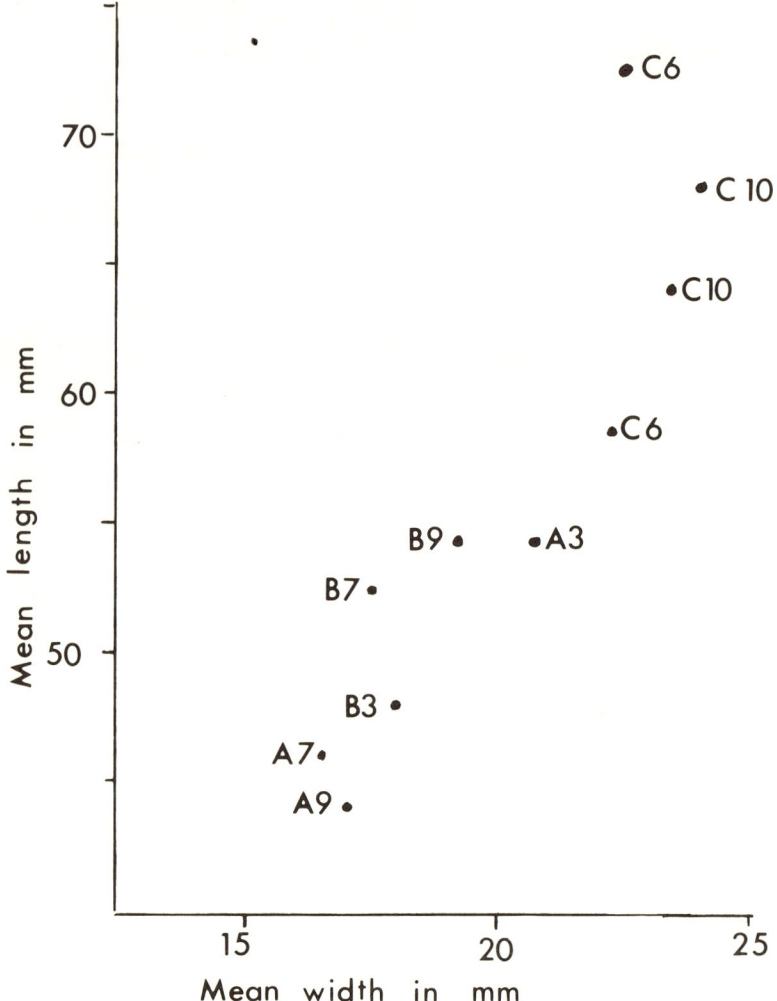

Fig. 17.6. Spatial variation in blade debitage dimensions at Rosh Ein Mor.

significant variation in index values among samples over space, but no patterning of the values comparing samples from areas A, B, and C. The small size of the samples of retouched tools (Tables 4 and 5) may account for the statistically significant but non-patterned variation.

Variation in technological indices over depth also was analyzed for each assemblage. A one-way ANOVA test was performed for each index, each artifact class, and each assemblage. For Rosh Ein Mor, samples from all spatial areas were analyzed both separately and collectively in examining stratigraphic

THE USE OF TECHNOLOGICAL INDICES 553

Table 17.4
Composition of Artifact Assemblages from Nahal Aqev

Artifact class	3b #	3b %	3c #	3c %	3d #	3d %	3e #	3e %	3f #	3f %
Flake debitage	28	58	39	75	21	44	31	52	28	76
Blade debitage	10	21	5	10	8	17	5	8	2	5
Levallois flakes	2	4	—	—	3	6	2	3	—	—
Levallois blades	4	8	—	—	8	17	4	7	1	3
Levallois points	1	2	6	12	2	4	4	7	2	5
Retouched tools	3	6	2	4	6	12	14	23	4	11
TOTAL	48		52		48		60		37	

Table 17.5
Composition of Artifact Samples from Rosh Ein Mor

Artifact class	B3 #	B3 %	A3 #	A3 %	C6 #	C6 %	C6 #	C6 %	B7 #	B7 %	A7 #	A7 %	B9 #	B9 %	A9 #	A9 %	C10 #	C10 %	C10 #	C10 %
Flake debitage	49	54	43	48	51	73	59	73	62	68	108	85	130	70	70	71	86	74	44	62
Blade debitage	19	21	15	17	4	6	10	12	4	4	19	15	26	14	19	19	12	10	13	18
Levallois flakes	7	8	7	8	4	6	2	2	5	5	—	—	5	3	5	5	8	7	10	14
Levallois blades	4	4	6	7	4	6	2	2	3	3	—	—	9	5	1	1	7	6	1	1
Levallois points	6	7	6	7	3	4	4	5	7	8	—	—	4	2	—	—	3	3	3	4
Retouched tools	5	6	13	14	4	6	4	5	10	11	—	—	11	6	3	3	—	—	—	—
TOTAL	90		90		70		81		91		127		185		98		116		71	

variation. For Nahal Aqev, samples from all spatial areas were combined in examining stratigraphic variation.

At Rosh Ein Mor, the width and thickness of *flake debitage* exhibit statistically significant variation through the levels (Table 3). However, no trend was observed in the width or thickness values over levels, either when all areas were combined or when they were analyzed individually. Thus, variation in flake width and flake thickness does not seem to be either spatially or temporally patterned at Rosh Ein Mor.

Despite marked differences in the individual dimensions of width and thickness for flake debitage, the relationship of width to thickness does not vary significantly through time for this artifact class (Table 3). The width/thickness index remains stable over both space and strata.

The length, width, and size of blade debitage varies significantly over depth at Rosh Ein Mor when collapsing samples across areas. The significance of these results, however, probably does not reflect large variations in the index values over depth, as initially might seem to be the case. Rather, it probably reflects a bias of the sample design in confounding spatial variation with stratigraphic variation (Fig. 2). This notion is supported by the fact that variations in these indices among levels is not significant when analyzing the areas individually, nor do the variations form a trend over depth. At the same time, these indices exhibit significant variability over space.

At Nahal Aqev, variation in the length and width of flake debitage is statistically significant through the strata of Level 3 (Table 6). Means of these measurements describe a trend toward smaller flake debitage through time (Fig. 7), suggesting an adjustment in core reduction strategies through the level. The significance of this trend is suggested by other ANOVA statistics. When flake debitage samples from the upper strata (3b-3d) are contrasted with those from the lower strata (3e-3f) results indicate that flakes in the upper strata are significantly shorter ($p = .0082$) and narrower ($p = .0050$) than those in the lower strata. It is noteworthy that these reductions in the length and width of flake debitage did not significantly affect the shape of flakes. Variation in the length/width and width/thickness indices are not statistically significant through time at Nahal Aqev.

Levallois points, on the other hand, do show a trend in shape variation over time at Nahal Aqev, becoming more elongate in the upper strata of Level 3 (Fig. 8a). When Levallois points from the upper (3b-3d) and lower strata (3e-3f) are compared, differences in the length/width index approach statistical significance ($p = .1157$). Given the small sample sizes, this difference would seem to be significant.

In summary, intra-assemblage temporal trends in artifact morphology occur only at Nahal Aqev. Here, a reduction in the size of flake debitage and an increase in the elongation of Levallois points are observed in the upper strata of Level 3.

Table 17.6

Intra-Assemblage Comparison of Artifact Dimensions at Nahal Aqev

Characteristics of Intra-site Variation		Artifact Classes					
		Flake Debitage	Blade Debitage	Levallois Flakes	Levallois Blades	Levallois Points	Retouched Tools
Significance	L	.0359*	.5671	.4937	.3955	.5734	.0738*
of index	W	.0746*	.7499	.8196	.6051	.4718	.9997
variation	T	.6274	.7764	.4484	.3120	.2994	.1423
among strata	Size	.2482	.7708	.7468	.4618	.3936	.2060
(F prob values)	L/W	.4819	.8621	.0393*	.7930	.3588	.2324
	W/T	.6857	.6386	.2501	.0035*	.9550	.5377
Trend in	L	Shorter thru time —		—	—	—	No trend
index over	W	Narrower thru time —		—	—	—	—
depth	T	—	—	—	—	—	—
	Size	—	—	—	—	—	—
	L/W	—	—	No trend	—	—	—
	W/T	—	—	—	No trend	—	—
Significance	L	.0082*	.3737	.5153	.3495	.5338	.3102
of index variation	W	.0052*	.6710	.9434	.2593	.5853	.9701
	T	.1759	.8897	.8364	.4318	.9684	.8515
between upper	L/W	.9896	.5664	.4093	.8947	.1157*?	.4005
(3b-3d) and lower strata (3e-3f)	W/T	.3877	.4916	.4709	.5174	.8116	.9289
Trend in	L	Shorter in upper —		—	—	—	—
index comparing	W	Narrower in upper —		—	—	—	—
upper and	T	—	—	—	—	—	—
lower strata	L/W	—	—	—	—	More elongate —	—
	W/T	—	—	—	—	in upper	—

*Significant at the .11 level or better

Discussion of the Intra-Assemblage Analyses

Intra-assemblage analyses of technological indices serve to resolve some of the five problems outlined in the introduction: 2) which indices exhibit spatial patterns at Rosh Ein Mor, reflecting activity-specific variation in index values; 3) which indices exhibit trends through time (depth), reflecting local temporal trends; and 4) which artifact classes are responsible for these patterns and trends. Indices and artifact classes not characterized by these patterns and trends, but instead showing stability, could potentially serve to "fingerprint" Levantine Mousterian industries. The analyses also have interpretive value(s).

Examination of the spatial variation of all six technological indices showed no patterning of index values relative to toolkit localities for each of the artifact

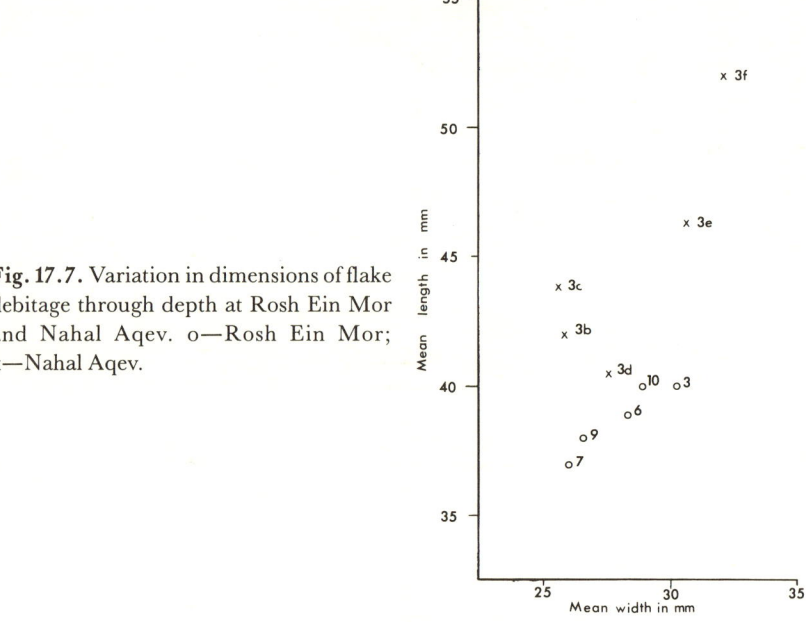

Fig. 17.7. Variation in dimensions of flake debitage through depth at Rosh Ein Mor and Nahal Aqev. o—Rosh Ein Mor; x—Nahal Aqev.

classes studied, with the exception of blade debitage. This suggests that for Rosh Ein Mor, and perhaps other Levantine Mousterian sites, technological indices for most artifact classes—flake debitage, Levallois flakes, Levallois

Fig. 17.8. Variation in the length/width index through depth at Nahal Aqev for Levallois points (A) and variation in the length/width index through depth at Nahal Aqev for Levallois flakes (B).

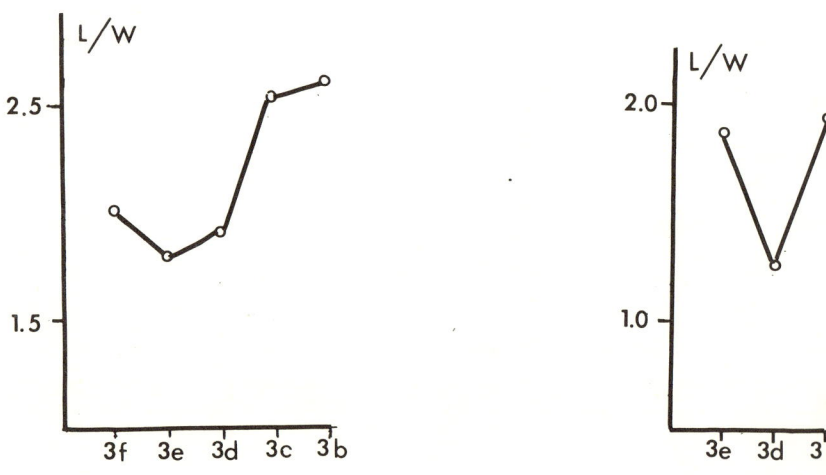

blades, and Levallois points—will exhibit stability over space, regardless of the patterning of activity centers within the site. This has major implications for the formulation of excavation sampling designs for Levantine Mousterian sites. Reliable estimates of technological indices for individual artifact classes can be obtained through the recovery of sufficiently large samples of artifacts, regardless of the spatial patterning of artifact classes. When restrictions are imposed on excavations, concern may be directed toward obtaining sufficiently large samples as opposed to sampling the range of activity areas.

Because most indices exhibit stability across the site of Rosh Ein Mor, it was possible to collapse samples over areas and compare levels of the site to isolate local temporal variation. The same could be done at Nahal Aqev, under the assumption of a similar lack of spatial structuring of the values of the technological indices examined. The comparisons made over depth for each assemblage showed that localized temporal trends occur only at Nahal Aqev. The index stability found at Rosh Ein Mor reflects a very conservative lithic technology throughout the 35 cm of cultural deposit. This technological stability is consistent with other evidence suggesting long term, semisedentary occupation of the site (Marks, 1977), or at least "tethered mobility," by a population maintaining a conservative strategy of lithic reduction.

The index stability through the levels of Rosh Ein Mor contrasts markedly with temporal trends in the size of flake debitage and elongation of Levallois points observed at Nahal Aqev. These intra-assemblage trends at Nahal Aqev can be examined in the context of the shift in reduction strategies described by Munday (1979).

In his analyses of intra-site variability at Nahal Aqev, Munday found that, on the whole, artifacts diminished in laminarity, coincident with a change in reduction strategies. Specifically, he proposes that a shift in reduction strategies occurred in the time represented by stratum 3c. In strata above 3c, dorsal scar patterns and platforms reflect a simpler core preparation technique (Munday, 1979). Results of the current study reveal that: (1) two phases of change, rather than one, can be isolated with regard to a shift in reduction strategies, and (2) only Levallois points, as opposed to all tool and debitage classes, exhibit a statistically significant trend in laminarity through the strata of Level 3, and these *increase* in laminarity.

In regard to the first of these points, it was found in this study that the size of flake debitage (length and width) diminishes markedly and significantly *prior* to the shift in platform facetting and dorsal scar patterns described by Munday. The initial modification occurs approximately in strata 3d-3e, as opposed to stratum 3c, where Munday observed a lower incidence of platform facetting and convergent dorsal scar patterns. Thus, the alteration of core preparation techniques identified by Munday was only the second phase of the shift in reduction strategies.

In regard to the second point, we can note that the temporal variation in dorsal scar patterns and platform facetting that Munday observed at Nahal Aqev correlates nicely with the temporal trends he describes for the length/width index for composite artifact class samples (Fig. 7). However, the temporal patterning of variation in the length/width index for composite artifact class samples, described by Munday, could not be duplicated by this author using the samples of artifacts employed here (Fig. 9). In addition, variation in the length/width ratio index for the composite samples was not found to be significant over the strata of Level 3 using Munday's published data (F ratio = 1.563 df = 6, 1489; Fig. 9). Moreover, after partitioning the assemblage into artifact classes, results of the current study indicate that only two artifact classes, Levallois flakes and Levallois points, change significantly in elongation through the strata of Level 3. Levallois points become more elongate in the upper strata, but Levallois flakes exhibit no trend in the variation of their length/width ratio (Fig. 8b).

In summary, localized temporal trends in artifact technology, detected in the current study, depict a slightly more complex picture of the process by which the reduction strategy was modified.

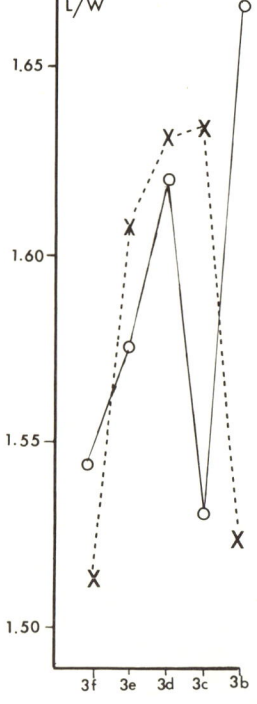

Fig. 17.9. Variation in the length/width index through the strata of Level 3 at Nahal Aqev, comparing Munday's observations (1979, 89) with those of the current study. x---x: Munday's observations, o——o: current study observations using the M method of measurement.

Inter-Assemblage Analyses

Having examined the six indices of interest for their variability over artifact classes, space, and/or depth within Rosh Ein Mor and Nahal Aqev, it is now possible to ask in a *meaningful* way which indices differ between the two sites, controlling for intra-assemblage variability. Inasmuch as the two sites differ in time, this is equivalent to asking which indices have the potential for aiding in seriating Levantine Mousterian assemblages.

In regard to their chronological placement, both Rosh Ein Mor and Nahal Aqev have been classified as early Levantine Mousterian sites. This is based on typological and technological similarities with the assemblage from Tabun, Bed 39, Uranium/Thorium dates, and paleoenvironmental data (Marks, 1977). The shift in reduction techniques at Nahal Aqev, however, has been interpreted as a technological response to deteriorating environmental conditions in the Central Negev and, thus, indicative of a slightly later date for the occupation of Nahal Aqev relative to that of Rosh Ein Mor.

Other considerations also suggest temporal as opposed to functional variation between the two sites (Munday, 1976a; 1976b). Although these arguments are presented in much greater detail elsewhere (Munday 1976a; 1976b), some factors which discourage a functional explanation of variation include similar core to debitage and tool ratios, a similar range and variety of tools at each site, and similar site settings relative to the availability of raw material and water. Moreover, these characteristics indicate that some control over curatorial and activity-specific variation is achieved when comparing the two sites. Geographic factors are controlled as well; the sites are separated by a distance of less than 6 km. Thus, Nahal Aqev may be considered slightly younger than Rosh Ein Mor.

In examining the several indices for their value as aids in seriating Levantine Mousterian sites, we will first focus on Jelinek's proposal of the significance of the mean and variance in the width/thickness ratio, and then on Munday's proposal of the significance of artifact elongation. Then we will turn to the significance of the other indices.

If the mean and variance figures for the width/thickness index have temporal significance among Levantine Mousterian assemblages, as Jelinek (1981) proposes, then both values should be higher at Nahal Aqev. Indeed, these values are higher at Nahal Aqev for assemblage samples composed of artifacts of *all* classes and spatial/stratigraphic proveniences. However, the question remains whether these values are meaningful in light of intra-assemblage index variation over artifact class, space, and depth.

First, consider the possible trend in the mean width/thickness index from Rosh Ein Mor to Nahal Aqev. Recall that the width/thickness index remained stable across space and/or through time at each site, for each individual artifact class, with the exception of retouched tools at Rosh Ein Mor and Levallois blades at Nahal Aqev. Inasmuch as intra-assemblage variation in regard to these two potential sources of variability is not statistically significant for almost all of the artifact classes, we can collapse across space and levels in order to compute mean indices for each assemblage and each artifact class. Reference to Table 5 indicates that the mean width/thickness index is greater at Nahal Aqev for each artifact class with the exception of retouched tools. The rise in this index, however, is statistically significant for only a *few* artifact classes: flake debitage, blade debitage, and Levallois points (Table 7, Fig. 10). Only the debitage classes and Levallois points vary significantly in shape between the two assemblages.

Thus, considering intra-assemblage variability, it can be concluded that the *mean* width/thickness index has the potential for serving as an aid in seriating Levantine Mousterin sites, but only after controlling for artifact class. The width/thickness index of each artifact class must be considered separately. More importantly, by considering each artifact class separately, the direction of technological change through the course of the Levantine Mousterian can be examined. Results of this study indicate that three classes of artifacts—blade debitage, flake debitage, and Levallois points—will show the most significant change through time with regard to the width/thickness index, at least in the Central Negev. In sum, the width/thickness index is sensitive to the proportions of artifact classes within an assemblage when calculated over all artifact classes and, thus, is not useful when it is derived from an entire assemblage.

Turning to the possible trend in the variance of the width/thickness index, it is necessary to test for the equality of variance between the two assemblages, considering the individual artifact classes separately. Considering all artifact classes in combination, variation in the width/thickness index is slightly greater at Nahal Aqev. However, the Bartlett-Box F test for equality of variation suggests that the differences between Rosh Ein Mor and Nahal Aqev are not statistically significant, except in the case of two artifact classes, flake debitage and Levallois points (Table 7, Fig. 10). Thus, the *variance* of the width/thickness index has the potential for aiding in the seriation of Levantine Mousterian sites, but only when artifact classes are considered separately and when attention is focused on flake debitage and Levallois points. The artifact class composition of assemblages affects the variance of the width/thickness index when it is calculated over all classes, so the index should not be employed in this way.

Munday's (1979) proposal of the significance of artifact elongation over time can be assessed in the same way as was Jelinek's proposal, controlling for intra-assemblage spatial and stratigraphic variability, and artifact class variability. The intra-assemblage analyses for Rosh Ein Mor and Nahal Aqev showed that the length/width index did not show patterning over space or a trend over depth at each site for most individual artifact classes. The exceptions are blade debitage, which systematically had a higher length/width ratio in area C of Rosh Ein Mor; retouched tools, which systematically had a lower length/width ratio in area C; and Levallois points, which showed a trend over depth toward a

Table 17.7

Inter-Assemblage Comparisons of Artifact Dimensions

			Artifact Classes					
Index/Site			Flake Debitage	Blade Debitage	Levallois Flakes	Levallois Blades	Levallois Points	Retouched Tools
Length	REM	$\bar{x}$	38.11	54.02	58.04	74.70	63.28	65.58
		s.d.	15.54	20.54	15.55	20.62	21.12	21.61
	NA	$\bar{x}$	45.00	54.50	59.00	69.70	63.67	65.45
		s.d.	14.87	24.04	16.01	16.21	17.75	22.57
		F prob	.0000*	.9106	.8786	.3826	.9503	.9796
Width	REM	$\bar{x}$	27.29	19.65	38.77	28.05	32.33	35.48
		s.d.	10.82	8.70	10.00	7.63	9.09	9.02
	NA	$\bar{x}$	28.37	19.70	36.43	24.82	30.13	32.34
		s.d.	10.38	10.01	8.77	5.46	8.45	7.87
		F prob	.2656	.9789	.5573	.1232	.4257	.1233
Thickness	REM	$\bar{x}$	6.69	6.98	7.61	7.02	6.23	8.48
		s.d.	3.38	4.22	2.65	2.67	1.61	2.46
	NA	$\bar{x}$	6.38	5.08	7.03	5.98	5.18	8.00
		s.d.	3.41	2.01	2.97	2.03	2.26	2.51
		F prob	.3208	.0172*	.5926	.1607	.0668*	.4046
Length/ Width	REM	$\bar{x}$	1.47	2.89	1.53	2.72	2.01	1.96
		s.d.	.60	.79	.32	.59	.64	.86
	NA	$\bar{x}$	1.71	2.86	1.64	2.86	2.19	2.14
		s.d.	.62	.68	.42	.63	.60	.93
		F prob	.0000*	.8436	.4124	.4571	.3727	.3716
Width/ Thickness	REM	$\bar{x}$	4.52	3.34	5.57	4.35	5.40	4.45
		s^2	3.80	3.02	5.56	2.08	3.38	1.92
	NA	$\bar{x}$	5.20	4.02	5.65	4.38	6.81	4.36
		s^2	5.43	1.98	2.91	1.11	14.82	2.06
ANOVA		F prob	.0002*	.0449*	.9299	.9350	.0835*	.7889
Bartlett-Box		F prob	.004*	.168	.343	.165	.001*	.834

*Significant at the .11 level or better

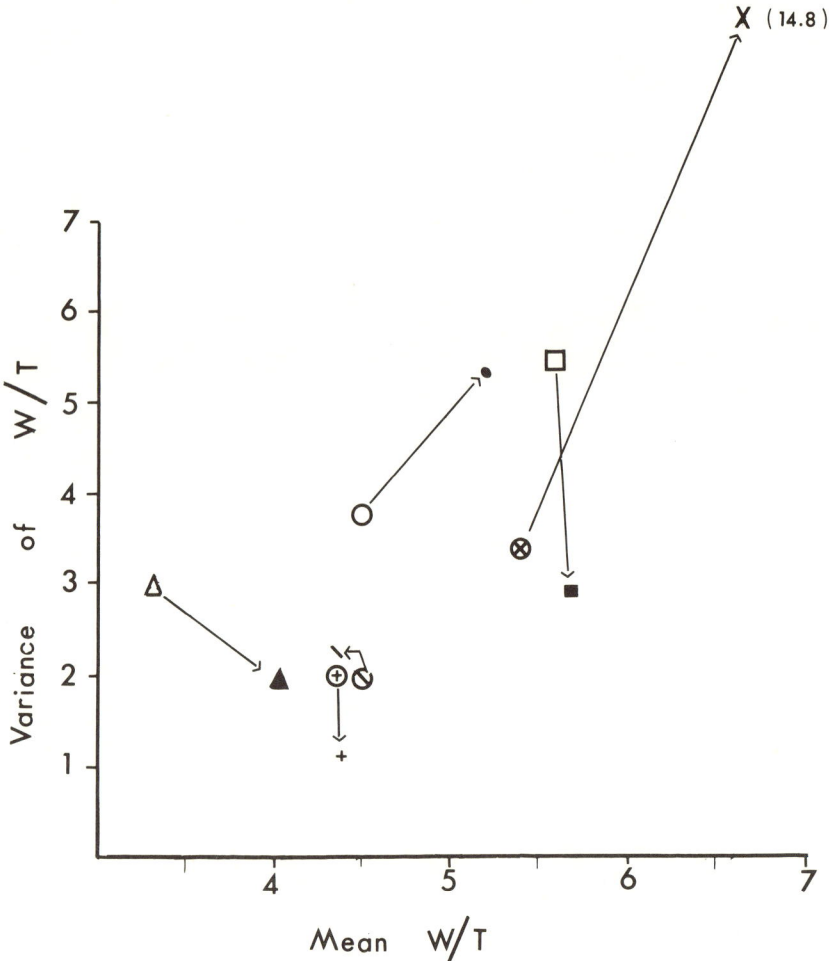

Fig. 17.10. Inter-assemblage variation in the mean and variance of the width/thickness index by artifact class. Open and circled symbols represent artifacts from Rosh Ein Mor; closed symbols represent artifacts from Nahal Aqev. Key: *dot*—flake debitage, *triangle*—blade debitage, *box*—Levallois flakes, *cross*—Levallois blades, *x*—Levallois points, *diagonal line*—retouched tools.

higher length/width ratio at Nahal Aqev. Inasmuch as intra-assemblage variation in the length/width ratio is not statistically significant over space and/or depth for most artifact classes at each site, one can collapse artifact samples over space and depth to compute mean indices for most artifact classes in each assemblage.

Reference to the inter-site comparisons of the length/width ratios (Table 7) show that this index is higher for nearly every artifact class at Nahal Aqev, with the exception of blade debitage. However, the only artifact class showing a statistically significant increase in elongation is flake debitage. Thus, the length/width ratio is most likely to have potential in seriating Levantine Mousterian assemblages when calculated for flake debitage alone, as opposed to all artifact classes combined. This trend, observed in the Central Negev, may be a very localized trend reflecting a local adjustment to deteriorating conditions rather than a pan-Levantine phenomenon.

Of the remaining indices, statistically significant differences in their values between the two assemblages for individual artifact classes were found for 1) the length of flake debitage, which increases over time, and 2) the thickness of blade debitage and Levallois points, which decreases over time. However, the reliability of the trend in thickness for blade debitage must be questioned, given that this index is not stable over space at Rosh Ein Mor (Table 3). Likewise, the significance of the trend in the length of flake debitage must be questioned, given the instability of this index over depth at Nahal Aqev (Table 6). Thus, of the remaining indices, only thickness, as applied to the individual artifact class of Levallois points, has a potential for aiding in the seriation of Levantine Mousterian sites.

DISCUSSION

The results of this study affect published works on inter-assemblage variability in the lithic tools and debitage of Levantine Mousterian sites in regard to both method and interpretation. First, concerning method, the study reveals the necessity of examining *intra-assemblage* variability in the values of an index— along the dimensions of artifact class, space, and depth—before drawing conclusions as to the significance of *inter-assemblage* trends. (Previous research does indicate, however, that variation in the availability of raw material and water can affect technological indices in inter-assemblage comparisons [Munday, 1976a].) For the Levantine Mousterian assemblages examined here, the necessity of partitioning assemblages into artifact classes prior to the evaluation of an index for inter-assemblage variation was demonstrated for every index considered (Tables 2, 3, 6). Lumping all classes together for purposes of comparison confounds the sources and meaning of variation in an index. On the other hand, spatial analyses of indices at Rosh Ein Mor suggest that for individual artifact classes, most of the indices examined are unaffected by activity-specific spatial variation at the site. Although blades from toolkit localities at Rosh Ein Mor are significantly shorter, narrower, and less elongate than those occurring outside the toolkit localities, this is the only artifact class to show such spatial (activity-specific) patterning and affording problems in their use. This assessment, however, was made possible only by detailed examination of the intra-assemblage variability of the indices.

Regarding interpretations, the notion of semisedentary occupation of Rosh Ein Mor, or at least tethered mobility, is further supported by the marked temporal stability of technological indices throughout the 35 cm of deposit.

In contrast to the temporal technological stability at Rosh Ein Mor, patterned variation in flake debitage and Levallois point dimensions through time at Nahal Aqev reflects an adjustment in reduction strategies. The results of the current study suggest a slightly different picture for this shift than that published by Munday. To monitor morphological trends leading to and directly resulting from the shift in core preparation techniques, only material from Level 3 at Nahal Aqev was analyzed for this study. An initial adjustment in the length and width of flake debitage was detected, preceding the more drastic shift in core preparation techniques observed by Munday (1979). Following this, the design of core preparation was altered as depicted in Munday's observation of a lower incidence of platform facetting and convergent dorsal scar patterns in the upper strata of Level 3. The only artifacts exhibiting significantly greater elongation after the shift in core preparation at Nahal Aqev are Levallois points (Table 6). Modification of the reduction strategy, therefore, may have been directed toward increasing the efficiency of Levallois point production.

Finally, the results of the inter-assemblage analyses not only support Jelinek's hypothesis that the mean and variance of the width/thickness index increase through time among Levantine Mousterian assemblages, but also partially reveal the dynamics of this trend. By partitioning the assemblages into artifact classes, results indicate that the width/thickness index is significantly higher at Nahal Aqev for only certain artifact classes: flake debitage, blade debitage, and Levallois points. Furthermore, tests of homogeneity of variance indicate that the source of the increased variation in the width/thickness index for composite artifact samples is not the result of growing morphological differentiation of artifact classes. Rather, the increased variation occurs *within* certain artifact classes (flake debitage and Levallois points) (Table 7).

In conclusion, results of this study indicate that the width/thickness index, when calculated over composite artifact samples, can easily be affected by variation among assemblages in their typological composition. It, therefore, is recommended that in further exploring this trend among Levantine Mousterian assemblages, comparison be restricted to the artifact class of flake debitage. The reasons should be clear. Flake debitage exhibits great spatial stability despite activity-specific variation within a site, yet is sensitive to changes in reduction strategies which are of concern in detecting temporal and geographic variation among Levantine Mousterian assemblages.

REFERENCES

Binford, L.R. (1982). The Archaeology of Place. *Journal of Anthropological Archaeology 1*(1), 5-31.
Binford, L.R., & Binford, S.R. (1966). A Preliminary Analysis of Functional Variability in the Mousterian of Levallois Facies. *American Anthropologist 68*(2), Part 2, 238-295.
Close, A. (1977). The Identification of Style in Lithic Artifacts from North East Africa. *Mémoires de l'Institut d'Égypte, tome 61*.
Crew, H.L. (1976). The Mousterian site of Rosh Ein Mor. In A.E. Marks (Ed.), *Prehistory and Paleoenvironments of the Central Negev, Israel, Vol. 1, Part 1, The Avdat/Aqev area* (pp. 75-112). Dallas: Institute for the Study of Earth and Man, Southern Methodist University Press.
Hietala, H., & Stevens, D. (1977). Spatial analysis: Multiple procedures in pattern recognition studies. *American Antiquity 42*(4), 539-559.
Jelinek, A.J. (1977). A Preliminary Study of Flakes from the Tabun Cave, Mount Carmel. *Eretz-Israel, Vol. 13*, 87*-96*.
Jelinek, A.J. (1981). The Middle Paleolithic in the Southern Levant from the Perspective of the Tabun Cave. Prehistoire du Levant. *Colloques Internationaux du Centre National de la Recherche Scientifique, No. 508*, 265-280.
Lubell, D. (1974). *The Fakurian: A Late Paleolithic industry from Upper Egypt* (Paper No. 58). Cairo: The Geological Survey of Egypt.
Marks, A.E. (1977). Prehistoric Settlement Patterns in the Avdat/Aqev Area. In A.E. Marks (Ed.), *Prehistory and paleoenvironments of the Central Negev, Israel, Vol. II, Part 2, The Avdat/Aqev Area and the Har Harif* (pp. 131-158). Dallas: Southern Methodist University Press.
Munday, F.C. (1976a). *The Mousterian of the Negev; A description and explication of intersite variability.* Unpublished doctoral dissertation, Southern Methodist University, Dallas.
Munday, F.C. (1976b). Intersite Variability in the Mousterian Occupation of the Avdat/Aqev Area. In A.E. Marks (Ed.), *Prehistory and Paleoenvironments in the Central Negev, Israel, Vol I, Part 1, The Avdat/Aqev Area* (pp. 113-140). Dallas: Southern Methodist University Press.
Munday, F.C. (1977). Nahal Aqev (D35): A stratified, open-air Mousterian occupation in the Avdat/Aqev area. In A.E. Marks (Ed.), *Prehistory and Paleoenvironments of the Central Negev, Israel, Vol. II, Part 2, The Avdat/Aqev Area and the Har Harif*, (pp. 35-60). Dallas: Southern Methodist University Press.
Munday, F.C. (1979). Levantine Mousterian technological variability: A perspective from the Negev, *Paleorient 5*.
Schwartz, H., Blackwell, B., Goldberg, P., & Marks, A. (1979). Uranium Series Dating of Travertines from Archaeological Sites, Nahal Zin, Israel. *Nature 277*, 558-560.

18

Projectile Point Maintenance and Typology: Assessment with Factor Analysis and Canonical Correlation

C. MARSHALL HOFFMAN

Projectile points, as an important focus of archaeological research, have been studied for several purposes. They are often: described by their morphological variability (e.g., Binford, 1963; Benfer, 1967; Faulkner & McCollough, 1973; Futato, 1977; Christensen & Read, 1977; Read, 1982); documented for their geographic and temporal distributions (e.g., Suhm, Krieger, & Jelks, 1954; Bell, 1958, 1960; Kneberg, 1956; Cambron & Hulse, 1964, 1975; Perino, 1968, 1971); analyzed for their function (e.g., Winters, 1969; Ahler, 1971, 1979; Ahler & McMillan, 1976); and used to model technological processes of point manufacture and maintenance (e.g., Frison, 1968, 1974; Ahler, 1971; Goodyear, 1974; Montet-White, 1974; Frison et al., 1976; House & Wogaman, 1978; Callahan, 1979; Miller, 1980; Bradley, 1982; Morrow, 1984).

The asymmetry, irregularities, and dynamic nature of point morphology, size, and edge angle, however, can make these goals difficult to achieve. Projectile points are not mass-produced to exact specifications, but tend to vary in shape and size (Goodyear, 1974). Furthermore, these tools can undergo varying degrees and kinds of changes throughout their life histories (Frison, 1968, 1974; Ahler, 1971; Goodyear, 1974; Frison et al., 1976; House & Wogaman, 1978; Miller, 1980). A point may be resharpened in a variety of ways, and edge damage or breakage commonly requires additional modifications for continued use of a tool. These processes can produce substantial and

---

I wish to thank Marvin Kay, James E. Dunn, David P. Braun, Allen P. McCartney, Teresa L. Hoffman, and especially Christopher Carr, for their helpful comments and criticisms on an earlier draft; also I wish to thank Michael P. Hoffman, Robert H. Lafferty III, W. Fredrick Limp, George L. Cowgill, Michael B. Schiffer, Sandra Parker, Deborah Sabo, and David Waddell. Carey Oakley provided access to the Brinkley site collections. The National Park Service Interagency Archaeological Services-Atlanta and the U.S. Army Corps of Engineers-Nashville District made research at the Brinkley site possible.

complexly interrelated variations in the sizes, morphologies, and edge angles of the blades of points before they finally enter the archaeological record.

The analysis of such variations is not a straightforward procedure. For example, point blade size is a composite concept embracing variation in the size and shape of an artifact that seldom has a simple geometric and symmetrical outline. Similarly, while blade edge angle usually refers to the average conditions along a blade edge, it may actually comprise considerable variation. Given the frequent irregularities and asymmetry in many chipped stone tools, their analysis may be approached more usefully as a multivariate problem rather than a univariate or bivariate statistical problem.

Multivariate techniques, such as factor analysis and canonical correlation, are useful in the analysis of chipped stone tools for summarizing large numbers of variables and for examining the basic dimensions of variation within a data set (Binford & Binford, 1966; Benfer, 1967; Ahler, 1971, 1979; Montet-White, 1974; Kay, 1975, 1980; Christenson & Read, 1977; Clarke & Kurashina, 1979). They provide an effective means for measuring and representing variation in chipped stone assemblages because they enable the use of multiple measures of tool morphology and size and allow the elimination of redundancies in the variables selected for analysis.

The appropriateness of any multivariate technique should be evaluated in reference to the goals of research and the nature of a specific data set to be examined. This chapter examines the effectiveness of R-mode factor analysis and canonical correlation for summarizing multiple measures of point blade size and blade edge angle within the context of constructing typologies of projectile points and analyzing tool maintenance. The utility of each technique in assessing relationships between variables is illustrated in an analysis that examines the relationship between blade size and blade edge angle over the course of a point's use-life. Additionally, the study suggests the importance of acknowledging manufacture, use, and maintenance processes in developing point typologies, and evaluates some traditional point typologies in this light.

THEORETICAL ORIENTATION

Because the focus of this chapter falls within the larger topic of archaeological classification and systematics, over which there is diverse opinion within the archaeological profession, it is necessary to present the view of archaeological classification taken here. Classification is "the creation of units of meaning by stipulating redundancies (classes)" (Dunnell, 1971, p. 44). It is arbitrary in the sense that any number and variety of criteria may be used to define classes. Classification is a matter of distinguishing qualities among objects that have relevance to a specific problem or serve a specific purpose for which a classification is constructed. Typologies are particular kinds of classifications in which classes of discrete objects (types) are defined by non-random clusters of attributes (Spaulding, 1953; Dunnell, 1971; Whallon & Brown, 1982). A type is a discrete unit that is differentiated from other units by a set of attributes and that has members that exhibit "internal cohesion and external isolation" (Doran & Hodson, 1975, p. 159).

The positivist model of systematics, classification, and typology is a useful approach in contemporary archaeology (Hill & Evans, 1972). It assumes that phenomena do not have a specific inherent meaning to be discovered, but rather are assigned meaning by the human mind and may have many meanings. There can be no "best," "all-purpose," or "natural" typology of materials, since the meanings one imposes on them depends on one's theoretical orientation, problems of interest, and goals (Dunnell, 1971; Hill & Evans, 1972; Christenson & Read, 1977).

The particular way a set of archaeological materials is classified depends on 1) the interpretive framework brought to the study by the researcher, reflecting his theoretical orientation, problems of interest, and goals and 2) the variables and procedures used in classifying the materials, as a function of all of the former. All classifications and typologies involve the selection of variables as criteria for class definition (Dunnell, 1971). Because it is impossible to record everything, choices and decisions have to be made about what variables should be considered in the development of any typology. The set of variables used to establish a typology should be those relevant to the researcher's goals and the meaning he wishes to impose on the materials.

Because archaeological materials can be classified in a variety of ways and have different meanings, depending on the particular variables chosen to define classes, during the classification process we must remain aware of why we are defining types and select our variables accordingly (Hill & Evans, 1972). We need conscious strategies for retaining and discarding information (Gardin, 1972), and should explicate the bridging arguments by which our variables are selected in relation to our theories and problems of interest. Thus, we find, for example, that Binford (1965, p. 205) argues that new classification schema, different from those used by normative archaeologists, are necessary for the explanation of culture process, and that the classes we construct "should be justifiable in terms of possessing common structural or functional properties in the normal operation of cultural systems." Vierra (1982, p. 163) also argues that "our systematics are procedures for understanding systemic behaviors [that should be] guided by theoretical principles or assertions about the organizational properties of cultural systems." Our ability to accurately assess the structure and organization of prehistoric human societies depends largely on the concordance of our classification schemes—and the variables upon which they are based—with our theoretical frameworks and analytical goals. This concordance can be achieved only by the researcher justifying, relative to his theoretical framework and goals, the variables he uses in creating a classification.

The process of selecting variables, however, must be justified not only in relation to theory and goals, but also in relation to the specific organization and content of the phenomenon under study (or its probable organization and content if they are not fully known; see Carr, chapter 1). Given the specific nature of the phenomenon under consideration, only some variables or combinations of variables may be useful in creating a meaningful typology and investigating the problem of interest.

In the classification of chipped stone tools, one's choice of variables for creating classes should be made in consideration of the *manufacture, maintenance, and use* of lithic tools, and the potential meaning of variables in relation to these processes. Such insights can be obtained by investigating the data for 1) constraints placed on the nature of tools by broadly applicable processes of tool maintenance, manufacture, and use as enumerated in accepted models of lithic technology, and 2) additional constraints placed by lithic processes active in more particular contexts (e.g., culture-specific or raw material-specific processes pertinent to more restricted areas and time periods).

In this regard, recent studies in lithic technology and archaeology provide several general models that are useful in developing classifications and typologies for chipped stone assemblages (Muto, 1971; Schiffer, 1972, 1976; Shafer, 1973; Collins, 1975; Bradley, 1975; Sheets, 1975; Patterson, 1977; Callahan, 1979; Ericson, 1984). These models provide a framework for defining the meaning of variables used to describe lithic tools and for interpreting the relationships among them in terms of manufacturing, use, and maintenance processes, thereby giving one insight into the organizational nature of the tools. On the basis of such insight, relevant variables can be chosen from the list of all potential variables that might be used for tool classification. It is in this capacity that models of lithic technology, in part, gain their importance.

Given this perspective on classification and the role of models of lithic technology in the classification process, the following sections 1) discuss and evaluate traditional point typologies constructed from a normative and empiricist standpoint without the benefit of such models, 2) summarize certain aspects of lithic technological models useful in developing classifications of points, and 3) offer and test a hypothesis on the processes responsible for point morphological variation that takes into consideration some principles of lithic technology and that stands in contrast to traditional classificatory interpretations of such variation. The utility and roles of factor analysis and canonical correlation in constructing lithic tool typologies become evident in the course of the test of the hypothesis.

PROJECTILE POINTS: DEFINITIONS AND TERMINOLOGY

In this chapter, the terms *projectile point* and *point* are used in a conventional sense to refer to a bifacially flaked implement with a prepared haft element, or stem, and a pointed distal end. Elsewhere, these items commonly have been called points (e.g., Clark & Kleindienst, 1974; Ahler & McMillan, 1976), projectile points (e.g., Binford, 1963; Ahler, 1971; Crabtree, 1972; Montet-White, 1974; Frison, 1974; Goodyear, 1974; Kay, 1975; Heizer & Hester, 1978; Thomas, 1981), projectile point/knives (e.g., Faulkner & McCollough, 1973; Chapman, 1975), arrowheads (e.g., Rau, 1876; Thruston, 1890; Van Buren, 1974), spearheads (e.g., Rau, 1876; Thruston, 1890; Van Buren, 1974), dart points (e.g., Schiffer and House, 1975), and biface tools (e.g., House & Wogaman, 1978), etc. Although these tools may have served as projectiles (Browne, 1938, 1940; Van Buren, 1974; Frison, 1974; Frison et al., 1976; Bradley, 1982), their utility as multifunctional tools is also well documented (e.g., Cushing, 1895; Ahler, 1971; Sollberger, 1971; Goodyear, 1974; Van Buren, 1974). Projectile points are comprised of two main elements: the blade and the stem, or haft element (Fig. 1). The blade contains the working edges of the tool, whereas the stem provides an area to be fastened to a handle, shaft, or foreshaft. These elements cannot always be distinguished precisely, but they can be differentiated satisfactorily in many point assemblages—particularly the one selected for this analysis.

NORMATIVE-EMPIRICIST POINT TYPOLOGIES OF THE SOUTHEASTERN UNITED STATES

Projectile point typologies became an important focus of research in North American archaeology as archaeologists began establishing chronologies and identifying prehistoric cultures in time and space (Willey & Sabloff, 1980). The historical relevance of types was a particular concern, as evidenced in the typological methods proposed by Rouse (1939), Krieger (1944), Taylor (1948), Spaulding (1953), and Ford (1954). In the southeastern United States, archae-

Fig. 18.1. The blade, stem, and other portions of chipped-stone points.

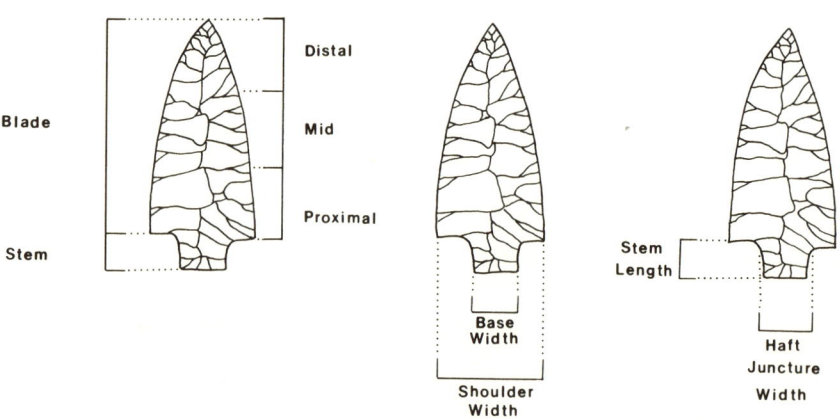

ologists developed point typologies to identify the shared styles of tools thought to reflect cultures and to have spatial, temporal, and functional significance (e.g., Newell & Krieger, 1949; Suhm, Krieger, & Jelks, 1954; Kneberg, 1956; Ford & Webb, 1956; Bell, 1958, 1960; DeJarnette et al., 1962; Coe, 1964; Cambron & Hulse, 1964, 1975; Perino, 1968, 1971).

These typologies employed a normative theoretical framework for the study of culture and material remains. From a normative standpoint, culture consists of shared mental constructs or norms (Binford, 1965; Krieger, 1944; Taylor, 1948; Ford, 1954). The shared characteristics of human behavior are emphasized because only they can reflect culture. From a normative perspective, the goal of the archaeologist is to identify or discover the shared preferences and techniques for designing and manufacturing artifacts (e.g., chipped stone points) that are diagnostic of past cultures. Variation per se is not an important concern since only norms can inform us about prehistoric cultural behavior (Binford, 1965).

The normative interpretation of culture and prehistoric cultural materials embraced an empiricist model of classification and typology (Hill & Evans, 1972), as opposed to the positivist one discussed above. The empiricist model considers all phenomena to have inherent meaning or significance within themselves. It is the task of the archaeologist to discover these meanings and the attributes of artifacts that indicate them. Usually, these inherent meanings are assumed to represent 1) ideas, customs, or mental templates; 2) functional significance; or 3) historical significance (Hill & Evans, 1972).

That artifacts have inherent meaning follows logically from the inductive scientific procedures stressed by the empiricists. In the empiricist viewpoint, inferences are to be derived from data and data should be gathered before inferences are made. Thus, research begins with data collection, proceeds to classification, and then to analysis and interpretation. That classification comes before analysis and interpretation implies that there must be a "natural" or "best" way to classify phenomena (Hill & Evans, 1972). Thus, the normative-empiricist theorists approached point typology with the purpose of identifying or discovering the "natural" or inherent shared tool types of prehistoric cultures in time and space.

In emphasizing the identification of shared cultural norms, researchers with a normative theoretical orientation focused on the discovery of distinct or recurring *clusters* of attributes, rather than the *processes* responsible for their presence. This is reflected in the structure of their typologies as well as the variables selected. Modes or ideal representations of selected attributes were sought. Chipped stone tools were viewed as static entities, and variation was partitioned into static classes thought to reflect normative tool styles. The variables selected to define classes were chosen without giving much attention to their sensitivity to maintenance processes.

Methodologically, this was accomplished by intuitively segregating classes of objects thought to be diagnostic of prehistoric cultures. Although archaeological contexts and associations were important (Krieger, 1944; Kneberg, 1956; DeJarnette, 1964), point types were defined primarily on the basis of distinctive or recurring combinations of attributes. Differences in tool morphology and size were relied upon to differentiate types, and certain technological or functional characteristics (e.g., beveling, serrations, fluting) were also considered. Variation in the stem and the blade were considered equally significant for defining types, and frequently subtle variations in either were used to define new types (Suhm, Krieger, & Jelks, 1954; Ford & Webb, 1956; Kneberg, 1956; Cambron & Hulse, 1964, 1975).

Unfortunately, this approach caused several problems. First, a large number of similar but slightly different point types were established, the interrelationships among which were not defined explicitly. Nor were the meanings of such interrelationships systematically explored. Types were intuitively determined, modal or eccentric combinations of attributes that were thought to be diagnostic of cultures because of their contextual associations.

Second, the point forms, not described as specific normative types, were either lumped into gross categories of "provisional" or "undifferentiated" types (Lewis & Lewis, 1961; DeJarnette et al., 1962; Cambron & Hulse, 1964, 1975), or classified as "left-overs" to be described and illustrated individually (Suhm, Krieger, & Jelks, 1954, p. 6-7). These were thought to be insignificant forms resulting from idiosyncratic variation (Krieger, 1944) or types not yet recognized because of insufficient research (Suhm, Krieger, & Jelks, 1954; Lewis & Lewis, 1961). As a result, much of the variation in point assemblages, which was not encompassed and explained by known types, was treated as largely irrelevant for understanding prehistoric human behavior.

However, an additional problem characterizes all of these typologies and is of perhaps greater significance than the problems previously discussed. The traditional point typologies were not founded on explicit principles for assessing the significance of and selecting specific variables as indicators of tool manufacture, use, maintenance, or cultural affiliation. Instead, the typologies were constructed intuitively. Because some of the variables that were chosen to differentiate types may reflect simply tool maintenance, some traditional types may not represent differences in cultural affiliation having spatial-temporal significance. Rather, they may represent a single continuum of variation resulting from differing degrees of use-life reduction.

For example, in forming traditional point types, some types were distinguished by an asymmetric blade (e.g., Ledbetter stemmed; Kneberg, 1956), others by narrow blade shoulders (e.g., Mulberry Creek; Cambron & Hulse, 1964), or bilaterally recurvate blade margins (e.g., Pickwick; DeJarnette et al., 1962). Although these criteria were chosen supposedly to define artifact types diagnostic of cultures in time and space, their selection did not consider the possibility of resharpening as a source of the variation observed in point sizes, morphologies, or technological characteristics. Thus, the variables and variable states selected intuitively to define types, as well as the types themselves, may reflect simply different stages of a tool's use-life or other dimensions of variation not controlled for explicitly, rather than cultural affiliation.

The following discussion examines research on the maintenance of chipped stone tools and explains some of the variation in point morphology, size, and edge angle that may result from their resharpening and modification. It lays the foundation for developing a hypothesis on point morphological variation that stands in contrast to traditional interpretations of such variation that have been used to construct point typologies.

POINT USE-LIFE AND MAINTENANCE

In the past, archaeologists were aware that lithic tools may require resharpening to maintain their use (Holmes, 1919; Krieger, 1952; Ford & Webb, 1956), but few typologies and classifications were concerned explicitly with this process (e.g., Ford & Webb, 1956). However, with the introduction of a functional and adaptive view of culture (Binford, 1962, 1965), attention became focused on the function and technology of stone tools, as well as their style (e.g., Frison, 1968, 1974; Ahler, 1971, 1979; Goodyear, 1974). The New Archaeology provided a view of culture that encouraged the study of tool manufacture, maintenance, and use, and the development of middle range theory for the study of lithic technology. Some of the research that has resulted addresses the resharpening and modification of chipped stone tools and in particular how point blade morphology and size may change over the life of a tool (e.g., Frison, 1968, 1974; Ahler, 1971; Goodyear, 1974; Frison et al., 1976; House & Wogaman, 1978; Miller, 1980).

The concept of tool use-life (i.e., life history) has been proposed by Schiffer (1972, p. 157) to describe their stages of "life" within a cultural system, and how this relates to the deposition of artifacts in the archaeological record. Several processes can be used to characterize tool use-life. These include procurement, manufacture, use, maintenance, and discard (pp. 157ff). Although all of these processes are important concerns, the present study is specifically concerned with tool maintenance.

The *maintenance* of a worn or damaged implement requires that its edge be resharpened or modified for continued use as a tool. *Resharpening* involves the removal of edge material to provide a new, but similar, edge for use (Collins, 1975, p. 23). *Modification*, on the other hand, consists of producing alternative functional tool forms on worn tools (e.g., scrapers, gravers, drills, etc.; Collins, 1975, p. 23) or reworking broken points into usable tools. For example, chipped stone points make effective tools but require resharpening to maintain efficient use. However, after repeated resharpenings, a point is eventually reached where resharpening no longer restores their utility, and the tool must be discarded or modified for another purpose (Frison, 1968).

Tool maintenance may significantly affect the morphology, size, and edge angle of chipped stone tools and is important to consider when identifying the life history of a tool. This is indicated by a number of different, but complimentary, approaches that have been undertaken for studying the use and maintenance of lithic tools (Frison, 1968, 1974; Ahler, 1971; Goodyear, 1974; Frison et al., 1976; House & Wogaman, 1978; Miller, 1980). In particular, research indicates that some portions of lithic tools change in different manners and at varying rates from resharpening, breakage, and modification. The blade element has been found to be particularly susceptible to reductions in size and changes in shape over the course of a tool's use-life (Ahler, 1971; Morse, 1971; Frison, 1974; Goodyear, 1974; Miller, 1980). The stem, on the other hand, is apt to undergo modification less frequently (Ford & Webb, 1956; Luchterhand, 1971; Goodyear, 1974).

Changes in the Stem

The stem of a projectile point is rarely affected significantly by the resharpening process (Ford & Webb, 1956; Goodyear, 1974). This proposition is generally supported by several analyses that have noted that the blade's characteristics are most significantly affected from resharpening, whereas the stem exhibits only occasional changes (Ahler, 1971; Luchterhand, 1971; Goodyear, 1974). This is not to imply that the stem never undergoes maintenance, but simply that it is required less frequently than for the blade of a tool. The reason for this circumstance is that the stem or haft element cannot be reworked until it is removed from its handle, shaft, or foreshaft; and there is no reason for doing this as long as the implement is hafted and remains serviceable. Therefore, we can conclude that tool maintenance causes varying rates of change for different tool elements over the course of a tool's use-life. This variation may be useful in identifying the life history of a tool.

Changes in the Blade

Reductions in Blade Size

Experiments in lithic technology have demonstrated that the resharpening of bifaces often causes gradual reductions in blade size. Frison (1968) performed resharpening experiments that suggest that during a single cycle of use and resharpening a single biface edge is reduced approximately 1-2 mm by use and approximately 2 mm by resharpening. This amounts to a total loss of 3-4 mm per edge during a single cycle, or potentially a 6-8 mm loss if both lateral margins are resharpened simultaneously. Goodyear (1974) also performed a resharpening experiment for Dalton blade element reduction. An initial-stage Dalton point was consecutively dulled and resharpened four times, with each resharpening resulting in a 2-5 mm loss of total blade width. These experiments demonstrate that point blade size is reduced gradually from resharpening over the course of a tool's use-life.

Archaeological evidence suggesting the cyclic use and resharpening of points has been found in a number of lithic assemblages. In the analysis of points from Rodgers Shelter, Ahler (1971) observed uniformity in the stem and blade width measurements for most point categories. However, blade length, shape, and edge angles varied considerably, leading Ahler to conclude the cyclical use and resharpening of points. Morse (1971) suggested that variation in Dalton point blade sizes from the Hawkins cache represents distinct stages of resharpening in Dalton point use-life. Similarly, Goodyear (1974) also observed variation in blade size, as well as blade morphology and edge angle that he interprets in terms of maintenance over the course of Dalton point use-life. These studies indicate that a point's blade size is likely to change from cyclic use and resharpening or modification, and that morphologically distinct kinds of points do not necessarily represent stylistic preferences of ethnic groups.

Alterations in Blade Shape

Variation in the morphology of point blade elements in addition to their size may occur within an assemblage for several reasons. One source of this variation is the use of different resharpening strategies suited for particular tool functions (Fig. 2). Miller (1980) proposed a model for point reduction that considers the effects of alternative tool functions in the morphology of reduced forms. Two patterns in the reduction sequence were recognized and distinguished by characteristics of morphology and edge wear. Points used more for scraping became progressively shorter from resharpening, while points used for cutting or sawing became progressively narrower.

Variation in point blade morphology and size may also occur from the modification of broken or damaged points during their use-life (Frison, 1968, 1974; Frison et al., 1976). Breakage does not always necessitate tool disposal because often it can be corrected with more intensive reworking. For example, a finished initial stage point may break across the tip and be modified into a smaller size point rather than being discarded (Fig. 3). Similarly, a point broken near the blade shoulders may simply require a new stem to maintain its use as a tool (Fig. 3).

A third factor that may be responsible for considerable variation in blade morphology and size results from idiosyncratic variation in the manners tools are used, resharpened, or modified (Gunn, 1975, 1977; Johnson, 1977; McGhee, 1980). Individuals have varying motor habits, experience, and capabilities for using and maintaining tools effectively and are not apt to resharpen or modify them in precisely the same manner (Goodyear, 1974). Therefore, we should expect some variation in point assemblages to result

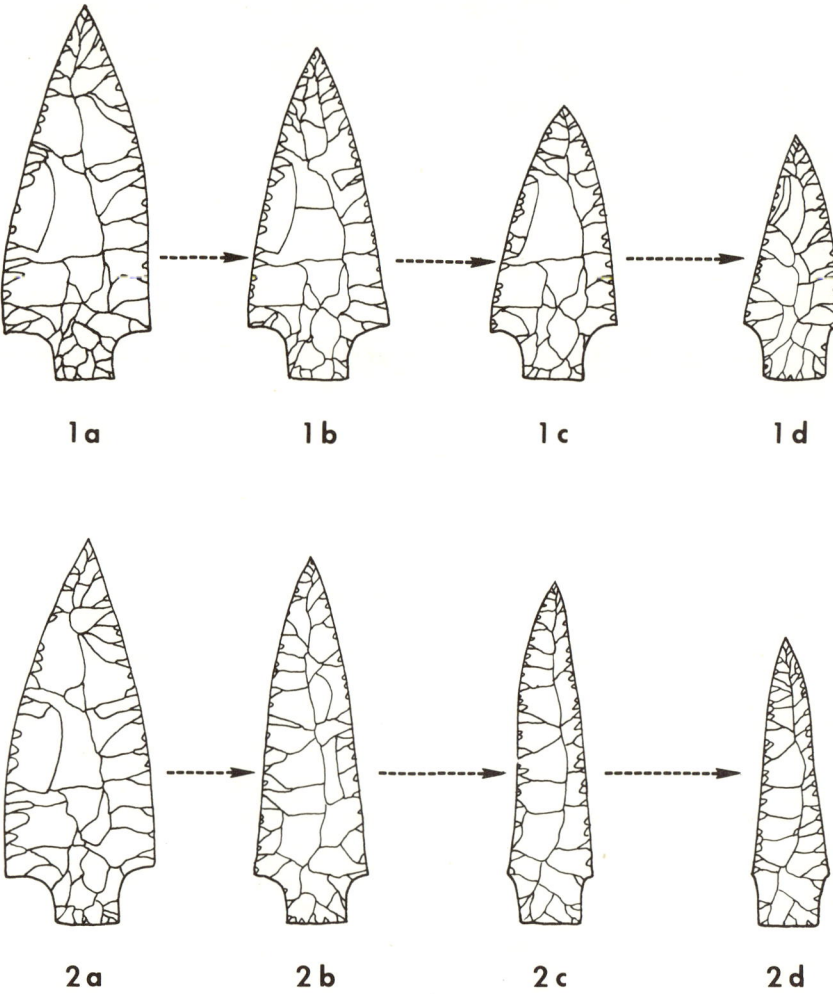

Fig. 18.2. Changes in morphology from different resharpening strategies. Row 1: Emphasis on resharpening the distal blade margins causes reduced blade length. Row 2: Emphasis on resharpening the lateral blade margins causes reduced blade width.

simply from the fact that they were made, used, and maintained by different individuals.

All of these factors can combine to make a tool's use-life complex and varied, and have the potential to produce a wide range of variation in point morphology and size, especially for a tool's blade. As a result, we can have little assurance that our point types have any spatial/temporal or functional significance unless

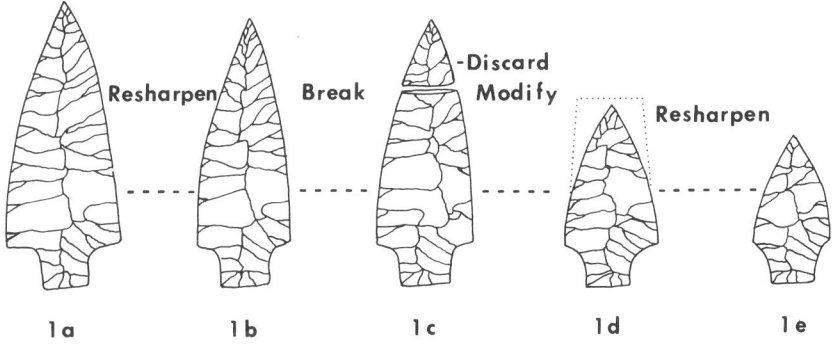

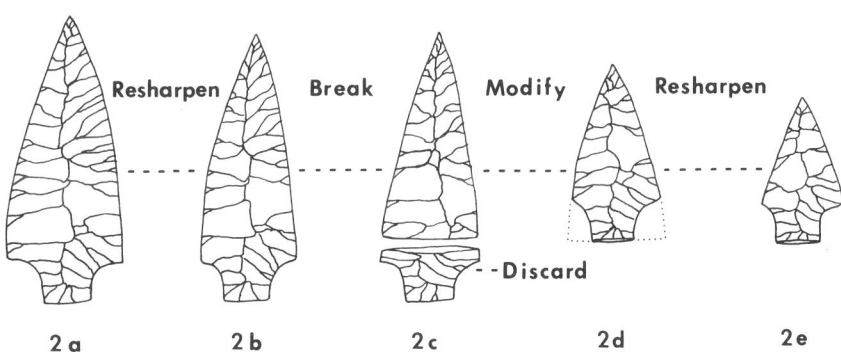

Fig. 18.3. Changes in morphology from tool breakage and modification. Row 1: The distal end breaks during use, and the blade is modified into a smaller form. Row 2: The proximal portion of the blade breaks and requires a new stem for continued use.

such principles are considered when we select the variables to be used in constructing them.

TOOL MAINTENANCE AND POINT TYPOLOGY: THE BLADE SHAPE/ POINT USE-LIFE HYPOTHESIS AND ITS TRADITIONAL ALTERNATIVE

The methods by which traditional point typologies were constructed are consistent with the normative theoretical framework for which they were designed. However, they are not consistent with the principles of lithic technology describing the effects of use and maintenance of chipped stone tools. Although there was some awareness by traditional typologists that resharpening and modification did occur, there were few discussions of tool maintenance in the literature (Holmes, 1919; Krieger, 1952; Ford, Phillips, & Haag, 1955; Ford & Webb, 1956). Generally, only extreme reductions in blade size were considered to provide evidence of resharpening or modification. The modification of broken points into alternative functional tools (e.g., scrapers, drills) was used frequently to explain the occurrence of certain tool forms (Ford, Phillips, & Haag, 1955; Ford & Webb, 1956; Kneberg, 1957; Lewis & Lewis, 1961; DeJarnette et al., 1962). Less extreme alterations usually were not attributed to successive tool use and resharpening (cf. Ford & Webb, 1956).

Although few of the normative-empiricist point typologies address the issue of tool maintenance explicitly, the organization of their typologies as well as the variables selected reflect certain implicit assumptions regarding the impact of tool maintenance on point morphology and size over the course of a tool's use-life. All of these typologies recognize a range of variation in the size for each type, which is not taken to indicate differences in cultural affiliation. However, the typologies do not specify the probable causes of this variation. Is it the result of tool maintenance, idiosyncratic variation in tool manufacturing, the availability of lithic raw materials, or different tool functions?

Another assumption evident in these typologies is that blade shape does not vary significantly over the course of a tool's use-life—that prehistoric social groups had specific normative blade styles that were considered important to maintain throughout the life of a tool. This is reflected in the traditional typological practice of differentiating types primarily by differences in blade shape. For example, in the Tennessee Valley, the Ledbetter, Pickwick, Little Bear Creek, and Cotaco Creek types all possess stems of a similar size and shape but are distinguished on the basis of blade size, shape, or symmetry (Cambron & Hulse, 1964, 1975). Similarly, in the Lower Mississippi Valley, the Macon, Pontchartrain, Carrollton, and Delhi types possess stems of a similar size and shape but are distinguished largely on the basis of blade size, shape, or the presence of shoulder barbs (Ford & Webb, 1956). Thus, differences between similar types were thought "to represent a style of a distinct function or a different origin" (Ford & Webb, 1956, p. 51), rather than the result of tool use and maintenance.

Traditional typologists expected the use-life sequence of a point to contain forms with similar blade shapes characterized by varying blade sizes (Fig. 4).

Contemporary theory on lithic technology, however, suggests that changes in blade size and shape may result from tool maintenance, as well as from the constraints of stylistic norms and the formal requirements of function on tool manufacture. Current research suggests that considerable variation in chipped stone tools may be due to their use, resharpening, and modification (Frison, 1968, 1974; Ahler, 1971; Morse, 1971; Goodyear, 1974; House & Wogaman, 1978; Miller, 1980). Reduction in the blade size and changes in the blade morphology of a point over the course of its use-life are likely to occur frequently and be pronounced, whereas size reductions and morphological changes in its

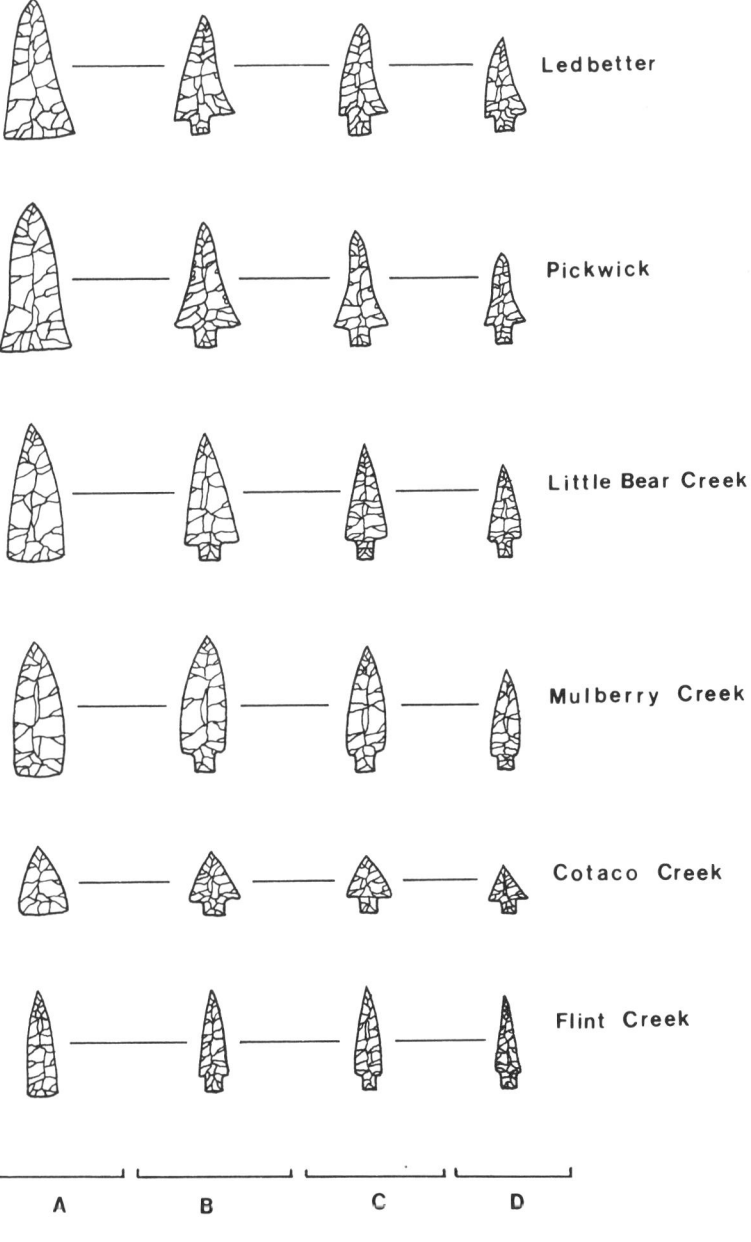

Fig. 18.4. The normative-empiricist model of tool use-life: Blade size decreases but point blade morphology remains unchanged.

stem may occur less frequently and be less pronounced. If this is the case, then we can expect the use-life sequence of a point to be similar to that shown in Figure 5.

Thus, we are presented with two *alternative hypotheses* concerning the variation of blade morphology and size over the course of use-life of a point. The traditional typologist would hold to a hypothesis stipulating that blade shape is not allowed to vary over a point's use-life, although blade size might exhibit reduction. Contemporary theory on lithic technology, on the other hand, suggests a hypothesis stipulating variation in both the shape and size of a point, with blade size exhibiting reduction.

But how can these hypotheses be operationalized? What measures are available that allow us to examine tool use-life and to evaluate the nature of point blade morphology over the course of a tool's use-life? One potential line of research concerns the relationship between blade size and blade edge angle that may result from tool resharpening and modification.

Fig. 18.5. A possible sequence of point reduction using the typology of Cambron and Hulse (1975). The normative types represent forms that may occur over the course of a tool's use-life.

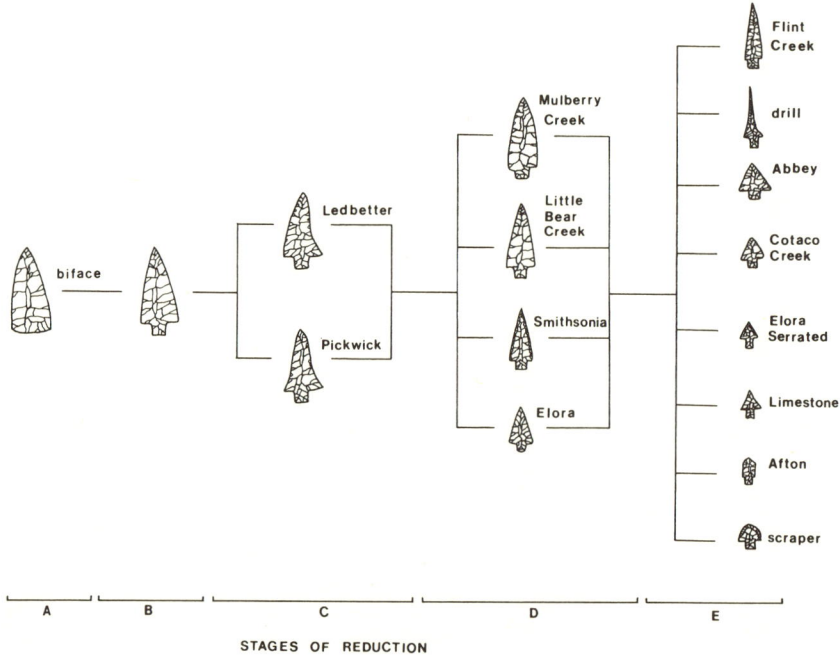

Operationalizing the Concept of Use-Life: The Point Blade Size/Blade Edge Angle Hypothesis

Observations in several recent lithic studies have suggested that blade edge angle may increase with successive tool resharpening (Ahler, 1971; Morse, 1971; Goodyear, 1974; House & Wogaman, 1978). Ahler (1971) found more intensively resharpened points to be characterized by steeper edge angles and suggested that changes in tool function may occur over the life of a tool. Similarly, Morse (1971) and Goodyear (1974) attributed sequential increases in Dalton blade edge angles to the process of resharpening, but also recognized that their functions may have changed over the course of tool use-life. House and Wogaman (1978) also examined the relationships between blade edge angles and use-life for Morrow Mountain points in South Carolina. Hypothesizing that blade edge angles increase with successive resharpenings, they derived the test implication that whole points, presumably discarded during the later stages of tool use-life in an exhausted form, generally should have less acute edge angles than broken points. This follows under the assumption that points are likely to be successively resharpened until they are either broken or exhausted. House and Wogaman's empirical results agreed with their expectations, giving support to the hypothesis that blade edge angle increases with successive point resharpenings.

None of these studies, however, clearly specify how resharpening a blade causes increases in its edge angle. It is possible to offer an explanation of this pattern if individuals in prehistoric societies attempted to extend the use-life and productivity of their lithic tools and were concerned with efficiently utilizing lithic raw materials, we can expect that they removed minimal amounts of edge material to resharpen their tools. We also can expect that they employed resharpening techniques that minimized the risk of seriously damaging or breaking their tools. Because of its greater precision and control, pressure flaking was frequently used to achieve these goals. However, a drawback of using pressure flaking techniques is that they frequently reduce blade width more rapidly than thickness. As a result, blade edge angles may increase with successive resharpenings (Fig. 6).

If the reduction of blade size from resharpening is a relatively gradual sequential process, we should then expect similar sequential increases in blade edge angle as tool use-life progresses. Furthermore, if we were to plot a population of points representing the reduction sequence of a single type, we may expect a linear trajectory to illustrate the use-life process (Fig. 7). Initial stage points should be characterized by a large blade size with acute blade edge angles, whereas more extensively used and resharpened points possess a smaller blade size with more obtuse edge angles. In other words, the relationship between blade size and blade edge angle defines a *dimension* or scale of variability that can be used (with some corrections) to measure the use-life of a point.

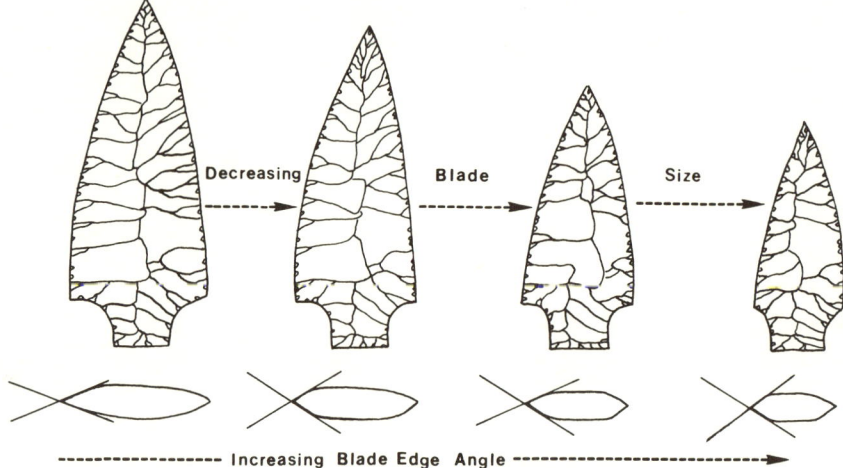

Fig. 18.6. Resharpening causes point width to decrease more rapidly than thickness and results in increased blade edge angles with successive resharpenings.

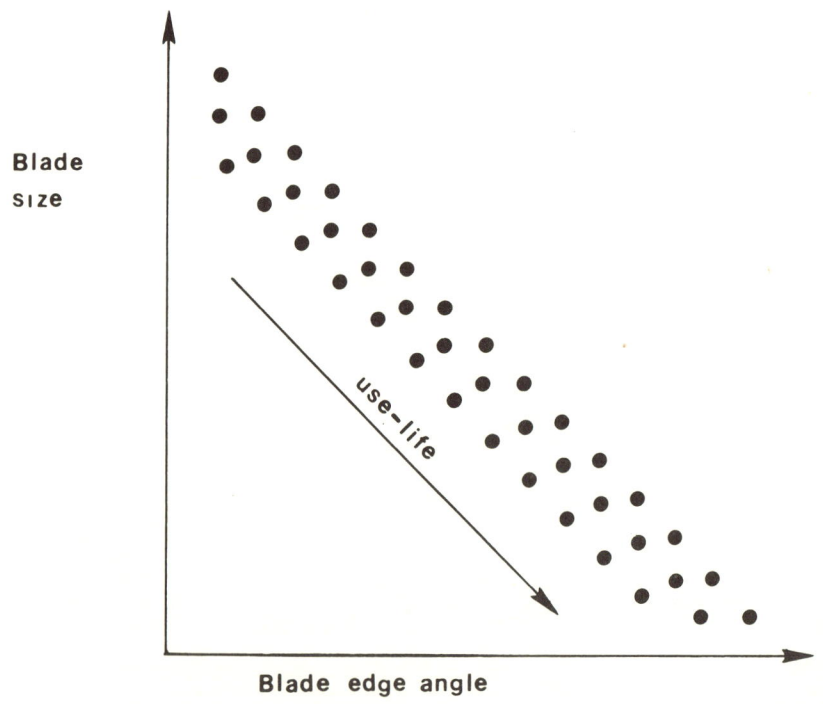

Fig. 18.7. Relationships between blade size and edge angle in a hypothetical assemblage of points representing all stages of use-life.

This scale of the use-life of a point can be used to operationalize the two alternative hypotheses on changing blade morphology and size suggested by normative-empiricist typologies and contemporary theory on lithic technology. If normative-empiricist point types represent distinct styles of tools maintained over the course of their use-lives, then each type should exhibit its own reduction sequence (Fig. 8). Furthermore, because each type should evidence varying degrees of blade reduction, there should be a trajectory of forms for each type, demonstrating gradual decreases in point blade size with gradual increases in blade edge angle. However, if the traditional types represent simply different stages of reduction for a single type, we should expect the traditional point types to occur along restricted portions of a single reduction trajectory (Fig. 8). Thus, by examining the distribution of the traditional types along the blade size and blade edge angle dimension, we can evaluate the two hypotheses of interest.

To accurately assess these test implications, we need variables and measurement techniques that will provide an *objective* and *comprehensive* measure of blade size and blade edge angle, despite the morphological irregularities that characterize individual points. The following section presents these variables and techniques in the context of an example analysis testing the two hypotheses of interest.

THE ANALYSIS

The Sample

The points for this analysis are from excavations at the Brinkley site (22TS729), a multicomponent accretional midden located on a tributary of the Tennessee River in northeastern Mississippi (Otinger & Hoffman, n.d.) (Fig. 9). The sample includes 80 points characterized by relatively straight narrow stems (Figs. 10 & 11). These points usually are described as Ledbetter, Pickwick, Little Bear Creek, Mulberry Creek, Cotaco Creek, and Flint Creek types (Kneberg, 1956; DeJarnette et al., 1962; Cambron & Hulse, 1964, 1975); as provisional or undifferentiated types (Lewis & Lewis, 1961; Cambron & Hulse, 1964, 1975); or as other functional tool forms (e.g., drills, gravers, burins). Whereas the stems of all of these tools are very similar in size and shape, substantial differences are reflected in the sizes and shapes of the blade. Most of these points were recovered from the plowzone at the Brinkley site and are thought to be associated with the Late Archaic and Early Woodland periods in this area (Kneberg, 1956; DeJarnette et al., 1962; Cambron & Hulse, 1975; Peterson, 1971; Faulkner & McCollough, 1973; and Jenkins & Curren, 1975).

Measurement Techniques

Meaningful analysis and typology require that variables be chosen carefully in relation to a specific problem or goal. As dictated by the hypotheses presented above, the initial goal of this analysis is to determine whether there is a

584   ARTIFACT ANALYSIS

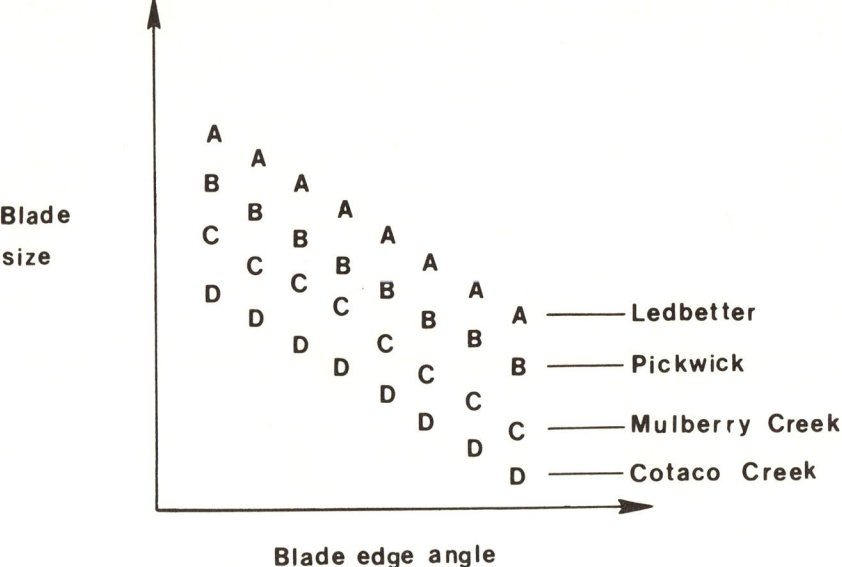

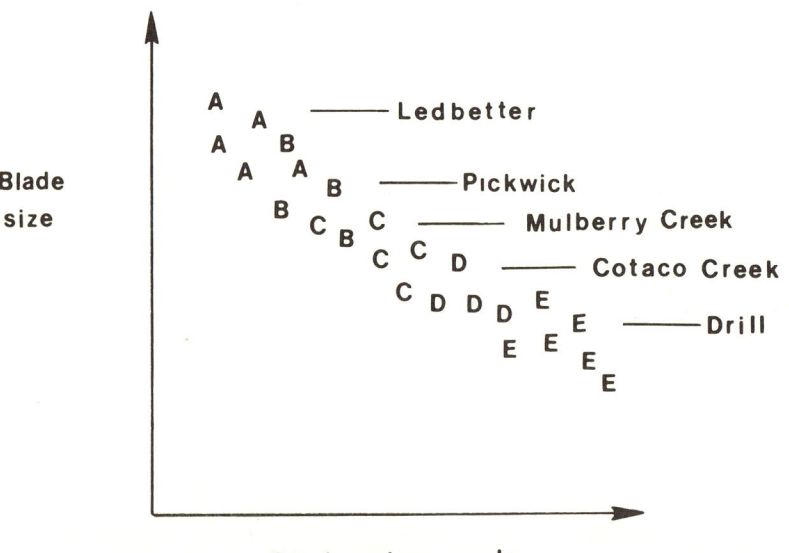

Fig. 18.8. A dichotomy of reduction sequences. Top: The normative model of tool use-life. Bottom: An alternative model of tool use-life.

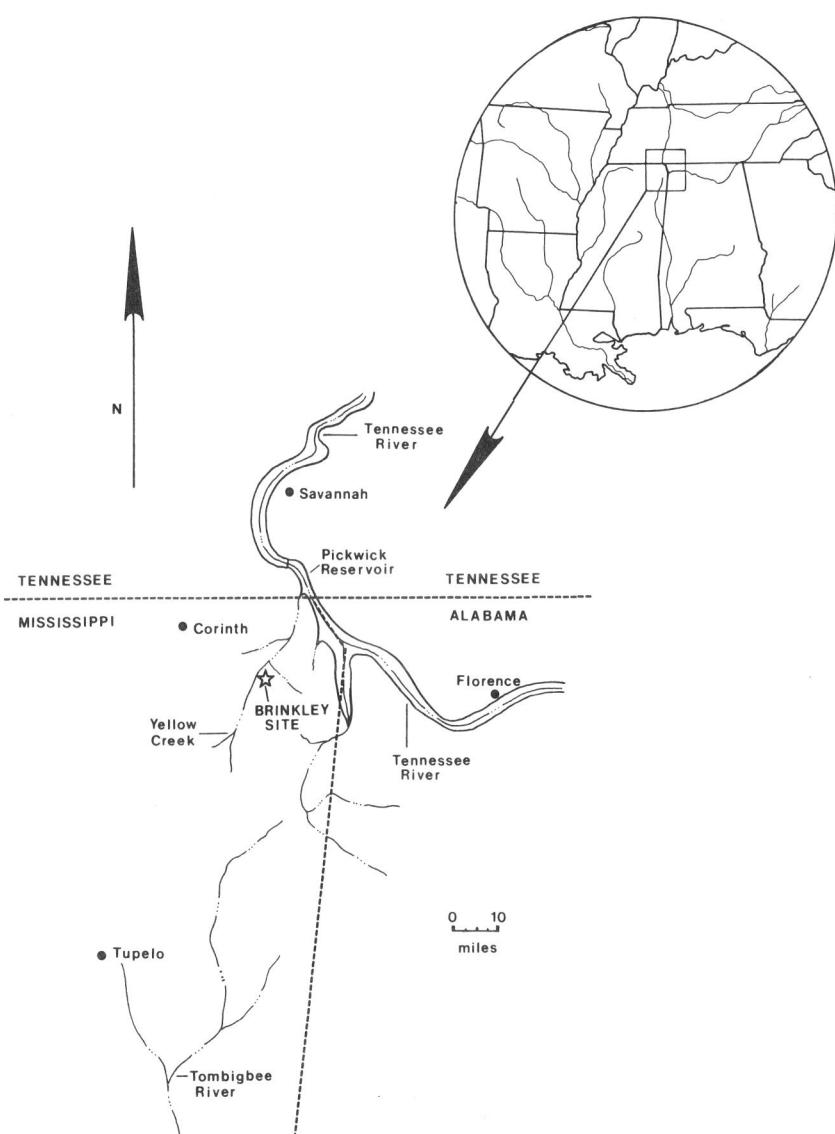

Fig. 18.9. Location of the Brinkley site (22TS729).

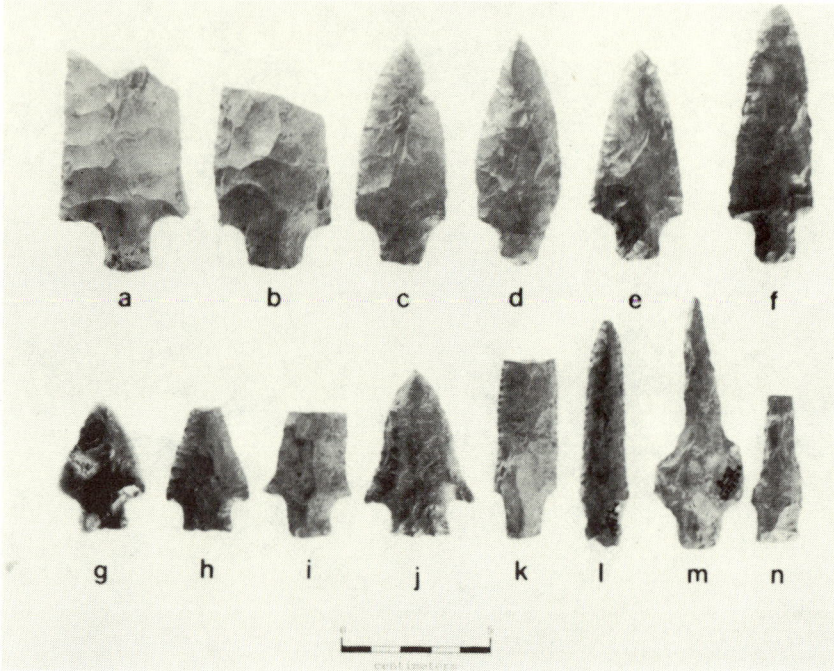

Fig. 18.10. Normative types identified at the Brinkley site. a-b Ledbetter, c-d Mulberry Creek, e-f Little Bear Creek, g-h Cotaco Creek, i-j Pickwick, k-l Flint Creek, m-n drills.

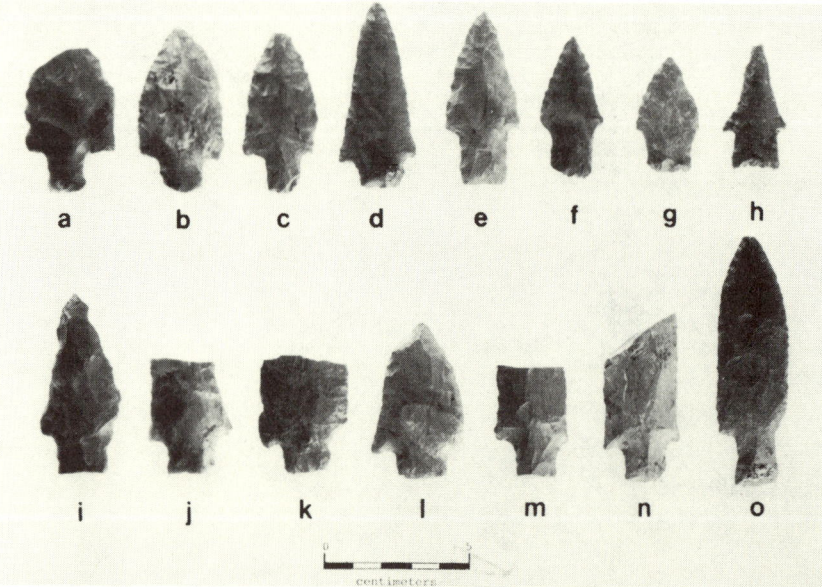

Fig. 18.11. Provisional types identified at the Brinkley site. a-i provisional type 1, j-l provisional type 4, m-o narrow stem undifferentiated.

systematic correlation between point blade size and blade edge angle. Therefore, a measurement technique must be selected that provides variables that sufficiently represent the variation in point blade size and edge angle commonly found in chipped-stone assemblages.

Traditionally, this has been accomplished with the use of two kinds of variables: 1) qualitative descriptions of ideal geometric forms and 2) quantitative measurements taken along Cartesian coordinate axes. These are useful kinds of variables for the typology and analysis of chipped stone points but may have limitations for certain kinds of research.

Perhaps the most common method of classifying chipped stone points is with qualitative attributes describing ideal geometric shapes (Rau, 1876; Fowke, 1896; Wilson, 1899; Strong, 1935; Black & Weer, 1936; Newell & Krieger, 1949; Suhm, Krieger, & Jelks, 1954; Ford & Webb, 1956; Kneberg, 1956; Cambron & Hulse, 1964, 1975; Bullen, 1975). This method involves the description of selected areas of points in reference to their geometric shapes. Attributes describing a blade edge as convex, concave, or straight, etc., or stem margins as expanding, contracting, or parallel, etc., are commonly employed to describe tool elements.

Qualitative variables are useful in a descriptive sense and provide an expedient method of assessing this morphological variation. However, being based in a nominal scale of measurement, the magnitude and direction of differences between attribute states are not specified or capable of objective evaluation. Continuous variation is forced into static classes representing intuitively defined modes or norms. Given that ideal geometric tool forms rarely, if ever, occur in the archaeological record, a discrepancy arises between our methods of analysis, on one hand, and the nature of the data, on the other.

Quantitative measurements taken along Cartesian coordinate axes are also commonly used to provide variables for point classifications and typologies (Finklestein, 1937; Suhm, Krieger, & Jelks, 1954; Ford & Webb, 1956; Kneberg, 1956; Binford, 1963; Cambron & Hulse, 1964, 1975; Benfer, 1967; Kay, 1975). This usually involves measuring the length and width of specific tool portions important for distinguishing types (e.g., blade width, stem length).

Variables based on Cartesian coordinate measures are useful for many purposes and have advantages over qualitative attributes. They reflect the continuous nature of the morphological variation of a tool, allowing precise measurements of specific tool portions. Also, multiple Cartesian variables can be used to represent the multivariate expression of the size of a tool or its shape, under conditions of tool morphological irregularity.

Nevertheless, Cartesian variables have limitations. First, they can be difficult to operationalize with types that are not characterized by discrete points of juncture in their morphology because the boundaries of elements must be defined explicitly if they are to be comparable. Second, as traditionally used in point typologies, Cartesian variables assume the bilateral symmetry of points. Measurements are usually taken from the outer margins or periphery, regardless of any asymmetry or irregularity in morphology. For example, blade shoulder width is a concept comprised of variation from the centerline to two opposing blade margins. However, by combining this variation into a single measure, one eliminates the ability to examine blade asymmetry—a form of morphological variation that can be important to document when considering tool manufacturing, use, and maintenance processes. Because balanced symmetry is rarely present in most point assemblages, the measurement technique is often inconsistent with the reality of the phenomena being examined, and alternative techniques may be required that can avoid this problem.

To avoid the erroneous assumption of bilateral symmetry and to overcome the restrictive requirement of well-defined points of juncture, an alternative technique for estimating point morphology and size can be used. This technique involves measuring distances along polar coordinate axes (Montet-White, 1974; Kay, 1980). The point is centered in a standard position on a polar coordinate graph, and the distance from that position to the tool periphery is measured along a series of chosen rays within a 360° radius. This allows measurement of continuous morphological variation and asymmetry, and provides multiple measures of complex tool forms. Additionally, the flexibility in choice of the number and positions of the rays allows an analysis to be as simple or detailed as desired.

For the present analysis, each point was centered on a polar coordinate graph so that the shoulders of the blade rested equally along the horizontal axis (Fig. 12). A series of distance measurements were then taken from the center of the polar coordinate grid to the margin of each point at 20° intervals from 30-330°. By centering the shoulders of the point on the horizontal axis, variables *A1, A2, B1, B2, C1, C2, D1*, and *D2* always refer to distances to the blade periphery, whereas variables *E1, E2, F1, F2, G1, G2, H1*, and *H2* always refer to distances to the stem periphery (Fig. 12). Distal portions of the blade were not measured because most points were broken and could not be estimated accurately.

Edge angle measurements were taken with a goniometer and rounded to the nearest degree. Instead of measuring a single representative angle for each tool, edge angles were measured at the 30°, 70°, 290°, and 330° axes of the polar coordinate grid (Fig. 12). If minor edge damage precluded measurement at these intervals, then edge angle measurements were taken at the nearest possible location along the blade edge. Additional measurements for maximum blade and stem thickness were taken with calipers and rounded to the nearest millimeter.

Data Screening

The polar coordinate and edge angle measures of the Brinkley site sample were analyzed using both factor analysis and canonical correlation analysis.

TOOL MAINTENANCE AND POINT TYPOLOGY 589

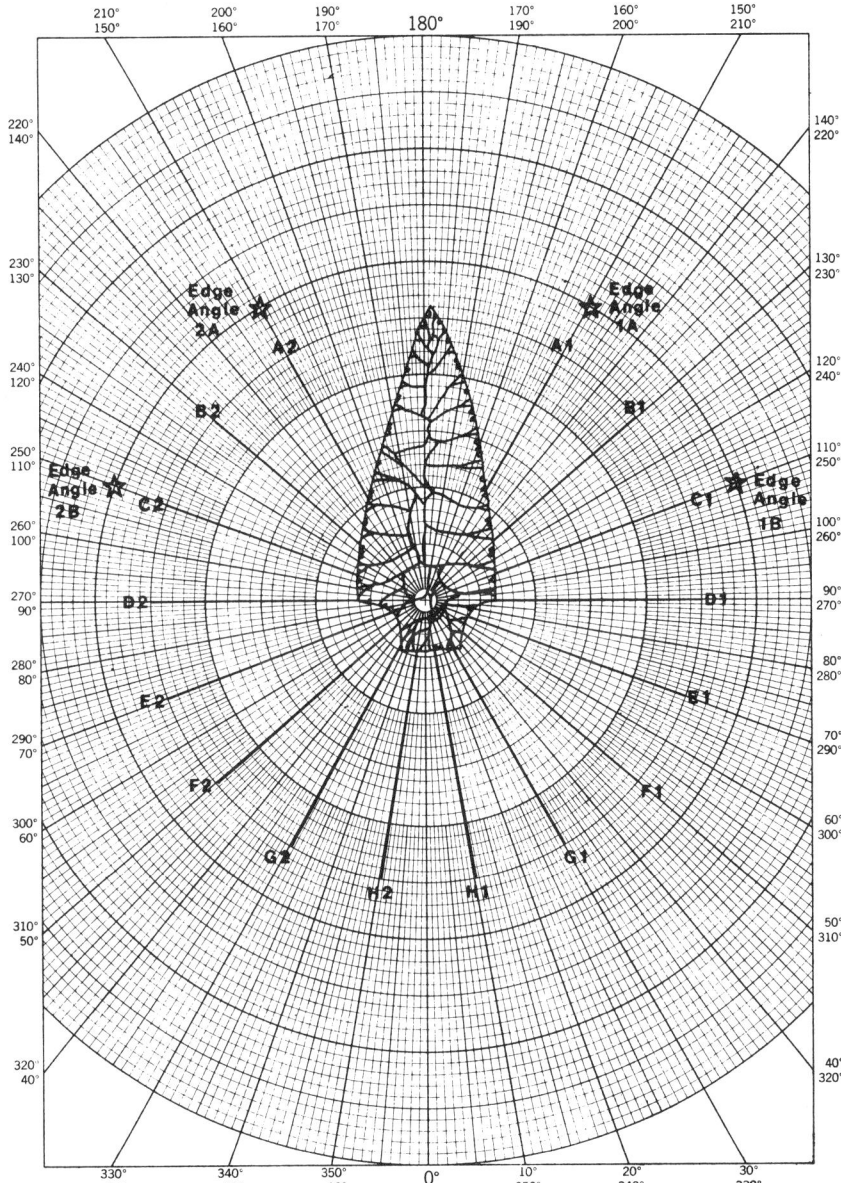

Fig. 18.12. Measurements selected for analysis.

This was done to evaluate the relationship between point blade size and edge angle over the course of a tool's use-life and to illustrate the relative appropriateness of these techniques in assessing relationships between such morphological variables of artifacts. In preparation for these analyses, however, it was desirable to first reach a general understanding of the behavior of the size and edge angle variables, and their congruence to the assumptions of factor analysis and canonical correlation.

To allow preliminary screening of the data set, histograms and bivariate scatterplots were examined for all variables. Histograms showed each of the variables to be unimodal and approximately normal in distribution. However, the distributions of most of the variables were slightly and positively skewed and leptokurtic (Table 1). Scatterplots between all variable pairs were also examined to ensure that their relationships were not curvilinear and that outliers were not present; both can distort correlations among variables (Speth & Johnson, 1976).

Descriptive statistics were also generated for each variable. Table 1 lists several statistics including the mean, standard deviation, variance, skewness, and kurtosis for each variable. Variables *E1, E2, F1, F2, G1, G2, blade thickness,* and *haft thickness* have the lowest standard deviations, indicating that the size and shape of the stem and overall point thickness exhibit the least variation among the tools present. This is expectable, given the sampling procedures and point maintenance processes described previously. Variables *A1, A2, B1, B2, C1, C2, D1, D2, Angle1A, Angle2A, Angle1B, Angle2B,* on the other hand, are characterized by much higher standard deviations, indicating that blade shape, size, and edge angle exhibit the most variation among these tools. Again, this is expectable given the previously described processes.

To assess the strength of the relationships between variables, Pearson's product-moment correlation coefficients were generated between all variable pairs. Several strong correlations are evident (Tables 2, 3, and 4). All of the variables measuring the size and shape of the blade are strongly or moderately positively correlated with each other (Table 2). *Blade thickness* exhibits moderate positive correlations with some of the blade size variables, but is more strongly correlated with *haft thickness*. A few of the edge angle variables exhibit moderately negative correlations with the blade size variables, as expected, but are strongly positively correlated only among themselves (Table 3).

Moderately strong positive correlations also are evident between some of the stem size variables (Table 4). However, a closer examination reveals two distinct trends. Variables reflecting stem width (*E1, E2, F1, F2*) are strongly correlated among themselves, but are not strongly correlated with the other stem size variables. This indicates that variation in stem width does not strongly influence variation in stem length, or vice versa, for this assemblage.

R-Mode Factor Analysis

At the beginning of this chapter, it was argued that the analysis of chipped stone tools can be undertaken more naturally in a multivariate rather than a univariate or bivariate framework. This circumstance arises from the asymmetry of and irregularities in morphology and edge angle that typify stone tools.

Table 18.1

Descriptive Statistics

Variables	Mean	Standard Deviation	Variance	Skewness	Kurtosis
Blade Size					
A1	2.49	0.65	0.42	0.28	−0.37
A2	2.31	0.61	0.37	0.41	0.82
B1	1.82	0.43	0.18	0.35	0.15
B2	1.72	0.36	0.13	0.18	0.07
C1	1.58	0.33	0.11	0.18	−0.27
C2	1.53	0.30	0.09	0.64	0.87
D1	1.51	0.34	0.12	0.21	−0.20
D2	1.46	0.27	0.07	0.32	0.15
thickness	0.97	0.19	0.04	0.86	1.64
Stem Size					
E1	0.93	0.12	0.02	0.18	−0.09
E2	0.88	0.11	0.01	−0.09	−0.47
F1	1.03	0.16	0.02	0.81	1.33
F2	0.97	0.14	0.02	0.97	2.07
G1	1.39	0.17	0.03	0.32	0.52
G2	1.36	0.17	0.03	−0.08	0.16
H1	1.43	0.20	0.04	−0.03	−0.32
H2	1.41	0.19	0.04	0.07	−0.13
thickness	0.77	0.13	0.02	0.11	−0.14
Edge Angle					
Angle 1a	56.13	10.89	118.62	0.05	0.10
Angle 2a	56.25	10.76	115.78	0.23	−0.05
Angle 1b	55.34	9.01	81.26	0.27	0.19
Angle 2b	55.29	10.23	104.71	0.50	−0.43

Table 18.2

Correlation Matrix for the Blade Size Variables

Variables	A1	A2	B1	B2	C1	C2	D1	D2
Blade Size								
A1	1.00	0.92	0.91	0.91	0.79	0.82	0.64	0.78
A2	0.92	1.00	0.90	0.95	0.75	0.88	0.63	0.78
B1	0.90	0.90	1.00	0.92	0.91	0.92	0.82	0.85
B2	0.91	0.95	0.92	1.00	0.82	0.92	0.68	0.84
C1	0.79	0.75	0.91	0.82	1.00	0.86	0.92	0.87
C2	0.82	0.88	0.92	0.92	0.86	1.00	0.80	0.93
D1	0.64	0.63	0.82	0.68	0.92	0.80	1.00	0.82
D2	0.78	0.79	0.85	0.85	0.87	0.93	0.82	1.00
Thickness	0.47	0.45	0.44	0.43	0.38	0.39	0.26	0.30
Stem Size								
E1	0.33	0.28	0.48	0.39	0.59	0.48	0.63	0.54
E2	0.38	0.36	0.43	0.44	0.48	0.52	0.49	0.57
F1	0.15	0.12	0.30	0.20	0.38	0.30	0.46	0.37
F2	0.25	0.23	0.34	0.29	0.39	0.38	0.45	0.44
G1	0.18	0.12	0.21	0.14	0.28	0.17	0.35	0.20
G2	0.36	0.33	0.35	0.35	0.36	0.34	0.40	0.35
H1	0.16	0.11	0.09	0.12	0.10	0.02	0.01	0.04
H2	0.20	0.15	0.12	0.16	0.11	0.06	0.02	0.07
thickness	0.18	0.18	0.17	0.18	0.12	0.14	0.08	0.04
Edge Angle								
Angle 1a	−0.50	−0.43	−0.41	−0.41	−0.35	−0.37	−0.24	−0.37
Angle 2a	−0.52	−0.50	−0.46	−0.48	−0.39	−0.42	−0.34	−0.40
Angle 1b	−0.38	−0.31	−0.29	−0.31	−0.26	−0.24	−0.16	−0.26
Angle 2b	−0.43	−0.37	−0.35	−0.37	−0.29	−0.33	−0.28	−0.37

Table 18.3

Correlation Matrix for the Edge Angle and Thickness Variables

Variables	Angle 1a	Angle 2a	Angle 1b	Angle 2b	Blade Thickness	Stem Thickness
Blade Size						
A1	−0.50	−0.52	−0.38	−0.43	0.47	0.18
A2	−0.43	−0.50	−0.31	−0.37	0.45	0.18
B1	−0.41	−0.46	−0.29	−0.35	0.44	0.18
B2	−0.41	−0.48	−0.31	−0.37	0.43	0.18
C1	−0.35	−0.39	−0.26	−0.29	0.38	0.12
C2	−0.37	−0.42	−0.24	−0.33	0.39	0.14
D1	−0.24	−0.34	−0.16	−0.28	0.26	0.08
D2	−0.37	−0.40	−0.26	−0.36	0.30	0.04
thickness	0.07	0.06	0.04	0.10	1.00	0.54
Stem Size						
E1	−0.14	−0.09	−0.01	−0.06	0.11	0.17
E2	−0.07	−0.03	−0.14	−0.03	0.17	0.06
F1	−0.10	−0.04	−0.02	−0.11	−0.18	−0.10
F2	−0.15	−0.08	−0.19	−0.14	−0.06	−0.10
G1	−0.04	−0.08	−0.19	−0.14	0.18	0.22
G2	−0.10	−0.13	−0.24	−0.15	0.14	0.13
H1	−0.02	0.04	−0.12	0.04	0.30	0.31
H2	−0.05	0.04	−0.18	0.02	0.30	0.30
thickness	0.09	0.08	0.06	0.23	0.54	1.00
Edge Angle						
Angle 1a	1.00	0.65	0.63	0.59	0.07	0.09
Angle 2a	0.65	1.00	0.64	0.74	0.06	0.08
Angle 1b	0.63	0.64	1.00	0.67	0.04	0.06
Angle 2b	0.59	0.74	0.67	1.00	0.10	0.23

Table 18.4

Correlation Matrix for the Stem Size Variables

Variables	E1	E2	F1	F2	G1	G2	H1	H2
Blade Size								
A1	0.33	0.38	0.15	0.25	0.18	0.36	0.16	0.20
A2	0.28	0.36	0.12	0.23	0.12	0.33	0.11	0.15
B1	0.48	0.43	0.30	0.34	0.21	0.35	0.09	0.12
B2	0.39	0.44	0.20	0.28	0.14	0.35	0.12	0.16
C1	0.59	0.48	0.38	0.39	0.28	0.36	0.10	0.12
C2	0.48	0.52	0.30	0.38	0.17	0.34	0.02	0.06
D1	0.63	0.49	0.46	0.45	0.35	0.40	0.01	0.02
D2	0.54	0.57	0.37	0.44	0.20	0.35	0.04	0.07
thickness	0.11	0.17	−0.18	−0.06	0.18	0.14	0.30	0.30
Stem Size								
E1	1.00	0.51	0.72	0.42	0.44	0.30	0.03	0.01
E2	0.51	1.00	0.45	0.72	0.21	0.42	−0.01	0.04
F1	0.72	0.45	1.00	0.63	0.35	0.20	−0.22	−0.23
F2	0.42	0.72	0.63	1.00	0.22	0.44	−0.21	−0.16
G1	0.44	0.21	0.30	0.22	1.00	0.63	0.37	0.34
G2	0.30	0.42	0.21	0.44	0.63	1.00	0.22	0.24
H1	0.03	−0.01	−0.22	−0.21	0.37	0.22	1.00	0.96
H2	0.01	0.04	−0.23	−0.16	0.34	0.23	0.96	1.00
thickness	0.17	0.06	−0.10	−0.09	0.22	0.13	0.31	0.30
Edge Angle								
Angle 1a	−0.14	−0.07	−0.10	−0.15	−0.04	−0.10	−0.02	−0.05
Angle 2a	−0.09	−0.03	−0.04	−0.08	−0.05	−0.13	0.04	0.04
Angle 1b	0.01	−0.14	−0.02	−0.19	−0.15	−0.23	−0.12	−0.18
Angle 2b	−0.06	−0.03	−0.11	−0.14	−0.15	−0.15	0.04	0.02

Under these conditions, it is advantageous to take multiple measures of each tool characteristic that is of interest at various positions, and then to summarize the measures of each characteristic into a single, composite measure using some multivariate, data reduction technique. The following sections evaluate the use of factor analysis and canonical correlation in achieving this aim, as well as in defining relationships among composite measures.

R-mode factor analysis comprises several techniques that are useful for transforming large numbers of variables into fewer new variables, or *factors*, that describe the main dimensions of variation within a data set. Each factor is a linear combination of variables that is designed to extract maximum amounts of variance while providing the "best" reproduction of the correlations between the observed variables (Harman, 1967, p. 14).

There are several techniques in factor analysis for rotating the original coordinate system to find an optimal orientation of the axes in factor space. Orthogonal solutions retain perpendicular axes during rotation and, under the assumption of normality, allow the derivation of factors that are linearly independent. Oblique solutions, on the other hand, permit the axes to take nonperpendicular orientations during rotation, allowing the definition of factors that are linearly dependent. As Rummel (1970, p. 386) has observed, orthogonal rotations are actually a subset of oblique rotation procedures: if the factors derived from an oblique solution are uncorrelated, the defined axes will be orthogonal.

For any given data set, it may be possible to justify the use of either orthogonal or oblique rotations. Choice will depend on 1) whether one holds to the philosophy that the fundamental processes of nature are always uncorrelated, or that they may be correlated, and 2) whether one is concerned with representing the empirical structure of the data in their own terms (inductively) or from the perspective of a factor model imposing constraints of dimensional independence (deductively). In the example presented here, I was concerned with representing the empirical structure of the Brinkley data in an unconstrained way, regardless of what the resultant solution might imply about the independence of lithic processes. Given this purpose and the fact that the correlation matrix of the original variables indicated moderate negative correlations between most of the blade size and edge angle variables, a factor model allowing for dependence between factors was considered more appropriate.

The eight blade size variables (*A1, A2, B1, B2, C1, C2, D1,* and *D2*) and the four edge angle variables (*Angle1a, Angle2a, Angle1b,* and *Angle2b*) were submitted to an R-mode factor analysis as implemented by the SAS 79.6 factor procedure (Helwig & Council, 1979). The analysis was based on the matrix of correlations among the variables rather than a variance-covariance matrix in order to give equal weighting to all the variables. The initial two-factor principal axes solution was subjected to an orthogonal rotation using the varimax criterion. The constraint of orthogonality of the axes was then relaxed to obtain the promax oblique solution.

Plots of the variables in factor space illustrate how successively better fits are obtained as we use the principal axis, varimax orthogonal, and promax oblique solutions to delineate variable clusters (Fig. 13). This also is shown by the correlations of each variable with the newly derived factors, represented by the loadings in the factor pattern matrix for the principal axis and varimax orthogonal rotations, and in the structure matrix for the promax oblique rotation (Table 5). The principal axis method tends to produce a solution that less clearly approaches "simple structure" (Thurstone, 1947), whereas the varimax orthogonal and promax oblique rotations provide solutions more clearly approaching this ideal. For the varimax orthogonal and promax oblique solutions, factor 1 accounts primarily for variation in blade size, whereas factor 2 accounts primarily for variation in blade edge angle. Although both solutions provide similar results concerning the patterning of variables, the promax

Table 18.5

Factor Loadings for the Original Variables

Original Variable	Principal Axis Pattern Matrix		Varimax Orthogonal Pattern Matrix		Promax Oblique Structure Matrix	
	Factor 1	Factor 2	Factor 1	Factor 2	Factor 1	Factor 2
A1	0.921	0.040	0.843	−0.372	0.907	−0.558
A2	0.912	0.119	0.870	−0.298	0.916	−0.493
B1	0.950	0.210	0.945	−0.233	0.973	−0.446
B2	0.935	0.159	0.908	−0.272	0.947	−0.475
C1	0.894	0.270	0.922	−0.154	0.932	−0.364
C2	0.930	0.252	0.945	−0.187	0.963	−0.401
D1	0.805	0.316	0.862	−0.073	0.855	−0.272
D2	0.898	0.230	0.907	−0.192	0.927	−0.398
Edge Angle						
Angle 1a	−0.562	0.610	−0.232	0.797	−0.411	0.829
Angle 2a	−0.627	0.615	−0.288	0.829	−0.473	0.874
Angle 1b	−0.460	0.732	−0.087	0.861	−0.285	0.857
Angle 2b	−0.537	0.682	−0.178	0.850	−0.370	0.868

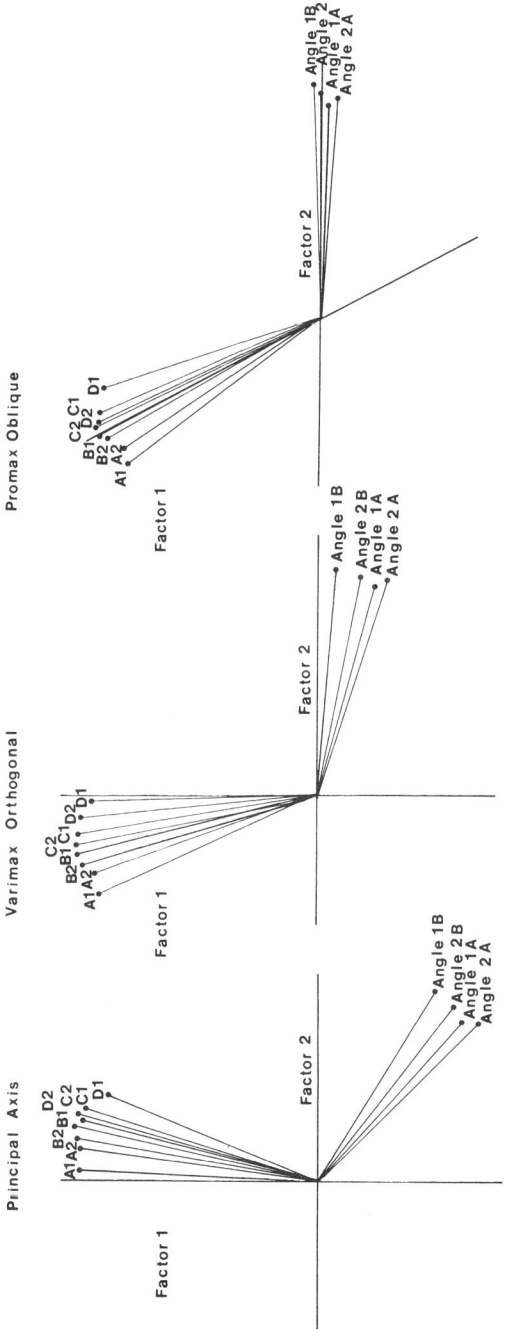

Fig. 18.13. Plots of the variables in factor space.

oblique solution generated factors more highly correlated with the original variables.

A plot of the factor scores for the promax oblique solution exhibits a negative linear relationship between the two factors representing blade size and blade edge angle (Fig. 14). An interfactor correlation of −0.452 indicates a moderately negative relationship between them and suggests that as blade size decreases, blade edge angle increases. An r^2 value of 0.204 indicates that approximately 20% of the variation in factor 2 (blade edge angle) can be explained by factor 1 (blade size). Thus, while some of the variation in blade edge angle can be accounted for by reductions in blade size, the analysis suggests that other elements are also responsible for much of this variation.

This example illustrates the most frequent use of factor analysis: as a pattern-searching or *variable clustering* technique, and for *summarizing* the variability encompassed by groups of related variables. The technique provides a concise

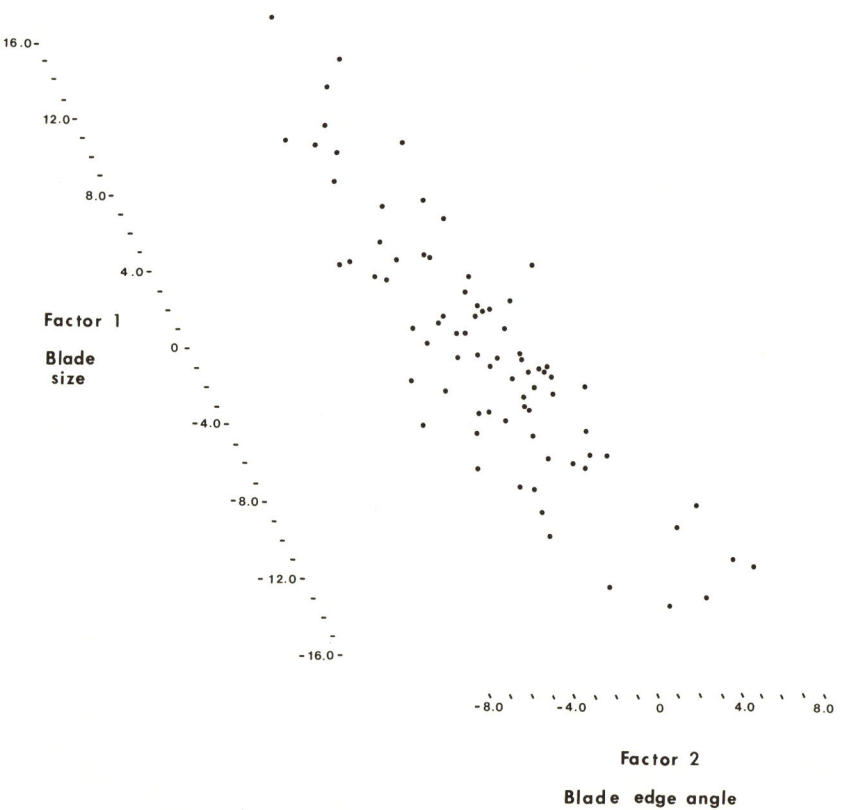

Fig. 18.14. Scatterplot of the factor score.

representation of the original variables and indicates which variables within a data set covary in similar or dissimilar manners.

It is useful to reconsider, however, whether factor analysis is the most appropriate method for this kind of study. In particular, it can be noted that factor analysis does not distinguish between independent and dependent variables as does regression analysis. As a result, if all variables of interest are submitted to analysis, including both dependent and independent variables that are strongly related, it is very probable that dependent and independent variables will hopelessly intermix (load highly on) the same factors. Thus, while factor analysis may be useful for defining the *dimensionality* of a data set and *summarizing* the variability encompassed by multiple, related variables, it is not particularly suited for *investigating the relationships* between groups of multiple related variables.

In this study, for example, the problem with using factor analysis for examining relationships between the groups of multiple variables jointly representing blade size or blade edge angle is that neither of the derived factors measure blade size or blade edge angle *exclusively*. Each factor is determined in relation to all of the variables in the analysis and provides a mixed measure of the variation present. The loadings in the oblique factor structure matrix (Table 5) indicate that while factor 1 measures primarily blade size, variation in blade edge angle is also measured. Similarly, while factor 2 measures primarily blade edge angle, some of the variation in blade size is also represented by this factor (Table 5). Neither factor reflects variation solely in point blade size or blade edge angle.

The original variables separately measure the two distinct kinds of variation we are interested in assessing (blade size and blade edge angle), whereas factor analysis transforms them into mixed measures of the variation in the data set. This forces us to question the utility of factor analysis for the purpose of this kind of analysis concerned with relationships among multivariate dimensions (e.g., blade size, blade edge angle) and to consider whether alternative multivariate techniques, such as canonical correlation, may be more effective.

Canonical Correlation Analysis

Canonical correlation is a multivariate statistical technique designed to find the maximum correlation between two sets of variables. A canonical analysis first defines a linear combination of variables, or *component*, for each set so that the correlation between the two components is maximized. It then proceeds successively to define other pairs of canonical components that are maximally correlated but under the constraint of being orthogonal to the previously defined canonical components (Cooley & Lohnes, 1971, p. 169). The successively defined pairs of components will be characterized by successively lower correlations, for a nonrandom data set. As in factor analysis, the component loadings represent the correlations of the original variables with their canonical components.

Whereas factor analysis attempts to find a few dimensions that account for as much of the *variance* represented *within one set* of variables, canonical correlation analysis selects a pair or a few pairs of dimensions that account for as much of the *covariance between two sets* of variables as is possible. It is clear that this goal of canonical correlation is more concordant with the problem at hand: defining the relationship between the multivariate but distinct measures of point blade size and blade edge angle.

Nevertheless, canonical correlation has a disadvantage compared to factor analysis. Whereas factors can be rotated so as to be oriented obliquely, different pairs of canonical variates cannot. Pairs of canonical variates are always extracted so as to be orthogonal, although the variates within a pair usually are obliquely oriented. In this way, canonical components may not necessarily represent the patterns of covariance within a data set in its own terms, just as orthogonal factors in factor analysis may not necessarily represent the patterns of variance within a data set in its own terms.

Given the concordance between the goals of canonical correlation analysis and those of the example presented here, the Brinkley data were further analyzed using this method. In preparation for the analysis, variations in the stem size variables ($E1$, $E2$, $F1$, $F2$, $G1$, $G2$, $H1$, $H2$) and the *stem thickness* and *blade thickness* variables were *partialled* out of the data. These variables were taken as indicators of the original (presharpened) morphology and sizes of points and their blades because they are not affected much by resharpening. By partialling them out of the analysis, it was possible to control analytically for the original sizes of blades, and thus to clarify the relationship between point blade size and blade edge angle. Partialling out the effects of these variables provided a canonical correlation between blade size and edge angle cast in a *residual space* that is independent of stem size and thickness and blade thickness.

The eight blade size variables were correlated with the four edge angle variables using the SAS 79.6 procedure CANCORR (Helwig & Council, 1979). The first pair of canonical variables have a correlation of 0.679 associated with an F statistic (32 d.f.) of 2.012 and p-value of 0.0018 (Table 6). A crossplot

Table 18.6

The Canonical Correlation Analysis

Canonical Variable Pair	Canonical Correlation	Canonical R-Squared	F Statistic	Degrees of Freedom	Probability F
1	0.679	0.461	2.012	32	0.018
2	0.434	0.189	1.007	21	0.456
3	0.302	0.091	0.643	12	0.802

of the observations using their component scores, which were scaled to unit variance for each component, shows a positive linear distribution (Fig. 15). However, because the blade size variables load positively on their canonical component while the edge angle variables load negatively on theirs, we can infer a negative linear relationship between point blade size and edge angle.

The first canonical variable for blade size accounts for 58% of the variation in the original blade size variables, and the first canonical component for edge angle accounts for 54% of the variation in the original edge angle variables (Table 6). As a result, we can conclude that the first pair of canonical components provides an adequate representation of the variability in the data set. The canonical R^2 indicates that approximately 46% of the variation in the canonical component for edge angle can be accounted for by variation in the canonical component for blade size.

It is possible for the canonical *correlation* between two canonical components to be high while very little of the *variability* in one set of variables is contingent upon variability in the other and vice versa. To determine whether or not the obtained R^2 is misleading in this way, a canonical redundancy analysis (Stewart & Love, 1968) can be performed. The generated statistics specify the proportion of the variability or *redundancy* in one set of original variables attributable to the opposite set, as transmitted through the canonical component pair. For the Brinkley data set, a canonical redundancy analysis (Table 7) shows that approximately 27% of the variation in the original edge angle variables is accounted for by variation in the original blade size variables as transmitted through the first canonical component pair. Approximatley 25% of the variation in the original blade size variables is accounted for by variation in the

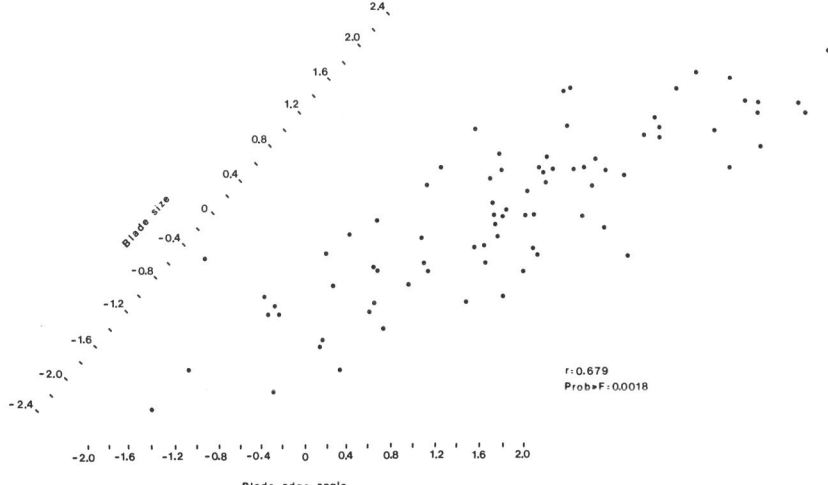

Fig. 18.15. Scatterplot of the canonical components.

Table 18.7

The Canonical Redundancy Analysis

Variance of the blade size variables explained by:

	their own canonical variables		the opposite canonical variables
	Proportion	Canonical[1]	Proportion
1	0.582	0.461	0.268
2	0.027	0.189	0.005
3	0.157	0.091	0.014

Variance of the edge angle variables explained by:

	their own canonical variables		the opposite canonical variables
	Proportion	Canonical[1]	Proportion
1	0.539	0.461	0.249
2	0.208	0.189	0.039
3	0.065	0.091	0.006

[1]R-squared

original edge angle variables as transmitted through the first canonical component pair. These redundancies are relatively high, suggesting the reliability and interpretability of the R^2 statistic.

The canonical analysis indicates that there is a significant negative correlation between point blade size and blade edge angle. Almost half of the summarized variation in blade edge angle can be accounted for by summarized variation in point blade size. This suggests that much of the variation in blade size and edge angle may be attributed to tool maintenance. These findings support those of other researchers (e.g., Ahler, 1971; Goodyear, 1974; Frison, et al., 1976; House & Wogaman, 1978; Miller, 1980) who have suggested that much variation in point blade size, morphology, and edge angle results from tool use, resharpening, and modification. It also suggests that for this data set, the relationship between point blade size and edge angle can be used as a dimension of variability for measuring the use-life of a point, when testing the two alternative hypotheses on morphological variation in points over their use-lives.

Comparison of Factor Analysis and Canonical Correlation

Different multivariate techniques are designed for different purposes. One should use a technique that is logically consistent with the specific goals of an analysis and the structure of a specific data set. Although factor analysis is used frequently to summarize large numbers of variables, it is particularly useful for defining the dimensional relationships between clusters of variables *within* a set. However, if the purpose of analysis is to summarize and examine *relationships* between sets of variables comprising conceptually *separate* dimensions, then other multivariate techniques, such as canonical correlation, may provide more direct measures of the relationships we wish to examine.

Because the latter goal pertains to this particular analysis, canonical correlation was preferred. It provided more sensitive summary measures of point blade size and edge angle by allowing us to exert more control over the sources of variation determining each canonical component. Moreover, it indicated a stronger negative relationship between blade size and edge angle than did factor analysis, although the conclusions from the two analyses are similar.

It should not be concluded, however, that the use of factor analysis and canonical correlation analysis need be mutually exclusive. As Christenson and Read (1977) have suggested, factor analysis may be useful for screening data prior to undertaking other multivariate analyses. The utility of factor analysis for the purpose of identifying clusters of variables measuring similar dimensions of variation in a data set is well known. *If factor analysis is used as a screening device prior to canonical correlation, we can ensure that each set of variables in the canonical analysis measures a single, coherent dimension of variation and that each canonical component measures a different dimension of variation in the data set.*

For the data set used in this analysis, such a stepwise analytic design was not necessary. The relation of the blade size variables to each other and their internal coherency was evident in the correlation matrix, as well as logically expectable. The same is true for the blade edge angle variables. In other lithic studies, however, where the technological processes responsible for artifact variation are less clear, such a stepwise analytic design may be very useful.

Evaluating the Hypotheses

The canonical analysis of the Brinkley data indicates that there is a significant negative correlation between point blade size and blade edge angle that may directly result from the resharpening process. Furthermore, the continuous and systematic nature of this relationship suggests that it can be interpreted as a dimension representing the use-life of points for this assemblage. Thus, it is possible to test the two hypotheses on blade shape variation over the use-life of a point.

The test implications of these two hypotheses, to which analytical results will be compared, can be summarized briefly 1) If the normative-empiricist point types represent distinct styles of tools maintained over the course of their use-lives, then each type should exhibit its own reduction sequence (Fig. 5). Because each type should demonstrate varying degrees of blade reduction, there should be a trajectory of forms for each type evidencing decreases in blade size associated with corresponding increases in blade edge angle (Fig. 8). 2) On the other hand, acknowledging current research in lithic technology, if the traditional types represent simply different stages of reduction for a single type (Fig. 4), we may expect the traditional types to occur along restricted portions of a single reduction trajectory (Fig 8). Therefore, by examining the distribution of normative types along the blade size and blade edge angle dimension, we can evaluate the two hypotheses of interest.

Figure 16 illustrates the distribution of the traditional morphological types of the Brinkley points over the dimension of covariation interpreted to represent a reduction sequence. It can be observed that each of the normative types extends over a restricted portion of the trajectory. While some types overlap considerably, others overlap very little. However, the types form only a single reduction sequence rather than a series of similar sequences. This pattern corresponds with the test implications of the hypothesis suggesting that variation in the shape of the point blades results primarily from the resharpening process, as opposed to the makers' attempts to reproduce stylistic norms. It suggests that the points at Brinkley probably represent a single, culture-specific type evidencing varying degrees of use-life reduction rather than several culture-specific types.

The distribution of the provisional point types is interesting to consider also. While one provisional group of points encompasses the complete range of variation for the use-life sequence, two others exhibit more localized distributions. Provisional type 1, the catchall category for variant stemmed forms, is distributed throughout the entire reduction sequence (Fig. 16). This indicates that variation not explained by the nonprovisional traditional types but encom-

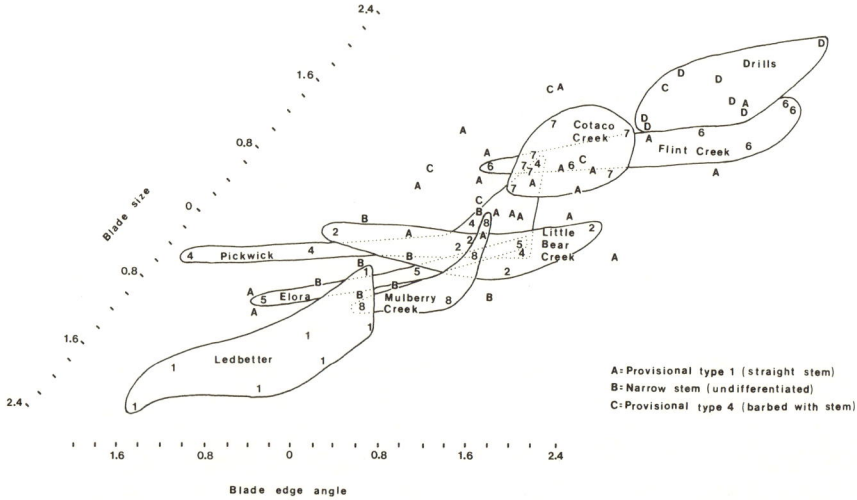

Fig. 18.16. The distribution of the normative-empiricist types in the use-life sequence.

passed by provisional type 1 is present throughout the entire use-life trajectory.

The provisional category for undifferentiated narrow stemmed points and provisional type 4 (barbed and stemmed), on the other hand, exhibit more localized distributions. Points classified as undifferentiated narrow stem types cluster with the Pickwick, Elora, and Little Bear Creek type points within the earlier portion of the reduction sequence (Fig. 16). Points classified as provisional type 4 cluster with the Cotaco Creek and Flint Creek types in the later portions of the trajectory (Fig. 16). These two provisional types express distributions similar to the normative types, but simply were not recognized as such.

Conclusions of the Analysis

The results of this analysis suggest that many of the traditional point types in the Tennessee Valley area may actually represent a single type evidencing varying degrees and manners of use-life reduction. Variation in point blade size and edge angle is apt to result from resharpening, and changes in blade morphology are apt to occur from alternative resharpening strategies or the modification of broken points into useful tools. As a result, it is probable that neither similarities in point blade size and shape nor types solely based on such similarities are useful indicators of spatially or temporally restricted cultural units, as traditional, normative-empiricist typologists have assumed. This suggests that the traditional point typologies for this area need to be revised, and that our behavioral interpretations of the point assemblages need to be reconsidered.

This analysis also has important implications for the functional analysis of chipped stone tools. Edge angle frequently is used as an index of tool function (Wilmsen, 1968a, 1968b). This is based on the assumption that the effectiveness of a tool for a certain task is significantly affected by the angle of its working edge. Thus, tools with different edge angles may have served different functions. Although distinct modalities of edge angles may imply functionally distinct groups of tools for some assemblages (Wilmsen, 1968a, 1968b), this analysis suggests that tool resharpening should be recognized as an equally important source of edge angle variability. Edge angle differences between tools (e.g., various classes of endscrapers) may represent differences in the degree of tool resharpening rather than functional differences between the tools. Therefore, the use of tool edge angle to distinguish tool functions should be employed carefully so as to avoid such problems.

PERSPECTIVE ON TYPOLOGY

The development of meaningful and useful classifications and typologies is dependent upon the selection of appropriate variables for defining classes. In the past, decisions on the selection of variables for creating typologies, such as point typologies in the southeast United States, have been made implicitly and applied inconsistently from type to type. Also, a mixed array of criteria have been used to define types, with some relating to tool manufacture, use, and maintenance, and others having temporal/spatial, and perhaps, cultural significance. These procedures for defining types have caused the significance and meaning of the derived types to be unclear.

In contrast, the process of selecting variables for creating classifications and typologies should be based on considerations of the meaning and appropriateness of variables, relative to our theories, the problem of interest, and the organization and content of the phenomenon to be examined. These considerations should be made explicit in the form of bridging arguments.

To understand the organization of individual lithic artifacts and to help in the selection of variables that can be used to create meaningful typologies, it is important that we also consider *general models* of lithic technology that specify how different variables are related to each other by tool manufacture, use, and maintenance. These models allow us to rank variables by their importance or relevance to specific problems.

For example, if we want to design a point typology having primarily cultural spatial/temporal significance, an important factor to control is the variation likely to occur from successive use and maintenance of a tool over its life. This can be accomplished by initially differentiating points on the basis of the size, morphology, and technological characteristics of the *stem* rather than on characteristics of the *blade*. The first group of criteria creates classes of tools sharing similar hafting requirements, techniques, or styles, which probably vary among cultural groups (Wiessner, 1983) and are less likely to reflect tool maintenance and use. The second group of criteria probably evidence varying stages, degrees, or manners of tool reduction during tool maintenance and use, or functionally distinct kinds of tools. These circumstances arise from the fact that the stem of a point, being fixed in a handle or shaft and less susceptible to damage and necessary maintenance, is altered less frequently than the blade. If so desired, the two sets of criteria could be applied sequentially to define a hierarchically structured classification of points reflecting both phenomena.

Constructing tool typologies that accurately reflect the prehistoric behavior we desire them to represent depends not only on selecting variables in relation to culture theory, but also on our understanding of the manufacture, maintenance, and use of these tools as one aspect of their organizational nature. Therefore, we need to develop more and better models for understanding these processes so our classifications can be made more relevant to our theoretical concerns. It is hoped that the analysis presented in this chapter provides a concrete illustration of this point, as well as a step toward improving such models.

CONCLUSION

This chapter has presented several important arguments concerning the analysis and classification of lithic tools, as exemplified by chipped stone points. These may be summarized briefly as follows:

1. The morphology, size, and edge angle of lithic tools often are more accurately expressed by multiple variables of a continuous nature than as single or several discrete measures, given the typical irregularities and asymmetry of these attributes over a tool. The multiple measures of each of these characteristics can be summarized as single dimensions of variability using multivariate, data reduction techniques, such as factor analysis or canonical correlation.

2. The analysis of multiple measures of the shape and size of tools for the purpose of defining tool classes that reflect a controlled range of behavioral phenomena can be achieved efficiently and accurately using a stepwise analytic design. For this analysis, this design involved (a) using factor analysis to determine the basic dimensions of variability within a data set and the variables most strongly representing them; (b) initial assignment of behavioral meaning to the dimensions on the basis of the factor analysis; (c) testing and refinement of the behavioral meaning of the dimensions (including the documentation of maintenance and use processes) through an investigation of the relationships among sets of variables representing different dimensions, using canonical correlation analysis; (d) selection of variables appropriate for creating a typology relevant to the behavioral phenomenon of interest; (e) creation of the typology using any of a large number of Q-mode techniques. The interpretation of dimensions in steps b and c are dependent on the availability of models of lithic technology and artifact style capable of subsuming and explaining the observed relationships, and points to the need for development of such models.

3. The development of explanatory models of lithic technological processes is necessary for the analysis and construction of typologies of points. To this end, this study suggested a negative relationship between the size and edge angle of point blades to be expectable, given certain aspects of point maintenance procedures. This relationship was documented in the Brinkley site data set.

4. The size, morphology, and technological characteristics of the stems of points, rather than their blades, may have more relevance in some assemblages for establishing point typologies reflective of social units possessing spatial-temporal significance.

5. Meaningful and useful types are likely to be created only if the variables used to define them are concordant with (a) one's theoretical orientation and goals of analysis, but also, importantly, (b) the organization and content of the phenomenon under investigation. It is in the latter issue that the normative-empiricist typologies were misguided.

Our ability to construct point classifications and typologies that accurately reflect prehistoric human behavior depends upon our theory, but it is also affected significantly by the models we use to select variables and structure our typologies. Only by developing explicit models that specify how different variables are related to each other by tool manufacturing, use, and maintenance can we provide a logical foundation for ranking and selecting variables by their importance or relevance to specific problems. By designing typologies that are concordant with our theoretical orientation and the organization and content of the phenomena under study, we can develop typologies that provide more sensitive measures of prehistoric human behavior.

REFERENCES

Ahler, S.A. (1971). *Projectile point form and function at Rodgers Shelter, Missouri* (Research Series No. 8). Columbia: Missouri Archaeological Society.

Ahler, S.A. (1979). Functional analysis of nonobsidian chipped stone artifacts: Terms, variables, and quantification. In B. Hayden, (Ed.), *Lithic Use-Wear Analysis*. New York: Academic Press.

Ahler, S.A., & McMillan, R.B. (1976). Material culture at Rodgers Shelter: A reflection of past human activities. In W.R. Wood & R.B. McMillan (Eds.), *Prehistoric man and his environment: A case study in the Ozark Highland* (pp. 163-199). New York: Academic Press, Inc.

Bell, R.E. (1958). *Guide to the identification of certain American Indian projectile points* (Special Bulletin No. 1). Oklahoma City: Oklahoma Anthropological Society.

Bell, R.E. (1960). *Guide to the identification of certain American Indian projectile points* (Special Bulletin No. 2). Oklahoma City: Oklahoma Anthropological Society.

Benfer, R.A. (1967). A design for the study of archaeological characteristics. *American Anthropologist 69*, 719-30.

Binford, L.R. (1962). Archaeology as anthropology. *American Antiquity 28*(2), 217-25.

Binford, L.R. (1963). A proposed attribute list for the description and classification of projectile points. In A.M. White, L.R. Lewis, & M.L. Papsworth, *Miscellaneous Studies in Typology and Classification* (Anthropological Papers No. 19). Ann Arbor: University of Michigan, Museum of Anthropology.

Binford, L.R. (1965). Archaeological systematics and the study of culture process. *American Antiquity 31*(2), 203-10.

Black, G.A., & Weer, P. (1936). A proposed terminology for shape classifications of artifacts. *American Antiquity 1*, 280-294.

Bradley, B.A. (1975). Lithic reduction sequences: A glossary and discussion. In E. Swanson (Ed.), *Lithic technology: Making and using stone tools* (pp. 5-13). The Hague, Netherlands: Mouton Press.

Bradley, B.A. (1982). Flaked stone technology and typology. In G.C. Frison & D.J. Stanfor (Eds.), *The Agate Basin Site: A record of the Paleoindian occupation of the northwestern High Plains* (pp. 15-34). New York: Academic Press, Inc.

Browne, J. (1938). Antiquity of the bow. *American Antiquity 4*, 358-359.

Browne, J. (1940). Projectile points. *American Antiquity 8*(3), 209-213.

Bullen, R.P. (1975). *A Guide to the identification of Florida Projectile Points*. Gainesville, FL: Kendall Books.

Callahan, E. (1979). The basics of biface knapping in the eastern fluted point tradition: A manual for flintknappers and lithic analysts. *Archaeology of Eastern North America 7*(1), 1-180.

Cambron, J.W., & Hulse, D.C. (1975). In D.L. DeJarnette (Ed.), *Handbook of Alabama Archaeology, part 1, point types* (rev. ed.). Moundville, AL: Archaeological Research Association of Alabama, Inc.

Chapman, J. (1975). *The Rose Island site*. (Rep. of Investigations No. 14). Knoxville: University of Tennessee, Department of Anthropology.
Christenson, A.L., & Read, D.W. (1977). Numerical taxonomy, r-mode factor analysis, and archaeological classification. *American Antiquity 42*(2), 163-179.
Clark, J. & Kleindienst, M.R. (1974). The Stone Age cultural sequence: Terminology, typology, and raw materials. In J.D. Clark (Ed.), *Kalambo Falls Prehistoric Site II: The Later Prehistoric Cultures*. London: University Press.
Clark, J. D. & Kurashina, H. (1979). An analysis of earlier stone age bifaces from Gadeb (locality 8e), northern Bale Highlands, Ethiopia. *The South African Archaeological Bulletin 34*(130), 93-109.
Coe, J.L. (1964). *The formative cultures of the Carolina piedmont* (Vol. 54). Philadelphia: Transactions of the American Philosophical Society.
Collins, M.B. (1975). Lithic technology as a means of processual inference. In E. Swanson, (Ed.), *Lithic Technology* (pp. 15-34). The Hague, Netherlands: Mouton Press.
Cooley, W.W., & P.R. Lohnes (1971). *Multivariate Data Analysis*. New York: John Wiley & Sons, Inc.
Crabtree, D.E. (1972). *An introduction to flintworking* (Occasional Papers No. 28). Pocatello: Idaho State University, Idaho State University Museum.
Cushing, F.H. (1895). The arrow. *American Anthropologist 8*(4), 307-349.
DeJarnette, D.L. (1975). Preface. In D.L. DeJarnette (Ed.), *Handbook of Alabama Archaeology, part 1, point types* (rev. ed.). Moundville, AL: Archaeological Research Association of Alabama, Inc.
DeJarnette, D.L., Kurjack, E.B., & Cambron, J.W. (1962). Excavations at Stanfield-Worley Bluff Shelter. *Journal of Alabama Archaeology 8*(1,2).
Dunnell, R.C. (1971). *Systematics in prehistory*. New York: Free Press.
Ericson, J.E. (1984). Toward the analysis of lithic production systems. In J.E. Ericson & B.A. Purdy (Eds.), *Prehistoric Quarries and Lithic Production*. Cambridge: Cambridge University Press.
Faulkner, C.H., & McCollough, C.R. (1973). *Introductory report of the Normandy Reservoir salvage project: Environmental setting, typology, and survey* (Rep. of Investigations No. 11). Knoxville: University of Tennessee, Department of Anthropology.
Finklestein, J.J. (1937). A suggested projectile point classification. *American Antiquity 3*(3), 197-203.
Ford, J.A. (1954). On the concepts of types. *American Antiquity 56*(1), 42-54.
Ford, J.A., Phillips, P., & Haag, W.G. (1955). The Jaketown site in west-central Mississippi. *Anthropological Papers of the American Museum of Natural History 45*, 1-164.
Ford, J.A. & Webb, C.H. (1956). Poverty Point: A Late Archaic site in Louisiana. *Anthropological Papers of the American Museum of Natural History 46*, 1-136.
Fowke, G. *1896 Stone art*. (13th Annual Rep.) (pp. 47-184). Washington, DC: Bureau of American Ethnology.
Frison, G.C. (1968). A functional analysis of certain chipped stone tools. *American Antiquity 33*(2), 149-155.
Frison, G.C. (1974). *The Casper Site: A hell gap bison kill on the high plains*. New York: Academic Press, Inc.
Frison, G.C., Wilson, M., & Wilson, D. (1976). Fossil bison and artifacts from an early Altithermal period arroyo trap in Wyoming. *American Antiquity 41*(1), 28-57.
Goodyear, A.C., III (1974). *The Brand site: A techno-functional study of a Dalton site in northeast Arkansas* (Series No. 7). Fayetteville: Arkansas Archaeological Survey Research.
Gunn, J. (1975). Idiosyncratic behavior in chipping style: Some hypotheses and preliminary analysis. In E. Swanson, (Ed.), *Lithic technology: Making and using stone tools*. The Hague, Netherlands: Mouton Press.
Gunn, J. (1977). Idiosyncratic chipping style as a demographic indicator: A proposed application to the South Hills region of Idaho and Utah. In *The individual in prehistory: Studies of variability in style in prehistoric technologies*. New York: Academic Press, Inc.
Harman, H.H. (1967). *Modern Factor Analysis*. Chicago: University of Chicago Press.
Heizer, R.F., & Hester, T.E. (1978). *Great Basin projectile points: Forms and chronology* (No. 10). Socorro, NM: Ballena Press Publications in Archaeology, Ethnology, and History.

Helwig, J.T., & Council, K.A. (Eds.) (1979). *SAS User's Guide, 1979 Edition*. Raleigh, NC: SAS Institute, Inc.

Hill, J.N., & Evans, R.K. (1972). A model for classification and typology. In D.L. Clarke (Ed.), *Models in archaeology*. London: Methuen.

Holmes, W.H. (1897). *Stone implements of the Potomac-Chesapeake tidewater province* (15th annual report of the Bureau of American Ethnology). Washington, DC: U.S. Government Printing Office.

Holmes, W.H. (1919). Handbook of aboriginal American antiquities, part 1: the lithic industries. *Bulletin of the Bureau of American Ethnology 60*.

House, J.H., & Wogaman, R.W. (1978). *Windy Ridge: A prehistoric site in the inter-riverine Piedmont in South Carolina* (Occasional Papers of Anthropological Studies No. 3). Columbia: The University of South Carolina, The Institute of Archaeology and Anthropology.

Jenkins, N.J., & Curren, C.B., Jr. (1975, November). *Archaeological investigations on the Central Tombigbee River, Alabama, chronology, subsistence, and settlement patterns: A preliminary report*. Paper presented at the 32nd annual meeting of the Southeastern Archaeological Conference, Gainesville, FL.

Johnson, L.L. (1977). A technological analysis of an Aquas Verdes quarry workshop. In *The individual in prehistory: Studies of variability in style in prehistoric technologies*. New York: Academic Press, Inc.

Kay, M. (1975). Social distance among central Missouri Hopewell settlements: A first approximation. *American Antiquity 40*(1), 64-71.

Kay, M. (1980). *The Central Missouri Hopewell subsistence-settlement system* (Research Series No. 15). Columbia: Missouri Archaeological Society.

Kneberg, M. (1956). Some important projectile point types found in the Tennessee area. *Tennessee Archaeologist 12*(1), 17-28.

Kneberg, M. (1957). Chipped stone artifacts of the Tennessee Valley area. *Tennessee Archaeologist 13*(1).

Krieger, A.D. (1944). The typological concept. *American Antiquity 9*(3), 271-88.

Krieger, A.D. (1952). [Review of *The Prehistoric Horizons of Northeastern Oklahoma*, by David Baerreis]. *American Antiquity 18*, 174-175.

Lewis, T.M.N., & Lewis, M.K. (1961). *Eva: An archaic site*. Knoxville: University of Tennessee Press.

Luchterhand, K. (1971) Early Archaic projectile points and hunting patterns in the lower Illinois Valley. In S. Struever (Ed.), *Illinois Valley Archaeological Program Research* (Papers No. 3). Springfield: Illinois Valley Archaeological Program.

McGhee, R. (1980). Individual stylistic variability in Independence I stone tool assemblages from Port Refuge, N.W.T. *Arctic 33*(3), 443-453.

Miller, P.A. (1980). Archaic lithics from the Coffey site. In A.E. Johnson, (Ed.), *Archaic prehistory on the prairie-plains border* (pp. 107-111). Lawrence: University of Kansas Publications in Anthropology.

Montet-White, A. (1974). Significance of variability in Archaic point assemblages. *Plains Anthropologist 19*(63), 14-24.

Morrow, C.A. (1984). A biface production model for gravel-based chipped stone industries. *Lithic Technology 13*(1), 20-28.

Morse, D.F. (1971). The Hawkins cache: A significant Dalton find in northeast Arkansas. *Arkansas Archaeologist 12*(1), 9-20.

Muto, G.R. (1971). *A Technological Analysis of the Early Stages in the Manufacture of Lithic Artifacts*. Unpublished master's thesis, Idaho State University, Pocatello.

Newell, H.P., & Krieger, A.D. (1949). The George C. Davis Site, Cherokee County, Texas. *Memoirs of the Society for American Archaeology No. 5*.

Oakley, C.B., & Futato, E.M. (1975). *Archaeological investigations in the Little Bear Creek reservoir* (Research Series No. 1). Tuscaloosa: University of Alabama, Office of Archaeological Research.

Otinger, J., & Hoffman, C.M. (n.d.). *Archaeological investigations at the Brinkley site, 22Ts729* (Report of Investigations No. 36). Tuscaloosa: University of Alabama, Office of Archaeological Research.

Patterson, P.E. (1977). A lithic reduction sequence: A test case in the North Fork Reservoir area, Williamson County, Texas. *Bulletin of the Texas Archaeological Society 48*, 53-82.

Perino, G. (1968). *Guide to the identification of certain American Indian projectile points* (Special Bulletin No. 3). Oklahoma City: Oklahoma Anthropological Society.

Perino, G. (1971). *Guide to the identification of certain American Indian projectile points* (Special Bulletin No. 4). Oklahoma City: Oklahoma Anthropological Society.

Peterson, D.A., Jr. (1973). *The Spring Creek site, Perry County, Tennessee: Report of the 1972-1973 excavations* (Occasional Papers No. 7). Memphis: Memphis State University, Anthropological Research Center.

Pond, A.W. (1930). Primitive methods of working stone based on the experiments of Halvor L. Skavlem. *Logan Museum Bulletin, Beloit College 2*(1).

Rau, C. (1876). The archaeological collection of the United States National Museum, in charge of the Smithsonian Institution. *Smithsonian Contributions of Knowledge 22*(4).

Read, D. (1982). Toward a theory of archaeological classification. In R. Whallon & J. Brown (Eds.), *Essays on Archaeological Typology*. Evanston, IL: Center for American Archaeology Press.

Rouse, I. (1939). Prehistory of Haiti: A study in method. *Yale University Publications in Anthropology 21*.

Shafer, H.J. (1973). *Lithic Technology at the George C. Davis Site, Cherokee County, Texas*. Doctoral dissertation, University of Texas, Austin. (University Microfilms. Ann Arbor, MI.)

Schiffer, M.B. (1972). Archaeological context and systemic context. *American Antiquity 37*(2), 156-165.

Schiffer, M.B. (1976). *Behavioral Archaeology*. New York: Academic Press, Inc.

Sheets, P.D. (1975). Behavioral analysis and the structure of a prehistoric industry. *Current Anthropology 16*(3), 369-91.

Sollberger, J.B. (1971). A technological study of beveled knives *Plains Anthropologist 16*(53), 209-218.

Spaulding, A.C. (1953). Statistical techniques for the discovery of artifact types. *American Antiquity 18*(4), 305-313.

Speth, J.D., & Johnson, G.A. (1976). Problems in the use of correlation for the investigation of tool kits and activity areas. In C.E. Cleland (Ed.), *Cultural change and continuity: Essays in honor of James Bennett Griffin*. New York: Academic Press, Inc.

Stewart, D., & Love, W. (1968). A general canonical correlation index. *Psychological Bulletin 70*, 160-163.

Strong, W.D. (1935). An introduction to Nebraska archaeology. *Smithsonian Miscellaneous Collections 93*(10).

Suhm, D.A., Krieger, A.D., & Jelks, E.B. (1954). An introductory handbook of Texas archaeology. *Texas Archaeological Society Bulletin 25*.

Taylor, W.W. (1948). *A study of archaeology*. Carbondale, IL: Southern Illinois University Press.

Thomas, D.H. (1981). How to classify the projectile points from Monitor Valley, Nevada. *Journal of California and Great Basin Anthropology 3*(1), 7-43.

Thruston, G.P. (1890). *The antiquities of Tennessee*. Cincinnati, OH: Robert Clarke.

Thurstone, L.L. (1947). *Multiple-factor analysis*. Chicago: University of Chicago Press.

Van Buren, G.E. (1974). *Arrowheads and projectile points, with a classification guide for lithic artifacts*. Garden Grove, CA: Arrowhead Publishing Company.

Vierra, R.K. (1982). Typology, classification, and theory building. In R. Whallon & J.A. Brown (Eds.), *Essays on archaeological typology*. Evanston, IL: Center for American Archaeology Press.

Whallon, R., & Brown, J. (1982). Preface. In R. Whallon & J. Brown (Eds.), *Essays on archaeological typology*. Evanston, IL: Center for American Archaeology Press.

Wiessner, P. (1983). Style and social information in Kalhari San projectile points. *American Antiquity 48*(2), 253-277.

Willey, G.R., & Sabloff, J.A. (1980). *A history of American archaeology*, (2nd ed.). London: Thames and Hudson, Ltd.

Wilmsen, E. (1968a). Functional analysis of flaked stone artifacts. *American Antiquity 33*(2), 156-161.

Wilmsen, E. (1968b). Lithic analysis in Paleoanthropology. *Science 161*, 982-987.

Wilson, T. (1809). Chipped stone classifications. In *Report of the U.S. National Museum for 1807* (pp. 887-944). Washington, DC.

Winters, H.D. (1969). *The Riverton Culture* (Monograph No. 1). Springfield: Illinois Archaeological Survey.

Index

abduction 21, 22, 23, 24, 37, 40
Accessible Space 230, 231, 232
activity area 302, 305, 307, 308, 321, 352, 353
activity set 328, 329, 330, 331, 333, 343, 350, 352
Activity Space 230, 231, 232
ADCLUS 375, 380, 455
algorithm 131, 132, 141, 163, 164
ALSCAL 408, 455
AMASDA-DELOS 89, 91, 103, 104, 106, 107, 109, 112
analogical argument 47, 48, 49, 51, 52, 82,.83
ANOVA 541, 542, 547, 548, 549, 552, 554
antimode 63
a priori hypotheses 319
archaeological domain 47, 49, 50, 51, 305, 312, 314, 321, 329, 330, 331, 333, 334, 340, 343, 345, 347, 348, 351, 352, 353, 354, 355, 356, 366, 452
archaeological model 47, 52
archaeological theory 46, 50, 51, 58, 81
archaeomagnetic dating 514
argumentation by principle 47, 51
Arkansas Archeological Survey 89, 91, 112
artifact analysis 502
association group 100
assumption 2, 5, 6, 7, 8, 9, 10, 12, 16
asymmetrical coarrangement 335, 337, 338, 339, 340
attainable set 133, 137, 138, 143
autocorrelation 204, 298, 299, 301, 474, 475, 476, 477, 478, 479, 480, 488, 489, 494, 495, 496, 498, 500, 501, 514, 515
auxiliary hypothesis 7, 16, 20, 24, 30
AVDISTGM 297
AVDISTGP 297, 359, 366, 367, 370, 371, 372, 378, 430, 436, 437, 439, 440
AVDISTLP1 297, 359, 366, 367, 368, 369, 370, 371, 372, 378, 396, 408, 413, 414, 415, 431, 437, 439, 440, 450
AVDISTLP2 297, 359, 366, 367, 371, 372, 373, 378, 408, 437, 440
AVDISTM 359, 360, 361, 363, 365, 366, 367
axiomatic choice theory 131, 132, 141, 143, 144, 168, 174
Bartlett-Box F test 568
Bartlett's test 74
base type 359

BASIN I 271, 281, 291
behavioral domain 304, 305, 312, 313, 314, 321, 329, 330, 331, 333, 334, 336, 347, 348, 351, 352, 353, 354
Bermuda Index 188, 189
big man 262
binding constraint 249, 252, 256
Black Mesa 514, 539
bottom-up organization 95
boundary condition 5, 302
boundary problem 476, 480, 487, 489, 494
box and whisker 31
bridging argument 2, 5, 20, 41, 297, 516
bridging principle 302, 308
Brinkley site 583, 588, 607, 611
canonical correlation 3, 567, 569, 588, 590, 595, 599, 600, 603, 607, 611
canonical redundancy analysis 601
capitalist society 268
Cartesian vs. polar coordinates 507, 587, 588
catchment analysis 116, 127, 150, 151, 152, 155, 156, 157, 172, 173, 207
Central Limit Theorem 533
ceramic technology 514, 515, 518, 525, 527
Chi-square test 187
choropleth 474, 475, 487, 489, 490, 492, 500
chronometry 510, 512, 513, 537, 538
classification 1, 2, 16, 17, 25, 30, 33, 35, 43, 44, 54, 59, 61, 63, 64, 65, 80, 82, 83, 84, 85, 86, 93, 94, 102, 103, 106, 107, 111, 112, 113, 277, 278, 279, 281, 292, 296, 502, 505, 506, 508, 567, 568, 569, 571, 573, 577, 583, 587, 605, 606, 607, 608, 609, 610, 611, 612
cluster analysis 30, 33, 66, 298
cognized environment 116
Cole's C_7 364
Cole-Wishart clustering 375
complex data set 19, 21, 24, 25, 34, 36, 37, 38, 39, 40, 41
computer 87, 88
conceptual domain 45, 46, 47, 48, 51, 53, 55, 58, 61, 63, 81
conceptual model 88, 89, 95, 96, 97, 98, 99, 100, 101, 102, 103, 104, 106, 107, 108, 109, 111
concordance 46, 48, 52, 58, 60, 61, 81, 150, 505, 507
conditional preference aspect 115, 116, 122, 124,

613

INDEX

134, 135, 136, 138, 139, 140, 142, 147, 148, 150, 155, 156, 157, 158, 159, 163, 164, 168
confidence limits 50
confirmation 50, 51, 53
constrained exploratory data analysis 3, 31, 33, 39, 41, 90, 502, 503, 506
contiguity-anomaly method 298, 299, 301, 475, 476, 480, 487, 489, 492, 493, 494, 495, 496, 499, 501
contingency table 125
correlation 3, 10, 66, 72, 74, 82, 85, 313, 314, 321, 567, 569, 587, 588, 590, 595, 596, 598, 599, 600, 601, 602, 603, 607, 611
cost/benefit analysis 264
cost function analysis 114, 151, 155, 156, 157
covariation 6, 9
covering laws 1, 17
CRM 117, 118, 119, 120, 124, 126
cultural formation process 297, 300, 306, 307, 308, 309, 310, 311, 316, 321, 325, 326, 353
cultural resource management 236, 275, 475
cumulative frequency diagram 65
curation 64, 82, 306, 307, 312, 326, 327, 353
currency 244, 252, 263, 264, 265, 266, 267, 272, 273
curve fitting 478, 517
data base 47, 48, 49, 50, 52, 57, 58, 59, 60, 61
data base management 87, 91, 92, 94, 95, 96, 98, 99, 100, 101, 102, 103, 107, 111
data base management system 92, 111, 112, 113
data documentation 96, 99, 106
data modeling 95, 99, 111
data observation 46, 58
data redundancy 96, 99
data screening 2, 19, 25, 31, 60, 61, 66, 80, 590, 603
data set 46, 49, 50, 57, 58, 60, 61, 63, 64, 65, 66, 68, 71, 72, 78, 79, 80, 81
data standardization 96, 99, 104, 107
data structure 2, 5, 6, 7, 8, 10, 11, 12, 13, 15, 16, 92, 93, 95, 96, 97, 101, 102, 104, 106, 108, 303, 304, 323, 330, 344, 345
dating associational error 525, 527, 534, 536
dating measurement error 512, 515, 525, 530, 533
debitage 547, 548, 552, 554, 556, 557, 558, 559, 560, 563, 564
decision making 2, 27, 29, 43, 129, 130, 132, 133, 134, 139, 140, 141, 144, 146, 147, 148, 149, 151, 152, 156, 158, 159, 161, 162, 166, 169, 170, 171, 172, 243, 257, 259, 260, 261, 263, 266, 267, 271
decision tree 140, 159, 160, 161, 162, 163, 165
deduction 1, 5, 25, 26, 27, 30, 31, 33, 34, 37, 38, 39, 40, 41, 42, 50, 53
dendrochronology 277, 523
depositional area 28
depositional set 297, 298, 299, 300, 301, 314, 315, 320, 321, 322, 324, 326, 327, 328, 329, 330, 331, 333, 343, 344, 345
description 46, 51, 52, 57, 58, 59, 66, 81, 85
Desert culture 279, 280
dialectical relationships 262, 267
diet problem 249, 252
dimensional analysis of variance 362, 454
dimensionality reduction 66, 76, 82
dimensional physical property 135, 160, 162
discriminant function analysis 119, 199, 200, 201
drop zone 387, 388, 425
dual simplex 251, 254
dummy variable 179
dynamic programming 257
Early Archaic 161, 162
Early Woodland 583
ecological niche 228, 229
ecological paradigm 104, 114
economic analysis 29, 115
economic theory 29, 43, 129, 130, 142, 143, 145, 150, 164, 168, 169, 170, 268
elementary event 53, 81
emic decision process 258
emic normative 79, 80, 81
emic symmetry 7, 115, 140, 150, 156, 162, 164, 165
entity 94, 100, 104, 105, 107, 108, 109
entropy 310, 342, 352
entry model 3, 22, 26, 34, 35, 36, 37, 38, 39, 299, 300, 301, 303, 324, 326, 327, 328, 330, 342, 343, 347
epistemological constraints 268
Es-Shubbabiq 65
etic coherence 7, 115, 150, 156, 163, 164, 165
Euclidean distance 359, 377, 380, 383, 415, 416
expected value 80
experiment 51, 54, 56, 57, 58, 59, 81, 84, 130, 131, 141, 146, 149, 152, 157, 165
explanation 1, 4, 17
exploratory data analysis 3, 25, 31, 33, 90, 300, 313, 318, 319, 320
extended activity sites 214, 220, 223, 224, 225, 226, 227, 228, 232, 234, 235
factor analysis 3, 16, 20, 25, 28, 29, 30, 33, 43, 61, 62, 63, 64, 65, 72, 81, 82, 83, 84, 276, 298, 321, 567, 569, 588, 590, 595, 598, 599, 600, 603, 607, 609, 611
feasible solution 246, 247
filtering 3, 19, 34, 203, 301, 305, 326, 345, 475, 488, 489, 514, 515, 517, 530, 531, 532
flat files 107, 108, 110
formalist-substantivist 142, 145, 166
formalist-substantivist debate 115
formation process 59, 303, 304, 305, 306, 307, 308, 309, 310, 311, 312, 316, 317, 318, 320, 321, 322, 323, 324, 325, 326, 327, 328, 330, 342, 343, 344, 347, 351, 352, 353, 354
Fourier analysis 19, 305, 326, 504, 515
fully enumerated matrix 96

fusion step 381, 382, 383, 415, 416, 420
game theory 146, 147, 166, 263
Geary's C 479, 480, 481, 485, 496, 498
generative theory 131, 132, 141
genetic theory 53, 54
Glenwood Springs 209, 210, 211, 213, 214, 215, 216, 217, 219, 220, 223, 224, 225, 228, 232, 234, 236, 237, 238
global choice set 133, 135
global organization 3, 121, 312, 313, 314
Goodman and Kruskal's gamma 361
GRIPHOS 108, 112
Great Basin 279, 280, 281, 285, 292, 293, 295, 296
hierarchical choice analysis 114
hierarchical decision making 140
hierarchical spatial organization 229, 231
hierarchical structure 102
histogram 63, 590
histogram equalization 326
homogeneous population 8, 11, 13, 46
Houppeville 65
human settlement niche 229
hypothesis-testing 3, 50, 125
identity matrix 72
idiosyncratic variation 572, 575, 578
independent dating 509, 510, 514, 515, 519, 524, 537
indifference 133, 134, 136, 138, 139, 158
induction 3, 5, 22, 24, 26, 31, 34, 38, 39, 40, 41, 42, 50, 51, 52, 58, 59
information accessibility 139, 142, 147, 148, 150, 156, 157, 163, 164, 165, 166, 167
information exchange theory 26, 27
information processing 91, 103
information processing capability 129, 147, 150, 156, 157, 165
inter-assemblage variation 544, 563
interpolation 528, 530, 533
interval scale 49, 62
intra-assemblage variation 541, 549, 559, 560, 562, 564
intrasite artifact distribution 1
intrasite spatial analysis 2, 28, 33, 224, 300, 304, 305, 306, 307, 308, 310, 311, 316, 319, 320, 322, 328, 345
intuition 276, 283, 285
isolated artifacts 211, 232, 235
isopleth 488, 489
ITREG 375, 380
Jaccard coefficient 361, 375
Jardine-Sibson clustering 375, 454
Jelinek's width/thickness ratio 541, 542
JOIN 109, 110
kaolin pipestem dating 514, 537
Kaupauku 262, 263, 272
Kendall's tau 356, 361, 364

kernel discriminant analysis 119
k-fold partitioning 117, 133, 134, 135, 140, 143, 157
Kolmogorov-Smirnov test 114, 117, 186, 220, 225
Kriging 114, 117, 199, 202, 203, 204, 206, 207
!Kung San 54, 81, 84, 86
land parcel 116, 118, 119, 122, 123, 125
Late Archaic 161, 162, 250, 251, 253, 259, 260, 583, 609
Late Woodland 161, 162
Leonard Haag site 252, 272
Levallois point 544, 547, 554, 557, 558, 560, 562, 563, 564
Levantine Mousterian 503, 541, 542, 544, 546, 555, 556, 557, 559, 560, 563, 564, 565
limited activity sites 214, 220, 223, 224, 225, 226, 227, 228, 232, 234, 235
linear programming 1, 17, 114, 124, 140, 164
linking identifier 96
lithic technology 28, 506, 557, 569, 573, 574, 577, 578, 580, 583, 604, 606, 607
local organization 3, 120
location choice 159, 160, 161, 162, 163, 171, 174, 175, 187, 188, 206, 209, 212, 215, 216, 227, 228, 229, 230, 232, 234, 237, 286
logical concordance 2, 4, 5, 6, 7, 8, 9, 10, 11, 16, 18, 19, 20, 21, 22, 23, 24, 25, 26, 27, 28, 29, 30, 31, 39, 40, 41, 42, 89
logical consistency 303, 304
Maasai 229
Magdalenian 304, 384, 385
magnetometry survey 474, 489
Mahalanski's D 71
management science 243
marginal cost 248, 256, 270
marginalism 115, 129, 138, 141, 143, 144, 168, 172
market economies 129, 144
maximizer 145, 146, 166
maximizer-satisficer debate 115
measurability 138, 139, 140, 142, 143, 148, 156, 164
median absolute deviation 33
median split procedures 356
methodological double bind 3, 19, 26
middle range theory 26, 28, 34, 39, 52, 507
midwest United States 510, 514, 518, 519, 524, 527, 537, 538, 539
Mississippian 161, 162, 172
mobility pattern 306, 310
modal values 260, 261
model 239, 240, 241, 242, 243, 245, 248, 249, 250, 251, 252, 253, 254, 255, 256, 257, 258, 259, 260, 261, 262, 263, 264, 265, 266, 267, 268, 269, 270, 271, 272, 273, 275, 277, 281, 292, 293, 295, 296
model free method 66
modeling 303, 304, 340
model validation 190, 192, 193, 205
modes of analysis 48, 60

616 INDEX

Monitor Valley 275
monothetic organization 6, 9, 11, 19, 35, 36, 125, 126, 277, 278, 279, 280, 286, 293, 300, 313, 315, 320, 321, 326, 330, 331, 333, 334, 335, 338, 339, 340, 342, 343, 348, 351, 352, 353
monotonic function 511
Monte Carlo simulation 376, 485, 487, 494, 495, 501
Moran's I 479, 480, 481, 496, 498
Morisita's method 363, 454
Mousterian 63, 65, 82
moving average 514
MRPP 224, 225, 227, 228, 234
multidimensional scaling 62, 298, 301, 374, 376, 377, 378, 379, 383, 384, 408, 409, 413, 415, 421, 423, 430, 439, 440, 441, 455
multinomial response variable 177, 178, 179, 202
multiple processes 18, 25, 47
multivariate logistic regression 114, 116, 117, 118, 119, 120, 121, 122, 123, 124, 179, 182, 187, 199, 202, 203, 204, 205, 225, 228, 234, 235, 236, 238
Munday's index of artifact elongation 541
Nahal Aqev 541, 544, 545, 546, 548, 549, 554, 557, 558, 559, 560, 562, 563, 564, 565
natural formation process 297, 300, 306, 308, 309, 310, 311, 325, 353
nearest neighbor 337, 339, 353, 476, 478, 500
neighborhood analysis 377
network structure 92
New Guinea 263, 272
noise 514, 517, 530
nominal scale 6, 9, 10, 11, 15, 16, 27, 30, 49, 62, 69, 70, 73, 77, 79, 90
nonlinear programming 256
"non-market" economies 129
nonoverlapping sets 303, 313, 319, 320, 321, 326, 330, 331, 333, 334, 343, 347, 348, 350
norm 141, 146, 148, 149, 155, 164, 169
normalization 95, 109, 110, 111
normative-empiricist classification 568, 569, 570, 571, 572, 577, 578, 583, 603, 604, 605, 607
normative-empiricist typology 505
Nunamiut 310
Nyquist frequency 517, 530
objective function 244, 245, 246, 247, 248, 249, 251, 256
open-ended system 93, 95, 97, 102, 107, 111
optimal foraging theory 259, 271
optimal solution 246, 247, 248, 249, 250, 251, 256, 257, 262
ordinal scale 49
outcome 48, 53, 54, 55, 56, 57, 58, 59, 60, 65, 78, 79, 80, 81
outlier 66, 67, 71, 76, 78, 486, 487, 489, 492, 496, 499, 500
OVERCLUS 298, 301

overlapping sets 28, 303, 313, 319, 320, 322, 326, 330, 331, 333, 334, 343, 347, 348, 350
Owen's Valley 275
palimpsest 34, 36, 42, 43, 304, 305, 314, 315, 320, 321, 322, 325, 326, 379, 384, 398, 407, 429, 453
paradigm 4, 13, 16, 17, 92, 97
paradigmatic classification 63
parallel data set 34, 36, 37, 38, 40, 299
parameters of production 137
parametric programming 251
path dependency 102
pattern recognition 209, 238, 316, 317, 318, 319, 320, 321, 322, 323, 324, 327, 328, 454
physical model 88, 90, 95, 97, 98, 107, 108, 111
physical property 115, 122, 134, 135, 136, 159, 160, 161, 162, 163, 168
Pincevent habitation no. 1 304, 344
plex structure 102, 103, 106, 108, 110
point based data 178
pointer 89
point morphology 507
point pattern analysis 479
Poisson distribution 192, 194
polythetic association 304, 314
polythetic organization 3, 6, 9, 11, 19, 28, 35, 36, 42, 114, 119, 125, 126, 275, 276, 277, 278, 279, 280, 283, 286, 288, 290, 292, 293, 299, 300, 303, 304, 307, 313, 314, 315, 319, 320, 322, 326, 330, 331, 333, 334, 335, 338, 339, 340, 342, 343, 345, 348, 351, 352, 353
POLYTHETIC1 360, 371
POLYTHETIC2 370, 371, 408
Pompeii effect 353
population 46, 47, 48, 49, 50, 51, 52, 53, 56, 57, 58, 59, 60, 61, 62, 63, 64, 65, 66, 69, 70, 71, 77, 78, 79, 80, 81, 84, 85
positivist classification 568, 571
post-depositional processes 6, 8
post optimal analysis 248, 250, 251, 259
predictive modeling 2, 118, 120, 126, 173, 174, 175, 176, 177, 179, 184, 186, 187, 190, 192, 196, 204, 206, 236, 238, 275
preference 132, 133, 134, 135, 136, 137, 138, 139, 142, 143, 145, 147, 148, 149, 159, 160, 161, 162, 163
preference ordering 135, 136, 147, 159, 160
preparation cost 265
primal problem 248, 251
primary physical property 136
principal components analysis 19, 66, 67, 69, 70
probability distribution 54, 56, 78, 81
probability surface 177, 178, 179, 190, 204
probability theory 47, 51, 53, 58, 81, 83, 84
problem domain 4, 8, 11, 12, 13, 14
PROBNORM 504, 530, 531, 532
production costs 151, 152, 157

projectile point 66, 68, 78, 80, 82, 85, 86, 567, 569, 570, 571, 573, 574, 587, 607, 608, 609, 610, 611
PROJECTION 109, 110
promax rotation 595, 596, 598, 599, 600
pure error 78
pursuit cost 265
quadrat based data 123
radioisotope 515
random variable 54, 55, 56, 57, 58, 59, 60, 78, 79, 80, 81
ranging analysis 251
ratio scale 6, 9, 11, 12, 16, 47, 49, 55, 56, 58, 59, 60, 62, 63, 64, 66, 67, 68, 71, 76, 77, 81, 82, 85
rectangular integration 528
Reese river, 275, 280, 281, 282, 283, 286, 287, 292, 293, 294
reference type 359
regional analysis 173, 209
regionalized variable theory 202
regression 8, 78, 83, 477, 478, 496, 514, 515, 516, 517, 532, 536, 539
relational data base 89, 96, 108, 109
relevant data structure 11, 13, 313, 323
relevant relational data structure 297, 300
relevant relational structure 11, 12, 15, 25, 36, 38, 42, 502, 504
relevant subset structure 11, 12, 15, 20, 115, 120, 121, 122, 502, 505
remote sensing 209, 238
resource density 265
resource mobility 265
retroduction 22
risk 243, 244, 264, 265, 266, 271
Rosh Ein Mor 544, 545, 548, 549, 552, 554, 555, 556, 557, 559, 560, 562, 563, 564, 565
sample 49, 50, 51, 52, 53, 54, 56, 65, 72, 76, 80, 81, 82
sample space 54
sampling 186, 199, 210, 211, 212, 213, 220, 223, 224
sampling theory 51
San 256, 261, 269, 270, 272, 273
SARG 145, 166, 170, 171, 172, 173, 208, 237
satisficer 129, 142, 145, 146, 147, 148, 166
scale of analysis 260, 261
scatterplot 33, 590
screening 90
search cost 265
segregation analysis 356
SELGEM 100
semantic integrity 96
sensitivity analysis 250, 251
separable programming 256
seriation 1, 17, 277, 502, 503, 504, 505, 509, 510, 511, 512, 513, 514, 516, 518, 519, 524, 525, 533, 534, 536, 538

settlement analysis 116, 127, 150, 158, 171
settlement archaeology 173
settlement pattern 1, 174, 187, 190, 202, 203, 206, 207
Settlement Space 230, 231, 232
settlement system 173, 174, 175, 187, 202, 205, 207
shadow cost 248
shadow price 248, 249
Shoshoneans 281, 284
simplex method 247, 248, 251, 254
simulation 56, 84
simultaneous decision making 158
single process 18, 24, 27, 46, 47, 48, 52, 55, 57, 58, 59, 60, 63, 65, 78, 81
sites vs. nonsites 175, 178, 190, 194, 199, 204, 212, 213, 214, 215, 217, 219, 220, 223, 224, 225, 227, 228, 232, 234, 235, 236
social cost 267
social exchange 169, 170, 262, 263, 269
social organization 26, 27, 28, 42
space contraction 378, 440
Sparta 179, 182, 183, 184, 185, 186, 187, 190, 192, 193, 194, 196, 198, 199, 206, 207
spatial arrangement 55, 57, 60, 100, 297, 298, 299, 300, 303, 304, 305, 307, 308, 310, 312, 315, 321, 323, 328, 334, 335, 336, 337, 338, 339, 340, 342, 356, 358, 360, 361, 362, 363, 364, 365, 366, 367, 368, 370, 371, 372, 373, 377, 378, 380, 382, 383, 387, 388, 406, 427, 430, 431, 436, 437, 438, 439, 440, 446, 453, 475, 476, 479, 492, 495, 504, 507, 544, 549, 552, 555, 557
Spearman's rho 217, 361, 362
spectral analysis 34, 305, 325, 326, 504
statistical decision theory 166
statistical domain 47, 49, 50, 51, 52, 53, 57, 59
statistical model 47, 52
statistical theory 45, 46, 47, 51, 58, 61, 81
status-quo theory 269
stepwise analysis 26, 31, 39, 40, 63, 66, 88, 124, 502, 506
stochastic error 515, 528, 534
Strahler method 185
style 512, 513, 514, 516, 517, 518, 525, 536, 537, 538
style analysis 26, 27
subsistence analysis 124, 150
subsistence system 1
substantive-formalist debate 269
SYMAP 488, 489
symmetrical coarrangement 337, 338, 339
Tabun Cave 541, 565
technological index 540, 541, 542, 543, 545, 547, 548, 549, 552, 555, 556, 557, 563, 564
tethered mobility 557, 564
theory 1, 2, 3, 4, 5, 7, 8, 12, 16, 17, 45, 46, 47, 48, 51, 52, 53, 54, 55, 56, 59, 61, 81, 82, 83, 84, 85,

86
time series analysis 3, 19, 504, 536, 538
tool kit 35, 36, 38, 42, 44, 63, 64, 65, 302, 307, 308, 312, 313, 314, 321, 328, 330, 344, 557
tool maintenance 566, 567, 569, 572, 573, 574, 575, 577, 578, 580, 581, 583, 595, 598, 600, 602, 603, 604, 605, 606, 607, 608, 611
tool use-life 567, 572, 573, 574, 575, 576, 577, 578, 580, 581, 583, 589, 602, 603, 604, 605
top-down organization 88, 94, 95, 96, 98, 111
toss zone 388
trade-off 136
transformation 46, 47, 51, 52, 53, 58, 79
transitivity 134
transportation costs 133, 152, 154, 155, 156

trend surface analysis 117, 199, 203, 206, 475, 488, 489
trimmed mean 33
unconstrained clustering 33, 298, 299, 312, 317, 318, 320
unexpected absences 353, 354
upper bound technique 254
varimax rotation 595, 596, 599, 600
Ven 39 66, 78, 80
water sources 209, 215, 216, 217, 220, 224, 227
Winzorized mean 33
Woodland 510, 514, 515, 518, 519, 524, 525, 526, 527, 528, 531, 532, 533, 534, 537, 538, 539
world systems theory 261
Zipf's Law 129, 148, 171, 252

About the Contributors

Robert L. Bettinger, Ph.D. is Associate Professor of Anthropology at the University of California, Davis, and a Research Associate of the American Museum of Natural History and the Museum of American Indian, Heye Foundation. His principal research is on prehistoric hunter-gatherers in western North America, specifically those in California and the Great Basin, about which he has written extensively. Equally interested in the more general problem of nonagricultural adaptations, Dr. Bettinger has been active in developing predictive models of hunter-gatherer behavior and exploring their application in archaeological settings.

David P. Braun, Ph.D. is Associate Professor of Anthropology at Southern Illinois University in Carbondale, Illinois, and Director for Publications in the Center for Archaeological Investigations. Since completing his doctorate at the University of Michigan, he has pursued research on social and cultural ecological change during the prehistoric transition from hunting-gathering to food producing subsistence economies, using the midwestern United States as his study area. Part of this research has focused on developing better methods and more reliable evidence for studying prehistoric social, ecological change, leading him to work on such diverse topics as burial practices, pottery decorative styles, pottery construction and use, and alternative approaches to seriation. Dr. Braun's articles on these topics and on his interpretations of midwestern prehistory have appeared in numerous journals, conference proceedings, and edited collections. Support for his work has come from several federal, state, and private grants and contracts, as well as from Southern Illinois University.

Christopher Carr, Ph.D. is Associate Professor of Anthropology and Director of the Institute for Quantitative Archaeology at the University of Arkansas, Fayetteville. He received his graduate and undergraduate degrees from the University of Michigan, Ann Arbor, and the University of Illinois, Chicago, where he was supported by a National Science Foundation Graduate Fellowship and nine additional national and regional scholarship funds. His current research includes the evaluation and development of quantitative methods for a variety of archaeological applications; the development of middle range theory for intrasite spatial analysis, artifact style analysis; mortuary analysis; ceramic and textile technology; and assessment of the role of ritual and belief in the development of hierarchical social structures and the formation of alliances in prehistoric Woodland, southern Ohio. Dr. Carr has ten seasons of field experience, primarily in the midwestern United States, and five years of experience in museum studies involving over twenty institutions in the midwestern and southeastern United States. His recent publications include a comprehensive evaluation of methods of intrasite spatial analysis (in *Advances in Archaeological Method and Theory*), a discussion of quantitative methodology in ethnoarchaeology (in *Method and Theory for Activity Area Research*), an assessment of exchange of meteoritic iron in the Middle Woodland (in *Southeastern Archaeology*), and a 678-page book on soil analysis and resistivity surveying (*Handbook on Soil Resistivity Surveying*, Center for American Archaeology). Dr. Carr has received research grants from the National Science Foundation, the Center for American Archaeology, Battelle Research Laboratories, and the Ohio Historical Society.

ABOUT THE CONTRIBUTORS

James A. Farley is the lead systems administrator for the Arkansas Archeological Survey where he has been since 1984. Farley received his M.A. in anthropology from the University of Arkansas in 1983 for his work in archaeological data base management. In his current position as systems expert in a small multiuser Unix environment, he is responsible for general systems administration in addition to cooperating in the design and development of archaeological data bases. Farley has presented and published a number of papers that focused on the application of data base management principles to the problems of archaeological analysis.

Bruce G. Gladfelter, Ph.D. received his Ph.D. in geography from the University of Chicago. His interests have been in relating physical geography and geomorphology to the interpretation of the contexts of artifacts and the archaeological record. He has participated in geoarchaeological excavations in the Old and New Worlds, ranging in time from the Lower Paleolithic to the Mississippian, respectively. This research has contributed to the authoring and coauthoring of more than two dozen reports, articles, chapters in books, and one book. Dr. Gladfelter is Assistant Professor of Geography and Affiliate, Department of Anthropology, at the University of Illinois at Chicago where he is currently corecipient of a grant to study Upper Paleolithic hunter-gatherer exploitation strategies in Southern Sinai.

C. Marshall Hoffman is a graduate associate in the Department of Anthropology at Arizona State University. He received his M.A. degree in anthropology from the University of Arkansas in 1983 and his B.A. degree in anthropology from Southern Illinois University in 1976. Hoffman's publications and papers have focused on lithic technology, typology and classification, the analysis of stylistic design, and quantitative methods. He has participated in field and laboratory research in the southwestern and southeastern United States, the Great Basin, and Alaska. Hoffman is a flintknapper interested in experimental approaches to lithic analysis. He frequently conducts workshops and demonstrations in lithic technology at local museums and schools.

Marcia L. Jones, Ph.D. is a Senior Analyst and is involved with the prehistory of the Levant and the designing of analytical and mapping software for archaeological applications. She received her Ph.D. in anthropology from Southern Methodist University. She has published several articles on paleolithic sites in southern Jordan and in the Central Negev, Israel. Dr. Jones' most recent research efforts involve restructuring the taxonomy used in classifying Epipaleolithic assemblages from the Levant.

Arthur S. Keene, Ph.D. is Assistant Professor of Anthropology at the University of Massachusetts-Amherst. Keene received his Ph.D. from the University of Michigan, where he developed mathematical optimization models for the study of prehistoric foragers. His research interests include epistemology in archaeology, subsistence change, and the ecology of small scale social formations. His current research focuses on intensification of production among prehistoric foragers in the eastern United States. Dr. Keene has authored two books, one on linear programming applications in archaeology and one (coedited with James A. Moore) on the relationship between method and theory in archaeology.

Kenneth L. Kvamme, Ph.D. is an Associate Archaeologist of Arizona State Museum at the University of Arizona. Dr. Kvamme received his Ph.D. in anthropology at the University of California, Santa Barbara, and has held positions at the University of Denver and with the U.S. Bureau of Land Management. His recent interests focus on geographic computer data bases and in the development of computer models of archaeological settlement systems. This research has culminated in a number of publications and research grants dealing with the Mesolithic of West Germany, prehistoric hunters-and-gatherers of Colorado, the Anasazi of northern Arizona, and methodological issues. Dr. Kvamme also has performed extensive work in the fields of intrasite spatial analysis, lithic analysis, and paleodemography. He has performed archaeological fieldwork throughout the western United States, and in Alaska, Mexico, and Europe.

W. Fredrick Limp, Ph.D. is Assistant Director of the Arkansas Archeological Survey and a researcher at the Institute for Quantitative Archaeology. Dr. Limp received his Ph.D. in anthropology with an emphasis in economics at Indiana University, Bloomington. He has published numerous articles on both economic analysis in archaeology and computer applications, and, with Dr. Sandra Parker, has reviewed numerous grants and contracts for computer applications in archaeology. Dr. Limp also serves as series editor for the Arkansas Archeological Survey Research Series, Research Reports, and Technical Papers.

Sandra Parker, Ph.D. is an Associate Archaeologist with the Arkansas Archeological Survey, where she has been since 1972. She holds an M.A. in anthropology and a Ph.D. in operations research from the University of Arkansas. She has published numerous articles and papers concerning computer and statistical applications in archaeology. Dr. Parker is a member of the International Union of Pre and Protohistoric Sciences Commission on Data Management and Mathematical Applications in Archaeology, and is a researcher at the Institute for Quantitative Archaeology at the University of Arkansas.

Dwight W. Read, Ph.D. is Associate Professor of Anthropology at the University of California, Los Angeles. Dr. Read received his Ph.D. degree in mathematics from the University of California, Los Angeles, and joined the anthropology department in 1970. He has done extensive work as a statistical consultant in archaeology and anthropology. Dr. Read was a co-Principal Investigator on the Chevelon Archaeological Research Project and has done ethnographic work among the !Kung San. His research interests are mathematical representation of anthropological constructs, quantitative procedures and formal models in archaeology, and models of hominid evolution. Dr. Read's publications include papers on kinship terminologies, artifact typologies, statistical sampling, and hominid evolution. Dr. Read is a Fellow of the Royal Anthropological Institute and the American Anthropological Association, and a member of the American Association for the Advancement of Science and the Society for American Archaeology.

David Hurst Thomas, Ph.D. is presently Curator of Anthropology at the American Museum of Natural History. Dr. Thomas received his Ph.D. in anthropology from the University of California, Davis, and previously taught at the City College of New York. His primary research deals with the archaeology of Native American people, and his fieldwork involves primarily two long-range projects: one in the Desert West, the other on St. Catherines Island, Georgia. Dr. Thomas was previously Chairman, Department of Anthropology, American Museum of Natural History. He has published over fifty scientific articles and monographs, edited two volumes, and written three textbooks.

Clifford E. Tiedemann, Ph.D. is Associate Professor of Geography at the University of Illinois at Chicago. He received his Ph.D. from Michigan State University and has maintained interest in the thrust of his dissertation—the casting of spatial-analytic models into inference or inference-like contexts while only minimally sacrificing the identity of data. These efforts are closely connected to his other professional foci: commercial, industrial, and public-facility site selection, and analysis of regional patterns of resource exploitation, as they provide intelligible evidence supportive of research findings and consultative recommendations to private and public decision makers. His continuing association with Dr. B.G. Gladfelter in the work reported herein follows that pattern. Recent activities involve retail and wholesale trade site-selection studies, school-development and school-closing studies, and school-district desegregation with a minimum commitment to transportation. Dr. Tiedemann's current work centers on the geography of opportunity costs confronting farmers, manufacturers, and businessmen.

Leonard Williams served as Assistant Director of the Museum of Man, Department of Anthropology, Central Washington University, and a member of the American Association of Museums. He was appointed Museum Scientist after receiving his M.A. in anthropology at the University of California, Davis, and has lectured and published a number of articles concerning museum ethics, museums and their role in tourism, and museums as interpretive centers. In addition, Williams has worked closely with Pacific Northwestern archaeologists, providing preservation techniques to include rock art by silastic casting.